THE SPECIAL EDUCATION HANDBOOK

THE SPECIAL EDUCATION HANDBOOK
An Introductory Reference

PHILLIP WILLIAMS

Open University Press
MILTON KEYNES · PHILADELPHIA

Open University Press
Celtic Court
22 Ballmoor
Buckingham MK18 1XW

and
1900 Frost Road, Suite 101
Bristol, PA 19007, USA

First Published 1991

British Library Cataloguing in Publication Data

Williams, Phillip, *1926–*
The special education handbook: an introductory reference.
1. Great Britain. Special education
I. Title
371.90941

ISBN 0-335-09314-0

Library of Congress Cataloging-in-Publication Data

Williams, Phillip.
The special education handbook: an introductory reference/Phillip Williams.
p. cm.
ISBN 0-335-09314-0
1. Special education–Dictionaries. 2. Handicapped children–Education–Dictionaries. I. Title.
LC3957,W55 1990
371.9–dc20 90-35680 CIP

Typeset by SB Datagraphics, Colchester, Essex
Printed in Great Britain by St Edmundsbury Press, Bury St Edmunds, Suffolk

CONTENTS

LIST OF ILLUSTRATIONS

PANEL OF CONSULTING EDITORS

ACKNOWLEDGEMENTS

First and foremost I want to acknowledge my gratitude to the Leverhulme Trust. The Trust's award of an Emeritus Fellowship in 1986 enabled me to proceed with the task of collecting material. It allowed me to make many visits to different libraries, and supported the mundane but essential office chores of photocopying, collating, typing, etc., that are involved in creating the Handbook. I particularly appreciated the Trust's attitude, both generous and undemanding, an ideal combination of virtues.

Library staff have been unfailingly helpful. Two libraries in particular have borne the brunt of the many requests for information. The National Library of Wales, apart from offering reading facilities, provided helpful computer-generated lists of recent publications by interest-area, and I am particularly grateful to David Jeremiah and Avril Thomas for enabling me to access the Library's collection productively in this way.

At the University College of North Wales, Bangor, the Education Library proved to be a most efficient and uncomplaining channel of communication with the inter-library loan service, a facility that was often and regularly used. The many different staff involved accepted this unusually heavy extra burden pleasantly and willingly.

Many sources other than those referenced in the body of the text were consulted. One in particular must be mentioned. While the Handbook was being prepared, the Reynolds and Mann encyclopaedia of special education was published.[1] This is not acknowledged in the body of the Handbook, but it is a unique and most useful reference work, and I gladly confirm its helpfulness at many points.

The role of the panel of consulting editors was invaluable. Between them, they read every entry, and the Handbook is a different and much improved publication as a result. Many authors make the comment that any flaws in the text are their own, while any felicities are due to the consultants. I gladly endorse this view.

Many individuals have helped in ways too numerous to mention. I have to single out David Mitchell and John Biggs, who provided glimpses of the special education scene in New Zealand and Australia respectively.

I remain indebted to the University College of North Wales and to the School of Education in particular for providing the facilities which enable a retired colleague to indulge his interests so freely. Iolo Williams has continued to offer accommodation when the School has passed through a period of reconstruction, and I do appreciate this.

Finally, Glenys has tolerated a husband who for nearly four years has retreated to library or study at almost every spare moment. Her forbearance over the neglected garden and house has been exemplary, and her encouragement of the task has been unfailing. The Handbook would never have been completed without her support.

Publishers' acknowledgement:
We are grateful to Somerset EA and Globe Education, Basingstoke, for permission to reproduce the illustrations on pp. 174 and 300.

[1] Reynolds, C.R. and Mann, L. (Eds.) (1987) *Encyclopedia of Special Education*, New York, Wiley.

INTRODUCTION

Purpose

This book is intended as a basic reference for people who carry – or intend to carry – professional responsibilities in special education. Those most likely to consult it are students of special education, particularly experienced teachers following inservice courses of special education, advisors on special education, and members of the many professions who work with children with special needs. The book is not and could not be a substitute for specialist publications in particular fields. But since any one field of special education inevitably overlaps with others, and practitioners increasingly work in an interdisciplinary format, it is hoped that the book will be useful to all as a desk reference.

In the last decade or so, Special Education has gone through a period of great change. The publication of the Warnock Report in 1978 generated a marked growth of interest in the education of children with special needs, and the new thinking of the report had to be disseminated through the education service. Warnock was followed by the Education Act 1981, which meant that substantial legislative changes had also to be accommodated. These developments led to a growth in the number of posts of Local Education Authority (LEA) advisors for special education: primary schools designated their special education coordinators, secondary schools reorganised their remedial departments and the further education sector appointed staff to increase its provision for students with special educational needs.

Training had to be offered for the holders of these new posts, and various kinds of INSET courses in Special Education were established by the LEAs, by establishments of higher education and by other providers. The growth of training facilities was paralleled by a growth in publications. (Phillips (1988) lists six new journals centrally concerned with special education which started publication in the UK between 1981 and 1988.)[1] During the 1980s several series of books dealing with topics in special education appeared, as did many individual books. No-one with a responsibility for special education lacks for published material for guidance.

The end of the 1980s has been marked by the passage into law of the Education Act 1988, and the belated recognition by authority of the

[1] Phillips, C.J. (1988) 'Editorial Reflections on the First Seven Years', *British Journal of Special Education*, 15, 2, 71–2.

many implications this has for the practice of special education. The spirit and attitudes of the post-Warnock period have had to adjust to yet another legislative framework. More courses and more publications!

As we enter the 1990s, there is nevertheless a new feeling of unity among special educators. This is not the reaction of a beleaguered profession. The emphasis on integration means that teachers who previously carried responsibilities for remedial classes now carry responsibilities for children with special needs. This is an altogether wider brief and one with more status. The courses now do justice to this wider concept. The abolition of categories of special education, advocated by Warnock and included in the 1981 Act, has drawn attention to the interdependence of special needs and to the importance of educating children as individuals, and not as members of artificially separate categories. At the time of writing the two main professional associations in special education, the National Council for Special Education and the National Association for Remedial Education, are engaged in forming a new National Association, which other bodies representing particular interest groups are considering joining.

In this climate of increasing cohesion, many courses for the teaching profession cover special education as a whole. Yet there is no British teaching text nor reference book which offers a view of the whole field at an appropriate level. This Handbook aims to meet the second of these two needs.

Construction

The author's Glossary of Special Education[2] was the main base from which this Handbook was developed. The Glossary has a different aim, offering simple explanations of the many terms that all teachers and parents of children with special needs might encounter in the specialist reports which they meet and the background material which they might read. To construct this Handbook, the Glossary entries were first pruned to exclude items which a more sophisticated readership would find superfluous, then extended to include additional terms which have acquired importance since the Glossary was prepared in 1987. The comments of various reviewers of the Glossary were helpful here. The new list was then rewritten for the different readership.

At this point the entries were allocated to twelve different fields of special educational need. This was done for the purpose of editing the Handbook efficiently. It was not an easy task, for independent categories of special educational needs are impossible to create. An expert in each of the fields agreed to act as a consulting editor. (Two editors jointly covered one of the fields.) The editors read the entries in their separate sections, and were also provided with a complete list of proposed entries in the Handbook. They

[2] Williams, P. (Ed.) (1988) *A Glossary of Special Education*, Milton Keynes, Open University Press.

suggested modifications to entries within their own field, including additional references where appropriate, advised on deletions and proposed a small number of additional entries, not restricted to their own section. While I acknowledge elsewhere my great debt to the editors, it must be emphasised that they are not responsible for the material in the Handbook, for the final draft was prepared by the author.

These changes were incorporated into a second draft, which itself received a further check for consistency, etc., before handover.

Content

The Handbook contains over a thousand terms. Entries on individuals, no matter how great their influence on special education, are excluded. So are entries on the very large number of societies and associations with concerns in the special education area; it would have been impossible to draw a satisfactory line of demarcation between those whose concern for special education is central and those whose concern is marginal. An exception has been made for a very few overseas organisations to which reference is sometimes made in the literature. There are a number of entries which are specifically concerned with overseas (mainly North American) topics; these are limited to legislation, projects, tests, reports etc., which have featured prominently in the international literature.

Readers may wish to know how the entries are distributed. It is not easy to provide this information. For a start, the twelve editorial categories used would not be everyone's choice, and given these categories, one person may allocate the entries quite differently from another. The distribution by number of entries may be (and in this case, is) quite different from the distribution by wordage. What is clear, however, is that educational terms – including learning difficulties but excluding the specialist reading terms – predominate, covering nearly a quarter of the wordage. The reading terms themselves cover about an additional 9%.

Another 9% or so of the content (by wordage) covers educational and psychological tests and associated terminology. The test part of this section could have been extended indefinitely, for virtually any test could at some time or other be used to assess a child with special needs. It was decided to limit these entries to short comments on those tests which are used in schools and in clinical assessments, and to which reference is made in the special education literature.

Terms which are mainly concerned with the education of children with emotional and behavioural difficulties and physical, neurological, sensory and mental handicaps cover between them about 32% of the total. Terms from medicine and psychology cover about 16%, and the remaining 10% represents terms with a social work, legal or overseas emphasis.

Using the Handbook

Entries appear in alphabetical order. Where an acronym is often used instead of the full term, the acronym usually appears as an additional entry, cross-referenced to the full term.

In the Glossary, terms which were used in the explanations and which were themselves glossed, were always italicised. This principle has not been followed slavishly in this Handbook. There are several reasons for this. First, terms often appear which are not central to the discussion in which they are used: to cross-reference these might irritate. Second, the large number of unnecessary italicised intrusions might be distracting: 'special educational need' would be italicised in very many entries, for example. So only those terms which extend the treatment of the topic under discussion have been italicised; other relevant terms are listed at the end of the entry. But this policy should in no way deter readers from looking up any other term which appears and with which they may not be familiar. In addition, many entries end with a short list of references, usually limited to three or four. Each list is a selection of the material used to compile the entry. If the reader wishes, these references can be used as sources for further reading.

The entries aim to provide information on the many and varied concerns of the fast-growing discipline of special education. Many entries also offer a brief discussion, alerting the reader to some of the issues and debates which enliven so many topics in special education. After a lifetime in education, I remain convinced that it is this sector of the educational enterprise that offers the greatest challenges, commands the most dedicated responses and yields the most profound satisfactions.

A

AAMD, American Association on Mental Deficiency, now *American Association on Mental Retardation.*

AAMD Adaptive Behavior Scale, an example of a rating scale designed to assess competence in skills and habits needed for the achievement of independent living. It originated in North America, and is designed for use with people with mental handicap who are three years old or more. The scale is in two parts, one covering the skills of daily living, such as handling money, leisure activities, etc., while the other covers personality characteristics, particularly maladaptive behaviours such as *hyperactivity, withdrawn behaviour,* etc.

See *adaptive behaviour scales.*

Reference:

Hallahan, D.P. and Kaufman, J. (1988, 4th edn.) *Exceptional Children: Introduction to Special Education,* Englewood Cliffs, Prentice Hall.

AAMR, see *American Association on Mental Retardation.*

AB design, simple experimental plan, often found in a *behaviour modification* project with a single child. A and B refer to the two phases of the project. In the A phase, which precedes intervention, baseline data are collected, usually by structured observation of the behaviour being targeted. The B phase represents the intervention period, during which data collection

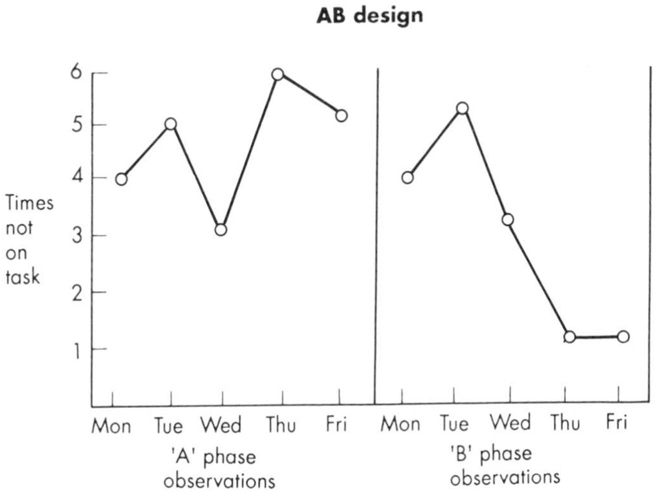

continues. The two sets of data are compared, often graphically, to judge the effect of the intervention. The advantage of this design is its simplicity. It is easy to understand and quicker to apply than other, logically sounder designs. Its weakness lies in the difficulty of imputing change to the intervention itself, when other influences might have been responsible. This difficulty can be eased by using a more sophisticated approach, for example an ABAB design. In this case, the first B phase is followed by a second A phase, i.e. the intervention is withdrawn, so the original conditions obtain. After a suitable period the B or intervention phase is reintroduced. The changes in behaviour that occur during these four phases enable better inferences about the effects of the intervention to be made.

See *multiple baseline design.*

Reference:

Alberto, P.A. and Troutman, A.C. (1986, 2nd edn.) *Applied Behaviour Analysis for Teachers,* Columbus, Merrill.

AB lists, set of fifteen word lists, each containing ten words (30 phonemes), used for speech *audiometry.* The child repeats each test word as it is presented and responses are scored phonemically. The results are shown as a speech *audiogram,* which can then be compared with the normal ear response.

Reference:

Tucker, I. and Nolan, M. (1984) *Educational Audiology,* Beckenham, Croom Helm.

ABA, see *Applied Behaviour Analysis.*

ABC, see *Adaptive Behavior Curriculum.*

Abecedarian Project, one of the few adequately controlled experimental investigations of the efficacy of intervention programmes for socially disadvantaged pre-school children. Developmental assessments were made at six months of age and at six-monthly intervals thereafter on a control and an experimental group of children, equally 'at-risk' of mild mental retardation. Significant differences in favour of the experimental group appeared at eighteen months of age and on every test occasion thereafter.

See *compensatory education.*

Reference:

Ramey, C.T. and Campbell, F.A. (1984) 'Preventive Education for High-Risk Children: Cognitive Consequences of the Carolina Abecedarian Project', *American Journal of Mental Deficiency,* 88, 5, 515–23.

ABIC, see *Adaptive Behavior Inventory for Children.*

ability, in a general sense, potential for school success, as in the phrase 'a pupil of considerable ability'. This is an educational usage and can carry overtones of a fixed, inherited intelligence – a capacity model of intelligence – and an intelligence that can be measured. For those who believe with Plutarch that 'a child's mind is not a vessel to be filled but a fire to be kindled', ability in this sense is not so important to determine, for it can be developed: other attributes such as motivation, teaching skill, experiences, etc., are involved in developing an ability which is not fixed.

Ability is also used in a narrower sense to refer to more precisely identified talents, for example perceptuo-motor ability, reasoning ability, verbal ability, etc., all of which can contribute to human intellectual performance. Note that these two usages parallel the factor structure of intelligence advanced by educational psychologists, the first resembling *general intelligence,* and the second *group* and *specific factors.*

Many programmes in special education are aimed at fostering the development of abilities in this second sense. For example the *Frostig Programme* is aimed at improving children's perceptuo-motor abilities.

Although ability is often used in an intellectual context, it is not restricted to it. For many children in special education the development of physical abilities, for example, is crucial.

References:

Gardner, H. (1990) 'Multiple Intelligences and Education', in Entwistle, N. (Ed.) (1990) *Handbook of Educational Ideas and Practices,* London, Routledge.

Vernon, P.E. (1960) *Intelligence and Attainment Testing,* London, University of London Press.

ability–attainment controversy, debate over the relationship between scores on tests of *ability*, e.g. *intelligence* tests, and tests of *attainment*, e.g. reading tests. It was argued that an attainment score lower than an intelligence score indicated that a child was underfunctioning, and that the size of the discrepancy was an index of need for special help. In the UK a *retardation* of two years, e.g. a reading age two years lower than mental age, was often used as a criterion for offering special educational help. This is open to criticism on various grounds:

a discrepancy of two years at one age level has quite different implications from a similar discrepancy at another age level;

a discrepancy based on age-scores, while simple to handle, is somewhat out of place when test scores are so often produced as *deviation quotients;*

this procedure does not identify a child whose performance may be average in one area, but nevertheless substantially below expectations – e.g. a gifted child with a significant reading problem.

For reasons such as these, supporters of the discrepancy principle have turned to regression-based formulae and other techniques to provide more precise indices of the significance of the differences between scores on ability and attainment tests. But the key criticism argues that the principle is based on an implied acceptance of the outmoded capacity model of *ability*; since as many children are advanced, with attainment scores above their ability scores, as are retarded, this model is seriously flawed.

For this reason it has been argued that a better criterion for special help would be attainment scores which are at least two years below chronological age, i.e. a criterion based on *backwardness* rather than retardation. This principle is still open to some of the criticisms listed above, but does avoid the capacity pitfall.

The main point to note is that procedures such as these may give a spurious precision to methods of identifying children with special needs, and in the end are no substitute for careful and detailed assessment.

References:

Curr, W. and Hallworth, H.J. (1965) 'An Empirical Study of the Concept of Retardation', *Educational Review*, 18, 1, 5–15.

Hallahan, D.P. and Kaufman, J.M. (1988) *Exceptional Children: Introduction to Special Education* (4th edn.), Englewood Cliffs, Prentice Hall.

Yule, W., Rutter, M., Berger, M. and Thompson, J. (1974) 'Over- and Under-Achievement in Reading: Distribution in the General Population', *Brit. J. Educ. Psychol.*, 44, 1, 1–22.

ability grouping, principle of allocating pupils to classes according to their *ability*. There are four main systems in use (though infinite variations are possible):

streaming, where a year-group is rigidly divided into classes by ability and remains so divided for all subjects;

setting, where the streamed pupils are reorganised for certain subjects, e.g. maths and foreign languages, by competence in the subject. A set can include members of any of the original streams;

banding, where the year-group is divided into two or three bands according to ability, each ability band then being divided into mixed-ability classes;

mixed-ability grouping, where pupils are allocated randomly to classes, so ensuring that each class is a reasonable cross-section of the whole ability range.

Arrangements of this sort apply in larger schools only, usually secondary schools and a few primary schools. The method used can have significant effects on the pupils, for it is claimed that classes designated as 'low-ability' in the streamed arrangement can generate an anti-school culture, fostering the development of emotional and behavioural difficulties as well as hindering the promotion of an atmosphere which helps children with learning difficulties. At the same time there is no clear evidence which unambiguously supports a case for instituting any one of the other possible arrangements.

References:
Galloway, D.M. (1985) *Schools, Pupils and Special Educational Needs,* London, Croom Helm.
Hargreaves, D.H. (1967) *Social Relations in a Secondary School,* London, Routledge and Kegan Paul.
Kelly, A.V. (1990) 'Mixed Ability Teaching in the Secondary School', in Entwistle, N. (Ed.) (1990) *Handbook of Educational Ideas and Practices,* London, Routledge.

abreaction, release from repressed fears and emotionally charged memories by bringing the original (unconscious) experience to mind and reliving it in the imagination; the technique is used in *psychoanalysis* and *psychotherapy.* See *catharsis.*

acalculia, extreme difficulties with number symbols and mathematical operations, generally more severe than dyscalculia, though both are often used interchangeably. The term is comparable with alexia, in that it was originally a medical description of a condition found in adult patients, later applied also to children's *learning difficulties.* Its use in special education is diminishing since it is descriptive rather than prescriptive: difficulties with mathematics are best dealt with by specially designed teaching programmes.

acceleration, advancing children through the school system faster than normal: it is one of the three main ways of providing for *gifted children,* the other two being *enrichment* and segregation. Acceleration can be effected by admitting gifted children before the normal school starting age, or by skipping a year, where the school is organised by age-groups. Either way, the children finish their school course ahead of their peers.

Acceleration may have advantages in that it offers gifted children a greater intellectual challenge. But this advantage may be gained at the risk of emotional and social stress that may arise from mixing with older pupils. For this reason, decisions about accelerating gifted children need to be taken with care: issues such as all-round maturity, position in the age-group, opportunity for individualised programming in the normal classes, school organisation, etc., all need to be taken into consideration. It is not a very common practice in either the UK or the USA.

References:
Alexander, P.A. and Muia, J.A. (1982) *Gifted Education: a Comprehensive Road-map,* London, Aspen Systems Corporation.
Freeman, J. (1990) 'Educating Gifted Children', in Entwistle, N. (Ed.) (1990) *Handbook of Educational Ideas and Practices,* London, Routledge.
Maltby, F. (1981) *Gifted Children and Teachers in the Primary School,* Lewes, Falmer Press.

ACE Centre, see *Aids to Communication in Education Centre.*

ACER, see *Australian Council for Educational Research.*

achievement, originally achievement was attainment in relation to potential. It was measured by an achievement quotient: thus a child with an arithmetic age of nine years and a mental age of ten years would be said to have an achievement quotient for arithmetic of 90 (9/10 × 100).

As the capacity model of ability has fallen from favour, so this use of achievement has declined; today it is often used in the same sense as *attainment.* But while attainment is often restricted to performance in school subjects, achievement is used more widely. Thus the *Hargreaves Report* identified four kinds of achievement, achievement in written tests, in practical skills, in personal and social skills and in motivation and commitment.

More recently, achievement has been used as the sum of a pupil's attainments in school, particularly in the components of the National Curriculum.

See *ability–attainment controversy, Record of Achievement.*

Reference:

Department of Education and Science (1990) *Education (Individual Pupils' Achievements) (Information) Regulations 1990,* London, Department of Education and Science.

achondroplasia, or chondrodystrophy, disorder which results in reduced height and various problems with bone development. It is usually inherited and is the most common form of dwarfism. The main educational needs are help to adjust to an unusual appearance and some modifications to furniture and equipment. Intellectual development is unaffected.

achromatic vision, see *colour vision.*

Active Tutorial Work, or ATW, planned programme of pastoral care, based on group activities primarily designed for pastoral care or tutorial periods. ATW moves pastoral care away from a 'crisis intervention' model and gives it a recognised place in the school timetable, with a curriculum to be followed. It is aimed at all mainstream pupils in the eleven to sixteen age-range, including those with special educational needs.

Reference:

Baynes, A. (1987) 'The Pastoral Role' in Hinson, M. (Ed.) (1987) *Teachers and Special Educational Needs,* Harlow, Longmans in association with NARE.

acoustic feedback, occurs as a disturbing high-pitched whistle when the earmould of a *hearing-aid* does not provide a good seal in the ear, leading to amplified sound leaking out around the earmould. This amplified sound is picked up again by the microphone of the hearing-aid.

acoustic impedance test, see *audiometry.*

acquired defect, defect not present at birth, but which develops as the result of injury or illness later. It is contrasted with *congenital defect.*

acrocephaly, *congenital* malformation of the skull, which in the past almost invariably led to severe *mental handicap.* Nowadays, surgery in the early years can reduce the physical deformities and the associated likelihood of mental handicap.

adaptive behaviour, those skills needed to manage one's own affairs and live an independent life; social competence. The main skills can usually be grouped into domains such as communication (e.g. speech, reading); physical functioning (e.g. mobility); self-help (e.g. toileting, dressing); vocational skills; etc.

Adaptive behaviour is a key concept in *mental handicap.* When *intelligence tests* were developed at the turn of the century, they were used to classify levels of mental handicap more precisely. Classifications based on intelligence tests were soon criticised, but it took a long time to wean practitioners away from a method which was reliable and familiar. Eventually the American Association on Mental Deficiency produced a manual which used both adaptive behaviour and IQ as joint principles for classifying levels of mental handicap. But there is still a debate as to whether these two principles provide a more appropriate way of defining mental handicap than IQ alone.

A similar situation obtained in relation to special education. In the UK, following the *Education Act 1944,* intelligence test performance was replaced by educational competence as the main determinant of need for special schooling for children with learning difficulties – though many professionals effectively continued to rely on IQ.

The increasing worldwide emphasis on *normalisation* has meant that IQ has become much more peripheral to decisions about educating children with special needs: behaviour in the normal environment is now central. This is one reason why interest in adaptive behaviour and its measurement has grown. For children with *severe learning difficulties,* the adaptive behaviour scales offer information which can relate directly to the developmental curriculum. They can indicate which skills have been mastered and which skills the curriculum should offer.

References:

Grossman, H.J. (Ed.) (1983) *Classification in Mental Retardation,* Washington, American Association on Mental Deficiency.

Raynes, N.V. (1987) 'Adaptive Behaviour Scales', in Hogg, J. and Raynes, N.V. (Eds) (1987) *Assessment in Mental Handicap,* London, Croom Helm.

adaptive behavior curriculum, detailed set of over three thousand teaching objectives or terminal behaviours, arranged in five skill areas – self-help, communication, perceptual–motor, socialisation and aquatics. For most behaviours, a *task analysis,* which usually incorporates behavioural principles such as *backward chaining,* lists the skills required.

This curriculum is designed for teachers working with children with *severe learning difficulties.* It is not intended to be prescriptive: teachers are expected to select those behaviours which are appropriate to their pupils' needs and stage of development.

Reference:

Popovich, D. and Laham, S.L. (Eds.) (1981) *The Adaptive Behavior Curriculum,* Baltimore, Brookes.

Adaptive Behavior Inventory for Children (ABIC), measure designed specifically for children, originally developed as part of the *SOMPA* (System Of Multicultural Pluralistic Assessment). It covers six different areas of *adaptive behaviour.* While the names of these areas may be a little different from usual, the items are familiar. Thus the self-maintenance area covers how well the child can manage essential daily living needs; the earner/consumer area covers the child's understanding and management of money – and so on.

See *adaptive behaviour scales.*

References:

Hallahan, D.P. and Kaufman, J. (1988, 4th edn.) *Exceptional Children: Introduction to Special Education,* Englewood Cliffs, Prentice Hall.

Mercer, J.R. and Lewis, J.E. (1977) *Adaptive Behavior Inventory for Children,* New York, Psychological Corporation.

adaptive behaviour scales, as the importance attached to *adaptive behaviour* – the key concept in *mental handicap* – has steadily increased in recent years, so the number of instruments available to measure it has also grown steadily. Adaptive behaviour scales usually provide measures of several different areas of behaviour, using items which are often behaviourally formulated. The scales use interviews with parents or other adults familiar with the child's behaviour to gain answers to items, though sometimes direct observation of the child is used. Since inter-rater reliability is not high, and also because the period of intensive development of these scales is, with few exceptions, relatively short, their reliability and validity are less than those of instruments such as most intelligence and attainment tests which rarely rely on raters and have a much longer period of development. On the other hand, adaptive behaviour scales offer the advantage of providing information which is often easily translatable into teaching activities. Thus where items concerned with self-help are not well answered, there is a clear indication of a curriculum area which needs further investigation and which could be improved.

Scale results are sometimes provided as age equivalent performances, and sometimes as norms for different groups.

See, e.g. *Vineland Scale, AAMD Adaptive Behavior Scale.*

Reference:
Raynes, N.V. (1987) 'Adaptive Behaviour Scales', in Hogg, J. and Raynes, N.V. (Eds.) (1987) *Assessment in Mental Handicap*, Beckenham, Croom Helm.

ADD, see *Attention Deficit Disorder.*

adolescence, the period between the onset of puberty and the achievement of maturity. Different societies define different limits to adolescence, though in most Western societies adolescence is used to describe the years between roughly twelve and twenty years of age, by which time major physical and psychological changes have occurred. Nevertheless there are considerable individual variations in the ages at which these changes happen and for these reasons as well as societal ones precise limits to adolescence cannot be stated.

The physical changes of adolescence include the staged development of the primary and secondary sexual characteristics, a spurt in growth, and changes in physique, sometimes accompanied by temporary coordination problems. The psychological changes include achieving independence from parents, making satisfactory sexual choices, working out a set of values and beliefs and preparing adequately for a career and a family.

The extent to which these changes lead to psychological difficulties, in the context of our society, is a question which is often debated. They can pose difficulties for some: in themselves they can lead to special educational needs, as witness the increase in provision for pupils with emotional and behavioural difficulties in the secondary school years. In addition, for a child who already has special educational needs, some of these changes pose special challenges. Thus the problems of gaining independence through finding and holding a job are certainly not easier; there are special problems for many seriously handicapped youngsters in making satisfactory sexual relationships; and so on. This is not to say that handicapped youngsters invariably have a difficult adolescence: it is to say that their extra problems must be anticipated, noticed, and handled sensitively.

References:
Hendry, L.B. (1990) 'Adolescent Needs and Priorities in Modern Society', in Entwistle, N. (Ed.) (1990) *Handbook of Educational Ideas and Practices*, London, Routledge.
Rutter, M., Graham, P., Chadwick, O. and Yule, W. (1976) 'Adolescent turmoil: fact or fiction?' *Journal of Child Psychology and Psychiatry*, 17, 35–56.
Widlake, P. (1983) *How to Reach the Hard to Teach*, Milton Keynes, Open University Press.

adoption, complete and irrevocable transfer of a child from one family group to another. An adoption order vests parental rights and responsibilities in relation to the child in the adoptive parents, who then have the same legal status as if the child were born to them legitimately. Various changes to the rules governing adoption are introduced by the Children Act 1989 and a review of adoption law is currently being carried out by the Law Commission.

While the main purpose of adoption is to provide a permanent, secure and loving home for the child, it is also a process through which many childless adults are able to experience the privileges and responsibilities of child-rearing. One of the many issues connected with adoption is the extent to which adopted children are likely to show *emotional and behavioural difficulties.* While there is evidence of a higher incidence of referral to *child guidance clinics* than would be expected, it is not easy to determine whether this is associated with adoption per se or with other factors such as the characteristics of the adoptive family, or the age at which adoption takes place.

Reference:

Richards, M. (1989) *Adoption,* Bristol, Jordan and Sons.

adult education, courses in broadly non-vocational activities, covering mainly hobbies and interests at a non-advanced level, though including some basic literacy and numeracy classes. Some providing institutes also hold *outreach* classes in *adult training centres* and *social education centres.* There is room for considerable growth in courses designed to accommodate students with special needs.

See *further education.*

Reference:

Dean, A. and Hegarty, S. (1984) (Eds.) *Learning for Independence,* London, Further Education Unit.

Adult Literacy and Basic Skills Unit (ALBSU), organisation providing help for adults with problems in skills such as reading, numeracy and communication. It was established in 1980, replacing, with extended terms of reference, the Adult Literacy Resource Agency, set up in the early 1970s. It is estimated by ALBSU that there are about two million adults in the UK with severe reading and writing problems.

Reference:

Hamilton, M. (1990) 'Adult Basic Education', in Entwistle, N. (Ed.) (1990) *Handbook of Educational Ideas and Practices,* London, Routledge.

adult training centre (ATC), establishment run by a local authority social services department and attended by adults and young people with *severe learning difficulties.* Its purpose is to provide training in social skills, including those needed for employment, though few trainees leave to take up work in the community. The opportunities provided by a centre may range from a *sheltered employment* environment to instruction in basic social skills.

There is a view, quoted in the Warnock Report, paras 10.52–3, that the facilities provided in some ATCs are poor in comparison with educational establishments and that these purposes would be better served if the training centres and their students were brought more clearly into the ambit of *further education*. (*Outreach courses* and *link courses* are examples of moves in this direction.) For this and other reasons, the *Warnock Report* proposed that adult training centres should be renamed social education centres. There is also a view that the needs of school leavers and young adults are sufficiently distinct from those of older persons to justify separate arrangements for them.

References:

Dean, A. and Hegarty, S. (Eds.) (1984) *Learning for Independence*, London, Further Education Unit.

Department of Education and Science (1978) *Special Educational Needs*, London, HMSO (Warnock Report).

Advisory Committee on Handicapped Children, advised the Secretaries of State for Education and for Wales on relevant educational matters, but was suspended when the Warnock Committee was established in 1974. The Warnock Report recommended that an advisory committee on special educational needs, with similar terms of reference, should then be established. Although this recommendation was not adopted, in the face of strong pressure the government funded a working party to consider the matter again. This group unanimously endorsed the Warnock recommendation, proposing that the advisory committee should be funded and appointed by government but housed and serviced elsewhere. The recommendation has not been implemented.

advisory service, see *support services*.

advocacy, speaking and acting on behalf of children with special needs – and their parents – to ensure that their interests are best served and their rights met. This role is distinguished from that of the expert witness, who gives a professional judgement and from that of the *named person*, who is essentially a counsellor and adviser.

The advocacy role has been extensively developed in the USA, where voluntary societies are widely involved in providing advocacy on behalf of individual children and their families, both in the courts and elsewhere, an activity which may well grow in the UK. Acting as a pressure group, seeking changes in policy and improvements in provisions, is a facet of advocacy with which voluntary societies here are more familiar. More recent developments in the advocacy role include the growth of self-advocacy for young people and adults; it is interesting in this context that the Education (Scotland) Act 1981, mentions consultation with over-16s with special needs, a situation where some skill in self-advocacy would be desirable.

Reference:

Russell, P. (1983) 'The Education Act, 1981', *Concern*, 49, 6–13; quoted in Cohen, A. and Cohen, L. (Eds.) (1986) *Special Needs in the Ordinary School*, London, Harper and Row.

affective disorder, serious emotional disturbance, for example a *depressive disorder.*

See *emotional and behavioural difficulties.*

age equivalent, age for which a *raw score* on a *standardised test* is the average performance. For example, a raw score of 73 on a certain test might be the average score obtained by children aged nine years and two months. This then is the age equivalent of a score of 73. The age equivalent is used to make comparisons between a child's performances in different skills, and his/her chronological age.

Age equivalents are attractive measurement units; they are easy to understand and demand little knowledge of statistics. But their simplicity is deceptive, for the units are not equal in value; put another way, the scale they form is not an interval scale. This is easily seen in relation to reading skills, though the point applies to the measurement of any quality. The growth in reading vocabulary between years seven and eight is enormous: between years fifteen and sixteen it is hardly measurable. Yet on an age-equivalent scale both differences are assigned the value of one year.

In addition, to say that a young person of eighteen has a mental age of five, say, on a test of intellectual development may be an accurate reflection of his test score, but makes an unhelpful comparison. For many purposes, standardised scores, which offer comparisons within the person's own age-group, and not between age-groups, have the advantage. In short, age-equivalent scores have to be interpreted with care and sensitivity.

See *norms.*

References:

Anastasi, A. (1982, 5th edn.) *Psychological Testing,* New York, Macmillan.

Davies, P. and Williams, P. (1974) *Aspects of Early Reading Growth: a Longitudinal Study,* Oxford, Blackwell.

age norms, see *norms*

agnosia, inability to recognise familiar images, sounds, etc. For example,

(1) visual agnosia, in which a child can see adequately, but cannot recognise what is seen, even though able to recognise it through the other senses;
(2) auditory (non-verbal) agnosia, in which the child is able to hear sounds, but cannot interpret their meaning;
(3) auditory (verbal) agnosia, in which the meaning of spoken words cannot be grasped, although there is no difficulty in hearing them adequately;
(4) tactile agnosia, in which familiar objects cannot be recognised by touch.

Agnosias may be some of the effects of brain damage.

See *Gerstmann Syndrome, perceptual disorder.*

Reference:
Campbell, R.J. (1981, 5th edn.) *Psychiatric Dictionary*, Oxford, Oxford University Press.

agraphia, inability to express thoughts in writing. This is a medical term for serious writing difficulties, which may be helped by educational procedures.
Reference:
Reason, R. and Boote, R. (1986) *Learning Difficulties in Reading and Writing: a teacher's manual*, London, NFER-Nelson.

AH tests, series of tests of reasoning and intelligence, devised by Alice Heim and others, some of which are used for the assessment of children with high ability, while others (AH1, X and Y) are intended for children with reading difficulties. They cover different age bands between school entry and university level.
Reference:
Levy, P. and Goldstein, H. (1984) *Tests in Education*, London, Academic Press.

aide, see *classroom assistant.*

AIDS (Acquired Immune Deficiency Syndrome), is an illness due to a virus infection, which can produce an asymptomatic carrier state or, in a minority of people, the full-blown clinical syndrome in which lowered immunity makes the sufferer succumb to a variety of infections.

It can be transmitted by sexual intercourse, the transfusion of infected blood, as in haemophilia, and the sharing of contaminated needles and syringes by drug addicts. Some babies can be infected in-utero, i.e. before birth, if their mother is carrying the infection.

All present evidence suggests that there is no risk in the school setting and no contraindication to the child attending school, with some precautions being taken.
References:
Department of Health and Social Security (1986) *Children at School and Problems Relating to AIDS*, DHSS letter CMO (86), 1st Jan. 1986.
National Children's Bureau, 'Aids and Children', *Highlight*, 75, London, NCB.

Aids to Communication in Education Centre (ACE Centre), facility offering help on the the use of microlectronics for children with communication disorders. The Centre disseminates information and provides opportunities for trying out various devices.

See *National Council for Educational Technology.*
Reference:
Bates, R. (1988) 'New Technology and Disability', *Educational and Child Psychology*, 5, 4, 66–8.

air conduction, see *audiometry, hearing impairment.*

albinism, inherited condition in which the pigmentation of the skin, hair and eyes is affected, sometimes recognised by fair hair, pale skin and pinkish eyes. Visual acuity can be severely impaired, *nystagmus* and squint, i.e. *strabismus*, may also be present and individuals with albinism are very sensitive to bright light. These visual problems can give rise to special needs, most obviously over levels of classroom lighting and the provision and use of correct visual aids. Some children are also sensitive to their unusual physical appearance.

Reference:

Chapman, E.K. and Stone, J.M. (1988) *The Visually Handicapped Child in Your Classroom*, London, Cassell.

alexia, inability or unusual difficulty in reading, as the result of brain damage such as injury or tumour. If the affected area includes the *angular gyrus*, alexia may result, often combined with other *language disorders*. It has been argued that the study of acquired alexia may shed light on developmental reading difficulties in children.

See *dyslexia*.

References:

Coltheart, M., Patterson, K.E. and Marshall, J.C. (Eds.) (1980) *Deep Dyslexia*, London, Routledge and Kegan Paul.

Pavlidis, G.T. and Miles, T.R. (Eds.) (1981) *Dyslexia Research and its Application to Education*, Chichester, Wiley.

All Wales Strategy, policy initiative instigated by the Welsh Office with the aim of providing better services in the community for people who are mentally handicapped. It seeks to encourage cooperation at county level among agencies such as social services, health and education authorities, and voluntary organisations. One important feature of the Strategy is the emphasis on integrating the planning and delivery of services. Another is the stress placed on participation by individuals who are mentally handicapped, and their families, in developing schemes tailored to meet their needs.

See *community care, Community Mental Handicap Team.*

References:

Humphreys, S. (1987) 'Participation in Practice', *Social Policy and Administration*, 21, 1, 28–9.

Welsh Office (1983) *All Wales Strategy for the Development of Services for Mentally Handicapped People*, Cardiff, Welsh Office.

allergy, unusually high sensitivity to an intrinsically harmless substance, resulting in physical upset and other adverse reactions. For example, hay fever may be due to a pollen allergy. The educational implications involve being aware of a child's difficulties in demonstrating normal competence when affected by conditions such as itchy skin, continuous sneezing bouts, etc. At the same time there is a considerable volume of research which attempts to implicate oversensitivity to certain types of foods in hyperactivity.

See *Attention Deficit Disorder, Feingold Diet.*

Reference:
Marsh, G.E., Price, B.J. and Smith, T.E.C. (1983) *Teaching Mildly Handicapped Children*, St. Louis, Mosby.

alpha wave, see *electroencephalogram.*

alphabetic method, out-dated method of teaching children to read by first learning the names of the letters and then learning to recognise words as combinations of letters and letter clusters, e.g. see – ay – tee = 'cat'. The method is a simplistic example of mediated learning and of learning by association.
See *phonic method, look-and-say method.*

amblyopia, poor visual acuity in one or both eyes after correction with glasses or otherwise. Suppression amblyopia, commonly known as lazy eye syndrome, occurs when the visual signals from one eye are suppressed or ignored in the brain, often to avoid the double vision which may otherwise be present in cases of *strabismus.*
Reference:
Chapman, E.K. and Stone, J.M. (1988) *The Visually Handicapped Child in Your Classroom*, London, Cassell.

American Association on Mental Retardation, formerly American Association on Mental Deficiency, the pre-eminent North American association in its field. It is responsible for numerous contributions to the study of learning difficulties generally, including a widely used definition of and classification system for *mental retardation,* and the *AAMD Adaptive Behavior Scale.* It also publishes a number of monographs and two research journals.
Reference:
Further information available from the Association at:
1719 Kalorama Rd., Washington, DC 20009, USA.

American Sign Language (Ameslan), see *sign language.*

Amerind system, set of hand-signals used by North American Indians for inter-tribal communication. The system has been used with some success by individuals with severe learning difficulties, since it is said to be easy to learn and particularly easy to understand in comparison with other sign systems.
See *sign language.*
References:
Kiernan, C., Reid, B. and Jones, L. (1982) *Signs and Symbols*, London, Heinemann for the Institute of Education, University of London.
McCartney, E. (Ed.) (1984) *Helping Adult Training Centre Students to Communicate*, Kidderminster, British Institute for Mental Handicap.

amniocentesis, taking a specimen of the liquid (amniotic fluid) surrounding the unborn baby in the womb. The fluid is analysed in order to determine whether the child is likely to be born with a specific congenital defect (e.g. *spina bifida* or a *chromosome* abnormality such as *Down's syndrome*). If so, the mother is then faced with the difficult decision of whether to have the pregnancy terminated or not, often quite late in the pregnancy. Although not all congenital disorders can be detected in this way, the number of those that can is increasing. This has considerable implications for the nature of the future population of children with special needs.

See *genetic counselling.*

Reference:

Harper, P.S. (1989) *Practical Genetic Counselling,* Bristol, Wright.

anal stage, see *Freudian theory.*

analysis of variance, technique of analysing data in order to see whether differences between groups of data (e.g. test scores) can be reasonably explained as chance fluctuations or not. The scores are grouped according to the experiences or treatments that are posited to have influenced them. Thus a number of equivalent groups of children with reading difficulties could each be taught by a different method. The variance, or spread, of their progress scores is then analysed to see whether or not the differences among the groups could reasonably be ascribed to the different treatments that the groups have experienced.

See *F-ratio.*

Reference:

Guilford, J.P. and Fruchter, B. (1978, 6th edn.) *Fundamental Statistics in Psychology and Education,* New York, McGraw Hill.

anarthria, or dysarthria, see *speech disorder.*

ancillary worker, see *classroom assistant.*

angular gyrus, part of the *brain* which is of considerable importance in the development of *language.* It relates ideas conveyed by speech to the written symbols which represent them: damage in this area is often associated with difficulties in written language.

aniridia, congenital absence of the iris, usually inherited and often associated with other visual problems. For example, the very large pupil which results from partial or total absence of the iris means that aniridic children dislike bright light. Various kinds of glasses or contact lenses help with managing school work. *Genetic counselling* is advisable later.

Reference:

Chapman, E.K. and Stone, J.M. (1988) *The Visually Handicapped Child in Your Classroom,* London, Cassell.

anorexia nervosa, eating disorder, characterised by an extreme fear of becoming obese. Eating is deliberately restricted and significant weight loss, in some instances as high as 50%, occurs. This can lead to other physiological complications.

The disorder is most frequently found in adolescent girls, twelve to eighteen years being described as the high-risk group. Estimates of prevalence range around one per 200, 95% of sufferers being girls, though the number of boys with anorexia is said to be increasing. (In effect, a comprehensive school of 1,500 or so pupils may expect around half a dozen anorexics on its roll, an indication of the need for teaching staff to be sensitive to the signs.)

Although there is a feminist view that anorexia is linked with the social and sexual role of women in society, most explanations for the condition are psychological, some psychoanalysts believing that the anorexic is unable to face the challenges of leaving the dependent state of childhood. Alternatively it has been suggested that the anorexic has learnt to associate slimness with desired qualities such as attractiveness and happiness. For these reasons treatment usually consists of *psychotherapy* or *behaviour therapy*.

It is a serious complaint: reports suggest that while most anorexics make a total or partial recovery after only a single bout, as many as 10–20% of anorexics die of the complaint. Referral to the medical or psychological services is essential.

References:

American Psychiatric Association (1980, 3rd edn.) *Diagnostic and Statistical Manual of Mental Disorders*, Washington, American Psychiatric Association.

Elston, T. and Thomas, J.B. (1985), *Anorexia Nervosa, Child care, health and development*, 11, 355–73.

Graham, P.J. (1986) *Child Psychiatry: a Developmental Approach*, Oxford, Oxford University Press.

ANSI, American National Standards Institute, body which specifies acceptable standards for *hearing-aids* in the USA.

anoxia, see *hypoxia*.

anticonvulsant, drug used to control epileptic and other convulsions. There has been considerable research into the effects of anticonvulsants on behaviour and intellectual performance. While any such effects are usually mild, and held to be preferable to the effects of the convulsions they control, teachers need to know which pupils are being treated in this way so that any changes of mood, intellect, etc., can be monitored.

Reference:

Simon, G.B. (1984) *A Teacher's Guide to Medication for Children with Special Needs and to Drug Misuse by Young People*, Stratford-upon-Avon, National Council for Special Education.

antisocial behaviour, behaviour which gives rise to social disapproval, e.g. vandalism, disruption, and in serious cases delinquency. It is commonly contrasted with *neurotic behaviour*: both these two major behavioural dimensions are measured by, e.g. *Rutter's Behaviour Questionnaire.*

Antisocial behaviour is described in many ways, e.g. conduct disorder, aggressive behaviour, disaffected behaviour, and in the school context is most frequently described as *disruptive behaviour*. Treatment for antisocial behaviour follows any of the major therapeutic lines, with behavioural therapy approaches increasing in popularity. At the same time it must be remembered that some medical conditions can be associated with antisocial behaviour. And there is the ecological view that the behaviour can be itself determined by the environment in which it occurs. Finally, studies of clinical populations usually show that the prognosis for children referred for antisocial behaviour is not as favourable as for those referred for neurotic behaviour, whether treatment is provided or not.

References:

Herbert, M. (1987, 2nd edn.) *Conduct Disorders of Childhood and Adolescence: a social learning perspective*, Chichester, Wiley.

Williams, P. (1985) 'Troubled Behaviour, Units 18/19', Open University Course E206, Milton Keynes, Open University.

anxiety disorders, category of behaviour problems. Anxiety – 'fear spread thin' – can be generalised, or specific to a particular situation, as in *separation anxiety* and *school refusal*, two conditions that many teachers are likely to meet. Anxiety disorders are usually explained through psychoanalytic or behavioural theory. Prevalence figures depend on the diagnostic criteria used: the *Isle of Wight Study* found about a 2% rate at both ten and eleven years and at fourteen years. Treatment programmes are generally based on *psychotherapy* or *behaviour therapy.*

References:

American Psychiatric Association (1980, 3rd edn.) *Diagnostic and Statistical Manual of Mental Disorders*, Washington, American Psychiatric Association.

Graham, P.J. (1986) *Child Psychiatry: a Developmental Approach*, Oxford, Oxford University Press.

Apgar Rating Scale, system used to evaluate a baby's physical condition, usually one and five minutes after birth, in order to assess rapidly whether intensive care or specialised treatment is needed. It is a measure of asphyxia, on a scale from 0–10, where 0 usually = stillborn, and 10 = in good health.

aphasia, or – especially in the UK – dysphasia, impairment of the ability to understand or use language, caused by damage to the *cerebral cortex*. It is distinguished from other *language disorders* caused, for example, by hearing loss or damage to the speech muscles. The type of aphasia and its severity depend on the location and extent of the cortical damage. Thus expressive aphasia, in which the sufferer has difficulty in producing language, even though aware of the words intended, is associated with damage to *Broca's area.*

As with all language disorders, one of the key considerations in treatment is whether the aphasia is acquired, i.e. due to damage occurring after some language skills have developed, or congenital, i.e. due to a defect present at birth.

Several different classifications of the aphasias are used, but the where and when of the damage are two of the most important features in classification systems. Knowing these, and after a full investigation, often involving a psychologist, neurologist and speech therapist, treatment can be devised. The teacher may be heavily involved with the treatment team, too, not least because of her opportunities for ongoing involvement with a pupil's language.

See *expressive language disorder, receptive language disorder.*

References:

Brain, W.R. (1977, 8th edn.) *Diseases of the Nervous System,* Oxford, Oxford University Press.

Crystal, D. (1988, 2nd edn.) *Introduction to Language Pathology,* London, Cole and Whurr.

appeals procedure, established for special education in England and Wales under the *Education Act 1981.* It covers situations when parents are dissatisfied with the Local Education Authority (LEA)'s decision over their child's *special educational needs,* after following the agreed consultation arrangements. Appeals can be made at two main points. The first occurs when the authority, having assessed a child, decides that no *Statement* is necessary, i.e. a child's needs can be met without special arrangements. A parent then has the right of appeal to the Secretary of State for Education and Science, who can direct the authority to reconsider its decision, but cannot overrule it. The second occasion occurs when the parent and authority disagree over the content of a Statement. In this case the parent has the right of appeal to an Appeal Committee, established by the authority, but whose composition is governed by legislation. The Appeal Committee can ask the authority to reconsider its view, but cannot overrule it. If the parent is still dissatisfied, there is a right of further appeal to the Secretary of State, who in these circumstances can require the authority to alter the Statement.

Although the Appeal Committee procedure was set up to ensure that parents have every chance to have their voices heard, nevertheless it has been criticised on two main counts. The first is the possible partiality of a committee, some of whose members are also members of a body (the LEA) which is party to the dispute. The second is the status of the committee's decision, which if it goes against the LEA, need not be implemented by it (unless a further appeal to the Secretary of State so requires.)

These arrangements do not affect the rights of parents of non-statemented children under the *Education Act 1980,* to appeal against an authority's decision on school placement.

See P.L. 94–142.

References:
Adams, F. (1986) *Special Education*, Harlow, Councils and Education Press for Longmans.
Cox, B. (1985) *The Law of Special Educational Needs*, London, Croom Helm.
Department of Education and Science (1989) *Circular 22/89, Assessments and Statements of Special Educational Needs: Procedures within the Education, Health and Social Services*, London, Department of Education and Science. (Joint circular with Department of Health.)
Goacher, B., Evans, J., Welton, J. and Wedell, K. (1988) *Provisions for Special Educational Needs: implementing the 1981 Education Act*, London, Cassell.
Scottish Education Department (undated) *Guidance Note – Rec 5*, Edinburgh, Scottish Education Department.
Swann, W. (1989) 'Appealing Against the System', *British Journal of Special Education*, 16, 4, 144.

apperception test, projective technique used in clinical work with children, for example by educational psychologists, in which the child is shown pictures and encouraged to make up stories about them. The stories are then analysed to gain insights into the child's personality.

See, for example, *Children's Apperception Test* and *Thematic Apperception Test*.

applied behaviour analysis (ABA), using the principles of learning theory to manage and change behaviour. *Fading, modelling, reinforcement, shaping,* and *time-out* are all examples of some of the principles followed. The use of social learning techniques such as modelling indicates that ABA is more broadly set in psychological theory than *behaviour modification*, which is heavily dependent on *operant conditioning* techniques. Like behaviour modification, however, ABA is widely used in classrooms and schools for dealing with learning and behaviour problems. There are similar steps to be followed in order to implement both techniques. These steps are described in different ways by different practitioners, but there are five important ones, *viz.*

(i) specify precisely the behaviour that it is intended to change;
(ii) record the frequency of the behaviour under normal conditions, i.e. obtain *baseline data*;
(iii) note what precedes and follows the behaviour, and, if possible, the desired behaviour;
(iv) on the basis of (iii), plan and carry out a programme of behavioural change, using appropriate psychological principles. Note that the programme may be more effective if applied in different environments, e.g. if both teachers in school and parents at home can collaborate in the programme;
(v) evaluate progress.

There is a considerable literature testifying to the value of applied behaviour analysis in education, perhaps mainly in teaching children with severe learning difficulties and/or emotional and behavioural difficulties, though its use has by no means been confined in this way.

References:

Alberto, P.A. and Troutman, A.C. (1986, 2nd edn.) *Applied Behaviour Analysis for Teachers*, Columbus, Merrill.

Gearheart, B.R. (1981) *Learning Disabilities: Educational Strategies*, London, Mosby.

apraxia, or dyspraxia, inability to carry out voluntary purposive movements when there is no paralysis or defect of muscular coordination. The sufferer may understand what movement is required but cannot perform it. Thus he or she may not be able to protrude the tongue on command, yet may freely lick ice-cream from the lips. There are several different varieties of apraxia, classified in different ways. In general, children with apraxia attain higher scores on verbal than performance tasks as assessed by the WISC (Wechsler Intelligence Scale for Children) for example, for their motor skills are affected. They need help in training or retraining skills that other children usually learn easily.

References:

Brain, W. R. (1977, 8th edn.) *Diseases of the Nervous System*, Oxford, Oxford University Press.

Crystal, D. (1988, 2nd edn.) *Introduction to Language Pathology*, London, Cole and Whurr.

aptitude, a particular *ability* or set of abilities, e.g. language aptitude or mechanical aptitude. In older usages an aptitude, like ability in general, was regarded as an inherent potential or capacity, and aptitude tests were used to measure this. Thus language aptitude tests were held to measure the potential a child had for learning languages: more recent views hold that performance on such a test reflects language experience as well as endowment.

Many aptitude tests have been designed to measure skills closely connected with occupations – e.g. clerical aptitude, musical aptitude – and hence are often used in *vocational guidance*. They differ from tests of *attainment*, which emphasise the measurement of performance in school subjects and courses.

Reference:

Anastasi, A. (1982, 5th edn.) *Psychological Testing*, New York, Macmillan.

arithmetical difficulties, have received far less attention than difficulties with reading. This has been explained on the grounds that the education system is predominantly a verbal system, using language as the method of instruction. Hence while language skills such as reading are essential for progress, mathematical skills such as arithmetic have been seen as important, but not essential. The advent of pocket calculators may have reinforced this view. It has also been argued that mathematics worries some teachers, who are themselves unsure and thus reluctant to try to help children.

On the other hand, the demand for a mathematically literate population that a technological society generates has recently focused more attention on mathematics teaching and attached more emphasis to it. The introduction of the National Curriculum, with mathematics as one of the core subjects, demonstrates this attitude.

The growth of a variety of mathematics schemes, with different aims and objectives, has reduced the usefulness of nationally normed tests of attainment in mathematics, though the National Curriculum may swing the pendulum back in this direction. Recently, several projects have been aimed at examining the nature of children's special needs in mathematics in general and arithmetical operations in particular. Many of the newer projects emphasise behaviourally based teaching methods, involving *mastery learning* techniques.

See *DISTAR*.

References:

Department of Education and Science (1982) *Mathematics Counts* (*The Cockcroft Report*), London, HMSO.

Larcombe, T. (1985) *Mathematical Learning Difficulties in the Secondary School*, Milton Keynes, Open University Press.

Womack, D. (1988) *Developing Mathematical and Scientific Thinking in Young Children*, London, Cassell.

art therapy, treatment of *emotional and behavioural difficulties*, using the materials and techniques of the visual arts, in particular drawing and painting. Art therapists may rely heavily on the psychoanalytic belief that creative productions can symbolise feelings that may not be easily put into words. The drawings are interpreted in order to help the child gain insight into his or her situation. At the same time a creative activity can of itself generate a sense of well-being, accompanied by a feeling of achievement and confidence, and a child's personal relationships may improve for this reason too.

References:

Dalley, T. (Ed.) (1984) *Art as Therapy: an introduction to the use of art as a therapeutic technique*, London, Tavistock.

Reynolds, M. (1979) 'Art', in Upton, G. (Ed.) (1979) *Physical and Creative Activities for the Mentally Handicapped*, Cambridge, Cambridge University Press.

Segal, S. (Ed.) (1990) *Creative Arts and Mental Disability*, Bicester, AB Academic Publishers.

articulation disorder, incorrect production of the speech sounds, or *phonemes*, leading to unclear speech. Since most young children make such errors as they learn to speak, the presence of an articulation disorder is often judged by comparing a child's speech pattern with normal expectations for the age group.

Articulation disorders are usually classified into substitutions (wobin for robin), omissions (ha for hat), distortions (a lisp, in which the s sound is attempted but produced incorrectly) and additions (chairn for chair). They are investigated and treated by speech therapists in the first instance.

See *Edinburgh Articulation Test, speech disorder.*

Reference:

Webster, A. and McConnell, C. (1987) *Children with Speech and Language Difficulties*, London, Cassell.

ascertainment, used to describe the process of identifying children needing special education, established by the regulations which followed the *Education Act 1944*. The term has now largely dropped out of use.

asphyxia, literally without breath, a condition which can occur during the birth process and which may be the cause of some of the handicapping conditions which lead to special educational needs. There are various possible reasons why asphyxia can occur during birth. Whatever the reason, the effects of asphyxia are serious. Obviously, prolonged asphyxia must result in death: shorter periods can result in different kinds of brain damage. For example, *cerebral palsy* can be caused in this way, as can *sensori-neural hearing loss.*

See *hypoxia.*

assessment, measuring and evaluating, used widely in education, but referring particularly to the assessment of a child's competencies, or a course's effectiveness, or an institution's success.

Assessment has always been a central educational activity, nowhere less than in special education. Indeed it has been argued that the whole edifice of educational and psychological assessment rests upon the use from 1905 onwards of the Binet-Simon test of intelligence, developed to provide equitable identification of mentally handicapped children. Like so many bold claims this is an oversimplification, but as with many oversimplifications, it is partly true.

The Binet-Simon test illustrates what was for many years the main role of assessment in special education, namely the use of standardised tests to assess children. The fact that many classroom activities – the daily use of question and answer sessions, the regular provision and marking of teacher-made tasks, for example – are equally examples of assessment, even though non-standardised, was largely ignored. This heavy reliance on standardised tests met with resistance: 'You can't make a child heavier by weighing him' was an argument relatively easy to counter. Nevertheless, it served to indicate that much of the standardised testing which passed for assessment in special education had little relevance to the teacher in the classroom. To put it another way, unlike some *diagnostic testing* it had no link with the curriculum: it was *norm-referenced* and not *criterion-referenced.*

Assessment certainly served one purpose, namely classifying children into the *categories of handicap* that were part of the legal framework of special education in the UK until the passing of the *Education Act 1981*. This was particularly important for the ascertainment of educationally subnormal children, now children with *learning difficulties*. In this procedure the individual intelligence test featured heavily, even though this was not required by the *Education Act 1944*: voices were raised against this, too.

The arguments levelled against categorisation; the increasing stress being placed on criterion-referenced assessment; unhappiness with the thoughtless use of intelligence tests – all these and other factors led to significant changes in assessment for special education in the 1970s and 1980s. In the USA, *Public Law 94–142* required that handicapped children should be provided with an *Individual Education Program*, or IEP. In other words assessment had to be for an educational purpose. Similar consideration in the UK led to the Education Act 1981 abolishing categories of handicap and requiring that, for children with more serious special needs, assessment should be directed towards providing a *Statement of Special Educational Needs* (in Scotland a *Record of Needs*).

The procedures for assessing a child when special educational needs may be present are laid down in the UK regulations and follow the five stages suggested in the *Warnock Report*. When a child's needs can be met from within the school's own resources, perhaps as a result of an assessment by the teacher, or with the support of an advisory teacher or educational psychologist, the procedures are less prescriptive than suggested in the Warnock Report, allowing schools and local education authorities to make their own arrangements for the progressive extension of professional involvement, according to circumstances. When formal procedures are required, perhaps to consider a child for placement elsewhere, or to consider the need for extra resources within the child's own school, these procedures, which often involve assessment by a team of specialists, are carefully stipulated. The rights of the parents to information and to participation in the assessment procedures are carefully set out and must be met. So too are the requirements for regular review of Statements. (Note that since *Local Management of Schools* was introduced by the Education Act 1988, the authority can delegate provision for children with Statements of special educational need in ordinary schools, though retaining the duty to ensure that appropriate provision is being made.)

These procedures, while intended for the protection of the child and the family, have proved to be unwieldy in practice, and have led to considerable complaint, most particularly over the time taken from starting the assessment procedure to implementing the Statement. This is one of the issues which is likely to lead to pressure for change in the legislation.

While the developments in assessment in special education have emphasised the need for criterion-referenced procedures, in which the child is led to concentrate on a programme of work tailored to his/her own development, recent changes in the UK may move counter to this. The *Education Act 1988* requires all children to take national tests in the curriculum (Standard Assessment Tasks, or SATs) in order to see how well they match up to attainment targets and to encourage competition between schools. Progress will be monitored, assessed, recorded and reported at ages seven, eleven, fourteen and sixteen years. The position of children with special needs in these developments is unclear. If those pupils with Statements are excused the tests, then it has been argued that they are as effectively labelled as if they were categorised. To allow them to take national tests when they have been following a modified curriculum may be damaging to them and also adversely affect the performance of their school, a performance which it is intended to make public. On the other hand, the agencies engaged in producing SATs have been charged with ensuring that they are suitable for – or can be adapted to – pupils with special educational needs. These are issues which have yet to be thrashed out adequately.

References:

Department of Fducation and Science (1989) *Circular 22/89. Assessments and Statements of Special Educational Needs: Procedures within the Education, Health and Social Services*, London, Department of Education and Science. (Joint circular with Department of Health.)

Galloway, D. and Goodwin, C. (1987) *The Education of Disturbing Children*, Harlow, Longman.

Goacher, B., Evans, J., Welton, J. and Wedell, K. (1988) *Policy and Provision for Special Educational Needs: implementing the 1981 Education Act*, London, Cassell 1990.

Reason, R., Farrell, P. and Mittler, P. (1990) 'Changes in Assessment', in Entwistle, N. (Ed.) (1990) *Handbook of Educational Ideas and Practices*, London, Routledge.

Ysseldyke, J.E. (1987) 'Do Tests Help in Teaching?' *Journal of the Association for Child Psychology and Psychiatry*, 28, 1, 21–5

Task Group on Assessment and Testing – A Report (1987) London, Department of Education and Science.

assessment centre,

(1) in special education a diagnostic unit, staffed by a team which usually includes a teacher, social worker, doctor and psychologist, with the intention of making decisions about the best educational arrangements for children whose learning difficulties or behaviour disorders are complex. Sound decisions may require lengthy periods of observation and children may remain in the assessment centre for some months or more, education being provided there too.

(2) unit run by the local authority for the team assessment of children at the point of entry into care.

association test, *projective technique* in which the child states the first idea that comes to mind in response to a picture or word. The answers help a skilled psychologist diagnose feelings and attitudes that the child might not be able to express openly. Association tests are often used in clinical work based on psychoanalytic principles.

asthma, constriction of the air passages in the lungs, leading to wheezing and breathing difficulties. It is a common disease of childhood, and while estimates of prevalence vary, it is probable that at least 5% of children in the UK suffer from some form of asthma.

The attainments and abilities of asthmatic children are broadly similar to those of their peers, except for the effects of the interruption of schooling that severe asthmatics suffer. In school, teachers need to be aware that asthmatic children may be on medication which affects their behaviour, making them drowsy, or perhaps more active, depending on the course of treatment. Since undue stress is one of the causes of asthma, this should be avoided as far as is consistent with a normal educational programme. And since asthma can be caused by allergies, teachers should be alert for any clue to an asthma-provoking substance or situation. Consultation with the parent or doctor is obviously important. Although asthma is a serious condition and an asthma attack can be frightening, the great majority of asthmatic children should be able to enjoy a normal education.

References:

Dinnage, R. and Gooch, S. (1986) *The Child with Asthma*, Windsor, NFER-Nelson.

Marsh, G.E., Price, B.J. and Smith, T.E.C. (1983) *Teaching Mildly Handicapped Children*, St. Louis, Mosby.

astigmatism, blurred, distorted vision due to an irregularly shaped eyeball. It can be corrected with special lenses.

Aston Index, a test designed at Aston University to identify children with language difficulties in general and *dyslexia* in particular. It is given at two levels; Level 1 is essentially a *screening test* for children between five and seven years, while Level 2 is essentially a *diagnostic test* for children from seven years upwards, intended to suggest an appropriate remedial programme. The Index assesses a number of verbal and performance skills associated with the development of literacy, and all the items are chosen for easy use by teachers. But many of the items have to be given individually, and hence one of the criticisms of the Index is the time required.

At Level 1 the effectiveness of the Index as a predictive device for screening young children with later literacy difficulties has been questioned. There are doubts, too, about the need to expose children to such a battery of tests at so early an age. At Level 2, there is little convincing evidence of the effectiveness of programmes built on the diagnostic findings. Nevertheless the Index is fairly widely used by teachers and others, who find that it does meet a need for a comprehensive instrument.

References:

Lindsay, G. (Ed.) (1984) *Screening for Children with Special Needs*, London, Croom Helm.

Pumfrey, P.D. (Ed.) (1985, 2nd edn.) *Reading: Tests and Assessment Techniques*, Sevenoaks, Hodder and Stoughton in association with UKRA.

Aston Portfolio Assessment Checklist, aims to link identified reading, spelling and writing problems with specific remediation procedures. Children deemed to be underachieving are assessed in order to identify which skills are weak. Teaching cards associated with particular skills provide programmes to be used by teacher.

The validity of the methods used for identification of weakness, resting on the ability–attainment discrepancy, is open to question, and although the Portfolio is popular with teachers, thorough evidence of its value is awaited.

Reference:

Pumfrey, P.D. (1985, 2nd edn.) *Reading: Tests and Assessment Techniques*, Sevenoaks, Hodder and Stoughton in association with UKRA.

at-risk register, or high-risk register, list of children identified as at-risk in some way and likely to need special attention later. In the 1960s many local authorities instituted registers of new-born children at risk developmentally, in order to ensure that their progress was carefully monitored. In some areas at-risk registers for particular conditions, e.g. *hearing impairment*, were compiled. Although the rationale for such registers is attractive, most have been abandoned, partly because of the possibility of overlooking other children with difficulties who are not included on the register in the first instance and partly because of the anxiety that a listing might cause to parents.

For these – and other – reasons, the Warnock Report recommended against the use of at-risk registers for children with educational difficulties, arguing that careful observation of all children was essential.

Nevertheless, mounting social concern over the ill-treatment of children has led social services to keep a register of children who are or might be in danger of physical, emotional or sexual abuse or mental cruelty within the family.

See *screening*.

References:

Committee on Child Health Services (1976) *Fit for the Future* (The Court Report), London, HMSO.

Lindsay, G. (Ed.) (1984) *Screening for Children with Special Needs*, London, Croom Helm.

ataxia, poor muscular coordination, characterised by lack of balance and an unsteady gait. It is the name given to a form of *cerebral palsy*, linked with damage to the brain, involving the functions of the cerebellum. Children who are ataxic will have some difficulties with many areas of the curriculum, most obviously those involving physical activity, not forgetting writing. The extent to which the curriculum has to be modified hinges on the severity of the ataxia; physiotherapy is certainly beneficial.

Reference:

Griffiths, M. and Clegg, M. (1988) *Cerebral Palsy; Problems and Practice*, London, Souvenir Press.

athetosis, form of *cerebral palsy*, characterised by slow, writhing movements of the limbs. The movements are involuntary, i.e. cannot be controlled. This is one difference between athetosis and other forms of cerebral palsy, in which there is often difficulty in initiating movement rather than stopping it. Children with athetosis may need help from therapists in order to manage adequately feeding activities such as chewing and swallowing. Speech may also be affected, perhaps by uncontrollable movements of the tongue. As with all children with cerebral palsy, vision and hearing will need careful examination and although intellectual skills may be good, in the majority of children with athetosis there will be learning difficulties.

Reference:

Griffiths, M. and Clegg, M. (1988) *Cerebral Palsy; Problems and Practice*, London, Souvenir Press.

attainment, performance in an educational skill and hence a central concept in special education and in *learning difficulties* in particular. Attainment is broadly distinguished from concepts such as intelligence and personality and its measurement has occupied educational psychologists for generations.

While an attainment test is essentially a measure of what a child has learnt, no more and no less, nevertheless the way in which that attainment is measured has been a source of concern. Thus many attainment tests are *norm-referenced*, encouraging comparison of a child's performance with that of others. While this has its place, making a fetish of such comparisons at the expense of devising a suitable programme for an individual does not.

As an example of norm-referenced procedures, many tests of reading attainment express their results as reading ages, enabling comparisons to be made between a child's performance and that of other age-groups. Thus a child with a reading age of 8.0 years is reading as well as the average child of that age on the test's standardisation sample.

Some attainment tests provide results in the form of attainment quotients, originally calculated as the ratio of the reading and chronological ages, expressed as a percentage. Thus a child aged 10.0 years, with a reading age of 8.0 years, would have a reading quotient of 80 ($8.0/10.0 \times 100$). This enables a child's performance to be compared with that of his own age-group, rather than others. More precise comparisons within the age-group are made through the use of deviation quotients, often based on a mean score of 100 and a standard deviation of fifteen points.

With the advent of the *Education Act 1988*, national standards for attainment in school subjects will be set, with regular assessments at specified ages. This approach can be contrasted with the importance of assessing the whole child in his/her environment, which has increasingly characterised the practice of special education; assessing attainment alone attaches undue importance to one segment only of the educational process. The effects of these developments on the education of children with special needs have yet to be seen.

See *ability–attainment controversy, assessment, mastery learning.*

References:

Reason, R., Farrell, P. and Mittler, P. (1990) 'Changes in Assessment', in Entwistle, N. (Ed.) (1990) *Handbook of Educational Ideas and Practices*, London, Routledge.

Task Group on Assessment and Testing – A Report (1987) London, Department of Education and Science.

attendance allowance, cash allowance paid to people who are physically or mentally severely disabled, and also in need of considerable attendance or supervision. To be eligible to receive the allowance, which will be paid to their parents, children must be two years of age or over, and must be in need of attention or supervision which is substantially in excess of that normally required by a child of the same age and sex.

Attendance allowance is not means-tested and is paid free of tax. The amount payable depends on the regulations currently in force.

Reference:

Department of Health and Social Security (1985, revised) *Non-contributory Benefits for Disabled People*, London, HMSO.

attendance officer, see *education welfare officer.*

attendance order, order served by a local education authority on parents requiring them to send their child to school regularly or otherwise satisfy the authority that suitable educational provision has been made for the child. If the parents fail to comply, the authority can take legal proceedings against them.

See *educational welfare officer.*

Attention Deficit Disorder (ADD), diagnostic category used by the American Psychiatric Association to define a group of symptoms roughly equivalent to the former 'hyperactive child syndrome'. The change in title reflects the view that lack of attention, rather than excess activity, is the key feature of this condition, though both are often present, when the preferred diagnosis on this system is 'Attention Deficit Hyperactivity Disorder', or ADHD. The category was formulated to lend order to an area of behaviour that had given rise to a variety of names, e.g. minimal brain damage, hyperkinetic child, minimal cerebral dysfunction, etc., as well as hyperactivity. In spite of the attempt to lend more precision to its diagnosis, the condition remains difficult to identify reliably. Indeed some findings suggest that lack of attention and hyperactivity may well be two separate dimensions, often accompanying each other, but nevertheless unrelated.

Teachers characterising a child as very restless, fidgety, unable to sit still, always 'on the go', impulsive and easily distracted, are describing the ADD syndrome. In the USA it is often assumed that aggressive, antisocial behaviour is an additional associated feature. These and other variations in criteria mean that large differences in prevalence rates are to be expected: figures ranging from 0.1% to 40% have been quoted, but 3 to 6% is a more usual finding, with sex (boys are significantly more vulnerable than girls) and age affecting rates.

Many causes have been suggested – neurological damage; food additives and other inappropriate diets; inadequate social training; etc. None is entirely satisfactory as an explanation. For example, while some children with brain damage may show ADD, not all do. Nevertheless, the probability that physiological conditions may be one of the causes has led to a variety of dietary and pharmacological treatments. While the dietary regimes have been controversial, the use of drugs has been a burning issue, regarded by some as an assault on the child's personality. In the classroom, because of the need to be sure that the physical possibilities have been investigated, medical involvement is important. Without sustained attention, educational progress can be seriously affected and these children can show significant learning difficulties. Their behaviour is an obvious source of concern, too, not only intrinsically, but also because of its effect on other members of the class. Teachers may well wish to air their concerns to the parents, only to find that parents themselves are equally concerned at the effect of their child's behaviour on their home and social life.

Behaviour therapy has been used with some success, both at school and in the home. In the end, a planned programme, often combining approaches drawn from different disciplines is most likely to improve matters.

See *Feingold Diet.*

References:

American Psychiatric Association (1987, 3rd edn. revised) *Diagnostic and Statistical Manual of Mental Disorders*, Washington, American Psychiatric Association.

Barker, P. (1988, 5th edn.) *Basic Child Psychiatry*, Oxford, Blackwell.

Egger, J., Carter, C.M., Graham, P.J., Gumley, D. and Soothill, J.F. (1985) 'Controlled Trial of Oligoantigenic Diet in the Hyperkinetic Syndrome', *Lancet*, 9th March 1985, 540–5.

Gearheart, B.R. (1981) *Learning Disabilities: Educational Strategies*, London, Mosby.

Holden, H. (1981) 'Hyperactive Children: a Review of Research', *Highlight*, 46, London, National Children's Bureau.

attitude scale, method of measuring the strength of an attitude, e.g. a pupil's attitude towards schoolwork. There are various kinds of scales, but most are composed of a series of simple and relevant statements, e.g.

Maths is an enjoyable lesson

which together constitute a scale of known validity and reliability.

The pupil is asked to check one of a number of possible responses to each statement, ranging from strong disagreement to strong agreement. The responses to the set of statements are converted into an attitude score.

Attitude scores are useful in various ways; as well as attitudes to schoolwork, a child's attitude to peers, to relations, to herself or himself, for example, can all be assessed by attitude scales and the scores can be helpful in counselling pupils with learning and behavioural difficulties. Nevertheless an attitude scale is only one method of enquiry, to be used judiciously and usually in combination with other observations and techniques.

Reference:

Pratkanis, A.R., Breckler, S.J. and Greenwald, A.G. (1989) *Attitude Structure and Function*, Hemel Hempstead, Erlbaum.

audiogram, graph of a child's hearing thresholds. A pure-tone audiogram is met most often, and on this (see illustration) the horizontal axis represents sound pitch, or *frequency*, measured in cycles per second (cps), or Hertz (Hz), while the vertical axis represents loudness, or intensity, measured in *decibels* (dB). Each point on the graph represents the intensity at which a

Pure-tone audiogram

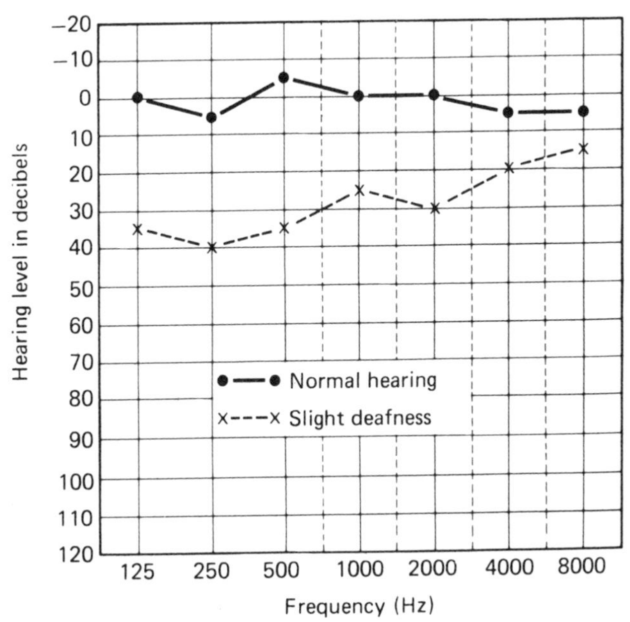

child can just hear sound of that particular pitch. Measurements are usually made at five or six different frequencies, and the hearing of the right and left ears shown separately.

Sound thresholds are usually measured for both air conduction and bone conduction. For air conduction, pure tones are presented through headphones into the ear canal, where the air-conducted signals vibrate the eardrum and middle-ear structures. For bone conduction the test signal is presented through a small vibrator placed on the skull, usually the mastoid bone behind the ear, thus reaching the inner ear through the bones of the skull and effectively by-passing the middle ear. A normally-hearing person will hear signals conducted through the air and bone at approximately the same level of intensity; any discrepancies therefore provide important diagnostic indicators, particularly about the workings of the middle ear.

In real life, pure tones are rarely encountered. The complex pattern of tones and overtones that constitute speech are met far more frequently. Although a pure-tone audiogram is important diagnostically, a speech audiogram (see illustration), which presents the results of testing a child's hearing for speech, is more relevant. Here, the horizontal axis represents the levels of intensity, or loudness at which standard lists of words are presented to the child, and the vertical axis represents the percentage of those words correctly heard. Audiograms such as these and the results of other tests enable a trained *audiologist* to make inferences about the nature and extent of a child's *hearing impairment*, and to suggest appropriate intervention.

See *audiometry*.

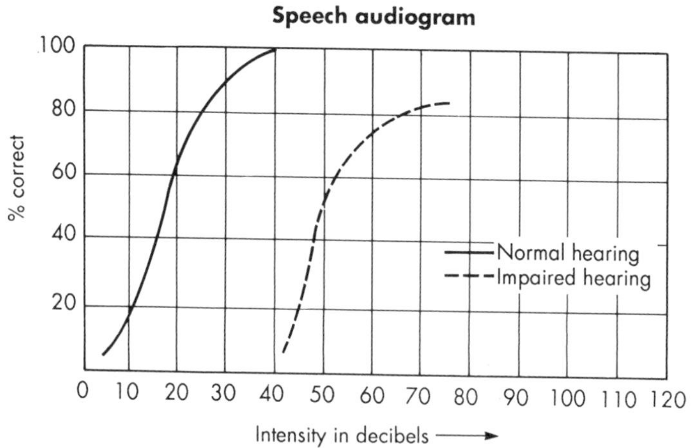

References:

Reed, M. (1984) *Educating Hearing-Impaired Children*, Milton Keynes, Open University Press.

Webster, A. and Ellwood, J. (1985) *The Hearing-Impaired Child in the Ordinary Classroom*, Beckenham, Croom Helm.

Webster, A. and Wood, D. (1989) *Children with Hearing Difficulties*, London, Cassell.

audiologist, non-medical specialist in the study and evaluation of hearing and *hearing impairment.* Audiologists carry out audiometric examinations, provide information for the diagnosis of deafness and the prescription and monitoring of hearing-aids, and can help teachers over classroom procedures for pupils with hearing loss. They are usually hospital-based, and work in close collaboration with medical and other colleagues.

Reference:

Foulkes, A. and Fitzsimons, R. (1986) 'The Role of the Linked Agencies', in Coupe, J. and Porter, J. (Eds.) (1986) *The Education of Children with Severe Learning Difficulties.*

audiometry, the measurement of hearing. This is usually associated with the pure-tone audiometer, an instrument for providing sounds of precise pitch and intensity in order to determine hearing thresholds, presented as an *audiogram.* It is the pure-tone audiometer which is usually used for screening schoolchildren in order to identify those who may need further hearing investigations.

Pure-tone audiometry can measure hearing thresholds for both air-conduction, when sound is conducted to the inner ear via air in the ear canal, and bone-conduction, when sound is conducted to the inner ear via the bones of the skull. Pure-tone audiometry is contrasted with speech audiometry, in which hearing for the complicated pattern of tones and overtones that constitute speech is measured. But these are only two of an increasingly sophisticated set of techniques for assessing hearing.

In impedance audiometry, an instrument is used to measure the amount of sound reflected by the eardrum when a sound wave reaches it, thus giving useful diagnostic information about the efficiency of the middle ear and possible conductive hearing loss. Brainstem electrical response audiometry (BSER, or *electric response audiometry*) is one of a number of specialised procedures which measure the tiny voltages generated in the nerves of the hearing system as they respond to sound.

For young children, and others who are difficult to test, conditioning techniques can be used. The examiner 'conditions' the child to respond to a stimulus (such as 'go') by dropping a brick into a box or fitting a peg into a board. Once the desired response has been established, sounds of different intensities and pitch can be used to determine whether they too produce the response. The hearing profile is again shown as an audiogram. The technique is often treated as an enjoyable game, but it is specialised and lengthy.

Very young babies may be tested in an auditory response cradle (ARC). A computer is used to present sounds to new-born babies. The baby lies in a special cradle, housing sensors which identify changes in bodily activity, head movement and breathing, in response to the sounds. The ARC has been heralded as the screening method of the future for early identification of hearing loss, but it is not entirely problem-free and other techniques such as auditory brainstem response screening may come to the fore.

What cannot be overemphasised in the assessment of hearing is the importance of careful observation of a child's response to sounds. It is this – qualitative audiometry, perhaps – which often provides the first clue that hearing impairment may lie behind the difficult behaviour, or lack of attention, or learning difficulties that concern the teacher in the classroom or the parent in the home.

See *ear, hearing impairment; visual reinforcement audiometry.*

References:

Bishop, J. and Gregory, S. (1986) 'Disorders of Language and Communication', in Gillham, W.E.C. (Ed.) (1986) *Handicapping Conditions in Childhood*, Beckenham, Croom Helm.

Tucker, I. and Nolan, M. (1984) *Educational Audiology*, Beckenham, Croom Helm.

Webster, A. and Wood, D. (1989) *Children with Hearing Difficulties*, London, Cassell.

auditory aphasia, see *receptive language disorder.*

auditory discrimination, ability to differentiate sounds. Although just noticable differences in loudness (intensity) or pitch (frequency) between pure tones can be used as measures of auditory discrimination, it is the ability to discriminate speech sounds which, perhaps, has most relevance. Clearly, this has great importance for language development: a child who cannot perceive the difference between the sounds of 'bat' and 'bad' may have problems with comprehension, speech, reading and other language skills.

There are a number of techniques available for testing the discrimination of speech sounds. One of the most popular classroom scales, used with children between five and eight years of age, is Wepman's Auditory Discrimination Test. The tester reads pairs of words from a given list. In some pairs, both words are identical, whereas in others they differ slightly (e.g. 'fit' and 'pit'). The child has to indicate whether the words are the same or not. If discrimination is poor, and hearing is satisfactory, a remedial programme has to be instituted.

See *auditory training.*

Reference:

Pumfrey, P.D. (Ed.) (1985. 2nd edn.) *Reading: Tests and Assessment Techniques*, Sevenoaks, Hodder and Stoughton, in association with UKRA.

auditory feedback, feedback through sound, as when we hear our own speech and so can correct its production. Hearing-impaired children may not have full auditory feedback; if they cannot hear the full range of speech sounds they produce, or the sounds heard are distorted, it is correspondingly harder for them to learn to produce clear speech. In delayed auditory feedback, equipment ensures that speech reaches the speaker's ear momentarily later than normal. This procedure can be used in the treatment of *stammering.*

auditory perception, the ability to extract meaning from sounds. Children may 'hear' sounds, in the sense that the hearing mechanism may detect them, but not be able to interpret them. Where one person hears a string of sounds, another may hear a musical theme. The musical analogy can be extended to spoken language. A child whose hearing is perfect on examination, who is intelligent and bright, may yet have significant difficulties in language development. Such a child may have problems with auditory perception. Auditory perception can be analysed into a set of component skills, including *auditory discrimination*, auditory recall, etc., each of which can be separately assessed and a remediation programme based on the findings.

See *language disorder.*

auditory response cradle, see *audiometry.*

auditory training, a teaching programme designed to improve listening skills and selective attention. A programme might start by presenting marked phonetic contrasts, then gradually minimising differences to sharpen a child's attention to relevant distinctions.

Augmented Roman, see *initial teaching alphabet.*

aura, sensation which may be experienced before an attack of *epilepsy* or migraine. For epilepsy, the aura is associated with the part of the brain in which the fit originates; if it starts within the temporal region, for example, lights, colours, sounds, smells or other sensations may occur, depending on the exact location involved. For migraine, the aura is usually characterised by dizziness and blurred vision. The aura is useful, for it enables a child to warn a teacher or parent and to prepare for an attack.

Australian Council for Educational Research (ACER), a national independent organisation which supports, conducts and publishes educational research. It is funded by grants from various sources, including the Commonwealth and State governments. It publishes a bulletin on special education for Australian educators and is the main source of supply in Australia for tests and other materials used in special education.

Reference:

Further details from Radford House, Frederick St., Hawthorn, Victoria 3122, Australia.

autism, a condition which appears in very young children, sometimes described as infantile autism or childhood autism, and sometimes as Kanner's syndrome, after the author of the classic paper on it.

Autism has been a controversial condition. Initially, many diagnosticians found it difficult to distinguish from mental retardation or language disorder, the former being often and the latter always present in autism. Moreover the bizarre behaviour which many autistic children show led some to consider it a variant of childhood schizophrenia. Recently, there is more general agreement that autism is a separate condition, identified by the presence together of four characteristics, *viz.* failure to develop normal social relationships, perhaps treating people as objects; poor communication skills, language development being both deviant and delayed; rigid, inflexible behaviour, resulting in bizarre mannerisms and habits; onset before 30 months of age. With these diagnostic criteria, the prevalence rate is about four or five per 10,000, boys outnumbering girls by about three to one.

Kanner believed that autism was mainly found in middle class families, caused by a cold and undemonstrative relationship between parents and children. More recent work has discounted this view. It is now believed that many different factors may be operating, and autism may be the outcome of a neurological impairment or a biochemical abnormality, perhaps genetic in origin, or the result of illness in infancy. In short there is no single, clearcut cause.

Since education depends so centrally on communication, autistic children obviously have special educational needs. Athough some autistic children are educated in the ordinary school, many attend special schools or units. Emphasis has been placed on the design of behaviourally-based programmes aimed at improving communication skills, and which involve parents as well as school staff. A structured educational environment, allied to systematic teaching, is better than a relatively free approach. Provision for autistic adolescents and adults, which has been a serious problem, is improving.

References:

Elgar, S. and Wing, L. (1977 reprint), *Teaching Autistic Children*, Stratford-upon-Avon, National Council for Special Education and the National Society for Autistic Children.

Graham, P.J. (1986) *Child Psychiatry: a Developmental Approach*, Oxford, Oxford University Press.

Rutter, M. and Schopler, E. (Eds.) (1978) *Autism: a Reappraisal of Concepts and Treatment*, New York, Plenum.

Wilson, D. (1986) 'Autism', in Gillham, W.E.C. (Ed.) (1986) *Handicapping Conditions in Childhood*, Beckenham, Croom Helm.

automatism, repeated behaviour, e.g. rocking, head banging, lipsmacking, which may be self-stimulating. Automatism is sometimes found in association with severe learning difficulties or severe emotional disturbance, and *behaviour modification* is frequently used to manage it.

See *self-injurious behaviour.*

autosome, any chromosome that is not a sex chromosome and which appears as one of an identical pair in the human body cell. Autosomal inheritance is the transmission of characteristics from parents to children through the pattern of genes carried on the autosomes. Many hereditary conditions, whether resulting in physical or mental impairment or both, are the result

of a defective gene on an autosome. *Cystic fibrosis* and *phenylketonuria* are two of many examples with implications for special education.
See *genetics*.

aversion therapy, a form of *behaviour therapy* in which unpleasant experiences are used to control unwanted behaviour. For example, an alcoholic may be made to feel nausea each time alcohol is taken. Aversion therapy has been used in the treatment of problems such as drug abuse, or sexual perversions. *Punishment,* for example slapping a child who is misbehaving, is a kind of aversion therapy which used to be practised in the classroom. While this can be effective, the disadvantages are serious. The use of aversion therapy with adults, though controversial, escapes most of the arguments against punishment when it is restricted to adults who have given permission for its use.
Reference:
Alberto, P.A. and Troutman, A.C. (1986, 2nd edn.) *Applied Behavior Analysis for Teachers,* Columbus, Merrill.

avoidant disorder, see *withdrawn behaviour.*

Ayres therapy, method of treating learning and behaviour problems, mainly by a pattern of movement exercises. Ayres found that occupational therapy for children's sensory integration problems improved their academic performances. She developed this finding into a theory that some learning disorders are linked to inadequate neurological functioning, in particular to inadequate sensory integration at a sub-cortical level. Ayres therapy provides tests to assess sensory integration and treatment procedures to stimulate it.
Reference:
Levitt, S. (Ed.) (1984) *Paediatric Development Therapy,* Oxford, Blackwell.

B

Babinski reflex, reaction to stroking the sole of the foot, causing the toes to move upwards and outwards. After the first year of life, or thereabouts, this is replaced by a downward movement of the toes, except in some pathological states. For this reason the reflex can be used diagnostically in medical examinations.

backward chaining, see *chaining.*

backwardness, educational attainments which are below the average of the age-group. The use of the word declined markedly after the 1960s, but it will be met in some of the classic texts on special education.

Backwardness could refer to low attainments in a single subject, e.g. reading, in which case the extent of the backwardness was the difference between a child's *reading age* and chronological age. Backwardness was sometimes regarded as a discrete condition, and in this case a criterion had to be laid down, often an eighteen-month or two-year gap in performance. This criterion had its roots in the age-based 'standards' for primary classes laid down by the Board of Education in the 19th century, for a child with low attainments could, it was argued, be taught with children a year or so younger, but not with those two years or so younger: in this latter case special (i.e. separate) education was required.

With the increasing use of concepts such as *criterion-referenced testing* and *mastery learning*, with less emphasis on group teaching, and also with the opprobrium that the word backwardness itself generated, it has fallen into disuse. Nevertheless there is an inherent appeal in comparing a child's performance with norms for age-groups, and the idea of backwardness still has considerable currency, even if the term itself does not.

See *retardation*, with which backwardness is sometimes (incorrectly) confounded.

References:

Burt, C. (1937) *The Backward Child*, London, ULP.

Tansley, P. and Panckhurst, J. (1981) *Children with Specific Learning Difficulties; a Critical Review of Research*, Windsor, NFER-Nelson.

Balthazar Scales of Adaptive Behavior (BSAB), scales standardised in the USA on institutionalised persons aged five to 57 years, with IQs below 35, and measuring functional independence (eating, dressing and toileting) and social adaptation (self-directed behaviour, interpersonal behaviour, play activity, response to instructions, personal care, etc.).

See *adaptive behaviour.*

Reference:

Raynes, N.V. (1987) 'Adaptive Behaviour Scales', in Hogg, J. and Raynes, N.V. (Eds.) (1987) *Assessment in Mental Handicap*, Beckenham, Croom Helm.

banding, see *ability grouping.*

barbiturates, group of drugs that act to depress the activity of the central nervous system. While their main use is as sedatives to promote sleep, the more rapidly-acting barbiturates (e.g. sodium pentothal) are used as anaesthetics, and the slower-acting ones (e.g. phenobarbitone) are used for the relief of tension and anxiety and also for controlling attacks of epilepsy. In children, phenobarbitone prescribed as an anticonvulsant often produces drowsiness, but may sometimes produce side effects of irritability and hyperactivity.

See *anticonvulsant.*

basal age, concept used in scoring educational and psychological tests which group items by age. In these tests, the highest age at which a child can pass all the items is the basal age. Thus if in a test of mathematics, a child passes all the items up to and including all those for ten-year-olds, but makes a first failure on one of the eleven-year items, then ten is that child's basal age for that test of mathematics. In arriving at the child's mathematics age, credit would be given for items passed above the basal age.

See *ceiling.*

basal reading program, see *basic reading scheme.*

baseline data, data obtained at or before the start of an experiment. In special education the term is largely used for the measurement of the behaviour to be changed through planned intervention, using behaviour modification principles. Thus if it is desired to reduce the frequency of a child's interruptions in class, a careful record of the frequency of those interruptions over specified periods (baseline data) would first be obtained. This would enable the effect of the intervention to be shown, both mathematically and diagrammatically. In effect baseline data resemble pretest scores, though pretest measures tend to be associated with classical experimental methodology involving groups of subjects and generalisable results, whereas baseline data tend to be associated with single-case experiments.

For baseline data to be sound, the behaviour to be measured should be carefully specified, and the data itself should be stable, i.e. not showing marked fluctuations in frequency. Allowable limits for data fluctuations are suggested in the literature.

See *applied behaviour analysis, multiple baseline designs.*

References:

Alberto, P.A. and Troutman, A.C. (1986, 2nd edn.) *Applied Behavior Analysis for Teachers,* Columbus, Merrill.

Shapiro, E.S. (1987) *Behavioral Assessments in School Psychology,* New York, Erlbaum.

basic reading scheme (USA basal reading program), a graded series of reading books and related materials for the systematic teaching of reading. Some commercial schemes provide a complete range of material for teaching reading, often including teachers' manual, graded readers, collections of supplementary stories, and in many cases tapes, work-books, diagnostic tests, etc.

Basic reading schemes, unfortunately, are the staple materials through which many children learn to read at school. Their attraction lies in the fact that they appear to demonstrate pupils' progress in reading: 'I'm on book three!' They are nevertheless open to criticism, not least on the grounds of their controlled vocabulary and word repetition, which does not suit all children and causes some to lose interest. Many of the older schemes have been criticised on the grounds that they offer stereotyped sex-roles, their largely middle-class values and experiences may be inappropriate for children from minority backgrounds, and because their controlled vocabularies result in unnatural language and deny pupils the opportunity to predict linguistic structures. Many more recent schemes are attractively designed and avoid these pitfalls, but are often over-elaborate. Many schools therefore eschew commercial schemes and select books to meet the developing interests, needs and abilities of their pupils.

See *individualised reading.*

Reference:

Department of Education and Science (1975) *A Language for Life*, London, HMSO (Bullock Report).

basic sight vocabulary, limited number of irregular words which appear frequently in early reading material, e.g. 'was', 'one', 'their', etc. Since they cannot be taught by phonic methods, children are taught to recognise them on sight.

basic skills, traditionally, the basic subjects of reading, writing and arithmetic, i.e. the skills deemed necessary to function in society. But changing emphases lead to different analyses, and many would want to add other language skills, such as proficiency in oral communication, or social skills to their list.

BATPACK, Behavioural Approach to Teaching Package, set of materials designed to underpin a course of six one-hour sessions for serving teachers. The course aims to develop competence in behavioural skills such as effective reinforcement, specifying behaviour, rule-setting, etc.

The materials, which were developed at the University of Birmingham, include a manual, video, work-books, and transparencies, and are available only to trained and registered tutors. BATPACK has been fairly widely used in recent years and there is evidence on its effectiveness for improving the set of skills it targets.

See *precision teaching.*

Reference:

Wheldall, K., Merrett, M., Worsley, M., Colmar, S. and Parry, R. (1986) 'Evaluating Effectiveness: a Case-study Evaluation of the Behavioural Approach to Teaching Package', *Educational and Child Psychology*, 3, 1, 33–44.

battered child syndrome, battered baby syndrome, see *child abuse.*

Bayley Scales of Infant Development, set of tests standardised on infants aged between two and thirty months and resulting from a long-standing research project. The material consists of an Infant Behaviour Record and two scales, the Motor Scale, which assesses skills such as sitting, standing, walking and manipulation, and the Mental Scale, which assesses memory, communication, problem-solving, etc. The tests are intended to provide a measure of current functioning, and while very low scores do indicate a high risk of mental retardation, prediction of future development based on a single assessment on these scales alone is extremely hazardous.

Reference:

Berger, M. and Yule, W. (1987) 'Psychometric Approaches', in Hogg, J. and Raynes, N.V. (Eds.) (1987) *Assessment in Mental Handicap*, Beckenham, Croom Helm.

Behavior Development Survey, modified and shorter form of the *AAMD Adaptive Behavior Scale.* Like its parent scale, the survey is in two parts, one covering the skills of daily living and the other personality characteristics.

Reference:

Raynes, N.V. (1987) 'Adaptive Behaviour Scales', in Hogg, J. and Raynes, N.V. (Eds.) (1987) *Assessment in Mental Handicap*, Beckenham, Croom Helm.

behaviour disorder, see *emotional and behavioural difficulties.*

behaviour modelling, learning a new skill by copying a model. Demonstrating 'how to do it' is one of the basic techniques of teaching, and some of the characteristics of successful modelling were pointed out by social psychologists. Since modelling has been incorporated into the repertoire of behavioural methods, it has been further analysed. Among the important points to consider are the status of the person providing the model (not necessarily the teacher), the reinforcement received for successful modelling, the kind of skills for which modelling is most suitable, etc.

Apart from its use in teaching, modelling has been used in the treatment of learning disorders and various emotional and behavioural disorders, notably fears and avoidance behaviour, social skill deficits and conduct problems.

See *behaviour modification.*

References:

Alberto, P.A. and Troutman, A.C. (1986, 2nd edn.) *Applied Behavior Analysis for Teachers*, Columbus, Merrill.

Herbert, M. (1987, 2nd edn.) *Conduct Disorders of Children and Adolescents; a social learning perspective*, Chichester, Wiley.

behaviour modification, the use of learning theory, in particular *operant conditioning* principles such as *reinforcement,* to change behaviour. *Time-out, chaining,* and *behaviour shaping,* are examples of some of the procedures used in behaviour modification, which has been widely used with children with special needs. There is now a vast literature detailing successes gained following the application of behaviour modification techniques to children's learning and behavioural disorders, both within school and without. At the same time the introduction of behaviour modification programmes has generated controversy, partly because techniques such as psychosurgery or electric shock treatment are sometimes quite incorrectly thought to be associated with them, leading to unjustified anxieties on the part of parents and teachers. It is partly to avoid these anxieties that those procedures based on operant principles are now often collectively referred to as *applied behaviour analysis*. Sometimes, too, behaviour modification procedures involving *aversion therapy* in particular have been insensitively and inappropriately designed: the steps that should be followed in implementing a behaviour modification programme are similar to those described under the *applied behaviour analysis* entry.

Other objections to the use of behaviour modification techniques rest on the belief that attempts to change behaviour are in some way immoral, since they contravene an individual's freedom and smack of indoctrination or even brainwashing. This view has to be reconciled with the purpose of teaching, which is itself to change behaviour, and with the limitations placed on an individual's freedom (and the freedom of others) by the continued exercise of antisocial behaviour, for example.

See *applied behaviour analysis, behaviour therapy.*

Reference:

Harrop, A. (1983) *Behaviour Modification in the Classroom*, London, Hodder and Stoughton.

behaviour shaping, reinforcing successive approximations to the desired outcome, so that eventually the final behaviour is learnt. For example, children can be taught to write their names by reinforcing the first attempt, then showing how the attempt can be improved and reinforcing the improvement, until a sequence of reinforced improvements leads to the desired level of accuracy.

Shaping thus allows new behaviour to be built, rather than waiting until the required behaviour appears before reinforcing it. The criterion for reinforcement must gradually change, lest the first approximation itself becomes the learnt behaviour: finally only the desired outcome is reinforced. The skill in shaping lies in deciding which behaviours will be reinforced and which will not, i.e. applying a successful pattern of differential reinforcement.

See *behaviour modification.*

References:

Harrop, A. (1983) *Behaviour Modification in the Classroom*, London, Hodder and Stoughton.

Wheldall, K. and Merrett, F. (1984) *Positive Teaching: the Behaviourist Approach*, London, Allen and Unwin.

behaviour therapy, the use of principles derived from the psychology of learning to treat human problems. Since the psychology of learning is itself a broad church, behaviour therapy encompasses techniques based on a variety of theories. The most prominent are techniques based on *classical conditioning* (e.g. *aversion therapy*), *operant conditioning* (e.g. *behaviour shaping*), as well as social learning theory (e.g. *behaviour modelling*).

Although behaviour therapy is sometimes used as a synonym for one or other of the many possible approaches, particularly behaviour modification, it is essentially an umbrella term. Moreover the techniques are not necessarily mutually exclusive, and behaviour therapists sometimes use a combination of approaches from the available repertoires.

Behaviour therapy has been widely practised with children with special needs. Here the various methods have been applied to managing children's learning and behavioural difficulties. The contrast with *psychotherapy* based on psychoanalytic theory has been a source of longstanding and sometimes bitter controversy. Apart from the debate over the relative success of the two therapies, behaviour therapy has the great advantage that it does not need a lengthy and expensive training: many of the basic principles can be learnt and applied by both teachers and parents.

References:

Harrop, A. (1983) *Behaviour Modification in the Classroom*, London, Hodder and Stoughton.

Herbert, M. (1987) *Behavioural Treatment of Children with Problems: a Practice Manual*, London, Academic Press.

behavioural objective, target that the teacher wants the child to attain. A behavioural objective may be an item of knowledge, a skill, an attitude – any aspect of behaviour that can be taught. Behavioural objectives should state precisely what the child should be able to do after instruction, and should be testable in an unambiguous way. Testing is essential, so that teacher knows exactly what the child can actually do, rather than assuming this. 'Bill will be able to spell better this week.' is not an appropriate behavioural objective: 'Bill will be able to spell correctly nine out of the ten words taught this week on each of two oral tests on Friday.' is. Note that this latter statement specifies the outcome of the learning, the standard to be achieved, the number of trials involved and the conditions required.

The use of behavioural objectives is one example of the application of behavioural psychology to education. It involves analysing the aims of the curriculum into carefully graded teaching steps, each specified as a behavioural objective and each testable as the child progresses.

The use of behavioural objectives has been criticised on the grounds that it leads to a mechanical, rote approach to teaching, useful for the acquisition of routine skills, but not much else. Nevertheless it is at the heart of both *Direct Instruction* and *precision teaching*, both widely and successfully used with children with learning difficulties. Behavioural objectives fit more readily with individual than group teaching, and the idea of an *Individualised Education Program* owes a debt to this approach.

See *task analysis*.

References:

Ainscow, M. and Tweddle, D.A. (1981) 'The Objectives Approach: a Progress Report', in Somerset Education Authority, *Ways and Means 2*, Basingstoke, Globe Education.

Brennan, W.K. (1985) *Curriculum for Special Needs*, Milton Keynes, Open University Press.

behavioural tests of hearing, methods of assessing the hearing of very young or severely handicapped children. In essence these tests involve careful observation by an experienced observer of a child's response to sounds under controlled conditions. These are usually screening tests, followed by more thorough investigations if they suggest the presence of any hearing impairment.

See *distraction test*.

Reference:

Tucker, I. and Nolan, M. (1984) *Educational Audiology*, Beckenham, Croom Helm.

bell and pad method, procedure based on *classical conditioning* principles which is used in the treatment of nocturnal enuresis, or bed-wetting. A pad, wired to a battery-operated bell or buzzer, is placed under the bottom bedsheet and over a rubber sheet. When the pad gets wet the electrical circuit is completed and the bell or buzzer sounds. This wakes the child, who has to get out of bed, switch the alarm off, and go to the toilet. This establishes the habit of going to the toilet after waking up. Since bladder pressure always immediately precedes being woken up, this becomes the conditioned stimulus to going to the toilet.

The apparatus is not usually suitable for children below six years of age. But when it is used properly with older children, including full discussion beforehand, success rates as high as 90% have been achieved.

Reference:

Barker, P. (1988, 5th edn.) *Basic Child Psychiatry*, Oxford, Blackwell Scientific Publications.

Bellak Children's Apperception Test, see *Children's Apperception Test.*

Bender Visual Motor Gestalt Test, often referred to as the Bender Gestalt, or most simply as the Bender, after its constructor, Lauretta Bender. This test measures visual-motor maturation through asking the subject to reproduce in turn each of a set of nine designs. The extent to which children's reproductions deviate from expectations for their age-level provides diagnostic information in various areas. While the most frequent use of the test has been in providing indications to psychologists of possible neurological abnormality, or brain damage, it has also been used as an aid in the diagnosis of emotional and other problems. It can be used either as an individual or group test.

References:

Anastasi, A. (1982, 5th edn.) *Psychological Testing*, New York, Macmillan.

Bender, L. (1938) *A Visual Motor Gestalt Test and its Clinical Use*, American Orthopsychiatric Association.

Bene-Anthony Test, see *Family Relations Test.*

bereavement, is associated with a number of conditions for which at least extra care in school is needed. After bereavement, many children show a drop in school performance, mild depression and some withdrawn behaviour. In some children these consequences are more severe. Other reactions such as temper tantrums and bed-wetting can also appear, depending to some extent on the age and sex of the child. The teacher has to remember that bereavement may be a cause of these conditions and be aware of the child's need for support.

Reference:

Van Eerdewegh, M.W., Clayton, P.J. and Van Eerdewegh, P. (1985) 'The Bereaved Child: Variables Influencing Early Psychopathology', *British Journal of Psychiatry*, 147, 188–94.

Bereiter and Engelmann Program, North American *compensatory education* programme, aimed at preschool disadvantaged children and designed to make rapid improvements in the skills important for school progress. The programme saw language development as critical, including early reading and number skills. The children are taught formally in small groups, with little opportunity for creativity or self-expression, and this rigidity led many traditional nursery school teachers to oppose the programme. Nevertheless children who followed the programme showed marked gains. The *Direct Instruction* movement owes a considerable debt to this pioneering 1960s work.

See *Distar, mastery learning.*

Reference:

Bereiter, C. and Engelmann, S. (1966) *Teaching Disadvantaged Children in the Preschool*, Englewood Cliffs, Prentice Hall.

beta wave, see *electroencephalogram.*

bibliotherapy, the use of reading matter which helps children gain a deeper understanding of their own and others' problems. Often fictional stories are read, involving characters with whom the child can readily identify, after which feelings are discussed. Bibliotherapy can be an informal arrangement, with teachers using suitable texts in normal reading or English lessons, or it can be a more structured procedure, with specially written texts which offer guidance on points for discussion or self-help treatment programmes. Since it can be used with groups of children and without the intervention of skilled therapists, one of its advantages is its cost-effectiveness.

Reference:

Herbert, M. (1987, 2nd edn.) *Conduct Disorders of Childhood and Adolescence: a Social Learning Perspective*, Chichester, Wiley.

bilingualism, ability to use two languages, usually with different facility. Educational difficulties arise where the child's home or dominant language is not the language of instruction: some argue that these children have special educational needs.

In the USA the Bilingual Education Act aims to ensure that equal educational opportunities are offered to children of limited English proficiency (LEP). In the UK there has been no legal recognition of these needs, other than that conferred by the broad requirements of the *Education Act 1944*, and which led to the establishment of many language classes and units for the 'immigrant' children of the 1950s and 1960s. Circulars explaining current policy in the UK specifically state that children whose home language is not the language of instruction should not be regarded for this reason as children with a learning difficulty in the terms of the Education Act 1981.

This raises several issues. First, these children's special needs have to be assessed in their home language, for measures of competence couched in English and standardised on pupils from an English-speaking culture will be invalid, i.e. assessment materials in the home language and culture have to be available, since *culture-fair tests* have their deficiencies. Then the assessor will have to be proficient in the child's home language. Finally, if the child is shown to have special needs, teaching materials in the home language will be needed. All these three requirements, assessment instruments, staff and teaching materials are usually in short supply. Hence special education for bilingual children is an area with very special problems.

See *Diana v. State Board of Education of California* (1970).

References:

Cummins, J. (1984) *Bilingualism and Special Education,* Clevedon, Multilingual Matters.

Department of Education and Science (1989) *Circular 22/89, Assessments and Statements of Special Educational Needs: Procedures within the Education, Health and Social Services,* London, Department of Education and Science. (Joint Circular with the Department of Health.)

Williams, P. (Ed.) (1984) *Special Education in Minority Communities,* Milton Keynes, Open University Press.

biofeedback, technique through which persons can monitor their own physiological processes, information on which is converted into a readily-perceived signal, such as a varying sound tone, or a pointer movement on a dial. In this way people can be made aware of their own condition, and thus may be able to control it. For example, adults have been helped to control their blood pressure by this means.

The technique has been used with children in the control of hyperactivity. Muscle tension was monitored electronically, and a tone sounded when the tension exceeded a set level. The child was asked to try to turn the tone off (and keep it turned off) by relaxing muscle tension.

Reference:
Gearheart, B.R. (1981) *Learning Disabilities: Educational Strategies*, London, Mosby.

blindness, visual acuity defined as less than 3/60 in the better eye, after correction (in the USA the figure is 20/200, and includes people with a severely restricted field of vision). See *Snellen chart.* This is a legal definition, and is the limit for registration as a blind person. It is not an educational definition of blindness, for many people with acuity less than 3/60 do have some sight which can be used for various purposes, including reading, even though large print or magnifying aids are used.

In educational terms a blind child is one who has to depend primarily on touch, e.g. *Braille,* or hearing, for learning. Blindness is not a common condition. The incidence in infants under one year of age is about four per 100,000, although this will rise slightly through accidents and other reasons in older age-groups. Blind children were almost invariably educated in special schools for the visually impaired. There is a debate as to whether the drop in numbers now attending these schools is due mainly to a drop in the numbers of visually impaired children or mainly to current pressures for integrated education, with appropriate support for children and teachers in ordinary schools. Probably both factors are implicated.

See *partial sight, visual impairment.*

References:
Dodds, A. (1986) 'Visual Handicap', in Gillham, W.E.C. (Ed.) (1986) *Handicapping Conditions in Children*, Beckenham, Croom Helm.
Low, C. (1983) 'Integrating the Visually Handicapped', in Booth, T. and Potts, P. (Eds.) (1983) *Integrating Special Education*, Oxford, Blackwell.

blindism, behaviour said (incorrectly) to be characteristic of blind children, e.g. rocking, eye-pressing or -rubbing, etc. In fact similar self-stimulating or self-comforting mannerisms can be observed in children without visual impairment, and some children with autism or severe learning difficulties may show such behaviour just as frequently as children who are blind.

Bliss symbol system, Blissymbolics, or semantography, set of signs or symbols originally intended by its Canadian author, Charles Bliss, to facilitate international communication. Its potential as a visual-graphic system for helping the communication skills of people with serious language difficulties was soon recognised. It has been used with children with physical handicaps and speech impairments since, in contradistinction to some other symbol systems, manipulation of materials is not necessary: the child can select a symbol by pointing, or indicating otherwise. It has also been used with children with severe learning difficulties. Each symbol represents a concept, and they can be combined to construct representations of complex ideas. The number of agreed symbols has increased and there is a dictionary and handbook available. While the

Some Bliss symbols

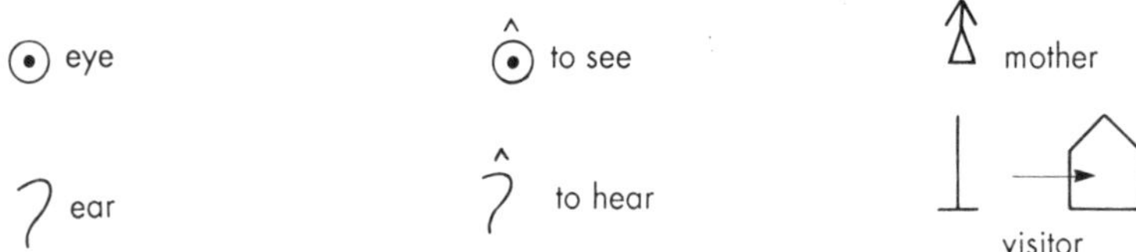

system possesses many advantages, it can be cumbersome in that the symbol board or display must be available. This is particularly true when two people using Blissymbolics wish to communicate with each other and need to have access to both boards.

Reference:

Kiernan, C., Reid, B. and Jones, L. (1982) *Signs and Symbols*, London, Heinemann for Institute of Education, University of London.

block design test, performance test of intelligence, originated by Koh. The problem is to copy a series of designs, using cubes with different patterns on their faces. While block design tests have been used as tests of non-verbal intelligence per se, they are more often found as subtests in a more comprehensive battery, for example in the Wechsler scales of intelligence. They are said to tap spatial abilities, but other competencies are also involved.

Block design example

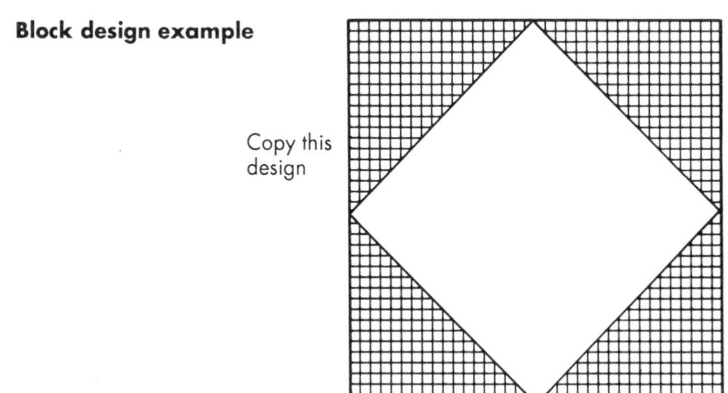

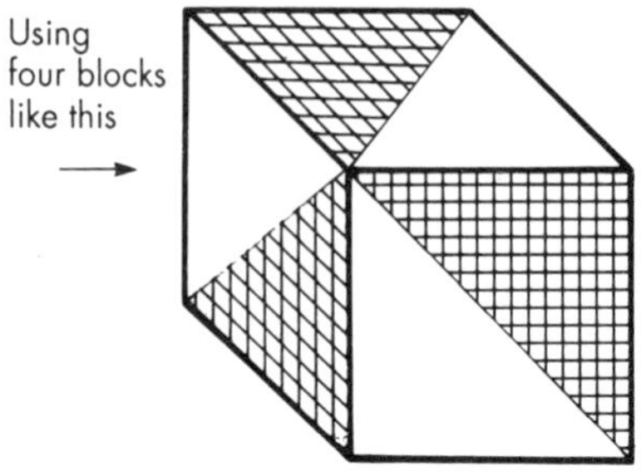

Bobath method, physiotherapy originated in the 1960s by Karel and Berta Bobath and devised for patients following a stroke. Since the patient's handicap is due to impairment of the central nervous system (cns), the therapist works on postural reactions mediated by the cns in order to stimulate muscle groups in everyday use, so helping to improve mobility in particular.

The treatment has been used with children with cerebral palsy, where again cns impairment is the cause, and the Bobaths have established a centre in London for this purpose. Teachers and parents are taught the Bobath techniques so that the child is exposed to them consistently.

References:

Bobath, B. and Bobath, K. (1975) *Motor Development in the Different Types of Cerebral Palsy,* London, Heinemann.

Levitt, S. (1982) *Treatment of Cerebral Palsy and Motor Delay,* Oxford, Blackwell Scientific.

Boehm Test of Basic Concepts, (BTBC), measures children's understanding of fifty concepts needed for success in the early years of schooling. The child responds to pictures, rather than spoken language. The test can be given to small groups, but is more often used as an individual, diagnostic test.

bonding, development of a warm relationship between a newborn infant and its parents, particularly mother. It has been argued that there is a sensitive period, just after birth, which is very important for facilitating an enduring warm attachment between parent and child. Seeing, hearing and holding the infant are essential to releasing parental feelings. But this is not a one-sided activity, for the infant's responses – smiling, gurgling, etc. – also play a part in what is a process of social interaction. Many believe this period to be important not only for emotional development, but also for the development of linguistic and other skills. Where bonding cannot take place, there is evidence that it may be more difficult to establish a normally loving mother–child relationship, with a greater risk of emotional difficulties later.

References:

Murphy, F. (1984) 'The Physiotherapist in the Neonatal Unit', in Levitt, S. (Ed.) (1984) *Paediatric Development Therapy,* Oxford, Blackwell.

Oates, J. (1985) 'Three Views of Infancy', Unit 3 of Open University Course E206, Milton Keynes, Open University.

bone conduction, see *audiometry, hearing impairment.*

bottom-up approaches, methods of learning to read which are essentially analytic, such as *alphabetic* and *phonic methods,* and which are contrasted with *top-down approaches,* which are essentially concerned with meaning, such as *look-and-say* and *Breakthrough to Literacy.*

Bottom-up and top-down approaches to learning to read

Top-down approach

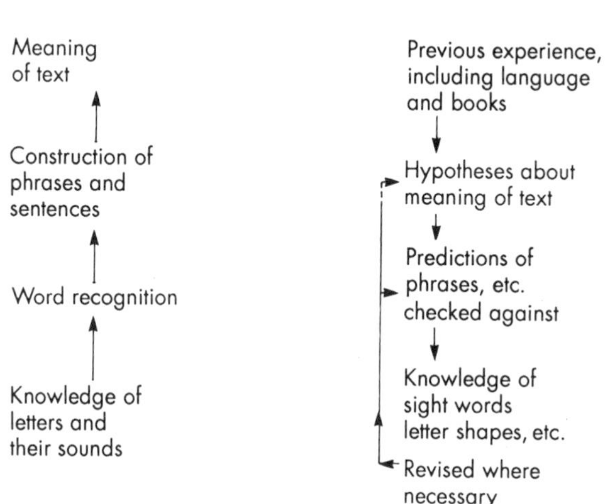

Bottom-up approach

The reader is taught such skills as decoding print, learning the letter shapes (*graphemes*), the sounds associated with them (*phonemes*), and how to synthesise the phonemes into words, so that the phrases and sentences can be read. Note that meaning comes as the end-product of this activity, and indeed one of the criticisms of children who have been taught to rely too heavily on a bottom-up approach is that their reading tends to be mechanical and lacking in fluency.

On the other hand, many children with reading difficulties do progress when introduced to a structured, bottom-up approach, for it gives a technique for tackling new words which builds confidence. In many ways the bottom-up/top-down debate resembles closely the earlier phonic/look-and-say debate. There is little doubt that children need both approaches to reading: holistic methods provide a variety of strategies appropriate to the child's competencies and learning style.

See *holistic method, top-down approaches.*

BPVS, see *British Picture Vocabulary Scale.*

braces, supports for children with physical impairments. Supportive braces help children stand and walk. In addition, corrective braces prevent deformities appearing while children grow, and control braces are used to prevent unwanted involuntary movements. Teachers need to be alert to any problems caused by braces, most obviously undue rubbing. Note that in the UK leg braces are commonly called calipers.

Reference:
Florence, J. (1984) 'Orthotics', in McCarthy, G.T. (1984) *The Physically Handicapped Child*, London, Faber and Faber.

Braille, tactile system used by blind people for reading and writing. The system is based on a set of six raised dots, whose different configurations represent letters, punctuation marks, numbers, etc. The meaning carried by a Braille configuration may also depend on its position in a word. Some configurations represent commonly occurring groups of letters and words, so that the speed of using Braille can be increased. In short, the Braille system is an intricate tactile orthography.

Grade 1 Braille uses twenty-six signs for the twenty-six letters, and sacrifices speed to simplicity; Grade 2 Braille uses the configurations for letter groups and words mentioned above, and is a more complex but quicker medium. Even so, the speed of a child's reading in Braille is about one-third that of a sighted child of the same age, a point which is important for teachers to note. Teaching Braille is a skilled activity, and there are reading schemes designed for this purpose.

Braille is written with a Perkins Brailler, a device with six keys which embosses paper with the Braille dots. Since this equipment is cumbersome, a slate and stylus, which is simpler but involves a more complex procedure, can be used. But new developments in electronics, linking Braillers to computers for example, are advancing the techniques used by blind people to communicate and many current devices may soon be obsolescent.

See *blindness, Versabraille.*

Reference:
Chapman, E.K. and Stone, J.M. (1988) *The Visually Handicapped Child in Your Classroom*, London, Cassell.

brain, see illustration.

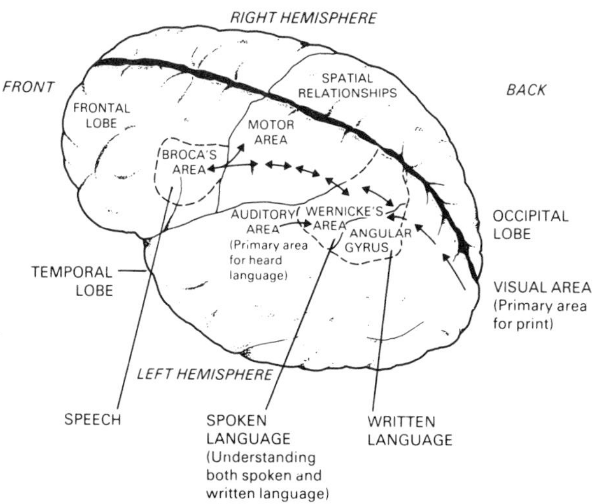

brain damage, can affect a child's education in many different ways – intellectual skills, emotional and social behaviour, motor and perceptual development can all be influenced, depending on the location of the injury, its extent, and the age at which it occurs. Early studies of the characteristics of brain-damaged adults led some workers to suggest that similar patterns of behaviour found in children, particularly a combination of perceptual problems, hyperactivity and some learning difficulties might also be due to brain damage, perhaps congenital. For this reason diagnoses such as 'minimal brain damage' or 'minimal cerebral dysfunction' found favour as explanations of some children's problems. The logic behind this approach is clearly weak and recent research suggests that it has been over-emphasised. Brain damage is a valid neurological diagnosis, but is not one which can be reached lightly and not on the results of psychological tests alone. The importance of a neurological component in children's educational problems cannnot be escaped. But for educational purposes a diagnosis of brain damage is not as important as a thorough assessment of a child's competencies and weaknesses so that a suitable educational programme can be planned.

References:

Quin, V. and MacAuslan, A. (1981) *Reading and Spelling Difficulties: a Medical Approach*, Sevenoaks, Hodder and Stoughton.

Rutter, M. (1981) 'Psychological Sequelae of Brain Damage in Children', *American Journal of Psychiatry*, 138, 1533–44.

brainstem electrical response audiometry (BSER), see *electric response audiometry*.

Breakthrough to Literacy, reading scheme devised by a Schools Council team set up to study linguistics and the teaching of English, and based on a *language experience* approach. Children make up their own sentences by placing a selection of the word-cards provided into the slots on a sentence track. Words that the child wants to use but which are not in the scheme vocabulary can be added by the teacher. The scheme thus develops individual reading material based on the child's own language and interests. Moreover it does not penalise children who might have difficulty in writing out their stories. It is a whole-word and look-and-say method of starting to read. The absence of early teaching of phonic skills, letter learning, etc. has been criticised, as it deprives children of the opportunity to learn new skills through the tracing and copying of words, which is an essential part of the language experience approach proper.

Reference:

Tansley, P. and Panckhurst, J. (1981) *Children with Specific Learning Difficulties; a Critical Review of Research*, Windsor, NFER-Nelson.

Bristol Social Adjustment Guides (BSAG), rating scale widely used by teachers for assessing a pupil's behavioural difficulties over the age-range five to fifteen years. It has also had wide application in research projects (e.g. the *National Child Development Study*). The scale consists of well over a hundred items, each of which is a phrase commonly used by teachers to describe a child's behaviour. Some items describe well-adjusted behaviour, others poorly-adjusted behaviour. The phrases are related to common social situations, and the rater is required to underline those that apply to the child. The 'poor adjustment' items are grouped into a number of core syndromes, e.g. unforthcomingness, which are combined into two adjustment scales, one measuring overreaction and the other underreaction.

The scale is easy to use and score and the familiarity of the descriptions gives it an appeal to teachers. The BSAG scores provide an assessment of a child's behaviour on the core symptoms and the two scales; the total score is also used as a measure of maladjustment.

Reference:

Levy, P. and Goldstein, H. (1984) *Tests in Education*, London, Academic Press.

British Ability Scales (BAS), individually administered battery for psychologists wishing to measure a child's cognitive abilities. It is the most ambitious instrument of its kind produced in the UK, consisting of twenty-three separate subtests, covering the age-range 2.5–17.5 years. The scales cover six process areas: speed of information processing; reasoning; spatial imagery; perceptual memory; short-term memory; retrieval and application of knowledge. These provide a general IQ and a profile of abilities; four scales only can be used for a short form IQ. The BAS has been carefully standardised. It includes two interesting elements: the use of Piagetian ideas on development in the test content and, more controversially, the use of the *Rasch Model* for item analysis.

The revised BAS appeared in 1983, partly in response to criticisms of complexity in administering a detailed and comprehensive test. The scales are used for assessing children with special needs, and are being adapted for use with people with visual handicap. They offer a flexible and sophisticated set of tools for the educational and clinical psychologist.

Reference:

Levy, P. and Goldstein, H. (1984) *Tests in Education*, London, Academic Press.

British Picture Vocabulary Scale (BPVS), measures receptive vocabulary, or comprehension of single words, over the age-range 2.5 to 18 years. It has been developed from the revised version of the Peabody Picture Vocabulary Test and standardised on a British population. A short form, used for screening, is available.

Children are shown a card with four illustrations. The child has to indicate, usually by pointing, but other movements can be used, which illustration corresponds to a test word. A series of cards covers a set of words of increasing difficulty.

The advantages of the BPVS are its speed and ease of administration.

Unlike older tests of vocabulary it neither requires a child to read the test words, nor to write or even speak in response. For these reasons it is useful with language-impaired children. The simple, gestural response means that it can be used with children who have severe physical disabilities. These practical advantages make it easy to forget that receptive vocabulary is only one narrow segment of language functioning, and that a full assessment of language requires a more detailed investigation.

See *language impairment.*

Reference:

Webster, A. and McConnell, C. (1987) *Children with Speech and Language Difficulties,* London, Cassell.

British Sign Language, see *sign language.*

brittle bones, osteogenesis imperfecta, a group of conditions in which the bones are particularly fragile, due to an inherited defect in collagen, a substance important for bone strength. The incidence is said to be about one in 20,000.

These children show a normal range of ability, but their education may be interrupted by periods in hospital and immobilisation in plaster. Their progress therefore needs regular and sensitive monitoring. Handwriting can present difficulties for more severely affected children, whose limbs may be short and who may need special equipment in class. Physiotherapy may be required. Although the limitations the condition places on a child's activities may occasionally lead to emotional difficulties, the main problem posed is the ever-present risk of fractures.

Reference:

Alston, J. (1982) 'Children with Brittle Bones', *Special Education – Forward Trends,* 9, 2, 29–32.

Broca's area, part of the brain's left hemisphere, closely associated with the ability to speak. This relationship between brain area and function was established by the French surgeon, P.P. Broca. Damage to Broca's area leads to loss of the ability to produce coordinated speech.

See *aphasia, brain.*

Bruininks-Oseretsky test of motor proficiency, an American (1978) version of a much older Russian scale. Eight subtests assess aspects of motor performance such as running speed, balance, coordination, dexterity, etc., providing measures of gross motor skills and fine motor skills, as well as an overall score. The test is well presented, and it is one of the few instruments in this field. Its standardisation characteristics have been criticised, as has the validity of providing separate fine and gross motor skills scores from the subtest results.

Reference:

Hattie, J. and Edwards, H. (1987) 'A review of the Bruininks-Oseretsky Test of Motor Proficiency', *British Journal of Educational Psychology,* 57, 104–13.

Buckley Amendment, see *Public Law 93-380.*

Bullock Report 1975, 'A Language for Life', report of the Committee of Enquiry into the Teaching of English, established to consider '. . . a) all aspects of teaching the use of English, including reading, writing, and speech; b) how present practice might be improved and the role that initial and in-service training might play; c) to what extent arrangements for monitoring the general level of attainment in these skills can be introduced or improved . . .' A chapter on children with reading difficulties is included in what remains the most comprehensive study of the subject available, covering the position in the 1970s.

The report offered a critique of the concept of *dyslexia,* proposing that the term specific reading retardation should be used instead, arguing that with skilled teaching most of these children would learn to read. It also recommended that every education authority should establish a reading centre or clinic where children with severe reading difficulties could be given intensive help.

Reference:

Department of Education and Science (1975) *A Language for Life,* London, HMSO (Bullock Report).

buphthalmos, see *glaucoma.*

Burt (Rearranged) Word Reading Test, is a graded word reading test, developed over the years from perhaps the oldest English word reading test, that produced by Burt in 1921. It was last restandardised in the UK in 1974. As with other graded word tests the child reads aloud a series of words of gradually increasing difficulty. The number of words pronounced correctly is converted into a reading age.

While the test has the advantages of familiarity attached to long usage in schools, the word selection reflects its early origin. It shares the virtue of simplicity with other *graded word reading tests,* but also possesses their disadvantages.

Reference:

Levy, P. and Goldstein, H. (1984) *Tests in Education,* London, Academic Press.

C

Cadman Report, 1976, 'Learning Difficulties in Children and Adults', report of the Australian House of Representatives Select Committee on Specific Learning Difficulties. The report, which was a landmark in Australian special education, gave thorough consideration to various approaches to defining the term *'specific learning difficulty'*. It concluded that a definition was not as important as ensuring that those who do not reach the educational standards consistent with obtaining a reasonable livelihood, enjoying reasonable social intercourse and achieving personal dignity, should be offered suitable educational help. The committee then abandoned the term 'specific learning difficulties' in favour of 'learning difficulties.'

The report made a series of recommendations geared to ensuring that this group received a more than equal share of educational and other resources, including proposals for regular surveys of the incidence of learning difficulties, and changes in the funding arrangements for special education in Australia.

References:

Parliament of the Commonwealth of Australia (1976) *Learning Difficulties in Children and Adults*, Canberra, Australian Government Printing Service.

Parmenter, T. (1979) 'Factors Influencing the Development of Special Educational Facilities in Australia for Children with Learning Disabilities/Learning Difficulties', *Australian Journal of Special Education*, 3, 1, 11–17.

Cain-Levine Social Competency Scale, was designed and standardised in the USA with five- to thirteen-year-old trainable mental retardates, i.e. children with severe learning difficulties. The scale is completed by interviewing a person familiar with the child's day-to-day behaviour, e.g. a teacher or parent. It measures *adaptive behaviour.*

Reference:

Raynes, N.V. (1987) 'Adaptive Behaviour Scales', in Hogg, J. and Raynes, N.V. (Eds.) (1987) *Assessment in Mental Handicap*, Beckenham, Croom Helm.

calipers, see *braces.*

CALL Centre, see *Communication Aids for Language and Learning Centre.*

calligrams, pictograms, or typograms are words or sentences made to look like their meanings. (See illustration.)

Some calligrams

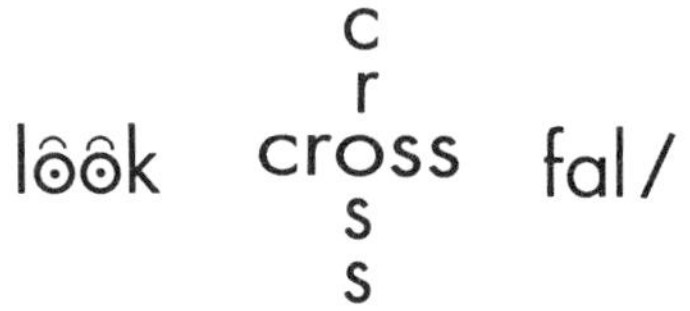

c
r
lôôk cross fal/
s
s

This visual form of *onomatopoeia* is a useful way of drawing pupils' attention to the appearance and meaning of words. By encouraging children to make their own calligrams of words or verses they may be helped to enjoy learning to write and spell.

Camphill Movement, movement founded by Karl Konig, which puts the principles of anthroposophy, the philosophy of Rudolf Steiner, into practice. These principles are complex, but central to them is Steiner's concern for the individuality of the person, no matter how malformed and damaged the body. This has led to the founding of residential schools dedicated to the full development of the potential of children with handicaps, often very severe learning difficulties, through the use of novel therapies based on music, rhythm and colour. In these schools the staff, irrespective of discipline, are expected to participate equally with the children in the creation of a therapeutic atmosphere.

The movement set up its first school in Camphill, near Aberdeen, in 1940. Since then similar schools have been established in other locations, both in the UK and abroad.

The Camphill Village Trust was set up to foster the growth of communities in which adults with and without handicaps live together, and the first such community was started at Botton village, North Yorkshire in 1954. The village idea has been developed to include the provision of town-based living and working together. As with the schools, the communities are expected to follow Steiner's fundamental social law, *viz*: 'The well-being of a community of human beings working together becomes greater the less the individual demands the products of his achievements for himself, that is, the more of these products he passes on to his fellow-workers and the more his own needs are not satisfied out of his own achievements but out of the achievements of others.' (Quoted in Camphill Village Trust, 1988.)

See *curative education, Rudolf Steiner schools.*

References:

Pietzner, C. (Ed.) (1966) *Aspects of Curative Education*, Aberdeen, Aberdeen University Press for Camphill Movement.

Camphill Village Trust (1988) *Association of Camphill Communities*, pamphlet available from Camphill Village Trust, Botton Village, Danby, Whitby, North Yorks.

cardiac disorders, heart problems, mainly congenital in origin, with an incidence of approximately eight to ten per thousand live births. In many cases the defect can be corrected surgically. Surveys of the intellectual status of children with cardiac problems place them within the average range for their age-group, though there are some variations, depending on the nature of the defect. Thus children whose heart defect is associated with cyanosis, i.e.blueness of the skin due to lowered levels of oxygen in the blood, tend to have lower scores on tests of intellectual performance, though still within normal limits. It is a moot point to what extent this is due to physiological causes, or to the limitations on experience that physical incapacity imposes.

Any physical incapacity, however slight, carries implications for school activities requiring exertion, and teachers need to be familiar with the medical recommendations for an individual child. While periods in hospital may temporarily hamper educational progress, a suitable programme should rectify this.

Reference:

Dinnage, R. (1986) *The Child with a Chronic Medical Problem*, Windsor, NFER-Nelson.

care order, order committing a child to the care of a local authority, usually as the result of care proceedings brought in the juvenile court under the Children and Young Persons Act 1969 by a local authority or, exceptionally, by the NSPCC or the police. If the court makes a care order, then while the order is in force the local authority is given rights and duties over the child which normally include the right to decide on the child's placement.

When section 31 of the *Children Act 1989* is brought into force, care (and supervision) orders will be governed by it. The court may only make an order if it is satisfied that the child is suffering or is likely to suffer harm from the care given or likely to be given, or is beyond parental control. 'Harm' means either (i) impairment of physical or mental health or of physical, intellectual, emotional, social, or behavioural development, or (ii) ill-treatment, which includes sexual abuse and forms of ill-treatment which are not physical.

Note that under the 1989 Act it will no longer be possible for the police to bring care proceedings, nor for a local education authority to do so on the grounds that a child is not being properly educated. But this latter allegation may be grounds on which a court might find that the child was suffering significant harm as defined above.

The Children Act 1989 will place a duty on local authorities to reduce the need to bring proceedings for care and supervision orders in relation to children in their area. There is a considerable body of work on the feelings of parents and children who have been involved in care proceedings. There is evidence on the feelings of powerlessness and inadequacy experienced by parents and on the surprising lack of understanding of the reasons for being in care on the part of children in long-term fostering. Most children felt stigma or discomfort over their situation, feelings of which foster parents and social workers were often unaware. These findings endorse the importance of participation by children and parents in planning placement decisions and of extensive explanations of them. There is surprisingly little published work on the educational characteristics of children in care.

See *child abuse, children in care, supervision order.*

Reference:

Gardner, R. (1985) 'Client Participation in Decision-Making in Child Care: a review of research', *Highlight*, 71, London, National Children's Bureau.

careers guidance, is given by the careers service, whose staff work closely with careers teachers in secondary schools. Advice is given on career entry requirements and job opportunities, and pupils are counselled over their career choice. Some careers officers specialise in working with young people with special needs, and the *Warnock Report* recommended planning for one such person per 50,000 school population. This recommendation has not been implemented, and there are far too few such specialists in post. Until their numbers can be substantially increased it has been argued that careers officers generally should receive extra training, and should help schools staff to gear their leavers' programmes more closely to the employment possibilities for young people with special needs.

References:

Adams, F. (Ed.) (1986) *Special Education*, Harlow, Councils and Education Press for Longmans.
Hegarty, S. (1987) *Meeting Special Needs in Ordinary Schools*, London, Cassell.

CARF, see *Council for the Accreditation of Rehabilitation Facilities.*

carrier,

(1) individual or animal who harbours and spreads an organism causing an infectious disorder without suffering from it personally.
(2) individual whose *chromosomes* carry a recessive gene for one of a wide variety of hereditary disorders. Where both parents are carriers of the recessive gene there is a one-in-four chance that a child of theirs will be affected by the disorder. This is the case in the vast majority of hereditary conditions. Where the gene is carried on the X chromosome, only females are the carriers; they may transmit the disease to their sons and the carrier state to their daughters, e.g. in Duchenne muscular dystrophy or haemophilia.
Reference:
Harper, P.S. (1989) *Practical Genetic Counselling*, Bristol, Wright.

cascade model,

(1) cascade of service model, usually attributed to Deno, is essentially a list of educational facilities, arranged from most integrated (children in normal classes, without extra services), to least integrated (children under medical care and supervision, with no education). The cascade model was important in that it diverted attention away from the stark alternatives of ordinary school or special school, and focused attention on providing a range of educational possibilities for children with special needs. It has been criticised in that it emphasises placement, rather than curriculum. Many variants of the model have since appeared, some simplifications, others extensions and developments. See illustration.
Reference:
Topping, K. (1983) *Educational Systems for Disruptive Adolescents*, London, Croom Helm.
(2) a cascade model of training in special education involves training one

Example of a 'Cascade of Service' Model

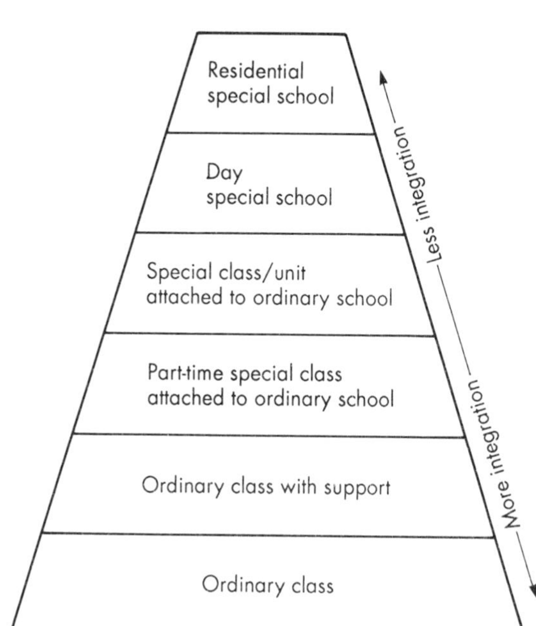

Note that the 'leaps' in the cascade can be graduated more finely with a more-developed range of provision

person who in turn trains others. Examples of this are the *SNAP* programme, or the *EDY* programme.

case conference, meeting of people involved with an individual's problems in order to reach a decision that takes into account as much relevant information as possible and which is acceptable to at least the majority of interested parties, and hopefully to all.

Conferences can be called at critical points in a child's life, for example when a change of school is being contemplated, or can be scheduled in advance, as when a termly conference is diaried to review a child's educational progress.

Membership of a case conference can be a thorny issue, in particular whether it should be offered to parents, either by invitation or by right; there are arguments for including some older pupils in discussions which concern their future, too.

Another issue relates to the efficiency of the case conference, both as a method of making decisions and also on the grounds of cost: the time of highly paid professionals is expensive.

case history, compilation of relevant data about an individual's life in order to deepen understanding of the problem under investigation. The case history is in effect an adjunct in diagnosis: supported by data obtained otherwise, e.g. through observation, it merges into the case-study, a basic method of experimental investigation. This is a weak method when judged by orthodox scientific criteria – e.g. historical data recalled from memory may be substantially inaccurate – but it can offer important insights.

The case history is widely used in therapeutic work based on psychodynamic principles: behaviourally based approaches work with current behaviours, regarding information on a child's life history as irrelevant.

See *psychotherapy.*

References:

Nisbet, J. and Watts, J. (1980) 'Case Study', *Rediguide 26*, Nottingham, Nottingham University School of Education.

Timms, N. and Timms, R. (1982) *Dictionary of Social Welfare*, London, Routledge & Kegan Paul.

casework, method of treating problems, widely used by social workers, and historically associated with a psychotherapeutic approach. It focuses on the individual or family in difficulties, rather than attempting to change the social conditions which might have brought these difficulties about. There is an analogy here with child-centred approaches as opposed to system-centred approaches in educational psychology and special education. In recent years a number of different theoretical approaches to casework have developed, e.g. *crisis intervention.*

Reference:

Timms, N. and Timms, R. (1982) *Dictionary of Social Welfare*, London, Routledge & Kegan Paul.

CAT and **CAT(H),** see *Children's Apperception Test.*

cataract, opacity of the lens of the eye, which in childhood is often associated with hereditary disorders and dealt with by surgery to remove the lens. Even with the strong glasses that are then needed, vision may still be poor. The level of lighting provided for the child is important, and the use of *low vision aids,* if recommended, needs monitoring. Since peripheral vision may be poor, there may be problems with movement around the school and classroom.

See *visual impairment.*

Reference:

Chapman, E.K. and Stone, J.M. (1988), *The Visually Handicapped Child in Your Classroom*, London, Cassell.

categories of handicap, the subgroups into which children with special needs were placed for the purposes of providing education.

The principle of categorisation has its roots in the *medical model* of dealing with an illness, essentially a diagnosis to identify the disease or condition, followed by the specific treatment for it. It was assumed that similar principles should apply to the education of children with learning difficulties: after the handicap had been diagnosed, the appropriate educational treatment could follow.

Since doctors held the key to medical diagnosis, the early categorisation of children with learning difficulties reflected those categories with which medicine was familiar, most obviously blindness, deafness and mental handicap. These were later refined and non-medical categories added. By the 1970s there were ten categories in use in the UK, viz. blind, partially sighted, deaf, partially hearing, delicate, educationally subnormal, epileptic, maladjusted, physically handicapped, and speech defects. In the USA, the Bureau for the Education of the Handicapped established eight broadly similar categories. In both these (and other) countries, educational provision was geared to the categories. Separate schools and classes for partially hearing children were established independently of similar provisions for other categories, for example.

But by this time not only had the centrality of a medical role in decisions affecting a child's education been challenged, but the idea of categorisation itself, whether based on medical or educational or indeed any other principle, was under attack. It is illogical to assume that children with the same medical condition necessarily pose the same or even similar educational problems, and equally illogical to suggest that they need the same educational programmes. It is also strange to suggest that children be allocated to a single category: some children with hearing impairment will also have difficulties in adjustment, or speech, or learning, for example. Even if hearing impairment is the root cause, they might also have been categorised as maladjusted, or speech defective, or educationally subnormal – and in some cases were. When the type of education depended on the category, this could be very damaging. At the same time, two other changes were occurring: sociologists in particular were drawing attention to the pervasive effects of *labelling* a child, and the attack against segregation was also developing. Categorisation is an invitation to label and to segregate.

For these reasons the movement to abolish categories grew in strength and in the UK abolition was a recommendation of the Warnock Committee, given legislative force by the *Education Act 1981*. Instead of allocating a child with special needs to a category, the assessment team is now required to provide a *Statement* or *Record* of educational needs. The emphasis is placed on an educational programme for an individual, similar to the provisions of PL 94–142 in the USA. The abolition of categories has not occurred totally nor without difficulty. It is still important to identify a child as blind, for example, but this is categorisation for medical and administrative, not educational purposes. The development of the replacement procedure of statementing has been widely criticised, too. But for most people in the field, the abolition of categories has been a move for the better.

See *classification*.

References:
Department of Education and Science (1978) *Special Educational Needs*, London, HMSO (Warnock Report).
Sabatino, D.A. and Miller, T.L. (Eds.) (1989) *Describing Learner Characteristics of Handicapped Children and Youth*, London, Grune and Stratton.
Van Etten, G., Arkell, C. and Van Etten, C. (1980) *The Severely and Profoundly Handicapped*, St. Louis, Mosby.

catharsis, technique for therapeutic release of repressed or pent-up emotions, perhaps by open discussion or by re-enacting a past situation. In psychoanalysis, *free association* is often used for this purpose, sometimes in conjunction with hypnosis and hypnotic drugs. Catharsis is sometimes used in the same sense as abreaction, though some distinguish method (catharsis) from product (abreaction).

CEC, see *Council for Exceptional Children.*

ceiling,

(1) upper limit of ability or skill that can be measured by a particular test, sometimes called the test ceiling.
(2) Ceiling age is a concept used in scoring tests which group items by age. Thus a child may pass all the items at the eight-year level on a test of mathematics, some of those at the nine-year level, but none at the ten-year level. The ceiling age for that child is ten years.

See *basal age.*

central nervous system (cns), the brain and spinal cord, the structures which are responsible for the coordination and control of human activity. While particular parts may be closely involved with particular functions, (e.g. *Broca's area*) the cns is best seen as an integrated whole, injury to any one part of which may have repercussions throughout the system, leading to complex learning problems.

See *brain damage.*

cerebral dominance, the control of function by one of the two cerebral hemispheres. Each cerebral hemisphere controls movement of the opposite side of the body: thus the left hemisphere controls movement of the right hand, leg, etc. When Broca demonstrated that speech appeared to be controlled by an area in the left hemisphere, it was assumed that the control of other cognitive functions could be located in one or other hemisphere, i.e. that one half of the cerebrum would assume a dominant role for each activity. This has since been shown to be an oversimplified view of the localisation of function in the brain.

Other investigators suggested that different patterns of dominance might be related to different learning difficulties. A common example of this is the view that crossed hand-eye dominance, e.g. a child whose right hemisphere controls hand movement (i.e. is probably left handed) and whose left hemisphere controls eye movements will have difficulties with activities that involve coordination of eye and hand, e.g. reading and writing. Research has not produced clear-cut evidence to support this view: indeed the great majority of children with unusual patterns of dominance do not have learning difficulties – though much of the early research used tests of laterality to measure cerebral dominance, not always a sound procedure.

Later work has supported the view that, broadly speaking, the left hemisphere is dominant in most people for activities that involve processing information in sequence, as in language skills. About 90% of right-handed people and about 65% of left-handed people are left-hemisphere dominant for speech; the remainder, 10% of right-handers and 35% of left-handers are right-hemisphere dominant for speech. The right hemisphere is usually dominant for nonverbal skills such as music, pattern recognition and orientation in space. More detailed elucidation of the patterns of cerebral dominance and their relation to educational difficulties is a matter of current research.

See *dichotic listening tests, laterality.*

References:

Pavlidis, G.T. and Miles, T.R. (Eds.) (1981) *Dyslexia Research and its Application to Education*, Chichester, Wiley.

Young, P. and Tyre, T. (1983) *Dyslexia or Illiteracy?*, Milton Keynes, Open University Press.

cerebral hemisphere, one of the two halves into which the brain is divided. Each hemisphere specialises in the control of different functions. See *brain illustration, cerebral dominance.*

cerebral palsy (CP), group of conditions in which the capacity to make voluntary movements is impaired due to brain damage, usually occurring before or during birth. The incidence varies according to the quality of obstetric care, but in most advanced countries is between two and five per thousand live births.

The cerebral palsies are classified by type and by effects. Six or more different types have been described, the three most prevalent of which are spasticity, athetosis and ataxia. *Spasticity* is most common, characterised by tight, rigid limb muscles, resulting in jerky, uncontrolled movements. *Athetosis* is recognised by purposeless, repetitive limb movements, which increase with anxiety or effort, but cease during sleep. *Ataxia* is a difficulty in coordinating movement, and is characterised by poor balance, high-step walking and *nystagmus.* Children can suffer from more than one type.

Various combinations of affected limbs occur in CP: monoplegia (one limb affected); hemiplegia (both affected limbs on the same side of the body); paraplegia (both legs affected); triplegia (three limbs affected); diplegia (all four limbs involved, but the arms less affected than the legs);

quadriplegia (all four limbs equally affected). In each case the impairment can range from mild to severe, and in more severe cases other effects are likely to be present. These depend upon the location and extent of the brain injury, but may include speech and hearing difficulties, problems with swallowing, chewing and drooling, problems with vision and visual perception, epilepsy, and intellectual deficits.

Cerebral palsy is not a disease which can be cured, but the obvious physical effects can be alleviated and helped considerably by specialised physiotherapy, particularly if started early, if the parents are closely involved and if a team approach is adopted, with other professionals such as speech therapists, psychologists, etc., collaborating as appropriate. The role of the education service is critical. While it is clear that any brain damage is likely to lead to intellectual damage, not all cerebral palsied children are mentally handicapped. The extent of the intellectual handicap is associated with the severity of the condition and also with its type. Thus there is evidence that children who are athetoid demonstrate the full range of ability, the spastic group are less able, while the ataxic group are most intellectually damaged. But it must be stressed that any one child with cerebral palsy, no matter how severe its extent, can be highly intelligent.

Educational attainment, even allowing for intellectual damage, has been shown to be retarded in most CP children. Absence from school, and the effects of the perceptual, speech and other problems mentioned above make this an unsurprising finding. But appropriate educational help can make a significant difference. With the increasing integration of cerebral palsied children into ordinary schools, the importance of extra support, both educational and medical, is of crucial importance.

See *brain damage, conductive education.*

References:

Dinnage, R. (1986) *The Child with Cerebral Palsy*, Windsor, NFER-Nelson.

Griffiths, M. and Clegg, M. (1988) *Cerebral Palsy; Problems and Solutions*, London, Souvenir Press.

McCarthy, G.T. (1984) *The Physically Handicapped Child*, London, Faber and Faber.

Pugh, G. (1980) *Children with Cerebral Palsy: a review of research*, London, National Children's Bureau. (Highlight No. 39.)

chaining, procedure for teaching a skill that involves a sequence of steps, or chain of behaviour. It is thus a technique for acquiring complex behaviour.

Backward chaining involves acquiring the components of the chain in reverse order. The last step is learnt first, i.e. the learner is placed in a position where only one step is needed to complete the task and gain reinforcement. Thus in learning to put on a coat, a child may be first taught to fasten the buttons. The preceding step, putting the second arm through the sleeve, is then taught and the task again completed. All the steps are taught in this reverse order until the child learns to put on a coat successfully on being asked.

Backward chaining is widely used for teaching self-care skills to children with severe learning difficulties, though it is a technique that has much more general application. It has the advantage that the learner has frequent experience of successfully completing the task being taught, and also knows what the result of each new step will be.

These particular advantages do not apply to forward chaining, in which the steps are learnt in the correct temporal sequence. This technique is less frequently used.

See *behaviour shaping.*

References:

Ainscow, M. and Tweddle, D.A. (1981) 'The Objectives Approach: a Progress Report', in Somerset LEA (1981) *Ways and Means 2,* Basingstoke, Globe Education.

Alberto, P.A. and Troutman, A.C. (1986, 2nd edn.) *Applied Behavior Analysis for Teachers,* Columbus, Merrill.

child abuse, physical or emotional injury, neglect, or sexual abuse of a child under eighteen years of age, usually by a person within the family household.

An earlier term, battered child syndrome, dates from the 1960s, when children with unexplained fractures were being seen by paediatricians. Non-accidental injury, as this is now more usually called, has been of increasing concern to professionals in the field, and many of the difficulties of dealing with such cases were highlighted by the reports of enquiries set up following some tragic child deaths. More recently, the emotional and physical damage caused by sexual abuse has been recognised, and the wide publicity given to alleged cases of sexual abuse led to the publication of the Cleveland Report (Butler-Sloss, 1988).

There is no clear view on the causes of child abuse, though it is more likely to occur in disadvantaged families where one or both parents were themselves abused as children. Treatment is a complex question. Programmes aimed at changing parental behaviour through behaviour modification techniques have had some success, but some workers see the problem as an unhealthy interaction between child and parent, rather than as a defenceless child being attacked by a vicious parent whose behaviour needs changing. Legally removing the child from the abusing environment is another option, for child abuse is a very serious issue. Children who are the victims of brutal parents may be disfigured, permanently damaged, or even die. Yet it is not a clearcut issue: parents have a right to discipline and punish their children, and the line between reasonable and excessive punishment is not always easy to draw.

In an emergency, a *place of safety order* or warrant can be obtained in order to remove the child from danger for up to twenty-eight days. Local authorities and the NSPCC can institute care proceedings in the juvenile court. The police can also bring criminal proceedings against the alleged instigator of the abuse. The education service has a key role to play, for teachers are in daily contact with nearly all children of school age, and at least one-third of child abuse cases come to light in school. Indeed, in the Jasmine Beckford Report (Blom-Cooper, 1985) it was recommended that there should be at least one teacher in every school who is responsible for liaison work with other professional groups in the handling of child abuse cases. But bringing parents to court is a major step, not to be taken lightly, and the harm to the family that this may entail has to be set against the relief that it affords to the child.

See *child assessment order, Children Act 1989, emergency protection order.*

References:

Blom-Cooper, L. (1985) *A Child in Trust: the Report of the Panel of Enquiry into the Circumstances Surrounding the Death of Jasmine Beckford,* London, London Borough of Brent.

Butler-Sloss, Dame Elizabeth (1988) *Report of the Inquiry into Child Abuse in Cleveland,* Cmd 412, London, HMSO.

Lindsay, G. and Peake, A. (Eds.) (1989) 'Child Sexual Abuse', *Educational and Child Psychology,* 6, 1.

Maher, P. (Ed.) (1987) *Child Abuse: the Educational Perspective,* Oxford, Blackwell.

Smith, J.E. (1986) 'Working with Child-Abusing Parents: Problems and Practices', *Educational and Child Psychology,* 3, 3, 169–76.

child assessment order, a new order created under the *Children Act 1989,* for which a local authority or other authorised person will be able to apply.

The purpose of the order is to provide access to a child where there are reasonable grounds for suspicion that a child is suffering or is likely to suffer significant harm, but not sufficient grounds to apply for an *emergency protection order,* a *care order* or a *supervision order,* and where those caring for the child are not willing to cooperate. The court may make the order only if it is satisfied that the grounds for suspicion are indeed reasonable, and that an assessment of the child's health, development or treatment is needed to determine the matter. In making its decision the court has to apply the 'welfare principle' (see *Children Act 1989*) and consider whether making the order is better for the child than making no order at all. An applicant for a child assessment order has to take all reasonable practical steps to give notice to a number of persons, most obviously the parents, and also the child if he or she is of sufficient understanding to make an informed decision on whether or not to submit to an assessment.

See *child abuse.*

child guidance, a movement which originated at the turn of the century, when the study of child development became an applied science. Laboratories in Europe and the USA offered parents assessments of their children's progress. Later, clinics for 'guiding' children were opened in major cities, and children with problems were referred there. The interdependence of medical, social and educational factors in these problems was soon recognised and the idea of a child guidance clinic, staffed by a team of three – child psychiatrist, psychiatric social worker and educational psychologist – took root. (Post-war development in Scotland, where Education Authorities were empowered to provide a child guidance service, was quicker than in England and Wales, where the legislation relating to special education made no mention of child guidance. Since 1986, the child guidance service in Scotland has been retitled, and is now known as the psychological service.)

Initially, child guidance clinics tended to follow a psychodynamic approach in their work with children's emotional difficulties. They were criticised on the grounds of expense and lack of evident effectiveness. It also became clear on logistical grounds that the intensive investigation followed by psychotherapy that characterised the classic child guidance case could only be made available to a very few children. For these reasons alternative developments occurred – in particular educational psychologists provided a more responsive service to schools. For a time the child guidance clinics, many of which moved into the hospitals, seemed to be distancing themselves from society's needs.

More recently, the child guidance movement has shown new life, growing out of the clinic framework and becoming increasingly involved in preventive work in schools and other community organisations. While severe problems still require a careful, multidisciplinary investigation, treatment has become more eclectic, with approaches from *behaviour therapy, family therapy*, etc. also being used. The team approach is still followed, but the original trinity is no longer seen as sacrosanct, and members of other disciplines participate.

See *emotional and behavioural difficulties, school psychological service.*

References:

Sampson, O. (1980) *Child Guidance: its history, provenance and future*, Leicester, British Psychological Society.

Tizard, J. (1973) 'Maladjusted children and the child guidance service', *London Educational Review*, 2(2), 22–37.

child guidance clinic, see *child guidance.*

Child Health and Education Study, third of the three major *longitudinal studies* of child development carried out in post-war Britain, based in this case at Bristol University. All children born in England, Scotland and Wales in the week of 5th–11th April, 1970 formed the cohort studied. Their later development was monitored in order to investigate its relationship with biographical data in general and social background variables in particular.

The study constructed a social index to measure social background. This offered advantages over the father's occupational classification, widely used in earlier investigations, in that it was based on a number of variables, provided a measure of social background for fatherless families, and was normally distributed.

Among the more interesting of the study's results so far, are the confirmation of earlier work demonstrating a high correlation between social background and educational performance (at five and ten years of age); the definite association found between mother's smoking in pregnancy and the child's limited later physical and educational development; the evidence that attendance at nursery schools and play-groups can have a positive effect on children's cognitive development.

The study has been criticised – for example educational performance and curriculum content are assessed by a limited range of instruments – but it has provided important information for influencing social and educational policy.

See *National Survey of Health and Development of Children, National Child Development Study.*

Reference:

Osborn, A.F. and Milbank, J.E. (1987) *The Effects of Early Education: a Report from the Child Health and Education Study,* Oxford, Clarendon Press.

child minder, person who looks after one or more children under five years of age for reward in the child minder's own home for periods totalling two or more hours a day, or for any longer period not exceeding six days. Responsibility for registration and inspection of child minders lies with the local social services. Some authorities offer a training programme for child minders. The current legal provisions are amended by the Children Act 1989.

See *day care.*

child psychiatrist, medical practitioner who has specialised in children's emotional and behavioural disorders. Child psychiatrists are usually employed by the Health Service, often based in hospitals, but are nevertheless key members of the local *child guidance* team.

child psychologist: in many countries this describes any psychologist trained to work with children. In the UK child psychologists working in the applied field are most commonly designated as *educational psychologists,* or *clinical psychologists* specialising with children, depending on whether they have been trained for work in the education or health service. Children with special needs who need a psychological opinion are much more likely to meet with an educational psychologist. The skills of the two groups are somewhat different, but are both underpinned by the principles and methods of the scientific study of children's behaviour. In some other countries child psychologists have formed a single profession, irrespective of occupational affiliation.

Reference:

Williams, P. (1977) *Children and Psychologists,* London, Hodder and Stoughton.

childhood psychosis, group of rare, serious personality disorders in which the characteristic feature is lack of contact with reality, demonstrated by behaviour which is strange and bizarre. It is this altered contact with reality which distinguishes psychotic behaviour from neurotic behaviour.

There is debate over the classification of childhood psychoses. Most authorities divide the group of illnesses into *childhood schizophrenia* on the one hand, and psychotic states induced by drugs, severe illness, metal poisoning (e.g. lead), etc., on the other. Some authorities include *autism* as a childhood psychosis, but others do not.

Children with marked psychotic conditions are rarely able to function effectively in mainstream education, if only because their thinking processes are so distorted. They are often managed in residential educational settings, where the medical treatment needed can be offered alongside suitable education.

See *neurosis, psychosis.*

Reference:

Barker, P. (1988, 5th edn.) *Basic Child Psychiatry,* Oxford, Blackwell.

childhood schizophrenia, serious developmental disorder, but also a controversial diagnostic category. Until the 1960s childhood schizophrenia and *autism* were often interchangeable terms for conditions characterised by the inability to develop normal interpersonal relationships, a withdrawal from reality and an inability to respond normally to events in the environment. Since then, they have increasingly been regarded as distinct conditions, for the following reasons. The onset of childhood schizophrenia tends to occur in adolescence, rather than in infancy: the prevalence of childhood schizophrenia is roughly the same in both sexes, rather than being about three times higher in boys: the symptoms differ, delusions and hallucinations being characteristics of childhood schizophrenia.

Treatment of childhood schizophrenia usually involves work with the family, medication, and long-term therapy. But it is not a condition which can be expected to respond quickly to treatment. There may well be educational problems; in some cases relief from the pressures of following a school curriculum being advisable, while in other cases education may be an important anchor to reality.

Reference:

Barker, B. (1988, 5th edn.) *Basic Child Psychiatry,* Oxford, Blackwell.

Children Act 1989, brings together the law relating to private individuals (e.g. issues resulting from divorce) with that relating to public authorities (e.g. the responsibilities of local social service authorities towards children and their families). One of the principal results of the new legislation will be to strike a new balance between the rights and responsibilities of parents, on the one hand, and the protection of children on the other. The Act is based on the premise that normally, children are best looked after by both parents within the family unit, and that as far as possible, law and practice should support that principle.

The primary duty of local authorities will be to provide support for children in need and their families. If a child in need requires to be accommodated by a local authority, then the Act insists that this should preferably be on the basis of a partnership between the authority and the parents, with parents retaining their parental responsibilities and the right to remove the child at any time, provided that it is in the child's welfare (the 'welfare principle').

This principle is applied in court proceedings, where the court should not make any order unless it considers that doing so would be better for the child than making no order at all. This principle should also be the paramount consideration in issues relating to a child's upbringing and property.

The Act provides for two forms of proceedings in relation to children. In family proceedings the court is empowered to make a number of orders, for example a contact order, governing access to a child, a residence order, determining with whom a child is to live, etc.

On the application of a local authority or the NSPCC the court may also make a *care order* or *supervision order*, either in other family proceedings, or separately, provided that it is satisfied of the existence of the grounds laid down by the Act. The current procedures for the emergency protection of children by *place of safety orders* are to be replaced by provisions for *child assessment orders* and *emergency protection orders.*

It is intended that the Act will be implemented as a whole in October 1991.

See *child abuse.*

Reference:

Russell, P. (1990) 'Introducing the Children Act', *British Journal of Special Education*, 17, 1, 35–7.

children in care, children who have been admitted into the care of a local authority either voluntarily or under a care order. The local authority is obliged to review their cases regularly, though there is evidence of considerable variation in the purpose and duration of reviews, the amount of child participation and indeed in the extent to which their frequency meets the legal requirements. Recent practice emphasises greater use of support systems at home before a child is taken into care.

Under the *Children Act 1989* this term will refer only to children being looked after under a *care order.* This Act states that it will be the local authority's duty to safeguard and promote the welfare of these children, and obliges the local authority to give due consideration to the wishes and feelings of relevant persons, most obviously the child and the parents. Due consideration must also be given to the child's religious persuasion, racial origin, and cultural and linguistic background.

Children in care normally attend the school in whose catchment area their foster home or residential establishment falls, though different arrangements are sometimes made, for example if special needs have to be met outside the mainstream or if it is advantageous to spread children between several different schools, or in the case of a short-stay centre, where education is provided on the premises.

The relatively few published studies of the educational characteristics of children in care generally agree that they are likely to show a higher prevalence of behavioural difficulties and lower educational attainments than would be expected for their age. Various explanations have been offered for this, including a poor start in life, the stresses of separation and entry into care, lack of interest from foster parents and social workers in their educational progress, and the sense of failure that is sometimes felt by children who may be moved from one foster placement to another several times.

See *children in need.*

References:

Gardner, R. (1985) 'Child Care Reviews – a review of research', *Highlight*, 70, London, National Children's Bureau.

Heath, A., Colton, C. and Aldgate, J. (1989) 'The Educational Progress of Children In and Out of Care', *British Journal of Social Work*, 19, 447–60.

Jackson, S. (1987) 'The Education of Children in Care', Bristol University, *Bristol Papers in Applied Social Studies*, 1.

National Institute for Social Work (1988). *Residential Care: a Positive Choice*, London, HMSO (Wagner Report).

children in need, are children who are unlikely to achieve or maintain a reasonable standard of physical or mental health, or physical, intellectual, emotional, social or behavioural development, or who are disabled. Under the provisions of the *Children Act 1989* local social service authorities are required to promote and safeguard the welfare of these children and to promote their upbringing by their families so far as that is consistent with their welfare.

To meet these duties, local authorities must provide, as appropriate: advice, guidance and counselling; occupational, social, cultural or recreational activities; home help; assistance to enable a child and the family to have a holiday. Local authorities will have to take reasonable steps to identify the number of children in need in their area. They will have to maintain a register of disabled children. They will have to publish information about the services available, both official and voluntary, and ensure that this information reaches those who might benefit.

While advice, guidance and counselling are free, a reasonable charge may be levied for other services, though this will not apply to families receiving Income Support or Family Credit.

See *Chronically Sick and Disabled Persons Act 1970, Disabled Persons* (*Services, Consultation and Representation*) *Act 1986.*

Children's Apperception Test (CAT), *projective technique* in which children aged three to ten years are asked to tell a story about each of ten different pictures. The original set, now called CAT-A, featured animals in various situations, designed to tap possible sources of concern to the child, such as sibling rivalry, night fears, etc. Since some older children found the animal pictures too babyish, a second set of pictures was produced, featuring humans, and called CAT-H. A third set is available, designed to tap more specific issues, such as pregnancy and divorce, and called CAT-S.

The test rests on the assumption that the stories will reflect the child's own anxieties and concerns. Interpreting the stories is a skilled clinical procedure, and the interpretation is used – in conjunction with other information – as an aid in the diagnosis of children's emotional difficulties and a guide to possible lines of treatment.

Children's Behaviour Questionnaire, see *Rutter's Behaviour Questionnaires.*

Children's Personality Questionnaire, set of four parallel questionnaires for assessing the personality of children aged eight to twelve years. Most items force a choice between two questions. The results provide scores on 14 personality dimensions, derived from analysis of the responses of the USA standardisation population.

Reference:

Levy, P. and Goldstein, H. (1984) *Tests in Education,* London, Academic Press.

chorea, rare disease of the central nervous system, associated with rheumatic fever. It is characterised by continuous involuntary movements, such as twitching of the muscles, which, together with the emotional stress and absence from school, can hinder educational progress. (Huntington's chorea is a different disease, appearing in middle age.)

chorionic villus sampling, technique for detecting defects such as chromosome abnormalities in the unborn foetus through analysing a very small amount of tissue taken from the placenta. This can be done as early as the ninth week of pregnancy, so offering advantages over other diagnostic methods, which cannot be employed until later in pregnancy.

See *amniocentesis.*

chromosome, threadlike structure in the nucleus of a cell, carrying the genes, the determinants of hereditary characteristics. In humans, the body cells normally contain forty-six chromosomes, arranged in twenty-two pairs, plus a pair of sex chromosomes. The immediate link with special education was the 1959 finding that *Down's syndrome* was associated with an abnormality in chromosome pair no. 21.

This finding demonstrated the presence of a third chromosome at this site, hence Down's syndrome is sometimes known as trisomy 21. Since then, various other kinds of chromosome abnormalities have been identified: mosaicism, in which an abnormal chromosome pair coexists with its normal version in the same person; translocations, in which a part of one chromosome is added to another at a different site; fragility, in which a constriction occurs along one of the chromosomes; etc.

Since 1959, a number of different chromosome abnormalities have been shown to be associated with educational problems, in particular with learning difficulties of various sorts. Techniques for identifying these abnormalities, and for identifying them earlier in pregnancy, have improved significantly in recent years. Thus genetic counselling may lead to a substantial drop in the prevalence of children whose learning difficulties arise for these reasons.

See *amniocentesis, chorionic villus sampling, fragile X syndrome.*

References:

Connor, M. (1990) *The Causes and Prevention of Handicap,* Stratford-upon-Avon, National Council for Special Education.

Harper, P.S. (1989) *Practical Genetic Counselling,* Bristol, Wright.

Chronically Sick and Disabled Persons Act 1970, legislated for the provision of services for disabled people at home and in the community. The Act required local authorities to identify the number and needs of disabled people and to inform them of the help that it is the authority's duty to supply where needed, e.g. meals, help in obtaining a telephone, special equipment, taking a holiday, access to public places and suitable toilets. Increasing concern about the lack of proper individual assessment under the Act led to the *Disabled Persons (Services, Consultation and Representation) Act 1986.*

While the 1970 Act did include a section specifying an education authority's duties in respect of children suffering from acute *dyslexia,* the 1986 Act has more substantial implications for special education generally.

classical conditioning, see *conditioning.*

classification, system of differentiating children's educational problems. Classification in special education evolved from the *medical model* of diagnosing a specific condition in order to develop and use a specific remedy. This approach has been criticised in special education, not least since the broad categories used for administrative purposes in education were largely medically determined and not necessarily relevant educationally. Moreover their validity was often called into question, since factors such as availability of places, parental pressures, social attitudes, professional preference, etc., affected the classification.

This is not to say that classification is unimportant. In order to obtain and compare prevalence rates meaningfully, for example, it is important to use an agreed system of classification, based on agreed terminology. There are various systems in use, usually more detailed and more subtle – sometimes multiaxial, i.e. using several dimensions – than the broad administrative categories which were so unsatisfactory. Some of these have been suggested by individuals, but others have been agreed by professional organisations. For example, the American Association on Mental Deficiency has produced a Manual on Terminology and Classification, the American Psychiatric Association has produced a Diagnostic and Statistical Manual of Mental Disorders, and the World Health Organisation has produced the International Classification of Diseases. These three texts are valuable contributions to the classification of those intellectual, emotional and physical conditions for which special education is needed.

See *categories of handicap, dimensional classification.*

References:

Evans, P. and Ware, J. (1986) *Special Care Provision: The Education of Children with Profound and Multiple Learning Difficulties*, Windsor, NFER-Nelson.

Tharinger, D.J., Laurent, J. and Best, L.R. (1986) 'Classification of Children referred for Emotional and Behavioral Problems: a Comparison of the PL 94-142 SED Criteria, DSM III and the CBCL System', *Journal of School Psychology*, 24, 111–21.

classroom assistant, member of the team responsible for the education of children with special needs. While ancillaries such as nursery nurses and classroom assistants have always had a place in nursery and special schools, their services are often required when children with special needs enter the mainstream. Their roles include general caring duties, such as dressing, feeding and toileting children where necessary, some broadly educational duties, such as helping the teacher prepare educational materials, hearing children read, etc., working with the advisory services, such as giving speech therapy exercises at the request of the speech therapist, etc.

No special training is at present required for this wide range of activities. But there is no doubt that the presence in the classroom of another adult to whom the children can relate, another person who can offer to meet those needs that a class teacher is often too busy to meet, is indispensable to the educational progress of many children with special needs.

Current proposals (not recommendations) for allocating classroom assistant (called special support assistant) time per pupil, suggest that this could depend on phase of education, primary children needing more support than secondary, and degree of learning difficulty. These proposals offer a range from 0.3 assistant per primary pupil with greatest difficulty to 0.05 assistant per secondary pupil with least difficulty.

References:

Bell, F. (1988) 'Support of Mainstreamed Children with Special Needs by Non-Teaching Assistants', Newsletter No. 29 of the Division of Educational and Child Psychologists, *British Psychological Society*, March 1988, 28–31.

Hegarty, S. and Pocklington, K. (1982) *Integration in Action*, Windsor, NFER-Nelson.

Clayton, T. (1990) 'The Training Needs of Special Welfare Assistants: What do Heads, Class Teachers and the Assistants themselves Regard as Important?' *Educational and Child Psychology*, 7, 1, 44–51.

Department of Education and Science (1990) 'Staffing for Pupils with Special Educational Needs', Circular Letter 10.1.1990, London, Department of Education and Science.

classroom management, see *room management.*

cleft lip; cleft palate, congenital conditions, hereditary in origin, in which the tissues of the lip and roof of the mouth fail to close properly. Either lip or palate can be affected, or both; the severity varies from child to child and the clefts sometimes appear with other congenital malformations. The incidence is about one per thousand births worldwide, but local prevalence is related to the extent of inbreeding in a community. The conditions are corrected by surgery, starting in the first few months of life, but treatment may continue for some years.

Children with cleft palate have no intrinsic intellectual difficulties. But as a group, they do show speech and language problems. These may be due to difficulties in managing the airflow needed for correct speech, leading to *articulation disorders,* or to weakness in the speech musculature, leading to nasal speech, or to *hearing impairment* linked to middle ear infections, to which children with cleft palate are vulnerable. Speech therapy is obviously helpful, and teachers need to be alert to any sensitivity children with cleft lip may show over their appearance.

Reference:

Webster, A. and McConnell, C. (1987) *Children with Speech and Language Difficulties,* London, Cassell.

clinical psychologist, applied psychologist, usually employed by the Health Service to work with patients and their problems. The activities of a Clinical Psychology Service serving a Health District have been roughly divided into work with patients with general psychological problems, work with patients with neurological problems, work with elderly patients, work with the adult mentally handicapped, and work with children and young people, particularly those with mental handicap. This represents a diversification from an earlier role, in which clinical psychologists were largely employed with psychiatric patients, and has been accompanied by a shift from a hospital to a community orientation.

Their activities with children and young people mean that some clinical psychologists are becoming more involved with children in special education. These psychologists may often have children with severe learning difficulties referred to them, though they may also deal with many other kinds of problem. Of the 1,700 or so clinical psychologists working in the UK in the mid-80s, only 15% worked with children.

Irrespective of their later field of work, all clinical psychologists follow a post-graduate generic training, usually with a behavioural emphasis.

See *educational psychologist.*

References:
Kat, B. (1989) 'Sharing Skills and Care', *The Psychologist*, 2, 10, 434 (and other articles on clinical psychology in the same issue).
Levick, M. (1986) 'Clinical Psychologists Working with Children, Young People and their Families', *Educational and Child Psychology*, 3, 3, 177–85.

cloze procedure, technique for assessing the readability, or level of difficulty of books in order to select those which match pupils' reading skills. It was devised by W.L. Taylor in 1953 and is based on the assumption that fluent reading requires the use of comprehension skills and contextual clues to predict missing material. Cloze procedures can also be used informally to assess a pupil's comprehension of reading matter, which some say is a more appropriate use for it.

Cloze procedure example

If you are unwell, the doctor takes your temperature with a clinical thermometer. Your temperature is usually 98.4 _____ on the Fahrenheit scale, written 98.4°F _____ short. This is called _____ normal temperature. A few _____ have their normal temperature _____ little higher or a _____ lower ... etc.

The technique involves deleting every nth word from a passage, and requiring the child to guess the deletions by using contextual clues. Different formats have been suggested. One often followed is to choose three representative passages of 100 words in length, one from each of the start, middle and end of the book. Every fifth word is then deleted, but retaining the first and last sentences of each passage in their entirety, the first word in each sentence, numbers and proper nouns. According to one set of criteria, if fewer than 44% of the deletions are completed correctly, the reading material is at frustration level, i.e. too hard; if between 45% and 57% are correct, then the material is at instructional level, i.e. can be used to help improve a child's reading skills; if over 57% are correct then the material is at independent reading level, i.e. the child can use it for recreational reading.

There is debate over whether the correct word only should be scored, or whether, as most teachers accept, reasonable synonyms should also score.

See *GAP Reading Comprehension Test, readability index.*

References:
Klare, G.R. (1982) 'Readability', in Mitzel, H.E. (1982, 5th edn.) *Encyclopaedia of Educational Research*, New York, Free Press.
Rye, J. (1982) *Cloze Procedure and the Teaching of Reading*, London, Heinemann, referenced in Pumfrey, P. (1985, 2nd edn.) *Reading: Tests and Assessment Techniques*, Sevenoaks. Hodder and Stoughton.
Stephens, T.M., Blackhurst, A.E. and Magliocca, L.A. (1982) *Teaching Mainstreamed Students*, New York, Wiley.

clumsy child, a child who is physically fit, but with coordination problems. As well as having difficulties with activities in which good motor development is essential, such as dressing or ball games, clumsy children often write badly and present work that is generally untidy.

It has been suggested that clumsiness may be due to minimal brain damage, too small to show overt neurological signs, and possibly associated with a difficult birth. This neurological damage may also be responsible for the reading and language difficulties some clumsy children show.

This explanation can be debated, but is of minor relevance educationally. Any language problems are dealt with by good teaching; physiotherapy and occupational therapy can help with the motor and coordination problems, which can be assessed by a test such as the *Bruininks-Oseretsky.* Finally, clumsiness is a relative concept: there is no such entity as a clumsy child per se, only children who are more or less clumsy.

See *brain damage, motor impairment.*

References:

Gordon, N. and McKinley, I. (1980) *Helping Clumsy Children*, Edinburgh, Churchill Livingstone.

Graham, P.J. (1986) *Child Psychiatry: a Developmental Approach*, Oxford, Oxford University Press.

Quin, V. and MacAuslan, A. (1981) *Reading and Spelling Difficulties: a Medical Approach*, Sevenoaks, Hodder and Stoughton.

cochlea, see *ear.*

Cocktail party syndrome, inability to keep talk relevant and meaningful, with a tendency to use language superficially and without true comprehension. It has been said to characterise children with spina bifida, who generally have good expressive language but may not have such good understanding as people are led to believe. It may arise because of the conceptual or spatial problems displayed by some children with spina bifida or hydrocephalus, or result from the difficulties children have in tying language to direct experience when their mobility is limited.

Reference:

Webster, A. and McConnell, C. (1987) *Children with Speech and Language Difficulties*, London, Cassell.

cognitive behaviour modification (CBM), changing behaviour through changing thinking processes. Contrary to orthodox *behaviour modification,* which deals with observable behaviour only, CBM rests on the belief that an individual's thinking or cognition can affect behaviour, and that individuals should be helped to control their own behaviour through learning to think about it. Various approaches have been described. For example, an adult may model an appropriate response to a situation, saying out loud the steps being taken. The child is then asked to replicate the model response. This approach is more successful with children who are not intellectually limited, and has been found most effective in coping with hyperactive behaviour.

Reference:
Hallahan, D.P. and Kaufman, J.M. (1988, 4th edn.) *Exceptional Children: Introduction to Special Education,* Englewood Cliffs, Prentice Hall.

cognitive development, the growth of the intellect. While education is inescapably concerned with the flowering of the whole personality, for most people, school is seen as centrally concerned with the development of a child's cognitive skills, though also involved in fostering social and emotional development.

Theories of cognitive development are – or should be – of great interest to special education, since learning difficulties and poor cognitive development are inextricably intertwined.

The fore-runners of modern behaviourists attempted to explain development as a steady accretion of learnt responses, shaped by considerations such as frequency of repetition and proximity in time. Later behavioural psychologists built in the importance of reinforcement and reward as explanatory principles, an emphasis which has been reflected in teaching procedures in many special education classrooms.

In contradistinction to these approaches, *Piagetian theory* is based on careful observation of children's thinking at different levels, emerging with a stage theory of cognitive development. One implication of this approach is to avoid introducing higher stage thinking until the child has passed through the stage below. Teaching materials and assessments based on the Piagetian approach have been familiar in special education for many years.

Other theories of cognitive development emphasise that learning can be a social activity; social learning theory argues that procedures such as modelling have a part to play in successful cognitive growth.

These and other theories of cognitive growth are not contradictory, but complementary. For example all accept that impaired senses will affect cognitive growth, though some have more obvious relevance to this than others. But all have insights to offer through which cognitive development can be facilitated.

Reference:
Child, D. (1986, 4th edn.) *Psychology and the Teacher,* London, Holt Rinehart and Winston.

cognitive modifiability, the belief that it is possible to change a person's cognitive development by altering basic thinking processes. The theory of *Instrumental Enrichment,* in which cognitive modifiability is a key concept, holds that learning difficulties are best helped by concentrating not on what we learn, but on how we learn. This involves changing basic thinking structures, how we act on and respond to information. Feuerstein, the author of Instrumental Enrichment, holds that, apart from severely organically impaired persons, the course of cognitive development can be modified for the better at any age. This optimistic stance, supported by case-studies, has proved a great attraction.

See *Learning Potential Assessment Device.*

Reference:
Feuerstein, R. (1980) *Instrumental Enrichment*, Baltimore, University Park Press.

cognitive style, characteristic ways of perceiving, thinking and learning. Originally cognitive styles were seen as personality variables, and different authors constructed different typologies. Often these were similar, though named differently. (Witkin's field-independent/field-dependent styles resembling Pask's holists/serialists, for example.) More recently it has been argued that some learning difficulties – e.g. dyslexia – may in part reflect a faulty or inappropriate learning style. Instruments for assessing learning styles have also been produced.
References:
Stott, D.H., Green, L. and Francis, J. (1988, 2nd edn.) *Guide to the Child's Learning Skills*, Stafford, National Association for Remedial Education.
Tansley, P. and Panckhurst, J. (1981) *Children with Specific Learning Difficulties; a Critical Review of Research*, Windsor, NFER-Nelson.

COHI, acronym for Crippled and Other Health Impaired children, used in the USA to describe those children whose main problem is medical, although they may also have associated educational problems, e.g. children with cerebral palsy. In the UK these children have often been loosely described as physically handicapped.

In the USA, the term 'physically handicapped' is sometimes used to refer to children whose main problem is a sensory impairment, e.g. a child with partial hearing: hence the need for a description such as COHI to differentiate the two groups.
Reference:
Van Etten, G., Arkell, C. and Van Etten, C. (1980) *The Severely and Profoundly Handicapped*, St. Louis, Mosby.

colour coding, the systematic association of colour with phonemes or language structures in order to help learning. The use of colour coding in reading schemes is an old cueing device, going back to readers used at the turn of the century and probably earlier. The simple procedures of printing vowels in one colour and consonants in another has been extended and developed so that some reading schemes include separate colour representation for voiced and unvoiced letters, common phonemes, etc.

The natural attraction of colours has led speech therapists, too, to employ colour coding of language structures, often in conjunction with other aids. As in the reading context, the important points to bear in mind are clarity, consistency, and fading colour out once skills develop.
Reference:
Stackhouse, J. (1985) 'Procedures for Assessment and Management', in Snowling, M.J. (Ed.) (1985), *Children's Written Language Difficulties*, Windsor, NFER-Nelson.

colour vision, is important where colour is used in teaching activities (e.g. *colour coding*), and defective colour vision (colour blindness) rules out

several careers. Defective colour vision occurs mainly in males, where roughly 10% suffer from it. Usually there is a difficulty in distinguishing the red and green parts of the spectrum, but a blue-yellow colour vision deficiency and, very rarely, a complete loss of colour vision are also known.
See *Ishihara Test.*

Coloured Progressive Matrices, see *Raven's Progressive Matrices.*

Columbia Mental Maturity Scale, individual test of reasoning ability in children aged three to ten years, originally produced for assessing children with cerebral palsy. The child has to choose the 'odd' drawing out of four or five, presented on a large card. The score from the set of cards is transformed into a standard score. The test is particularly useful for assessing the development of children with severe motor problems, since a choice can be indicated by simply pointing or nodding.
Reference:
Anastasi, A. (1982, 5th edn.) *Psychological Testing,* New York, Macmillan.

Committee of Enquiry into Special Education, incorrect but frequently-used title for the Committee which produced the *Warnock Report.*

Committee on Accreditation of Rehabilitation Facilities (CARF), attempts to upgrade the quality of services provided in the USA by organisations such as *sheltered workshops.* Thus CARF expects that sheltered workshops should provide, as a minimum, adequate vocational evaluation, work adjustment, medical services, psychological services, social work services and job-placements.
Reference:
Brolin, E. (1982, 2nd edn.) *Vocational Preparation of Persons with Handicaps,* Columbus, Merrill.

Communication Aids Centres, aim to provide people with speech impairments with communication aids. They were funded by a voluntary organisation (Royal Association for Disability and Rehabilitation) and the Department of Health and Social Security. Originally there were six centres, but their number has since grown.
Reference:
Hope, M.H. (1987) *Micros for Children with Special Needs,* Souvenir, London.

Communication Aids for Language and Learning (CALL) Centre, offers assessment and provides information and training in the use of microelectronics for learners with communication impairment. It is jointly funded by the Scottish Education and Social Work Departments.
Reference:
Hope, M.H. (1987) *Micros for Children with Special Needs,* Souvenir, London.

community care, support that enables a person to live in society, rather than in an institution such as a residential school, hospital or children's home.

In many respects, community care has been the least developed aspect of social policy, with practice falling short of the standards set by government guidelines, and with considerable variation from region to region. Indeed the Griffiths Report spoke of community care as 'a poor relation, everybody's distant relation, nobody's baby'. But paying lip-service to the principle of community care has led to the closure of many hospital wards for the psychologically disturbed and the mentally handicapped. In special education the effect of this movement has been most clearly seen in the running down of hospital beds and hospital schools for children with serious mental handicap, who are then often expected to attend schools for children with severe learning difficulties while living at home.

The government has now published its proposals for the provision of community care, based on the Griffiths Report and the White Paper 'Caring for People'. These proposals set out six key objectives for service delivery in the community. These are: the development of domiciliary day and respite services to enable people to live in their own homes wherever feasible and sensible; that residential, nursing home or hospital care should be a positive choice for those who really need it; to ensure that practical support for carers has a higher priority than at present; to make proper assessment of need and good case management the cornerstone of high quality care; to promote the development of a flourishing independent sector alongside quality public services, and to clarify the responsibilities of agencies and make them more accountable; to secure better value for money and maximise social care by introducing a new funding structure.

To meet these objectives entails some basic changes to the functions of social service authorities. In addition, new arrangements are required to fund individuals needing financial support for social care, including residential and nursing-home care.

One criticism of these proposals is that they contain no provision for a specific annual grant to be made to local authorities in the context of community care. The emphasis placed upon the independent sector as the key provider of community care has also given rise to disquiet, since there is considerable doubt as to its ability or willingness to undertake this considerable task.

References:

Department of Health (1989) *Caring for People – Community Care in the Next Decade and Beyond*, Cmd 849, London, HMSO (Griffiths Report).

Department of Health and Social Security (1988) *Community Care: Agenda for Action*, London, HMSO.

community medical officer, sometimes known as clinical medical officer, is a medical practitioner usually specialising in child health. His/her considerable influence on special education is exercised through

a. liaising between the medical and education services over pre-school children with special needs;

b. coordinating medical assessment and advice to the Local Education Authority;
c. advising teaching staff and parents over health factors that might play a part in a child's educational difficulties, and
d. contributing as a member of the *District Handicap Team* and other services for children with special needs.

Note that there are two main types of health provision for children, the hospitals and primary care teams, with an emphasis on treatment, and the community health services, with an emphasis on prevention. But the integration of the two services is being encouraged through joint appointments and shared responsibilities. Consultant community paediatricians are increasingly being appointed to lead the community child health services and to link their work with that of hospital consultants and general practice.

References:

Adams, F. (Ed.) (1981) *Special Education*, Harlow, Councils and Education Press for Longmans.

Powell, R. (1984) 'Medical Screening and Surveillance', in Lindsay, G. (Ed.) (1984) *Screening for Children with Special Needs*, London, Croom Helm.

Community Mental Handicap Team, was set up to coordinate the somewhat fragmented services for the mentally handicapped of all ages and to provide practical support at home for individuals who are mentally handicapped and their families. The composition of the team varies from area to area and within an area, depending on the particular function being exercised at the time. But there is usually a core team of a social worker and a community psychiatric nurse. This team is augmented by a psychiatrist, psychologist and medical officer (mental health) to form the clinical team, though therapists, health visitors and teachers are also co-opted, according to the needs of the person and the family.

The community mental health teams have no special provision for dealing with children, and their composition and function should be compared with that of the *District Handicap Teams.*

References:

Cotmore, R. (1986) 'The District and Community Mental Health Team', in Coupe, J. and Porter, J. (Eds.) (1986) *The Education Of Children with Severe Learning Difficulties*, Beckenham, Croom Helm.

Furneaux, B. (1988) *Special Parents*, Milton Keynes, Open University Press.

Grant, G., Humphreys, S. and McGrath, M. (Eds.) (1986) *Community Mental Handicap Teams: Theory and Practice*, Kidderminster, British Institute of Mental Handicap.

companion reading, combination of *Direct Instruction* and *peer tutoring* of reading, used for initial reading teaching as well as with older children with reading difficulties. It aims to develop reading proficiency through clear modelling of demonstrated skills, overt responding, checking by mastery tests, followed by systematic review.

Children are divided into pairs by inverse matching, i.e. the least able is paired with the most able and so on. Teacher first demonstrates the required skill on the board, the children responding in unison. This is followed by a short period of companion study, in which the members of a pair take it in turn to tutor each other, having learnt the importance of *Pause, Prompt and Praise* techniques. A short period of individual study follows, after which mastery checking occurs.

Companion reading is planned as a ninety-minute-a-day activity, five days a week, parents being invited to share in the process through asking the child to read the worksheet that is taken home weekly.

See *paired reading*.

Reference:

Pitchford, M. and Story, R. (1988) 'Companion Reading: Group Instruction, Peer tutoring and Inservice for Teachers', *Educational and Child Psychology*, 5, 4, 29–34.

compensation, see *defence mechanism*.

compensatory education, originally extra preschool education for children from poor families, intended to improve the relatively slow growth in their attainments after entering school. In part compensatory education was a celebration of the environmentalist's belief in the importance of nurture for intellectual growth, of the theoretician's belief in the importance of the early years for later development and of the educational philosopher's belief in the capacity of education for changing the human condition.

Compensatory programmes were targeted at the young child, for the effectiveness of preschool programmes for disadvantaged children had been demonstrated in the 1950s. The *Head Start* programme in the USA was the first attempt to exploit these findings through a coordinated national effort. As part of President Johnson's 'War on Poverty' the programme offered extra health care and extra support from the social services, as well as a compensatory education component: in the event, the typical educational component was a summer school of some six weeks or so.

Given this short experience it was hardly unexpected when the first evaluations of the compensatory education programmes subsumed under the Head Start banner appeared to show that they had had little or no educational effect. More careful analyses showed that some programmes were effective, in particular those which worked with the parents as well as the children, started when the children were very young, often in infancy, enjoyed very low staff–student ratios, concentrated on language development, and worked intensively and over far longer periods than the typical Head Start six weeks. More recent analyses have shown that even if it is difficult to show academic gains for the children of the normal, relatively cursory Head Start programme, there is evidence that by school leaving age they have been retained in their grade less frequently, referred to special class less frequently, and have been in trouble with the law less frequently than similar children who did not participate in Head Start. In short their attitudes to school and society have improved.

The compensatory movement was introduced into the UK with the *Swansea Project.* Unlike many of the programmes in the USA it aimed at influencing the curriculum throughout the three years of infant schooling, developing assessment procedures for identifying individual children at risk, rather than working with a whole area, and linking these activities to ongoing research findings in the British context. Apart from four interlinked projects started shortly afterwards by the Department of Education and Science, little further specific work into compensatory education has been instituted, though the movement has had effects on educational policy and practice in various ways – the current emphasis on language work in infant schools is entirely consistent with the compensatory approach. More fundamentally, there is now less faith in the ability of education to effect significant alterations in society.

Compensatory education has direct relevance to special education, since so many children with learning difficulties grow up in disadvantaged homes. Anything that can be done to help their response to school is a contribution to meeting their special needs.

See *disadvantage, Milwaukee project, sleeper effect.*

References:

Chazan, M. and Williams, P. (Eds.) (1978) *Deprivation and the Infant School*, Oxford, Blackwells.

Nisbet, J. and Watts, J . (1984) *Educational Disadvantage: Ten Years On*, Edinburgh, HMSO.

Woodward, M. (1986) 'Early Intervention', Unit 27, Course E206, Milton Keynes, Open University.

comprehension, understanding the meaning of a situation, however presented.

A comprehension test is used as part of many tests of intelligence, often presenting a social situation in the form of a series of pictures, which the child has to interpret. Alternatively, the child may be asked to rearrange a set of pictures so that the sequence has meaning. *Factor analyse*s have shown that this kind of comprehension test measures verbal as well as nonverbal abilities: this is explained on the grounds that internal language may be used in ordering the pictures, even though the verbal component appears at first glance to be confined to understanding the basic instructions.

Reading comprehension, the extent to which a pupil grasps the meaning of a printed passage, is the central reading skill, distinguished from others such as *word recognition*, or *fluency*. Tests of reading comprehension usually require the pupil to read a series of sentences, either separately or forming a passage, and then answer questions on them, though tests based on the cloze procedure are also used.

Oral comprehension, or listening comprehension, is a measure of the child's understanding of the spoken word. Again, tests of oral comprehension can use a sentence by sentence format, or a longer, passage format. Either way, the child is asked questions on the meaning of what he has heard. The Wechsler Intelligence Scales for Children include such a comprehension test among their verbal subtests.

Tests of reading vocabulary and oral vocabulary are particular examples of reading and oral comprehension tests, focused on single words, and widely used in the assessment of children's language skills.

See *GAP reading comprehension test, Neale Analysis of Reading Ability.*

References:

Flood, J. (Ed.) (1984) *Understanding Reading Comprehension,* Newark, International Reading Association.

Lunzer, E., Waite, M. and Dolan, T. (1979) 'Comprehension and Comprehension Tests', in Lunzer, E. and Gardner, K. (Eds.) (1979) *The Effective Use of Reading,* London, Heinemann.

Niles, O.S. (1972) 'Comprehension Skills', in Melnik, A. and Merritt, J. (Eds.) (1972) *The Reading Curriculum,* London, ULP.

compressed speech, method for conveying information to the visually impaired. Since Braille is a slow way of reading, much material for the visually-impaired is recorded on tape. While speech recorded at normal speed still conveys information faster than a person can read Braille, any technique that speeds this up is advantageous. In compressed speech very small segments of the speech are discarded, for example through a computer programme eliminating vowel sounds, so permitting material to be covered at a faster rate without losing meaning.

The technique depends on a high level of listening skill.

Reference:

Hallahan, D.P. and Kaufman, J.M. (1988, 4th edn.) *Exceptional Children: Introduction to Special Education,* Englewood Cliffs, Prentice Hall.

computer-assisted learning (CAL), can be considered under four headings:

(1) Instructional, where the computer is used to present teaching material to the pupil, whose response is then reinforced or not, depending on its accuracy. This is immediately recognisable as learning in the behaviourist mode, advantageous for children with learning difficulties since the pupil controls the pace, a suitable difficulty gradient can be followed, perhaps using branching programmes, and the tutor (computer) is infinitely patient. But instructional CAL is knowledge-orientated.

(2) Revelatory, where CAL provides opportunities for learning experiences not normally possible. Simulations fall into this category, for example simulating the long-term effects of weather on scenery via the computer. This approach affords a range of interesting possibilities for providing access to the curriculum for children with special needs.

(3) Conjectural, where the computer is used to encourage higher-level thinking, perhaps allowing the pupil to test out the effects of hypotheses and ideas. Note that in this case the learner is firmly in charge of the learning, a situation which can help to build self-confidence.

(4) Emancipatory, where the computer is a mechanical device used by the teacher to help with record keeping, filing reports, statements, etc.

Reference:

Reid, D.J. and Hodson, D. (1987) *Science for All: teaching science in the secondary school*, London, Cassell.

concept keyboard, device which replaces the standard qwerty keyboard on a computer with touch-sensitive pads. With an appropriate overlay, the set of pads can represent a set of concepts, not letters. An overlay will provide concepts relating to a particular lesson or group of lessons, and with a suitable program, the child can access a database from which information can be gained. Different overlays are available commercially, or can be made by the teacher to fit the curriculum being followed. Synthetic speech allows children who are visually handicapped to use the device.

Reference:

Reid, D.J. and Hodson, J. (1987) *Science for All: teaching science in the secondary school*, London, Cassell.

concrete operations stage, see *Piagetian theory.*

conditioning, the central explanatory principle of learning for the behaviourist school of psychology. It implies that learnt behaviour is behaviour which depends on (i.e. is conditional on) events in the environment. These can be either events which precede the behaviour (classical conditioning) or events which follow it (operant conditioning). Concepts such as motivation, discovery learning, interest, etc., all of which feature prominently in other theories of learning, are regarded as redundant or of marginal usefulness by behavioural psychologists, who prefer to work with observable behaviour only. Even complex behaviour is explained through conditioning, the bedrock on which the behavioural house has been erected.

Classical conditioning rests on the set of reflexes with which a baby is born. An example is the sucking reflex; placing a teat in the infant's mouth automatically produces sucking behaviour. If the arrival of the teat is regularly preceded by the sound of the bottle being prepared, the infant will start to suck on hearing the bottle sounds. From such simple pieces of learning, the behaviourist uses classical conditioning (Pavlovian conditioning) to try to explain many complex behaviours – an attempt which does not satisfy everyone.

Nevertheless, it has considerable application to special education. For example, classical conditioning is used in *audiometry* with very young children; it is used in a number of *behaviour therapy* procedures, particularly those dealing with inappropriate fears and other emotions; it is used in teaching simple responses to children who are severely mentally handicapped.

Operant conditioning explains learning through the events which follow behaviour. Whereas classical conditioning is seen as mechanical, operant conditioning (Skinnerian, or instrumental conditioning), starts from the assumption that the child emits voluntary behaviour. Whether that behaviour is learnt or not depends upon whether what follows it is reinforcing or not. If staying in one's seat is reinforced with praise, the pupil is likely to learn to remain in the seat. That which is reinforced is learnt; that which is not reinforced is not learnt. This relatively simple principle has also been advanced as a building block from which the learning of complicated behaviour can be explained. Complicated behaviours can be constructed by stringing together separate learnt reactions, rather like stringing beads on a chain. The principles of *reinforcement* enable the stringing to be accomplished effectively.

Operant conditioning, too, has had great influence on special education; for example, *behaviour modification* programmes have been based on it; the token economy system has been developed from it; motivation to learn has been facilitated through it. Perhaps its greatest contribution to special education has been its emphasis on the importance of the teacher's response to the child's behaviour. In operant conditioning theory, this is a key element in the child's learning at school, whether learning scholastic skills or emotional behaviours.

References:

Child, D. (1986, 4th edn.) *Psychology and the Teacher*, London, Holt Rinehart and Winston.

Devereux, K. (1982) *Understanding Learning Difficulties*, Milton Keynes, Open University Press.

Evans, P. (1986) 'The Learning Process', in Coupe, J, and Porter, J. (Eds.) (1986) *The Education of Children with Severe Learning Difficulties*, Beckenham, Croom Helm.

conduct disorder, broadly, persistent serious antisocial behaviour. Children's behaviour problems are sometimes divided into conduct disorders on the one hand and emotional disorders on the other. This conduct disorder/emotional disorder dichotomy parallels the antisocial/neurotic dichotomy used in *Rutter's Behaviour Questionnaires*, and is similarly supported by *factor analysis* of behaviour intercorrelations. (This does not imply that a child's behaviour cannot show both conduct and emotional problems: simply that this division is helpful for classification purposes.)

The conduct disorders themselves can be further subdivided, but here the ground is less sure, different authorities providing different subclassifications. For example, Herbert offers three: serious antisocial behaviour; overactivity; aggression. The American Psychiatric Association also offers three: a group type (conduct problems occurring as a group activity with peers); a solitary aggressive type (physical violence initiated by the individual); an undifferentiated type (those that cannot be classified in either of the first two categories).

Since there are no agreed criteria for diagnosing a conduct disorder, it is not possible to give a meaningful prevalence rate. But whatever criteria are used, conduct disorders are significantly more prevalent in boys than girls, overall figures of three to one having been reported, in contrast to emotional or neurotic behaviour. The preponderance of boys itself varies with the kind of conduct disorder, and for delinquency a ratio of up to ten boys to one girl has been reported: note that these ratios appear to be changing as sex-roles alter.

Conduct disorders are among the least responsive to treatment, which may partly account for the growth in the number of *units for disruptive pupils.* Moreover the prognosis is not good, for most studies of disruptive, aggressive children show that these behaviour patterns are likely to persist into adolescence and beyond.

References:

Barker, P. (1988, 5th edn.) *Basic Child Psychiatry,* Oxford, Blackwell.

American Psychiatric Association (1987, 3rd edn. Rev.) *DSM IIIR, Diagnostic and Statistical Manual of Mental Disorders,* Washington, American Psychiatric Association.

Herbert, M. (1987) *Behavioural Treatment of Children with Problems: a Practice Manual,* London, Academic Press.

conductive education, aims to teach adults and children to overcome the effects of motor disorders, particularly those associated with *cerebral palsy.* It emphasises the attainment of orthofunction, which involves learning to gain control of afflicted limbs, rather than using aids, and learning to sit, stand and walk without the use of wheelchairs, ramps or other special equipment or support. A success rate of over 70% of children entering the normal setting of school or work is claimed by the Petö Institute in Budapest. Much less dramatic improvement has so far been obtained elsewhere.

The method was developed in Hungary by Petö, who believed that for the approach to succeed, it had to be applied consistently and intensively throughout the day. This argued against conventional methods of managing these conditions, where a set of different specialists – speech therapist, physiotherapist, teacher, occupational therapist, nurse, care attendant, etc. – all work with the same child, often using different techniques and for practical reasons often finding it difficult to meet to collaborate.

To overcome this, Petö founded a new profession, that of the 'conductor'. The conductor is trained to teach the child important skills, such as dressing, feeding, walking, sitting, grasping, and handling early reading and number. The conductor is not a polymath who combines the skills of all the professions noted above, but rather a specialist in those parts of their skills which apply to children with cerebral palsy. Two or more conductors work with a group of children from waking to sleeping. Parents are involved from an early stage so that they can take the work over when the child leaves the Institute.

The basis of conductive education is purposive learning. Movements and exercises are not taught for their own sakes, but in order to fulfil a function; the child may be taught to hold on in order to learn to sit. The child is taught to use speech to help control the function; external speech is later replaced by inner speech, which in turn disappears as the function becomes automatic.

Conductive education raises several interesting theoretical points. The relationship between the details of Petö's approach and Vigotsky's theories of the development of thought and language are matters of considerable interest. The emphasis placed on the role of the parents is very much in line with the view that parents should be partners in special education. But note too that the method involves the residential education of children with special needs in a separate establishment, an approach which is contrary to the principles of integration.

The first Centre for Conductive Education in the UK was started in Birmingham in 1986.

Note that the Children Act 1989 inserted a provision in the Education Act 1981 enabling a local authority to make payments for children with special needs to attend an establishment outside England and Wales. This was specifically designed to meet the expenses of children attending the Petö Institute.

References:

Cottam, P.J. and Sutton, A. (1989, 2nd edn.) *Conductive Education: a System for Overcoming Motor Disability*, London, Croom Helm.

Hari, M. and Akos, K. (1988) *Conductive Education*, London, Routledge.

Jernqvist, L. (1986) 'Conductive Education: an Educational System for Children with Neurological Disorders', *European Journal for Special Needs Education*, 1, 1, 3–12.

New Law Journal, 17.11.1989, p.1568.

Sutton, A. (1986) 'Conductive Education: A Challenge to Integration?', *Educational and Child Psychology*, 3, 2, 5–12.

conductive hearing loss, impaired hearing caused by difficulties in sound transmission into the ear canal or across the middle ear system. It is distinguished from *sensorineural hearing loss*, caused by damage to the inner ear and/or auditory nerves. Conductive hearing loss may be due to obstructions such as wax or foreign bodies in the the ear. But middle ear infection – *otitis media* – which may prevent the mechanism of the ear from working properly, is the main cause of conductive hearing loss and is readily treated medically. Many young children suffer from these conditions from time to time and teachers should be alert to the hearing difficulties that may ensue.

Difficulties in sound transmission are sometimes due to malformations in the outer/inner ear: these can often be dealt with by surgery. But whatever the cause of conductive hearing loss, it affects equally all parts of the sound spectrum, both high and low frequencies, leading to dampening of hearing sensitivity at all levels of pitch, rather than distortion of sounds.

Children who suffer from conductive hearing loss may show some evidence of delayed language development; even mild temporary losses can have effects on language, though ground lost can be made up. Use of language structures as well as speech may be affected. Poor and intermittent hearing means that children may find difficulty in discriminating sounds, which may well hinder learning to read. It also means that they pay less attention in class, hence distractibility and poor concentration may also be signs of hearing loss, to which teachers need to be alert.

Conductive hearing loss may arise in conjunction with other problems, such as general ill-health, poor nutrition, low birth weight, poor family environment, which also predispose children to developmental problems. It can thus be difficult to pinpoint conductive hearing loss as the exact cause of any learning difficulties, when it is associated with many other risk factors.

See *ear, hearing impairment.*

References:

Webster, A. and McConnell, C. (1987) *Children with Speech and Language Difficulties*, London, Cassell.

Webster, A. and Wood, D. (1989) *Children with Hearing Difficulties*, London, Cassell.

conductor, see *conductive education.*

confidentiality, an ethical principle that has caused considerable concern. Some sensitive information about a child's background and development may be essential for a thorough understanding of his or her needs, yet a parent may volunteer the information without wishing it to be passed on. In this situation, if persuasion is unsuccessful, confidences must be respected.

By the same token, professionals may not want their reports on children to be revealed fully to parents (or occasionally even to other professionals), for some findings, it is argued, may be better not known, perhaps on the grounds that they may cause unnecessary anxiety and be actually counter-productive.

Before the Education Act 1981, parents had no right of access to the reports made to the education authority and on which the educational future of their child was decided. Since the 1981 Act this has changed, and parents now have the right to see the professional advice on which the education authority bases its statement of special educational needs. Note that (unless an authority decides otherwise) this does not convey the right to see all notes, reports, documents that a professional might have compiled; only those reports that are made to the authority. But while complete freedom of information is not usually available, the key Department of Education and Science circular, Circular 1/83, enjoins authorities to be as frank and open as possible.

See *medical records.*

Reference:

Adams, F. (Ed.) (1986) *Special Education,* Harlow, Councils and Education Press for Longmans.

congenital defect, defect present at birth. This includes hereditary disorders, as well as those which arise at conception (e.g. some chromosome abnormalities) and those which are due to damage to the foetus during pregnancy.

The incidence of congenital defects is said to be about 3% of live births. However not all infants with congenital defects survive to school age, not all congenital defects are severe enough to require special education, and the advances in techniques of prenatal screening may significantly reduce this incidence in the near future.

Contrast *acquired defect,* see *genetic counselling.*

conjoint family therapy, see *family group therapy.*

consonant digraph, see *digraph.*

contextual clue, guide to word recognition, based on the sense and syntax of a passage. There are many ways in which a reader may recognise a word: its shape is important; so is its phonic structure. But good readers are often able to anticipate what a word may be before meeting it: their experience of linguistic probabilities can be put to good use. Thus a possessive s is nearly always followed by a noun, as in 'John's coat; the dog's tail'. This immediately narrows the range of possible words which a reader can expect to meet after reading a possessive: from the meaning of the story in the passage, the range of possibilities is still further narrowed. These are the contextual clues which help a reader, particularly when meeting a new word, and which have led to reading being described as a 'psycholinguistic guessing game'. Other kinds of clues, familiar letters or strings of letters, for example, help still further to read the word correctly.

Fluent readers use contextual clues to great effect. Children with reading difficulties may need help to learn how to use them.

See *cloze procedure, top-down approach.*

contingency management, arranging *reinforcement* so that behaviour is changed. Where positive reinforcement is contingent on certain behaviour appearing, the likelihood of that behaviour being maintained or strengthened is increased; for contingent negative reinforcement the converse applies. 'Managing the contingencies' is thus the central principle of *behaviour modification.*

contracting, form of *behaviour modification* in which agreed *contingencies* are specified, usually in writing, and signed by both parties. Thus a teacher and pupil may draw up a contract specifying that:

'Each day, for the week beginning (date), (pupil's name) will arrive for the start of lessons at or before the bell. For each day that this is done, a token shall be awarded by (teacher's name). Tokens will be exchangeable at the standard rate at end of the week, when this contract will be reviewed.'

A contract requires negotiation between pupil and teacher: it has been argued that involving the pupil in this way leads to increased motivation. A contract should set goals that are realisable, the contingencies should be precisely defined, the reward immediate (in the example, daily, at the start of lessons), the performance should be recorded (again daily, at the start of lessons) and the contract should apply for a short period only, after which it should be cleared and then reviewed. Contracting is clearly more suitable for older children, and the behaviour to which it applies must be observable by both parties to the contract. Given these points, and the conditions mentioned above, contracting is a useful string to the bow of the behaviour modifier.

References:

Marsh, G.E., Price, B.J. and Smith, T.E.C. (1983) *Teaching Mildly Handicapped Children*, St. Louis, Mosby.

Wheldall, K. and Merrett, F. (1984) *Positive Teaching: the Behaviourist Approach*, London, Allen and Unwin.

control group, group of individuals who match as nearly as possible a similar group or groups who are the subjects of an experiment. Members of the control group are not exposed to the experimental treatment and so provide a basis for evaluating its effects. Since research in special education is usually carried out in the field, not the laboratory, and usually lasts over a period of time, it is not always easy to provide equivalent groups (children move; are exposed to extraneous influences over which the investigator has no control, etc.). Random allocation of children to groups helps to ensure similar vulnerability to these effects, as well as providing initial equivalence on qualities central to the investigation, so increasing the chances of an investigator being able to draw robust conclusions.

See *experimental group.*

Reference:

Christensen, L.B. (1988, 4th edn.) *Experimental Methodology*, New York, Allyn and Bacon.

convulsion, alternative term for fit or seizure, effectively caused by a sudden rapid electrical discharge in the brain resulting in physical symptoms varying from brief loss of attention to loss of consciousness and continence.

A convulsion is often assumed to be due to *epilepsy*, but this is not always so: epilepsy implies the presence of convulsions, but the presence of convulsions does not necessarily imply epilepsy – there are other conditions which could be responsible.

See *anticonvulsant.*

cooperative test of hearing, used with children approximately eighteen to thirty months of age. This is a screening test of hearing, requiring the child to be able to understand language and carry out prescribed actions with toys. It is simple in conception but difficult in execution.

See *audiometry, screening.*

Reference:

Tucker, I. and Nolan, M. (1984) *Educational Audiology*, Beckenham, Croom Helm.

coordinator of special needs, teacher responsible to the Head for ensuring that a school meets the special educational needs of its pupils. In a secondary school, organised by departments, this person is sometimes designated 'Head of Special Needs', but in primary schools where there is unlikely to be a special needs department, the coordinator title is usually used.

While every teacher has to share responsibility for the education of children with special needs, there should be one person on the staff with training and experience to take the lead. Such a person – the coordinator – has many duties, and these will vary from school to school. But they would normally include working with colleagues over the assessment of special needs, developing suitable teaching and support programmes, liaising with outside agencies, representing special education in the school management team's meetings and facilitating inservice training for colleagues in special education. In secondary schools the coordinator may also have to lead a small team of special education teachers.

References:

Hinson, M. (Ed.) (1987) *Teachers and Special Educational Needs*, Harlow, Longmans in association with National Association for Remedial Education.

National Association for Remedial Education (1985) *Guidelines No. 6, Teaching Roles for Special Educational Needs*, Stafford, National Association for Remedial Education.

Copewell System, basic tool for teacher-instructors working with adolescents and adults with mental handicap. Its basis is a complete curriculum, divided into four sections: self-help skills, social and academic skills, interpersonal skills, and vocational skills. The system consists of three elements: a filebox (containing the complete set of 174 numbered curriculum cards, grouped into subject areas within each of the four sections); 174 corresponding teaching packages, containing teaching plans plus visual aids; a recording system for individual trainees.

The system was developed at the Hester Adrian Research Centre in consultation with staff of *adult training centres* in order to extend and develop the skills used in teaching adults with mental handicap.

Reference:

Whelan, E., Speake, B. and Strickland, T. (1984) 'The Copewell Curriculum: Development, Content and Use', in Dean, A. and Hegarty, S. (Eds.) (1984) *Learning for Independence*, London, Further Education Unit.

copy forms test, assessment of a child's ability to copy a set of simple shapes, such as a circle, square, triangle, divided rectangle and diamond, an ability which develops with age. Hence one or more of these shapes are used as items in some intelligence tests, the child's performance being compared with that of peers. Since form-copying involves visuo-motor abilities, significant difficulties may imply neurological problems. Hence some tests of neurological impairment are based on a detailed assessment of the ability to copy forms, and the errors made.

See *Bender Visual Motor Gestalt Test.*

corrective reading, US programme of reading tuition for children aged eleven upwards to adults, who have made a start with reading but who are still at a 'remedial' level. The programme is based on the same principles as the *Distar* programme (which is not intended for children more than nine years old).

Corrective reading involves teaching in groups of fifteen or less, and is organised in three levels: Decoding A, containing sixty lessons on basic reading skills; Decoding B, containing 140 lessons covering word attack skills and comprehension; Decoding C, containing 140 lessons on skill application.

One lesson is taught each day, the teacher's approach being described and scripted. British evaluations reported so far are encouraging, but few in number.

Reference:

Gregory, R.P., Hackney, C. and Gregory, N.M. (1982) 'Corrective Reading Programme: an Evaluation', *British Journal of Educational Psychology*, 52, 33–50.

correlation, the way in which sets of measures vary together. For example, younger children tend to be lighter and older children heavier: there is a correlation between age and weight in children. The correlation in this case is said to be positive, since low values of one measure tend to be accompanied by low values of the other; similarly for high values. Where low values of one measure are accompanied by high values of the other, the correlation is negative. An example of negative correlation is the relationship between age and dependency on parents: young children are very dependent, older children less dependent.

The size of this co-variation, or correlation, is called the coefficient of correlation, often represented by the letter r. Conventional formulae lead to values of +1.0 for perfect positive correlation, and −1.0 for perfect negative correlation. A correlation coefficient of 0 represents no clear relationship between the two sets of measures.

There are different types of correlation coefficient, depending on the nature of the measurement data, but all values fall between +1.0 and −1.0.

correspondence schools, are a feature of the education systems of many countries. Using distance teaching techniques, correspondence schools fulfil several different functions. Some countries, notably Australia and New Zealand, established correspondence schools to meet the needs of isolated children, living in remote areas, and so unable to attend school.

Later, these schools were used to teach children with special needs, who might be prevented from attending ordinary school by disability.

Since 1977, the New Zealand correspondence school has developed the system of 'dual enrolment', in which a child who may be attending a public school can receive extra support for special needs through the correspondence school. With increasing emphasis on integration, dual enrolment has grown rapidly.

Correspondence schools devise a programme for a child in consultation with the parents and the local services, including the local school where appropriate. The programme is delivered through the post, and includes print materials, audio and visual resources, and in Australia may involve radio programmes from the School of the Air. Assignments are set, marked and returned through the postal services.

Distance teaching techniques have been used in various countries to help prepare and deliver educational materials for small groups of children whose special needs are uncommon. For example, in the UK the education of children with visual disabilities has been supported in this way.

Reference:

Rego, M. and Short, P. (1987) 'The Correspondence School', in Mitchell, D. and Singh, N.N. (Eds.) (1987) *Exceptional Children in New Zealand*, Palmerston North, Dunmore Press.

COSPEN, Committee on Special Educational Needs, a Scottish group, which reports to the Consultative Committee on the Curriculum. Its main remit is to identify requirements and develop initiatives in relation to special educational needs; to examine existing provision for and report on the needs of pupils with a *Record of Need* in mainstream schools; and to encourage other bodies to develop pedagogy that takes account of pupils at all stages and levels of ability. It operates in the Scottish educational system.

co-teaching, two or more teachers, one of whom is a special education teacher, sharing their work in order to teach more effectively. There are two main forms of co-teaching. In the first, the special education teacher spends time in classes taught by colleagues, helping children with learning difficulties to master the content. In the second, the special education teacher is a member of a small team of teachers, usually two or three, who plan their teaching programme together, and are jointly responsible for a group of children, some of whom have special needs.

Co-teaching is an alternative to the special class or the withdrawal system for children with learning difficulties. Clearly it offers all children the advantages of integration in the ordinary class. Under the withdrawal system, children might miss an important or enjoyable lesson, as well as feeling stigmatised by being withdrawn: co-teaching avoids this. Moreover teachers learn from each other.

But there are disadvantages, relating mainly to the staff. There can be personality clashes. Teachers are not used to sharing a classroom with a colleague, and some feel threatened by this. In secondary schools in particular, where the subject specialist is responsible for the content of the lesson, the special education teacher may feel a loss of status.

These points indicate that co-teaching is not an easy system to introduce, but that it needs careful planning to gain the advantages that it offers.

See *support teaching*.

References:

Ferguson, N. and Adams, M. (1982) 'Assessing the Efforts of Team Teaching in Remedial Education: the Remedial Teacher's Role', *Remedial Education*, 17, 1, 24–30.

Fish, J. (1985) *Special Education: The Way Ahead*, Milton Keynes, Open University Press.

Hodgson, A., Clunies-Ross, L. and Hegarty, S. (1984) *Learning Together*, Windsor, NFER-Nelson.

Council for Exceptional Children (CEC), the main North American organisation for workers (primarily teachers) in special education. CEC has over 40,000 members, and is organised into geographical groups, as well as on a divisional basis. The divisions meet the needs of members with particular interests – e.g. in educating children with communication disorders, or in training for special education. CEC's activities include publishing journals, holding conferences, etc., as well as lobbying nationally for special education.

Reference:

Hallahan, D.P. and Kaufman, J.M. (1988, 4th edn.) *Exceptional Children: Introduction to Special Education*, Englewood Cliffs, Prentice Hall.

counselling, helping persons to cope more effectively with their problems through skilled discussion.

There are a variety of counselling systems. For example, the non-directive counselling of Carl Rogers uses a quite different theoretical framework from behavioural counselling, and emphasises a different set of skills. These and other systems have been used in work with adults: they are used too in counselling in the school context.

Although much informal counselling takes place, unrecognised as such, in primary schools, counselling is usually regarded as a secondary school activity. In many countries secondary schools include one or more specially-trained school counsellors on the staff. The full-time school counsellor is found in few schools in the UK. Some schools employ a teacher-counsellor, i.e. an experienced teacher with extra training, who spends part of the time teaching and part available for consultation by pupils, but the majority rely on the *pastoral care* system.

Counselling pupils encompasses three main functions: guidance over choice of courses, with future career possibilities in mind; help over learning problems in school; help over personal problems. The latter two functions begin to overlap with meeting pupils' special education needs, stressing the importance of close collaboration between special needs and counselling staff in school. It has also been argued that in our concern to meet the curricular needs of pupils with disabilities we often overlook their emotional needs, and that schools should be sensitive to the value of counselling for these pupils in particular.

Finally, anyone who works closely with parents of children with special needs will from time to time be in a counselling situation with the parents, and should be aware of the basic tenets of the counselling relationship.

References:

Cunningham, C. and Davies, H. (1985) *Working with Parents*, Milton Keynes, Open University Press.

Galloway, D.M. (1990) *Pupil Welfare and Counselling*, Harlow, Longman.

Jones, A. (1984) *Counselling Adolescents: school and after*, London, Kogan Page.

Lowe, P. (1988) *Responding to Adolescent Needs: a pastoral care approach*, London, Cassell.

counter-conditioning, eliminating unwanted behaviour by strengthening alternative behaviour, in particular behaviour that is incompatible with it. For example, hyperactive, out-of-seat behaviour can be reduced by reinforcing desk-work. Behaviour therapists often prefer counter-conditioning to other methods of handling unwanted behaviour, such as *extinction* procedures or *punishment*.

See *behaviour therapy*.

Reference:

Herbert, M. (1987, 2nd edn.) *Conduct Disorders of Childhood and Adolescence: a social learning perspective*, Chichester, Wiley.

cretinism, or hypothyroidism, condition resulting from inadequate action of the thyroid gland in early life. This produces varying degrees of mental retardation, with short stature and a variety of less serious symptoms. Early diagnosis and treatment lead to virtually normal physical growth and negligible or very minor mental retardation. Routine screening of infants by blood testing helps to detect this disorder, which is now very rare in Western Europe.

crib-o-gram, or auditory response cradle, see *audiometry.*

Crichton Vocabulary Scale, measures the comprehension vocabulary of children between four-and-a-half and eleven years of age. The child is required to define in his own way a word spoken by the examiner. There are two parallel sets of stimulus words, forty in each set, arranged in order of difficulty. Although the test norms are based on a limited sample, the reliability is said to be satisfactory. The Crichton Scale is often used in conjunction with *Raven's Progressive Matrices,* the two scores offering an estimate of both verbal and non-verbal intelligence.

Reference:

Pumfrey, P.D. (1985, 2nd edn.) *Reading: Tests and Assessment Techniques,* Sevenoaks, Hodder and Stoughton in association with the UKRA.

crisis intervention, group of techniques that seek to use a client's personal and educational crisis in a constructive way. The common element in these techniques is that intervention takes place when feelings are out in the open, before the client has been able to erect defences, as happens when the immediate crisis is past. Some American schools have appointed a crisis teacher to deal with behaviour problems.

Crisis teachers do not represent authority as does the Principal. They have additional training in applied psychology and usually operate from a small classroom where they can work with no more than one or two children at a time. The immediate intervention should lead to a management plan, including possible changes to the curriculum, when learning difficulties are associated with the behavioural problems.

References:

Feingold, T.W. (Ed.) (1986) *Crisis Intervention Strategies for School-Based Helpers,* Springfield, C.C. Thomas.

Marsh, G.E., Price, B.J. and Smith, T.E.C. (1983) *Teaching Mildly Handicapped Children,* St. Louis, Mosby.

criterion-referenced tests, measure how well a person has mastered set skills. If a teacher seeks to teach an arithmetical operation, she needs to know whether a child has mastered that skill before moving on to the next teaching objective. So she sets a test to find this out.

Note that a criterion-referenced test is not designed to compare a child with his/her peers: this information is provided by *norm-referenced tests.* The child's performance is compared with the teaching objectives only; whether this performance is better or worse than that of others is of little relevance to learning arithmetic.

Criterion-referenced tests have many advantages. Although some are commercially available, often in the form of checklists – for language skills, for example – most are set by teachers to fit their own curriculum. A teacher can set an appropriate 'passing standard' – it might be that 80% success or more on this arithmetic test means that, in the teacher's view, the child's performance is satisfactory, and so the next teaching objective can be introduced. If performance is below the standard set, then the teacher can decide whether to repeat the teaching unit or to vary it to help the child learn better. The results provide a useful record of a child's learning. Criterion-referenced tests are tied to the immediate curriculum in a way that few if any published tests are.

Note that the old concepts of reliability and validity cannot be ignored – the results of criterion-referenced tests must be meaningful. The tests are not an easy option; they require careful preparation, and are an integral part of a well-designed curriculum.

See *curriculum-based assessment, precision teaching.*

References:

Black, H.D. and Dockrell, W.B. (1984) *Criterion-referenced Assessment in the Classroom*, Edinburgh, Scottish Council for Research in Education.

Department of Education and Science and Welsh Office (1987) *National Curriculum Task Group on Assessment and Testing*, London, DES and WO.

Hinson, M. (1987) 'Assessment and Intervention: a key role for SEN support teachers', in Hinson, M. (Ed.) (1987) *Teachers and Special Educational Needs*, Harlow, Longman in association with NARE.

Kiernan, C. (1987) 'Criterion-referenced Tests', in Hogg, J. and Raynes, N. (Eds.) (1987) *Assessment in Mental Handicap*, Beckenham, Croom Helm.

crossed laterality, preferred use of different sides of the body for different purposes. In special education the term is nearly always confined to hand and eye dominance, e.g. a child whose dominant hand (usually for writing) is the right hand and whose dominant eye (usually for sighting) is the left eye is said to be a crossed lateral.

Although it used to be thought that crossed laterality was a cause of reading difficulties, there is no evidence to suggest that there is a significant association between the two conditions. Crossed laterality is in fact fairly common, one investigation finding 34% of primary school children to be crossed laterals, though the proportion will vary depending upon the criteria used to decide dominance.

See *cerebral dominance, dichotic listening test.*

Reference:

Clark, M.M. (1979, 2nd edn.) *Reading Difficulties in Schools*, London, Heinemann.

cross-sectional study, collecting information on child development from groups of children of different ages. The central point about a cross-sectional study is that the information on all ages is collected at or about the same time. Thus the height of separate age-groups of children from birth to maturity would be measured in order to obtain information on how height changes with age. The data might be gathered in a matter of weeks, and this economy of time (and money) can be contrasted with the eighteen years or so that would be required to gain the same information by regular measurements of the same group of children from birth to maturity (*longitudinal study*).

But a cross-sectional study cannot provide data on individual development. Its use of group means results in a smoothed and reduced gradient of growth and leads to an underestimation of the rates of development of individuals. Moreover there are logical difficulties in combining data from children of different ages and hence with different experiences in order to chart a curve of development.

Cross-sectional investigations have been used to chart the development of psychological and educational qualities, such as intelligence, language skills, emotional characteristics, reading skills, etc., as well as physical attributes.

References:

Tanner, J.M. (1961) *Education and Physical Growth*, London, University of London Press.

Fischer, K.W. and Lazerson, A. (1984) *Human Development*, New York, W.H. Freeman.

Croydon Check List, widely used procedure for screening young children for learning problems, requiring systematic observation of a child's behaviour and progress.

It includes items assessing speech, perceptual, motor, emotional and social development. It suggests helpful exercises and activities for improving listening skills, the use and understanding of words and concepts, etc.

Reference:

Wolfendale, S. and Bryans, T. (1979) *Identification of Learning Difficulties: a model for intervention*, Stafford, National Association for Remedial Education.

cued speech, uses a system of single hand shapes around the lips to differentiate speech sounds which are visually similar, e.g. p and b, and to identify sounds that are invisible, e.g. k. There are four hand signals for vowels and eight for consonants. Cued speech is said to improve both accuracy and intelligibility of lipreading, and to give children access to the phonetic basis of reading.

Reference:

Reed, M. (1984) *Educating Hearing-Impaired Children*, Milton Keynes, Open University Press.

cueing, signalling to a child in order to encourage a response. In the behavioural approach, responses are strengthened through reinforcement. But if responses are not forthcoming they have to be encouraged. Techniques such as *behaviour shaping* or *behaviour modelling* can be used; cueing is an alternative.

Cueing uses *prompts*. These can be verbal, as when a teacher encourages a quiet child to respond by calling his or her name; or visual, as when pointing to the open door encourages the child to close it. It is important that the behaviour is reinforced after it has occurred. The prompt can be faded out as the desired behaviour becomes established.

References:
Alberto, P.A. and Troutman, A.C. (1986, 2nd edn.) *Applied Behaviour Analysis for Teachers*, Columbus, Merrill.
Wheldall, K. and Merrett, F. (1984) *Positive Teaching: the Behavioural Approach*, London, Allen and Unwin.

Cuisenaire rods, see *structural apparatus.*

cultural deprivation, some loss of the normal experiences of childhood through crowded living conditions, poverty at home, lack of adult interest, etc. Cultural deprivation is traditionally associated with the inner city poor, but neither poverty nor urban life are necessary conditions, for children from wealthy homes and children living in rural areas can both be deprived of normal childhood experiences.

Cultural deprivation is likely to lead to limited development, perhaps both physically and intellectually. Most children with moderate learning difficulties are children who can be loosely described as culturally deprived. The important features from the school point of view are poor motivation and limited language development, resulting in a gap between achievement and expectation which widens as the child progresses through school. The language issue in particular has been controversial, some arguing that much of the observed language deficit is an artefact: the child from a deprived background being an effective communicator in his own language system or code, albeit different from the middle-class linguistic standards that educators assume to be required.

Another issue relates to the relevance of educational procedures to offsetting the effects of cultural deprivation. Some have argued that cultural deprivation is a social phenomenon which will respond to social, not educational measures. For a discussion of this point, see *compensatory education.*

References:
Chazan, M. and Williams, P. (Eds.) (1978) *Deprivation and the Infant School*, Oxford, Blackwell.
Nisbet, J. and Watts, J. (1984) *Educational Disadvantage: Ten Years On*, Edinburgh, HMSO.

cultural–familial retardation, North American term for mild to moderate *mental handicap*, with no obvious biological cause, usually characterised by an IQ in the 55–70 range; another person with mental handicap in the family; a home of poor socioeconomic status.

Since cultural–familial retardation often appears in successive generations, it used to be ascribed to hereditary causes. Nowadays more attention is paid to the influence of a poor environment on development. A child growing up in poverty, with a mother who may herself be handicapped, poorly nourished, perhaps a member of a large family, living in overcrowded conditions, not enjoying suitable health care – such a child is clearly at risk intellectually. Since some children do develop well in spite of conditions such as these, it is argued that the retardation is probably due to the interaction of genetic and environmental factors. One problem is that the children themselves may become the parents of families growing up in similarly discouraging conditions, linking the generations in a cycle of deprivation.

See *cultural deprivation.*

Reference:

Grossman, H.J. (Ed.) (1983) *Classification in Mental Retardation,* Washington, American Association on Mental Deficiency.

culture-fair tests, claim to be equally valid for children from any cultural background. Since traditional intelligence tests contain items which depend on knowledge and experience familiar to the constructor, who is usually from a white, middle–class cultural background, it is argued that these tests are biased in favour of children from similar backgrounds. Attempts have been made to produce tests which avoid or at least reduce this bias. These tests omit items which have overt language content, such as vocabulary items, and items which rely on culturally-loaded information, such as general knowledge, but rely heavily on abstract and symbolic reasoning items as in the *Raven's Progressive Matrices.* In fact, no test can be completely culture-fair, though some are more so than others.

More recently, in view of the controversy over the intellectual level of minority groups, some psychologists have constructed tests which are deliberately biased towards the minority culture. Such a test might include vocabulary items from the argot of the minority community, for example, and so produce scores which show the minority group to possess an intellectual advantage. Such scales clearly point up the issue of cultural bias in testing.

See *SOMPA.*

Reference:

Hegarty, S. and Lucas, D. (1978) *Able to Learn? The Pursuit of Culture-fair Assessment,* Slough, National Foundation for Educational Research.

curative education, 'the doctrine of the scientific approach to a study of the causes and effects of the physical, emotional and mental conditions and symptoms of behaviour in retarded children and juveniles, and to methods of teaching, educational guidance and attention to their special needs.' (Hanselmann, quoted in Piezner, p.3.)

Curative education is closely associated with Rudolf Steiner's philosophy. It works with the disciplines of psychiatry, paediatrics, psychology, sociology and education, but believes that these can do no more than offer help towards giving children the right guidance, which must be based on the best possible knowledge of Man.

While there are chairs of curative education on the mainland of Europe, it has no similar academic roots in the UK. Here some schools and villages for individuals who are mentally handicapped have been based on curative education principles.

See *Camphill Movement, Rudolf Steiner schools.*

Reference:

Piezner, C. (Ed.) (1966) *Aspects of Curative Education,* Aberdeen, Aberdeen University Press for Camphill Movement.

curriculum, the total of a pupil's planned learning experiences in school: while the curriculum is often taken to mean the content of lessons, more broadly it also encompasses those attitudes, interests, etc., that the school aims to engender through less formal experiences.

The curriculum for children with special needs starts as the curriculum for all children. The purpose of special education is to try to make that curriculum as accessible as possible to everyone. There are various ways in which this is achieved.

First, the teaching arrangements can be modified. For example, children with physical or sensory disabilities may be able to manage the ordinary curriculum with teaching aids to help overcome hearing impairment, or aides in the classroom to help with physical limitations. This is known as a 'mainstream-with-support' curriculum.

Second, since some children learn more slowly – children with moderate learning difficulties – it may be necessary to modify the curriculum objectives for them. They will follow the same curriculum, but the objectives reached at the end of their school years will be less ambitious. These variations will be noted in the child's Statement. This is known as a 'modified curriculum'.

Third, some children, for example children with severe and complex learning difficulties, will need a curriculum which is significantly modified, starting from the pupil's special needs. For example, one pupil may need extensive help to learn normal social skills: another may need extensive help with motor coordination. This is known as a 'developmental curriculum'.

These three kinds of approaches to the curriculum for special needs follow the suggestions of the Department for Education and Science. The National Foundation for Educational Research has refined this further into a five-point scale, dividing each of the second and third approaches into two, depending on the extent of the variation from a normal curriculum.

Whatever curriculum is planned for a child with special needs, regular assessment of progress will be required. This demands that teaching objectives have been carefully specified beforehand.

The introduction of the *National Curriculum* for all children, together with school-by-school assessments, established by the *Education Act 1988,* has placed the curriculum for children with special needs under sharp scrutiny. In certain circumstances, children with special needs can be partly or fully exempted from the National Curriculum and from the associated assessments at seven, eleven, fourteen and sixteen years of age. On the one hand this arrangement appears necessary: if the National Curriculum is not fully followed, then the national assessments are inappropriate. On the other hand, exemption implies separation, and the ideal of an integrated school community may be dealt another blow. The effects of these provisions have yet to be determined.

References:

Brennan, W.K. (1985) *Curriculum for Special Needs,* Milton Keynes, Open University Press.

Daniels, H. (1990) 'The Modified Curriculum: Help with the Same or Something Completely Different?' in Evans, P. and Varma, V. (Eds.) (1990) *Special Education: Past, Present and Future,* London, Falmer Press.

Department of Education and Science (1989) *Circular 5/89 Education Reform Act 1988: The School Curriculum and Assessment,* London, Department of Education and Science.

Hegarty, S. (1990) 'The Curriculum in Special Education', in Entwistle, N. (Ed.) (1990) *Handbook of Educational Ideas and Practices,* London, Routledge.

National Curriculum Council (1989) *Curriculum Guidance 2: a Curriculum for all,* York, National Curriculum Council.

curriculum-based assessment (CBA), a halfway house between *criterion-referenced assessment* and *norm-referenced assessment.* Like criterion-referenced assessment, CBA is closely tied to the objectives of the immediate classroom programme, and not to national norms: teachers themselves usually construct the tests. But like norm-reference tests, a pupil's performance is intended to be compared with others in the class, or indeed in the locality, if several schools combine to produce a joint curriculum.

Usually several short parallel tests are produced, so that progress can be assessed frequently.

Reference:

Hallahan, D.P. and Kaufman, J. (1988, 4th edn.) *Exceptional Children: Introduction to Special Education,* Englewood Cliffs, Prentice Hall.

custodial mentally retarded, US term for individuals with profound mental handicap, essentially people with IQs below 25. This condition was contrasted with that of people with IQs between 25 and 50, designated 'trainable mentally retarded', and that of people with IQs between 50 and 80, designated 'educable mentally retarded'. This method of classification was adopted since it had implications for school systems, as it was believed that people with IQs below 25 required institutional care, rather than education or training.

With the knowledge that all individuals can benefit from some form of education, the term has been largely replaced in the US literature by 'profoundly mentally retarded', or 'profoundly mentally handicapped'.

Reference:

Van Etten, G., Arkell C. and Van Etten, C. (1980) *The Severely and Profoundly Handicapped,* St. Louis, Mosby.

custodianship, order granting legal custody to a non-parent, such as a relative, step-parent or foster-parent who is currently looking after a child and has been for some time. Custodianship will disappear under the provisions of the *Children Act 1989.* However, any person with whom a child has lived for the previous three years may apply for a residence order under the conditions specified in the 1989 Act. A residence order has much the same effect as a custodianship order.

cystic fibrosis, inherited disorder that causes excessive secretion of mucus in the lungs and other organs. The incidence is one in about 1,500 live births.

The disease has no direct effect on intellectual development, but periods of absence from school are likely to pose educational problems. Special diets may be prescribed, and advice on appropriate physical exercise should be sought. Teachers should also be sensitive to the probable stress on the child and family. Better medical management of cystic fibrosis means that many children with the disease are now living into adulthood, instead of dying in childhood.

Reference:

Marsh, G.E, Price, B.J. and Smith, T.E.C. (1983) *Teaching Mildly Handicapped Children*, St. Louis, Mosby.

D

Daniels and Diack Reading Tests, see *Standard Reading Tests.*

DARBAS, Developmental Age-Referenced Breakdown Assessment Schedule, a particularly thorough and detailed set of developmental schedules, incorporating over 1,500 items drawn from over a hundred scales. The items are arranged by developmental age in six subscales: gross motor, fine motor, cognitive/academic, language, self-help, socialisation. The items are also arranged in seven age-levels, spanning the period from birth to five years of age. Since so many items are used, it is possible to assess children's current *developmental quotients* and their progress over relatively short time intervals with some precision. The scales have been used in New Zealand in assessment and teaching centres for people who are intellectually (i.e. mentally) handicapped.

Reference:

Bridgeman, G.D. (1981) 'An Evaluation of One Year of using the Darbas Schedule in the Developmental Assessment and Teaching Centres of the Auckland Branch of the Society for the Intellectually Handicapped': paper presented to the Annual Conference of the New Zealand Association for the Advancement of Research in Education, August 1981.

DATAPAC, Daily Teaching and Assessment – Primary Age Children, set of resource materials, offering programmes in reading, handwriting, spelling and arithmetic. The programmes are based on an assessment through teaching approach, but allowing a choice between three levels of detail: a sequence of objectives only, in which teacher controls the content and progress of the lesson; objectives with suggested teaching steps; and completely scripted lessons. The materials were produced by a group of educational psychologists at the University of Birmingham, and courses are held to train potential users. The users in turn train DATAPAC coordinators in individual schools.

The materials have some similarity to *DISTAR,* but the three-level structure allows greater flexibility. The whole DATAPAC set of materials is cumbersome, but different programmes can be selected according to need. It has not as yet been published, but cyclostyled copies are provided for course members, who can photocopy materials for school coordinators.

See *precision teaching.*

References:

Ackerman, T. and eleven co-authors (1984) *The DATAPAC Users Guide,* Birmingham, Birmingham University.

Pearson, L. and Lindsay, G. (1986) *Special Needs in the Primary School,* Windsor, NFER-Nelson.

day care, social facilities which might include education, training or medical care, provided on a daily basis by health and social service authorities, voluntary organisations, or others. Day care offers contact for some people with handicaps who might otherwise be homebound and isolated. Many young people with severe learning difficulties experience day care through attending *adult training centres,* currently strengthening their educational programmes through forging links with the further education service.

Following the *Children Act 1989,* local authorities will have to provide appropriate day care for *children in need* who are aged five or under and not yet attending school. For children in need who are attending school, local authorities will have to provide appropriate care and supervised activities outside school hours, including school holidays.

The 1989 Act also changes the law relating to the registration of *day nurseries* and play groups. Registration will be necessary if the care relates to children under the age of eight years who are looked after for more than two hours in toto per day.

See *child minder.*

day nursery, form of *day care* provided by social service departments, voluntary organisations or others. Every local authority must keep a register of independent day nurseries in its area: the provisions for registration and the general rules relating to day nurseries have been changed by the Children Act 1989.

Many day nurseries give priority to admitting children from families under stress. Some take a quota of children with special needs or contain a unit designed specifically for them.

The *Warnock Report* recommended that day nurseries should develop closer links with the education service, particularly in relation to children with special needs and also recommended an increase in the number of combined day nurseries and nursery schools.

See *nursery education, pre-school education.*

Reference:

Robson, B. (1989) *Pre-school Provision for Children with Special Needs*, London, Cassell.

DD, see *developmentally disabled.*

deaf-blind, see *dual sensory impairment.*

deafness, see *hearing impairment.*

decibel, measure of physical intensity of sound, which is experienced psychologically as loudness. We hear sound by interpreting pressure

Approximate decibel values of some common sounds

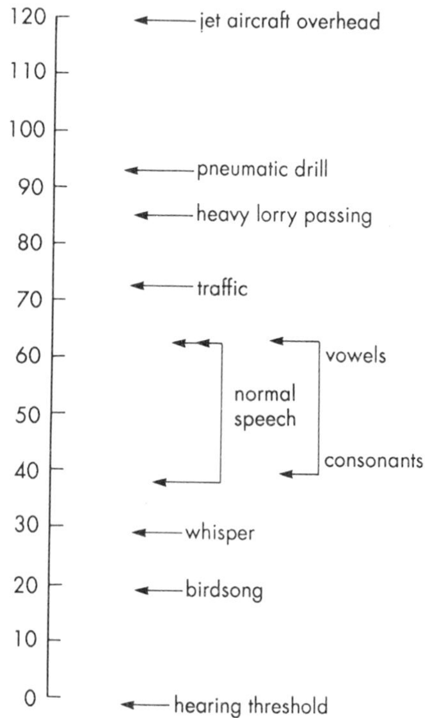

waves, usually in air, signalled to the brain by our hearing mechanism. The pressure waves can vary in frequency, interpreted as pitch of sound; they may also vary in amplitude, or intensity, interpreted as loudness of sound.

Very loud sounds, high energy pressure variations, may be as much as ten million times the energy of the quietest sounds we can hear. To measure loudness on a scale from one to ten million would be cumbersome and difficult to interpret. So a logarithmic ratio scale, the decibel scale, has been introduced. On this scale the quietest audible sound has been allocated a decibel value of 0; a tenfold increase in sound energy is then represented by an increase of 20 decibels; this means that the loudest sound attains a decibel value of about 140.

Some intermediate points will add meaning to the 0–140 decibel scale. Thus a close whisper measures about 30 decibels; normal speech about 60 decibels; nearby heavy traffic about 90 decibels. The decibel scale is used in the measurement of *hearing impairment*, usually indicated as 'decibel loss'. A 60 decibel loss thus implies that, without aid, normal speech will be barely audible; but this is a guide only, and more sensitive assessment will reveal the nature of the loss in more detail.

See *audiometry*.

decoding, perceiving and interpreting signals in order to gain meaning from them.

For education, listening and reading are two very important decoding skills. In listening, the signals are not only the speech sounds, but also their intonation, stress, sequence and context, as well as any accompanying gestures and facial expression. The listener 'decodes' these signals to make sense of speech.

In reading, the signals are the *graphemes*, arranged in words, whose sequence, together with punctuation marks, spacing, context, etc., enable the reader to make sense of print.

Some children have difficulty in learning to decode, and at one time tests of decoding ability were in vogue as part of the process of diagnosing reading and language disabilities. The value of this approach has since come into question. Contrast *encoding*.

defectology, term used in the USSR for the interdisciplinary study of all aspects of handicap. The Scientific Research Institute of Defectology in Moscow is the body with main responsibility for planning and coordinating research on handicapped children and for training teachers for special schools in the USSR.

defence mechanism, or mental mechanism, method of protecting oneself from psychological hurt, such as loss of self-esteem or anxiety. Defence mechanisms were described by Freud, and are used by psychoanalysts and others to understand behaviour.

The major mechanisms include:

- compensation, reacting to feelings of inadequacy or incompetence in one activity by concentrating on prominence in another. Thus a child with poor academic attainment may try to compensate for this through other attention-seeking activities in the classroom.
- displacement, transferring feelings from one person to another, where they may be more acceptably placed. Thus a child who has strong feelings of hate for his father, which he feels to be wrong and is unable to express, may displace these feelings on to a male teacher.
- projection, accusing others of one's own unacceptable feelings. Thus a person who feels aggressive, but cannot admit to this, may project the unacceptable feelings on to someone else, claiming that they feel aggressive.
- rationalisation, denying a true, but unacceptable reason for an action and substituting an alternative one. Thus a child may not attend school, claiming to feel unwell, whereas in reality he cannot admit to fear of being bullied.
- repression, refusing to allow unacceptable thoughts or wishes into consciousness. The thoughts may appear in other ways, for example in dreams, or in slips of the tongue, when, in *Freudian theory*, the control of the unconscious is temporarily relaxed.

Reference:

Barker, P. (1988, 5th edn.) *Basic Child Psychiatry*, Oxford, Blackwell.

deficit model, deficit theory, seeing people with special needs in terms of weaknesses. Much earlier work with deprived children suggested that their language usage was limited, i.e. showed a deficit in comparison with their peers, and accounted for their poor performance in school. This view was later attacked by those who believed that the deficit theory was misplaced, that deprived children had a rich language of their own to which middle-class teachers and examiners did not have access, a language which was not in deficit, but different.

The deficit model was later applied to attitudes outside the language field. The use of a category to describe someone is an illustration, e.g. 'she's an epileptic', rather than 'she's a child with epilepsy'. The former construes the person in terms of the disorder and its limitations, the latter puts the person first.

Attempts to help children with learning difficulties by diagnosing weaknesses within the children, and constructing special (i.e. limited) curricula for them, rather than concentrating on teaching them, have also been considered examples of the use of the deficit model: but it is sometimes easy to stigmatise well-intentioned practice unfairly.

Reference:

Barton, L. and Tomlinson, S. (Eds.) (1984) *Special Education and Social Interests*, Beckenham, Croom Helm.

delinquency, see *juvenile delinquency.*

delta wave, see *electroencephalogram.*

Denver Developmental Screening Test (DDST), designed to help in the early identification of young children with developmental problems, but also used in the assessment of individuals with severe and profound learning difficulties.

It covers four areas of development: personal-social; fine motor skills; gross motor skills; language. Norms are provided for the age-range one month to six years. Some items are completed from direct observation of the child, others by information from mother or other adult.

The test is said to have acceptable validity and reliability, to be easy to administer, but complicated to score.

Reference:

Sabatino, D.A. and Miller, T.L. (Eds.) (1979) *Describing Learner Characteristics of Handicapped Children and Youth,* London, Grune and Stratton.

depressive disorder, emotional state characterised by long-lasting feelings of sadness, worthlessness and hopelessness that are out of all proportion to reality. A depressive disorder is a serious illness, in which the risk of suicide is often present, and is quite different in kind from the 'feeling depressed' which everyone experiences from time to time. There are two main types: endogenous depressions, brought on for no apparent reason, and often found in conscientious – sometimes obsessive – personalities; reactive depressions, which follow hard knocks, perhaps a bereavement, or a period of financial stress. (But both types can coexist.)

It used to be thought that depressive disorders (from which more women suffer than men) were mainly illnesses of adults, and especially the elderly. More recently an increasing number of adolescents and even quite young children have been diagnosed as sufferers. There is disagreement among psychiatrists on the diagnosis and the prevalence of depressive disorders, especially in pre-adolescent children. One authority (Graham) cites prevalence rates of 'pure' depressive disorders of 1% before puberty, rising to 2 to 5% in adolescence, with higher prevalences for less serious conditions.

The main methods of treatment involve drugs and psychotherapy, separately or in combination. Teachers should recognise the warning signs, which might include falling off with work, loss of concentration, tiredness, inability to sleep, lack of appetite, withdrawal – or sometimes aggression. The child should be referred to the medical or school psychological services, for there is always the danger of a suicide attempt.

References:

Blagg, C. (1980) 'Depression', in Varah, C. (Ed.) (1980) *The Samaritans in the '80s,* London, Constable.

Graham, P.J. (1986) *Child Psychiatry: a Developmental Approach*, Oxford, Oxford University Press.

deprivation, see *cultural deprivation, maternal deprivation, sensory deprivation.*

deprived area, see *Educational Priority Area.*

Derbyshire Language Scheme, set of activities designed to improve children's receptive and expressive language skills. The scheme was based on experience with children with learning difficulties and with language delay, attending a special school, but has much wider application. It aims to cover language usages up to the four-and-a-half-year level, dealing particularly well with the one-and-a-half to two-and-a-half-year range.

The scheme is based on careful observation and assessment. The assessments and activities are linked, so giving direct teaching suggestions for helping with acquiring particular grammatical structures, for example. The scheme emphasises interactive play activities, which children find enjoyable, and is deservedly popular. But the presentation and complexity of the guidelines have been criticised.

Reference:

Webster, A. and McConnell, C. (1987) *Children with Speech and Language Difficulties*, London, Cassell.

desensitisation,

(1) procedure used in *behaviour therapy*, particularly in dealing with abnormal fear reactions – for example fear of leaving home, or fear of swimming. The feared situation is introduced very gradually, perhaps at first in fantasy. Training in relaxation skills is sometimes given beforehand. The child's responses are managed by the usual behavioural techniques of modelling, shaping, reinforcement, etc. As appropriate responses are produced, so a closer approximation to the feared situation is introduced, and the procedure repeated.

Compare *flooding*.

Reference:

Walker, S. (1975) *Learning and Reinforcement*, London, Methuen.

(2) method of treating some allergies, e.g. hayfever, by giving the patient gradually increasing doses of allergen, e.g. pollen, over a long period. Partial or complete immunity can be established.

developmental delay, slow acquisition of skills, both physical and psychological. In the USA the term is used to identify young children who are developing slowly, despite the absence of chromosome abnormalities, neurological or sensory impairment, and where there is no evidence of neglect or deprivation.

Developmental schedules are widely used in the assessment of young children, usually offering comparisons with expected development for a given age. The assessments are usually broken down into areas such as motor development, language development, social development, etc. Developmental delay can thus be general or specific.

There are several problems with the term. For example, it elevates the average (i.e. the norm) to an expectation, yet half the population are by definition below average in any normally-distributed skill. As with all inferences from norm-referenced testing, attention has to be paid to how large a gap between performance and expectation should cause concern, and in this case be formally classified as a 'developmental delay'. It is also important to remember that developmental delay is a description, and not a diagnosis: it should be the starting point for a remedial programme, not just the terminus of diagnosis. Nevertheless, the idea that specific developmental delays in, for example, neurological organisation, may be responsible for some specific learning difficulties is intriguing, though controversial.

Reference:

Keogh, B.K. and Bernheimer, L.P. (1987) 'Developmental Delays in Preschool Children: Assessment over Time', *European Journal of Special Needs Education*, 2, 4, 211–20.

developmental disability, severe, longstanding condition which significantly limits normal functioning. In the USA the term has legal status; a person who is developmentally disabled is entitled to certain services.

Originally people with developmental disabilities were assumed to be found among those suffering from mental handicap, or neurological conditions such as cerebral palsy, autism, etc. But the term has proved difficult to define satisfactorily, some arguing that the condition should be defined by function, not by diagnostic category. Two agreed criteria are that the condition has to appear before maturity, and has to be expected to continue indefinitely.

Reference:

Thompson, R.J. and O'Quinn, A.N. (1979) *Developmental Disabilities*, Oxford, Oxford University Press.

developmental disorder, diagnostic category used by the American Psychiatric Association for what is more commonly known in the UK as a *specific learning difficulty*.

Some examples are:

developmental arithmetic disorder, see *arithmetical difficulty*;
developmental articulation disorder, see *speech disorder*;
developmental language disorder, see *language disorder*;
developmental reading disability, see *dyslexia*.

Reference:

American Psychiatric Association (1980, 3rd edn.) *DSM III, Diagnostic and Statistical Manual of Mental Disorders*, Washington, American Psychiatric Association.

developmental quotient (DQ), the results of developmental assessments of young children are usually expressed as developmental quotients, usually covering cognitive, language, motor and social skills. In older tests the developmental quotient was obtained by expressing developmental age as a percentage of chronological age: newer tests transform test scores into a DQ which is a standardised score, or *deviation quotient.*

A very low DQ is useful as a signal that a young child needs careful investigation: more generally, DQs bear little relation to future intellectual development until after the age of two years.

Reference:

Berger, M. and Yule, W.M. (1987) 'IQ and Developmental Assessment', in Hogg, J. and Raynes, N. (Eds.) (1987) *Assessment in Mental Handicap*, Beckenham, Croom Helm.

Developmental Test of Visual-Motor Integration (VMI), fairly widely-used in the USA for children between the ages of four and thirteen years. The child is required to copy a set of 24 designs, increasing in complexity. The quality of the performance is assessed against set scoring criteria in order to provide a standardised score.

Reference:

Gearheart, B.R. (1981) *Learning Disabilities: Educational Strategies*, London, Mosby.

Developmental Test of Visual Perception (Frostig Test), measures separately the following visual perceptual skills over the age range four to eight years:

eye–motor coordination;
figure ground perception;
form constancy;
position in space;
spatial relationships.

The test was developed in the belief that impaired visual perception is responsible for some learning difficulties in children. It is accompanied by a training programme in perceptual skills (the Frostig Programme) for teachers to use, on the assumption that remedying the perceptual deficits revealed by the test will improve learning skills.

The test was a pioneering instrument, which has been widely used. The standardisation data have been criticised and the independence of the five separate perceptual areas is questionable. Although the exercises in the Frostig Programme have been found useful, and improve performance on the skills measured in the test, their effect in improving children's learning is controversial.

References:

Gearheart, B.R. (1981) *Learning Disabilities: Educational Strategies*, London, Mosby.

Levy, P. and Goldstein, H. (1984) *Tests in Education*, London, Academic Press.

deviation quotient, form of test score which relates a child's performance to that of peers in a meaningful way. Scores on tests of intelligence, attainment, development, etc., were originally transformed into age-equivalent values (mental ages, reading ages, etc.). To better appreciate a child's performance, age scores were expressed as quotients, i.e. percentages of chronological age. Thus a child of ten years of age with a reading age of eight years would have a reading quotient of 80. A ten-year-old with an average performance for his age, i.e. a reading age of ten years, would have a reading quotient of 100.

This system had several weaknesses. For example, the spread of quotients differs, depending on the age; one-fifth of one age-group might have quotients less than 85, whereas, even on the same test, one-sixth of another age-group might fall below the same quotient of 85. This made scores difficult to interpret. Then, since intellectual growth begins to level off after adolescence, there is a problem in calculating a meaningful quotient for mature people (what chronological age and what reading age should be used?).

Between the two world wars, test constructors began to transform raw scores from tests into distributions with a mean of 100 and a standard deviation of 15 points for each age group. A value on this distribution was

Deviation quotients, standard scores and percentile ranks in a normal distribution of test scores, with a standard deviation of 15 points

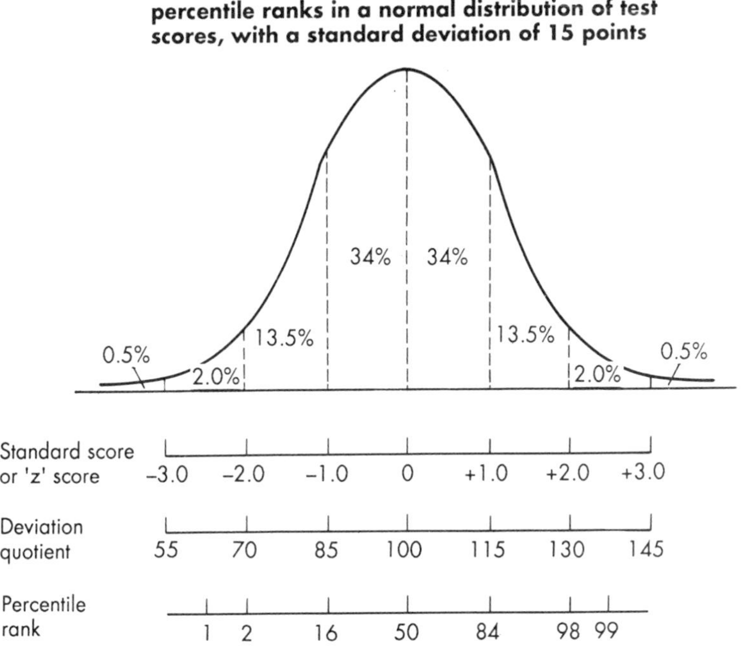

known as a deviation quotient, a quotient since it still represented a comparison between a child's performance and his own age-group, and a deviation quotient since the standard deviation was fixed.

A deviation quotient has immediate meaning, for knowing the mean and standard deviation (usually, but not always 100 and 15 respectively) the child's position on the age-group can be located, and comparisons between scores on different tests are meaningful. For example, a deviation quotient of 130 indicates a score which is better than 97.5% of the age group – irrespective of the test.

See *Intelligence Quotient, standard deviation.*

Reference:

Aiken, L.B. (1986, 5th edn.) *Psychological Testing and Assessment,* New York, Allyn and Bacon.

diabetes, metabolic disorder in which sugar cannot be utilised properly, due to a deficiency of insulin. The prevalence in school-children is about one per thousand.

It is managed medically by insulin injections and control of diet and exercise. Older children are able to handle this programme themselves, but with younger children in particular, teachers may have a role in monitoring it. Teachers should also be alert to two possibilities. The child may have too much insulin, the sugar level already having been reduced through over-exercise or under-eating. This is countered by taking sweet food or drink. The child may have too little insulin, the sugar level being high through over-eating, under-exercising or failing to inject insulin, in which case the child is at risk of slowly entering a diabetic coma. An injection of insulin is needed.

In both cases the child will first begin to feel unwell and teachers should know where to turn for guidance.

There is no reason why diabetic children should not be able to participate in all normal school activities. Intellectually they mirror the normal distribution and there is no evidence to suggest that diabetes causes learning difficulties. There may be some sensitivity over the condition, however, and it is important to keep in touch with parents.

References:

Dinnage, R. (1986) *The Child with a Chronic Medical Problem,* Windsor, NFER-Nelson.

Marsh, G.E., Price, B.J. and Smith, T.E. (1983) *Teaching Mildly Handicapped Children,* St. Louis, Mosby.

diacritical marking, marks added to letters (graphemes) to indicate pronunciation values (phonemes). Some languages, such as Czech, for example, use accents as diacritics (č = ch; š = sh).

Diacritical systems have been used as cueing techniques (see *colour coding*) for helping children learn to read, in particular to help them overcome the difficulty experienced when the same grapheme signifies different phonemes in different contexts. Note that new graphemes are not introduced, nor is the spelling changed, but special marks are added. For example letters which are not pronounced may be crossed out (~~h~~our); two letters which are pronounced as one phoneme may have a bar under them (shut); a long vowel may be given a bar over it (mē).

It is argued, on the one hand, that the regularity provided by the system facilitates learning to read and that there is little difficulty in making the transition from print with diacritics to print without. On the other hand, there is no need for teachers to be tied to elaborate schemes, nor for pupils to be kept in lock-step with them, whilst over-emphasis on phonemes may detract from attention to meaning and delay rapid and effective reading.

Reference:

Department of Education and Science (1975) *A Language for Life*, London, HMSO (Bullock Report).

diagnostic testing, aims to identify problems or weaknesses, whether medical, psychological or educational. For many years diagnosis in special education followed the medical model of attempting to allocate a child to a particular category of handicap, on the analogy of identifying a disease entity, for which a specific treatment existed. In special education the treatment involved signposting a child to one of the various special schools, units, etc., for particular handicaps.

As dissatisfaction with this approach grew, so diagnosis procedures moved away from the *medical model*, but retained the scientific approach. Hypotheses were erected and tested, and algorithms for the logical exploration of perceptual, emotional, linguistic and other possible causes for learning difficulties were devised.

The implication of this approach was that within-child deficits were responsible for learning difficulties and that remedying the deficit would solve the problem. This deficit model has in turn proved unsatisfactory, and diagnostic assessment has now become closely linked with the curriculum, and less dependent on standardised tests. Whether the assessment of a child's development in a curricular area, followed by teaching the skills needed for success, followed by reassessment, should be called diagnostic testing is a matter of semantics: it is certainly a long way from the orthodox conception of diagnostic testing as practised in other professions. But whatever it is called, it is a model that holds out hope of better progress.

See *assessment, curriculum-based assessment.*

References:

Reason, R., Farrell, P. and Mittler, P. (1990) 'Changes in Assessment', in Entwistle, N.E. (1990) *Handbook of Educational Ideas and Practices*, London, Croom Helm.

Shapiro, E.S. (1987) *Behavioral Assessment in School Psychology*, New York, Erlbaum.

Wedell, K. (1972) 'Diagnosing Learning Difficulties: a Sequential Strategy', in Reid, J.F. (1972) *Reading: Problems and Practices*, London, Ward Lock.

Diana v. State Board of Education of California (1970), important case in USA special education legislation, which led to a stipulation that children enrolled in classes for the educable mentally retarded (mild and moderate learning difficulties) should be re-assessed in their primary (first) language, using non-verbal tests and an interpreter where appropriate, and returned to the ordinary class if necessary.

The decision was important. It marked a recognition that the over-representation of children from minority cultures in special classes was a well-founded grievance, and instituted procedures for dealing with it.

References:

Cook, R.E. and Armbruster, V.B. (1983) *Adapting Early Childhood Curricula,* St. Louis, Mosby.

McLoughlin, J.A. and Lewis, R.B. (1986, 2nd edn.) *Assessing Special Students,* London, Merrill.

dichotic listening tests, ascertain how individuals recall information such as digits or syllables presented in balanced pairs to both ears simultaneously. If the recalled information demonstrates an advantage for one ear over the other, it is argued that inferences can be drawn about the lateralisation of language function in the brain. But the application of these tests and *visual half-field tasks* to children with reading difficulties has produced tentative findings only so far.

Reference:

Tansley, P. and Panckhurst, J. (1981) *Children with Specific Learning Difficulties; a Critical Review of Research,* Windsor, NFER-Nelson.

Dienes Apparatus, see *structural apparatus.*

differential reinforcement, technique used in behaviour therapy for reducing unwanted behaviour by reinforcing behaviour which is alternative to it. Some authorities include reinforcing incompatible behaviour under the general heading of differential reinforcement, whereas others prefer to regard both procedures as examples of *counter-conditioning.*

However the terms are classified, it is generally agreed that these procedures are preferable to other techniques of reducing unwanted behaviour, such as *aversion therapy* or *punishment.*

References:

Alberto, P.A. and Troutman, A.C. (1986, 2nd edn.) *Applied Behaviour Analysis for Teachers,* Columbus, Merrill.

Herbert, M. (1987, 2nd edn.) *Conduct Disorders of Childhood and Adolescence: a social learning perspective,* Chichester, Wiley.

digraph, sometimes diagraph, a pair of letters that in combination function as a single phoneme, different from either letter individually. There are consonant digraphs, e.g. 'ch' or 'th', and vowel digraphs, e.g. 'ea' or 'ai'. Note that digraphs, like single letters, may have different phonemic values, e.g. 'ch' in choose and 'ch' in chauffeur; 'ea' in each and 'ea' in head.

The sound values of digraphs are examples of the many departures from complete phonetic regularity which may impede learning to read English. Children have to learn to distinguish the digraph sound values: *colour coding* and a *diacritical marking* system may help, but these in turn add to the number of symbols a child has to learn and serve to divert attention from the meaning of the text.

See *bottom-up approaches.*

dimensional classification, method of describing children's behaviour disorders. It was developed as a reaction to the inadequacies of the diagnostic approach, based on the *medical model.* Instead of attempting to allocate children to such categories as neurotic, autistic, etc., this system establishes (by factor analysis of questionnaire items) four dimensions of disturbed behaviour, conduct disorder, anxiety-withdrawal, immaturity, and socialised aggression. Behaviour is then described in terms of its severity on each of the four dimensions, so yielding a better picture of a child's difficulties than a traditional diagnosis. The dimensional description serves as a baseline against which behaviour change can be evaluated.

Note that different types of analysis will yield different dimensions. Thus the neurotic and antisocial subscales of *Rutter's Behaviour Questionnaire* can be regarded as a two-dimensional classification system for behaviour disorders.

Reference:

Hallahan, D.P. and Kaufman, J.M. (1982, 2nd edn.) *Exceptional Children in the Schools,* Englewood Cliffs, Prentice Hall.

diplegia, see *cerebral palsy.*

Direct Instruction, teaching method originating in work with disadvantaged children following the *Bereiter and Engelmann Program.* Direct Instruction is based on the philosophy that all children can learn – 'a child who fails is a child who has not been taught'. It represents a departure from much traditional special education in that it shifts the focus from studying the child to analysing the teaching process.

Here it follows behavioural principles, breaking down the material to be learnt into small, easily managed steps, with speedy reinforcement of success. It is argued that children whose attainments are below those of their peers have not only to learn at the same rate; they must actually learn at a faster rate if they are to catch up. For this reason direct instruction focuses on the basic subjects, which are taught in small groups of three to eight children. The lessons are fast and concentrated; for example hand-signals are used to indicate the kind of response required from the child so that no time is wasted on oral instructions and that attention is maintained at a high level throughout the lesson. Unison responding is frequently practised, and considerable attention paid to error correction.

The success of direct instruction procedures led to the production of DISTAR materials, Direct Instruction System for Teaching And Remediation (sometimes incorrectly given as Direct Instruction System for Teaching Arithmetic and Reading). DISTAR materials for teaching reading, language skills and arithmetic have been produced. They include a sequence of lesson plans, based on a careful analysis of material to be taught. The lessons are scripted, teachers being required to follow word for word the given questions, instructions, etc.

Direct instruction is now being used more widely than with the culturally deprived children of primary age for whom it was originally designed. Various evaluations have demonstrated its effectiveness. But the approach is not one which suits every teacher. Moreover training in DISTAR before using it is strongly advised; it is more effective if used where other colleagues are equally committed to it, rather than by a single, isolated teacher. With these reservations, it has unquestionable value as a teaching method for children with learning difficulties.

See *corrective reading, mastery learning, precision teaching.*

References:

Fields, B.A. (1986) 'Direct Instruction and the Practicality Ethic: a Case Study and Position in Curriculum Innovation', *Australian Journal of Remedial Education,* 18, 1, 17–22.

Hart, K. (1981) 'SRA: the Distar Instructional System', in Somerset LEA *Ways and Means,* 2, Basingstoke, Globe.

Solity, J. and Bull, S. (1987) *Special Needs – Bridging the Curriculum Gap,* Milton Keynes, Open University Press.

directionality, understanding the right-left relationship of features of the environment. Children learn to identify their own *laterality,* right hand, left foot, etc.; when this understanding can be transferred outside their own body, so that they can identify which of two objects is on the right of the other and which on the left, they have acquired directionality, an important step educationally.

The directionality of print is also important in reading and writing; scanning from left to right (see saccadic *eye movements*) and writing from left to right are skills which have to be both acquired and automatised.

disability, one of three key interlocking terms in special education, the others being impairment and handicap. Impairment is a pathological condition, a loss of physiological, psychological or anatomical function; an example is damaged vision, or neurological damage. Disability is the effect the impairment has on an individual's capacity to function normally. These effects appear in the individual's behaviour, ability to communicate, personal care, mobility, etc., in fact in the activities of daily living. Handicap refers to the social consequences of disability for the individual, its cultural, social and economic effects.

Thus for a child with loss of bowel control, the condition causing this is the impairment, the incontinence is the disability, and any restrictions this imposes on normal social and academic activities are the handicap. Note that identical disabilities may result in different handicaps, depending on the different circumstances of the individuals. Note too that the handicaps associated with a disability may change over time, as an individual's circumstances change. This clearly applies as a child matures. The bowel control (disability) mentioned above may not be a significant handicap in a young child. As the child grows older the social consequences of the disability change, opportunities for recreation which are available to other children may be restricted and there is thus a growing handicap. But the extent of the handicap depends on the kinds of activities in which the individual is engaged and on the success of efforts made to manage the incontinence.

In the UK the extent of disability is assessed for benefit purposes. A comparison is made between the activities that the person with a disability can perform and those that are expected normally.

References:

Fish, J. (1985) *Special Education: the Way Ahead,* Milton Keynes, Open University Press.

Wood, P. for World Health Organisation (1980) *International Classification of Impairments, Disabilities and Handicaps,* Geneva, World Health Organisation.

Disabled Persons (Services, Consultation and Representation) Act 1986, requires (among other stipulations) local education authorities to notify social services departments of all children aged fourteen and over who have special educational needs. Notification has to be made at specified times, so that an officer from the social services department can give an opinion as to which children are disabled under current legislation. Those deemed disabled must be notified again to the social services about nine months before leaving school or college so that their needs for statutory services such as provision of recreational activities, home helps, meals, travelling assistance, holidays, etc., can be met.

One effect of this Act is to ensure that education and social service departments collaborate more closely over the school-leaving transition point than has usually been the case hitherto. Another effect is likely to be an increased demand for occupational therapists to carry out the assessments now required by law. But most importantly, young people with special needs should not now fall into an administrative limbo on leaving school.

Reference:

Peter, M. (1986) 'Editorial', *British Journal of Special Education,* 13, 2, 49.

Disabled Persons Community Welfare Act 1975, New Zealand legislation that committed the government to a policy of *normalisation* for people who are handicapped and to the provision of community-based care services for them.

Reference:

New Zealand Board of Health (1982) *Child Health and Child Health Services in New Zealand*, Wellington, Board of Health.

Disabled Persons' Register, is for people who are substantially handicapped by injury, disease or deformity and have difficulty in securing employment suited to their age, qualifications and experience. The disability must be likely to continue for at least twelve months.

Registration, which is voluntary, depends upon a Disablement Resettlement Officer confirming that the person is disabled within the meaning of the legislation. It enables a listed person to gain help with fares to and from work, special equipment at work, sheltered employment, and access to those jobs reserved for the disabled. This last can be advantageous, for all organisations employing more than 20 people have a duty (though an escapable one) under the Disabled Persons (Employment) Act to employ a quota – at present 3% – of disabled people. Note that registration as a Disabled Person under employment legislation is distinct from registration with the social service authorities under the Chronically Sick and Disabled Persons Act 1970.

See *Quota Scheme.*

References:

Furneaux, B. (1988) *Special Parents,* Milton Keynes, Open University Press.
Thompson, M. (1986) *Employment for Disabled People,* London, Kogan Page.

Disablement Resettlement Service, aims to provide advice and help over employment for disabled people. The key person in the Service is the Disablement Resettlement Officer, or DRO, who can be contacted through the local jobcentre. The DRO works with people with all kinds of disabilities except the blind and some people with partial sight (who are served by Blind Persons Resettlement Officers), and can advise over training, admission to sheltered employment, job modification, local employment opportunities, etc. A few DROs are hospital-based. The DRO has access to specialist medical advice, and is supported by the local Disablement Advisory Committee, which liaises with both DROs and employers over local problems, and has some responsibilities for the functioning of the *Disabled Persons' Register* and the related quota arrangements.

The Service has been criticised in the past, mainly on the grounds that DROs have a highly skilled and onerous task for which little training has been available, and with poor career prospects. They often work on their own and have to be familiar with the range of employment possibilities and special needs of a wide spectrum of disabilities.

References:
Darnborough, A. and Kinrade, D. (1981) 'The Disabled Person and Employment', in Guthrie, D. (Ed.) (1981) *Disability – Legislation and Practice*, London, Macmillan.
Hutchinson, D. (1982) *Work Preparation for the Handicapped*, London, Croom Helm.

disadvantage, essentially the effect of *cultural deprivation*. There are different kinds of disadvantage: educational disadvantage is the limitation placed by adverse circumstances on a child's expectations of normal educational progress and development; these same adverse circumstances may also result in other disadvantages, e.g. in health, through inadequate provision and use of medical services, or poor nutrition. In these terms disadvantage is a relative concept; it requires agreement about what are normal expectations of progress.

The view, common in the 1960s and early 1970s, that schools, through *compensatory education* programmes, were central to efforts to improve the life-chances of disadvantaged children, has changed. Emphasis has now switched to themes such as vocational training, the education service being seen in a supportive role. But schools and colleges retain the basic function of improving the educational chances of disadvantaged children through meeting their learning and behaviour needs. The ethos of the school as a social institution is one of the key factors in the effectiveness with which this responsibility is discharged.

See *whole-school approach*.

References:
Essen, J. and Wedge, P. (1982) *Continuities in Childhood Disadvantage*, London, Heinemann.
Nisbet, J. and Watt, J. (1984) *Educational Disadvantage: Ten Years On*, Edinburgh, HMSO.
Rutter, M., Maughan, B., Mortimore, P. and Duston, J. (1979) *Fifteen Thousand Hours: Secondary Schools and their Effects on Children*, London, Open Books.

disapplication (of the National Curriculum), lifting the requirement for a pupil to follow the *National Curriculum*. This form of exemption can be offered when the content is considered of low priority; for example learning a foreign language may be considered a low priority for a child with severe learning difficulties: it can also be offered when a child's attainments are below level 1 on an attainment target in one of the core or foundation subjects. Disapplication is distinguished from modification, the other form of exemption from the National Curriculum, in which the subject requirement is retained, but attainment targets may be varied to ones outside the expected range for the child's age. The disapplication and modification procedures are governed by regulations.

Disapplication can be seen as a form of labelling. The possibility of introducing a curriculum with attainment targets below level 1 has been put forward as one way of avoiding this, and the issue is currently being reviewed.

References:

Department of Education and Science (1989) *Circular 22/89, Assessments and Statements of Special Educational Needs: Procedures within the Education, Health and Social Services*, London, Department of Education and Science. (Joint circular with the Department of Health.)

Department of Education and Science (1989) *Circular 15/89, The Education Reform Act 1988: Temporary Exceptions to the National Curriculum*, London, Department of Education and Science.

Norwich, B. (1989) 'How Should We Define Exceptions?' *British Journal of Special Education*, 16, 3, 94–7.

discrimination, differential treatment of individuals, typically through restrictions against them in housing, public services and employment, usually on grounds of race, religion or sex. It is argued that handicapped people are discriminated against in many different ways; for example public buildings are not always designed so that they are accessible to people in wheelchairs. Educating children with special needs in special schools and units is also sometimes considered to be discriminatory, since they are thereby denied a normal education.

Discrimination on the grounds of colour, race or national origin was made illegal in 1968 and 1976 by the Race Relations Acts. The Sex Discrimination Act 1975, applies similar principles to discrimination on the grounds of sex or marital status.

Positive discrimination aims to improve the opportunities of some sections of society, e.g. by providing more resources and a better pupil–teacher ratio for schools attended by disadvantaged children, or by seeking to appoint a better proportion of teachers from ethnic minorities. One of the earliest examples of the application of positive discrimination in education was the introduction of *Educational Priority Areas* following the publication of the *Plowden Report* in 1967.

displacement, see *defence mechanism.*

disruptive behaviour, an educational descriptor for behaviour that is out of place in school. It became fashionable to talk of disruptive behaviour, rather than disruptive or difficult children, when attention was drawn to the variation in behaviour that children show: a difficult child in one class may be entirely amenable in another. Teachers vary in the kind of classroom climate that they create as do the relationships that are forged between them and their pupils. (But it must not be forgotten that there are a few children who do not conform in any situation.)

Not only do individual teachers affect the prevalence and nature of what can be described as disruptive behaviour, so do individual schools. School organisation, staff attitudes and values, all those innumerable qualities that together constitute the ethos of a school, contribute to the variation in disruptive behaviour between schools.

Yet another point makes disruptive behaviour an elusive concept. To describe behaviour as disruptive depends not on the behaviour itself, but on its context. Shouting is appropriate at a football match, but not in a science lesson.

For these reasons it is difficult to study disruptive behaviour objectively. Nevertheless most investigators agree that disruptive behaviour in school is rarely the violence or aggression against teachers that the popular media report. Rather it is a series of incidents involving rowdiness, bad language, talking, refusing authority, etc.

Various methods of managing disruptive behaviour exist. Units for pupils whose behaviour is persistently disruptive are popular, but have been criticised, mainly on the grounds of their limited curricula and the principle of segregation involved. Moreover their record of successful return to the ordinary school is not high. Counselling and behaviour modification techniques also have their supporters but require work with individuals and so are time-consuming. More recently attention has been paid to the social psychology of the school, modifying its organisation and management so as to alter the contexts in which behaviour might be seen as disruptive.

See *emotional and behavioural difficulties.*

References:

Chisholm, B., Kearney, D., Knight, G., Little, H., Morris, S. and Tweddle, D. (1986) *Preventive Approaches to Disruption: developing teaching skills,* Basingstoke, Macmillan.

Cohen, L. and Cohen, A. (Eds.) (1987) *Disruptive Behaviour: a Sourcebook for Teachers,* London, Harper and Row.

Department of Education and Science (1987) *Education Observed 5: Good Behaviour and Discipline in Schools,* London, HMSO.

Various authors (1990) 'Disruptive Behaviour', *Educational Psychology in Practice,* 5, 4 (whole issue)

Williams, P. (1985) 'Troubled Behaviour', Units 18/19 of Course E206, Milton Keynes, Open University.

distance vision, the ability to see distant objects clearly; one of the four characteristics of vision commonly measured, the other three being near vision, colour vision and field of vision. Distance vision is usually measured by the *Snellen chart,* though for young children and older children with severe learning difficulties the *Stycar tests* are sometimes employed.

Reference:

Chapman, E. K. and Stone, J. M. (1988) *The Visually Handicapped Child in Your Classroom,* London, Cassell.

DISTAR, see *Direct Instruction.*

distractibility, inability to concentrate on an activity, a difficult concept to measure since it varies with the activity and the nature of the distraction.

But in the classroom it is a characteristic which is closely associated with learning difficulties.

Although all children are easily distracted on occasion, some are chronically distractible, for example some children suffering from neurological damage, or mental handicap. Diet is sometimes assumed to be a cause, it being argued that some children cannot metabolise certain foods correctly, distractibility being one of the behavioural consequences. Hyperactivity is closely associated with distractibility, but although both are often present together they need not necessarily be.

See *Attention Deficit Disorder, Feingold Diet.*

Reference:

Hallahan, D.P. and Kaufman, J.M. (1988, 4th edn.) *Introduction to Special Education*, Englewood Cliffs, Prentice Hall.

distraction test, routine screening test of hearing, carried out by health visitors on all babies attending child health clinics from about six to eighteen months of age. The tester gains the baby's attention until, at a suitable moment, a controlled sound signal is supplied by a second tester, out of the baby's immediate vision. The test is repeated for high and low frequencies and for both ears separately, at about 35 decibels. The responses (head turning) are used to indicate whether a more specialised hearing examination is needed.

Distraction testing is difficult to carry out, for it is hard to ensure that only auditory stimuli (and not visual, tactile or olfactory ones) are presented, and that they are presented at the correct intensity. As many as 40% of infants with significant hearing impairments are not identified by this screening procedure.

References:

Tucker, I. and Nolan, M. (1984) *Educational Audiology*, Beckenham, Croom Helm.

Webster, A. and Wood, D. (1989) *Children with Hearing Difficulties*, London, Cassell.

distractor, one of a number of incorrect but usually plausible answers to a multiple choice item on a standardised test. The greater the number of distractors, the less the likelihood that the correct answer will have been given by guessing.

District Handicap Team (DHT), group of specialists set up to improve the health service provided for all handicapped children and their families. These teams were established following one of the recommendations of the 1976 Court Report on Child Health Services. The *Warnock Report* endorsed this development but suggested that membership should be extended to strengthen the teams' educational expertise, and argued that teams should work mainly at centres other than hospitals.

In practice, most health districts have established DHTs, but their functions and composition vary considerably. Some carry out assessment only, others carry out both assessment and treatment, still others see themselves in a coordinating role. The core membership is likely to include a doctor, nurse, psychologist, social worker and therapist, but not all teams cover the full range of specialisms.

There is some overlap of function between the DHT and the *Community Mental Health Team,* since support for young children with mental, handicap could fall within the terms of reference of both groups.

Reference:

Cotmore, R. (1986) 'The District and Community Mental Health Team', in Coupe, J. and Porter, J. (Eds.) (1986) *The Education of Children with Severe Learning Difficulties,* Beckenham, Croom Helm.

Doherty Report 1982, report of a working party set up to consider planned proposals for special education in New South Wales and to make recommendations. It presented a structured plan for improving services, but omitted to examine educational problems related to cultural background, considering aboriginal or migrant children with developmental disabilities or learning difficulties as part of the total number of children in need.

Domain Phonic Test, set of five subtests aimed at assessing a child's knowledge of letter names, sounds, blending ability and phonemic discrimination. The test provides diagnostic information on problems in applying a phonic approach to reading, but is not standardised. No data on reliability are given and validity is based on content validity only. The test is given individually and is used for children with reading difficulties, and with a reading age of less than eight-and-a-half years. Useful guidance on interpreting results and suggestions for appropriate remedial work are also given.

Reference:

Levy, P. and Goldstein, H. (1984) *Tests in Education,* London, Academic Press.

Doman-Delacato method, programme of therapy for ameliorating the learning difficulties of neurologically damaged children. The programme is based on the belief that the neurological development of the individual recapitulates that of the race (ontogeny recapitulates phylogeny). Problems with late-developing functions such as reading and language arise when earlier-developing functions have been incompletely organised. Hence treatment on this method involves diagnosing the level at which damage has occurred and then patterning surviving brain cells to take over the organising roles of those damaged or destroyed. The patterning involves intensive exercises linked with simple movements and requires total commitment from the family.

The programme has generated much controversy, and in 1968 a group of professional bodies in the USA published their concern about the methods used to promote the treatment, the effect of the intensive treatment on other family members, the restriction on normal activities, the lack of validity of the diagnostic methods used and the undocumented claims for cures.

Reference:

Gearheart, B.R. (1981) *Learning Disabilities: Educational Strategies*, London, Mosby.

dominance, see *cerebral dominance.*

Down's syndrome, the most common identifiable cause of mental handicap, named after J. Langdon Down, the physician who first described it in 1866. The prevalence is between one and two cases per thousand live births. However, prevalence rates are affected by procedures such as *amniocentesis* and by factors such as the age of the mother – it has been reported that the prevalence rate rises to about one per eighty births in women over forty years of age.

Down's syndrome is caused by any one of three different types of chromosome abnormalities: trisomy 21, in which the twenty-first set of chromosomes is a triplet, and not the usual pair; mosaicism, when some cells show trisomy 21 but others do not; translocation, when parts of one chromosome pair are wrongly attached to another. Trisomy 21 is the most common form, accounting for about 95% of the Down's population; mosaicism is characterised by a higher intelligence range; translocation is the only hereditable form of Down's syndrome.

Children with Down's syndrome are recognisable by their physical features – slanting eyes; skinfold across the inner eye-corners, small heads, short necks, flattened noses and a single palmar crease instead of the usual double one, etc. (The complete constellation of features does not always appear.) In addition many suffer from respiratory complaints and cardiac conditions.

Most children with Down's syndrome have learning difficulties, either moderate or severe. But it is wrong to assume that this is necessarily so: children with Down's syndrome show a wide range of ability, with a few showing IQs falling in the average range. Nearly all function in the education system, with or without support.

It used to be thought that children with Down's syndrome were characterised by cheerful, pleasant temperaments. More recently this has been shown to be incorrect and it was held that they showed the same range of behaviour difficulties as any group of children. More recent work still (Gath and Gumley) suggests that in fact they may demonstrate a significantly greater incidence of behaviour difficulties than would be expected on the basis of their age and background.

References:

Gath, A. and Gumley, D. (1986) 'Behaviour Problems in Retarded Children with Special Reference to Down's Syndrome', *British Journal of Psychiatry*, 149, 156–61.

Gillham, W.E.C. (Ed.) (1986) *Handicapping Conditions in Childhood*, Beckenham, Croom Helm.

Hallahan, D.P. and Kaufman, J.M. (1988, 4th edn.) *Exceptional Children: Introduction to Special Education*, Englewood Cliffs, Prentice Hall.

DRO - Disablement Resettlement Officer, see *Disablement Resettlement Service.*

drug misuse, harmful and socially unacceptable use of chemical substances. This may lead to dependence on the substance, followed in turn by addiction.

Accurate data on the prevalence of drug abuse in pupils and students are difficult to obtain, but surveys have estimated that about 10% of pupils have taken drugs other than alcohol and tobacco. The figure rises to as much as 40% in some institutions of higher education. These figures do not, of course, represent the prevalence of addiction.

According to the World Health Organisation, addiction has four characteristics: first an intolerable craving for the drug; second, an increasing tolerance, so that larger quantities of it are required to produce the same effect; third, physical dependence on the drug, which becomes an essential part of body physiology, leading to the physical illness and distress known as withdrawal symptoms when it is discontinued; and fourth, harmful effects on the user's mental and physical health, together with long-term social problems.

It is the effects on behaviour which will alert teachers to the possibility of drug abuse in pupils. Some of the signs are a decline in school performance, unwillingness to participate in school activities, irritability, stealing money or goods, and loss of interest in food and personal appearance.

Cannabis (pot, hash, marijuana) is the most widely used drug. It does not produce addiction as defined above, but some regard the psychological dependence that it causes as equally dangerous; it is also held that use over a long period increases the likelihood of using hard drugs. These are usually defined as the narcotics, opium and heroin, and do produce true addiction.

Discussions on drug abuse in class, and counselling individual pupils may help to limit drug-taking. But where drug misuse is suspected, a professional adviser such as the school medical officer should be consulted immediately.

See *solvent abuse.*

References:

Department of Education and Science and Welsh Office (1985) *Drug Misuse and the Young*, London, HMSO.

Home Office (1988, 3rd edn.) *Tackling Drug Misuse: a summary of the Government's strategy*, London, Home Office.

Simon, G.B. (1984) *A Teacher's Guide to Medication for Children with Special Needs and to Drug Misuse by Young People*, Stratford-upon-Avon, National Council for Special Education.

drug treatment, is used to manage many conditions that teachers meet, for example insulin is used in the control of diabetes. The use of a substance such as insulin which the body itself produces naturally, albeit sometimes insufficiently, is rarely the subject of debate. However, the use of synthetic drugs for the control of inappropriate or unwanted behaviour, as when amphetamines were used for the treatment of hyperactivity, is more controversial.

In that particular example it was later found that some children so treated were at risk of dependency, and so alternative treatments have been developed.

While drug treatment has been widely used for managing behaviour, it has had little success in ameliorating learning difficulties, other than indirectly, as when stimulants have been used to improve behaviour such as ability to concentrate.

The use of any drug poses ethical problems: it is also usually accompanied by side effects, which vary from individual to individual. From the teacher's point of view it is essential to know which child is on medication so that the results can be monitored and any side effects detected.

References:

Simon, G.B. (1984) *A Teacher's Guide to Medication for Children with Special Needs and to Drug Misuse by Young People*, Stratford-upon-Avon, National Council for Special Education.

Tansley, P. and Panckhurst, J. (1981) *Children with Specific Learning Difficulties; a Critical Review of Research*, Windsor, NFER-Nelson.

DTVP, see *Developmental Test of Visual Perception* (*Frostig Test*).

dual sensory impairment, condition of children otherwise known as deaf-blind. There is no official definition of deaf-blindness in the UK, but as in other countries it is generally applied to people whose vision and hearing are both so severely impaired that they cannot automatically use services for people with visual impairments or hearing impairments. Maternal rubella is one of the main causes. The prevalence of dual sensory impairment is not accurately known, but is low enough to argue for provision to be coordinated nationally, rather than relying on individual local authorities, as is currently the case, and where the absence of local facilities may lead to an inappropriate placement.

A deaf-blind child is not a deaf child who cannot see, nor a blind child who cannot hear. The loss of the two major senses leads to difficulties in other areas – distance perception for example is absent and children who are deaf-blind acquire a distorted view of the world. For these reasons some authorities prefer to use the term multi-sensory deprivation, rather than dual sensory impairment. Some residual vision and hearing is sometimes present, but assessing its extent is a complex and skilled task.

These difficulties pose great problems of communication and demand very skilled teaching. A particularly important role, especially in the early years, is played by the parents, who themselves need great help in learning to relate to their child. Advice is provided by the Family Advisory Service of SENSE, the National Deaf-Blind and Rubella Association.

Reference:

McInnes, J.M. and Treffry, J.A. (1982) *Deaf-Blind Infants and Children: a Developmental Guide*, Milton Keynes, Open University Press.

Duchenne muscular dystrophy, see *muscular dystrophy.*

dwarfism, limited growth, resulting in reduced body height. There is no absolute height below which an individual is classified as a dwarf and hence it is not possible to give a prevalence figure that has meaning. The condition is usually due to disturbance of function of the pituitary gland, although it is also seen as a possible manifestation of abuse and neglect.

Limited stature may cause some social and emotional problems, but otherwise there are usually no special educational needs. In some instances other disabilities are present, including mental handicap.

Treatment with human growth hormone helps to improve height in cases where dwarfism is associated with endocrine disturbance.

dys- prefix, usually implies 'damage to', or 'difficulty with', as in dyspepsia, difficulty with digestion, or indigestion. The dys- prefix is contrasted with the a- prefix, which usually means 'complete loss of' or 'total inability to'. Thus dysphonia usually implies difficulty with producing speech sounds, whereas aphonia means inability to produce any speech sounds at all. But these conventions have to be treated with care, for two reasons.

First, usages change over time. Thus in older textbooks dyslexia meant difficulty in developing reading skills, and alexia inability to read at all, both as a result of brain damage. But in modern usage dyslexia means difficulty in developing reading skills, neurological evidence of brain damage not being a necessary condition, whereas alexia now means total or partial loss of existing reading skills as the result of brain damage through accident or disease.

Second, such inconsistencies have led some authorities to use the prefixes interchangeably. Thus dysgraphia and agraphia are both used for difficulties with writing.

For both these reasons the sense in which terms using the dys- or a- prefix are used should always be clearly stated.

dysarthria, see *speech disorder.*

dyscalculia, difficulty with mathematics in general, but particularly operations involving number, as in arithmetic. Dyscalculia is usually assumed to be associated with impairment of neurological structures relevant to mathematics, even though this cannot be demonstrated conclusively. It is distinguished from acalculia, often used to describe damage to existing mathematical abilities following confirmed brain damage. (Sometimes the terms are used interchangeably.)

Dyscalculia is much less frequently diagnosed than *dyslexia* and there is much less political pressure to provide appropriate special education, though this may change. Whether a child is diagnosed as dyscalculic or not, the essential educational issue is to identify the precise learning problems and to institute appropriate teaching procedures.

See *arithmetical difficulties, dys- prefix.*

dysgraphia, see *writing difficulty.*

dyslalia, see *speech disorder.*

dyslexia, essentially difficulty with reading. This simple definition conceals one of the fiercest controversies in special education.

Originally dyslexia was a term used by neurologists for reading difficulties caused by brain damage, usually in adult patients. (It was seen as a less serious form of alexia, inability to read at all, for the same reason.) There was a large increase in reported cases of dyslexia after 1914, as a result of the many head injuries suffered by military personnel during the first world war. Interest in dyslexia grew, and some neurologists suggested that the origin of some reading difficulties in children could also be explained by neurological abnormality, not necessarily acquired through injury, but probably congenital and perhaps inherited. As a result, some children with reading difficulties who happened to see neurologists were diagnosed as dyslexic.

There was neither then, nor is there today, agreement on either the cause or the characteristics of dyslexia: one definition simply emphasises the child's inability to reach appropriate standards of reading, writing and spelling, notwithstanding conventional classroom experience, whereas another states that intellectual limitations, sociocultural opportunities, emotional factors or known brain defect should also be absent. Other investigators stress the importance of a variety of other features, including right-left confusion, difficulty in repeating a sequence of digits in reverse order, etc. Since there is no agreement over diagnosis, there is no reliable incidence figure.

Educators had previously described all such children as retarded in reading. They could see no advantages in any of the various dyslexia diagnoses, for the 'treatment' proposed seemed no different from teaching procedures already in use. Similar conclusions were reached in both the *Tizard Report, 1972,* and the *Bullock Report, 1975,* which recommended the use of the term *specific reading difficulty.* Nevertheless some parents undoubtedly found comfort in the diagnosis, for it suggested that their children were suffering from a handicap, and not to be stigmatised as 'merely slow'. Moreover, before the 1981 Education Act, to be categorised as having a particular handicap improved opportunities for special education, and it is understandable that many parents argued that their children were handicapped by dyslexia. Since the 1981 Education Act this is no longer necessary.

Those who are convinced of the existence of a dyslexia syndrome, distinguishable from other reading difficulties, have continued to press their case. Perhaps the most productive result has been the strenuous research attempts to determine the psychoneurological organisation underlying reading ability. The roles of the hemispheres, the development of cerebral dominance, the effects of lesions in specific areas – in all these fields of research, knowledge has increased. As yet there is little pay-off in improved teaching methods, and reading difficulty, whether described as dyslexia or not, remains a predominantly educational problem. This was the line adopted in the *Warnock Report, 1978,* which discussed dyslexia under the heading of *specific learning difficulties,* not marked off by ability level, social class, nature of causation, or any syndrome pattern. The advantage of this approach is that it requires the educational needs of the child with a reading difficulty to be determined and met, irrespective of any diagnosis. In its treatment of dyslexia the Warnock Report is consistent with its general approach, avoiding medical labels and stressing educational solutions.

See *reading difficulties.*

References:

Miles, T. (1987 edn.) *Understanding Dyslexia,* Bath, Bath Educational Publishers.

Pavlidis, G.T. and Miles, T.R. (Eds.) (1981) *Dyslexia Research and its Application to Education,* Chichester, Wiley.

Tansley, P. and Panckhurst, J. (1981) *Children with Specific Learning Difficulties: a Critical Review of Research,* Windsor, NFER-Nelson.

Young, P. and Tyre, C. (1983) *Dyslexia or Illiteracy? Realizing the right to read,* Milton Keynes, Open University Press.

dysmorphism, the occurrence in a child of multiple congenital abnormalities, some of which may be relatively minor and common, such as the encurved little finger of a child with Down's syndrome. Such collections of abnormalities are recognised as constituting a syndrome which may be linked to chromosomal alterations. It may then be possible to give a genetic prediction and suggest a likely pattern of intellectual development. An example is the *Fragile X syndrome.*

Reference:

Harper, P.S. (1989) *Practical Genetic Counselling,* Bristol, Wright.

dysnomia, or anomia, difficulty in finding and using a wanted word, even though the word is known. It is thus a form of expressive *aphasia,* and is sometimes known as nominal aphasia.

dysphasia, used interchangeably with *aphasia,* though sometimes used to describe a milder rather than a more severe condition.

dysphonia, see *speech disorder.*

dyspraxia, used interchangeably with *apraxia.*

E

ear, contains the mechanism through which pressure waves, usually in the atmosphere, are transformed into nerve impulses. These nerve impulses are then interpreted by the brain as sounds.

The ear is usually divided into three parts, outer, middle, and inner. The outer ear consists of the auricle and the auditory canal. After travelling along the auditory canal, sound waves reach and vibrate the eardrum, which in turn vibrates three linked tiny bones, the malleus, incus and stapes. The eardrum (tympanic membrane) and these three bones (ossicles) constitute the middle ear. The stapes transfers these mechanical vibrations via the oval window to the cochlea, which converts them into electrical impulses, picked up by the nerve endings of the auditory nerve, the transmission pathway to the brain. The cochlea, together with the semicircular canals, which provide the sense of balance, constitute the inner ear.

See *audiometry, decibel, ear illustration, hearing impairment.*

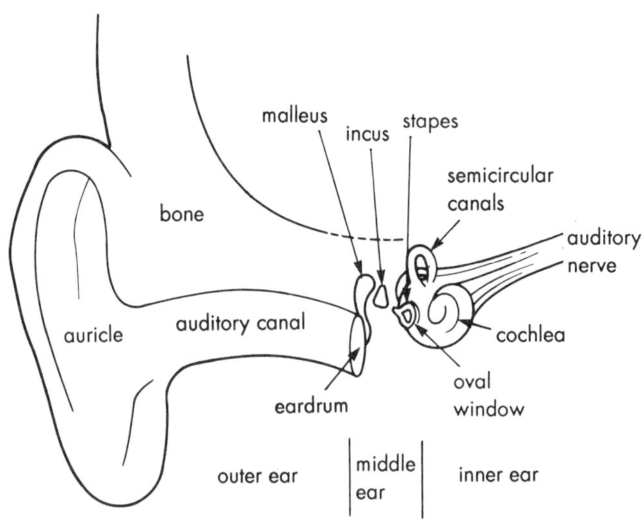

Eardmark Reading Program, US behaviourally-designed scheme based on a task analysis of reading. It aims to teach 150 words through learning sequences using methods such as discrimination techniques, cueing, fading, shaping and appropriate reinforcement. The program has had considerable success with children who are mentally retarded.

Reference:

Marsh, G.E., Price, B.J. and Smith, T.E.C. (1983) *Teaching Mildly Handicapped Children*, St. Louis, Mosby.

early identification, reflects the view that the sooner suitable special education is available, the better for the child. Special education has always attached great importance to early education. When, out of concern over the alleged effects of maternal deprivation, many educators were arguing that to start school at five years of age was disadvantageous, parents of hearing-impaired children, for example, were arguing for education to start as early as possible. Research findings emphasising the importance of the early years to later development in all children then led to calls for a change in educational policy, involving an earlier start to formal education, and more pre-school play groups, nursery schools and classes. Although these facilities are still not universally available, nevertheless there is a legal obligation on education authorities to provide education for children with special needs as soon as these are apparent. Early identification of special needs is important.

Before school age it is usually children with sensory and physical impairments and more serious mental retardation who can be identified with reasonable validity. Indeed, in some instances – genetic abnormalities are a good example – identification can occur before birth. Identifying young children with less serious learning difficulties is an uncertain activity, since developmental tests of pre-school children have low predictive validity. For this reason many education authorities have introduced screening procedures at school entry, so that children's special needs can be met as early as possible in their school career. While this is often a helpful procedure, it is not a complete solution. For example, reading difficulties do not usually appear in the first few months at school and early identification of reading difficulties should take place a little later. In short, 'early' has meaning only in relation to the nature of the special needs being identified. Too early runs risks of misidentification, just as too late limits the effectiveness of remediation.

See *screening*.

References:

Clarke, A.M. and Clarke, A.D.B. (Eds.) (1976) *Early Experience: Myth and Evidence*, Shepton Mallet, Open Books.

Lindsay, G. (Ed.) (1984) *Screening for Children with Special Needs*, London, Croom Helm.

Early Learning Skills Analysis (ELSA), scheme designed to identify a child's skills in those curriculum areas important in the early stages of schooling, e.g. various language, number and motor skills. The scheme provides clear objectives for each area with the skills required defined and graded. A criterion for success is specified and must be reached before progressing to the next stage.

Reference:

Ainscow, M. and Tweddle, D.A. (1984) *Early Learning Skills Analysis*, London, Fulton.

earmould, part of a hearing-aid moulded to fit the wearer's outer ear. The quality of fit is very important; the poorer the fit the greater the likelihood of *acoustic feedback*, usually recognised as a high-pitched howl.

Earmoulds are made from an impression of an individual's ears, usually taken by syringing a soft silicone rubber solution into the ear and leaving this to harden,. In growing children earmoulds need frequent replacement.

Reference:

Tucker, I. and Nolan M. (1984) *Educational Audiology*, Beckenham, Croom Helm.

earshotting, technique designed to help a child develop desirable behaviour patterns. A positive comment is made about the child's behaviour within the child's hearing. If John has been noisy in class then teacher may say to a visitor within John's earshot, 'John is working well and is much quieter'. This helps build up a child's self-concept. Note that this is a somewhat different technique from operant conditioning, where desired behaviour is reinforced when emitted.

EAT, see *Edinburgh Articulation Test.*

ebd, see *emotional and behavioural difficulties.*

echolalia, automatic repetition of words and phrases without necessarily understanding them. Imitation of sounds, words, etc., is a normal stage in speech development, particularly during the second year of life, when the sound patterns of the language are acquired, forming the basis of adult speech. But while echolalic speech normally disappears, in some conditions such as autism and severe mental retardation it frequently remains. Delayed echolalia describes the repetition of words or phrases heard hours or even days previously.

ED/BD, or emotionally disturbed/behaviorally disordered, term in use in the USA, equivalent to ebd, emotional and behavioural difficulties, used in the UK. Both can be regarded as transitional terms, reflecting a move from unsatisfactory attempts to define emotional disturbance to an emphasis on definition via observable behaviour.

Reference:

Hallahan, D.P. and Kaufman, J.M. (1988, 4th edn.) *Exceptional Children: Introduction to Special Education*, Englewood Cliffs, Prentice Hall.

Edinburgh Articulation Test (EAT), assesses the phonology of three- to six-year-old children by analysing their production of single consonants and consonant clusters. The test is based on the view that consonants are more reliable indicators of phonological development than vowels.

The accuracy with which children can vocalise names of pictures of common objects provides an articulation score, which can be converted into an 'articulation age', based on the performance of a sample of Edinburgh children. Qualitative evaluation of the responses is additionally helpful.

The test requires a knowledge of phonetic symbols, and is used mainly by speech therapists.

See *articulation disorder, speech disorder.*

References:

Beveridge, M. and Conti-Ramsden, G. (1987) *Children with Language Disabilities*, Milton Keynes, Open University Press.

Webster, A. and McConnell, C. (1987) *Children with Speech and Language Difficulties*, London, Cassell.

Edinburgh Reading Tests, cover the age range seven to sixteen years in four separate age-bands, or stages. At each stage there are up to six subtests, each measuring a different reading skill: these range from vocabulary and comprehension to retention of ideas and reading for facts. Results are given as standard scores for each stage and each subtest; reading ages can also be derived. The test was standardised on children in England, Scotland and Wales. While the wide range of reading skills assessed is valuable, the high intercorrelations of the subtest scores make the use of subtest differences hard to interpret. Hence the test is better as a survey instrument than a diagnostic tool.

References:

Levy, P. and Goldstein, H. (1984) *Tests in Education*, London, Academic Press.

Pumfrey, P. (1985, 2nd. edn.) *Reading: Tests and Techniques*, Dunton Green, Hodder and Stoughton in association with UKRA.

Edith Norrie Letter Case, box of solid letters and constant digraphs, colour-coded. Thus vowels are coded red, voiced consonants green, unvoiced consonants black. The consonants are also grouped according to method of articulation. Thus labials (m, b, p, v, w, f) are placed together, as are gutterals (k, g, q, x, h, y, ng) etc.

Using the Letter Case to construct words enables the child to learn phonic rules, e.g. that every syllable must contain a vowel (red letter). It also requires the child to think how a phoneme is produced, so that the correct letter-group is chosen. This is an additional aid in identifying and in sequencing the letters needed to build up words and sentences. The Case also contains a mirror to help the child see how the letter sounds are produced and there are advised procedures for using the Case as a teaching aid. It has been successfully used in teaching children with visual and auditory recall and sequencing problems and severe reading difficulties. It was devised by Edith Norrie, a Danish teacher, who founded the Copenhagen Word-Blind Centre in 1939.

See *colour coding*

References:

Tansley, P. and Panckhurst, J. (1981) *Children with Specific Learning Difficulties; a Critical Review of Research*, Windsor, NFER-Nelson.

Educable Mentally Retarded, category of *mental handicap* used in the USA.

It is part of a simple educational classification system, distinguishing children who are educable mentally retarded, and can be taught in the school system, from children who are *trainable mentally retarded* and *custodial mentally retarded.* Note that more recent classification systems in use in mental handicap rely more heavily on child-centred criteria such as adaptive behaviour and/or intellectual performance, and not outcome criteria such as educational placement.

As with all classification systems, there are dangers, e.g. of allowing the category boundaries to become too rigid, and of *labelling.*

See *classification.*

References:

Hallahan, D.P. and Kaufman, J.M. (1988, 4th edn.) *Exceptional Children: Introduction to Special Education*, Englewood Cliffs, Prentice Hall.

Grossman, H.J. (Ed.) (1983) *Classification in Mental Retardation*, Washington DC, American Association on Mental Deficiency.

Education Acts, all Acts refer to England and Wales unless otherwise stated. (USA legislation appears under its Public Law designation.)

Education Act (1964) New Zealand, contains the legislation relating to special education in New Zealand. This legislation defines special education as 'education for children who because of physical handicap or of some educational difficulty, require educational treatment beyond that normally obtained in an ordinary class in a school providing primary, secondary or continuing education'. The definition avoids the pitfalls of classification at the expense of precision.

The interesting feature of this legislation is that there is no obligation on the New Zealand education service to provide special education; the appropriate sections of this Act are permissive, not mandatory. While permissive legislation remains, there are no overwhelming reasons for specifying special needs more exactly. Although the various Ministers of Education have used the Act to provide special schools, classes, supporting services, etc., it has been argued that the absence of mandatory legislation with accompanying regulations has disadvantaged children with special needs.

References:
Singh, N.N. and Wilton, K.M. (1985) *Mental Retardation in New Zealand*, Christchurch, Whitcoulls.
Sleek, D. and Howie, D. in Mitchell, D.R. and Singh, N.N. (Eds.) (1987) *Exceptional Children in New Zealand*, Palmerston North, Dunmore Press.

Education (Handicapped Children) Act 1970, endorsed the right of every child to education by requiring local authorities to provide education for severely mentally handicapped children. Previously, such children had been earlier described as 'ineducable', then later as 'unsuitable for education at school'. They were the last group of children to whom education had been denied, and had been the responsibility of Health Authorities who had usually provided places for them in junior training centres, special care units and hospitals.

This legislation had several effects. First, the training centres were redesignated as special schools, for which education support services were made available. Staffs who were not qualified teachers were accorded qualified teacher status, usually provided they successfully completed an approved inservice course. Existing courses of training for the work became incorporated in the pattern of initial training for teachers, thus changing previous arrangements for entry to training in special education, which normally required a period of experience as a trained teacher in ordinary schools beforehand.

The change in status of schools and staff met with broad approval, particularly on the part of the parents. But the change in training arrangements proved more contentious and was finally removed when every teacher was required to obtain initial training in an approved, broad course before specialising in work with children with special needs.

See *initial training of teachers.*

Reference:
Department of Education and Science (1970) *Circular 15/70, Responsibility for the Education of Mentally Handicapped Children.*

Education (Mentally Handicapped Children) (Scotland) Act 1974, introduced legislation for Scotland broadly similar to that provided for England and Wales in the *Education (Handicapped Children) Act 1970*. The junior training centres attended by children previously described as 'ineducable but trainable' were designated as schools and teachers appointed in addition to the instructors already in post. Those children previously described under Scottish legislation as 'ineducable and untrainable' became the responsibility of the education authorities, so securing, as in England and Wales, that every child was entitled to an education.

Reference:
Department of Education and Science (1978) *Special Educational Needs*, London, HMSO.

Education Act 1976, dealt mainly with the reorganisation of secondary schools into comprehensive schools. But in the House of Lords supporters of integration succeeded in introducing Section 10, which required all special education to be provided in ordinary schools, subject to certain provisos. Section 10 was never implemented, the then Secretaries of State preferring to await the report of the Warnock Committee and the results of the consequent consultations. The Education Act 1981 eventually included clauses (Section 2) which met the aim of Section 10, with provisos which were virtually identical.

Reference:

Department of Education and Science (1978) *Special Educational Needs*, London, HMSO.

Education Act 1980, among other provisions required all schools, including special schools, to have parent and teacher representatives as members of their governing bodies. But the continuing dominance of education authority nominees was criticised as a retreat from the principles of partnership which had been advocated in the *Taylor Report* on school management. The responsibilities of governing bodies, including those in relation to special education, have since been modified by the *Education Act 1988.*

The 1980 Act also gave all parents, except the parents of children attending nursery and special schools, some rights over choice of school.

See *Education* (*No.* 2) *Act 1986, school governors.*

Education Act 1981, the major piece of legislation governing special education in England and Wales. It came into force on 1st April, 1983, repealing provisions of previous Education Acts relating to special educational treatment. It established a new framework for special education, replacing *categories of handicap* with the concept of *special educational need.*

Under the Act, Local Education Authorities (LEAs) have a duty to identify children with special educational needs from two years of age, and from birth if the parents agree. Identification is based on assessment arrangements designed to protect parents' rights and to give them a greater role in their child's education. The assessment process includes *appeals procedures.* These formal assessment arrangements are followed if an LEA thinks a child may have special needs which cannot be met within the ordinary school without extra resources, either material or human. They are distinguished from the normal, ongoing assessment of children's progress, which may also lead to special needs being determined but which the school can meet from normal resources. If, after formal assessment, the LEA believes that special needs exist for which extra provision is necessary, these needs and the means of meeting them are to be specified in a *Statement* of Special Needs, which has to be regularly reviewed. This is intended as a protection for the child, for the LEA is obliged to arrange the special provisions detailed in the Statement.

The Act also stipulates that given certain provisos, special education should be provided in the ordinary school, with the child engaging in school activities with other children without special educational needs, so far as is practicable. The provisos applying to this duty to integrate are that the parents should agree, that the child's needs can be met in the ordinary school, that efficient education can be provided for the other pupils and that resources are used efficiently.

The Act also contains clauses on a number of other topics, including the closure of special schools, approval of non-maintained special schools and independent schools offering places for children with special needs, etc.

The implementation of the Act has been carefully monitored, though the extent to which changes are due to the Act itself, to the earlier *Warnock Report*, or to a changing climate of opinion is difficult to decide. Broadly, the majority of people professionally involved with special education regard its provisions as an improvement on previous practices. The abolition of categories has been welcomed, but the concept of special educational need has been criticised by some as too imprecise.

More is now being done in the ordinary school to meet children's special needs, although the emphasis on *integration* has not led to the expected reduction in special school rolls. Advocates of greater integration believe that the provisos mentioned above substantially weaken the LEA's duty to integrate.

The improvement effected in the position of parents has been welcomed, although information for parents on special education facilities has been criticised as inadequate, as has help with completing parental contributions to assessment. Parents from ethnic minorities, where the home language is not English, have found the procedures particularly hard to follow.

Probably the greatest criticism has been levelled at the statementing procedure. While the intentions behind this have been supported, its execution in some LEAs has proved unwieldy and very time-consuming. Some of the long delays between starting to identify a child's special needs and starting to meet them have been ascribed to staff shortages, but the complex procedure itself, with its various checks and safeguards, also contributes. Finally, the Act can be criticised for what is absent as well as what is present. It makes no attempt to legislate for further education, nor to improve teacher training, both of which were priority recommendations of the Warnock Report. Improvements in both these areas have occurred as a result of local and central initiatives, but in spite of and not because of the Act.

Most significantly it makes no mention of the extra resources which most practitioners feel are needed to implement its provisions fully. In the end, the changes of the years since the Act reached the statute book have been built on local goodwill and the redistribution of resources within LEAs rather than support from central government.

See *Education Act 1988, school governors.*

References:

Adams, F. (Ed.) (1986) *Special Education*, Harlow, Councils and Education Press for Longmans.

Goacher, B., Evans, J., Welton, J. and Wedell, K. (1988) *Implementing the 1981 Education Act*, London, Cassell.

Hogg, R. and Green, L. (1988) *Reactions to the Act*, National Council for Special Education Research Exchange, 9, 2–4.

House of Commons Education, Science and Arts Committee (1987) *Special Educational Needs: Implementation of the Education Act 1981*, London, HMSO.

Newell, P. (1983) *ACE Special Education Handbook*, London, Advisory Centre for Education.

Education (Scotland) Act 1981, dealt with a range of issues in Scottish education. Sections 3 and 4 and schedules 2, 3 and 8 contain the legislation which now governs special education in Scotland. This legislation broadly parallels the 1981 Act for England and Wales. There are differences in the appeals procedures, the provisions for integration in the English Act have no equivalent in Scottish legislation, and the Scottish Act uses the term 'Record of Need', instead of 'Statement'.

The Act has met with a similar response to that outlined for the Education Act, 1981.

References:

Adams, F. (Ed.) (1986) *Special Education*, London, Longman for Councils and Education Press.

Riddell, S., Dyer, S. and Thompson, G. (1990) 'Parents, Professionals and Social Welfare Models: The Implementation of the Education (Scotland) Act 1981', *European Journal of Special Needs Education*, 5, 2, 96-109.

Scottish Education Department (1981) *Circular No. 1074*, Edinburgh, Scottish Education Department.

Thomson, G., Budge, A., Buultjens, M. and Lee, M. (1986) 'Scotland and the 1981 Education Act', *British Journal of Special Education*, 13, 3, 115.

Education Order (Northern Ireland) 1984, created a framework for special education which broadly parallels that obtaining in the rest of the UK. One outstanding anomaly was the position of children with severe mental handicap, who were taught in *special care schools*, controlled by the Health and Social Services Boards. From April 1987 this anomaly was rectified when legislation bringing these schools into the Northern Ireland education service was implemented.

Reference:

Adams, F. (Ed.) (1986) *Special Education*, London, Longman for Councils and Education Press.

Education (No. 2) Act 1986, covered a number of detailed administrative issues such as the role of Local Education Authorities and *school governors* in determining school terms and holidays, grants for teacher training, etc. It also included a number of more controversial sections requiring that a 'balanced view' of political issues be provided in schools, empowering arrangements for teacher appraisal, abolishing corporal punishment, etc. But the heart of the Act were the changes made to the composition of school governing bodies. These changes effect a parnership between representatives of the local education authority (LEA), the teachers, the parents and the local community and so remove the continued dominance of the LEA, one of the features of the Education Act 1980.

The Act's provisions on governing bodies apply equally to special schools. It has been argued that these provisions offer opportunities for schools, both ordinary and special, to meet special needs more effectively. Thus the increased community involvement is one example of an opportunity which could be seized for this purpose. Another is the greater voice given to parents, which should provide more opportunities for developing the partnership principle advocated in the Warnock Report.

The responsibilities that the Act laid on school governors have now to be seen in the light of the provisions of the Education Act 1988.

References:

Sallis, J. (1987) *Education (No. 2) Act 1986*, London, Advisory Centre for Education.

Sayer, J. (1987) *Secondary Schools for All? Strategies for Special Needs*, London, Cassell.

Education Act 1988 (Education Reform Act, ERA), effected the greatest changes in the education service since the Butler Act of 1944.

These changes include:

- introducing a *National Curriculum;*
- testing pupils' attainments at ages seven, eleven, fourteen and sixteen;
- publishing the results of testing;
- devolving major responsibilities for financial management to individual schools;
- allowing individual schools to apply to opt out of Local Education Authority (LEA) control and receive finance direct from central government.

These arrangements have significant implications for special education. Consider the National Curriculum; the entitlement of all children to the same curriculum could help to ensure that children with special needs enjoy the broad educational experiences available to others. But the National Curriculum emphasises the central importance of academic subjects, particularly the core subjects of English, Mathematics and Science; personal, emotional and social development, which underpin so much of the curriculum for many children with special needs are significantly underplayed. The dilemma has been resolved by allowing the requirements of the National Curriculum to be either modified or disapplied for children whose Statements specify this. Children who are not statemented, but who have learning difficulties, can also be exempted at the discretion of the Head, but for limited periods only, as set out in regulations.

These arrangements have direct implications for the assessment procedures – if a child is not following the National Curriculum then the national assessments do not apply. But where children are integrated in the educational mainstream it has been argued that this policy of exemption from the curriculum and the assessments that are obligatory for other children will lead to the discriminatory situation that the 1981 Act attempted to eliminate.

The publication of attainments, especially where results are published by individual schools, has led to a different concern. The purpose of this part of the Act is to introduce a degree of accountability by teachers and schools to parents. Under the arrangements for Local Management of Schools, introduced by the Act, a school's budget is based mainly on pupil numbers. Since better published results may attract more pupils, how will this affect the position of children with learning difficulties? Will schools want to admit children with learning difficulties? Will they press for children with learning difficulties already on roll to be statemented, perhaps with a requirement for attendance at a special school? The National Curriculum Council has indicated that statementing should not be used as pretext for transferring to special schools pupils who might not perform well on national assessments, so these questions may be redundant. Moreover LEAs have a continuing responsibility to ensure that proper provision is made for pupils with special needs in their area.

Under the Education Act 1988, the devolution of finance from LEAs allows schools more freedom to choose what staff, services, etc., they buy. This will have considerable implications for ways in which schools use staff and other resources to meet special needs. Under the new arrangements for local financial management of larger schools, LEAs allocate a budget to each school, for which the governing body is ultimately accountable. The Act specifies that in the allocation of a school's budget an LEA may take into account the number of pupils with special needs and the nature of the provision made for them. But this section of the Act is permissive, not mandatory. How these arrangements work out for children with special needs remains to be seen.

Schools who apply to opt out of LEA control will, if successful, receive their funds direct from central government. Will this greater independence mean that they evolve into elite establishments, leaving the LEA-controlled schools to educate all children with special needs, whether statemented or not? One of the conditions attached to opting-out is that the school should not change its character; it remains to be seen how this condition is put into practice.

The 1988 Act has introduced a sea-change in the education service. How its many clauses are interpreted in relation to special needs will not be apparent for some time. The main obligations of the 1981 Act are unaffected by it: what matters is the effect it has on the attitude with which the education service discharges those obligations. Notwithstanding the pressures of the new, competitive ERA, it is hard to believe that the education service will suddenly be motivated primarily by competitive and financial considerations only, and entirely lose its concern for individual pupils.

See *Inner London Education Authority.*

References:

Department of Education and Science (1989) *Circular 22/1989, Assessments and Statements of Special Educational Needs: Procedures within the Education, Health and Social Services,* London, Department of Education and Science.

National Curriculum Council (1989) *A Curriculum for All,* York, National Curriculum Council.

Peter, M. (1989) 'Local Management and Schools', *British Journal of Special Education,* 16, 2, 75–6.

Wedell, K. (1988) 'The New Act: a Special Need for Vigilance', *British Journal of Special Education,* 15, 3, 98–101.

Education Authority, Scottish equivalent of Local Education Authority in England and Wales, with broadly similar responsibilities for special education.

Education Board, body responsible for administering most special education services in New Zealand. There are ten Education Boards, which deal with most special schools, units and special classes. Other special services are provided through secondary school boards, voluntary organisations and by the New Zealand Department of Education itself. But the administration of special education in New Zealand is currently being re-examined.

Reference:

Hyman, P. (1981) *Economic Aspects of Special Education in New Zealand,* Wellington, New Zealand Council for Educational Research.

Education for All Handicapped Children Act (USA), see *Public Law 94–142.*

Education of the Developmentally Young (EDY), inservice training programme in the use of behavioural methods, designed for staff working with children and adults with severe learning difficulties. The course is delivered through a pyramid training model; the original trainees were eighty educational psychologists and twenty senior advisers in special education who returned to their various parts of the country after training, in order themselves to train key staff.

The first phase of the programme consists of ten workshops, each at least an hour in length, and each covering a specific behavioural technique, e.g. reward assessment, task analysis, shaping, etc. One instructor usually works with two trainees only. Typically, each workshop begins with a videotape of a teacher using the technique, followed in turn by roleplay, practice in using the technique with a child, and feedback. Successful students receive a certificate, and move on to the second and third phases, in which they plan their own programmes of behavioural teaching with children with severe learning difficulties, with gradually decreasing support from the instructors. *Room management* skills are covered in the fourth and last phase of the programme.

The pyramid approach has meant that the programme has been very widely disseminated. The various evaluations of EDY are strong in its support, though with minor criticisms, such as the use of psychological jargon in the phase one workshop material. More importantly, evaluations reveal that the majority of those who complete phase one do not go on to complete later phases of the training programme. The reasons are mainly practical, such as other commitments, lack of time or non-availability of instructors, etc. Most would have liked to proceed.

These points argue for further strengthening of a widely-approved programme.

References:

Farrell, P. (Ed.) (1985) *EDY: Its Impact on Staff Training in Mental Handicap*, Manchester, Manchester University Press.

McBrien, J., 'Introducing the EDY Project', *Special Education: Forward Trends*, 8, 29–30.

Robson, C. (1988) 'Evaluating the education of the developmentally young (EDY) course for training staff in behavioural methods', *European Journal of Special Education*, 3, 1, 13–32.

Education Reform Act, see Education Act 1988.

education supervision order (ESO), has been created by the Children Act 1989. It can be made on the application of a local education authority, on the grounds that a child is of compulsory school age and is not being properly educated. It will be presumed that a child is not being properly educated where a school attendance order has not been complied with, or where a child is not regularly attending the school at which he or she is a registered pupil.

Where an ESO is in force the supervisor has a duty to advise, assist, befriend and give directions to the child and the parents in order to ensure that proper education is secured. The wishes and feelings of the child and the parents must also be taken into consideration.

educational audiologist, see *audiologist.*

educational diagnostician, is employed by education services in the USA for the assessment and treatment of children's learning difficulties. The educational diagnostician is usually an experienced teacher with additional training, and often works with school psychologists.

educational guidance, consultations over such matters as choice of school, choice of course and subjects, etc. It is often provided by teachers and educational psychologists, but is also regarded as one of the main activities of school counsellors. See *counselling*.

Educational Priority Areas (EPAs), were set up following the *Plowden Report*, which recommended a policy of positive *discrimination* for primary schools in deprived areas. An area was accorded EPA status if it met certain conditions such as high levels of supplementary benefit, poor standard of housing, school buildings in poor condition, high proportion of children from ethnic minority groups, etc. Schools in these areas were given favourable treatment over staffing, facilities and equipment, and special allowances were added to teachers' salaries. While the EPA programme had an effect on teaching conditions and morale in some very deprived schools, the boundary of the EPA, with the advantages that it conferred, was a bone of contention. Some education authorities preferred to identify individual schools of 'exceptional difficulty'. The criteria used varied, too, and this led to anomalies.

See *Swansea Project*.

Reference:

Widlake, P. (1973) 'Educational Priority Areas: Action Research', in Chazan, M. (Ed.) (1973) *Compensatory Education*, London, Butterworths.

educational psychologist, psychology graduate with initial training and experience as a teacher, followed by postgraduate qualifications (usually a master's degree) in educational psychology: the key member of a *school psychological service*.

Educational psychologists carry out a wide variety of tasks, but the heart of their activities is the management of individual children's special educational needs. How this is achieved varies from psychologist to psychologist and from one school psychological service to another. Traditionally this has involved assessing the needs of individual children and making recommendations. The effectiveness of working mainly in this way has been criticised, not least because of the impossibility of a small number of educational psychologists having the time to work with a large number of individual children. For this reason some psychologists have placed more emphasis on trying to ameliorate children's learning and behavioural difficulties by changing the approaches and attitudes of those who are closely involved with the children, particularly teachers and parents. This involves educational psychologists in an educative, consultative role, using skills derived from social psychology as much as from educational psychology itself. Many educational psychologists contribute to courses, for example, as well as holding seminars and discussion groups.

Senior educational psychologists have a managerial function in their school psychological service, as well as helping with the planning and policy of their Local Educational Authority's services for children with special needs.

The effect of the 1981 Act, with its statutory requirements for statementing, reviews, etc., led perforce to more time having to be devoted to the older practice of assessing individual children with special needs and making recommendations on their education. Many educational psychologists regret the time which now has to be spent on the administrative chores of report writing, etc., and the consequent restrictions on opportunities to develop new methods of working.

Since the 1944 Act, which laid the foundations for the education service's current responsibilities for special education, the number of educational psychologists in post has increased dramatically. At that time there were fewer than a hundred educational psychologists in post in England and Wales. The growth in concern for the education of children with special needs (handicapped children, then) and a chronic shortage of educational psychologists led to the establishment of the Summerfield Working Party, which recommended a ratio of one educational psychologist per 10,000 pupils. When the Warnock Committee reported in 1978, a ratio of one educational psychologist per 11,000 had been reached, though in Scotland the ratio was then one per 4,000. The Warnock Report recommended a ratio of one educational psychologist per 5,000 children and young people in England and Wales and one per 3,000 in Scotland. This was no over-estimate: the demands of the 1981 Act led to many more educational psychologists being recruited.

The 1988 Act will bring changes, perhaps profound changes, in the way educational psychologists work. Local financial management may mean that some schools will decide how much educational psychologist time to buy: educational psychologists may have to sell their services in competition with others. But the statutory duties of education services in relation to children with special needs still remain. How these different philosophies will run in harness, and the resulting effects on the work of the educational psychologist, remain to be seen.

See *Education Act 1981, 1988, Summerfield Report, Warnock Report.*

References:

Association of Educational Psychologists (1990) *The Educational Psychologist: A Career Information Sheet,* Durham, Association of Educational Psychologists.

Department of Education and Science (1968) *Psychologists in Education Services* (Summerfield Report), London, HMSO.

Farrell, P. (1986) 'The Educational Psychologist', in Coupe, J. and Porter, J. (Eds.) (1986) *The Education of Children with Severe Learning Difficulties,* Beckenham, Croom Helm.

Galloway, D. (1982) 'Deviance in Secondary Schools: a Question of Political and Educational Priorities for Educational Psychologists, Occasional Papers of the Division of Educational and Child Psychology', *British Psychological Society,* 6, 3, 7–13.

Quicke, J.C. (1982) *The Cautious Expert,* Milton Keynes, Open University Press.

educational welfare officer (EWO), person employed by a local education authority, originally to ensure that parents met their legal obligations to secure their children's right to education, normally through attendance at school. While that duty is still the basis of the educational welfare officer's role, this has widened considerably. Advising parents of their rights over assistance with travel to school, welfare grants, etc., also fall within the EWO's responsibilities. This development into social work has extended in some instances to casework with children and families, perhaps particularly with some emotional and behavioural difficulties. In some areas the EWO is seen as the education service's social worker, leading to a demand for social work qualifications to be held by recruits to the service.

The casework activity of the EWO can sometimes clash with basic duties. Children with *school phobia* provide an example of this, for the EWO as caseworker may want to deal with such problems very differently from the EWO as the education service's attendance officer. This emphasises the importance of collaboration between the education welfare service and other organisations, such as the school psychological service or the social services.

The position of the education welfare service, following the *Education Act 1988*, will be affected by the financial and administrative implications of Local Management of Schools. How the service will develop remains to be seen.

References:

Department of Education and Science (1984) *The Educational Welfare Service*, London, HMSO.

Galloway, D.M. (1990) *Pupil Welfare and Counselling*, Harlow, Longman.

EDY, see *Education of the Developmentally Young.*

eeg, see *electroencephalogram.*

elective mutism, the silence of a child who is able to speak, but does not. Often the condition depends upon the situation; many elective mutes talk normally at home but not at all at school. There is no physical or intellectual cause.

The prevalence rate varies with the criterion used. In one investigation, cited in Graham, seven per thousand children did not speak at all during their first term at school. Using the criterion of no speech for at least a year, a rate of about one per thousand is usually quoted for infant school children, which is when the prevalence rate is at its highest. The condition appears slightly more frequently in girls than boys – one of the few language problems for which this obtains.

Both psychodynamic and behavioural explanations have been proffered, the former in terms of distorted family relationships such as repressed hostility towards a parent, perhaps following a separation, and the latter in terms of learnt behaviour, silence offering some kind of reward to the child. Psychotherapy or behaviour therapy can be used to encourage speech, though it has been argued that sometimes this may of itself exacerbate the problem, in which case the best treatment is no treatment – acceptance and no pressure. This may not be an easy course to follow, for a child who refuses to speak in school can be a source of considerable irritation.

References:

Graham, P.J. (1986) *Child Psychiatry: a Developmental Approach*, Oxford, Oxford University Press.

Lumb, D. and Wolff, D. (1988) 'Mary Doesn't Talk', *British Journal of Special Education*, 15, 3, 103–6.

electric response audiometry (ERA), set of procedures used to test the functioning of the nerves of hearing. It is known that tiny electrical events occur, physiologically, in the cochlea and auditory pathways, when a sound stimulus is presented to the normal ear. Using computers, these nerve impulses or action potentials can be measured. The process may involve the child having a general anaesthetic, so that an electrode can be passed through the eardrum to the covering of the cochlea. More often, the test uses non-invasive electrodes attached to the skull when the child is asleep.

The technique is sophisticated, and is usually found in specialised audiology centres only. It is useful in the audiological examination of children who are difficult to test, perhaps because their responses to normal procedures are unreliable, and is an important supportive means of identifying hearing loss.

See *audiometry.*

References:

Tucker, I. and Nolan, M. (1984) *Educational Audiology*, Beckenham, Croom Helm.

Webster, A. and Wood, D. (1989) *Children with Hearing Difficulties*, London, Cassell.

electroacoustic impedance bridge, technique for testing the functioning of the middle ear. The extent to which sound energy is transmitted to the inner ear or absorbed (lost) by the middle ear is measured by a probe placed at the end of the ear canal. The probe picks up and records middle ear activity at different air pressures.

The technique is objective, requiring no response from the child, and is important in that it helps to distinguish between conductive and sensorineural hearing losses.

See *audiometry.*

Reference:

Tucker, I. and Nolan, M. (1984) *Educational Audiology*, Beckenham, Croom Helm.

electrocochleography, highly specialised audiometric procedure. The child is anaesthetised in order to insert a tiny electrode through the eardrum, to be placed on the covering of the cochlea. This assesses the electrical activity at the cochlea in response to sound stimuli.

See *ear, electric response audiometry.*

electroencephalogram (eeg), recording of the electrical activity of the brain. This is obtained from electrodes placed at standard positions on the scalp, via a machine called the electoencephalograph, which amplifies the small voltage fluctuations picked up. These fluctuations are usually classified into four groups: alpha waves, the slow frequencies which are characteristic of the normal waking state; beta waves, which are most obvious when a person is mentally active, as when solving a puzzle; delta waves, the slowest of the frequency groups, normally obtained from a person in deep untroubled sleep; and theta waves, whose frequency lies between delta and alpha.

The eeg shows characteristic abnormalities in a number of disorders. It was widely used in the localisation of brain damage until more sophisticated imaging techniques such as computerised tomography appeared. Its main application is in the assessment of epileptic seizures, where expert interpretation is essential.

See *epilepsy.*

Reference:

Department of Health and Social Security (1986) *Report of the Working Group on Services for People with Epilepsy,* London, HMSO.

Elton Report 1989, 'Discipline in Schools', report of a committee set up to consider responses to disruptive behaviour in schools. Although recognising widespread concern with indiscipline, the enquiry found that less than 2% of staff were affected by serious physical aggression from pupils. Pupils talking out of turn represented the biggest problem for teachers, of whom only one in six thought indiscipline to be a serious problem in their school.

The report made 173 different recommendations for dealing with disruption. As with most educational reports, the main point of attack was teacher training. The government responded by stating that practical class management would be a required component in courses of initial teacher training, and that grants would be made for in-service courses in the same area. Training courses for Heads and other senior staff would cover similar territory, and teacher appraisal schemes would be expected to pay close attention to class management. Financial support for action against *truancy* would also be available.

Other recommendations have so far been ignored by government. These included suggestions for making parents legally liable for their children's behaviour in school, and offering legal, financial and personal support for teachers who have been attacked.

One of the more interesting findings of the report is the teachers' view that introducing the *National Curriculum* is likely to increase rather than decrease disciplinary problems among low-achieving pupils in the upper secondary school. The National Curriculum requirements may not allow them to take the reduced range of subjects allied to vocational courses that are proving popular: the report did not discount this view. Another interesting finding is the strength of the teachers' view that increasing the number of *units for disruptive pupils* would help ease disciplinary problems: this approach was not endorsed by the report.

References:

Department of Education and Science (1989) *Discipline in Schools*, London, HMSO (Elton Report).

Editorial (1989) 'Discipline: Lord Elton is Long on Diagnosis, but Short on Cures', *Education*, 17 March 1989, 173, 11, 249–50.

Gray, P.J., Pike, R. and Maddox, B.L. (1990) 'In Response to Elton', *Educational Psychology in Practice*, 6, 1, 35–8.

emergency protection order, a new short-term order for the emergency protection of a child, replacing *place of safety order*. It is effective for a period of up to eight days, and may be extended once only for a further period of up to seven days.

The court will make the order if it is satisfied that there are reasonable grounds for believing that the child is likely to suffer significant harm unless placed urgently in suitable accommodation. But the court has to apply the welfare principle, i.e. no order will be made unless the court is satisfied that making an order would be better for the child than not making one at all.

See *Children Act 1989*.

emotional and behavioural difficulties (ebd), cover a wide range of psychological problems, ranging from chronic disorders, such as autism or depression, through specific conditions such as school phobia, enuresis, stealing, anxiety, withdrawn behaviour, etc., to temporarily troubled behaviour associated with, for example, a change of class. Attempts to classify ebd usually rely on factor analysis to identify groups of maladaptive behaviours which co-exist. These attempts have resulted in two generally agreed broad groupings, *antisocial behaviours* and *neurotic behaviours*, found useful in differentiating studies of treatments and outcomes. Antisocial behaviours usually have poorer prognoses than neurotic behaviours.

Ebd is a relatively new term in a field that is bedevilled by terminology. It is not difficult to recognise emotional and behavioural difficulties, but very difficult to define them. This is reflected in the number of alternative terms existing, such as maladjusted (for many years the official term in the UK), psychologically disordered, emotionally handicapped, socially maladapted, emotionally disturbed, etc. The introduction of the word 'behaviour' into the term represents an attempt to gain clarity by the use of observable characteristics. Most of the alternative terms have been criticised on the grounds that they are not only imprecise, but also exemplifications of the medical model of thinking, implying that the condition is located in the child, whereas current thinking emphasises the importance of the relationship between the child and the environment as a determining factor in ebd. Behaviour that is acceptable in one context will be regarded as a sign of emotional problems in another. Moreover in the same situation, behaviour acceptable to one person will be regarded as maladaptive by another.

These relativities mean that little significance can be attached to early estimates of prevalence. In fact figures ranging from 6% to 50% of schoolchildren have been reported. The use of newer behaviourally-based schedules, though improving the reliability of estimates, still does not escape criticism, for validity is a problem: changing attitudes and tolerances in society mean that some previously unacceptable behaviours are now acceptable, whereas new behaviours may not be assessed. For example, solvent abuse is an example of a behavioural difficulty that was too rare to be included in behavioural schedules until very recently.

Ebd are managed in various ways. Psychotherapy, behaviour therapy, support teaching, counselling, placement in special units or special schools are all examples of the many different procedures being used, separately or in combination. Considerable research has gone into evaluating their relative effectiveness, but much hinges on the purposes being met. Broadly speaking, placement in separate units or schools succeeds in improving behaviour (while the pupil is there). But this is gained at the expense of a restricted curriculum, and the rate of successful reintegration into the ordinary school is not very high.

The effectiveness of other procedures depends on factors such as the intensity with which they can be offered, the age of the pupil, the extent of parental collaboration, etc.

Finally, special needs due to ebd often occur in association with other special needs, most particularly learning difficulties. This association has also been the focus of much research, most particularly into the direction of any possible causality. 'Does reading retardation cause ebd, or vice versa?' is an interesting question, but, like so many questions in this fascinating field, much too complicated to permit a straightforward, unequivocal answer. A recent study (Mortimore et al.) of the relationship between ebd and reading difficulties, using a longitudinal approach, showed that for some children ebd preceded reading problems, whereas for others the sequence was reversed.

See *disruptive behaviour.*

References:

Bowman, I. (1990) 'Curriculum Support and the Continuum of Emotional and Behavioural Difficulties', in Evans, P. and Varma, V. (Eds.) (1990) *Special Education; Past, Present and Future,* London, Falmer Press.

Department of Education and Science (1989) *Circular 23/89, Special Schools for Pupils with Emotional and Behavioural Difficulties,* London, Department of Education and Science.

Kolvin, I., Garside, R.F., Nicol, A.R., MacMillan, R., Wolstenholme, F. and Leitch, I.M. (1981) *Help Starts Here,* London, Tavistock.

Laslett, R. (1982) *Maladjusted Children in the Ordinary School,* Stratford-upon-Avon, National Council for Special Education.

Mortimore, P., Sammons, P., Stoll, L., Lewis, D. and Ecob, R. (1988) *School Matters: the junior years*, Wells, Open Books.
Moses, D., Hegarty, S. and Jowett, S. (1988) *Supporting Ordinary Schools: LEA initiatives*, Windsor, NFER-Nelson
Williams, P. (1985) 'Troubled Behaviour', Units 18/19 of Open University Course E 206, Milton Keynes, Open University.

Emotionally disturbed/behaviorally disordered, see *ED/BD.*

Employment Rehabilitation Centre (ERC), offers assessment and training for disabled men and women of employable age who have been referred by a Disablement Resettlement Officer. The Centres provide special help for people to adapt physically and mentally to return to or prepare for work. Although their main purpose is to provide for people who have become disabled because of sickness or injury, they also serve young people with special needs. They aim to build confidence, improve physical skills and to give sensible vocational guidance. Courses usually last for six to eight weeks, but can be extended up to twenty-six weeks.

Although there is much satisfaction with the work of ERCs, it has been argued that they are geared towards industrial and commercial employment, and that there is a need for additional provision to serve the needs of able people, e.g. the disabled professional.

See *Disablement Resettlement Service.*

References:

Hutchinson, D. (1982) *Work Preparation for the Handicapped*, London, Croom Helm.
Thompson, M. (1986) *Employment for Disabled People*, London, Kogan Page.

empty language, literally not knowing what stands behind many word meanings. This may be characteristic of some visually-impaired children who have a superficial oral facility but lack the everyday experience necessary to form concepts, e.g.:

CHILD: 'Putting the dishwasher on'
ADULT: 'What does it do?'
CHILD: 'Buzz'
ADULT: 'What do you put in the dishwasher?'
CHILD: 'Pyjamas'

Reference:

Webster, A. and McConnell, C. (1987) *Children with Speech and Language Difficulties*, London, Cassell.

EMR, see *Educable Mentally Retarded.*

encephalitis, acute inflammation of the brain, caused by a group of viruses, some of which are rare and cause encephalitis only, whereas others, e.g. mumps, measles and chickenpox, are common, but occasionally cause encephalitis as well as normal symptoms. The brain damage which sometimes results from encephalitis can lead to disturbances of intellect and behaviour, and special education may be required.

encoding, the process of transforming thoughts, experiences, etc. into spoken or written codes, as part of a communication system. Thus thoughts are encoded in language, language is encoded in print, mathematics is encoded in symbols and formulae, music is encoded in notes, etc. Encoding skills, in an educational context, usually refer to the skills of encoding language in the alphabetic system of print.

See *decoding.*

encopresis, or soiling, passing faeces in clothes or elsewhere, rather than the toilet. Most children are 'clean' by about three years of age: if soiling continues after the age of four years, it is called encopresis.

Prevalence depends on sex and age. The rate in boys is about three times that in girls. Studies of children aged five to seven years give overall prevalence figures of 1 to 2%, but by sixteen years of age prevalence is virtually zero. It mainly affects primary school pupils, and if the soiling occurs in school, can strain relationships with teachers and peers.

There are some physical causes, dealt with medically. But if these are ruled out, the cause may be inadequate toilet training, which must then be provided effectively, or emotional problems, usually dealt with by psychotherapy, often involving the family.

See *enuresis.*

Reference:

Barker, P. (1988, 5th edn.) *Basic Child Psychiatry*, Oxford, Blackwell.

Engelmann-Becker Program, see *Oregon Direct Instruction Model.*

English Picture Vocabulary Tests (EPVT), measure comprehension of spoken words by requiring the child (or children, for the tests covering the older age-ranges can be given to groups) to identify which one of four pictures best represents the word spoken. They are similar to the *British Picture Vocabulary Scale*, covering between them the same age-range, but derived from an earlier version of the Peabody Picture Vocabulary Test, and open to a similar evaluation.

References:

Levy, P. and Goldstein, H. (1984) *Tests in Print*, London, Academic Press.

Pumfrey, P. (1985, 2nd edn.) *Reading: Tests and Assessment Techniques*, Sevenoaks, Hodder and Stoughton in association with UKRA.

enrichment, learning experiences additional to those normally offered. The term is used for giving deprived children activities usually provided at home, but which they have failed to experience, but is more commonly used in the education of *gifted children.*

There are three main approaches used in the education of gifted children. *Acceleration* can pose administrative problems, as well as possibly causing social and emotional stress. Segregation, via special classes or schools, raises socio-political issues. Enriching the normal curriculum while the child stays in the ordinary class is not as vulnerable to these criticisms, and is popular with the teaching profession.

Enrichment can take various forms. Existing subject matter can be studied to a greater depth, or new topics can be introduced. The main problem is the work involved in preparing advanced teaching materials and activities, which usually falls on the teacher. However, this can be eased, though not removed, by such measures as the use of specially designed teaching packages, independent study programmes, and support teaching.

References:

Alexander, P.A. and Muia, J.A. (1982) *Gifted Education: a Comprehensive Roadmap*, London, Aspen Systems Corporation.

Maltby, F. (1981) *Gifted Children and Teachers in the Primary School*, Lewes, Falmer Press.

enuresis, incontinence of urine, either at night (more common: bed-wetting, or nocturnal enuresis) or by day (diurnal enuresis). Primary enuresis means that the child has never been 'dry', whereas secondary enuresis means that bladder control has been gained, but has lapsed. Most children are dry both by day and night by four years of age, and if they are still not dry (apart from the occasional lapse) after five years of age, some authorities diagnose enuresis. Bed-wetting does pose problems for the child and family. There are practical difficulties over staying away from home, extra laundry, etc., as well as psychological pressures which the child may have to endure at home. Diurnal enuresis leads to social problems with teachers and peers.

Prevalence varies with sex and age and also with the criteria used. But the rate in boys is roughly twice that in girls; one study reported that at age five, 18% of boys and 10% of girls wet the bed at least once a month. By late adolescence, the complaint has virtually disappeared for both sexes.

Most cases of enuresis are not associated with any relevant physical condition. Children can be helped by restricting the intake of fluids, being woken at night, and generally encouraged. Drugs are sometimes used, but probably the most effective treatments are those based on conditioning techniques. Variants of the *bell and pad method* often secure bladder control quite quickly.

See *encopresis.*

Reference:

Barker, P. (1988, 5th edn.) *Basic Child Psychiatry*, Oxford, Blackwell.

epilepsy, recurrent seizures (or fits, or convulsions – the words mean the same) caused by recurrent electrical disturbances in the brain, often associated with a damaged area or areas. Not all children with fits suffer from epilepsy. The term epilepsy is used appropriately only when the fits are recurrent.

There are four common kinds of seizures in epilepsy, grand mal, petit mal, temporal lobe, and focal. Grand mal seizures last from seconds to minutes, and are often preceded by an *aura*. The sufferer loses consciousness quite suddenly, makes jerky limb movements and may temporarily lose bowel and bladder control. Some time may be taken to recover. A prolonged grand mal seizure, termed status epilepticus, demands immmediate medical attention. Petit mal seizures last no more than a few seconds, with a very brief loss of consciousness. The sufferer is often unaware that they have occurred. Temporal lobe epilepsy results in bizarre activity during a fit; e.g. a child may walk off with a fixed stare. Often there are signs of disordered personality characteristics between fits, which are frequently preceded by an aura. Focal (or Jacksonian) seizures cause involuntary movements in one part only of the body initially, but may spread. The sufferer is usually conscious.

Prevalence rates for epilepsy vary from three to twenty per thousand, the highest rates usually being found in preschool children. Lower prevalence rates sometimes result from mild cases being unreported. A recent report of the total school population in an urban area in the UK quoted a prevalence of five known cases per thousand.

Most people with epilepsy have their seizures controlled by drugs. However the drugs may make children drowsy, and this in turn may affect their school work. Several studies of the intelligence levels of children with epilepsy have found a distribution that is lower overall than the normal population, and skewed to the left; i.e. with a higher than expected proportion of children with lower IQs. At the same time, a higher incidence of epilepsy is found in the mentally handicapped population. However, the *Isle of Wight study*, which covered a population of children with mainly uncomplicated cases of epilepsy, found a similar distribution of IQs to the rest of the school population. Note too that several great thinkers – e.g. Dostoevsky, Petrarch, Pascal – have been epileptic. Studies of the attainment levels of epileptic children find a high incidence of retardation, perhaps because of the loss of attentiveness caused by anticonvulsant drugs, or possibly by unnoticed petit mal. Epileptic children also show a higher incidence of ebd than average – which itself may be causally linked with lower attainment.

Most children with epilepsy attend ordinary schools, though teachers need to be aware of any restrictions on activities which may be dangerous, such as unsupervised swimming. There are however a few residential special schools designated for children with epilepsy, usually attended by pupils with multiple handicaps, and sometimes with family problems as well.

Reference:

Besag, F.M.C. (Ed.) (1989) *Educational and Child Psychology*, 6, 2 (whole issue).

Department of Health and Social Security (1986) *Report of the Working Party on Services for People with Epilepsy*, London, HMSO.
Dinnage, R. (1986) *The Child with Epilepsy*, Windsor, NFER-Nelson.

EPVT, see *English Picture Vocabulary Tests.*

ERC, see *Employment Rehabilitation Centre.*

ethnic minorities, the issues arising from children with special needs in ethnic minorities were first addressed in the UK in the Welsh-speaking areas of Wales. Here, education for children with special needs had to be provided for a population whose first language (Welsh) was not that of the majority (English) and whose culture was demonstrably different. Whether special education should be bilingual or monolingual; if monolingual which language should be used; could residential schooling in a special school in England be balanced against the emotional shock of leaving home for an alien culture – to these and other questions there were no straightforward answers.

Similar questions arose in the English conurbations in the 1960s and 1970s when ethnic minority children entered schools in large numbers. Immigrant education, as the issue was then inappropriately called, was conceived as special programmes emphasising English language, communication and communication skills, largely taught in reception centres and language units. Some communities were distressed by the high proportion of their children placed in special classes and schools for the educationally subnormal and maladjusted, and political pressure led to the establishment of the committees which produced the *Rampton* and *Swann Reports.*

Emphasis has now shifted to mainstream teaching of ethnic minorities through their home language and culture initially, introducing the majority language later. The approach stresses the different needs of a multiethnic population. But in special education, the Welsh issues already mentioned now appear in England, sharpened there by the existence of a number of different cultural backgrounds, not just two. Special education in ethnic minorities is a universal problem, usually inextricably bound up with *bilingualism.* Wherever it is examined, three main concerns arise. First, a shortage of professional personnel who are at home in the minority culture. Second, a dearth of assessment materials constructed from the perspective of the minority culture and not merely modifications or translations of existing English language tests. Thirdly, a shortage of appropriate teaching materials.

Some ethnic minorities are also deprived communities, in which case there are special needs arising from poor nutrition, poor use of the medical services, etc. Where the community is bilingual these problems are added to those arising from meeting learning difficulties in two languages. There has been pressure to acknowledge that the need to acquire a bilingual facility is itself a special need, a policy of some states in the USA, But this is not educational policy in the UK.

See *PL 94–142.*

References:

Williams, P. (Ed.) (1984) *Special Education in Minority Communities*, Milton Keynes, Open University Press.

Williams, P. and Varma, G. (1986) 'Ethnicity', Unit 23 of Open University Course E206, Milton Keynes, Open University.

eugenics, science concerned with improving the genetic characteristics of a species, originally through selective breeding. The eugenics movement of the latter 19th and early 20th century made claims, later discredited, that many human social ills, ranging from poverty to prostitution, were due to inherited mental retardation. These views led to policies to prevent the mentally retarded from producing children by confining them in institutions and by sterilisation.

The results of policies based on eugenics by the Nazi party in Germany in the 1930s led to a widespread change of attitude and eugenics fell into disfavour. Current developments in *genetics,* though not universally approved, offer more generally acceptable ways of improving inheritance. Genetic engineering may enable some disadvantageous genes to be eliminated, and genetic counselling and in vitro fertilisation offer parents choices over their future children which were not available previously.

See *heredity.*

exceptional children, North American term for children with special educational and/or developmental needs.

experience class, New Zealand special class for pupils with learning difficulties in secondary schools. The curriculum is closely geared to work in the community.

Reference:

Mitchell, D.R. and Singh, N.N. (Eds.) (1987) *Exceptional Children in New Zealand,* Palmerston North, Dunmore Press.

experimental group, a group of subjects differing from a *control group* in respect of the variable whose effects the experiment has been designed to test, but otherwise as similar as possible.

The experimental/control group design is one of the classic paradigms of educational research, based on the hypothesis-testing logic of traditional scientific methodology. It has fallen somewhat out of favour in recent years, partly because of a keener awareness of the limitations of generalising from controlled experiments. A greater volume of research work based on insights gained from the interpretative tradition of ethnography and participant observation has been published latterly.

Reference:

Christensen, L.B. (1988, 4th edn.) *Experimental Methodology,* New York, Allyn and Bacon.

expressive language disorders, problems in producing language. These can be classified according to the medium of transmission; thus speech problems and writing problems are both expressive disorders. They can also be classified according to the point in the communication chain responsible for them. Thus some problems of producing language may be linked with reception difficulties; the speech problem of a deaf child is the obvious example. The expressive *aphasias* are speech difficulties associated with neurological damage, i.e. with the centre of the communication chain. Some severe articulation problems are not associated with neurological damage, but with damage to the speech musculature, the chain's final link.

There are problems with this, as with any classification. Most obviously, one child may suffer from several expressive language disorders at the same time. Moreover, although expressive language disorders are contrasted with *receptive language disorders*, the presence of one does not exclude the other. Indeed the example of the deaf child shows how closely they can be associated. And it is not always easy to find any medical disability at all underlying some expressive language disorders. In these cases in particular, speech and language therapists may prefer to concentrate on the description and treatment of the child's language pattern, rather than strive to find a spuriously precise diagnostic category.

See *Reynell Developmental Language Scales, speech disorder.*

Reference:

Crystal, D. (1984) *Language Handicap in Children*, Stratford-upon-Avon, National Council for Special Education.

extinction, withdrawal of reinforcement, leading to behaviour being eliminated. Extinction is a procedure based on behavioural principles. It is usually considered as a method for eliminating unwanted behaviour; if restlessness in class is being reinforced by the attention gained from teacher, then ignoring the behaviour removes the reinforcement and leads to extinction. (But the principle of extinction cannot be disregarded in procedures aimed at maintaining desired behaviour, too: if reinforcement schedules are inappropriate, extinction – in this case to be avoided – may occur.)

As a technique of behavioural change, extinction is effective, particularly if used in conjunction with other approaches such as differential reinforcement of other behaviours. But there are three main problems. First, it is important to ensure that the correct reinforcement has been identified. Ignoring behaviour will not help to reduce it if adult attention is not the reinforcer. Secondly, the behaviour being extinguished may increase in frequency before being extinguished. Thirdly, extinction may take a long time to achieve. The teacher or therapist must be prepared for these last two points; the effects of extinction do not usually appear immediately.

See *behaviour therapy.*

References:

Alberto, P.A. and Troutman, A.C. (1986, 2nd edn.) *Applied Behavior Analysis for Teachers*, Columbus, Merrill.

Wheldall. K. and Merrett, F. (1984) *Positive Teaching*, London, Allen and Unwin.

eye, the organ of vision. Light passes through the cornea, the transparent outer layer of the eyeball. It then reaches the lens via the pupil, the variable opening in the iris. The lens focuses the light on the retina, the very specialised layer of light-sensitive cells which line the back of the eyeball. Cells in the retina convert the light into electrical impulses, transmitted to the brain by the optic nerve.

The importance of the eye for education, which is so heavily visual, cannot be underestimated. But even where the eye functions perfectly, what is seen depends on the interpretation of visual signals by the brain: perception depends on central structures as well as the eye.

See *eye illustration, visual impairment.*

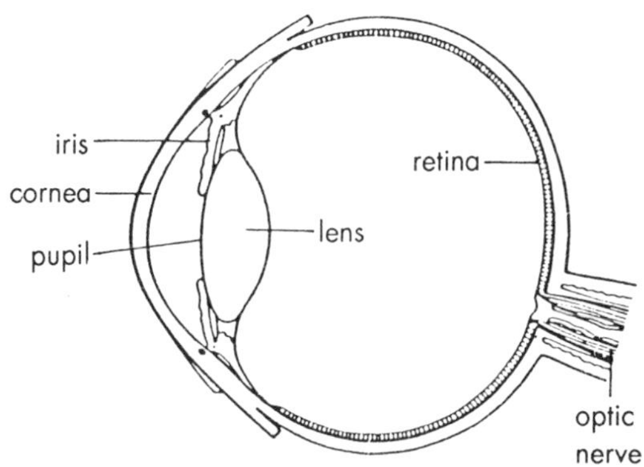

Reference:

Chapman, E.K. and Stone, J.M. (1988) *The Visually Handicapped Child in Your Classroom*, London, Cassell.

eye movements are characteristics of the left-to-right traverse of the eye as it follows print across the page. The gaze moves from point to point (fixation points) in quick jumps, known as saccadic movements, or saccades, during which no reading takes place. These saccades are punctuated by tiny fixation-pauses, during which recognition of words occurs. Regressions, or backward (i.e. right-to-left) eye movements also occur, though for most readers these form a small proportion (10%–25%) of the forward movements. While the eye specialist distinguishes many different kinds of eye movements, all of which have their place in effective vision, fixations, regressions and saccadic movements are probably of greatest interest to the reading specialist.

The recording and analysis of the eye movements of children with reading difficulties was a lively research area, but one which became increasingly disregarded as few practical applications for education emerged. Recently, dyslexia researchers have reactivated the field, revealing differences in movement patterns which, they argue, could be used as criteria for the diagnosis of dyslexia.

Reference:

Pavlidis, G.Th. (1981) 'Sequencing, Eye Movements and the Early Objective Diagnosis of Dyslexia', in Pavlidis, G.Th. and Miles, T.R. (Eds.) (1981) *Dyslexia Research and its Application to Education*, Chichester, Wiley.

eye-contact, meeting another person's gaze, so creating an extra channel of communication. Eye-contact is an important factor in *bonding* between mother and infant. Autistic children's withdrawal from personal relationships may be accompanied by an inability to look at people with a steady gaze, and therapy based on forcing eye-to-eye contact is said to be of some benefit.

eye-pointing, method of communication used by some severely handicapped children, which involves directing the gaze to a particular point, perhaps to indicate a need.

F

factor analysis, group of statistical techniques for reducing a large number of variables to a much smaller number of underlying factors. The techniques rely on mathematical transformations of the correlations between the original variables. The resulting factors are hypothetical constructs, useful for explaining the relationships between the variables in a parsimonious way.

In one of the earliest applications of factor analysis in education, Spearman showed that the correlations obtained between measures of cognitive skills could be explained if we were willing to accept the existence of a general factor, g, related to all such skills, and a number of specific factors, one for each. Later, Thurstone used factor analysis to reduce the correlations between measures of cognitive skills to nine primary mental abilities, a different solution from Spearman's to the same problem. These two and other solutions are valid; each has led to its own genre of psychological tests, aimed at measuring the factors that each identify as underlying human intellectual activity.

Factor analysis is widely used in educational research. One of the problems of correlational research is the difficulty of imputing cause. When studies show that reading difficulties and emotional and behavioural difficulties (ebd) are related, this alone does not indicate whether reading difficulties cause ebd, or vice versa, or whether another, third variable, related to both, is responsible for their relationship. The technique of 'linear structural relations' (Lisrel) has recently been developed to enable the direction of causality to be better inferred.

See *correlation.*

References:

Child, D. (1970) *The Essentials of Factor Analysis*, London, Holt, Rinehart & Winston.

Saris, W.E. and Stronkhorst, H.L. (1984) *Causal Modelling in Non-experimental Research*, Amsterdam, Sociometric Research Foundation.

fading, gradually removing the various supports (reinforcements, prompts, cues, etc.) that have been used to help a pupil produce desired behaviour, so that the behaviour can be produced unaided.

Skill is needed in deciding the best rate of fading. If support is removed too rapidly, the behaviour may not occur and the teaching procedure has to start again. If the rate is too slow, pupils may become dependent on the support. One of the key factors in this decision is the level of the pupil's learning difficulty.

Fading can be accomplished in different ways. For example, the amount of support can be gradually decreased, or the arrival of the support can be increasingly delayed.

Note too that the term is used more generally for many procedures which require gradual introduction (fading-in) or gradual removal (fading-out).

References:

Alberto, P.A. and Troutman, A.C. (1986, 2nd edn.) *Applied Behavior Analysis for Teachers*, Columbus, Merrill.

Wheldall, K. and Merrett, E. (1984) *Positive Teaching: the Behaviourist Approach*, London, Allen and Unwin.

false negative, missed identification. A child who has reading difficulties, not picked up on assessment, would be considered a 'false negative'.

A moment's reflection will reveal that this is one of four possible situations, illustrated by the 'Identification Possibilities' figure. The child without reading difficulties, correctly identified as such on assessment, is a true negative, i.e. the condition is genuinely absent.

The child without reading difficulties, but wrongly assessed as showing them, is described as a false positive.

The child with reading difficulties, wrongly assessed as without, is a false negative. The last category, the child with reading difficulties, correctly assessed as such, is of course a true positive.

Note that the ratio of correct identifications (true positives plus true negatives) to incorrect ones (false positives plus false negatives) is sometimes used as an index of the efficiency of an assessment procedure. Note too that this analysis depends on the assumption that all children can

Identification possibilities

Identified as	Children with special needs	Children without special needs
having special needs	True positive	False positive
not having special needs	False negative	True negative

and should be described as showing or not showing the condition under consideration, i.e. there is no allowance for uncertainty.

Reference:

Bansell, R.B. (1986) *A Practical Guide to Conducting Empirical Research*, London, Harper and Row.

false positive, see *false negative.*

familial mental retardation, usually equivalent to *cultural–familial retardation.* But the term is sometimes used for mental handicap which is unambiguously hereditary, and therefore clusters in families, whereas cultural familial retardation clusters in families, but is not necessarily hereditary.

family centre, base providing services for families with a child with special needs. These centres have usually been set up at the instigation of parents of children with similar needs, and/or with the support of one of the national associations for the welfare of children with special needs. They may provide education, therapy, advice and guidance on management, counselling, and may offer residential facilities for parents coming from a distance. But most of all they are a source of support for parents and children who might otherwise feel very isolated.

Under the provisions of the *Children Act 1989*, local authorities will be obliged to provide family centres as they consider appropriate. The centres will offer the services mentioned above.

Reference:

Furneaux, B. (1988) *Special Parents*, Milton Keynes, Open University Press.

family group therapy, form of *group therapy* which recognises that some emotional and behavioural difficulties, even if present outside the family context, as in the school situation, are nevertheless located in the relationships between family members. Treatment therefore involves all the significant members of the child's family.

Family group therapy has been widely used in child guidance clinics, and was originally based on psychoanalytic techniques. Like child guidance methods generally, it has developed to include approaches derived from other theoretical persuasions. One of the interesting points to note is the emphasis on relationships as the main focus of treatment, and not the child. The emotional and behavioural difficulties which led to the referral are thus not located in the child, but in the psychological environment shared with others.

Family group therapy is normally carried out by a single therapist: when two therapists jointly manage the treatment, so that two perspectives are gained, it is known as conjoint family therapy.

See *medical model.*

References:

Minuchin, P. (1985) 'Families and Individual Development: Provocations from the Field of Family Therapy', *Child Development*, 56, 289–302.

Street, E. and Dryden, W. (Eds.) (1988) *Family Therapy in Britain*, Milton Keynes, Open University Press.

Family Relations Test, measures a child's relationships with and feelings about different members of the family. As well as the child's own feelings, the tester is able to assess the child's perceptions of the feelings others hold about him or her.

A set of cardboard cutouts is presented, from which the child first constructs a representative family. A set of printed statements of emotions and attitudes are then provided and the child allocates statements to the family members. A statement could be of the form 'This person is always nice to me'.

The number of statements allocated to different family members is totalled to give a measure of the child's involvement with them. The statements are also analysed to indicate whether they represent positive or negative feelings. These analyses offer information on which treatment can be based.

There are two versions of the test, covering between them the age-range three to fifteen years. Note that relationships are explored without the child having to verbalise feelings, a considerable clinical advantage, particularly with younger children. The test is mainly used in child guidance and school psychological services.

family support unit, means of offering *respite care* to families with a child with special needs, often children with severe learning difficulties and those with other complex disabilities. Support is usually offered through a hostel, or home in the community, where the child is admitted for a specific time, so affording relief to the parents. Care is provided by the residential social work staff.

The alternative method, in which staff from the support unit go into the family's home itself, has the advantage that the child does not have to leave home, but has the disadvantage of a number of different professionals coming to and going from the house.

Reference:

Buggy, J. (1986) 'The Support Unit', in Coupe, J. and Porter, J. (Eds.) (1986) *The Education of Children with Severe Learning Disabilities*, Beckenham, Croom Helm.

family therapy, see *family group therapy.*

feedback, returning part of the output of a system. It then acts as input, to modify the system's operation.

The concept of feedback, although derived from engineering, has many educational applications. At its simplest, marks and comments on exercises provide feedback to pupils, so that performance can be improved. Feedback from the senses are important for many skills: the acquisition of good speech patterns is heavily dependent on hearing one's voice, for example.

The concept of feedback is used extensively in therapy for children with motor disabilities. Here the normal sensory feedback may be altered or damaged, and the therapist's task may be to provide alternative or additional feedback, so that effective movement patterns can be acquired.

See *postlingual deafness.*

Reference:

Levitt, S. (1982, 2nd edn.) *Treatment of Cerebral Palsy and Motor Delay*, Oxford, Blackwell.

Feingold Diet, special diet devised by Dr Ben Feingold in 1973, and used in the treatment of children with learning and behavioural difficulties, particularly *hyperactivity.* The diet is based on research linking food additives to allergies, and the belief that hyperactivity may be a symptom of an allergic reaction.

The diet aims at eliminating all food flavourings and colourings, as well as two preservatives. In addition naturally occurring salicylates, found in some fresh fruit and vegetables, are banned.

Feingold claimed that about 50% of hyperactive children show marked improvement when placed on his diet, which is popular with many parents. Feingold's findings have not been substantiated by later investigators. But there is evidence that a minority of children who are hyperactive do improve, though whether this is due to the diet itself or to other influences, e.g. the Hawthorne effect, has not been demonstrated conclusively. Concerns at the nutritional effects of such a rigorous diet have also been expressed.

References:

Barker, P. (1988, 5th edn.) *Basic Child Psychiatry*, Oxford, Blackwell.

Egger, J. Carter, C.M., Graham, P.J., Gumley, D. and Soothill, J.F. (1985) 'Controlled Trial of Oligoantigenic Treatment in the Hyperkinetic Syndrome', *Lancet*, 9th March 1985, 540–5.

Marsh, G.E., Price, B.J. and Smith, T.E.C. (1983) *Teaching Mildly Handicapped Children*, St. Louis, Mosby.

Fernald method, technique for teaching reading in particular, devised by Grace Fernald. It is an example of the marriage of a *whole-word approach* to a multisensory method.

The technique emphasises learning to read single words, rather than letters, digraphs or other possible units. A word is written by teacher on a card. The child then traces the word with a finger, saying it at the same time. This is repeated until the word can be written without looking at it.

Most reading methods use vision and hearing, the sight and sound of print, as the senses through which learning occurs. Fernald was one of the first to articulate the view that children with reading difficulties may not learn easily through these two main senses. Hence she added learning through touch (tracing) and kinaesthesis (writing movements), so that reading could be experienced through as many different senses as possible. The Fernald method is thus an example of a multisensory method, in particular a VAKT – Verbal Auditory Kinaesthetic and Tactile – method. It can be varied in different ways. Thus the tactile element can be strengthened by requiring words to be traced on sandpaper, or felt as plasticine shapes: the words themselves can be the components of a child's own story, so introducing a *language experience* element. Moreover it need not be confined to teaching reading, for though this has been its main application, the Fernald method has also been applied to teaching spelling and number.

The method has been widely used with children with severe reading problems. While some teachers are strong supporters of the Fernald method, and can quote individual examples of its value, sound research evidence for its success is difficult to find. As with so many reading methods, it works for some children, but not for others.

References:

Fernald, G.M. (1943) *Remedial Techniques in Basic School Subjects*, New York, McGraw Hill.

Tansley, P. and Panckhurst, J. (1981) *Children with Specific Learning Disabilities; a Critical Review of Research*, Windsor, NFER-Nelson.

FIE (Feuerstein's Instrumental Enrichment), see *Instrumental Enrichment.*

fine motor skills, see *motor skills.*

finger agnosia, inability to tell which finger has been touched by the examiner. The finger localisation test, in which patients have to identify the location and number of fingers touched by an examiner, is used by neurologists. Incorrect responses are said to be indications of minimal cerebral dysfunction.

Finger agnosia is one of the four symptoms of the *Gerstmann syndrome.* Its main educational relevance lies in its association with reading and other language difficulties.

See *agnosia, brain damage.*

References:

Kinsbourne, M. and Warrington, E.K. (1962) 'A Study of Finger Agnosia', *Brain*, 85, 47–66.

Masland, R.L. (1981) 'Neurological Aspects of Dyslexia', in Miles, T.M. and Pavlidis, G.T. (Eds.) (1981) *Dyslexia Research and its Applications to Education*, Chichester, Wiley.

finger localisation test, see *finger agnosia.*

fingerspelling, or dactylology, communicating by spelling out individual letters on the hands. Each of the twenty-six letters of the alphabet has been allocated a different hand-pattern, using one hand only in the American alphabet, but two in the British. The shapes of the hands represent roughly the consonant shapes, whilst vowels are indicated on the five fingers of the left hand in Britain.

Finger spelling is used in *sign languages,* but clearly it is a more laborious method of communicating than using signs which convey meanings of whole words or concepts without recourse to spelling. In effect fingerspelling is an adjunct to signing, used to spell out words when the need arises, e.g. introducing an unusual word or name.

See *fingerspelling illustration.*

Reference:

Miles, D. (1988) *British Sign Language: a beginner's guide*, London, BBC Books.

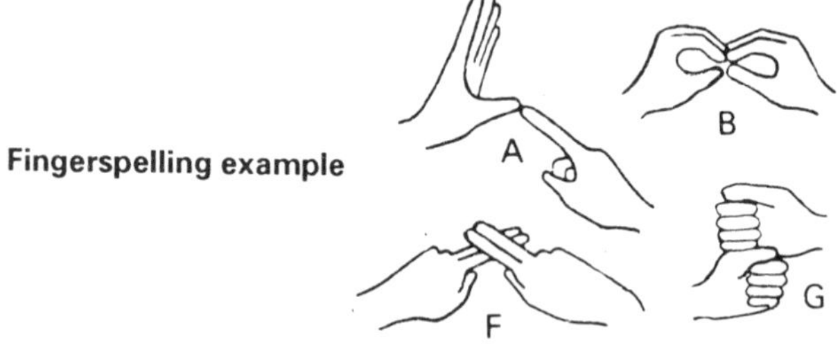

Fingerspelling example

Fish Report 1985, 'Educational Opportunities for All?', probably the best-known of the consultative documents on special needs, policies and provisions produced by education authorities in the wake of the *Warnock Report* and the *Education Act 1981.* The *Inner London Education Authority,* the ILEA (to be abolished later by the Education Act 1988) set up a committee chaired by John Fish, formerly HM Staff Inspector for special education, with a brief to 'review the range, quality and coherence of provision to meet special educational needs in the Authority...' The brief specifically required that the review should take place in the light of the ILEA's policy of promoting equal opportunities and combating under-achievement in children from all backgrounds. This emphasis was not unexpected in view of the multiethnic nature of the school population in ILEA schools, and its socio-economic characteristics, but it did strike a different chord from those sounded in the Warnock Report itself.

Like Warnock, Fish endorsed the view that the aims of education for all children are identical. It went on to argue that all children, irrespective of disability and special needs, had equal rights to the education provided by the authority, as had already been affirmed for children irrespective of race, gender or social background. This argument was of course entirely consistent with the ILEA's policy of comprehensive education, and led to a much stronger statement on integration than appeared in Warnock.

The Fish Report thus defined special educational provision as the technology and methodology required to provide access to the comprehensive curriculum and emotional and social climate in which education takes place.

The corollary of this emphasis on integration was that all teachers become teachers of children with special needs and should be given the support necessary to cope with these new demands.

While the Fish Report is based on consistent argument, it did not reach the conclusion demanded by its logic, namely recommending the abolition of special schools and units. It has also been criticised on the grounds that its recommendations for turning principles into practice lacked detail. But it does provide a framework from which the ILEA, had it remained in existence, could have developed a coherent policy for special educational needs.

References:

Galloway, D. and Goodwin, C. (1987) *The Education of Disturbing Children,* London, Longman.

Inner London Education Authority (1985) *Equal Opportunities for All?,* London, ILEA (Fish Report).

fixation-pause, see *eye movements.*

fixed role therapy, variant of *psychodrama,* derived from *personal construct theory.* The subject writes a character sketch of himself or herself, from the perspective of an intimate acquaintance. A role is then prepared which requires the subject to demonstrate an unusual dimension to the character; for example a timid person may be asked to enact an aggressive character. The role is maintained for a period of two weeks, say, during which time therapy sessions are conducted in role.

This form of psychotherapy is said to be less threatening than some others, for the subject is playing a role, rather than accepting that a real change in personality is taking place. Nevertheless it is said to be effective in modifying personality, though it is not appropriate for younger children.

Reference:

Van Meerts, M. (1983) *The Effective Use of Role-Play: a handbook for teachers and trainers*, London, Kogan Page.

flooding, technique used in *behaviour therapy*, usually for the treatment of neurotic conditions such as phobias. The therapist aims to maintain a high level of anxiety in the subject until the anxiety starts to subside through the subject realising that the fears are groundless. The therapist arranges for the subject (with consent) to be placed in a most-feared situation, and to remain there for a period. An alternative is imaginary flooding, in which the subject is asked to imagine being placed in the most-feared situation.

Since the procedure causes distress, it can only be used when controlled by a skilled and sensitive therapist. Note the difference between it and *desensitisation*, which is usually a preferred technique for these purposes.

Reference:

Walker, S. (1975) *Learning and Reinforcement*, London, Methuen.

foetal alcohol syndrome, pattern of symptoms said to appear in the children of mothers who drink alcohol heavily during pregnancy. The three main symptoms are facial deformities, poor physical development and mental retardation. Note too that behavioural difficulties, particularly attention deficit disorders are frequently present.

Incidence figures vary depending on the criteria used: although the condition is rarely reported in the UK, perhaps because of relative lack of publicity, rates of up to three per thousand live births have been reported elsewhere. The rate rises where populations of heavy-drinking mothers have been studied. The effects of other contributory factors such as smoking in mothers, dietary deficiencies, etc., are difficult to separate from the effects of alcohol. Nevertheless foetal alcohol syndrome has been described as a significant cause of mental handicap.

While there is still debate over the existence and cause of the condition, and consequently over a permissible level of drinking for mothers, the only safe way of avoiding the condition is total abstinence from alcohol during pregnancy.

Reference:

Cooper, S. (1987) 'The Fetal Alcohol Syndrome', *Journal of Child Psychology and Psychiatry*, 28, 223–7.

Jobling, M. (1982) 'The Fetal Alcohol Syndrome: a review of research', *Highlight*, 48, London, National Children's Bureau.

Fog index, one of a number of methods of assessing the difficulty of reading material. For a few sample passages of 100 words calculate (a) the average sentence length in words and (b) the percentage of words of three or more syllables. (a+b) × 0.4 is the Fog index, the *grade equivalent* for which the material is suited. To convert to an approximate reading age in years, add 5.0.

See *readability index.*

formal operations stage, see *Piagetian theory.*

formative assessment, refers to assessment designed to help a pupil's work improve. Constructive feedback on a child's performance is an example of formative assessment. Diagnostic testing is sometimes given as another example of formative assessment – provided that the information obtained is put to good purpose. Formative assessment should be an on-going process. It is contrasted with *summative assessment,* where a pupil's attainments are recorded and reported at a particular time, often at the end of a course.

The original formative–summative distinction was applied to the evaluation of new curriculum materials, the formative evaluation taking place during the development phase, with the intention of improving the final product. The evaluation of the effectiveness of the final product was called the summative evaluation. The distinction has been found useful in considering assessment procedures for individual pupils.

forward chaining, see *chaining.*

fostering,

(1) boarding out with foster parents a child in the care of a local authority;
(2) caring for and maintaining a child below the age of sixteen by someone who is not a relative, guardian or custodian (Foster Children Act 1980). The Act excludes children who are fostered for not more than six days or, when they are being looked after by someone who is not a regular foster parent, for not more than twenty-seven days. Children looked after in some other contexts are also excluded. Although there is no need for any reward to be paid, many foster parents are paid, for example those who look after children in the care of the local authority.

Boarding out, or foster care, has increasingly been accepted as the best way of looking after children in care, replacing residential care for this purpose. This view is held notwithstanding the prevalence of breakdown, or disruption in fostering, rates for which vary between 11 and nearly 50%, depending on a number of factors. For example, disruption is most common among adolescents in the thirteen to sixteen age group, being fostered for the first time. In general, lower disruption rates seem to appear in the later studies, perhaps because of the greater attention now paid to the recruitment, selection, training and support provided for foster parents.

These points have particular importance for the fostering of children with special needs. Here, foster parents taking children with severe behavioural problems, for example, may receive additional payment.

The new relationships to be formed in fostering can impose a period of stress on any child. Teachers, as adults closely involved with the child, though outside the family, may have an important part to play, in consultation with the social services, in helping a child adjust to a new situation.

Under the Children Act 1989 the rules governing private fostering are amended. The new rules apply to a child who is under sixteen years of age, and to a disabled child under eighteen. Local authority fostering arrangements will be governed by the Boarding-out of Children (Foster-Placement) regulations 1988; the placement of children by voluntary organisations will be subject to similar conditions.

See *care order.*

References:

Berridge, D. and Cleaver, H. (1987) *Foster Home Breakdown*, Oxford, Blackwell.

Birchall, D. (1983) 'Foster parents, their recruitment, selection and training', *Highlight*, 56, London, National Children's Bureau.

Jobling, M. (1985) 'Disruption in Foster placements', *Highlight*, 69, London, National Children's Bureau.

fragile X syndrome, genetic abnormality seen as a break or constriction on one of the arms of the X-chromosome. It is a fairly recently described condition, requiring a special chromosome test for identification, but is now said to be second only to Down's syndrome as a cause of mild or moderate learning difficulties. The prevalence in males has been reported as up to two per thousand live births, and affected individuals have particular difficulty with expressive language. Behavioural difficulties can also be present, and a higher than expected incidence of fragile X has been reported in autism.

Physically, males are characterised by prominent ears, elongated face and large testes.

Females may also suffer from fragile X, but usually show mild learning difficulties only, presumably since the second, normal X on the chromosome pair in females is able partially to compensate. But females are of course carriers and teachers in special education may have a responsibility to alert parents to the availability of genetic counselling.

See *genetics.*

Reference:

Barker, P. (1988, 5th edn.) *Basic Child Psychiatry*, Oxford, Blackwell.

fragilitas ossium, another name for *brittle bones.*

F-ratio, key statistic calculated in an *analysis of variance,* and named after its originator, Sir Ronald Fisher. It often appears in reports of educational research. Effectively it is an index of the significance of the difference between two variances, obtained by dividing the larger variance, or spread, by the smaller. The larger the ratio, the greater the likelihood that the difference has not arisen from chance influences and that the variables built into the research procedure are responsible. The significance of the F-ratio is interpreted by reference to appropriate F-ratio tables, which have to take into account the degrees of freedom of the two variables whose variances are being examined.

Reference:

Guilford, J.P. and Fruchter, B. (1978, 6th edn.) *Fundamental Statistics in Psychology and Education,* New York, McGraw Hill.

free association, originally a form of interview developed by Freud. Questioning his patients directly did not lead to an understanding of their difficulties, and hypnosis sometimes was ineffective. Freud therefore resorted to encouraging patients to speak whatever came into their minds, whether relevant or not, and uncensored by convention or any desire to please or say the right thing. The resulting unstructured, uncensored flow of thoughts and ideas enabled him to gain access to the inner conflicts and desires that underlay their neuroses.

This kind of interview is called a free association interview and its use is generally restricted to therapies based on psychoanalytic techniques.

The approach has since been modified for use in personality assessment, and a number of devices based on free association principles have been developed. For example, word association tests require the child to say the first word that comes into mind on hearing a set stimulus word. The responses can be scored for rarity, and can be interpreted clinically by psychologists to give insights into the child's personality. Tests such as this are used in the clinical treatment of more serious emotional difficulties.

Reference:

Holt, R. (1971) *Assessing Personality,* New York, Harcourt Brace Jovanovich.

frequency, as used in hearing, rate of vibration of sound waves, usually measured in cycles per second (cps), or Hertz (Hz). The character of sound is measured in two dimensions, amplitude, perceived as loudness, and frequency, perceived as pitch. Rapidly vibrating sound waves are perceived as high-pitched sounds, slowly vibrating waves as low-pitched sounds. The normal human ear responds to sounds between 60 and 16,000 cps, approximately, but is most responsive to the band-width from 500 to 4,000 Hertz. Speech sounds occupy different frequency bands within this range, as shown in the *Frequencies of speech sounds* illustration. Note that speech

Frequencies of speech sounds

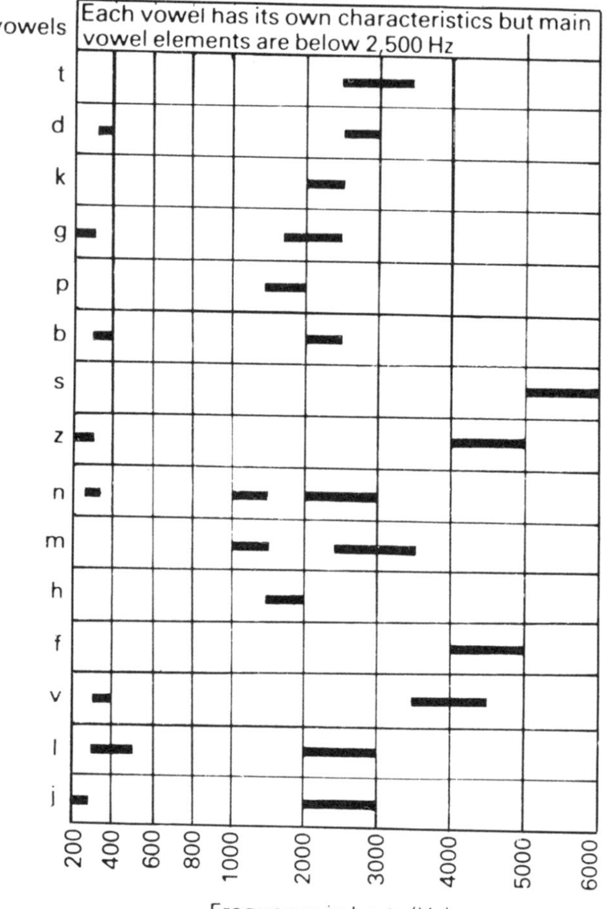

(Note that this illustration is only a rough guide to the frequencies contained in the various sounds)

sounds rarely occupy single band-widths, but are usually made up of a mixture of frequencies.

A hearing loss can affect all frequencies equally, in which case increasing the loudness by raising the voice or amplifying the sounds electronically is a simple means of compensating. But most hearing losses rarely affect all frequencies equally and in these cases hearing is distorted. Thus a child with high frequency hearing loss will find high-pitched speech sounds such as sibilants (s, sh) hard to hear, whereas a child with a low frequency loss will have difficulty with low frequency sounds, such as vowels. Broadly speaking, the latter problem is less serious than the former, for whereas the vowels supply power, the consonants, which use higher frequencies than the vowels, add intelligibility to speech.

See *audiometry, hearing impairment.*

References:

Webster, A. and Wood, D. (1989) *Children with Hearing Difficulties*, London, Cassell.

Reed, M. (1984) *Educating Hearing-Impaired Children*, Milton Keynes, Open University Press.

Freudian theory, major personality theory, with considerable influence on the understanding and treatment of emotional difficulties.

From his clinical work with patients, Sigmund Freud developed a range of ideas and explanations of the human condition, covering such apparently diverse topics as dreams, neuroses, aggression, the structure of personality, etc. The importance of his theory to emotional difficulties in childhood rests primarily on two contributions: his explanation of their aetiology, and the methods he developed for their treatment.

According to Freudian theory, most emotional difficulties have their origin in repressed infantile sexuality. Repression is one of the *defence mechanisms* that Freud described, and infantile sexuality covers the early period of Freud's theory of psychosexual development. This is a stage theory, starting with the oral-erotic phase, occurring from birth up to about two years of age, when the child derives pleasure from sucking and biting. This is followed by the anal-erotic stage, from about two to four years of age, when pleasure, achievement or possibly guilt are all related to the expulsion or retention of faeces.

When toilet training is complete the child enters the phallic stage, showing sexual curiosity and interest in the genitalia. During this period the Oedipus complex, rivalry between the male child and his father for the mother's affections, is experienced. Girls work through the Electra complex, in this case a rivalry with the mother for the affections of the father.

These situations end with the latency period, when sexual conflicts are subdued, until the child begins to enter the genital stage at puberty, when adult sexual feelings begin to be established.

Freud believed that emotional difficulties would arise if any of these stages were mismanaged. For him, the first five years or so of life were critical for the development of stable personalities. He related particular adult problems to particular stages: believing, for example, that an over-emphasis on toilet-training at the anal stage would lead to the development of miserly, obstinate character traits.

Freud believed that successful treatment of emotional difficulties depended on being able to work through the feelings and emotions associated with the early parent–child relationships, possibly leading to *abreaction.* To enable him to reach a patient's memories of, and feelings from, these all-important childhood years, often heavily repressed, Freud developed different methods. Some, such as hypnosis and the analysis of dreams, are techniques for the trained psychoanalyst. Others, such as *free association* and *projection* have been developed and turned into techniques used by psychologists who may not themselves follow a psychoanalytic approach.

Although Freud is viewed as the founding father of psychoanalysis, many different psychoanalytic schools have since been formed. Some place more stress on current relationships and less on early childhood experiences, and the specialised field of psychoanalysis now shades imperceptibly into the more general field of *psychotherapy,* using psychological techniques derived from Freud's work but not classically Freudian. Particular developments have occurred in work with children with emotional difficulties. New techniques for psychotherapy with young children were worked out by psychoanalysts such as Melanie Klein. Since young children do not find it easy to discuss their feelings, *play* has been developed as a means of therapy and the profession of play therapist has been established.

The early heavy reliance on Freudian psychoanalysis and its derivatives in treating children with emotional difficulties has now lessened considerably. Freudian theory itself has been heavily criticised. On practical grounds, doubts over the efficacy of psychotherapy, combined with the expense of treatment, have led to a much greater reliance on behavioural and other therapies. Today, classic psychoanalysis, derived from Freud, is usually reserved for a small minority of the more serious emotional and behavioural difficulties.

See *child guidance clinic, psychotherapy.*

Reference:

Barnes, P. (1985) 'Personality and Change', Unit 15 of Open University Course E206, Milton Keynes, Open University.

Friedreich's ataxia, inherited disease of the central nervous system, with its onset in late childhood or adolescence. The early stages are characterised by unsteadiness in walking and stumbling, leading eventually to inability to walk, skeletal deformities, nystagmus, and slurred, indistinct speech.

Reference:

Russell, P. (1984, 2nd edn.) *The Wheelchair Child,* London, Souvenir Press.

Frostig Test, Frostig Program, see *Developmental Test of Visual Perception.*

Fry readability formula, actually a readability graph. To estimate the readability of materials, three samples of a hundred words are taken. The number of syllables and the number of sentences per hundred words are counted, and the readability then read off from the graph.

See *readability index.*

Reference:

Klare, G.R. (1974–5) 'Assessing Readability', *Reading Research Quarterly*,10, 1, 62–102, reprinted (abridged) in Chapman, L.J. and Czerniowska, P. (Eds.) (1978) *Reading from Process to Practice*, London, Routledge & Kegan Paul, in association with the Open University.

functional curriculum, North American term describing a programme of education that emphasises *social competence,* learning to cope with the recurring problems of living and how to adapt to life in the community. This curriculum is commonly applied with children with serious learning or behavioural difficulties. It is at variance with the curriculum legislation contained in the Education Act 1988, and dispensation to modify or disapply the *National Curriculum* has to be sought before such a programme can be implemented.

functional hearing loss, apparent inability to hear, arising from psychological causes. Functional hearing losses are contrasted with the more usual organic hearing losses, due to pathology of the hearing system.

Among children referred for audiological assessment, a prevalence rate of 7.5% for functional hearing loss has been reported. Inconsistencies in results of tests are often key features in identification. It is important to detect functional hearing loss, since for these children, fitting hearing aids, etc., is clearly superfluous.

Reference:

Tucker, I. and Nolan, M. (1984) *Educational Audiology*, Beckenham, Croom Helm.

functional literacy, term first used by Gray in his UNESCO study to describe the minimal level of efficiency acceptable to the society in which the individual lives. The more complex and cultured a society the greater the demands for higher levels of reading and writing skills. Today in the UK a reading and writing ability equivalent to that of the average fifteen-year-old represents the minimal level of efficiency or functional literacy.

See *literacy.*

Reference:

Gray, W.S. (1956) *The Teaching of Reading and Writing: an International Survey*, Paris, UNESCO and London, Evans Bros.

functional vocabulary, words that have to be read to manage everyday activities. These include the vocabulary of survival (e.g. danger, warning, toilet), of travel (e.g. timetable, bus stop) and key words met at work, recreation, etc.

These words are then taught in reading lessons. Note the difference between functional vocabulary and *basic sight vocabulary.*

further education, includes three main areas of post-secondary education. Vocational education covers courses leading to vocational qualifications for specific fields of employment, normally based at colleges of further education and polytechnics. Non-vocational adult education covers all other classes for adults, and is provided at evening classes. Educational, social and recreational activities for young people are organised through the Youth Service.

Until the spur of the Warnock Report, the availability of further education for people with special needs was minimal. Much of the little on offer was vocational, geared to work-training for people with sensory and physical handicaps, and provided at residential colleges run by voluntary bodies. The striking absence of opportunities for the vast majority of school-leavers with special needs led the Warnock Committee to place the expansion of post-sixteen opportunities as one of its three main priority areas. This recommendation came at a time when, partly as a result of sharply increasing unemployment, there was considerable expansion in courses and training opportunities for all school leavers, and provision for students with special educational needs grew rapidly.

As well as recommending a sharp growth in the development of courses for students with special needs at further education colleges, Warnock advocated that there should be at least one special unit in each region which offered courses for young people with more severe difficulties or disabilities. While some such units have been established, and some students with severe disabilities have also been integrated in mainstream college provision, the main growth in further education colleges has been in courses for students with mild and moderate learning disabilities. This has meant that colleges have had to adapt in various ways. New curricula have been developed, new organisational arrangements have been created, new links with other educational establishments have been fashioned, and staff roles have changed in greater or lesser degree. Some government organisations have provided financial support for individual courses and for facilities such as microelectronic equipment. But notwithstanding the legal and moral right of all individuals to an education up to eighteen years of age, much of this development has been built on the goodwill of those concerned.

See *adult training centre, link course*.

References:

Adams, F. (Ed.) (1986) *Special Education*, Harlow, Councils and Education Press for Longmans.

Betts, D. (1989) 'Further Education and the 1988 Act', *British Journal of Special Education*, 16, 3, 123–5.

Cooper, D. for Further Education Unit (1986) *A College Guide: Meeting Special Educational Needs*, York, Longman.

Dean, A. and Hegarty, S. (1984) (Eds.) *Learning for Independence*, London, Further Education Unit.

Department of Education and Science (1987) *A 'Special' Professionalism*, London, HMSO.

Department of Education and Science (1989) 'Students with Special Needs in Further Education', *Education Observed*, 9, London, HMSO.

National Curriculum Council (1990) 16–19: *Core Curriculum*, York, National Curriculum Council.

G

'g' (general factor), general intellectual ability. In 1904 Spearman used the then novel technique of *factor analysis* to isolate one factor common to all measures of intellectual performance. Those activities which loaded most highly on 'g' involved abstract reasoning, and Spearman described 'g' as the ability to educe relationships and deduce correlates.

Other methods of factoring the correlations between tests led to alternative factorial solutions in which the existence of 'g' was concealed in a set of *group factors*, primary mental abilities.

Many held that 'g' was inborn, not amenable to improvement through education, and a search for a test of pure 'g', or for the identification of a biological equivalent, has continued. Others regard this as a fruitless pursuit and prefer to work with the abilities children possess, whether or not they are hereditarily determined.

See *'s'*.

References:

Child, D. (1986, 4th edn.) *Psychology and the Teacher*, London, Holt Rinehart and Winston.

Vernon, P. (1971, 2nd edn.) *The Structure of Human Abilities*, London, Methuen.

galactosaemia, hereditary disease in which sugar cannot be metabolised in the usual way. If it is not identified and treated soon after birth by a controlled diet, mental retardation and sometimes visual impairment and liver damage can result. Even after treatment, many galactosaemic children experience mild learning difficulties.

Game Oriented Activities for Learning (GOAL), programme from the USA for developing language skills in children with limited ability and speech and language difficulties. The programme uses games to teach the ten different skills assessed by the *Illinois Test of Psycholinguistic Abilities* (ITPA).

While the activities offer a useful classroom resource, there is doubt whether the analysis of language skills on which the ITPA is based is a very effective model for a programme of language improvement.

Reference:

Webster, A. and McConnell, C. (1987) *Children with Speech and Language Difficulties*, London, Cassell.

GAP and GAPADOL reading comprehension tests, measure comprehension over the age range seven to seventeen years, through a form of *cloze* *procedure*. Children have to supply words which have been deleted from print passages. The raw scores are converted into reading ages.

Since the responses are creative, some children supply responses that make sense, even though different from the 'correct' answers given in the test manual, and have to be penalised. This criticism apart, the test is simple and appealing, though more standardisation data could be provided.

Reference:

Pumfrey, P. (Ed.) (1985, 2nd edn.) *Reading: Tests and Assessment Techniques*, Sevenoaks, Hodder and Stoughton in association with UKRA.

Gates, McKillop, Horowitz Reading Diagnostic Tests, a battery of 15 tests from the USA, designed to provide a profile of a child's reading skills, in order to diagnose reading difficulties in children between the ages of six-and-a-half and twelve years. Not all the tests are intended to be given to every child. The tests are based on a 'deficit' view of children's difficulties; the aim is to identify a child's weaknesses so that suitable remedial programmes (insufficiently specified) can be instituted.

The full battery takes at least an hour to administer, and the tests are therefore more suitable for the investigation of an individual child with serious reading difficulties than for general classroom use.

Reference:

Levy, P. and Goldstein, H. (1984) *Tests in Education*, London, Academic Press.

gender differences in special educational needs. Boys outnumber girls in nearly every kind of special need. In children with specific reading difficulties, a ratio of ten boys to one girl has been reported, though this is unusually high. For children with mild and moderate learning difficulties the preponderance is not so marked, a ratio of around three to two being fairly typical. For children with severe and profound learning difficulties, there are still more boys than girls, though here the ratio drops still further to perhaps seven boys to five girls. Boys also are referred to child guidance clinics for behaviour problems more frequently than girls, and population studies of emotional disturbance have produced ratios of nearly two to one.

Various explanations for this male preponderance have been advanced. Biological explanations suggest that the male is somehow more vulnerable to damage, or alternatively more variable, on the argument that there seem to be more gifted males than females. Psychological explanations suggest that males are less willing to conform than females, and hence resist expectations both of good behaviour and of satisfactory attainment. Social explanations suggest that behaviours are learnt from gender role-models, leading to children being offered different experiences: if the role-models were to be changed, so would be the ratios.

All these explanations have some credibility, though none fully accounts for the observations. Note that in the population as a whole there are only tiny (but statistically significant) differences in attainment between boy and girl populations, girls showing a slight advantage in language skills and boys in spatial-mathematical abilities. A simple explanation accounting for all the observed facts has yet to be constructed.

References:
Czerniewska, P. (1985) 'Gender', Unit 22 of Open University Course E206, Milton Keynes, Open University.
Sutherland, M. (1990) 'Education and Gender Differences', in Entwistle, N. (Ed.) (1990) *Handbook of Educational Ideas and Practices*, London, Routledge and Kegan Paul.
Tansley, P. and Panckhurst, J. (1981) *Children with Specific Learning Disabilities; a Critical Review of Research*, Windsor, NFER-Nelson.

gene, the biochemical unit of heredity. Genes are molecules of deoxyribonucleic acid which are located at specific points on the chromosomes. The genes are responsible for the transmission of traits – including many conditions requiring special education – from parents to children through the heredity mechanism. When fertilisation occurs, half the chromosomes in the new organism are provided by the father, half by the mother. A gene from one parent will be matched with a gene from the other parent.

If both genes are disease-bearing, the child will have the disease. If the gene from one parent is disease-bearing and the other is not, the nature of the gene will determine whether the child has the disease or not: if it is a dominant gene, the disease will appear, if a recessive gene it will not. Knowing whether a gene is dominant or recessive, and whether one or both parents carries it, the likelihood of the condition associated with that gene appearing in children of the union can be determined.

The example given is that of a condition carried by a single gene, the simplest example possible. Many of the behavioural and learning difficulties for which special education is needed are probably carried by patterns of genes, where the heredity mechanism is correspondingly more complex.

See *genetics.*

References:
Connor, M. (1990) *The Causes and Prevention of Handicap*, Stratford-upon-Avon, National Council for Special Education.
Harper, P.S. (1989) *Practical Genetic Counselling*, Bristol, Wright.

genetics, the science of the transmission of hereditary characteristics. The hereditary characteristics, both psychological and physical, are carried by the genes. Some of the conditions for which special education is required are carried by a single faulty gene, e.g. PKU, whereas others are polygenic, caused by the interaction of several genes, e.g. some neural tube defects. Yet others are caused by abnormal development of the gene-bearing structures, the *chromosomes,* as in Down's syndrome.

The mechanisms through which these conditions are transmitted from parents to children lie in the province of genetics. As genetics develops, the genes responsible for an increasing number of the intellectual and behavioural conditions that lead to special educational needs are being identified. These conditions are more often caused by a pattern of interacting genes than by a single gene. While genetics has no direct implications for educational procedures, its applications will result in limiting the number of children born with special needs.

See *genetic counselling.*

References:

Connor, M. (1990) *The Causes and Prevention of Handicap*, Stratford-upon-Avon, National Council for Special Education.

Harper, P.S. (1989) *Practical Genetic Counselling*, Bristol, Wright.

genetic counselling, specialised family planning activity, provided by a trained geneticist. This is usually initiated when prospective parents or marriage partners seek advice over the likelihood of a particular condition appearing in their children and perhaps in future generations.

In the past, genetic counselling stopped at that point, i.e. before conception. More recently, new techniques such as amniocentesis have enabled the existence of disabling conditions to be detected after conception but before birth. The decision on whether to terminate pregnancy, in order to avoid giving birth to a handicapped child, is difficult for the parents, and the subject of ethical and political controversy. Sensitive counselling helps.

Newer techniques still may offer possibilities of dealing with a defective gene before the foetus starts developing, but these applications lie in the future.

Reference:

Harper, P.S. (1989) *Practical Genetic Counselling*, Bristol, Wright.

genital stage, see *Freudian theory.*

genius, see *gifted children.*

German measles, see *rubella.*

Gerstmann syndrome, pattern of symptoms first noted by Gerstmann in patients with damage to the left parietal lobe of the brain. The four main symptoms usually recorded are a right–left confusion, *finger agnosia,* writing difficulties and arithmetical difficulties.

Later investigations showed that a number of children diagnosed as dyslexic also showed similar symptoms, leading to the suggestion that some cases of *dyslexia* might be associated with abnormal development of or congenital damage to similar structures, in particular the *angular gyrus.* This is a hypothesis, not verified by medical investigation. At the same time, there is some doubt over the existence of the symptom itself, some neurologists believing that the particular combination of symptoms described by Gerstmann occur together no more frequently than many other behaviours resulting from brain damage.

Reference:
Masland, R.L. (1981) 'Neurological Aspects of Dyslexia', in Pavlidis, G.Th. and Miles, T.R. (Eds.) (1981) *Dyslexia Research and its Applications to Education*, Chichester, Wiley.

Gesell Developmental Schedules, were constructed in the USA to assess four areas of child development:

(1) motor behaviour, including postural reactions, head balance, standing, creeping, walking and fine motor coordination;
(2) adaptive behaviour, covering eye–hand coordination, e.g. handling objects, ringing a bell, simple drawing;
(3) language behaviour, covering all means of communication, e.g. facial expression, gesture, postural movements;
(4) personal social behaviour, covering the child's reactions to the expectations of the culture in which he lives, e.g. feeding, toilet training, play.

The tests, which are used with infants and young children, involve careful observation and are usually supplemented by an interview with the mother. They provide a *developmental quotient.*

As well as offering a good description of current functioning, it is claimed that they detect severe mental handicap in the first year of life, although the rate of misclassification remains high.

References:
Berger, M. and Yule, W.M. (1987) 'IQ and Developmental Assessment', in Hogg, J. and Raynes, N. (Eds.) (1987) *Assessment in Mental Handicap*, Beckenham, Croom Helm.
Gesell, A. (1971) *The First Five Years of Life*, London, Methuen.

Gifted and Talented Children's Act, see *Public Law 95-561.*

gifted children, children who stand out from their peers by virtue of special talents. Giftedness is a thorny topic for two main reasons. First, what is a satisfactory definition? Second, do gifted children have special educational needs?

The early definitions of gifted children took high IQ as their criterion. In Terman's classic study, children with intelligence quotients of 140 or higher on an individual intelligence test were defined as gifted. (Early attempts to identify 'genius' took the same route. Burt, reworking Galton's definition, set a criterion of an IQ of at least 150.) When the children of Terman's study were followed up into later life, it was found that other characteristics such as motivation and confidence were as important as IQ for the success that they achieved.

Interest then moved to the concept of creativity. The argument that creativity was an essential component of giftedness led to a broadening of the definition, though studies investigating the relationship between creativity and intelligence did not always succeed in demonstrating their independence to everyone's satisfaction. More recent work has broadened the definition of giftedness still further. In the USA, *Public Law 95-561* used outstanding potential in intellectual. creative, specific academic, leadership, or performing and visual arts areas as the criterion for identifying giftedness. Similarly in the UK, the main studies of the 1970s all used definitions of giftedness that enabled children who were outstanding in any particular academic or aesthetic area or physical skill to be included.

In short, definitions have broadened considerably, but since many of the activities are not assessed by standardised tests, subjective judgement now plays a much greater role in the identification of giftedness than hitherto.

Gifted children were not included in the categories of handicapped children requiring special education that were established after the 1944 Education Act. But there are two main arguments in favour of changing this view. First, there is evidence that unless special opportunities are provided, gifted children may not develop their talents as fully as possible. Second, a number of able individuals in later life report feelings of boredom, isolation and special anxieties in childhood, feelings which might have been avoided if attention had been paid to their educational needs. (But there is no evidence for the view that gifted children are more prone to emotional problems than their peers.)

The legislation following the *Education Act 1981*, abandoning the concept of handicap, more readily enables the needs of the gifted to be met. Education authorities have to identify any child with special educational needs, irrespective of the kind of need, and of course to meet those needs. In the case of gifted children, needs have been met in one of three different ways. The first method is through establishing special classes or schools, a method that is clearly open to the criticisms levelled against any form of segregated education, and which in this case has led to the additional charge of elitism – though strangely enough this is rarely applied to schools which cater for excellence in, for example, the performing arts.

The second method is through *acceleration*. Here, a gifted child is advanced through the school system faster than his or her age-group. It brings greater intellectual challenges, but risks the social and emotional problems of continual association with children whose attitudes and interests may be more mature.

The third method is *enrichment*. Here the child stays with the age-group, but various methods are employed to provide a curriculum more suited to his or her needs, perhaps through individual programmes, extra tuition, etc. This is generally regarded as the most effective method of providing a satisfactory education for gifted chidren needs, but is probably the most difficult to arrange.

References:

Alexander, P.A. and Muia, J.A. (1982) *Gifted Education: a Comprehensive Roadmap*, London, Aspen Systems Corporation.

Dinnage, R. (1981) 'Gifted Children: a Review of Research', *Highlight*, 47, London, National Children's Bureau.

Freeman, J. (1989) 'Educating Gifted Children', in Entwistle, N. (Ed.) (1989) *Handbook of Educational Ideas and Practices*, London, Routledge.

Maltby, F. (1981) *Gifted Children in the Primary School*, Lewes, Falmer Press.

Gillingham method, sometimes called Gillingham–Stillman method or Orton–Gillingham method, method of teaching reading, widely used with children with reading difficulties. In essence, the Gillingham method is a multisensory method, emphasising the importance of visual, auditory and kinaesthetic associations in learning to read. (The kinaesthetic element includes tactile sensations from the feel of letter shapes.) It is differentiated from the other main multisensory method, the *Fernald method*, by its stress on phonics, its structured approach, and its accompanying materials, such as drill-cards.

Specific instructions as to which letters are to be learnt first and how they are to be taught are followed by exercises in learning three-letter words, spelling the word orally while writing it (simultaneous oral spelling).

The Gillingham method is popular in teaching children with dyslexia.

References:

Gearheart, B.R. (1981) *Learning Disabilities: Educational Strategies*, London, Mosby.

Tansley, P. and Panckhurst, J. (1981) *Children with Specific Learning Difficulties: a Critical Review of Research*, Windsor, NFER-Nelson.

Gittins Report 1967, 'Primary Education in Wales', the Welsh equivalent of the *Plowden Report*. Among other recommendations, it argued for a fully bilingual education. For children with learning difficulties, the report recommended increased provision for special units and classes, to be integrated in the main school, and for flexible transfer between special and ordinary schools. These recommendations have since been overtaken by the Warnock Report and subsequent legislation.

Reference:

Central Advisory Council for Education (Wales) (1967) *Primary Education in Wales*, London, HMSO.

glaucoma, pressure within the eye, caused by faulty internal drainage of liquid; one of the rarer *visual impairments* in children. In some cases the pressure causes the eyeball(s) to bulge (buphthalmos, or ox-eye).

Although children with glaucoma may have reduced fields of vision, and difficulty with dimly-lit areas, they are usually taught in ordinary classrooms, and the condition managed by regular checks on the eye pressure, with operations to relieve pressure if necessary. In school, teachers should ensure that any eye-drop prescription is carefully followed, and that any complaint of pain, discomfort, etc., is investigated.

Reference:

Fitt, R.A. and Mason, H. (1986) *Sensory Handicaps in Children*, Stratford-upon-Avon, National Council for Special Education.

glue ear, fluid in the middle ear, which may thicken into a glue-like consistency, preventing the tiny bones of the middle ear from moving freely and dampening the sound signals. It is treated medically by antibiotics if there is infection, and by decongestants to dry out the middle ear. In persistent cases the fluid can be drained surgically and a *grommet* placed in the eardrum to keep the middle ear ventilated.

Glue ear is a commmon cause of *conductive hearing loss* in young children, sometimes associated with *otitis media*. It may come and go over a period of time, making it difficult for teachers to identify hearing impairment. Although the hearing loss itself may be mild, it is important to realise that it is most likely to occur at a time of rapid language development, and if not detected may have serious effects on a young child's development.

See *ear*.

References:

Webster, A. and McConnell C. (1987), *Children with Speech and Language Difficulties*, London, Cassell.

Webster, A. and Wood, D. (1989) *Children with Hearing Difficulties*, London, Cassell.

Goldman-Fristoe tests, a group of three tests of aspects of language, constructed in the USA, and covering articulation, auditory skills and auditory discrimination respectively. They are used to investigate speech difficulties in children.

governing bodies, see *school governors*.

grade equivalent, measure of educational performance, based on the attainment of 'grades' in the USA school system. In most States, children enter Grade 1 at the age of six-plus and normally progress by one grade each year until they enter the last year of High School at age seventeen-plus years. Thus a reading performance of grade equivalent 3.5 is the median performance of children halfway through Grade 3.

As with interpreting any test score, the norms refer to the standardisation sample. In the case of grade equivalents this is almost certain to be a sample of American children. Moreover a system of measurement by grade equivalent has similar strengths and weaknesses to any system of scaling which uses age-performance as its unit of measurement.

See *age equivalent*.

graded reader, component book of a reading series or reading scheme which offers a gradually increasing level of reading difficulty. The series or scheme generally indicates the difficulty level of each reader, usually as a reading age.

See *basic reading scheme.*

graded word reading test, measures word recognition skills by requiring the child to read aloud a set of words of gradually increasing difficulty. The number of words correctly pronounced is usually converted into a reading age. The format of allocating ten words to each year of reading age was originated by early test constructors and has been largely followed since.

Graded word reading tests have been for many years among the most popular tests of reading performance used in British classrooms. Those produced by Burt and Schonell are two obvious examples. They are quick and easy to administer and the reading age which results is easily understood.

These advantages have to be set against some serious drawbacks. The skill of word recognition is important, but so are other reading skills such as comprehension and fluency, which these tests do not measure. Nor do they give much help with the diagnosis of reading difficulties, although clues can be picked up from the nature of the miscues, etc. The reading age score is open to the criticisms levelled against all *age equivalent* scores. In short, a graded word reading test should be used as one of a number of methods of assessing reading performance, and with due awareness of its limitations.

See *Burt (Rearranged) Word Reading Test, Schonell reading tests.*

Reference:

Pumfrey, P.D. (1985, 2nd edn.) *Reading: Tests and Assessment Techniques,* London, Hodder and Stoughton in association with UKRA.

grand mal seizure, see epilepsy.

grandparents, often have close and regular contact with families of children with special needs, can be influential in the relationships which develop within the family system, yet are infrequently seen by professionals. It has been suggested that grandparents may be more positive than the parents in their attitude to a child with a special need, perhaps indicating that the grandparents are more ready to accept the problem, or alternatively more ready to deny it.

Reference:

McConachie, H. (1986) *Parents and Young Mentally Handicapped Children: a Review of Research Issues,* London, Croom Helm.

grant-maintained schools, are schools whose applications to opt out of Local Education Authority (LEA) control have been permitted, and which will be funded directly by the Secretary of State.

The intention is that they will receive similar funding to that which they would have received had they remained under the LEA umbrella. But, subject to certain conditions set out in DES Circular 10/88, the governors will effectively have independence in running the school.

The application for grant-maintained status should indicate the provision that the school intends to make for pupils with special needs, both those with Statements and those without. The application should describe how these pupils will be taught, staff involved and resources provided.

LEAs are expected to provide services (e.g. school psychological services) for pupils attending grant-maintained schools on the same basis as for pupils in other schools.

See *Education Act 1988.*

References:

Department of Education and Science (1988) *Circular 10/88*, London, Department of Education and Science.

Department of Education and Science (1989) *Circular 21/89 Grant-Maintained Schools: Financial Arrangements*, London, Department of Education and Science.

grapheme, one or more written letters representing a single speech sound, or *phoneme*. A grapheme can have various forms, e.g. the capital, lower case and cursive forms of a letter are examples of allographs of the one grapheme, as in C, c and *c*.

The relationship between grapheme and phoneme, grapheme–phoneme correspondence, is at the heart of the phonic approach to teaching reading skills.

See *initial teaching alphabet.*

Griffiths Mental Development Scales, measure development in babies and young children. The first scale, the 'infant development scale', was published in 1954 and covers the age-range from three months to two years. In 1970 the age-range was widened to cover children up to the age of eight years, with the publication of the 'abilities of young children scale', which includes a modified version of the earlier material for infants. Either scale can thus be used for infants, but the second scale has to be used for older children.

Four of the areas of development covered are similar to those assessed in the *Gesell Developmental Schedules,* viz. locomotor behaviour, hand–eye development, hearing and speech and personal–social behaviour. In addition both Griffiths Scales include a performance subscale, and a practical reasoning subscale is incorporated in the second scale.

The Griffiths scales are available to individuals who have taken a course of training in their use. They were pioneering instruments when first produced, and still offer advantages, being relatively quick to use, for example. But the construction and content may be dated by modern standards.

Reference:
Levy, P. and Goldstein, H. (1984) *Tests in Education*, London, Academic Press.

GRIST, Grant Related Inservice Training, programme of inservice education which places responsibility for deciding the aims and format of inservice training firmly in the hands of Local Education Authorities, (LEAs). Previously, inservice education had been funded by a pooling arrangement, under which LEAs who seconded teachers on to approved courses, usually full-time courses provided by institutions of higher education, were able to obtain from central funds up to 90% of the costs of the replacement teacher. Under GRIST, LEAs prepare a plan for inservice education, based on consultations between advisers and schools, for which central financial support can be provided. The extent of the support depends on the extent to which the authority's plans reflect needs as perceived by the Department of Education and Science. Thus in 1987, five areas affecting special needs were designated as areas of national priority, for which 70% financial support was available. Four were concerned with special needs in schools and one with special needs in further education. Any other area in which an LEA chose to provide inservice training would count as an area of local priority, eligible for 50% central funding.

The main effect of GRIST has been to provide INSET courses whose content and format reflect more directly the needs of the LEA as seen by the education advisers and the schools. This has resulted in a more flexible pattern of courses. Many more short courses, not necessarily award-bearing, often school-based, and part-time rather than full-time, are now being offered. Many areas prefer to fund evening or weekend courses, rather than courses that take teachers away from the classroom. Some of the prominent victims of these changes have been the one-year full-time courses leading to an M.Ed in special education, which were for many years the route to advanced qualifications in special education, and the flagships of the INSET work of departments of special education in institutions of higher education. These courses provided the leaders of the profession. The qualifications are still available, but on a modular basis, with teachers now taking longer to obtain the qualification, but perhaps more candidates being able to take advantage of the new arrangements. Special arrangements had to be made for the one-year inservice courses for intending educational psychologists, which had always been seen as serving national rather than local needs.

See *Inservice education and training.*

References:
Department of Education and Science (1986) *Circular 6/86, The Local Education Authority Training Grants Scheme: Financial Year 1987–8*, London, Department of Education and Science.
Department of Education and Science (1989) *Circular letter 17.2.1989, Local Education Authority Training Grants Scheme and Education Support Grants:*

National Curriculum Development Plans, London, Department of Education and Science.

Mittler, P. (1987) 'From Warnock to GRIST', *Times Educational Supplement*, 24.6.1987, p.4.

grommet, small tube placed in the eardrum to ventilate a malfunctioning middle ear. Eventually the grommet will fall out or be removed and the incision will heal. This is a procedure used in the treatment of *glue ear*, in order to alleviate conductive deafness.

References:

Bishop, J. and Gregory, S. (1986) Hearing Impairment, in Gillham, B. (Ed.) (1986) Handicapping Conditions in Childhood, Beckenham, Croom Helm.

Webster, A. and Wood, D. (1989) Children with Hearing Difficulties.

group hearing-aid, classroom-based amplification system, used in units and schools for children with impaired hearing. The main advantage of the system in comparison with individual hearing-aids is the much better sound quality that it provides. But this is achieved at the expense of mobility, for unlike systems relying on induction loops/radio transmission, which have other drawbacks, each child's station is physically connected to the teacher's station by wire leads.

Reference:

Tucker, I. and Nolan, M. (1984) *Educational Audiology*, Beckenham, Croom Helm.

group factor, in *factor analysis*, a factor common to a group of measurements, but not to all. In the case of cognitive abilities, for example, the positive relationships existing between all tests can be explained by '*g*'. But there still remain relationships between groups of tests, in particular those measuring linguistic abilities on the one hand, and those measuring spatial abilities on the other. These clusters of subsidiary abilities are called group factors. Like the general ability, 'g', they are given letters to identify them, 'v' for the verbal group factor and 'k' for the spatial one. This structure of a general ability, supported by two major group factors, in turn supported by minor group factors and then specific factors is the pattern of intellectual abilities recognised by most British educational psychologists, in comparison with alternative models from across the Atlantic.

References:

Child, D. (1986, 4th edn.) *Psychology and the Teacher*, London, Holt Rinehart and Winston.

Vernon, P.E. (1971) *The Structure of Human Abilities*, London, Methuen.

group test, test designed for administration to a group of children simultaneously, as opposed to an individual test. The advantages of economy possessed by the group test have to be offset against the loss of information gained from contact with and observation of a single child that the individual test offers. Note that some tests can be used both as individual and group tests. In these cases separate norms for the two different modes of administration should be provided.

group therapy, treating children (or parents) in groups, instead of individually. Therapeutic groups can be based on many different theoretical standpoints. Much early group therapy was used in child guidance clinics with a psychoanalytic approach, but transactional analysis, counselling, etc. can also be used as the basis for group therapy. Not everyone is suited to group therapy, nor to a particular group, and therapists have to make careful evaluations before deciding preferred treatments.

Group therapy has two main advantages, intrinsic and economic. The process enables group members to help each other, both by offering mutual support and by interpreting each other's situation and reactions to it: it also enables the time of a trained therapist to be spread among a greater number of clients.

With young children, group therapy takes the form of play sessions, but with adolescents, as with adults, group therapy is based on discussion.

See *family group therapy.*

guidance counsellor, North American equivalent of a *school counsellor.*

H

habit disorder, behavioural difficulty in which a normal habit fails to become established or, if established, is broken, e.g. enuresis affecting the habit of bladder control, or stammering affecting speech habits. Habit disorders form a category of an older classification system for emotional and behavioural difficulties, and have been described as affording relief from fears by shunting them into a physical symptom.

Reference:

Ministry of Education (1955) *Report of the Committee on Maladjusted Children,* London, HMSO.

haemophilia, inherited disorder in which the blood does not clot normally, and hence sufferers are at risk of episodes of serious bleeding, both internal and external, from normally trivial cuts and bruises. The condition is carried by the female, but commonly found only in the male. Severe haemophilia is said to affect one in about 25,000 persons. Modern treatment methods, including injections of clotting agents, have substantially improved the quality of life for haemophiliacs.

Most children with haemophilia attend normal school, though a few who are very seriously affected have to combine education with lengthy hospital treatment. The main difficulties educationally are the loss of school time through illness – there are no intellectual effects – the need to avoid contact sports, and special help over vocational guidance. The absences from school should be dealt with by home tuition, but this has not always been provided as rapidly or as intensively as is needed.

Recently, attention has been drawn to some children who have contracted *AIDS* from treatment with contaminated blood. All present evidence suggests that there is no increased risk of transmission in the school setting.

References:

Department of Health and Social Security (1986) 'Children at School and Problems Relating to AIDS', DHSS letter CMO (86) 1st Jan. 1986.

Dinnage, R. (1986) *The Child with a Chronic Medical Problem*, Windsor, NFER-Nelson.

Russell, P. (1984, 2nd edn.) *The Wheelchair Child*, London, Souvenir Press.

HAIC, Hearing Aid Industry Conference, body which issues specifications for the conditions under which the performance of hearing-aids is tested and reported.

Reference:

Tucker, I. and Nolan, M. (1984) *Educational Audiology*, Beckenham, Croom Helm.

halo effect, one of a number of possible sources of error in assessments using rating scales, in this case a tendency to be biased by an irrelevant characteristic when rating an individual. Judgement is coloured, often by whether the rater likes the person or not. Some teachers are influenced by pupils' docility, consistently rating obedient pupils more highly when making assessments of intelligence, reliability, etc., and disruptive pupils lower. If the trait being assessed is defined in behavioural terms this reduces the halo effect but does not eliminate it.

Reference:

Anastasi, A. (1982, 5th edn.) *Psychological Testing*, New York, Macmillan.

Halsey Report 1972–1975, description of a three-year action research project which took place in four *Educational Priority Areas* located in Birmingham, Liverpool, London and the West Riding of Yorkshire. There was also a parallel experiment in Scotland. The aim of the project was to explore different ways of countering deprivation and to make recommendations for appropriate educational and social policy.

While the project team found the use of the educational priority area concept convenient, it also stressed the importance of work with schools, school classes, individuals and families in order to realise an effective policy of positive *discrimination*.

Five different volumes were published, one for each area, and each separately authored. They are sometimes known collectively as the Halsey Report after the project leader, and the reference below is to the last publication.

See *compensatory education.*

Reference:

Smith, G. (1975) *Educational Priority*, Vol. 4: the West Riding EPA, London, HMSO.

handedness, the preferred use of either the left or right hand. For almost all children, this has developed before school entry. Most authorities suggest that between 5% and 10% of the population are lefthanded: however it is important to remember that an individual's preferred hand may depend on the activity, and someone righthanded for writing may be lefthanded for throwing, for example. An 8% prevalence of lefthanded writers in the school population was reported in one survey. The National Children's Bureau survey found 6% of lefthanded pupils in 1964, but 10% in 1976 in the 11-year-old age group.

Handedness is one example of *laterality*, the preferred use of one side of the body for different activities, and is thus associated with the *cerebral dominance* pattern. There is little doubt that hand preference has a genetic component, but it is also heavily influenced by environmental factors such as the attitude of society, training, etc.

Lefthandedness occurs more frequently in boys than girls (12.8% against 9.6% in a recent study) and more frequently in children with special needs. Here again, overall prevalence figures are suspect, for they depend not only on the activity, but also on the nature of the special need. For children with severe learning difficulties and for children with autism, prevalence figures approximately twice those found in the general population have been reported.

Early investigators believed that lefthandedness was associated with reading difficulties, but later work has failed to find definite confirmation of this. *Crossed laterality* and other unusual patterns of handedness, vision and hearing dominance were then suggested to occur more often in populations of children with reading difficulties, but here too the evidence is inconclusive, with the possible exception of a link with ambidexterity. In any case, an association, even if conclusively demonstrable, does not necessarily imply a causal relationship. Probably the only certain special need shown by lefthanded children is in relation to *handwriting.* Here, suggestions on seating, on posture, on the position of the paper, and on the grip of the pen, enable writers to see what has been and is being written and to make the fine motor movements with the fingers which will obviate their minor difficulties.

References:

Clark, M.M. (1974) *Teaching Lefthanded Children*, London, Hodder and Stoughton.

Pavlidis, G.Th. and Miles, T.R. (1981) *Dyslexia Research and its Application to Education*, Chichester, Wiley.

handicap, see *disability.*

handwriting, traditionally one of the three 'Rs', but perhaps the least valued. Yet handwriting is an important means of communication even in times of typewriters and wordprocessors. There are some particular problems in teaching handwriting skills to pupils with special needs.

The simplest problem faces children with learning difficulties, many of whom acquire writing skills like their peers, but more slowly.

Then children with coordination problems, particularly in the area of fine motor control will have difficulty in producing legible script. Exercises in hand-movements, starting with double-handed grasping, and moving on through stages such as controlled finger painting, until single-handed pencil gripping and use are reached, have been described for children whose fine motor disabilities are associated with cerebral palsy.

Lefthanded children also have difficulties with writing, caused largely by the left hand having to push the pen across the paper, instead of pulling it. The pen digs in, and if a nib is used, splutters and blobs occur. The writing hand, which follows the pen, instead of preceding it, is liable to cause smudging. These difficulties can be lessened if the paper is swivelled to replicate the natural arc of movement of the left hand, rather than the right, if ballpoint pens are used, or specially cut nibs for lefthanders, if the pen is held higher up the shaft, so that the following hand avoids the script, and if pairs of children are seated so that the left-hander has the writing hand on the outside of the pair!

See *clumsy child, handedness.*

References:

Aubrey, C. and Sutton, A. (1986) 'Handwriting: one measure of Orthofunction in Conductive Education', *British Journal of Special Education,* 13, 3, 110–14, Research Supplement.

Reason, R. and Boote, R. (1986) *Learning Difficulties in Reading and Writing,* Windsor, NFER-Nelson.

Hargreaves Report 1984, 'Improving Secondary Schools', one of three major reports – the other two were the Fish and Thomas reports – commissioned by the Inner London Education Authority, all of which were published a few years before the Authority's abolition by the Education Act 1988. The Hargreaves Committee was charged with considering the curriculum and organisation of secondary schools, with special reference to underachieving pupils. It defined achievement broadly, taking it to include achievement in practical skills, in personal and social skills, and in motivation and commitment as well as in written tests.

Its main recommendation for meeting pupils' special needs was that in-class support was a more productive way of offering special help than special units and schools. But it also recognised that difficulties in personal relationships between pupil and teacher might lead to other arrangements having to be made.

Reference:

Inner London Education Authority (1984) *Improving Secondary Schools*, London, ILEA (Hargreaves Report).

Haringey Reading Project, pioneer investigation of the effectiveness of using parental assistance with children's reading. The project aimed to organise planned help with reading from parents over a two-year period for children learning to read. It started when the children were six years of age and finished when they were eight.

At the end of the project, the children whose parents had participated in the project were reading at significantly higher levels than the controls, and the improvement was sustained at follow-up investigation at age eleven. This latter point is particularly interesting since the fall-away of reading improvement after traditional remedial help is withdrawn is well known.

The Haringey project gave a considerable impetus to the development of *paired reading* in the UK, and some striking increases in reading performance have been reported. But not all investigations of the effect of parental involvement in learning to read have shown the improvement reported by the Haringey project and other studies. This has led to speculation as to which of the various elements involved in the Haringey work (the role of the researchers in home visiting, the choice of materials by the schools, etc.) might have contributed to the improvement shown.

References:

Hewison, J. (1988) 'The Long Term Effectiveness of Parental Involvement in Reading: a Follow-up to the Haringey Reading Project', *British Journal of Educational Psychology*, 58, 184–90.

Topping, K. and Wolfendale, S. (Eds.) (1985) *Parental Involvement in Children's Reading*, London, Croom Helm.

Harrison-Stroud Reading Readiness Profiles, were standardised on six-year-olds, and are intended to measure whether a child has the skills necessary for starting formal reading lessons. The material originates from the USA, but has been widely used in this country. It consists of six subtests, covering skills such as using symbols, making visual discriminations, etc., and is attractive to children. The technical details are open to criticism, however. For example the interpretation of the profile of subtests rests upon their reliability and validity, for which adequate data are not provided.

See *reading readiness.*

Reference:

Pumfrey. P.D. (1985, 2nd edn.) *Reading: Tests and Assessment Techniques*, Sevenoaks, Hodder and Stoughton in association with UKRA.

Harris Tests of Lateral Dominance, assess hand, eye and foot dominance. For example manual dominance is assessed by tests of hand preference, left–right knowledge, tapping, card dealing, etc. The test does not provide an overall score, but enables the examiner to judge the extent of lateralisation.

See *handedness.*

Hawthorne effect, producing a spurious experimental finding through uncontrolled variables such as the novelty of the experiment, or the attention it creates, contaminating the results. Thus the interest created by introducing a new teaching method might be responsible for any improvement shown in children's attainment, rather than the method's intrinsic worth. The interest would drop with time; conclusions drawn from the experiment would then be rendered invalid.

These effects can be minimised by careful experimental design: thus *control groups* should receive experiences which are similar in novelty and interest to those planned for the *experimental groups.*

Reference:

Christensen, L.B. (1988, 4th edn.) *Experimental Methodology,* New York, Allyn and Bacon.

Head Start, federally (i.e. nationally) funded programme in the USA which started in 1965. The issue which, more than any other, led to Head Start was concern over the deprivation of the children of the inner cities. The solution proposed was rooted in the environmentalist's belief that early experience was the key to healthy later development – physical, educational and intellectual. The Head Start programme, 'an idea whose time had come', initially provided disadvantaged pre-school children with medical, nutritional and social benefits, as well as early education. Later, a proportion of handicapped children had to be included if proposed programmes were to be eligible for grants.

Early evaluations cast doubt on the hope that the programme would lead to measurable intellectual and educational gains. But supporters of Head Start argued that since many of the early programmes were hastily implemented, with poorly trained staff, and in some cases lasted for little more than a few weeks, these were great expectations. This argument was strengthened in two ways. First, some substantial gains were registered by children who participated in programmes which started in the first year of life, which offered intensive intervention, often several hours a day, and which captured the parents' support. Second, more recent evaluations have shown that even for minimal Head Start programmes, there is evidence that children who participated are less likely to have required special education, more likely to have completed high school and more likely to attend college. In short they appear to have gained in motivation at least.

The controversy which surrounded the Head Start programme in its first two decades has now quietened, and its advantages, though not as great as some had hoped, are less frequently questioned.

See *compensatory education, early identification, Milwaukee project, sleeper effect.*

References:
Woodhead, M. (1985) 'Early Intervention', Unit 27 of Open University Course E206, Milton Keynes, Open University.
Zigler, E.F. and Valentine, J. (Eds.) (1979) *Project Head Start: a Legacy of the War on Poverty*, New York, Free Press.

Health Service, through the District Health Authority (DHA), is responsible for both pre-school and school health services, which offer a wide range of screening and care functions. Each DHA must appoint a person (usually a community paediatrician, or principal school medical officer) to take charge of these services, who is effectively the pivot of the relationship between health and education in a given area. He or she is the channel through which specialist services such as speech therapy are normally provided, and the link with *Community Mental Health* and *District Handicap Teams.*

Under the Education Act, 1981, the DHA must inform the parents and the education authority if they believe that a child has or probably has special educational needs.

Reference:
Powell, R.M. (1984) 'Medical Screening and Surveillance', in Lindsay, G. (Ed.) (1984) *Screening for Children with Special Needs,* Beckenham, Croom Helm.

health visitor, state registered nurse with intensive extra training. Health visitors are members of the community health teams, engaged particularly in preventive medicine. Among other duties, they visit all homes with a child under five years of age, screening for special needs, counselling parents, giving information on health and welfare services, and providing support and informed reassurance for parents. Thus they form a very important link between families with children with special needs and the education and health services. This was recognised in the Warnock Report, which suggested that the health visitor could act as a *named person.*

Reference:
Jennings, K. (1984) 'The Role of the Health Visitor', in Lindsay, G. (Ed.) (1984) *Screening for Special Needs,* Beckenham, Croom Helm.

hearing-aid, provides hearing-impaired children and adults with experiences of sound that they would otherwise miss. Essentially a conventional hearing-aid consists of a microphone to pick up sound, an amplifier to increase it, and a receiver to transmit the signals from the amplifier into the ear. The system is powered by a battery. Most hearing-aids in use are self-contained, being worn entirely on the listener, but some systems involve others, e.g. a radio system in which the microphone component is worn by teacher, whose voice is broadcast over a transmitter.

Hearing-aids do not restore a child's hearing to normal in the way that spectacles might be considered to 'correct' poor vision. They make sound louder, but do not select the sounds which are most important for the child to hear. Conventional hearing-aids (post-aural: behind the ear; or body-worn) are most effective in good acoustic conditions within about two metres of a speaker. As the communication distance increases other nearer or louder sound sources will be picked up by the aid. Children usually find advantages in listening when two aids are prescribed because it is much easier to locate and attend to a sound with binaural listening; but two aids may be resisted on the grounds that they signify a double handicap.

While special centres advise over hearing aid choice and over changing *earmoulds* as the child grows, teachers have responsibilities for ensuring that hearing-aids are working satisfactorily and are being used effectively. This is easy to overlook when children with hearing impairment are educated in mainstream classes, particularly when they are taught by a number of different teachers.

See *radio aids.*

References:

Tucker, I. and Nolan, M. (1984) *Educational Audiology*, Beckenham, Croom Helm.

Webster, A. and Ellwood, J. (1985) *The Hearing-Impaired Child in the Ordinary Classroom*, Beckenham, Croom Helm.

hearing impairment, covers *conductive hearing loss*, in which there is damage to the outer or middle ear, and *sensori-neural hearing loss*, in which damage occurs at the inner ear or beyond. In a central hearing loss, the sound signals, though carried to the brain by an intact auditory nerve, are not properly perceived or heard as sound; this is thus a subdivision of the sensorineural category.

Hearing impairment arises for various reasons, and is often a complication of other conditions such as cerebral palsy. Prenatal causes, either hereditary conditions or diseases such as rubella, are frequently implicated. Other causes occur during birth, e.g. hypoxia, and postnatal causes, particularly the effects of illnesses such as meningitis, account for most other cases. In addition many young children suffer from periods of temporary conductive deafness associated with colds and conditions such as otitis media.

One way of describing hearing impairment is in terms of *decibel* (dB) loss. The system recommended by the British Association of Teachers of the Deaf and most frequently used in the UK lists four categories, dB loss referring to the average loss at five different frequencies, measured for the better ear:

slightly hearing impaired, i.e. not exceeding 40dB loss;
moderately hearing impaired, i.e. 41 to 70dB loss;
severely hearing impaired, i.e. 71 to 95dB loss, and postlingual losses greater than 95db;
profoundly hearing impaired, i.e. at least 96dB loss, acquired prelingually.

Note that these categories bring out the difference between hearing impairment present before children start to use speech (prelingual) and hearing impairment that occurs after speech has developed (postlingual). This difference can be very important for learning to communicate; clearly a child who has had the experience of hearing and using speech may already be communicating orally and will probably want to continue to do so, whereas a child with a similar loss acquired prelingually will find this much more difficult.

Prevalence figures for hearing impairment depend on the criterion used. Estimates usually suggest approximately one in five children with conductive hearing losses, with peak prevalence under two years of age, but most losses resolve without lasting difficulties. Sensori-neural losses affect about one per thousand, with many of those affected experiencing both sensori-neural and conductive losses.

The effects of hearing impairment are complex, depending not only on the size of the loss, but also on the frequencies affected. The approximate frequencies of speech sounds are shown on the accompanying illustration, and a child's *audiogram* will indicate which of the various speech sounds will cause most difficulty. That is not the whole story, however, for the child's understanding of and production of speech will also be affected by any perceptual (central) damage, by past experience, including teaching, by age at which the hearing impairment occurred, and many other factors.

How to teach children with hearing impairment to communicate has been a matter of perennial debate. Broadly, a choice between manual methods (*sign languages*) and oral methods (speech) has been posed. By and large, the greater the hearing impairment the less the likelihood that an oral method will be chosen, but even so, the choice has sometimes depended as much on the advocacy of individual teachers as on other factors. More recently 'total communication', using a combination of both main methods has become more popular.

Children with hearing impairment are educated in special schools, in units attached to ordinary schools and in mainstream classes. This last option has been increasingly advocated recently. It demands appropriate support from the peripatetic teachers and advisers of the authority's service for the hearing impaired, both for the children and for the staff of the ordinary school.

See *oral–manual controversy*.

References:

Fraser, B. (1990) 'The Needs of Hearing-Impaired Children and Integration', in Evans, P. and Varma, V. (Eds.) (1990) *Special Education: Past, Present and Future*, London, Falmer Press.

Hodgson, A. (1984) 'How to Integrate the Hearing Impaired', *Special Education: Forward Trends*, 11, 4, 27–9.

Moses, D., Hegarty, S. and Jowett, S. (1988) *Supporting Ordinary Schools: LEA Initiatives*, Windsor, NFER-Nelson.

Reed, M. (1984) *Educating Hearing-Impaired Children*, Milton Keynes, Open University Press.

Webster, A. and Ellwood, J. (1985) *The Hearing-Impaired Child in the Ordinary School*, Beckenham, Croom Helm.
Webster, A. and Wood D. (1989) *Children with Hearing Difficulties*, London, Cassell.

hemianopia, loss of half the field of vision in both eyes. The left-hand sides of the retinas of both eyes are connected to the right cerebral hemisphere; the right-hand sides to the left hemisphere. Consequently damage to the visual cortex of one hemisphere will affect vision in part of both eyes.

Children will have problems in mobility, sport and school subjects, including reading (finding the start of a line of print if the left field is affected, for example), not helped by glasses or low vision aids. But they can be taught to move head and eyes to compensate for the field loss.
Reference:

Chapman, E.K. and Stone, J.M. (1988) *The Visually Handicapped Child in Your Classroom*, London, Cassell.

hemiplegia, see *cerebral palsy.*

hemisphere, see *cerebral hemisphere.*

Her Majesty's Inspectorate, body of several hundred inspectors (HMIs), based on the Department of Education and Science and responsible for providing independent advice to the Secretary of State on the education service in England. One of the Chief Inspectors has responsibility for special education. There are parallel bodies of HMIs in Wales and Scotland, based on the Welsh and Scottish Offices respectively.

Inspectors assess course content, teaching methods and working conditions in any phase of education that is directly funded by the state, though the Warnock Report recommended that they should be also involved in monitoring standards in non-maintained special schools. They have also insisted on being invited by universities to inspect courses of teacher training there. Their reports on schools and other bodies are published and are influential in effecting changes. The inspectorate also produces its own publications on matters of educational interest, including issues in special education.
References:

Department of Education and Science (1983) *HM Inspectors Today: Standards in Education* (*Raynor Report*), London, HMSO.
Lawton, D. and Gordon, P. (1987) *HMI*, London, Routledge & Kegan Paul.

high frequency hearing loss, reduced ability to hear higher tones; in particular the sounds of sibilants and fricatives, such as s, sh, f, th, etc. Vowels, which tend to occupy the lower region of the speech frequency range, may be heard normally. This distorted hearing will be reflected in the child's own distorted speech pattern. A hearing-aid matched to the loss pattern can help, depending on the extent of the loss.

See *audiometry, frequency, hearing impairment.*

Reference:

Reed, M. (1984) *Educating Hearing-Impaired Children,* Milton Keynes, Open University Press.

High School Personality Questionnaire, HSPQ, measures fourteen of R.B. Cattell's primary personality dimensions for the age-range twelve to fifteen years, e.g. warmth, intelligence, emotional stability, etc. The questionnaire has been used for counselling adolescents. As each personality dimension is measured by a scale of ten questionnaire items only, the administration time of about forty-five minutes is acceptable, but the technical data have been criticised.

Reference:

Levy, P and Goldstein, H. (Eds.) (1984) *Tests in Education,* London, Academic Press.

higher education, advanced education beyond school, is in theory available to all students who meet entry requirements, whether with special needs or not. In practice, much depends on the availability of services such as provision of transcripts for the hearing impaired, readers for the visually impaired, etc. Universities and colleges, like other educational establishments, were required by the Chronically Sick and Disabled Persons Act 1970, to provide facilities for the disabled, including access, in their buildings. But this requirement has never been enforced and many older buildings in particular still present access problems.

Although a survey in the 1970s found that only a small minority of universities and polytechnics had set up a body to consider the needs of their disabled students, the impetus given to special education by recent legislation probably means that that position has now changed for the better. Most institutions of higher education do provide student counselling services which offer support for students with personal problems.

The Open University's contribution in this field is outstanding, for its open entry arrangements, combined with its distance teaching system, has attracted many students with special needs, to whom it pays particular attention.

References:

Russell. P. (1984, 2nd edn.) *The Wheelchair Child,* London, Souvenir Press.

SKILL (National Bureau for Students with Disabilities) (1988) *Provision for Students with Disabilities in Higher Education,* London, SKILL.

higher-order reading skills, include those of literal and inferential comprehension, the evaluation of what is read and its appreciation: the reader needs to know how and when to skip and skim, to find facts, follow a story line or argument, grasp key ideas and concepts, carry out instructions and read selectively, critically and reflectively. These skills entail competence in both the primary reading skills of recognising the shapes of letters, letter groups and words, and of associating appropriate sounds with them, and also in the intermediate reading skills of handling sequences of words and larger units of meaning, which lead to fluent reading.

Reference:

Department of Education and Science (1975) *A Language for Life*, London, HMSO (Bullock Report).

Hiskey-Nebraska Test of Learning Aptitude (HNTLA), individually administered scale for use with hearing-impaired and language-impaired children and adolescents between three and seventeen years of age. The responses to the items are entirely nonverbal, made by pointing, manipulation, etc., and the whole test can be administered in mime. For children without hearing loss, verbal instructions can be used.

It is a widely used instrument in assessing the educational possibilities for children with hearing loss. The twelve subtest scores are converted into a single deviation quotient.

Reference:

Salvia, J. and Ysseldyke, J.E. (1985, 3rd edn.) *Assessment in Special and Remedial Education*, Boston, Houghton Mifflin.

Holborn Reading Scale, popular individual test of word recognition and comprehension for children aged between five-and-a-half and eleven years. It consists of thirty-three sentences arranged in increasing order of difficulty, each sentence representing a reading age three months higher than the preceding one.

The test is easy to give and simple to use. These characteristics probably account for its popularity, for the technical data are poor.

Reference:

Pumfrey, P.D. (1985, 2nd edn.) *Reading: Tests and Assessment Techniques*, Sevenoaks, Hodder and Stoughton in association with UKRA.

holistic method, an approach to reading based on the concept that the whole is greater than the sum of its parts. It emphasises that pupils need a variety of strategies to gain meaning from print and to encode their thoughts in writing. Rather than teach one method of reading, it is argued, we need to give pupils opportunities to use the language experience approach, to learn to spell by writing and thus become familiar with digraphs and phonemes etc., and to master the subskills and higher-order skills of reading to the point where they become automatised. Throughout, the emphasis is on gaining meaning from print by the quickest method the individual finds appropriate. Thus paired reading and motivation, memory games and writing patterns, phonics and calligrams and clear articulation in speech all have a part to play if they facilitate learning.

The holistic approach has been used with the generality of pupils as well as those with severe reading and spelling difficulties, including dyslexia. It is essentially both a *top-down* and a *bottom-up approach.*

Reference:
Young, P. and Tyre, C. (1983) *Dyslexia or Illiteracy?* Milton Keynes, Open University Press.

Holter valve, sometimes Spitz-Holter valve, see *shunt*.

home tuition, traditionally, providing education at home for pupils who are unable to attend school, perhaps through longterm illness, injury or emotional and behavioural difficulties. Home tuition is arranged through local education authorities, usually for up to five half-days a week. Home teachers should keep in contact with the pupil's regular school in order to minimise the effect of the period at home on the pupil's learning. Nevertheless, since pupils taught in this way lose the opportunities of social intercourse and a full curriculum that school provides, home tuition has been seen as a 'second-best' alternative to attending school.

In recent years, home visiting programmes for young children have developed, based on research findings demonstrating the importance of the family in supporting children's learning. Most of the early programmes, such as *Head Start* in the USA and the compensatory projects in this country, aimed at disadvantaged children, but later ones were aimed at children with special needs, irrespective of socioeconomic background, for example the *Portage project*. In many of these schemes, teachers visit homes, not so much to teach the child, as to collaborate with the parents. The degree of collaboration ranges from the minimal, up to the parents participating in planning a programme of work at home, and learning how they themselves can put the programme into operation. Broadly speaking, the greater the degree of partnership with the parents, the more enduring the gains.

The strategies adopted in home visiting are spreading to the orthodox home tuition, and the two programmes are now characterised by an increasingly similar approach.

See *parents*.

References:
Birchall, D. (1982) 'Home Based Services for the Under Fives: a review of research', *Highlight*, 54, London, National Children's Bureau.
Fish, J. (1985) *Special Education: the Way Ahead*, Milton Keynes, Open University Press.
Cunningham, C. and Davies, H. (1985) *Working With Parents: Frameworks for Collaboration*, Milton Keynes, Open University Press.

home visiting, see *home tuition*.

homebound instruction, North American term for *home tuition*.

hospital school, provides education for children who are hospital patients. The teachers are usually employed by the local education authority.

The Platt Report on the Welfare of Children in Hospital Recommended that all children in hospital should be taught. Since then (1959), the pattern of hospital stay has changed, children now spending much less time on average in hospital. Nevertheless schooling is still important: it provides a link with normality both for children and their families, a link between the hospital teacher and the child's own school helping to minimise the effects of a break from normal school work. The stimulating effects of a good educational experience also helps to avoid the boredom that children can otherwise experience in hospital wards. There can of course be problems in marrying the school experience to the hospital routine, and offering a significant educational experience under unusual conditions is a challenge to the hospital teacher.

References:

Oswin, M. (1978) *Children Living in Long-Stay Hospitals*, London, Heinemann.

Wiles, P. (1988) 'Teaching Children in Hospital', Research Supplement, *British Journal of Special Education*, 15, 4, 158–62.

Hurler's disease, actually covers several different forms of an inherited metabolic disorder. Characteristic physical symptoms include widely-spaced eyes, flattening of the nasal bridge and a protruding forehead. Various organs, particularly the liver and spleen, are affected. Sufferers are retarded mentally and, if seriously affected, may not live beyond their teens. Amniocentesis now offers the possibility of prenatal diagnosis.

Reference:

Brain, W.R. (1977, 8th edn.) *Diseases of the Nervous System*, Oxford, Oxford University Press.

hydrocephalus, condition in which the rate of production of cerebrospinal fluid in the skull exceeds the rate of absorption. If this is not treated, increased pressure may result in physical symptoms, most obviously an enlarged head, and also in educational difficulties.

The commonest treatment procedure consists of inserting a valve into the head which 'shunts' the excess fluid into the bloodstream by various methods. This is an efficient procedure, but there is a risk of valve blockage due to bacterial colonisation and for other reasons.

Hydrocephalus is often found as a complication in children who suffer from *spina bifida*. The presence of hydrocephalus increases the likelihood of intellectual retardation, with non-verbal skills being more adversely affected than verbal skills.

Until the late 1950s, children with hydrocephalus and spina bifida were rarely treated, and most died in infancy. During the 1960s nearly all spina bifida babies were treated, and many seriously handicapped children survived. This resulted in many severe social and educational problems for families and services, and so in the 1970s the policy was changed again, only less-severely handicapped babies then being selected for treatment. Consequently the children with hydrocephalus coming to the attention of the education service were less seriously handicapped than previously. These changes obviously posed sharp ethical issues for the medical profession: for special education, it means that research findings on populations of children with spina bifida and hydrocephalus need to be interpreted partly in the light of their dates of birth. One effect of the selection policy is that a much higher percentage of children with hydrocephalus and spina bifida now attend ordinary schools.

Improved antenatal screening procedures now mean that a proportion of children with spina bifida and/or hydrocephalus can be identified early in pregnancy, and hence the incidence rate is likely to drop. At the same time, recent developments in foetal surgery could well result in earlier and better control of hydrocephalus, with consequently improved outcome.

See *neural tube defect, shunt.*

References:

Dinnage, R. (1986) *The Child With Spina Bifida,* Windsor, NFER-Nelson.

Gillham, B. (1986) 'Spina Bifida', in Gillham, B. (Ed.) (1986) *Handicapping Conditions in Childhood,* London, Croom Helm.

hyperactivity, see *attention deficit disorder.*

hyperkinetic syndrome, see *attention deficit disorder.*

hypermetropia, or hyperopia, commonly called long sight or far sight. Light which should focus on the retina actually focuses behind it, perhaps because the eyeball is unusually short. The effect is that light from distant objects can focus properly, but to bring near objects into focus requires a greater modification of the lens of the eye than is possible, so near objects are blurred. This results in difficulty with school work in general and reading in particular. Children complain of headaches.

Convex lenses are used to correct hypermetropia.

See *eye.*

Reference:

Chapman, E.K. and Stone, J.M. (1988) *The Visually Handicapped Child in Your Classroom,* London, Cassell.

hypertonicity, unusually high muscle tension, sometimes called spasticity, and clearly seen in some children with cerebral palsy. This may result in the child's joints being pulled into abnormal positions, with deformities possibly ensuing. Physiotherapy is usually helpful, though in severe cases other medical and surgical procedures are used.

References:

Griffiths, M. and Clegg, M. (1988) *Cerebral Palsy: Problems and Practice,* London, Souvenir Press.

Levitt, S. (Ed.) (1984) *Paediatric Development Therapy,* Oxford, Blackwell.

hypoglycaemia, physiological disorder in which the body reacts unusually to some carbohydrates, leading to periods of abnormally low levels of blood sugar. The only significant cause is a dose of insulin (in a diabetic) not accompanied by sufficient intake of food. There are associated behavioural changes, varying from weakness, confusion and depression to hyperactivity and aggression. Where the hypoglycaemia has been sufficiently severe to have resulted in coma there may be permanent physical and mental damage.

See *diabetes.*

Reference:

Brain, W.R. (1977, 8th edn.) *Diseases of the Nervous System,* Oxford, Oxford University Press.

hypotonicity, unusually low muscle tone, seen as flaccidity or floppiness, and which, unless treated, may lead to deformity. Some children with cerebral palsy show hypotonicity; treatment might involve surgery or physiotherapy, for example. There are educational effects, for sitting and working at a desk or table may be difficult.

Compare *hypertonicity.*

Reference:

Levitt, S. (Ed.) (1984) *Paediatric Development Therapy,* Oxford, Blackwell.

hypoxia, deprivation or reduction in the normal supply of oxygen. It refers particularly to the short period immediately before, during and immediately after birth, when the supply of oxygen to the infant's brain may be wholly or partially interrupted. The effects may be serious, leading for example to cerebral palsy, with its physical problems and possible intellectual damage (although only about 10% of cerebral palsy is due to perinatal disturbance).

I

identification:

(1) recognition of children's special needs; the result of *assessment.*
See *screening.*

(2) assimilating characteristics of others into the child's own personality. This is a key process in some psychoanalytic views of personality development, originating with Freud. On this view, the Oedipal (Electra) conflict normally ends with the boy (girl) identifying successfully with the father (mother), allowing the superego or conscience to start to develop and the child to enter the latency period. Other psychoanalysts believe that successful personality development depends on the child also identifying with other authority figures, such as teacher.

See *Freudian theory.*

Reference:
Klein, P. (1976) 'Personality Theories and Dimensions', Block 2 of Open University Course E201, Milton Keynes, Open University.

identity crisis, upsurge of doubt during which abilities, aims and values are all questioned in an attempt to establish an inner confidence and authority, often accompanied by experiments with different roles. The identity crisis plays an important part in Erikson's view of personality development. This attaches lesser significance to infancy and greater significance to adolescence than classic psychoanalytic theories of development, such as Freud's.

The identity crisis will be familiar to teachers of adolescents. For adolescents with special needs it may well be a particularly painful time, over which counselling will be helpful. But it must be remembered that epidemiological work does not altogether support Erikson's views on the importance of the identity crisis, for it seems that many adolescents do not experience it.

Reference:
Erikson, E. (1963, 2nd edn.) *Childhood and Society*, New York, Norton.

idiot savant, see *savant.*

IEP, see *Individualised Education Program.*

IHC, see *intellectual handicap.*

Illinois Test of Psycholinguistic Abilities (ITPA), a pioneering attempt from the 1960s to link language theory with practical educational problems. The ITPA is based on analysing a child's language skills in three different ways, by the communication channel, or sense, used (auditory–vocal; visual–motor), the processes involved (reception; organisation; expression), and the level of organisation required (automatic or representational). Ten different language skills are defined in terms of this model, each measured as a separate subtest; there are two supplementary subtests.

The result is a profile of language skills in children aged from two to ten years, intended as a basis for remedial work. Although the test has enjoyed wide popularity, there are questions on the wisdom of applying its norms to children from ethnic minorities and from deprived areas. Moreover the model of language on which the test is based is dated, as is the assumption that language can be best improved by identifying a specific weakness and remedying it. Evaluations of the effects of remedial programmes linked to the ITPA philosophy have been disappointing.

See *Game Oriented Activities for Learning, language development.*

References:

Anastasi, A. (1982, 5th edn.) *Psychological Testing,* New York, Macmillan.

Naylor, J.G. and Pumfrey, P.D. (1983) 'The Alleviation of Psycholinguistic Deficits and some Effects on the Reading Attainments of Poor Readers', *Journal of Research in Reading,* 6, 2, 129–53.

illiteracy, the state of 'One who is not as literate as someone else thinks he ought to be', as a Ministry of Education pamphlet put it in 1950. Complete illiteracy is very rare in developed countries, and in an NFER study published in 1972 in this country illiteracy was defined as the inability to read above the level of the average seven-year-old. This study found that just over 3% of fifteen-year-olds fell in this category. The Bullock Report found some subsequent improvement in standards, but drew attention to the increased numbers of seven-year-olds leaving infant school unable to read.

See *functional literacy, literacy.*

References:

Department of Education and Science (1975) *A Language for Life,* London, HMSO (Bullock Report).

Start, K.B. and Wells, B.K. (1972) *The Trend of Reading Standards: 1970–1971,* Windsor, NFER.

ILSA, see *Interpersonal Language Skills Analysis.*

immigrant education, see *ethnic minorities.*

impairment, see *disability.*

impedance audiometry, see *audiometry.*

in care, describes a child who has been admitted to the care of a local authority, usually under section 2 of the Child Care Act 1980, or by means of a care order made under section 1(2) of the Children and Young Persons Act 1969. The right to decide upon a child's placement when in care is normally vested in the local authority.

See *Children Act 1989, children in care, children in need.*

incidence, the number of new cases in a specified population over a set period. Incidence is often quoted as rate per thousand population. Thus the incidence of spina bifida per random sample of one thousand live births of the population over a recent period has been quoted as between two to three cases. But the incidence of spina bifida per thousand children in the year following their fourth birthday is probably very close to zero, nearly all spina bifida children being identified at birth.

Incidence is distinguished from *prevalence,* the number of existing cases in the specified population over a set period. Thus the prevalence of spina bifida per thousand children in the year following their fourth birthday is presently less than one, many of those born not having survived. For those responsible for delivering special education services, clearly prevalence is far more important than incidence. The two factors determining prevalence are incidence itself and the length of time that a condition persists.

incus, one of the three small bones in the middle ear which transmit sound vibrations from the eardrum to the cochlea.

See *ear.*

independent schools, now have to be approved by the Secretary of State for Education and Science before a Local Education Authority can place a child with a statement of special needs there. These arrangements apply following the Education Act 1981, and independent schools which provide wholly or mainly for children with special educational needs have been invited to apply for approval.

The Department of Education and Science keeps a list of schools approved for this purpose.

Reference:

Department of Education and Science (1984) *Special Education Letter* (84) 1, London, Department of Education and Science.

Individualised Education Program (IEP), written statement of the educational needs of a handicapped child required by USA legislation. (*Public Law 94–142.*) The IEP has to be prepared following a meeting of a representative of the local education agency, the teacher, the parent(s) or guardian and, where appropriate, the child. It must include details of the child's present educational performance, short- and long-term educational goals, the special services needed and the extent to which the child will be able to participate in normal educational activities, the date at which the program will start and plans for evaluating progress.

Although the IEP itself originated in the USA, similar but not identical procedures have been introduced in many other countries. In England and Wales the *Statement of Special Educational Needs* is the equivalent, but note that in practice the Statement rarely contains specific suggestions for teaching the pupil, and is usually limited to describing the areas of difficulty and the services needed. The IEP is more teacher-directed. It also seems to be administered more rapidly. A survey in the USA found a mean time of six weeks between identification and placement, a time which compares very favourably with the time taken to provide and implement Statements in the UK.

Criticisms of IEPs in action have focused on the lack of preparation of parents, preventing them from contributing as effectively to the initial planning meeting as they would have liked. Teachers found the time taken in activities such as meetings and paper work irritating. Children's participation in the process was low, but increased with age.

On the positive side, many teachers believe that the IEP process helps their teaching and many parents appreciate the requirement that their voices be heard. Notwithstanding the criticisms, the IEP represents a significant step towards ensuring that the education of children with special needs is given at least a minimum of special consideration by the parties concerned.

References:

Hallahan, D.P. and Kaufman, J.M. (1988, 4th edn.) *Exceptional Children: Introduction to Special Education*, Englewood Cliffs, Prentice Hall.

Pyl, S.P., De Graaf, S. and Emanuelsson, I. (1988) 'The Function of Individualized Education Programmes in Special Education: a Discussion of Premises', *European Journal of Special Education*, 3, 2, 63–74.

Taylor, J. (1981) *Speech-Language Pathology Services in the Schools*, New York, Grune and Stratton.

individualised reading, programme for teaching reading in which each child in a class has a different book and progresses at a different rate. The teacher provides books of varying degrees of difficulty, covering a variety of subjects. Each child chooses and reads a book until the teacher calls upon the child to read. Teacher checks the pages read, questions the child on the content and meaning of the story, gives help where needed and plans suitable follow-up activities. Note the difference between this approach and the use of a *basic reading scheme*. It is a specific example of *individualised teaching* in practice.

Reference:

Smith, N.B. (1966) 'New Forms of Classroom Organisation as Related to Reading', in Melnik, A. and Merritt, J. (Eds.) (1966) *The Reading Curriculum*, Milton Keynes, Open University.

individualised teaching, using the widest selection of available techniques to meet the identified special needs of the individual pupil. The educational aims for different pupils may be the same, but the routes through which they are met will be different. Individualised teaching does not mean one teacher to each pupil. Neither does it mean a completely separate programme for each member of a class: education includes acquiring social skills, and these are gained through interaction with fellow-pupils. Individualised teaching means varying the teaching approach to suit individual pupils, while retaining their sense of belonging to the same social unit.

See *individualised reading*.

Reference:

Brennan, W. (1985) *Curriculum for Special Needs*, Milton Keynes, Open University Press.

induction loop system, means of teacher–child communication, used in classrooms with children with hearing impairment. The amplified signals from teacher's microphone flow around a wire loop which traverses the classroom. The signals are picked up directly by the child's hearing aid, without interference from extraneous noise sources.

The system has disadvantages, most obviously that while it facilitates teacher–child communication, it does not enhance child–child communication. Some other problems are caused by the effects of the system being picked up in adjacent rooms, the presence of 'dead spots' in the classroom and the possible production of random internal noise in the child's hearing-aid. For these reasons induction loop systems have tended to fall out of favour.

Reference:

Tucker, I and Nolan, M. (1984) *Educational Audiology*, Beckenham, Croom Helm.

infantile autism, see *autism.*

Infant Rating Scale (IRS), aims to give teachers a straightforward but comprehensive instrument that they might use in the classroom to help in the analysis of their children's strengths and weaknesses, so offering early identification of special needs. This aim is met by providing twenty-five items, covering five developmental areas, *viz.* language, early learning, behaviour, social integration and general development for Level 1, used with five-year-olds. Another set of twenty-five items is used for seven-year-olds, covering broadly the same areas, except that a fine motor skills area is introduced, covered by two items.

Each item is rated by teacher on a five-point scale, the points being defined. There are no tests as such; the scale depends entirely on the teacher observing the child and rating the behaviour.

The IRS is widely used on account of its simplicity, but has been criticised on technical grounds. About half the children who are placed in the 'at risk' category are *false positives,* i.e. misclassified. However the author states that it is to be used as part of an on-going system of monitoring by teacher.

See *early identification.*

References:

Levy, P. and Goldstein, H. (Eds.) (1984) *Tests in Education,* London, Academic Press.

Lindsay, G. (Ed.) (1984) *Screening for Children with Special Needs,* London, Croom Helm.

inferiority complex, loosely used to describe a feeling of inadequacy. In its original sense an inferiority complex refers to the aggressive boastful behaviour that sometimes is shown as compensation for a subconscious or unconscious feeling of inadequacy.

Inferiority is a key concept in Adler's psychoanalytic theory of personality development.

informal reading inventory (IRI), aims to assess whether the difficulty level of a particular text matches a child's developing reading skills. The procedure is informal in the sense that it does not rely on standardised tests for this purpose. The goodness of the match is determined by a direct and clear method, an 'on-the-job' trial, with recommended guidelines.

These guidelines enable teachers to determine which of four reading levels characterises the child's reaction to the text:

- independent level, reached when the child reads with enjoyment and without the need for supervision: it may be defined by less than 1% error in reading individual words in context and less than 10% error in answering comprehension questions;
- instructional level, reached when the material is within the child's grasp, but some help from teacher is required: it may be defined as less than 5% error with individual words and less than 25% comprehension error;
- frustration level, too difficult and leading to negative attitudes to reading; it may be defined as more than 5% error with individual words and more than 25% comprehension error;
- capacity level, estimates how well a child is suited to the story content by listening to parts of the text read by teacher and answering questions on it. It is suggested that if the listening comprehension error is greater than 25% there is little point in asking the child to try to read the material.

Different authorities set slightly differing limits for the four levels, and give slightly different guidelines for the selection of test reading passages and comprehension questions.

The weaknesses of IRIs are mainly technical; evidence of the reliability of the procedure is hard to find and the latitude allowed in framing comprehension questions does not suggest that this will be high. The validity of the criteria used appears to be based on subjective judgement.

But IRIs have the advantages of flexibility, being adaptable to any textual material. They are prime examples of criterion-referenced assessment procedures, which also enable a teacher to note a child's reading strategies and attitudes to reading during the assessment. Their great advantage is to provide a means of avoiding the mistake of giving a child reading material which frustrates through being too difficult or bores through being too easy.

References:

King, C. and Quigley, S. (1985) *Reading and Deafness*, London, Taylor and Francis.

Pumfrey, P.D. (Ed.) (1985, 2nd edn.) *Reading: Tests and Techniques*, Sevenoaks, Hodder and Stoughton in association with UKRA.

information processing, explanation of learning by processes such as memory, reasoning, etc., which operate on the input from the senses. Note that all these processes are internal, in that they proceed 'inside the head', and none are directly observable. The information processing approach is thus quite different from the behaviourist approach which has underpinned so much work in special education in recent decades.

While research into the information-processing skills of children with special needs is a rapidly developing area, perhaps particularly in relation to children with specific learning difficulties, there is as yet little benefit in terms of direct help for the teacher. To determine that a child with reading difficulties has problems with short-term memory does not as yet easily help in planning a teaching programme. Where successful programmes have claimed to be based on information-processing models, it is sometimes difficult to see how they differ in principle from traditional remedial teaching methods, even if in practice they are more thorough in their application. The dangers of adopting a deficit model, too, are present.

See *reading recovery.*

Reference:

Tansley, P. and Panckhurst, J. (1981) *Children with Specific Learning Difficulties; a Critical Review of Research*, Windsor, NFER-Nelson.

initial blend, the combination of two or more sounds, usually consonants, at the start of a word, e.g. combining the sounds of the letters 's' and 't' to make the initial blend 'st', which starts many words. Learning initial blending is an important step in learning to read, particularly emphasised in phonic methods.

initial teaching alphabet (ita), medium for reading and writing, devised by Sir James Pitman, and developed from an earlier version known as Augmented Roman (AR). By modifying the English alphabet, ita aims to provide a single symbol for each of the forty-four main sounds of the language, thus providing a regular correspondence between symbol (grapheme) and sound (phoneme). In this way reading becomes a phonically regular activity and the vagaries of English spelling ('the world's most awesome mess') are avoided.

Some examples of the ITA medium

othodox version	ita version
hope	hœp
hop	hop
through	thrꞷ
bough	bou
cow	cou
reed	reed
read	reed

There is evidence that ita can be helpful in learning to read and write, and that the transition from ita to traditional orthography (t.o.) is not a great obstacle. There is disagreement as to how much of the improvement is attributable to ita itself and how much to the possibility that teachers choosing to use it may have been more energetic and more interested in teaching reading.

There is also evidence of some success when ita is used with children with learning difficulties. But ita is not a method of teaching: it is a medium through which the basic methods for teaching reading still have to be applied. Ita offers an easier introduction to the essential reading process of acquiring meaning from written symbols. But this has to be set against the practical problems of re-equipping classrooms with readers and teaching materials in ita. Although many teachers chose to try ita in the 1960s, its popularity has waned in recent years.

References:

Downing, J.A. (1964) *The ita Reading Experiment*, London, Evans for University of London Institute of Education.

Ravenette, A.T. (1968) *Dimensions of Reading Difficulties*, Oxford, Pergamon.

initial training (for teachers), became a focus of interest as pressures in the 1970s, culminating in the publication of the Warnock Report, swung attitudes in favour of recognising that up to 20% of children had special educational needs, and that most of them should be educated in the mainstream. The corollary of this view is that every teacher is in effect a teacher of children with special needs, and so every intending teacher should be prepared for this at the initial training stage.

The Warnock Report recommended that every course of initial training should contain a special education element. This should aim to develop:

- practical skills in child observation;
- an appreciation of the needs of children with developmental difficulties and of their parents;
- an understanding of the need to modify school and classroom organisation and, if need be, the curriculum;
- an awareness of the range of specialist services available.
- an appreciation of the career opportunities in special education.

While neither the substantive recommendation nor the detailed suggestions on content have been given legislative force, the body which validates courses leading to qualified teacher status, the Council for the Accreditation of Teacher Education, is most unlikely to approve a course of initial training unless it contains what it deems to be a satisfactory special education component.

See *inservice education and training.*

References:

Adams, F. (Ed.) (1986) *Special Education*, Harlow, Councils and Education Press for Longmans.

Department of Education and Science (1978) *Special Educational Needs*, London, HMSO.

Thomas, D. and Smith, C. (1988) 'Special Educational Needs and Initial Training', in Sayer, J. and Jones, N. (Eds.) (1988) *Teacher Training and Special Educational Needs*, London, Croom Helm.

inner ear, see *ear.*

inservice education and training (INSET), for teachers, is the route through which serving teachers gain special education skills. The Warnock Report accepted the view that about 20% of the school population had special educational needs and that most would be taught in mainstream education. One corollary of this belief is that every teacher is in effect a teacher of children with special needs, and consequently a programme of inservice education of all teachers should be organised nationally. This recommendation was not accepted by Government, and local education authorities (LEAs) were left to devise their own programmes, with varying degrees of success, often using a *cascade model* of training for this purpose.

The Warnock Report recommended that teachers with defined responsibilities for special education should be required to hold an additional recognised qualification, and that support for teachers to obtain this through INSET arrangements should be increased. This recommendation was again left to LEAs to implement, though from 1983 special education was one of a number of priority areas for INSET, which allowed central funding for a number of one-term full-time courses, or their equivalent, in universities and polytechnics. But the number of places is small in relation to national needs and their geographical distribution is uneven.

Since 1987, INSET has been controlled by the *GRIST* arrangements, which place control more firmly than ever in the hands of the LEAs. While this has some advantages, the emphasis which LEAs place on short courses has meant that the one-year full-time course, based at an institution of higher education, which has been the traditional route to an advanced qualification in special education, is at risk, being replaced by a mixed economy of part-time and full-time modules.

It is difficult to forecast the pattern of INSET for special education which will emerge from the current state of flux. What is certain is that the opportunity to build a rational pattern of training, ranging from short courses for all teachers, through a recognised qualification for those with defined responsibilities for special education, to advanced courses for teachers and advisers working in fields where special expertise is required, has been lost for at least a decade.

See *initial training, Open University, SNAP.*

References:

Hegarty, S. (1987) *Meeting Special Needs in Ordinary Schools: an Overview*, London, Cassell.

Hegarty, S. and Moses, D. (1988) *Developing Expertise: INSET for Special Educational Needs*, Windsor, NFER-Nelson

Mittler, P. (1987) 'From Warnock to GRIST', *Times Educational Supplement*, 24.8.1987.

Inspectors of Special Education, see *Her Majesty's Inspectorate.*

Inspectors Supervising Special Education (ISSE), senior administrators with responsibilities for the management of special education in New Zealand.

Reference:

Mitchell, D.R. and Singh, N.N. (Eds.) (1987) *Exceptional Children in New Zealand*, Palmerston North, Dunmore Press.

institutionalisation, concept based on the sociological assumption that the extent to which individuals become adjusted to their environment depends by and large on their status within a group. Thus the least powerful are likely to be those most influenced by their immediate environment. In an institution, the inmates (e.g. patients; pupils) are least powerful and are vulnerable to what Barton described as the disease of 'institutional neurosis', induced in particular by loss of contact with the outside world, enforced idleness and by the behaviour of staff.

Early studies of children in institutions such as hospitals and orphanages showed a higher incidence than expected of behaviour problems such as restlessness, distractibility and withdrawn behaviour and of restricted intellectual development. These effects were associated with lack of the stimulation and individual care to be found in most family environments but which a large institution may find hard to provide.

Present policy emphasises placing children for *fostering* within families wherever possible, and hospital stays are now much shorter and often accompanied by a parent.

References:

Barton, R. (1959) *Institutional Neurosis*, London, Wright and Son.

Bowlby, J. (1965, 2nd edn.) *Child Care and the Growth of Love*, Harmondsworth, Penguin.

Rutter, M. (1972) *Maternal Deprivation Reassessed*, Harmondsworth, Penguin Education.

Instrumental Enrichment, Feuerstein's Instrumental Enrichment, FIE, a programme of more than 500 pages of pencil-and-paper exercises, arranged in fifteen 'instruments', or sets of lessons. The purpose of the programme is to modify the thinking of children with learning difficulties, so that instead of being passive, dependent thinkers, they can make inferences, draw conclusions and so learn more effectively. It has been developed from work with retarded persons in Israel. Feuerstein believes that many learning difficulties arise because children have never learnt how to learn. The object of FIE is to remedy this, or in Feuerstein's terminology, to modify their cognitive structures.

Essentially the programme requires the learner to carry out a wide variety of intellectual exercises (e.g. finding patterns) in content-free material (e.g.

dots) in order to modify thinking skills. Each instrument covers a different cognitive skill, and provides material for a one-hour lesson three to five times a week for two to three years. Decisions as to which instruments are to be used with a child are based on an assessment with the *Learning Potential Assessment Device*. The instruments are not intended as substitutes for but as supplements to normal school lessons.

Observers have been impressed with the level of commitment and motivation shown by children working with FIE, and its essentially optimistic approach to learning difficulties is refreshing. But few research studies giving objective data on the effects of FIE have yet been published. It is in essence an attempt to identify a child's cognitive weaknesses and to remedy them through direct teaching, an approach which has not always proved successful in the past. Notwithstanding the subjective evidence mentioned above, it would be wise to suspend judgement on the value of FIE until clear evidence on its results is available.

See *cognitive modifiability*.

References:

Burden, R.L. (1987) 'Feuerstein's Instrumental Enrichment Programme: Important Issues in Research and Evaluation', *European Journal of Psychology of Education*, 2, 1, 3–16.

Feuerstein, R. (1980) *Instrumental Enrichment*, Baltimore, University Park Press.

Sharron, H. (1987) *Changing Children's Minds*, London, Souvenir Press.

integration, educating children together, whether they have special needs or not, as part of the general principle that those with special needs should enjoy the same opportunities as the rest of society. In some countries the application of this philosophy to education is known as mainstreaming; in others both terms are used but in slightly different senses. (See *mainstreaming*.)

The debate about the principle and practice of integration is not new. The integrationist and segregationist philosophies, both of which are means towards ends, not ends in themselves, have competed since education existed, with fluctuating fortunes. The Warnock Report intended to tilt the balance towards integration, while recognising that special schools would always be needed.

It has been argued that those in favour of separation are realists, looking at the advantages of concentrating special services in special schools and units, whereas those in favour of integration are idealists, believing that social considerations and opportunities should be paramount and that any special services needed should be provided in as normal a setting as possible. This bald sketch does not do justice to a complicated question, coloured by many other considerations. For example, it has been argued that children with special needs can be seen in the same way as ethnic groups, with the same right to receive an education that preserves their own culture and group identity as any minority community: the educational model should be a multicultural one, not an assimilation one. Perhaps children with severe hearing impairment are the best example, where the hearing-impaired community is well-established and the analogy extends even to the existence of a separate language (signing). This argument is not widely accepted, and the more common view is that expressed at the start of this entry.

The Warnock Report described three forms of integration:

(1) locational, where children with special needs are educated on the same site as others, but in separate units or schools and hence have little contact;
(2) social, where regular social interchange occurs, e.g. at mealtimes, in play areas and in out-of-school activities, although formal education is still separate;
(3) functional, where children with special needs attend regular classes and participate in other activities. The curriculum is shared.

The Education Act 1981 placed a duty on Local Education Authorities (LEAs) to ensure that children with special educational needs were educated in their local primary and secondary schools, provided that their parents were in agreement, that it was practicable, that it was educationally efficient, and that it was not unreasonably expensive.

Many supporters of integration felt that these conditions would enable LEAs to avoid their obligations to integrate children where possible. Investigations since the Act show that by 1986, with allowance for factors such as the changing size of the school population, there was only slight evidence of a fall in the number of children being educated in special schools. In interpreting this, two points have to be remembered. First, the prevalence figure of 20% of children with special needs, which the Warnock Report suggested, has gained broad acceptance. This means that many children in the mainstream whose special needs would have been unrecognised previously, have been identified and can now be said to be integrated much more effectively. Secondly, integration is not solely a matter of numbers of children: there has been development in the integration of schools and of teachers. A study of all special schools in a 25% sample of LEAs revealed that 85% had implemented or were in process of implementing a link with a neighbouring school. The links were diverse, and varied from the tenuous to the strong; for example where teachers from the special school worked in the link school, the time involved ranged from less than three hours per week to over twenty-five.

Following the Education Act 1988, the future pattern for these developing schemes is now uncertain, as is the movement towards a *whole school approach* in the ordinary school. The introduction of a National Curriculum, with national monitoring of educational standards, may make Heads of ordinary schools reluctant to take children with special needs, and eager to statement those pupils who in the past would not have been considered for special school placement. Integration is at any time a complex concept, often value-laden: more than ever it now needs careful monitoring.

See *least restrictive environment.*

References:

Cole, T. (1989) *Apart or a Part? Integration and the Growth of British Special Education,* Milton Keynes, Open University Press.

Goacher, B., Evans, J., Welton, J. and Wedell, K. (1988) *Policy and Provision for Special Educational Needs: Implementing the 1981 Education Act,* London, Cassell.

House of Commons Education, Science and Arts Committee, 1986–7, (1987) *Special Educational Needs: Implementation of the Education Act 1981,* London, HMSO.

Jowett, S., Hegarty, S. and Moses, D. (1988) *Joining Forces, a Study of Links between Special and Ordinary Schools,* Windsor, NFER-Nelson.

Mitchell, D. (1990) 'Integrated Education', in Entwistle, N.J. (Ed.) (1990) *Handbook of Educational Ideas and Practices,* London, Routledge.

Swann, W. (1988) 'Trends in Special School Placement to 1986: measuring, assessing and explaining segregation', *Oxford Review of Education,* 14, 2, 139–61.

Intellectual handicap, term used in Australia and New Zealand, roughly equivalent to moderate, serious or profound *mental handicap.* The IHC is the Society for the Intellectually Handicapped, whose New Zealand membership established centres for those children who were not admitted to special schools on grounds of low ability, and for whom no educational provision was available.

References:

Mitchell, D.R. and Singh, N.N. (Eds.) (1987) *Exceptional Children in New Zealand,* Palmerston North, Dunmore Press.

Singh, N.N. and Wilton, K.M. (1985) (Eds.) *Mental Retardation in New Zealand,* Christchurch, Whitcoulls.

intelligence, the ability to learn, solve problems and deal with new situations. The concept has long been used as a dimension for describing individuals, often in the sense of an inborn quality, which with the advent of intelligence tests became measurable. Intelligence then became a key concept in special education, low intelligence being advanced as an explanation of learning difficulties, and categories of mental handicap being defined in terms of scores on intelligence tests. This almost fatalistic attitude did little to promote the cause of education for the mentally handicapped.

With the resurgence of the view that intelligence could be developed through experience, there was a period during which the long-standing debate on the relative importance of heredity and environment to intelligence was revived, often using evidence from the analysis of differences in the development of identical twins reared together and apart. Attempts to measure the relative effects of heredity and environment are of theoretical rather than practical importance to the educator, who is by definition an environmentalist.

The nature of intelligence has occupied many investigators. The use of *factor analysis* provided different views of its structure, ranging from Spearmann's early advocacy of a general intelligence, '*g*', underpinning all intellectual activities, through elaborated hierarchical structures, involving group factors, to the 120 or more intellectual skills modelled by Guilford. These structures have led to the development of tests aimed at assessing children's performance in their different components – e.g. tests of spatial ability, reasoning ability, etc., sometimes used in special education.

The idea of a single, unitary intelligence is too simple to explain children's intellectual skills satisfactorily. The categories of skills produced by the factorial approach may be too complicated and too removed from everyday tasks to be of great use to teachers. For these reasons interest has shifted to the theory of multiple intelligence, the view that there is a variety of intelligences, e.g. musical intelligence, linguistic intelligence, etc., fundamentally different from each other. This view has some attractions for special education, enabling the phenomena of *savants*, effects of brain damage, etc., to be understood. But from the educator's point of view, understanding the structure of intelligence may be less important than understanding the processes underlying intelligent behaviour.

See *'g', intelligence test, nature–nurture controversy.*

References:

Gardner, H. (1990) 'The Theory of Multiple Intelligences', in Entwistle, N. (Ed.) (1990) *Handbook of Educational Ideas and Practices*, London, Routledge.

Pyle, D.W. (1979) *Intelligence: an introduction*, London, Routledge & Kegan Paul.

Pyle, D.W. and Nuttall, D.L. (1985) 'The Nature of Intelligence', Unit 11, Open University Course E206, Milton Keynes, Open University.

Stott, D.H. (1983) *Issues in the Intelligence Debate*, Slough, NFER-Nelson.

Intelligence Quotient (IQ), one of the various ways of indexing relative performance on an *intelligence test*. Originally, IQs were calculated as the ratio of mental age to chronological age, multiplied by 100. In this way, a child whose mental age was the same as his or her chronological age would have an IQ of 100. IQ 100 thus represents an average performance.

There are problems with this simple index; for example, intellectual growth begins to level off after adolescence, and many tests cease to provide mental ages higher than the late teens. Hence the use of a simple ratio for mature age-groups, whose mental ages are all below their chronological ages, leads to ratios which are largely devoid of meaning. This and other problems led to the introduction of the more satisfactory *deviation quotient*. Today most intelligence tests are standardised to produce distributions of IQs with means still set at 100 and standard deviations of fifteen points.

Note that an IQ is only one means of expressing test results. Intelligence test scores can be expressed as *percentile ranks*, or other measures, such as stanines: hence to use the phrase 'IQ test' as synonymous with 'intelligence test' is misleading.

Note too the common misconception that an IQ is a fixed and inalienable property of a person. Like all other psychological and educational characteristics of children, IQs vary according to the test used, vary over time and in many other ways. This is particularly important to remember when interpreting reports of psychological assessments of children.

Notwithstanding the objections raised against intelligence tests in general and bald IQ figures in particular, the IQ continues to be used and, in some circumstances, has quasi-official status. For example, both the two major systems of classification in mental handicap, the International Classification of Diseases and the Manual on Terminology and Classification of the American Association on Mental Deficiency use an IQ as a necessary but not sufficient condition for identifying categories of mental handicap. In other words professionals in this particular field of special education find it difficult to dispense with the notion of IQ.

See, for example, *custodial mentally retarded, normal curve.*

References:

Anastasi, A. (1982, 5th edn.) *Psychological Testing,* New York Macmillan.

Cronbach, L.J. (1984, 4th edn.) *Essentials of Psychological Testing,* New York, Harper and Row.

intelligence test, standardised method of measuring intelligence, widely used by psychologists and teachers. The popularity of intelligence tests has declined recently, partly because of misconceptions about their purposes and functions and partly because they have been superseded by more useful procedures. Nevertheless they still enjoy wide use.

Until the 1960s, most assessments of children needing special education included an intelligence test. Placements for handicapped children depended partly on their IQ, and psychologists included an individual intelligence test, usually a Terman Merrill or a Wechsler Intelligence Test, in their interviews. As lay persons tended to use IQs as inflexible labels, so resistance to the use of intelligence tests increased. In this country the inclusion of an intelligence test was one objection against the 11+ selection examination for secondary education, largely abandoned during that decade. In the USA some states prohibited the use of intelligence tests in the public schools. In both countries the use of intelligence tests for assessments for special education continued, probably because these were individual tests and not group tests, administered by specially trained personnel who were able to interpret the results sensitively and informatively.

There are difficulties inherent in the use of intelligence tests, for example with minority populations and subcultures, particularly where the home language is different from that of the test and of the standardisation population – though it is interesting to remember that one of the purposes in introducing tests of intelligence in the first place was to offset the educational disadvantages of children from deprived backgrounds. There is no point in requiring a child to take an intelligence test – or any test – unless it is clear beforehand why the test is to be given and the possible actions that might flow from it. For many educational purposes assessments of attainments and skills such as aspects of language development, perhaps in relation to educational objectives, are more helpful than a global intelligence test, which offers norm-referenced information rarely directly related to the teacher's concerns.

See *bilingualism, British Ability Scales, SOMPA.*

References:

Anastasi, A. (1982, 5th edn.) *Psychological Testing,* New York, Macmillan.

Gipps, C., Steadman, S., Blackstone, T. and Stierer, B. (1983) *Testing Children: Standardised Testing in Local Education Authorities and Schools,* London, Heinemann.

Pyle, D.W. and Nuttall, D.L. (1985) 'The Nature of Intelligence', Unit 11, Open University Course E206, Milton Keynes, Open University.

interactive theories of reading, represent a half-way house between bottom-up and top-down theories of the reading process, neither of which is entirely satisfactory. Interactive models stress that the reader is a processor of information, information derived both from the structure of the print and also from previous background knowledge. The acquisition of meaning from text is thus driven by the data provided by the text as well as by expectations based on previous experience.

Reference:

King, C. and Quigley, S. (1985) *Reading and Deafness,* London, Taylor and Francis.

intermediate reading skills, see *higher order reading skills.*

Intermediate Treatment (IT), programme of activities which represents a middle way of dealing with children and young persons in difficulties, avoiding the two extremes of compulsory removal from the family on the one hand and leaving circumstances unchanged on the other.

IT is often a requirement of a supervision order made in care proceedings, when 'complying with the directions of a supervisor' can include participating in IT schemes as well as meeting other requirements. An IT programme may include a short residential element, as well as required attendance at activities while living at home.

Reference:

Makin, K. (1985) 'Heading for the Rocks? Intermediate Treatment', *Community Care,* 18.7.1985. 22–3.

Interpersonal Language Skills Assessment (ILSA), offers a framework for observing and categorising the social language skills of children aged eight to fourteen years, on the basis of taped samples of interactions with peers. The categories include advising/predicting, commanding, commenting, criticising, informing, justifying, requesting and supporting. This enables social and conversational disability to be identified, and so suggests where remedial efforts might be directed.

See *language development.*

Reference:

Beveridge, M. and Conti-Ramsden, G. (1987) *Children with Language Disabilities,* Milton Keynes, Open University Press.

interval reinforcement, see *reinforcement.*

IQ, see *Intelligence Quotient.*

Irlen lenses, coloured lenses said to be helpful in some severe reading difficulties/dyslexia. The rationale for the use of the lenses rests on the belief that some reading difficulties are caused by visual dysfunction not normally detected by eye tests. Helen Irlen, the originator of the Irlen lenses, argues that the ophthalmologist rarely tests for dysfunctions which occur once the image has been correctly focused on the retina, *viz.* scotopic sensitivity.

Scotopic sensitivity is assessed by the Irlen Differential Perceptual Schedule, which notes features such as pulsation and differential shadowing of letters, etc. Where scotopic sensitivity exists, tinted lenses (Irlen lenses) are prescribed. An alternative and simpler method uses coloured overlays, placed over the reading material.

While early results offer some promise, long-term findings are needed for a proper evaluation.

Reference:

Robinson, G.L. and Miles, J. (1987) 'The Use of Coloured Overlays to Improve Visual Processing – a Preliminary Survey', paper obtainable from the authors at the Special Education Centre, Newcastle College of Advanced Education, New South Wales.

Ishihara Test, test of *colour vision,* consisting of a set of cards on which numbers or patterns are portrayed in small spots of contrasting colours. Different patterns are seen, depending on whether the individual has normal colour vision or not, and if not, the nature and degree of the individual's visual anomaly can be identified.

Isle of Wight Survey, classic 1964–5 epidemiological survey of the education, health and behaviour of children aged nine to twelve years, living on the Isle of Wight. A more intensive study of the health of the whole of the then compulsory school age-range of five to fifteen years was also carried out. The purpose of the survey was to provide a comprehensive picture of three sorts of handicap or special need:

(1) educational or intellectual retardation,
(2) emotional or behavioural problems,
(3) chronic or recurrent physical disorders.

The main conclusion was that in a population of children slightly above average in intelligence and standard of living, one child in six had a chronic handicap of moderate or severe intensity.

The survey was characterised by careful design and execution and by careful choice of the criteria used to define handicap in each of the three categories mentioned. Nevertheless the choice of criteria had to be subjective to some extent, most particularly in the diagnosis of psychiatric disorder – a problem which is not specific to this survey. The survey also brought out the exent to which behavioural disorder is a function of the situation, as much as of the child.

The overall *prevalence* figure found by the survey has been influential in shaping services for children with special needs, and was used by the Warnock Report. Comparative data from other areas (London, for example), demonstrate how prevalence data vary geographically, and a modern replication of a study as detailed as this would be valuable.

References:

Galloway, D. and Goodwin, C. (1987) *The Education of Disturbing Children: Pupils with Learning and Adjustment Difficulties*, Harlow, Longman.

Rutter, M., Tizard, J. and Whitmore, K. (Eds.) (1970) *Education, Health and Behaviour*, London, Longman.

Williams, P. (1985) 'Troubled Behaviour', Units 18/19 of course E206, Milton Keynes, Open University.

isolate, see *sociometry.*

IT, see *Intermediate Treatment.*

ita, see *initial teaching alphabet.*

itinerant teacher, North American term for a *peripatetic teacher.*

ITPA, see *Illinois Test of Psycholinguistic Abilities.*

J

Jaeger chart, test of near vision, consisting of lines of print in different type-sizes. This gets over one of the difficulties of the *Snellen chart,* namely that it measures visual acuity for distant, not near vision. and hence is not a good indicator of vision for reading. The results of testing on the Jaeger chart can be directly interpreted in terms of the kind of reading material that can be used by a visually impaired person – newspapers, large-print books, etc.

Reference:

Hallahan, D.P. and Kaufman, J.M. (1988, 4th edn.) *Exceptional Children: Introduction to Special Education,* Englewood Cliffs, Prentice Hall.

Jay Report 1979, Report of the Committee of Enquiry into Mental Handicap and Nursing Care. The Committee, chaired by Peggy Jay, recommended inter alia that all people with mental handicap should live in the community, with help and support from the professional services. Later, government adopted a policy of transferring about a third of the residents in long-stay hospitals into community care, while restricting new admissions. In this way the intentions of the report would be met gradually. In fact, while the number of residents has shown a decrease in the 1980s, the number of new admissions has risen, mainly due to the use of the hospitals for short-stay admissions, e.g. for *respite care.* The operation of the policy has been controversial, not least because of charges of inadequate funding for the *community care* alternative.

References:

Department of Health and Social Security (1981) *Care in the Community,* HMSO, London.

Furneaux, B. (1988) *Special Parents,* Milton Keynes, Open University Press.

JEPI, see *Junior Eysenck Personality Inventory.*

Jesness Inventory, a self-completion questionnaire, consisting of 155 true–false items, providing a general 'asocial index' derived from a set of ten subscales. The subscales offer a profile of social behaviour, covering areas such as social maladjustment, alienation, aggression, etc.

The inventory originated in the USA, but has been adapted for use elsewhere, including the UK. It has been used for the identification of delinquent tendencies in children and adolescents between eight and eighteen years of age, but is probably better employed as a research instrument.

Jim's People, language kit originally designed for teaching children with severe learning difficulties, but since used more widely with any children with language and communication problems.

The kit consists of cards depicting situations with a central character, Jim, and his family. The accompanying booklets present exercises on the cards, using language patterns of gradually increasing complexity, and aimed at developing understanding, speech and feedback. Teachers can use the material flexibly, however.

Jim's People was a pioneer attempt to produce an attractive programme for teaching early language skills. It is popular with teachers, though many other materials have since appeared.

See, for example, *Derbyshire Language Scheme.*

Reference:

Webster, A. and McConnell, C. (1987) *Children with Speech and Language Difficulties,* London, Cassell.

Junior Eysenck Personality Inventory, measures two dimensions of personality, *viz:* extraversion–introversion and neuroticism–stability through a pencil-and-paper questionnaire requiring a 'Yes' or 'No' answer to each of sixty items. (These also provide a short *lie scale*.) The age-range is seven to sixteen years.

The test has been widely used in research enquiries, although its validity in particular has been questioned. It is a group test and it appears of little use in work with individuals.

Reference:

Levy, P. and Goldstein, H. (1984) *Tests in Education*, London, Academic Press.

juvenile court, consists of local magistrates, appointed to the juvenile court panel as especially qualified to deal with proceedings involving juveniles. These include care proceedings and most criminal proceedings in relation to children and young persons between the ages of ten and seventeen years. The public is excluded, and the court structure is intended to be informal and suited to children's needs, though in some courts the trappings of the law are still much in evidence. In Scotland most of the functions of the juvenile court have been replaced by children's panels. The courts may require reports to be provided by the child's school, a psychologist, psychiatrist, or other person.

When the relevant parts of the Children Act 1989 are in force, all proceedings under it, including care proceedings, will be heard in the High Court, the county court or the magistrates' court. Criminal proceedings in relation to children and young persons will continue to be heard in the juvenile court.

An alternative to a juvenile court appearance is to regard the child as suffering from an emotional and behavioural disorder (ebd), which needs special educational provision. Thus some children placed in residential schools for ebd might in other circumstances have made court appearances. Many factors affect which course of action is followed, including the attitude of the local magistrates, whether the child is attending a child guidance clinic, etc. It is sometimes argued that the social background of the parents influences this decision, ebd being regarded by some middle-class parents as a 'condition' and less of a stigma than a juvenile court appearance.

References:

Anderson, R. (1978) *Representation in the Juvenile Court*, London, Routledge and Kegan Paul.

Morris, A. and Giller, H. (1987) *Understanding Juvenile Justice*, London, Croom Helm.

Parker, H., Casburn, M. and Turnbull, D. (1981) *Receiving Juvenile Justice*, Oxford, Blackwell.

juvenile delinquency, in essence the criminal behaviour of a juvenile, dealt with by the *juvenile courts*. In fact the term has become broadened in popular usage to include children's antisocial, deviant acts which may not be in themselves criminal, e.g. running away.

What is criminal and what is deviant varies between societies and within the same society over time. So too does the age at which a child can appear before a court. In short, juvenile delinquency is a social concept and cannot be defined objectively.

Juvenile delinquency is thus a subcategory of *antisocial behaviour*. If we take the incidence of court appearances as an index, then it rises to a peak in mid-adolescence. Truancy and stealing are more characteristic of early adolescence, aggressive behaviour and violence more characteristic of later adolescence. The incidence of delinquency in boys has always been significantly higher than in girls, but the difference is diminishing.

School and the education service have been implicated, for the delinquency statistics peak in the last full year of schooling, the peak age changing when the school leaving age was changed, so supporting the argument that the frustration caused by an inappropriate education programme eventually causes some children to protest through delinquency. The presence of different deliquency rates between schools with similar catchment areas supports the view that schools are influential.

Many other environmental causes have been advanced – material, such as poverty, psychological, such as lack of love – and there is some evidence to suggest that genetic factors may be implicated in some instances, e.g. chronic aggressive behaviour. In effect, every instance of delinquent behaviour has to be considered separately; there is no single cause and no single remedy.

Delinquents are often regarded as children with *emotional and behavioural difficulties* (ebd) and thus the education service is involved in remedial work. Education cannot cure social ills. Nevertheless sympathetic teachers and schools can play a significant part in providing both stable relationships with adults and also stable environments, sometimes therapeutically orientated, which can help to offset the damaging circumstances which delinquents may have endured.

See *disruptive behaviour.*

References:

Galloway, D., Ball, T., Blomfield, D. and Seyd, R. (1982) *Schools and Disruptive Pupils*, London, Longman.

Rutter, M., Maughan, B., Mortimore, P. and Ouston, J. (1979) *Fifteen thousand Hours: secondary schools and their effects on children*, London, Open Books.

K

k, symbol for the spatial ability factor. This is held to be the ability underlying competence in handling two- and three-dimensional structures, in particular the imagination required to be able to visualise the effects of manipulating shapes in space. With mechanical ability, m, it forms km, the main non-verbal group factor in the hierarchical model of human abilities advanced by British psychometrists.

There has been debate about the age at which the presence of k can be clearly detected, the extent to which km features more prominently in boys' abilities than girls, and the school subjects which require high km for proficient performance. In these debates, however, it has to be remembered that different methods of *factor analysis* produce different factor patterns.

Contrast *v.ed.*

References:

Smith, I.M. (1964) *Spatial Ability*, London, University of London Press.

Vernon, P.E. (1971, 2nd edn.) *The Structure of Human Abilities*, London, Methuen.

Karmel Report 1973, Schools in Australia, report of the Interim Committee of the Australian Schools Commission. The Committee's terms of reference were to examine the state of primary and secondary education in Australia: this remit included schools for the handicapped.

Previously, many schools for the handicapped had been established by voluntary bodies, in lieu of official provision. The Karmel Report recognised the right of all Australian children to education, and recommended that the Federal Government should assume the responsibility for meeting this obligation. The Government accepted the recommendation, and granted funds to enable States to implement it.

The report also had a view on where handicapped children should be educated, believing that as many handicapped children as possible should be educated in normal groups, influential support for the integration of children with special needs in Australian schools, later to become official policy.

Reference:

Elkins, J. (1985) 'Disability and Disadvantage: Special Education in Australia – Past, Present and Future', in Palmer, I. (Ed.) (1985) *Melbourne Studies in Education*, Carlton, Melbourne University Press.

Karnes Preschool Program, set of highly-structured activities aimed at improving the educational development of disadvantaged children aged three to five years. The program, which originated in the USA, includes daily work in language, science, and maths, based partly on the *ITPA* model of psycholinguistic abilities and the model of *intelligence* provided by the Guilford cube. It also aims to improve children's self-concept.

See *compensatory education.*

Reference:

Hare, B.A. and Hare, J.M. (1977) *Teaching Young Handicapped Children*, New York, Grune and Stratton.

Keele Preschool Assessment Guide, consists of a short series of items divided into two scales, one covering social behaviour and the other covering cognitive, physical, social and linguistic skills. It is intended for nursery school staffs who wish to ascertain the needs of their children and record their progress.

The material is simple to use, but unsophisticated: for example no details on standardisation or reliability appear.

Reference:

Birchall, D. (1982) 'Preschool Activity and the Curriculum', *Highlight*, 55, London, National Children's Bureau.

Kendall Toy test, is used to assess the hearing of young children in the age-range two to four years, approximately. The child is asked to point to different toys in turn, after the examiner has checked that the child is familiar with them.

The examiner's voice level required for the child to participate in the game is measured for each ear on a sound level indicator.

See *audiometry.*

Reference:

Tucker, I. and Nolan M. (1984) *Educational Audiology*, Beckenham, Croom Helm.

key words, words which represent the central concepts or terms in a subject area and which must be read and fully understood if the pupil is to benefit from reading it, e.g. 'precipitation' and 'isobar' in a passage about meteorology.

key words to literacy, the 200 most frequently used words which account for half to three–quarters of the running words occurring in everyday reading matter. Most of these words are short – e.g. 'and, but'; and many are phonically irregular – e.g. 'because, their'. Children's reading fluency increases if their responses to them are automatic. Hence many teachers of beginning reading encourage instant recognition of these words through flash cards and games.

Note the difference between this approach and those methods which start reading by introducing nouns which, although familiar, are not necessarily met with frequently in reading matter. The key word approach emphasises word frequency, and in practice is usually used in conjunction with other approaches.

See *sight vocabulary.*

Reference:

McNally, J. and Murray, W. (1962) *Key Words to Literacy*, London, Schoolmaster Publishing Co.

kinaesthetic method, teaching technique using kinaesthesis, the sense of position and body movement, and usually also involving touch. Kinaesthetic methods are used in teaching reading, often in association with methods using vision and hearing, when the combined approach is known as a multisensory method. The kinaesthetic component usually consists of tracing the letter and word shapes to be learnt, sometimes on paper and sometimes in the air, and writing them. Some children are helped if the teacher 'writes' a letter on the child's back while he or she attempts to write it. Most children are helped to learn to spell when they receive kinaesthetic feedback as they write. The input from several different sense channels is helpful for children who have difficulty in learning to read.

See, for example, *Fernald method.*

Reference:

Young, P. and Tyre, C. (1983) *Dyslexia or Illiteracy?* Milton Keynes, Open University.

km, see *k.*

Klinefelter's syndrome, chromosome abnormality in which a male possesses an extra female sex chromosome, i.e.the sex chromosomes are not the normal XY pair but an XXY complement. Physically, the male shows some feminine characteristics, particularly evident after puberty, and leading to normal adolescent worries being exacerbated. Counselling may be helpful.

Sometimes this condition is also associated with below average school performance in general and poor language abilities in particular. For this reason boys with Klinefelter's syndrome may appear more frequently in groups of children screened for learning difficulties than in the general population, where the incidence is said to be between one and three per thousand male births.

Reference:

Barker, P. (1988, 5th edn.) *Basic Child Psychiatry,* Oxford, Blackwell.

Kurzweil reading machine, converts printed material into synthetic speech, so enabling visually impaired persons to 'read' print. Most type faces are machine-readable, though illustrations are obviously not manageable. The speech speed of up to 250 words per minute enables print to be processed considerably more quickly than with the *Optacon.*

Reference:

Chapman, E.K. and Stone, J.M. (1988) *The Visually Handicapped Child in Your Classroom,* London, Cassell.

kyphoscoliosis, deformity of the spine in which there is both kyphosis, or hump-back, and scoliosis, or lateral curvature.

kyphosis, hump-back, curvature of the spine in which the vertebrae project outwards, forming a hump, often associated with spina bifida.

L

labelling, assigning an individual to a category and, by extension, attributing to that individual all the characteristics of the category, regardless of evidence. Note that categories are set up for administrative purposes, whereas labels are attached to individuals. But the categories have to exist, formally or informally, for the labels to have meaning. Labelling can apply to persons or establishments, but the discussion below uses persons only.

Labelling is a sociological process which has educational effects, not least in the education of children with special needs. In principle, labels can be positive or negative, leading to good effects or bad, stigmatising effects; in special education we are mainly concerned with the latter.

Labelling behaviour as deviant tends to perpetuate that behaviour. If a child is admitted to a school with the label 'troublemaker' then staff may expect difficulties in behaviour, attitude, work – all the many features which often characterise pupils with behavioural difficulties, whether or not they apply to the particular individual in the particular situation. Reputation matters, as well as character. The process also works both ways, for once labelled, children may respond to fill the roles in which they have been cast.

The effects of labelling are held to apply to attainment in school subjects, as well as other behaviour. Researchers have investigated the effects of children being labelled as more able than their performance on tests would suggest. This is said to lead to demonstrable intellectual growth, a *self-fulfilling prophecy,* though attempts to demonstrate this experimentally have been controversial.

See *classification.*

Reference:

Hargreaves, D.H., Hester, S.K. and Mellor, F.J. (1975) *Deviance in Classrooms,* London, Routledge and Kegan Paul.

Rogers, C. (1990) 'Teachers' Expectations and Pupils' Achievements', in Entwistle, N. (Ed.) (1990) *Handbook of Educational Ideas and Practices,* London, Routledge.

Rosenthal, R. and Jacobson, L. (1968) *Pygmalion in the Classroom,* London, Holt, Rinehart and Winston.

labyrinth, alternative name for the *inner ear.*

LAD, see *Language Acquisition Device.*

lalling, a disorder of speech in which a single speech sound, usually the 'r' phoneme, is poorly articulated, often being replaced by the 'l' or 'w' phonemes. Thus 'pretty red rose' might be pronounced as 'pletty led lose', or 'robin' as 'wobin'. This is a common stage in the development of speech and only becomes a problem if it continues beyond the age of five years or so. If language skills are otherwise normal, then this is then considered an example of a developmental articulation disorder. Lalling conveys an impression of baby-talk, amusing to some adults, whose reactions may reinforce the misarticulation, rather than encouraging better speech.

Compare *lisping;* see *speech disorder.*

LAMP,

(1) Less Academically Motivated Pupils, project which produced a science course for secondary school pupils of low motivation and poor attainment, conditioned to accepting low success in school work. The project was sponsored by the Association for Science Education.

Reference:

Reid, D.J. and Hodson, D. (1987) *Science for All*, London, Cassell.

(2) Low Attainers in Mathematics Project, established by the Department of Education and Science and a group of six Education Authorities as a follow-up to the Cockcroft Report on Mathematics Teaching, 'Mathematics Counts'. The project involved release for one day each week so that groups of teachers could develop ideas and methods suitable for work with pupils with learning difficulties. It recommended that this arrangement should be an accepted feature of a teacher's week, with a consequent increase in the teaching force to give the teaching cover needed.

See *mathematics difficulties.*

Reference:

Department of Education and Science (1988) *Better Mathematics*, London, HMSO.

language, means of communication. This can involve the use of words, symbols, and gestures enabling an individual to interpret experiences and communicate with others. This definition of language is broad enough to include body language, *non-verbal communication*, etc.

Without communication, education is impossible, and hence the centrality of language to learning has long been recognised. The problems of children with obvious communication problems, such as those with hearing and speech impairments, led to early studies of the role of language in education. When the compensatory education movement pinpointed language usage as a key element in the poor school performance of disadvantaged children, this led to an upsurge of interest in the assessment and remediation of language performance.

For assessment and remediation to be meaningful, some structure was needed. Language has thus been considered from various standpoints, or along different axes. First is the transmission axis, divided into speech, print or gesture. Speech and print surround us: transmission of meaning by gesture is not as important in English as in some other languages, but reaches a highly-developed form in the sign languages used by the hearing-impaired population.

Then there is the activity axis, divided into the receptive and expressive (or productive) modes. The act of writing involves the expression of meaning through print; listening involves the reception of meaning through speech.

Finally, in this attempt to simplify a most complex topic, there is the structural axis, divided into the grammar and semantics of language.

Children may have difficulty in any or all of these areas. Thus poor grammar may colour a child's expressive language in both speech and writing, so leading to educational problems.

How language develops is a controversial area. The main debate engages a psychobiological explanation, arguing for an inbuilt faculty (a *language acquisition device*, or LAD) for learning and using language, and an environmental explanation, relating language development to a behavioural system of reinforcement, nowadays stressing interaction with adult caretakers in social contexts (Language Acquisition Support System, or LASS). Although the debate has shed more heat than light, nevertheless it offers a convenient structure for considering a child's language difficulties: these may be biological or experiential. Biological causes include hearing impairment, leading to problems with the reception of language conveyed through speech, which will in turn pose problems for speech expression. Coordination difficulties are another example, leading to difficulties in producing written language. Some neurological impairments are a third example – even with auditory, visual and speech mechanisms intact, there may still be difficulty in communicating meaningfully.

The experiences valuable for satisfactory language development have attracted much research. The importance of an environment in which language, both speech and print, plays a prominent and stimulating part, is well understood. The contribution of the mother in pre-linguistic 'conversations' with infants is recognised. The development of discourse in older children leads to an understanding of the way language organisation differs according to the social context. The roles of reinforcement, modelling and other mechanisms are as important here as in any learning activity. All these lines of enquiry help to fill in the skeleton of our knowledge of language development and offer explanations of and ultimately remedies for the language disorders that children show.

References:

Child, D. (1986, 4th edn.) *Psychology and the Teacher*, London, Holt Rinehart and Winston.

Crystal, D. (1984) *Language Handicap in Children*, Stratford-upon-Avon, National Council for Special Education.

Czerniowska, P. (1985) 'Language and School', Unit 24, Open University Course E206, Milton Keynes, Open University.

Downes, G. (1978) *Language Development and the Disadvantaged Child*, Edinburgh, Holmes McDougall for the Schools Council.

language acquisition device (LAD), innate mechanism that facilitates language learning. This is the cornerstone of the biological theory of language development (sometimes described as the 'miracle' theory). It is essential for the view that language learning is governed by an inherited predisposition to understand the universal features of languages, such as noun phrases, verb phrases, etc. It stands in stark contrast to the associationist view that language develops through regular conjunctions of sound and situation, and that the behaviourist mechanism of reinforcement encourages correct expression (sometimes described as the 'impossible' theory).

The LAD mechanism is hypothetical: it is criticised in that it ignores the environmental and social components of language learning, i.e. the LASS, or Language Acquisition Support System. Moreover the existence of a universal language mechanism, responsive to any language, irrespective of its idiosyncrasies, is somewhat farfetched.

Reference:

Czerniowska, P. (1985) 'How is Language Learned?' Unit 12 of Open University Course E206, Milton Keynes, Open University.

Language Assessment, Remediation and Screening Procedure (LARSP), method for analysing and profiling the grammar of a child's speech. It postulates seven stages of grammatical development, listing the structures which occur at each stage and identifying those features which are well-established, those still emerging and those requiring remediation. It does offer suggestions for the next phase of work for a child whose language is delayed.

The profile is obtained from a detailed analysis of a transcript of samples of speech. The analyst has to be familiar with the various grammatical concepts used in the analysis, though these can be taught to the unsophisticated. LARSP is particularly helpful for those with some background in linguistic terminology, e.g. speech therapists and language specialists, working with children with fairly severe language disorders.

References:

Crystal, D., Fletcher, P. and Garman, M. (1976) *The Grammatical Analysis of Language Disability*, London, Edward Arnold.

Webster, A. and McConnell, C. (1987) *Children with Speech and Language Difficulties*, London, Cassell.

language code, language forms used by a particular group. The sociologist Bernstein provided an account of two codes in particular, a restricted code (previously called public language), and an elaborated code (previously called formal language). The restricted code is characterised by short, simple utterances, often ambiguous and heavily dependent on context: the elaborated code is characterised by longer sentences, grammatically more complex, and using more qualifiers, i.e. adjectives and adverbs.

The codes are not different languages, but different patterns of the same language, differing not in kind but in degree. Children acquire these patterns from the language experiences gained in their own families. In Bernstein's account they differentiate the social classes, working class children tending to use the restricted code, whereas middle class children use both codes, depending on the situation. Since teachers largely use an elaborated code, it is argued that the working class child is disadvantaged educationally. This is not to imply that the elaborated code is necessarily superior: many follow Labov, who argued that both codes are equally valid linguistically.

Reference:

Stubbs, M. (1980) *Language and Literacy*, London, Routledge and Kegan Paul.

language delay, see *language disorder.*

language development, is often used to refer to the acquisition of speech. In fact, the various aspects of language are themselves acquired in a particular sequence. The traditional view that speech reception (comprehension) precedes expression, and reception of print (reading) precedes expression (writing), has recently been modified so that receptive and expressive language are felt to develop interactively, with expressive language ahead of receptive for some of the time. For example, children may often say words they do not understand.

The importance of speech has led to a very careful study of the stages through which children pass as they gain proficiency. After the important first year of life, during which sounds and intonations are differentiated and practised, the first words begin to appear at about twelve to thirteen months. At eighteen months children begin to combine two or more words into brief but meaningful phrases, and the mean vocabulary sizes and sentence lengths characteristic of different ages have been determined.

Other studies have charted the development of phonology, the growth in the ability to recognise and produce the sound contrasts which enable the phonemes of the language to be properly utilised. For example, the p and b sounds are used early in the second year, but the r sound does not necessarily appear before the child is four.

Similarly the growth of grammatical structures leads to the identification of stages and milestones of development – the use of sentences with more than one clause, for example, appearing at about the age of three to three-and-a-half.

These developmental studies of language acquisition provide a most useful backcloth against which to evaluate a child's progress. But more important than the mean values which are usually given are their standard deviations. Children are individuals whose language acquisition patterns vary; a child who is not using two-word combinations at eighteen months does not give cause for alarm, for if that is the mean age at which this language feature occurs, then by definition half the child population will not demonstrate it until later.

The identification of language delay or language disorder serious enough to require therapy requires careful evaluation by a skilled therapist, using careful assessments that are sensitively interpreted.

References:

Crystal, D. (1982 version) *Child Language, Learning and Linguistics*, London, Arnold.

de Villiers, P.A. and de Villiers, J.G. (1979) *Early Language*, London, Fontana/Open Books.

Hallahan, D.P. and Kaufman, J.M. (1988, 4th edn.) *Exceptional Children; Introduction to Special Education*, Englewood Cliffs, Prentice Hall.

Webster, A. and McConnell, C. (1987) *Children with Speech and Language Difficulties*, London, Cassell.

language disorder, any disturbance in normal *language* functioning significant enough to affect a child's social, emotional or cognitive skills. Language difficulty, language defect, language deficit, language pathology, language disability, language dysfunction are some of the many alternative terms which appear for very similar conditions.

Language disorders are very important educationally, for language is central to the education process. They are classified in various ways.

One approach follows the division of language into receptive or expressive activity. In this system, hearing impairments are examples of receptive disorders, whereas speech problems, such as articulation difficulties, are examples of expressive disorders. (Both often coexist, of course.)

Language disorders can also be classified according to transmission mode, those involving speech (e.g. stuttering), those involving print (e.g. reading difficulties) and those involving gesture (e.g. dyspraxia).

Sometimes language disorders are classified into organic as opposed to functional groups. Organic disorders are those for which an obvious medical pathology can be identified, e.g. speech problems associated with a cleft palate, or a receptive aphasia linked to neurological damage. Functional language disorders are the miscellany of problems for which no pathology can usually be identified, e.g. dyslexia or the language patterns of autistic children.

Yet another classification attempts to distinguish between language delay, a normal pattern of language, but which is slow in developing, and language deviance, an abnormal language feature occurring within otherwise normal development.

Each of these different ways of describing language disorder can be encountered in the literature and each has value.

Estimates of the prevalence of language disorders in the child population depend heavily on the criteria adopted. Estimates are reported in the literature for individual conditions, so we limit our consideration here to noting estimates for the broad divisions of print-based and speech-based disorders. For *reading difficulty* the *Isle of Wight Survey* is an example of a reputable investigation, which offered a 4% prevalence rate. One of the most widely-quoted estimates of speech difficulty was given in the *Quirk report*. This concluded that overall, about 3% of children in ordinary schools suffered from a *speech disorder*. Three points need to be made about both of these estimates. First, as already emphasised, if different criteria are used, different prevalence figures emerge. Second, the figures quoted themselves vary considerably between ages and between social backgrounds. Thirdly, and more importantly, children with learning difficulties will show a substantially higher incidence of both speech and reading difficulties – indeed this is only common sense, for speech and reading, examples of the expressive and receptive aspects of language, are the very warp and woof of education. The ratios are nevertheless interesting; thus Quirk estimated that 50% of children attending special schools for severe learning difficulties (then described as ESN(S)), required speech therapy. *Speech therapists* in sufficient numbers to service a population of this size are unlikely to be forthcoming. This emphasises the role of the teacher – in collaboration with the therapist – in offering regular help to children with language disorders in special education.

See *language development, pragmatics.*

References:

Crystal, D. (1988, 2nd edn.) *Introduction to Language Pathology,* London, Cole and Whurr.

Hallahan, D.P. and Kaufman, J.M. (1988, 4th edn.) *Exceptional Children: Introduction to Special Education,* Englewood Cliffs, Prentice Hall.

Webster, A. (1988) 'The Prevalence of Speech and Language Difficulties in Childhood: some brief research notes', *Child Language Teaching and Therapy,* 4, 1, 85–91.

language experience approach, method of teaching reading that uses the child's own language and stories as text. Children are invited to give titles to their own pictures, and the teacher then writes these out for the pupils to trace and copy and read. Later, children are invited to relate a personal experience or their own stories, which the teacher writes down for the child to copy and read.

The advantage of this approach lies in the fact that the children's own language is used and that there is immediate motivation to read and write. Writing and spelling are facilitated from the outset. Children read their own words in their own sentence structures and can claim that 'they know what they mean when they read because they know what they meant when they said it'.

Most teachers using this method encourage children to enter new words in their own vocabularies or dictionaries, which can be used when they begin to write on their own.

Although it has been argued that the self-created reading material lacks the structure of the carefully-graded, controlled vocabulary found in reading schemes, children do tend to use the same basic vocabulary, and frequent repetition, an important feature in early readers, does occur naturally in the stories.

The language experience method can be developed as a class activity, producing class stories. It can be used as a vehicle for encouraging listening and conversational skills, etc. In later stages, spelling can be fostered through it. But like all reading approaches, it needs complementing with other methods.

See *Breakthrough to Literacy.*

Reference:

Goulandris, N. (1985) 'Extending the Written Language Skill of Children with Specific Learning Difficulties – Supplementary Teaching Techniques', in Snowling, M.J. (1985) *Children's Written Language Difficulties*, Windsor, NFER-Nelson.

Language Master, modified tape recorder used in teaching language and reading skills. The equipment includes cards with tape strips. A card might carry the picture of an 'apple' which the child identifies. To check, the tape strip on the card is then fed into the Language Master, which plays out the word.

Printed words, phrases and sentences can be handled similarly as an aid to improving reading skills, and there are several matching games for which the machine can be used.

Reference:

Reason, R. and Boote, R. (1986) *Learning Difficulties in Reading and Writing: a Teacher's Manual*, Windsor, NFER-Nelson.

language therapist, see *speech therapist.*

Language Through Reading (LTR), a reading scheme in three parts, with a linguistic base. Thus instead of the usual emphasis on word-frequency for governing content, in this scheme the content is also determined by level of grammatical complexity. The seven grammatical stages of the *Language Assessment, Remediation and Screening Procedure* (*LARSP*) are used as a guide. Thus the fifty-two units of LTR-I introduce thirty-seven clause structures and take the child up to the fourth of the seven LARSP stages, using a vocabulary of ninety-seven words. It also deliberately incorporates a high ratio of verbs to nouns.

LTR-II and -III increase the level of grammatical complexity in a controlled way, paying special attention to the concept of time involved in tense use.

Although the scheme was designed at a special school for use with children with serious language disorders, it has been used much more widely, in both ordinary and special schools.

References:

Crystal, D., Fletcher, P. and Garman, M. (1976) *The Grammatical Analysis of Language Disability*, London, Edward Arnold.

Gillies, M. (1986) 'Language through Reading', *British Journal of Special Education*, 13, 2, 71–3.

language unit, special provision for children with language disorders, including speech difficulties, more serious than can be managed in an ordinary classroom, even with some support. Most language units are attached to ordinary schools, though some are based on other facilities such as child guidance centres. They are usually staffed by specialist language teachers and speech therapists, the latter usually part-time only.

The key to the success of the unit often hinges on the quality of the working relationship established between teacher and therapist, both of whom can learn from each other, to the advantage of the children.

References:

Hegarty, S., Pocklington, K. and Lucas, D. (1981) *Educating Pupils with Special Needs in the Ordinary School*, Windsor, NFER-Nelson.

Pocklington, K. and Hegarty, S. (1982) *The Development of a Language Unit*, Slough, NFER.

LAPP, see *Lower-Attaining Pupils Programme.*

Larry P. v. Riles (1972), important USA case which had a significant effect on the assessment of pupils with special educational needs from minority communities. The court ruled that intelligence tests were culturally biased and therefore must not be used in assessing black pupils for placement in classes for children with mild retardation.

This situation was remedied to some extent by the passage in 1975 of *PL 94-142.* First, it adopted the AAMD (now *AAMR*) definition of mental retardation which requires, essentially, co-occurring deficits in intellectual performance and adaptive behaviour. Second, the law specified a set of special education procedures requiring that children be tested in their first language, that no single test score could be used as the basis for determining educational placement and that measures used be valid and non-discriminatory.

(Note that in later USA litigation it has been ruled that intelligence tests are not racially or culturally biased.)

See *ethnic minorities.*

References:

Cook, R.E. and Armbruster, J.B. (1983) *Adapting Early Childhood Curricula*, St. Louis, Mosby.

McLoughlin, J.A. and Lewis, R.B. (1986, 2nd edn.) *Assessing Special Education Students*, London, Merrill.

LARSP, see *Language Assessment, Remediation and Screening Procedure.*

larynx, or voice-box, casing of muscle and cartilage, visible as the 'Adam's apple'. It contains the vocal cords, whose actions help to produce most of the sounds needed for speech. The vibrations of the vocal cords give speech some of its characteristic timbre, and abnormal laryngeal conditions are associated with disorders such as dysphonia.

See *speech disorder.*

Reference:

Crystal, D. (1988, 2nd edn.) *Introduction to Language Pathology*, London, Cole and Whurr.

latency period, see *Freudian theory.*

laterality,

(1) the preference for using one side of the body rather than the other. In this sense laterality often refers to handedness and eyedness, hence crossed laterality, where the dominant eye and hand are on opposite sides of the body. But laterality is a feature of other activities, too, notably the use of the ear and foot. Note that a lefthanded individual will not necessarily exhibit a similar preference for hand, eye or foot: the laterality pattern need not be consistent.
Lateralisation is the process of establishing laterality, usually complete for both hand and eye preferences before children enter school. This does not mean that children prefer the same hand, for example, for every activity, but that one hand is usually dominant for most activities, whereas the other hand is preferred for the remainder.
The influence of laterality patterns on learning difficulties has been carefully studied, particularly in relation to reading. Most large-scale surveys have failed to find an association between patterns of laterality and reading difficulty – indeed the great majority of children with unusual laterality patterns have no reading difficulties. Nevertheless, it is possible that laterality patterns may be significant in some children with special needs.

See *handedness.*

(2) awareness of the difference between right and left, sometimes called *directionality.* This develops later than laterality in sense (1), and it is not until the age of eight or so that the great majority of children can distinguish right from left on their own body, e.g. pointing to the right foot with the left hand on request. (The ability to distinguish right from left on another person develops later.)
Laterality (2) is important in education. While the terms 'right' and 'left' are often used in communicating in the classroom, they also have specific importance in the early stages of reading, writing and number. In reading and writing, children have to learn to attack print from left to right, while many arithmetical operations (e.g. addition) have to be performed from right to left. These skills are normally acquired in the early stages of education, and with most – but not all – children rapidly become automatised.

References:

Clark, M.M. (1974) *Teaching Left-handed Children*, London, Hodder and Stoughton.

Faas, L.A. (1981, 2nd edn.) *Learning Disabilities: a Competency-Based Approach*, Boston, Houghton Mifflin.

Tansley, P. and Panckhurst, J. (1981) *Children with Specific Learning Difficulties; a Critical Review of Research*, Windsor, NFER-Nelson.

Laws, see under specific Act, e.g. Education Act 1981, Chronically Sick and Disabled Persons Act 1970, etc.

Lawther Report 1980, 'Lead and Health', report of the DHSS working party on lead in the environment. Much of the report deals with the damaging effects of lead on the behaviour, intelligence and attainment of children. The report was criticised for using a concept of 'safe' blood–lead levels in children and generally under-estimating the size of the problem of lead pollution. In the same year the Conservation Society published 'Lead or Health', which concluded that many children in the UK (and elsewhere) suffer from an epidemic of low-grade *lead poisoning.*

Reference:

Swann, W. (Ed.) (1981) 'The Effects of Lead Pollution on Children's Development: the Lawther Report and the Conservation Society Report', in Swann, W. (Ed.) (1981) *The Practice of Special Education,* Oxford, Blackwell in association with the Open University.

lead poisoning, causes damage to children's intellect and behaviour. Lead is inhaled through petrol fumes, or ingested through lead-based paints and cosmetics. Drinking water which has been carried by lead pipes or percolated through lead-rich soil can also be implicated.

There is no doubt that high levels of lead, such as are found in children who have eaten lead paint or old battery plates, can lead to permanent mental handicap and serious emotional and behavioural difficulties.

The effects of low levels of lead on children's development is a source of some controversy. Some investigators report a clear association between learning difficulties, distractible, hyperactive behaviour, and lead at all levels. Others believe that there is a limit below which little if any relationship can be established. Early work was criticised on the grounds that the effects of social class were not always controlled; children in environments with high lead levels coming from lower social classes, an alternative explanation for their intellectual and behavioural difficulties. More careful investigations do show small associations at even low levels, and attempts to reduce environmental lead, for which car petrol exhausts are most responsible, can do children's development nothing but good.

See *Lawther Report, pica.*

References:

Barker, P. (1988, 5th edn.) *Basic Child Psychiatry,* Oxford, Blackwell.

Swann, W. (Ed.) (1981) 'The Effects of Lead Pollution on Children's Development: the Lawther Report and the Conservation Society Report', in Swann, W. (Ed.) (1981) *The Practice of Special Education,* Oxford, Blackwell in association with the Open University.

learning difficulty, is defined in the Education Act 1981, as applying to a child who has a significantly greater difficulty in learning than the majority of children of his age, or cannot use the educational facilities provided in schools. (A learning difficulty arising because the language of the home is different from the language of the school is specifically excluded.) It is an important term, for it is effectively the legal basis for the identification of all *special educational needs.* Although the term has been extended to adults, it has status in relation to school pupils only.

However, the Warnock Report used learning difficulty in a narrower sense, i.e. to describe the problems of children whose special needs were not primarily associated with physical and sensory disabilities or with maladjustment (ebd). The term is there a replacement for the old 'educationally subnormal' (esn) category, which Warnock criticised on the grounds of imprecision, child centredness and stigma. The possibility that these criticisms will in time apply with equal force to 'learning difficulty' was recognised by Warnock. Indeed the history of similar terms shows that 'mental deficiency' was first introduced in the hope that its resonance with the then current 'physical deficiency' would remove stigma: mental deficiency was itself replaced with 'educationally subnormal' after that hope eventually proved illusory.

Learning difficulties in the narrower, Warnock sense, are divided into four groups, mild, moderate, severe and specific, the first three paralleling the divisions of the old esn category. Unlike the esn term they do not comprise a statutory category, categories of handicap having been abolished in the *Education Act 1981,* but a description.

The fourth group, specific learning difficulties, covers the needs of children who previously were often the concern of remedial services.

Children with learning difficulties in this narrower sense comprise the majority of the 20% of children estimated by Warnock as having special educational needs at some time or other during their school careers.

Mild learning difficulties require extra help, usually more teaching support from the school's own resources, to enable the child to progress satisfactorily with the National Curriculum.

Children with moderate learning difficulties are characterised by a significantly lower level of attainment, and may need a statement of special needs, specifying the extent to which the National Curriculum should be modified, or disapplied. In some cases they may be educated in special schools or classes, and services from outside the school will be involved in their assessment and their progress. Often adverse social and environmental conditions will be present.

The extent to which children with severe learning difficulties can follow the National Curriculum is currently a matter of intensive review. They are likely to have substantial problems with speech and the development of social skills, competencies that are normally learnt easily outside school: these children will need a curriculum that gives due weight to these competencies. They are often taught in special schools, although experiments in integration are occurring. They usually are children damaged by illness, e.g. encephalitis, or by a chromosomal abnormality, e.g. Down's syndrome, or birth injury.

Children with specific learning difficulties make good progress with most but not all the curriculum. An example is a child with a spelling difficulty, or a child with an arithmetical problem, both of whom make good progress otherwise. These children are taught in the ordinary school but with extra support from the school's own resources.

It is important to realise that these are descriptions, not categories, and that they are written in terms of the way the child copes with the curriculum: i.e. they are school-centred, not child-centred. It is this last point in particular which distinguishes learning difficulty, a UK term, from learning disability, a USA term.

See *mental handicap.*

References:

Brennan, W. (1987) *Changing Special Education Now,* Milton Keynes, Open University Press.

Gulliford, R. (1985) *Teaching Children with Learning Difficulties,* Windsor, NFER-Nelson.

Williams, P. (1990) 'Children with Learning Difficulties', in Entwistle, N. (Ed.) (1990) *Handbook of Educational Ideas and Practices,* London, Routledge.

learning disability, term originating in the USA to cover a group of children whose behaviour was reminiscent of adults with neurological damage and who had previously been described as children with perceptual handicap, dyslexia, minimal brain damage, developmental aphasia, etc. Although the condition has legal standing in the USA, no really satisfactory definition has emerged. Earlier definitions, e.g. that given in PL 94-142, emphasised the presence of language disorder in some form. In 1981 the National Joint Committee on Learning Disabilities stated:

'Learning disabilities is a generic term that refers to a heterogeneous group of disorders manifested by significant difficulties in the acquisition and use of listening, speaking, reading, writing, reasoning, or mathematical abilities. These disorders are intrinsic to the individual and presumed to be due to central nervous system dysfunction. Even though a learning disability may occur concomitantly with other handicapping conditions (e.g. sensory impairment, mental retardation, social and emotional disturbance) or environmental influences (e.g. cultural differences, insufficient/inappropriate instruction, psychological factors) it is not the direct result of these conditions or influences.'

Note that a specific learning disability is intrinsic to the child and linked to neurological dysfunction, whereas a specific *learning difficulty* (UK term) is seen as a school issue, a mismatch between the child's performance and the curriculum offered. In the UK approach the cause is less important than the cure.

Because of the difficulty in agreeing on a precise definition, estimates of prevalence vary widely; the expression 'significant difficulty' in the National Joint Committee definition (which does not appear in the PL 94-

142 definition) allows considerable latitude. A 2% to 3% prevalence is often accepted, but estimates as high as 30% have appeared.

Since learning disability is an umbrella term, there is no 'best buy' as a teaching method: children are assessed individually and separate programmes designed.

References:

Elliott, C.D. (1990) 'The Definition and Identification of Specific Learning Disabilities', in Pumfrey, P.D. and Elliott, C.D. (Eds.) (1990) *Children's Difficulties in Reading, Spelling and Writing*, London, Falmer Press.

Hallahan, D.P. and Kaufman, J.M. (1988, 4th edn.) *Exceptional Children: Introduction to Special Education*, Englewood Cliffs, Prentice Hall.

Kavale and Forness (1985) *The Science of Learning Disabilities*, Windsor, NFER-Nelson.

Wallach, G.P. and Butler, K.G. (Eds.) (1984) *Language Learning Disabilities in School-Age Children*, London, Williams and Wilkins.

Wiig, E.H. and Semel, E. (1984, 2nd edn.) *Language Assessment and Intervention for the Learning Disabled*, Columbus, Merrill.

Learning Potential Assessment Device (LPAD), the assessment instrument which, together with *Instrumental Enrichment*, forms the toolkit for Feuerstein's approach to learning difficulties. Feuerstein worked originally with deprived Israeli adolescents, but the LPAD is used with children and adults too, and in many different countries.

The material usually demands non-verbal responses, as in so-called culture-fair tests, but unlike many other assessment instruments, the LPAD claims to measure not what has been learnt, but how learning takes place, in other words, learning potential. This is done through a series of short tasks and reasoning problems in which the person is first tested, then taught, then tested again to determine learning potential. It is administered individually or in group form.

The LPAD does not produce a conventional IQ. Its results are intended to lead directly into the Instrumental Enrichment program. The introduction of the LPAD and the Feuerstein approach in the UK is relatively recent and evaluations are awaited.

See *cognitive modifiability*.

References:

Feuerstein, R., in collaboration with Rand, Y. and Hoffman, M.B. (1979) *The Dynamic Assessment of Retarded Performers: the Learning Potential Assessment Device, Theory, Instruments and Techniques*, Baltimore, University Park Press.

Feuerstein, R., in collaboration with Rand, Y., Hoffman, M.B. and Miller, R. (1980) *Instrumental Enrichment*, Baltimore, University Park Press.

least restrictive environment, phrase used in the USA to give effect to the principle that children with special needs should be educated in surroundings as normal as possible. This was a theme in some court judgements in the 1970s and was included in the provisions of *Public Law*

94-142. Like the emphasis on *integration* in the Education Act 1981, there are some qualifications to the requirement, in particular the needs of other children in the class and the competence of the teachers involved have to be considered.

Note that the term 'least restrictive environment' is used in place of the more customary 'mainstreaming'. The former provides more flexibility, and allows a number of possibilities to be examined by the team of professionals and parents involved in deciding placement. But the term is open to various interpretations. For example, the mainstream may be less physically restricting than a special class, but is it necessarily less psychologically restricting?

While the overall proportion of handicapped pupils taught in different settings has remained relatively stable, the overwhelming majority being taught in the regular classroom, the development of a range of placement options has meant that more children with visual, auditory and physical impairments and more children with emotional and behavioural difficulties have been taught in less restrictive settings since the Act became law.

References:

Stephens, T.M., Blackhurst, A.E. and Magliocca, L.A. (1982) *Teaching Mainstreamed Students*, New York, Wiley.

US Department of Education (1984) 'Executive Summary of Sixth Annual Report to Congress on the Implementation of Public Law 94-142', *Exceptional Children*, 51, 3, 199–202.

left-eyed, natural dominance of the left over the right eye, present in about a third of the population.

See *crossed laterality*.

lefthandedness, see *handedness*.

left hemisphere, see *cerebral dominance*.

Legg-Perthe's disease, see *Perthe's disease*.

Leiter International Performance Scale (LIPS), individual, non-verbal performance test, in which instructions are mimed. The child carries out matching, completion, analogies and classification items through placing blocks in a frame. The test has had numerous revisions and adaptations: the current version can be used between the ages of two and eighteen years.

The test was originally designed for use with children who might have difficulty in responding to items involving the use of English, e.g. children with hearing impairment, language disorder, or children for whom English is not the first language. This last group has given the test a long history of use in the assessment of children from minority cultures.

Criticisms of the LIPS centre on the inadequacy of the standardisation and the poverty of the reliability and validity data. But the long life of the test (it was first published in 1929) testifies to the usefulness of the approach it follows.

See *culture-fair test.*

References:

Anastasi, A. (1982, 5th edn.) *Psychological Testing,* New York, Macmillan.

Salvia, J. and Ysseldyke, J.E. (1981, 2nd edn.) *Assessment in Special and Remedial Education,* Boston, Houghton Mifflin.

Lesch-Nyhan syndrome, condition characterised by severe mental retardation, aggressive behaviour and self-mutilation, biting the lips and fingers in particular. The behaviour is due to a metabolic disorder, inherited as an X-linked recessive condition.

See *self-injurious behaviour.*

Reference:

Graham, P.J. (1986) *Child Psychiatry: a Developmental Approach,* Oxford, Oxford University Press.

leukaemia, usually described as cancer of the blood cells. In fact there are several different kinds of leukaemia, broadly divided into acute and chronic forms. Unfortunately, leukaemias in children are almost always acute, rapid in onset and quickly fatal unless treated. The prevalence rate of leukaemia in children is about one per 25,000, the most common age of onset being between two and five years.

As normal an educational programme as possible is recommended, subject to medical agreement. The treatment can be distressing to child and parents, and will involve periods off school, with consequent effects on school attainments. There are side effects such as hair-loss, which some children find upsetting, particularly in adolescence, and which may need to be handled sensitively in school. It is also important that teachers are aware of the dangers that childhood illnesses pose for some children with leukaemia. Medical advice should be sought if there has been a possible contact with an infectious child.

The main positive feature of childhood leukaemia is that treatments are steadily improving and the outlook for remission and possible cure is steadily brightening.

References:

Graham, P.J. (1986) *Child Psychiatry: a Developmental Approach,* Oxford, Oxford University Press.

Lansdown, R. (1980) *More than Sympathy,* London, Tavistock.

Lewis Counselling Inventory, questionnaire intended to identify adolescent pupils needing counselling and guidance. The first part of the questionnaire contains forty-six items covering six areas, *viz:* irritability, social confidence, health and relationships with teachers, family and peers, and includes a six-item lie scale. The second part allows pupils to expand freely on their problems.

The inventory was standardised on pupils in the third year of secondary school, but is used more widely. It is one of the few such personality inventories standardised in the UK. Administration (group or individual) is quick and easy, but the technical detail has been criticised. Recently a version that can be used in a computer administration, scoring, analysis and recording system has been developed and tested.

lie scale, subset of items in a personality test or questionnaire which helps to detect whether the questions are being answered honestly. The scale might consist of pairs of parallel, rephrased items, scattered through the main test. The extent to which items disagree with their partners indicates how much weight can be attached to the main responses.

Alternatively a lie scale might consist of a subset of items which, if checked in a certain way, represent an impossibly virtuous person. People responding thus are clearly trying to present the best possible picture of themselves rather than the truth, and again the validity of the main responses can be queried in the light of lie scale answers.

A lie scale is probably the best-known of a number of validity scales inserted into personality questionnaires in order to provide checks on the integrity of the answers.

Reference:

Cronbach, L.J. (1984, 4th edn.) *Essentials of Psychological Testing*, New York, Harper and Row.

life skills, those skills needed to function in society as an independent adult. They include personal skills such as hygiene and body care, domestic skills such as cookery and household management, as well as the ability to understand and deal with the institutions of society. For a young person with special needs, training in life skills involves learning those skills which are needed to overcome any existing handicap as well as those which may be required for dealing with situations which lie in the future – as when a child suffers from a condition in which sight will deteriorate to such an extent that it is advisable to learn Braille now.

Life skills often feature in courses for leavers, and courses offered at colleges of further education.

References:

Bradley, J. and Hegarty, S. (1982) *Stretching the System*, London, Further Education Curriculum Review and Developmental Unit.

Dee, L. (1988) *New Directions*, London, Further Education Curriculum Review and Development Unit.

life-space interview, technique originated by Redl and developed by Morse, among others, to help emotionally disturbed children. When the child is involved in a flare-up, an adult talks with the child about the crisis while feelings are still strong. The adult can be a therapist, but in the school situation is more likely to be a teacher. The interview can have two main objectives, to offer on-the-spot emotional support through empathy and calmness or to provide insight through talking the child through the events that caused the situation and interpreting them, what Redl called the clinical exploitation of the crisis.

The value of this technique, which is rooted in the psychoanalytic approach, lies in its use of the immediacy of the crisis to advantage. It does not take the child out of the classroom and into the clinic.

There are two main problems. First, it may not always be convenient for a busy teacher to take the child aside when the moment demands, nor may a classroom assistant be available. Second, the detachment and neutrality that the approach requires may be more easily demonstrated by a therapist than a teacher.

See *crisis intervention.*

Reference:

Marsh, G.E., Price, B.J. and Smith, T.E.C. (1983) *Teaching Mildly Handicapped Children*, St. Louis, Mosby.

lightwriter, communication aid for people who cannot speak. Messages are typed on a keyboard and displayed on two screens, one for the transmitter and one for the receiver. A speech synthesizer enables the lightwriter to be used for telephone conversations.

linguistic method, method of teaching reading which stresses the importance of learning the most frequent and most regular grapheme–phoneme correspondences in English. This means that simple patterns (e.g. three-letter consonant-vowel-consonant combinations, 'the tan man ran to the van') are learnt first, followed by patterns of gradually increasing complexity. Whereas in the phonic method pupils are taught to sound the letters and build up words, the linguistic method relies on frequent repetition forming an automatically recognised association betweeen pattern and sound.

Note that this emphasis leads to reading material in which interest and meaning are sacrificed to simplicity. The supporters of the linguistic method regard this as an advantage, claiming that it enables the learner to concentrate on the mechanics of reading, i.e. decoding skills, without the distractions of struggling after comprehension. However it has frequently been demonstrated that children find it more difficult to distinguish words with minimal contrast (bad, bed, bid, bud) than contrasting words and letter patterns (The big elephant's trunk).

The linguistic method probably reached its heyday in the 1960s, and is the antithesis of the language experience approach, now much more popular with teachers of reading. It should not be confused with linguistics and linguistic approaches to reading, both of which continue to provide insights into the development of children's language which have application to the development of reading skills.

See *Language Through Reading.*

References:

Goodacre, E. (1971) 'Linguistics and the Teaching of Reading', in Melnik, A. and Merritt, J. (Eds.) (1971) *The Reading Curriculum,* Milton Keynes, Open University Press.

Marsh, G.E. Price, B.J. and Smith, T.E.C. (1983) *Teaching Mildly Handicapped Children,* St. Louis, Mosby.

link course, see *link schemes.*

link schemes, arrangements in which pupils, staff or resources are shared between special schools and ordinary schools and colleges. They include link courses, provided by colleges of further education for students with severe learning difficulties, usually in their last year at special school. Sometimes students at adult training centres attend, too.

A recent survey showed that nearly three-quarters of special schools had link schemes operating with ordinary schools. Two-thirds of the schools had staff going into ordinary schools, either on a regular weekly basis or less frequently. Over half the special schools had pupils going into the ordinary schools, and nearly a third reported that they had resources that were shared with ordinary schools. There was movement of staff, pupils and resources in the reverse direction, i.e. from ordinary to special school, but this was less marked.

Although many link schemes were tenuous, involving no more than a few hours contact per week, nevertheless they represent a form of *integration* that is often overlooked in the debate over whether to mainstream or not. Moreover they offer integration for staff, as well as pupils.

To some pupils, link schemes can be a step to full-time placement in the ordinary school, reached through a process of gradual acclimatisation. To others, they offer the chance of a broader curriculum than would otherwise be available. And they extend children's social contacts in beneficial ways.

The difficulties are mainly organisational – meshing the timetables of two different schools presents obvious problems. There are problems, too, of pupils' adjusting to the different atmospheres and expectations of two different schools, but these can be eased by careful preparation beforehand and support during the link arrangement. And of course the arrangements are beneficial to the pupils and staffs of the ordinary schools also.

References:

Dean, A. and Hegarty, S. (Eds.) (1984) *Learning for Independence,* London, Further Education Unit.

Jowett, S., Hegarty, S. and Moses, D. (1988) *Joining Forces,* Windsor, NFER-Nelson.

lipreading (USA speechreading), understanding a spoken language by following the lip movements of the speaker. (Some extend lipreading to include the interpretation of facial muscles and body gestures.) Since less than half the speech sounds of English appear on the lips, this is a difficult skill to acquire, particularly for prelingually deaf children. Where language knowledge is extensive amd where some residual hearing remains, satisfactory lipreading skills can be acquired. However, lipreading does have limitations – unlike some other communication devices it helps with receptive language only, it demands a good light, a view of the other person's face and reasonably acute vision. In short, it is far from a complete answer to the problem of communication and probably is most effectively used in conjunction with other methods.

See *total communication.*

References:

Miles, D. (1988) *British Sign Language: a Beginner's Guide*, London, BBC Books.

Reed, M. (1984) *Educating Hearing-Impaired Children*, Milton Keynes, Open University Press.

lisping, disorder of speech in which some or all of the sibilants, sounds with a characteristic hiss, such as s, z, sh, are poorly articulated. The substitutions, e.g. 'thaw' for 'saw', give the impression of baby talk. The sibilants are among the later acquired speech sounds, and lisping occurs in the speech of many young children, usually to disappear naturally. Reinforcement by amused parents can be responsible for its continuation, or in a few cases there may be a physical cause to be found in the speech musculature or mouth structure. Advice from a speech therapist may be needed.

Compare *lalling;* see *speech disorder.*

listening, paying attention selectively to sound, the basic skill in language acquisition. If children have not learnt to listen well, their education will be hampered. At primary level an average of about 60% of classroom time is spent in listening, while at secondary level this rises to about 90%, though the range is considerable in both cases.

Three groups of children in particular will have listening difficulties, hyperactive children, those with hearing impairment and those from some disadvantaged backgrounds. In this last case, overcrowded home conditions may generate a confusion of sounds from traffic, television, radio and people, leading to children 'switching off'. Limited experience in listening to stories and in conversations with adults will not have encouraged listening skills.

An acoustically-controlled environment, in which sound conditions are optimal (extraneous noise reduced through careful soundproofing, reverberation reduced through sound-absorbent surfaces, etc.) makes listening easier, particularly for children with hearing impairment. But children have also to be taught to pay attention selectively, to attend to some sounds and to disregard others. Listening games for young children provide systematic practice in discriminating sounds in general, helping with the more complex skills required to listen to speech.

See *auditory training.*

References:
Downes, G. (1978) *Language Development and the Disadvantaged Child*, Edinburgh, Holmes McDougall.
Webster, A. and McConnell, C. (1987) *Children with Speech and Language Difficulties*, London, Cassell.

literacy, essentially, adequate reading and writing skills. This is an important concept internationally; the success of worldwide attempts to improve educational standards of whole populations is often expressed in terms of the improvement in the literacy rate. But how is 'adequate' defined? Subjective estimates were followed by the development of standardised tests of reading, which allowed literacy/illiteracy to be objectively defined in terms of reading ages. In the UK, a reading age of nine years was considered the bench-mark for literacy, reading ages between nine and seven defined semi-literacy and a reading age below seven represented illiteracy. In the USA literacy was similarly defined in terms of grade equivalent. But these definitions and the concept of reading age are of course open to criticism; as reading standards improve so does the literacy touchstone – the definition is not as objective as it seems. The levels chosen are in any case arbitrary, and different bodies hold different views; a person with a reading age of nine years would not be sufficiently literate for a job as a publisher's reader for example.

These criticisms led to the development of the concept of *functional literacy,* the view that persons are literate if they have the reading and writing skills which allow effective participation in their culture or group. Some authorities add the phrase 'appropriate to the age group'. This gets round the problem of labelling a bright seven year-old, reading children's stories with enjoyment and understanding, as illiterate.

References:
Hillerich, R.L. (1976) 'Towards an Assessable Definition of Literacy', in Chapman, L.J. and Czerniowska, P. (Eds.) (1976) *Reading from Process to Practice,* Milton Keynes, Open University Press.
Pumfrey, P.D. (1990) 'Literacy and the National Curriculum: the Challenge of the 1990s', in Pumfrey, P. D. and Elliott C.D. (Eds.) (1990) *Children's Difficulties in Reading, Spelling and Writing,* London, Falmer Press.
Young, P. and Tyre, C. (1982) *Dyslexia or Illiteracy?* Milton Keynes, Open University Press.

Little's disease, former name for cerebral palsy, so called after the surgeon, W.J. Little, who first described it fully.

Local Financial Management of Schools (LFM), see *Education Act 1988.*

Local Management of Schools (LMS), implies local financial management. See *Education Act 1988.*

longitudinal study, sometimes called cohort study, investigates aspects of the development of individuals over time. Longitudinal studies underpin some of the major investigations of children's development, for example the *Child Health and Education Study.* Unlike a *cross-sectional study,* a longitudinal study assesses the same group of individuals (or single individual) at intervals over the period of the investigation.

Longitudinal studies have several disadvantages. First, they are time-consuming and therefore expensive. To plot change in height from birth to eighteen years of age by a longitudinal study takes the full eighteen years. (A cross-sectional study would take groups of children at each of a number of selected ages, measure their heights, and produce a result within a matter of weeks.) Then 'mortality' occurs during the period of the study, i.e. the availability of individual members of the sample reduces, for some may move away, contact may be lost for other reasons, or some may die. This wastage can be circumvented statistically or by replacement, but it is still a weakness. Thirdly, regular assessment over a period of time may have its own effect on the sample, leading to a loss of validity in the findings. Again, this can be checked to some extent by using a control group, though this is a refinement that rarely appears for reasons of practicability.

A longitudinal study has two central and very important advantages. First, it enables individual growth curves to be produced. These demonstrate the authentic rates of growth of characteristics. For example, the tremendously rapid growth spurt in the rate at which individual children acquire reading vocabulary is revealed by a longitudinal study, whereas cross-sectional studies mask the effect by smoothing the growth spurt.

Second, it enables the influence of changes in conditions to be studied over time. Thus the cumulative effects of social class on educational attainment and on behavioural characteristics can be clearly illustrated. The different experiences of the different groups of a cross-sectional study would not allow equally firm conclusions to be drawn.

References:

Cohen, L. and Manion, L. (1989, 3rd edn.) *Research Methods in Education,* London, Croom Helm.

Davies, P. and Williams, P. (1975) *Aspects of Early Reading Growth: a Longitudinal Study,* Oxford, Blackwell.

Plewis, I. (1985) *Analysing Change: Measurement and Explanation Using Longitudinal Data,* Chichester, Wiley.

look-and-say method, look-say method, teaches reading by emphasising recognition of the pattern of whole words. It came into favour as a reaction against learning to read by methods which emphasise learning the sounds of the letters, such as the phonic approach. It avoids the difficulties of trying to learn to read irregular words such as 'yacht' through a phonic approach. It also helps to avoid the boredom of phonically-based reading materials which continually stress regular, similar words. In short it offers more interest, particularly when used in conjunction with a language experience approach.

Since words are learnt by their length and their configuration, this method does not offer a method of attacking new words, as does the phonic method. It does not provide a logic to help the adventurous reader: the mental attitude of thinking about words as composed of letters is not reinforced.

Clearly children eventually learn to read print both by configuration and by structure. The real debate between the look-and-say advocates and the phonic advocates is not which method to use, but which method to use first and when to introduce the other. To this debate there is no clear answer, notwithstanding the many investigations that have taken place. There are suggestions that children from deprived backgrounds and children with dyslexia learn better with a structured, phonic approach initially, but these findings may be explained in other ways. As with so many educational questions, method is less important than the quality of the teaching and the previous experiences of the child.

See *top-down approaches.*

References:

Goodacre, E.J. (1971) 'Methods of Teaching Reading', in Melnik, A. and Merritt, J.E. (Eds.) (1971) *The Reading Curriculum,* Milton Keynes, Open University.

Sheldon, S. (1985) 'Learning to Read', Unit 13 of Open University Course E206, Milton Keynes, Open University.

low birth weight, usually weight at birth below 2,500 grams, regardless of length of pregnancy. There are many possible reasons for low birth weight, e.g. diet in pregnancy, insufficient nourishment of the foetus for other reasons, smoking, drug addiction, etc. A higher incidence of low birth weight infants is found in lower social classes, poorer use of the prenatal services being yet another reason which might contribute to explaining this. Most low birth weight infants thrive successfully, but there is a slightly greater risk of developmental problems, the lower the weight the greater the risk. Sometimes low birth weight occurs in conjunction with abnormalities in the baby.

Reference:

Davie, R., Butler, N. and Goldstein, H. (1972) *From Birth to Seven,* London, Longman.

Low Vision Aid (LVA), optical equipment for helping children with visual impairment, usually involving some form of magnification. A large number of devices are available, ranging, for example, from a simple magnifying glass through glasses with telescopic attachments to the electronic enlargement of printed material through a closed circuit TV.

Children who have been prescribed LVAs may need encouragement to use them, sensitively offered. Children should also have received training in using their LVAs.

Reference:

Fitt, R.A. and Mason, H. (1986) *Sensory Handicaps in Children*, Stratford-upon-Avon, National Council for Special Education.

Lower-Attaining Pupils Programme (LAPP), series of projects aimed at improving the attainments, motivation and self-respect of lower-attaining pupils in the last two years of compulsory education, and at preparing them better for adult life. The programme was funded mainly (up to 75%) by government, and LAPP represents the first curriculum programme managed by the Department of Education and Science. Seventeen different Local Education Authorities (LEAs) participated, providing a variety of different schemes. These often involved practical projects, accentuating oracy, personal and social education and life skills, rather than the more conventional skills of literacy and numeracy.

Many of the children taking part in the LAPP schemes were children with special needs, often with moderate learning difficulties, in the ordinary schools. In some LEAs special schools have been incorporated in LAPP, and in some cases this has led to substantially increased collaboration between special and ordinary schools.

A major problem was the difficulty many schools found in setting realistic individual learning targets for pupils. There was little evidence of sustained improvement in motivation for most pupils. But confidence and articulation improved for many, and many teachers want the principles of LAPP extended to younger children.

Reference:

Harland, J. and Weston, P. (1987) 'LAPP: Joseph's Coat of Many Colours', *British Journal of Special Education*, 14, 4, 150–2.

LPAD, see *Learning Potential Assessment Device.*

LVA, see *Low Vision Aid.*

M

mainstreaming, educating children with special needs alongside their non-handicapped peers. It is the application of the principle of normalisation to the education system.

Mainstreaming is often considered to be an American synonym for *integration*, but this is not quite correct. In the USA, as in some other countries such as Canada and Australia, a distinction is drawn between the two terms. Integration usually describes children with special needs being fully enrolled at an ordinary school and participating fully, whereas mainstreaming describes children with special needs spending most of their time in ordinary classes, but being given extra help through withdrawal classes or in other ways.

See *least restrictive environment.*

Reference:
Mitchell, D. (1990) 'Integrated Education', in Entwistle, N. (Ed.) (1990) *Handbook of Educational Ideas and Practices*, London, Routledge.

mainstream-with-support curriculum, see *curriculum.*

Makaton, a 'vocabulary' of some 350 manual signs, taken from British Sign Language, and sometimes called BSL(M). The vocabulary is arranged in nine stages, stages one to six being based on the vocabulary development of children aged one to four-and-a-half years, stages seven and eight adding some more complex concepts, and stage nine providing an extended word bank. The first eight stages are taught in order.

Makaton was developed for use with hearing-impaired, mentally handicapped adults. Its advantages are its staged introduction, with a low 'floor' age, easy recognition of signs – precise coordination not being required, and availability of staff training courses. It has been criticised for lacking a sound linguistic rationale, and inexact correspondence with the grammatical structure of the English language.

But its success in facilitating effective communication in the subjects of the original project has led to its becoming widely used as a communication system for severely language-impaired children, not necessarily deaf. For example it is now the most widely-used non-vocal communication system in schools for children with severe learning disabilities.

See *Paget-Gorman Sign System.*

References:
Armfield, A. and Walker, M. (1981) 'What is the Makaton Vocabulary?' *Special Education: Forward Trends*, 8, 3, 19–20.
Byler, J.K. (1985) 'The Makaton Vocabulary: an Analysis Based on Recent Research', *British Journal of Special Education*, 12, 3, 113–120.
Kiernan, C., Reid, B. and Jones, C. (1982) *Signs and Symbols*, London, Heinemann for Institute of Education, University of London.

maladjustment, one of the official categories of handicap prior to the passing of the Education Act 1981. It has been largely replaced by the term *emotional and behavioural difficulties.* Objections to its use centred on its exemplifying the use of the *medical model* of special needs – implying a condition located within the child, basing 'treatment' on this premise and tacitly encouraging the neglect of environmental issues. Not everyone agreed with this criticism, some seeing value in the use of maladjustment as an administrative category, for which estimates of size could be used to argue for better support for children, irrespective of the philosophy underpinning the method of support offered.

References:
Bowman, I. (1981) 'Maladjustment: a History of the Category', in Swann, W. (Ed.) (1981) *The Practice of Special Education*, Oxford, Blackwell.
Ministry of Education (1955) *Report of the Committee on Maladjusted Children*, London, HMSO (The Underwood Report).

malleus, one of the three small bones in the middle ear which transmit sound vibrations from the eardrum to the cochlea.

See *ear*.

Manchester Scales of Social Adaptation, measure social competence in children aged six to fifteen years of age, are based on the *Vineland Social Maturity Scale*, and are individually administered. There are two main scales, a social perspective scale and a self-direction scale, each covering five short subscales. Tables of percentiles are provided for each age, allowing profiles of competence to be constructed.

Although the test has been useful in that it provides a social competence measure with a British (albeit North-West England) standardisation, it has been criticised on the grounds that the selection of items is subjective and that many of them need updating/changing in the light of the many social changes that have occurred since it was standardised in the late 1950s.

Reference:

Levy, P. and Goldstein, H. (1984) *Tests in Education*, London, Academic Press.

manual communication, manual English, the collective term for the many different systems using gestures, hand signs and movements, fingerspelling, etc., to communicate non-vocally.

Reference:

Reed, M. (1984) *Educating Hearing-Impaired Children*, Milton Keynes, Open University Press.

Marfan's syndrome, inherited condition in which the bones are elongated (long, tapering fingers, for example) and the muscles weak. Children may suffer from curvature of the spine and from heart conditions. Many have associated visual impairments, often a dislcation of the lens, which may lead to special educational needs, requiring care with the management of both academic and physical activities.

Reference:

Chapman, E.K. and Stone, J.M. (1988) *The Visually Handicapped Child in Your Classroom*, London, Cassell.

Marland Report, USA enquiry into the education of gifted children, conducted by Commissioner for Education Marland at the request of Congress, and published in 1972.

The report was a landmark in the history of the education of gifted children. It painted a picture of a tremendous waste of potential through inadequate services failing to meet the needs of the nation's most talented children. It led to the development of a number of programmes aimed at rectifying the situation. More importantly it resulted in the Federal Office of Education taking on new responsibilities in an area which it had previously neglected.

Reference:

Alexander, P.A. and Muia, J.A. (1982) *Gifted Education: a Comprehensive Roadmap*, London, Aspen Systems Corporation.

masking,

(1) since sound delivered to one ear may stimulate the other (for example a headphone at one ear may transmit sound to the other by bone conduction) there are problems in determining accurate hearing thresholds for each ear separately. These can be overcome by masking, i.e. delivering a continuous noise into the non-test ear while testing the other.

Reference:

Tucker, I. and Nolan, M. (1984) *Educational Audiology*, Beckenham, Croom Helm.

(2) a similar principle, i.e. introducing an extraneous sound into the ears, is sometimes used as a treatment for tinnitus, i.e. constant whistling and other noises, caused internally.

Reference:

Reed, M. (1984) *Educating Hearing-Impaired Children*, Milton Keynes, Open University Press.

mastery learning, rests on the belief that nearly all children can learn the skills taught in the school curriculum if taught appropriately. What matters is not children's abilities but the quality of the teaching.

Mastery learning principles demand that the curriculum is broken up into small, easily-managed steps. Children are taught each step until they have reached a pre-determined competency level, and so mastered the skill.

They can then move on to the next stage. Extra teaching approaches have to be devised for those pupils who take longer to reach mastery level, so offering challenges to the teacher's skill.

Note that since pupils will vary in the time they take to master a given stage, mastery learning is inconsistent with the idea of a set period of compulsory education: further education should take over the teaching process when school finishes. There are problems, too, in reconciling mastery learning with the concept of expected standards of attainment at certain ages, deriving from the national curriculum. Note too that mastery learning is essentially individualised instruction: the lockstep of a uniform class progression through a set curriculum, some children being bored and others failing, is broken. It is this demand on the resources of the teacher that has led to a reluctance to introduce mastery learning generally. It is more evident in special education settings, where class sizes are usually smaller.

See *precision teaching*.

Reference:

Brennan, W.K. (1985) *Curriculum for Special Needs*, Milton Keynes, Open University Press.

matched group, see *control group*.

maternal deprivation, the absence of a close relationship with mother for a significant period in early childhood. Bowlby's view that maternal deprivation could be responsible for far-reaching detrimental effects on children's personalities, leading in extreme cases to children developing into affectionless psychopaths, had enormous impact on child care practices in the 1950s and 1960s. Authorities were reluctant to separate children from their natural mothers, even where conditions were otherwise intolerable. Where children had to be taken into care they were placed in foster care rather than institutions, in the expectation that substitute mothering would compensate for the separation. Arrangements for visiting children in hospital were altered and joint admissions of mothers and young children introduced.

Later work challenged some of the inferences that had been drawn from Bowlby's work, while not detracting from his general conclusion of the importance of early mother–child relationships, nor denying the beneficial effects of many of the consequent changes. The age at which separation occurred, its duration, the support offered by father and the family, were some of the issues examined. While the long-term effects of maternal deprivation are still controversial, the distress and despair that are the short-term effects of separation on young children have been well documented. Perhaps the most important conclusion is not that deprivation of mother per se is necessarily detrimental to the child in the long-term, but that good mothering throughout childhood gives a stability which helps children weather some of the emotional storms that are met later.

See *bonding*.

References:

Bowlby, J. (1965, 2nd edn.) *Child Care and the Growth of Love*, Harmondsworth, Penguin.

Rutter, M. (1972) *Maternal Deprivation Reassessed*, Harmondsworth, Penguin.

Schaffer, R. (1977) *Mothering*, Douglas, IOM, Fontana/Open Books.

mathematics difficulties, have generated substantially less interest than reading difficulties, a difference reflected in the lesser national and international concern with numeracy as opposed to literacy. It is difficult to give a sensible estimate of the prevalence of mathematical difficulties, partly because expectations of the skills which should be acquired at particular ages are highly dependent on the maths curriculum which has been followed: the traditional curriculum is still being followed in some areas, in others it has been replaced by the so-called 'new maths', while the advent of Piagetian ideas has introduced different concepts into the curriculum. But whatever the nature of the maths being taught, as a subject it does cause difficulties, often associated with strong feelings of dislike and anxiety.

To some extent this is understandable. Take notation, the basis for representing number concepts in written form. Only a few centuries ago, when the notation we use today was coming into use, it was regarded as such a difficult system to use that German Universities specialised in teaching multiplication and Italian Universities division. Yet virtually all schools teach these processes to infants today: perhaps curriculum designers are over-optimistic over young children's grasp of difficult ideas.

The choice of topics for children with learning difficulties has occupied some investigators, hoping to design a curriculum concentrating on skills needed in work and home, appealing through its relevance. A foundation list of topics was provided in the Cockcroft Report for pupils in the lowest 40% of maths attainment. But irrespective of content, method is important. Children do need help to grasp the concepts they manipulate; the use of practical activities and of language, talking through the operations as they are performed, are both important processes in helping to grasp mathematical concepts.

See *LAMP* (2).

References:

Denvir, B., Stolz, C. and Brown, M. (1982) *Low Attainers in Mathematics 5–16,* London, Methuen.

Department of Education and Science (1982) *Mathematics Counts,* London, HMSO (Cockcroft Report).

Department of Education and Science (1988) *Better Mathematics,* London, HMSO.

Gulliford, R. (1985) *Teaching Children with Learning Difficulties,* Windsor, NFER-Nelson.

matrices test, see *Raven's Progressive Matrices.*

mbd (minimal brain damage), see *brain damage.*

McCann Report 1975, 'The Secondary Education of Physically Handicapped Children in Scotland', accepted that there would be a continuing need for special schools, but advocated that more integration should take place and that children should be educated in ordinary schools where possible.

It also pointed to the limited opportunities for further and higher education for young people with physical handicaps, and to the need for independent study arrangements linked to schools and colleges.

Reference:

Scottish Education Department (1975) *The Secondary Education of Physically Handicapped Children in Scotland,* Edinburgh, HMSO (McCann Report).

mcd (minimal cerebral damage), see *brain damage.*

mean, or arithmetic mean, one of a number of measures of the 'central tendency' of a set of scores, obtained in this case by summing the scores and dividing by the number of observations: i.e. the average.

See *median, mode.*

Mean Length of Utterance (MLU), measure of language development, essentially the average number of words a child produces at a time, i.e. before speech is interrupted by silence or another speaker. It is measured using a standard kit of toys and books, encouraging the child to respond until at least sixty consecutive utterances are tape-recorded. The first ten are disregarded and the mean length of the remaining fifty calculated.

The MLU is a simple index of language development: more sophisticated assessments take into account other elements, such as grammatical complexity.

See *Language Assessment and Remediation Procedure.*

Reference:

Gillham, B. (1986) 'Disorders of Language and Communication', in Gillham, B. (Ed.) (1986) *Handicapping Conditions in Childhood,* Beckenham, Croom Helm.

median, measure of central tendency of a set of scores: middle point in the set such that exactly half the scores lie above it and half below.

See *mean, mode.*

Mediated Learning Experience (MLE), principle on which Feuerstein's theory of *Instrumental Enrichment* is based.

Feuerstein believes that individuals develop intellectually as a result of two different processes. First, the individual learns through direct interaction with the environment. Second, the individual learns through interacting with stimuli which have been selected and modified (i.e. mediated) by others. These mediating agents, be they parents, siblings, teachers or others, enable the child to acquire behaviour patterns which maximise the effectiveness of the first process of development, direct interaction with the environment. MLE, in Feuerstein's view, induces the pattern of learning sets and strategies that form the basis of proper cognitive functioning.

Lack of or reduced exposure to MLE is a characteristic of cultural deprivation, leading to retarded intellectual performance. Conversely, providing effective MLE enables the normal patterns of cognitive growth to be restored. The Instrumental Enrichment program is the selection of learning experiences developed by Feuerstein and colleagues to enable children to learn more efficiently.

The extent to which the MLE principle represents a significant advance on earlier conceptualisations of learning in children depends in no small measure on evaluations of the IE program. These we await.

See *Learning Potential Assessment Device.*

Reference:

Feuerstein, R. (1980) *Instrumental Enrichment,* Baltimore, University Park Press.

medical model, the belief that learning and behavioural problems are analogous to diseases, located in the child, characterised by recognisable and specific symptoms, and once diagnosed, treatable by acknowledged methods.

This was the thinking of those who, in the handicapped pupils regulations which followed the 1944 Education Act, placed maladjustment as a category of handicap. This is a productive way of proceeding for many physical complaints and for some learning and behavioural problems. For example, hyperthyroidism leads to restless behaviour and poor concentration: once the condition is diagnosed, appropriate medication or other treatment can be prescribed and the condition will improve.

The appealing logic of the medical model and its clearcut effectiveness in some instances have led to its wide application, often to the exclusion of alternative approaches. The danger in the use of the 'symptom, syndrome, diagnosis, aetiology, pathology, therapy, cure' thinking lies particularly in focusing attention on individuals who are presumed to 'have' the condition, and who may need segregation for this reason. Possible social explanations in terms of relationships with others, including teachers, or psychological explanations in terms of reinforcement theory, for example, may be disregarded.

The continued use of the medical model, notwithstanding its relative lack of success in dealing with so many learning and behavioural difficulties has been ascribed to the longstanding influence of the medical profession in the field of special education.

References:

Ford, J., Mongon, D. and Whelan, M. (1982) *Special Education and Social Control: Invisible Disasters*, London, Routledge Kegan Paul.

Williams, P. (1985) 'Troubled Behaviour', Units 18/19 Open University Course E206, Milton Keynes, Open University.

medical officer, see *community medical officer.*

medical records, written source of a child's medical history. The primary medical record is that kept by the family practitioner with whom the child is registered. A secondary medical record is kept by the local authority clinic staff (*community medical officers*). A third set of records is kept by the hospital consultants by whom the child may have been seen.

In accordance with the Education Act, 1981, parents are entitled to see reports on a child for whom a statement of special needs is required, but there is no mandatory access to any of the three medical records described. These are confidential. Nevertheless some medical practitioners are willing to collaborate as fully as possible in sharing information for the benefit of the child.

Recently, parent-held records have been introduced. These are intended to be the main medical record on which any professional seeing the child may write. Parents can make these available to teachers if they wish.

Reference:

Hall, D.M.B. (Ed.) (1989) *Health for all Children; a Programme for Child Health Surveillance*, Oxford, OMP, Oxford University Press.

Melville Report 1973, 'The Training of Staff for Centres for the Mentally Handicapped.' The Melville Committee was set up by the Secretary of State for Scotland, following concern over the staffing of junior occupation centres, where children who had been ascertained as unsuitable for education at school were trained by instructors.

The report recommended that all children should be educated, bringing Scotland in line with the situation in England and Wales following the Education (Handicapped Children) Act 1970. It further recommended that the occupation centres should be designated as schools, and that teachers should be appointed to the staffs in addition to instructors. Teachers should also be appointed to the staffs of adult training centres, and new courses of training should be instituted for instructors of children and of adults. The report also made recommendations on staff–pupil ratios.

The Melville Report was followed by the *Education (Mentally Handicapped Children) (Scotland) Act 1974,* which required all children to be educated, and instituted other recommendations of the report.

References:

Department of Education and Science (1978) *Special Educational Needs*, London, HMSO.

Scottish Education Department (1973) *The Training of Staff for Centres for the Mentally Handicaped*, Edinburgh, HMSO (The Melville Report).

meningitis, inflammation of the meninges, the three membranes covering the brain and spinal cord. It is most common in children, about half the cases occurring in under-fives, with premature infants and the new-born being particularly affected. While some forms of meningitis were usually fatal, modern treatments are much more successful. However, there are effects which have implications for children's education. For example, the high temperatures associated with the disease can cause lasting intellectual damage: neurological damage (e.g. cerebral palsy) may occur, depending on the kind of infection. Meningitis is also the main cause of post-natal deafness, capable of damaging hearing both centrally and peripherally. Many of the young children who now survive will be pre-lingually deaf, needing to learn language without the benefit of having already acquired it.

Reference:

Tucker, I. and Nolan, M. (1984) *Educational Audiology*, Beckenham, Croom Helm.

meningocele, small sac that protrudes through the back of the spine, present at birth. Unlike a *myelomeningocele* it contains only the meninges and cerebrospinal fluid, and may therefore be associated with only minor disturbances of neurological functioning. It may be possible to remove it without any noticeable consequences.

mental age (MA), measure of intelligence which has the advantages and disadvantages of the *age equivalent* principle. Scores on early intelligence tests (e.g. the Stanford-Binet Intelligence Scale) were often transformed into mental ages, which could also be converted into ratio intelligence quotients.

The disadvantages of the mental age system generally outweigh the advantages, and so modern intelligence tests usually provide a *deviation quotient.* But in some instances – for example the assessment of the development of the profoundly handicapped – a scale providing mental ages, such as the Merrill-Palmer Scale, is still found useful.

Reference:

Hogg, J. and Raynes, N.V. (Eds.) (1987) *Assessment in Mental Handicap,* Beckenham, Croom Helm.

mental handicap, umbrella term covering a range of different conditions, all characterised by impaired intellect. The extent of the impairment and the meaning of intellect are not specified: effectively the use of the term is a matter of personal judgement. Children with mental handicap are more accurately described as children with *learning difficulties,* a term with legal status, used in the Education Act 1981. There are three levels of learning difficulties, mild, moderate and severe (sometimes known as profound), but mental handicap would be rarely used for mild learning difficulties. (This is an example of the personal judgement mentioned above.) Adults with mental handicap are described as adults with *mental impairment* or severe mental impairment, again terms with legal status, appearing in the Mental Health Act 1983.

Mental handicap is analogous to physical handicap, covering a similarly broad range of conditions, and also with a variety of causes. Note too that physical and mental handicap may well co-exist in the same person – a point that applies particularly to children with severe learning difficulties. In the USA the equivalent term is mental retardation, which is more tightly defined by IQ and adaptive behaviour.

See *disability.*

References:

Gillham, B. (1986) 'Mental Handicap', in Gillham, B., (Ed.) (1986) *Handicapping Conditions in Childhood,* Beckenham, Croom Helm.

Gostin, L. (1983) *A Practical Guide to Mental Health Law,* London, MIND.

Mental Health Act 1983, currently governs the reception, care and treatment of people who are mentally disordered and compulsorily detained in hospital or received into guardianship. Under the Act's definition of mental disorder, four categories are specified: mental illness; mental impairment (replacing subnormality); severe mental impairment (replacing severe subnormality); psychopathic disorder.

The Act reaffirms the central principle of the 1959 Mental Health Act, namely that as far as possible, care should be provided informally. However, it also strengthens the rights of the compulsorily-detained patient in matters such as admission to hospital, care while in hospital and discharge from hospital. The rights of persons detained in hospital are extended in relation to matters such as consent to treatment, correspondence, right of access to a Mental Health Review Tribunal, and after-care in the community.

See *mental impairment.*

References:

Anderson-Ford, D. and Halsey, M. (1984) *Mental Health Law and Practice for Social Workers*, London, Butterworths.

Gostin, L. (1983) *A Practical Guide to Mental Health Law*, London, MIND.

Russell, P. (1986) 'The Mental Health Act, 1983: a summary', *Highlight*, 73, London, National Children's Bureau.

mental illness, legally, one of the four categories of mental disorder specified in the Mental Health Act 1983, though not defined there. In effect it can be argued that it is defined by exclusion, a mental disorder which is neither one of the two levels of mental impairment nor a psychopathic disorder.

Medically, mental illness refers to any psychiatric disorder. It differs from mental handicap in that it usually has a recognisable time of onset, which can be sudden, and is usually temporary, for it can be cured or alleviated by treatment. Conversely, mental handicap is usually considered a permanent disability, often present at birth.

Mental illnesses fall into two main groups, the psychoses and the neuroses. Both cause difficulties in social adaptation, particularly evident in the problems sufferers have in their personal relationships. Psychoses (e.g. schizophrenia, paranoia) are less common and more serious, whereas neuroses (e.g. anxiety neurosis, obsessions) are more common and less serious.

With the current emphasis on describing behaviour, rather than labelling a condition, the term 'mental illness' has fallen somewhat out of favour. Although drugs are often used to treat some of these conditions, many are seen as reactions to social stresses, rather than as medical conditions, and the central role of the medical profession in their management is being increasingly challenged.

See *medical model.*

Reference:

Hargreaves, D. (1978) 'Deviance, the Interactionist Approach', in Gillham, B. (1978) *Reconstructing Educational Psychology*, London, Croom Helm.

mental impairment, one of the four categories of mental disorder specified in the *Mental Health Act 1983*. In this Act, mental impairment is defined as 'a state of arrested or incomplete development of mind (not amounting to severe impairment) which includes significant impairment of intelligence and social functioning and is associated with abnormally aggressive or seriously irresponsible conduct on the part of the person concerned'. Severe mental impairment is defined in the same terms, 'severe impairment' being substituted for 'significant impairment'.

An application for admission to hospital for treatment can be made voluntarily, or by the person's nearest relative, or by an approved social worker. It must be supported by two medical recommendations in the prescribed form. Note that the Act uses 'mental impairment' as a replacement for the term 'subnormality'. To this extent the Mental Health Act parallels the Education Act 1981, which similarly removed the term educationally subnormal from the statute book.

See *mental handicap, mental retardation.*

Reference:

Gostin, L. (1983) *A Practical Guide to Mental Health Law*, London, MIND.

mental retardation, the USA equivalent of *mental handicap.* It is defined by the American Association on Mental Deficiency thus: 'Mental retardation refers to significantly sub-average general intellectual functioning existing concurrently with deficits in adaptive behaviour, and manifested during the developmental period.'

Note that the definition is based on both intellectual and behavioural considerations, i.e. the condition is not defined by performance on intelligence tests alone.

In the definition, 'significantly sub-average intellectual functioning' refers to a score of IQ 70 or below on an individually administered general intelligence test; 'adaptive behaviour' refers to the effectiveness with which individuals meet the standards of independence and responsibility appropriate to their age and culture; 'developmental period' refers to the period from birth to eighteen years of age.

Prevalence figures for mental retardation vary according to the survey methods used, as well as by age and social group. For example, prevalence climbs during the school years, as the greater intellectual and social demands of school activities set standards of adaptive behaviour which some find it increasingly difficult to meet. Prevalence rates between 1 and 3% have been quoted, with boys generally outnumbering girls by two to one.

There is no single cause. Genetic abnormalities, perinatal damage, limited environmental stimulation – one or all of these and other factors may be responsible. The main point for educators is that the poorer the previous environment, the more likely it is that a rich educational experience will bring improvement: where a child has been damaged biologically the challenge for the educator is correspondingly harder.

Two separate classification systems for mental retardation have evolved. The medical/psychological system offers four subgroups, mild, moderate,

Mental retardation classification in the USA

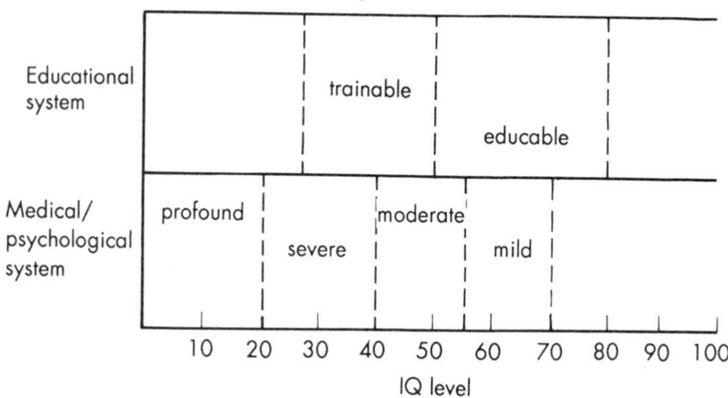

Note that IQ levels are used as guides only

severe and profound mental retardation, differentiated by IQ levels. The educational system offers two subgroups, educable mental retardation and trainable mental retardation, roughly equivalent to moderate and severe learning difficulties as used in England and Wales. Note that the use of trainable as opposed to educable does not mean exclusion from the public school system.

See diagram. See *custodial mentally retarded.*

References:

Grossman, H. (Ed.) (1983) *Classification in Mental Retardation,* Washington, American Association on Mental Deficiency.

Hallahan, D.P. and Kaufman, J.M. (1988, 4th edn.) *Exceptional Children: Introduction to Special Education,* Englewood Cliffs, Prentice Hall.

Merrill-Palmer Preschool Performance Scale, an individual test of verbal and non-verbal (but predominantly non-verbal) performance in children aged from eighteen months to just over five years. It provides mental ages which can be converted to ratio IQs and percentile ranks.

The Merrill-Palmer is one of the earliest tests designed for young children, having been used for over half a century. The materials are still attractive and children find the tasks enjoyable. One of its useful attributes is the ability to take account of refused or omitted items in arriving at a final score. It is sometimes used with older children with severe learning difficulties, where the test performance can, with careful interpretation, provide helpful information.

Reference:

Hogg, J. and Raynes, N.V. (Eds.) (1987) *Assessment in Mental Handicap,* Beckenham, Croom Helm.

MESU, Microelectronics Educational Support Unit, see *National Council for Educational Technology.*

metabolic disorders, result from malfunctioning of some of the biochemical processes which enable the body to break down nutrients and use them in different ways for growth, energy, etc. Metabolic disorders are often genetically-determined deficiencies in essential enzymes. An example is phenylketuria, PKU, in which the enzyme which converts the aminoacid phenylalanine into harmless products is absent. Unless identified and treated with an appropriate diet, the resulting high concentrations of phenylalanine cause damage to the brain, leading to severe mental handicap.

PKU is one example of many metabolic disorders of concern to special educators. Not all result in intellectual damage. Cystic fibrosis and diabetes are examples of metabolic disorders which have no intellectual implications but which can cause stresses on children's education for other reasons.

metacognitive skills, knowledge of one's own cognitive processes: for example the ability to 'stand back' and observe how much better one learns one activity than another. This feedback may enable more productive learning to take place.

There is evidence that children with learning difficulties are deficient in metacognitive skills and find difficulty in applying them. Programmes designed to offer training in metacognition are said to have made significant improvements in children's learning.

Reference:

Hallahan, D.P. and Kaufman, J.M. (1988, 4th edn.) *Exceptional Children: Introduction to Special Education,* Englewood Cliffs, Prentice Hall.

microcephaly, congenital abnormality, characterised by an exceptionally small head and underdeveloped brain, usually resulting in severe learning difficulties. In some cases the condition is hereditary, but in others environmental factors, e.g. rubella in pregnancy are responsible.

Children with microcephaly are found in special care units for children who are profoundly handicapped, where microcephaly is one of the more frequent causes of handicap.

See *special care provision.*

References:

Evans, P. and Ware, J. (1987) *Special Care Provision,* Windsor, NFER-Nelson.

Robinson, H.B. and Robinson, N.M (1965) *The Mentally Retarded Child: a Psychological Approach,* New York, McGraw-Hill.

Microelectronics Educational Support Unit (MESU), see *National Council for Educational Technology.*

middle ear, see *ear, otitis media.*

mild mental retardation, see *mental retardation.*

milieu therapy, involves all aspects of a child's environment, treatment and social experiences alike, in an attempt to effect behaviour change. Milieu therapy was used originally in hospital and other residential settings, but has been developed as a method of intervention in schools and classrooms. This may involve manipulating the school organisation and the social structure, and perhaps altering activities of family members, so that the whole social experience is geared towards modifying behaviour in the required direction.

Some regard milieu therapy as a psychoanalytic strategy, while others see it as an ecological or environmental strategy. The implication is that, for milieu therapy, the philosophy of treatment is less important than the determination to maximise the opportunities to modify behaviour that can be provided by any setting.

Mills v. Board of Education of the District of Columbia, landmark USA law suit brought on behalf of seven Washington children who had been excluded from school and were receiving no education. The court ruled that the Board of Education had to provide education for exceptional children – i.e. children with special needs – even though it pleaded shortage of funds. In effect this case established the constitutional right of all children to a public – i.e. state – education.

Reference:

Stephens, T.M., Blackhurst, A.E. and Magliocca, L.A. (1982) *Teaching Mainstreamed Students*, New York, Wiley.

Milwaukee Project, important but highly controversial investigation into the effects of early intervention on the intellectual development of deprived children. In 1965, forty children from Milwaukee families were chosen on deprivation indices such as poverty, poor housing, limited maternal intelligence, etc., and randomly assigned to either an experimental or a control group. The experimental children were given extensive stimulation, first in their own homes, from the age of a few months, and then in small nursery groups by project members. Their mothers were also involved in an education programme.

While both groups were shown to have similar IQ levels at the start of the experiment, they showed an increasing divergence (in favour of the experimental group) as the project progressed. By the time the children entered school, a mean IQ difference of 30 points was reported, the control group in the low average range, the experimental group in the superior range. The difference seemed to be sustained during the early years at school, when the experimental intervention had ceased.

These results were given great international prominence, for the experiment met the (expensive) criteria said to be needed for countering poor environment, namely extensive and regular intervention from infancy, based on a one-to-one child–adult relationship, sustained over the pre-school years and supported by work with the parent(s). Not only did the experiment meet these criteria: a growth of 30 IQ points amply demonstrated in practice the soundness of the theorists' arguments. The environmentalists' position on intellectual growth seemed to be confirmed.

But the investigators were unable to publish accounts of the project in detail sufficient to satisfy critics. There was a subsequent financial scandal which cast a cloud over the project and its findings, which have remained controversial. But it is nevertheless interesting to note that the main parallel investigation, the *Abecedarian Project,* has emerged with similar, if somewhat less remarkable, results.

See *compensatory education.*

References:

Garber, H. (1988) *The Milwaukee Project,* Washington, American Association on Mental Retardation.

Page, E.B. and Grandon, G.M. (1981) 'Massive Intervention and Child Intelligence: the Milwaukee Project in Critical Perspective', *Journal of Special Education,* 15, 2, 239–56.

minimal brain damage (mbd), see *brain damage.*

minimal cerebral dysfunction (mcd), see *brain damage.*

mirror writing, true mirror writing is the reflection of normal writing and can be read by holding it up to a mirror. A single letter formed in this way, e.g. writing 'b' for 'd', is called a *reversal.* Sometimes transpositions, such as writing 'was' for 'saw' are called examples of mirror writing, but this is incorrect.

There are many explanations of mirror writing. Some are neurological, one view being that the centres for motor and visual control may be functioning independently. Orton argued that if the 'writing centre' was located in a different hemisphere from that from which its visual cues were received, mirror writing would result: this view is based on the belief that there are two images of objects in the brain, one in each hemisphere, each the mirror image of the other.

Another view invokes laterality, arguing that our natural movements are from the midline of the body outwards, i.e. our right hand moves naturally towards the right and our left hand to the left. Since English writing involves movement to the right, natural lefthanders (perhaps even if writing with the right hand), may revert to their more natural movement flow and produce mirror writing.

Many children reverse individual letters when they learn to write, and a small proportion (an early investigation found one in 500), mostly lefthanders, produce full mirror writing, which with good teaching soon disappears. The key to preventing it becoming a habit is to ensure that the mirror writer always starts at the lefthand side of the page, perhaps indicating the start with a mark. Mirror writing is not a problem unless it persists for a few years after writing instruction has started.

See *dyslexia*.

References:

Burt, C. (1950, 3rd edn.) *The Backward Child*, London, University of London Press.

Clarke, M.M. (1974) *Teaching Left-handed Children*, London, Hodder and Stoughton.

Young, P. and Tyre, C. (1983) *Dyslexia or Illiteracy?* Milton Keynes, Open University Press.

miscue analysis, method of assessing children's oral reading. Miscue analysis was developed by Goodman, who argued that the ways in which children's reading deviated from text should not be regarded as errors, but rather as miscues, offering clues to the strategies adopted for extracting – or constructing – meaning from print and hence providing valuable diagnostic information to teachers. 'Oral reading miscues are the windows on the reading process at work.'

Goodman's original system classified miscues into a number of categories, such as substitutions, omissions, additions, refusals, reversals, etc. Substitutions were further classified as: graphophonemic, the substitution having a similar sound to the original word; syntactic, the substitution making grammatical sense; semantic, the substitution making contextual sense. Simpler systems of miscue analysis have since been developed, and teachers can devise their own.

Teacher asks the child to read a passage of about 200 to 300 words. This should be sufficiently difficult (instructional level) to generate a reasonable number of miscues, but not too difficult (frustration level). The miscues are recorded, usually as the child reads, or later if the reading is tape-recorded. Interpreting the miscues enables teacher to help the child adjust to a more effective reading strategy. For example, omissions may suggest a problem with speed of reading, semantic substitutions may suggest insufficient attention paid to the phonic structure of the word, and so on.

Note that miscue analysis emphasises diagnosis, and offers a quite different approach from that underpinning most standardised tests of reading. It differs, too, from older diagnostic techniques, which often assessed psychological qualities such as visual or auditory memory. Its strength is that it starts from the reading process itself. But it is limited to oral reading, and makes no claim to assess other, perhaps more important aspects of reading, most obviously comprehension.

See *informal reading inventory*.

References:

Goodman, K.S. and Goodman, Y.M. (1977) 'Learning about Psycholinguistic Processes by Analyzing Oral Reading', *Harvard Educational Review*, 47, 3, 317–32, in Chapman, L.J. and Czerniewska, P. (Eds.) (1977) *Reading: from Process to Practice*, Milton Keynes, Open University Press.

Gulliford, R. (1985) *Teaching Children with Learning Difficulties*, Windsor, NFER-Nelson.

Pumfrey, P.D., (1985, 2nd edn.) *Reading Tests and Assessment Procedures*, Sevenoaks, Hodder and Stoughton.

mixed ability grouping, see *ability grouping.*

mixed dominance, preferred side of the body not always the same; for example a child may prefer to use the right hand, but the left foot and left ear. The term is sometimes used as an alternative to *crossed laterality,* though the latter is nearly always applied to the particular example of mixed dominance in which the preferred hand and eye are on opposite sides of the body. Early suggestions that mixed dominance might be responsible for some learning difficulties have now been discarded. What does appear significant is unresolved dominance/laterality, when through lack of instruction or maturity, directional skills have not become automatised and pupils have no preferred hand/eye/ear for specific tasks.

MLE, see *mediated learning experience.*

MLU, see *mean length of utterance.*

mobility allowance, cash allowance for disabled people who are unable or virtually unable to walk and are likely to remain so for at least a year. It is payable to people aged between five and sixty-five years of age.

Mobility allowance replaces and extends the help previously available under the invalid vehicle scheme. It is intended to help with extra transport costs, but may be spent otherwise. It is payable whether the person is living at home or in an institution such as a hospital or special school. The rules governing payment are published by the Department of Social Security.

Reference:

Department of Health and Social Security (1985, revised) *Non-contributory Benefits for Disabled People,* London, HMSO.

mobility training, training in posture, orientation, locomotion and navigation for the visually impaired. These are skills which sighted people virtually take for granted, but which form a significant part of the curriculum for children who are visually impaired. Mobility confers independence, and the ability to move safely and confidently from one place to another is an essential skill to acquire.

From an early age, no opportunity to give informal mobility training should be lost. For example, children should be encouraged to move about the home independently, and helped to explore the world outside: positional terms such as 'in front', 'side by side', will need extra explanation – and so on. Later, formal mobility training in the use of the Hoover cane will be given, though there is debate about the age at which formal training is best started. In special schools for the blind there is a mobility officer, who can provide such training. Guide dogs are not available until schooldays are over.

References:

Chapman, E.K. and Stone, J.M. (1988) *The Visually Handicapped Child in Your Classroom*, London, Cassell.

Corley, G., Robinson, D. and Lockett, S. (1989) *Partially Sighted Children*, Windsor, NFER-Nelson.

Dodds, A. (1986) 'Visual Handicap', in Gillham, B. (Ed.) (1986) *Handicapping Conditions in Children*, Beckenham, Croom Helm.

modality, any one of the sensory systems for receiving, processing and responding to sensation, e.g. vision, touch, etc.

mode, measure of central tendency of a set of scores. The mode is the most frequently occurring measurement. In the normal distributions to which most tests are standardised, the *mean, median* and *mode* will be set at the same value, usually 100.

modelling, see *behaviour modelling.*

moderate mental retardation, see *mental retardation.*

modification (of National Curriculum), see *disapplication.*

monoplegia, see *cerebral palsy.*

monosomy, occurs where a single chromosome replaces the usual pair. *Turner's syndrome,* in which typically one X (female) chromosome is absent, is an example. Chromosome abnormalities as serious as this usually lead to mental and physical impairments. Thus individuals with Turner's syndrome typically show mild learning difficulties and reduced height, among other characteristics. Compare *trisomy.*

Mooney Problem Check List, US personality inventory for self-completion. There are four forms available, intended for junior high school, high school, college and adults. The problems listed are subdivided into areas, e.g. problems at school, personal problems, health and personal development, etc., which vary somewhat according to the form.

The Mooney Check List has proved valuable for counselling in particular, where pupils who cannot readily articulate their worries in an interview situation may find checking a statement easier. Analysis of the number of problems checked (about 10% of the total problems listed is said to be a reasonable expectation) and of the areas in which they fall gives a basis for starting a counselling interview.

The Mooney is an old test, which omits some of the problems concerning young people today (e.g. drugs; alcohol). There are few psychometric data provided, though face validity is clearly present. It also contains a number of Americanisms, and the ability to read the items is needed if it is to be used in group form.

See *Lewis Counselling Inventory*.

References:
Anastasi, A. (1982, 5th edn.) *Psychological Testing*, New York, Macmillan.
Levy, P. and Goldstein, H. (Eds.) (1985) *Tests in Education*, London, Academic Press.

morpheme, the smallest unit of language which has a grammatical function; e.g. the two morphemes 'girl' and 's' in the word 'girls'; the three morphemes 'look', 'ing' and 'ed' in the words 'looking' and 'looked'. Morphemes carry meaning, and are thus distinct from phonemes and graphemes, which represent sound only. The importance of prefixes (e.g. dis-, un-, im-, etc.) and suffixes (e.g. -able, -ly, -ology, etc.), which are also morphemes, is often overlooked, but these units of language are semantically consistent, always mean the same and, once known, aid the reader to gain more meaning from print and facilitate fluency.

mosaicism, presence in a single person of two or more (often three) kinds of cells with different chromosomal counts. A cell may divide atypically at an early stage of an embryo's development, perhaps giving rise to two cell populations. The best known example is in *Down's syndrome*, where most Down's children show trisomy 21, i.e. a faulty chromosome pattern for all cells was laid down at conception. In a few individuals, about 1%, a trisomy 21 population of cells is formed at a later stage, so that the child has the Down's pattern of chromosomes coexisting with a normal pattern.

This means that the Down's features are less prominent: learning difficulties are less marked and physical characteristics not so obvious. The principle that individuals with mosaicism are more 'normal' than those who show a typical chromosome abnormality makes sense, and applies generally. It emphasises the need to treat children whose condition is due to a chromosome abnormality as individuals, rather than stereotyping them.

See *chromosome*.

Reference:
Connor, M. (1989) *The Causes and Prevention of Handicap*, Stratford-upon-Avon, National Council for Special Education.

motor aphasia, inability to speak sensibly, due to injury to Broca's area, which coordinates and controls movements of the face and mouth. The words may be known and communication by gesture may be entirely practicable, but normal speech is not. There is no single accepted classification of the aphasias: motor aphasia is also an example of an expressive aphasia.

See *aphasia, expressive language disorder*.

Reference:
Crystal, D. (1988, 2nd edn.) *Introduction to Language Pathology*, London, Cole and Whurr.

motor impairment, inability to demonstrate the motor skills commensurate with age. Motor development is usually divided into the growth of gross motor skills and fine motor skills. These are often considered to proceed through a sequence of well-recognised milestones, though there are dangers in thinking of highly complex patterns in this way. Gross motor development includes such skills as sitting, standing, walking, etc., in young children, later running, skipping. riding, etc. The skills of fine motor development are equally important though not usually so well-recognised. They include such activities as holding a crayon, cutting with scissors, threading, buttoning and unbuttoning, tying knots, etc.

Motor development can be assessed by standardised tests, e.g. the *Bruininks-Oseretsky Test*. Children whose motor development is impaired may not only need physiotherapy; they may also have learning difficulties. This is most clearly seen in the case of individuals with cerebral palsy: the same neurological damage that causes the physical condition may also cause some mental handicap, and the damage may affect language and extend to the senses. Moreover the motor impairment itself may impose restrictions on a child – difficulties in gaining tactile experience through limited mobility, difficulties in gaining spatial experience through limited manipulation of objects, etc. – which may themselves place additional constraints on the development of full intellectual powers.

The same principles which lead to children with cerebral palsy having special educational needs may also apply to children with less obvious motor impairment. There is evidence that clumsy children show greater difficulties with reading, and there is some evidence that these difficulties may extend to other learning tasks. These findings have not always been replicated, however.

Some believe that good motor development is the foundation for successful learning and remedial programmes have been designed on these lines.

See *conductive education*.

References:

Bobath, B. and Bobath, K. (1975) *Motor Development in the Different Types of Cerebral Palsy*, London, Heinemann.

Tansley, P. and Panckhurst, J. (1981) *Children with Specific Learning Difficulties: a Critical Review of Research*, Windsor, NFER-Nelson.

Webster, A. and McConnell, C. (1987) *Children with Speech and Language Difficulties*, London, Cassell.

movement therapy, sometimes motor therapy, improving motor skills through creative activities such as dance and physical education exercises. This has two main aims. The skills gained assist in the development of confidence, and the opportunity for release of energy and tension can be therapeutic.

The first aim is valuable for all children, but particularly so for those whose opportunities for play and for learning physical skills have been restricted, for whatever reason. Children with physical and sensory handicaps are helped by exercises designed to improve body awareness and self-image: these help academically, too, by bringing extra understanding to positional concepts such as 'above', 'behind', etc.

The second, therapeutic aim, is partly derived from the psychoanalytic belief in the importance of expressing emotions. For those children who find expression through speech difficult, expression through body activities is one of a number of different routes to releasing feelings (creative art is of course another). For this reason creative dance is sometimes used as a therapy for children with emotional and behavioural difficulties.

References:

Sanderson, P. (1988) 'Physical Education and Dance', in Roberts, T. (Ed.) (1988) *Encouraging Expression: Arts in the Primary Curriculum*, London, Cassell.

Upton, G. (Ed.) (1979) *Physical and Creative Activities for the Mentally Handicapped*, Cambridge, Cambridge University Press.

msd, multisensory deprivation, see *dual sensory impairment.*

mucopolysaccharidoses, group of inherited metabolic disorders, characterised biochemically by an inability to control carbohydrate balance, due to an enzyme abnormality. Hurler's disease is an example.

The mucopolysaccharidoses are nearly all associated with mental retardation, behavioural difficulties and physical impairments. Life expectancy is reduced. Children suffering from them are typically educated in special care units; where schools with special care units do not exist they may well be found in the main stream of the special school.

See *special care provision.*

References:

Evans, P. and Ware, J. (1987) *Special Care Provision*, Windsor, NFER-Nelson.

Graham, P.J. (1986) *Child Psychiatry: a Developmental Approach*, Oxford, Oxford University Press.

multibase apparatus, see *structural apparatus.*

multidisciplinary team, group of professionals meeting, sometimes with parents, to assess and follow up children with special needs. It is based on the principle of interprofessional collaboration, which has underpinned the theory – if not always the practice – of work in special education for many years. Membership varies according to the child's needs, but usually includes a medical consultant (paediatrician or child psychiatrist), educational psychologist and social worker, though contributions from disciplines such as teacher or therapist are equally important.

There are undoubted advantages in teamwork, but there are economic drawbacks in bringing together a group of often highly-paid specialists. Such an approach can only be used for the more serious special needs. The criticism levelled against the unthinking use of *child guidance* teams to treat widely-occurring problems is a case in point. At the same time it is interesting to note that the supporters of *conductive education* have adopted a different strategy, preferring to combine the roles of several different specialists in one person, arguing that this makes treatment more consistent and less confusing for the child and family.

In short, multidisciplinary teams are most effective when employed judiciously.

See *Community Mental Handicap Team, District Handicap Team.*

Reference:

Fish, J. (1985) *Special Education: the Way Ahead,* Milton Keynes, Open University Press. (Ref. under professionals; relationships between.)

multiple baseline design, experimental design used in some behaviour modification procedures when the authenticity of the effect of the intervention cannot be satisfactorily demonstrated. Since an AB design is inherently weak logically (any effects might have been due to contemporary chance factors, rather than the intervention itself), this is usually replaced by the logically more satisfactory ABAB design. However, there are circumstances in which a behaviour, once removed, is difficult to reinstate, i.e. reverting to the A phase has little meaning. For example, intervention may have succeeded in eliminating a child's mathematical

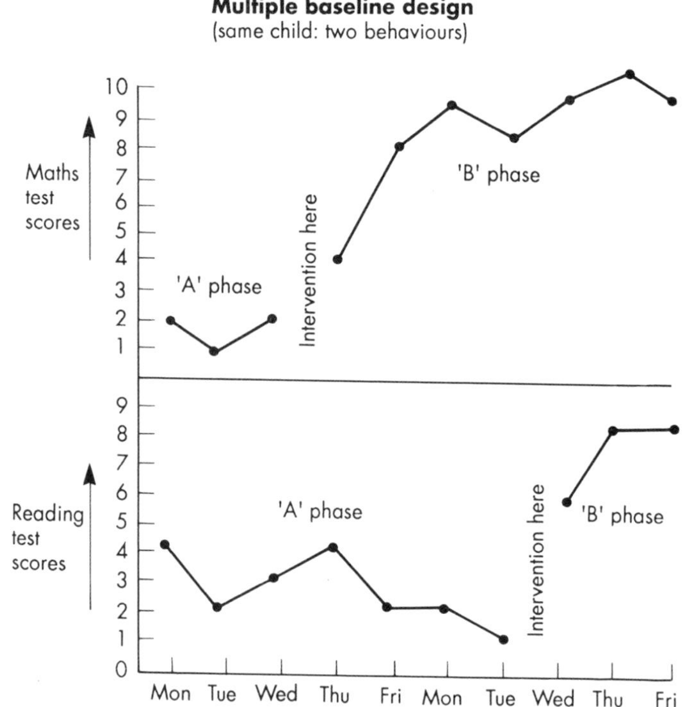

errors. Removing the modification procedure is unlikely to result in the maths errors, once overcome, returning: we cannot conclude that the intervention alone has necessarily been successful.

This logical weakness can be overcome by using the same intervention for another behaviour in the same child. If the intervention is again successful, we are on firmer ground in attributing behaviour change to it. Effectively, two (or more) sets of base-line data are gathered simultaneously, one for each behaviour. Intervention is then instituted for one, and data gathering continues for all. After criterion has been reached for the first behaviour, intervention is applied to the others in sequence. Examination of the graphed results enables a judgement to be made on the effectiveness of the intervention.

Alternative procedures involve using the same intervention with the same behaviour in the same setting on two (or more) children, or the same intervention on the same behaviour with the same child in two (or more) different settings – though data gathering in this last example cannot be simultaneous.

The effect of these designs is to provide better control of the experimental variables through repetition under as similar a set of conditions as possible, so strengthening the logic of the enquiry.

See *AB design.*

Reference:

Alberto, P.A. and Troutman, A.C. (1986, 2nd edn.) *Applied Behaviour Analysis for Teachers,* Columbus, Merrill.

multiple intelligence, see *intelligence.*

multiple sclerosis (ms), disease of the central nervous system, which damages and scars the sheaths surrounding the nerve fibres, so impairing control of the muscles. As well as muscular weakness, symptoms include visual disturbance, dizziness and balance problems, speech difficulties, tremors, etc.

Although ms is progressive, long periods of remission may alternate with episodes of symptoms. It affects older adolescents and young adults, and hence is rarely seen in children of school age, though it sometimes starts during college years. There are no learning difficulties specific to the condition as such, though sufferers can be helped considerably by counselling. The Petö Institute in Budapest has used *conductive education* to attempt to ameliorate the problems associated with ms.

Reference:

Russell, P. (1984, 2nd edn.) *The Wheelchair Child,* London, Souvenir Press.

multisensory deprivation (msd), see *dual sensory impairment.*

multisensory method, see *Fernald method.*

muscular dystrophy, group of progressive diseases characterised by muscular weakness. The most frequent and also the most severe form is Duchenne's muscular dystrophy, a sex-linked hereditary form, which affects males only, but is carried by females. Although the condition is present at birth it is not usually noticed until the child is at least two years old or more. The first signs appear as weakness in the leg and pelvic muscles, spreading then to the rest of the body. It is primarily the voluntary striped muscles (biceps, calf, thigh, etc.) which degenerate and are replaced by fibrous tissue and fat.

Most children with this condition need a wheelchair by the age of ten years or so, and usually die from heart failure or lung infection in late adolescence or early adulthood.

Female carriers can be identified by blood tests, and *genetic counselling* helps parents and prospective parents. The disease is managed by physiotherapy and regular exercise, especially swimming: occupational therapists can advise on home arrangements, and many families find counselling helpful with the strain of coping with a progressively more severely-handicapped child at home.

Nearly all muscular dystrophy children attend the early stages of school normally, and teachers should be familiar with any special equipment that the child may need, for example braces, standing tables, etc. As the disease progresses, the advisability of a special class or school usually has to be considered, and eventually education is continued at home or in hospital. Most children show mild learning difficulties, not related to the degree of physical handicap, and there is some evidence that verbal abilities are more affected than performance abilities. But it may be more important for their learning to be pleasurable rather than efficient, and lengthy educational and psychological assessments, which may be frustrating, should be avoided. The central point is that health is deteriorating, and help and encouragement are important. There may be emotional problems, too, for which teachers should be prepared.

References:

Brain, W.R. (1977, 8th edn.) *Diseases of the Central Nervous System*, Oxford, Oxford University Press.

Dinnage, R. (1985) *The Orthopaedically Handicapped Child*, Windsor, NFER-Nelson.

Russell, P. (1984, 2nd edn.) *The Wheelchair Child*, London, Souvenir Press.

music therapy, the use of music in the treatment of children with special needs. Music teaching can be adapted to enable children with special needs to benefit; for example instruments can be modified so that children with physical impairments can make music to the satisfaction of all – and indeed there are many examples of outstanding musicians with disabilities of various kinds. But music therapy, the deliberate use of music to promote emotional adjustment and to improve other skills is a different activity, one with a clinical perspective.

Music offers a means of engaging the interest of children with whom normal communication is impossible: its melodies and harmonies can quieten and relieve emotional tensions. Making one's own music is an act of creative expression which can be as effective as expression through the visual and movement arts in releasing feelings and helping children's emotional and behavioural difficulties.

References:

Eisler, J. (1990) 'Creative Music Therapy for the Mentally Handicapped or Emotionally Disturbed Child', in Segal, S. (Ed.) (1990) *Creative Arts and Mental Disability*, Bicester, AB Academic Publishers.

Hunt, A. (1979) 'Music', in Upton, G. (Ed.) (1979) *Physical and Creative Activities for the Mentally Handicapped*, Cambridge, Cambridge University Press.

Nordhoff, P. and Robbins, C. (1971) *Therapy in Music for Handicapped Children*, London, Gollancz.

Turnbull, J. (1988) 'Music', in Roberts, T. (Ed.) (1988) *Encouraging Expression: Arts in the Primary Curriculum*, London, Cassell.

mutism, literally absence of speech. There are several possible reasons for this condition. Profound deafness is one; severe mental retardation is another. But the most likely cause in children in the ordinary school is psychological, relatively easily distinguished from physical causes.

See *elective mutism.*

myelomeningocele, one of the more common and more severe forms of *spina bifida.* The developing neural tube fails to close, and the child is born with part of the spinal cord and its membranes protruding from the back in a sac-like bulge, the myelomeningocele. This can be repaired by surgery, but the child is likely to be incontinent. There may be other damage, depending on the site of the myelominingocele, and hydrocephalus may be an associated condition.

myopia, or shortsightedness, occurs when light is brought to a focus before the retina, resulting in blurred distance vision. It is often due to an unusually long eyeball. This can be corrected with concave lenses, but these have to be changed as the child grows.

For a small number of children with a more serious condition known as high myopia, abnormal eyeball growth stretches the retina, leading to the risk of retinal damage in vigorous activity. For this reason, medical advice about physical education, games, etc., should be sought.

See *eye;* contrast *hypermetropia.*

Reference:
Fitt, R. and Mason, H. (1986) *Sensory Handicaps in Children,* Stratford-upon-Avon, National Council for Special Education.

N

NAI, non-accidental injury, see *child abuse.*

named person, role proposed in the Warnock Report for an individual who could serve as a guide to parents of children with special educational needs. Research for the Warnock Committee highlighted the confusion felt by many parents in trying to make best use of the various services provided and the many different persons involved. The named person was intended to be the link between the family and this plethora of professionals, perhaps accompanying parents to interviews, perhaps visiting them to ensure that procedures were understood, suggesting what help and advice could be gained and where to get it.

In the event the named person as such did not appear in the Education Act 1981. It may well be that the voluntary societies, with the interests of the child their central concern, will take on the activities for which the named person was originally proposed.

Note that the Education (Scotland) Act 1981 does refer to a Named Person to advise and support parents, and states the arrangements for making the appointment.

References:
Adams, F. (Ed.) (1986) *Special Education,* London, Councils and Education Press for Longmans.
Department of Education and Science (1978) *Special Educational Needs,* London, HMSO (The Warnock Report).

National Child Development Study (NCDS), the second major longitudinal study of child development in the UK, which monitored the growth of virtually all the 17,000 children born in the first full week of March, 1958. The first data collection examined the operation of the maternity services, while follow-ups during the school period at ages seven, eleven and sixteen examined social and educational characteristics, including tests of reading and mathematics and teachers' estimates of behaviour. The findings, including post-school studies, provide a mine of data, much of which has relevance for special education.

For example, at sixteen years of age, just under 2% of the cohort were in special schools, while of those in the ordinary schools, 7% were receiving special help for learning difficulties, 5% for behavioural difficulties and 1% for physical or sensory disabilities. In addition, teachers estimated that another 5–6% needed special help. This total of approximately 20% is close to the Warnock estimate of one in six pupils needing special help at any one time.

Other data shed light on the relationship between home circumstances and learning, and how this effect changes over the years. The incidence of maladjustment and unsettled behaviour was studied, using a teacher-rated behavioural questionnaire. Some special subgroups were picked out for extra study; for example children living in one-parent families were studied when they were fourteen years old; samples of the children who had been receiving or in need of special help in school were followed up when they were eighteen years of age in order to look at their employment situation; at twenty-three years of age, 13% considered that they had difficulties with reading, writing or number work in their everyday lives.

While longitudinal studies of whole populations provide complete or nearly complete (a few children were not traced at follow-up, in spite of strenuous efforts) pictures of child development, large cohorts have disadvantages. Thus their very size means that data collection usually has to be restricted to questionnaire and other data that can be readily gathered by personnel in the course of their daily tasks: detailed assessment by specially-employed personnel has to be excluded on grounds of cost. They provide good broad-brush pictures: the detail requires finer-grained, smaller enquiries.

See *Child Health and Education Study, National Survey of Health and Development of Children.*

References:

Essen, J. and Wedge, P. (1982) *Continuities in Childhood Disadvantage*, London, Heinemann.

Fogelman, K. (Ed.) (1976) *Britain's Sixteen-Year-Olds*, London, National Children's Bureau.

Hamilton, M. (1987) 'Literacy, Numeracy and Adults. Evidence from the National Child Development Study', London, ALBSU; quoted in Entwistle, N. (Ed.) (1987) *Handbook of Educational Ideas and Practices*, London, Routledge.

Walker, A. (1982) *Unqualified and Underemployed*, London, National Children's Bureau.

National Council for Educational Technology (NCET), was formed in 1988 when the Council for Educational Technology amalgamated with the Microelectronics Educational Support Unit (MESU). As part of its general aim to develop the use of Information Technology in schools, NCET has carried forward MESU's responsibilities in special education, which included coordinating the work of the *Aids for Communication in Education Centre* (*ACE*) and of the Special Education Microelectronic Resource Centres (SEMERCS). Since central funding for the SEMERCS ceased, NCET has coordinated the development of a regional network of new centres.

The use of microelectronics in special education has been mainly geared towards improving access to the curriculum for children with special needs, perhaps most particularly for children with severe physical and communication difficulties. NCET disseminates information, develops curriculum materials and funds projects. The opportunities that microelectronics offers for broadening the curriculum have yet to be fully exploited, but the field is developing very rapidly.

References:

Brennan, W. (1985) *Curriculum for Special Needs*, Milton Keynes, Open University Press.

Fowler, P. (1989) 'A New IT network for Special Education', *British Journal of Special Education*, 16, 4, 148.

Hope, M.H. (1987) *Micros for Children with Special Needs*, Souvenir, London.

National Curriculum, was imposed by the Education Act, 1988. It aims to:

(1) promote the spiritual, moral, cultural, mental and physical development of pupils at school and of society; and

(2) prepare such pupils for the opportunities, responsibilities and experiences of adult life.

To meet these aims, the curriculum in maintained schools (private schools are exempted) must comprise a basic curriculum, including Religious Education, three core foundation subjects, English, Mathematics and Science, and other foundation subjects, History, Geography, Technology, Music, Art and Physical Education. These are to be available at all stages, and another foundation subject, a modern language, at key stages three and four, i.e. approximating the secondary school years. For each subject, ten levels (i.e. a ten-point attainment scale) are to be specified, and targets set for each of four key stages, viz. ages 5–7; 7–11; 11–14; and 14–16.

The legislation dealing with the National Curriculum, while not prescribing teaching methods and materials, does give central government through the Secretary of State for Education and Science, new powers in determining what shall be taught, to whom, and at what level. These affect pupils with special needs in several ways. First, it is the intention that the curriculum shall be available to all pupils. There are some worries here that the intended publication of attainments, aggregated by school, may lead to pressure for exempting children with special needs from some or all of the curriculum, under the arrangements noted below.

Second, although the National Curriculum applies to all pupils, there are flexible arrangements for it to be modified or disapplied – at present for individual pupils. A statement of special educational needs can specify changes which would be in the interests of the pupil – the parents' rights of appeal under the Education Act 1981 still stand, of course. Head teachers can also lift or modify the national curriculum for individual pupils, up to a maximum period to be set out in regulations, but not longer than six months initially. This provision can be used where the school believes that a child needs a statement of special needs and is waiting for the local education authority's assessment procedures.

Third and less importantly, the phasing in of the National Curriculum, which began in the Autumn term, 1989, may be delayed for a year for statemented pupils.

These are substantial changes; their effects will not be fully appreciated for some years and not until some time has passed will it be possible to assess their full significance for pupils with special needs. Initial concern at lack of awareness of the possible implications for special education has been allayed to some extent. Official publications now reiterate the importance of access to the National Curriculum for all pupils, and the first documents produced by subject working groups show a clear awareness of this principle.

See *assessment, curriculum, disapplication.*

References:

Department of Education and Science (1989) *Circular 5/89, Education Reform Act 1988: The School Curriculum and Assessment*, London, Department of Education and Science.

Department of Education and Science (1989) *Circular 22/89, Assessments and Statements of Special Educational Needs: Procedures within the Education, Health and Social Services*, London, Department of Education and Science.

Department of Education and Science (1989) *National Curriculum: From Policy to Practice*, London, HMSO.

National Curriculum Council (1989) *Two: A Curriculum for All. Special Educational Needs in the National Curriculum*, York, National Curriculum Council.

Wedell, K. (1988) 'The National Curriculum and Special Educational Needs', in Lawton, D. and Chitty, C. (Eds.) (1988) *The National Curriculum*, London, University of London Institute of Education.

National Foundation for Educational Research in England and Wales (NFER), conducts research into educational issues. It is funded by contributions from local education authorities, which support a small permanent staff, but most of its income derives from other activities. These include research projects commissioned by various bodies, including the Department of Education and Science, the sale of books and other publications and the construction and sale of educational and psychological tests, for which its test agency is the main UK supplier.

A substantial proportion of the NFER's recent activities have been devoted to special education issues, partly because the publication of the Warnock Report, followed by the Education Act 1981, generated intense public interest in the effects of new ideas, attitudes and policies.

Reference:

Hegarty, S. (1989) 'Past, Current and Future Research on Integration: an NFER perspective' in Jones, N. (Ed.) (1989) *Special Educational Needs Review*, Lewes, Falmer Press.

(Further details available from NFER, The Mere, Upton Park, Slough, Berks. SL1 2DQ.)

National Survey of Health and Development of Children, pioneer longitudinal study of child development in the UK, which monitored a stratified sample of over 5,000 children, selected from all births in Great Britain in the first week in March, 1948. It was particularly effective in documenting the relationship between family background and school progress.

See *Child Health and Education Study, National Child Development Study.*

Reference:

Douglas, J.W.B. (1964) *The Home and the School*, London, MacGibbon and Kee.

nature–nurture controversy, long-standing debate over the extent to which individual characteristics are determined by heredity or experience.

While the question arises for any human trait, its implications for human *intelligence* have attracted most work, with significant consequences for education. Put baldly, hereditarians support investment in the identification of gifted children, and in carefully tending Ashby's 'thin clear stream of excellence'; environmentalists advocate investment in compensatory education, positive discrimination and projects such as Head Start.

While it is indisputable that genetic causes are being found for an increasing number of serious mental handicaps, these constitute a numerically small proportion of the general population. Studies of identical twins, separated and reared in different circumstances, have provided the main source of data for the debate, some authorities interpreting the results as indicating that most of the variation in human intelligence is genetically determined. But the findings have been questioned in various ways and are not clear-cut.

Obviously the two influences interact, and for this reason many have argued that the debate is actually pointless, offering the analogy of the futility of arguing over the relative contributions of the length and breadth of a rectangle to its area. Until society is comfortable with possible manipulations of human genetic constitutions, the only way to foster children's qualities is through improving the environment – of which the educational experience is a highly influential component.

References:

Jensen, A.R. (1969) 'How much can we boost IQ and scholastic achievement?' *Harvard Educational Review*, 39, 1–123.

Stott, D.H. (1983) *Issues in the Intelligence Debate*, Windsor, NFER-Nelson.

NCDS, see *National Child Development Study.*

Neale Analysis of Reading Ability, individual oral reading test, covering the age-range six to twelve years, and providing measures of reading rate, accuracy, and comprehension as well as a procedure for analysing reading errors.

The original test has been widely used by educational psychologists, teachers and research workers. Three parallel forms, each measuring three reading dimensions, as well as providing diagnostic information, and attractive to children, comprised an outstanding package.

The Neale has been criticised on technical grounds – in particular inadequate standardisation data – and for the fact that materials have dated and reading standards have changed since its earlier versions were produced.

A completely revised version was developed in the early 1980s, but standardised on an Australian population. It retains the Neale format of parallel forms, now reduced from three to two, each containing six graded passages, so forming a continuous reading scale. There is a clear need for this to be available with British norms, so that the appeal of the Neale package can be maintained.

There is also a Braille version of the original Neale Test, intended for use with blind children.

References:

Neale, M.D., McKay, M.F. and Childs, G.H. (1986) 'The Neale Analysis of Reading Ability – Revised', *British Journal of Educational Psychology*, 56, 346–56.

Pumfrey, P.D. (1985, 2nd. edn.) *Reading: Tests and Assessment Techniques*, Sevenoaks, Hodder and Stoughton in association with UKRA.

near vision, sight for close work, and hence important for classroom activities such as reading and writing. The *Snellen Test*, perhaps the most familiar of vision tests, actually assesses distance vision. Near vision is assessed by asking the child to read passages (or single letters) of gradually decreasing print size. These are graded N36 (the largest print used in beginning readers) to N5 (the print used in a telephone directory). The N number (after correction) reported for a child's near vision gives an indication of his/her visual acuity for close work.

See *Jaeger Chart*.

Reference:

Chapman, E.K. and Stone, J.M. (1988) *The Visually Handicapped Child in Your Classroom*, London, Cassell.

Nebraska Test of Learning Aptitude, see *Hiskey-Nebraska Test of Learning Aptitude*.

negative reinforcement, see *reinforcement*.

nerve deafness, see *sensori-neural hearing loss*.

neural tube defects, group of congenital abnormalities, characterised by defects in the spinal column and skull, caused by failure of the neural tube – the formation which develops into the brain, spinal column and central nervous system – to close before birth. Neural tube defects include *meningocele*, *myelomeningocele* and *spina bifida*, and children born with them are always at risk of serious mental and physical handicap.

Many neural tube defects can now be detected in pregnancy by techniques such as amniocentesis or ultrasound scanning.

References:
Anderson, E. and Spain, B. (1977) *The Child with Spina Bifida*, London, Methuen.
Halliday, P. (1989) *Children with Physical Disabilities*, London, Cassell.

neurologist, medical practitioner with additional specialised training in the diagnosis and treatment of diseases of the central nervous system. Epilepsy is an obvious example of a condition where neurological expertise is essential, but since learning is clearly dependent on the integrity of the central nervous system, child neurologists play an increasing part in the assessment of children with many other conditions causing special educational needs.

A number of educational treatments claim to be founded on neurological principles, some soundly based, others less so.

See *Bobath method, Doman-Delacato method.*

neurosis, neurotic behaviour, broad term for a variety of psychological conditions. Many authorities prefer 'neurotic behaviour' to 'neurosis' as a descriptor. Like Agag, venturers have tread with care: school refusal can be a neurotic reaction (school phobia), but in some circumstances it is a rational response. Behaviour has to be carefully described if the distinction between rational and neurotic is to have meaning.

Neurotic behaviour is commonly contrasted with antisocial behaviour, these two groups of conditions covering between them most psychological disturbance in children. (Psychosis, which is much more serious, occurs much less frequently in children.)

Neurotic behaviour usually includes anxieties, fears, obsessions, eating and sleeping disorders, withdrawn behaviour, etc. The prevalence depends heavily on the criteria adopted for definition, but also on factors such as age, sex, and situation. In the careful and classic Isle of Wight Study, a prevalence rate of 2.5% was found in ten- to eleven-year-olds, taking into account behaviour both at home and school, anxieties and phobias being the most frequent conditions. Other investigations have found other, usually higher rates.

Neurotic behaviour is modified in various ways. Notwithstanding criticisms of the effectiveness of 'pure' psychoanalytical therapy, methods based on psychotherapy as well as those based on behaviour therapy have been used successfully, as have counselling techniques with older pupils.

See *antisocial behaviour.*

References:
Barker, P. (1988, 5th edn.) *Basic Child Psychiatry*, Oxford, Blackwell.
Kolvin, I., Garside, R.F., Nicol, A.R., MacMillan, R., Wolstenholme, F. and Leitch, I.M. (1981) *Help Starts Here*, London, Tavistock.
Rutter, M., Tizard, J. and Whitmore, K (Eds.) (1970) *Education, Health and Behaviour*, London, Longman.

NFER, see *National Foundation for Educational Research.*

NMR, see *nuclear magnetic resonance.*

nocturnal enuresis, see *enuresis.*

nominal aphasia, difficulty in retrieving words, usually nouns. The word was known and used previously, but cannot be recalled and spoken.
See *aphasia.*

non-directive counselling is derived from the client-centred approach to personal problems, associated with Carl Rogers. The intention is that the client – pupil or parent – should be helped to make his/her own decisions, so building up his/her own self-concept. The counsellor accepts all the client says, never disagreeing, but rather acting as a sounding-board from which the client's own views and comments are reflected. The client therefore takes the lead in the counselling session, the counsellor providing a climate of unconditional acceptance.
Two points need to be made. First, this is a role which is at variance with the traditional role of the teacher, which is one reason why it has been argued that it is difficult for one person to combine both roles. Second, although this approach probably underpins most counselling in British schools, this is not the only model of counselling: for example behavioural counselling is an alternative.
See *counselling.*

References:
Rogers, C. (1951) *Client-Centred Therapy,* Boston, Houghton Mifflin.
Nelson-Jones, R. (1983) *Practical Counselling Skills,* London, Holt, Rinehart and Winston.

non-language test, psychological test requiring no written or spoken language from child or examiner. Instructions might be given in mime, and responses might involve manipulating objects. Such tests – the Hiskey-Nebraska is an example – can be used for children with speech and hearing problems, children who are illiterate, or for whom there is no test in their first language. This is not quite the same as a non-verbal test, in which responses are non-language, though instructions often use speech. Note that this classification is open to criticism, for it is based on the assumption that language is a verbal activity: non-verbal communication systems are also languages.

non-maintained special schools, non-profit making schools which have to meet conditions for approval as special schools laid down in regulations. In return they receive some government grant. They also receive financial support from charities or trusts, but most of their running cost comes from the fees paid by local authorities for the education of pupils placed there.
Non-maintained special schools form a substantial part of residential education for pupils with special needs, providing about a third of the

places. This proportion varies according to the disability; in 1983 over 80% of blind pupils in residential special education were educated in non-maintained schools: for the deaf the corresponding figure was over 50%.

In view of this large contribution the Warnock Report recommended much closer links between the non-maintained schools and the rest of the education system, with more visits from the Inspectorate and with local authority representation on governing bodies.

References:

Cole, T. (1986) *Residential Special Education*, Milton Keynes, Open University Press.

Department of Education and Science (1978) *Special Educational Needs*, London, HMSO (Warnock Report).

non-verbal communication, sometimes non-vocal communication, communication system other than speech or written language. This definition includes symbol systems such as pictograms, systems using gestures, and most obviously the sign languages used by the deaf.

Everyone uses some non-verbal communication, perhaps body language to emphasise a point, perhaps a sign to communicate at a distance. These are examples of non-verbal systems being used in conjunction with the use of spoken or written language. But for some pupils with severe hearing impairment, or severe mental handicap, signs and symbols are the main means of communication.

The use of the various systems with children with special needs has developed markedly in recent years. The systems' grammar and syntax, sometimes different from English and sometimes deliberately similar, have been carefully studied. Data on the relative effectiveness of different systems with different populations is also becoming available.

See, for example, *Bliss Symbol System, Makaton.*

References:

Kiernan, C., Reid, B. and Jones, L. (1982) *Signs and Symbols*, London, Heinemann.

Remington, B. and Light, P. (1983) 'Some Problems in the Evaluation of Research on Non-Oral Communication Systems', in Hogg, J. and Mittler, P. (Eds.) (1983) *Advances in Mental Handicap Research*, Chichester, Wiley.

normal curve, normal distribution, Gaussian curve, bell-shaped curve which fits the distribution of many human characteristics, e.g. height. Most people are close to average height; the proportion of the population gradually declines at heights further from the average, in either direction. Since, for any age-group of young children, the distribution of mental ages is roughly normal, tests of intelligence and many educational attainment tests have been constructed so that the raw scores are transformed into a normal distribution of standardised scores, often *deviation quotients.* This is helpful for comparing performances between children on the same test and between tests on the same child (particularly if the standard deviations and means are identical). But it must be remembered that the comparison is made on an artificial scale, which might not represent the distribution as experienced in reality. Differences may be most apparent at extremes.

See *deviation quotients* illustration.

normalisation, the belief that persons with handicaps should enjoy the same privileges, rights and opportunities as persons without handicaps. Fewer young people with handicaps are entering large institutions – more are living on their own or in small groups in specially adapted houses; changes in transport arrangements and building access confer greater mobility; facilities for holidays for the handicapped are greatly improved. These examples of ways of increasing the independence of people with handicaps all reflect a sea-change in society's attitudes, gradual but none the less fundamental. In education it is demonstrated in the movement towards integration, which is in effect the application of the principle of normalisation to the education system.

See *community care.*

References:

Fish, J. (1985) *Special Education: the Way Ahead,* Milton Keynes, Open University Press.

Marsh, G.E., Price, B.J. and Smith, T.E.C. (1983) *Teaching Mildly Handicapped Children,* St. Louis, Mosby.

Wolfensberger, W. (1972) *The Principle of Normalisation in Human Services,* Toronto, National Institute on Mental Retardation.

norm-referenced tests, measure a person's competency by comparing it with that of others – the standardisation sample of the test. The pre-eminence of norm-reference testing has been increasingly under attack by the advocates of *criterion-referenced tests,* which compare a person's competency with a specified set of skills, rather than a specified set of persons.

While there are undoubted advantages to the teacher in using criterion-referenced tests, the advantages of norm-referenced tests should not be forgotten. A teacher's knowledge of child performance is restricted to the children encountered in a teaching career: we are the prisoners of our own limited experience. A well-standardised norm-referenced test will be based on the performance of a much larger group of children: it extends our experience, providing a backcloth against which unusual performance, unusually high or unusually low, can be assessed.

In short, both norm- and criterion-reference tests have their uses; they are complementary and not necessarily antagonistic procedures.

Reference:

Anastasi, A. (1982, 5th edn.) *Psychological Testing,* New York, Macmillan.

norms, means of summarising the test performances of the norm or standardisation sample. For any test the norms can be reported in several different ways. The most common is probably a table of standard scores, enabling any child's performance to be compared with the average performance of the appropriate age-group in the reference population. The comparison could be made by percentile ranks, or deviation quotients, or other descriptive statistics.

Alternatively the norms could be given as a table of the average scores obtained by each age-group in the standardisation population. This table of age-norms enables a child's score to be expressed as an age-equivalent (e.g. mental age; reading age). Developmental norms, which provide ages at which developmental milestones, such as grasping, walking, first word, occur, are particular examples of age norms.

Before using a test, its norms should be evaluated against three main criteria. The norms of many tests in use are not recent; changing educational standards may then lead to incorrect inferences being drawn. They may not be representative: if the standardisation sample is improperly constructed, then the norms will not reflect the population to which the test is intended to apply. Finally, they may not be relevant. If we need to assess the development of a hearing-impaired child, then for some purposes it may be more sensible to use norms based on performances of a hearing-impaired, rather than a hearing population.

Reference:

Aiken, L.R. (1986, 5th edn.) *Psychological Testing and Assessment*, New York, Allyn and Bacon.

Nuclear Magnetic Resonance (NMR), specialised diagnostic technique for obtaining images of the interior of the body. It is used to obtain images of the brain in investigations of epilepsy. No X-rays are involved and hence there are no radiation dangers.

nursery education, education intended for the under-fives, in nursery schools and classes. The nursery classes can be attached to infant schools or to special schools, in which case they cater only for children with special needs.

Nursery education, whether full-time or part-time, has been a bone of contention for many years. Its value has been widely applauded, but successive governments have been unable to find the funding to increase provision. Fewer than a quarter of children receive nursery education, and demand is far from satisfied.

If nursery education is worthwhile for most children, for many children with special needs it becomes vital. Many local authorities offer priority admission to nursery education, on grounds of social needs and of special educational needs, though in some cases there are conditions, which often mean that children who make greater demands are not admitted. Few nursery schools and units do not enrol a significant proportion of children with special needs – between 15% and 20%, according to a survey by HMI. In addition, nursery units attached to special schools provide early education for children with more severe and complex handicaps.

One of the problems identified by the survey was the limited contact between the special education advisory and support services and the staff of nursery classes. Another was the difficulty of identifying the special needs of young children from a different culture, with a mother tongue other than English. These problems have to be set against the obvious goodwill and concern of all involved in nursery education, identified in several studies.

See *preschool playgroups.*

References:

Chazan, M., Laing, A.F., Bailey, M.S. and Jones. G. (1980) *Some of our Children,* London, Open Books.

Chazan, M. and Laing, A. (1982) *The Early Years,* Milton Keynes, Open University Press.

Department of Education and Science (DES) (1983) *Young Children with Special Educational Needs,* London, DES.

Robson, B. (1989) *Pre-school Provision for Children with Special Needs,* London, Cassell.

nursery nurse, works in day nurseries, nursery schools and units, and in residential homes. The nursery nurse has responsibilities for child care, though in the educational situations nurses and teachers usually jointly plan the daily programme.

Extra nurses are sometimes allocated where children with special needs are being educated. People with nursery nurse qualifications, usually the certificate of the National Nursery Examination Board (NNEB), are sometimes found as *classroom assistants* for older children with special needs; the 'nursery' designation is then inappropriate.

See *nursery education.*

Reference:

Robson, B. (1989) *Pre–school Provision for Children with Special Needs,* London, Cassell.

nurture group, small group, usually of primary school pupils, given special attention in order to counteract the effects of social and emotional deprivation. The nurture groups aim to provide the normal warm relationships and experiences of childhood that some children have missed. Nurture groups have been used with some success for managing children with emotional and behavioural difficulties.

Reference:

Kolvin, I., Garside, R.F., Nicol, A.R., MacMillan, R., Wolstenholme, F. and Leitch, I.M. (1981) *Help Starts Here,* London, Tavistock.

nystagmus, oscillatory eye-movements, usually lateral, sometimes in a vertical plane and sometimes in both. It is often involuntary, but can sometimes be eased when the head is held in certain positions. Visual acuity is affected, and advice over this and its implications for classroom seating, etc., should be sought.

Reference:
Chapman, E.K. and Stone, J.M. (1988) *The Visually Handicapped Child in Your Classroom*, London, Cassell.

O

obesity in children, is sometimes equated with being overweight, defined as 20% above standard weight for height and age. Whatever the definition used, and there are several, obesity has both physical and psychological consequences.

There are various causes. Genetic make-up, overfeeding, lack of exercise, metabolic disorder, psychological factors have all been supported, separately and together. Note that children whose mobility is restricted by physical disability may be at some risk for this reason.

The prevalence of obesity has increased since the end of the second world war, though the reasons are not clear. Prevalence varies with age and sex: as an example of the latter, cited in Jobling, 32% of fourteen-year-old girls were found to be overweight compared with 4% of boys of the same age.

The health risks associated with obesity – heart disease, high blood pressure, etc. – are well known. Psychologically, fat children are sometimes teased by their peers for their slowness and clumsiness, as well as their appearance, and sometimes excluded from activities. This rejection may in turn lead to eating more food as a compensation, as well as aggressive or withdrawn behaviour.

In short, obesity should be considered as a possible cause when children show emotional and behavioural difficulties, though the topic needs handling with considerable tact.

References:
Graham, P.J. (1986) *Child Psychiatry: a Developmental Approach*, Oxford, Oxford University Press.
Jobling, M. (1985) 'Obesity in Children: a Review of Research', *Highlight*, 65, London, National Children's Bureau.

objective, see *behavioural objective.*

Object Relations Technique (ORT), projective test used to investigate interpersonal relationships in adolescents and adults with personality problems. The test consists of a set of twelve plates with deliberately ambiguous figures. Some plates depict a solitary situation, others two- or three-person relationships, others group situations.

The subject's interpretation of the plates is itself interpreted by the psychologist or psychoanalyst, in the light of the object relations theory developed by Melanie Klein as a derivative of classic Freudian theory.

This test is based on a particular approach, not acceptable to all. As with many projective techniques it has little truck with basic psychometric canons; it is intended to reveal glimpses of the ways in which the subject views the social world, so that counselling or therapy based on psychoanalytic principles can be started.

References:

Osborne, E.L. (1982) 'Using Projective Techniques to Evaluate Adolescents' Feelings about Themselves: with specific reference to the ORT', *Occasional Papers of the DECP*, 6, 3, 67–8, Leicester, British Psychological Society.

obsessive behaviour, unwanted, compulsive, repetitive actions, persisting despite awareness of their redundancy. Rituals at bedtime, touching lamp-posts, etc., are harmless examples which most children show at times. But obsessional behaviour severe enough to interfere with normal living occurs much more rarely and is a recognised neurosis, often associated with anxiety and sometimes with depression.

Prevalence rates of less than 1% are usually reported, but much depends on the diagnostic borderline of severity used: the Isle of Wight Survey reported seven children diagnosed as obsessional/anxiety disorder among 2,199 ten- and eleven-year-olds, a prevalence of approximately 0.03%.

Various treatments are used, but behaviour therapy is said to be more effective than treatment based on psychoanalytic principles.

See *neurosis*.

References:

Barker, P. (1988, 5th edn.) *Basic Child Psychiatry*, Oxford, Blackwell.

Rutter, M., Tizard, J. and Whitmore, K. (1970) *Education, Health and Behaviour*, London, Longman.

occupational classification, system of grading the status of occupations so that they form a scale. The long scale provided by the General Register Office is often condensed into five categories, viz: professional and managerial; skilled nonmanual; skilled manual; semi-skilled manual; unskilled and unemployed.

Occupational classification is significantly associated with school attainment, even after IQ and other variables have been controlled. This relationship can be seen in special education. For example, more children with mild and moderate learning difficulties come from homes where the main bread-winner works in the less-well-off occupations than would be expected on chance grounds. The effect is weaker or absent when the prevailing cause of the handicap is biological, as is often the case in children with severe learning difficulties.

References:

General Register Office (various dates) *Classification of Occupations*, London, HMSO.

Rutter, M., Maughan, B., Mortimore, P. and Ouston, J. (1979) *Fifteen thousand Hours*, London, Open Books.

Williams, P. and Gruber, E. (1967) *Response to Special Schooling*, London, Longman.

occupational therapist (OT), non-medical professional who works with people requiring assistance with activities of successful everyday living. Those working with children are sometimes called paediatric occupational therapists, and as well as normal OT training are expected to have made an additional study of childhood disabilities, their assessment and treatment.

Most OTs are employed in the health services, but a minority work with the social services. They may be members of teams working with children with special needs. Their skills include suggesting specialised aids and equipment (e.g. special seats, grab-rails) that a child may need to gain independence in self-help skills such as washing, toileting, etc. Mobility and communication devices are other areas where OTs can give assistance.

More recently OTs have become involved with programmes for children whose needs are less obviously physical and more psychological, e.g. perceptual training for clumsy children. The current emphasis on integrating children with special needs, who have to function in the real world of the ordinary school, has made greater demands on the OT's resourcefulness.

References:

McElderry, F. (1988) 'The Occupational Therapist and the Child with Special Needs', University of London Institute of Education Policy and Provision for Special Needs Project, *Newsletter No. 6*, 6–8.

Penso, D.E. (1987) *Occupational Therapy for Children with Disabilities*, London, Croom Helm.

Oedipal phase, see *Freudian theory*.

Office of Special Education and Rehabilitation Services (OSERS), USA government body which replaced the Bureau of Education for the Handicapped in 1980. It represents the interests of people with handicaps, and has responsibility for administering Federal programs for them.

onomatopoeic words, imitate the sound or action they stand for, e.g. hiss. Whereas the majority of words have no sound/sense corespondence, and many may not have grapheme/phoneme correspondence, onomatopoeic words are not only phonetically consistent, but also mean what they sound. Additional examples are: Baa, clang, flop, hum, rap, wheeze, zoom. For this reason they are excellent for introducing many graphemes, phonemes and digraphs to pupils in simple, amusing and significant ways.

See *calligrams*.

Open University (OU), was founded in 1969, originally to enable adults aged twenty-one years or more to study for degrees at a distance. Since study is mainly carried out at home, it offers particularly suitable arrangements for higher education for many people with special needs, who can be admitted from the age of eighteen. Many different programmes are offered, ranging from single, 'personal interest' courses to honours degrees and postgraduate study. Some courses cover aspects of handicap and special educational needs. Entry is not based on formal qualifications, but on a first-come-first-served basis. Teaching uses a mixture of correspondence texts, television programmes, audio cassettes and personal tuition.

The OU makes special provision for students with disabilities, for example providing audiotapes and transcripts for students with visual and hearing impairments, arrangements for companions to attend summer schools, special induction courses, etc.

Reference:

Thompson, M. (1986) *Employment for Disabled People*, London, Kogan Page.

Further information available from:

Office for Students with Disabilities, Open University, Walton Hall, Milton Keynes, MK7 6AN.

operant conditioning, see *conditioning*.

ophthalmologist, medical practitioner with additional specialised training in the structure, functioning and diseases of the eye. An ophthalmologist's activities include conducting diagnoses, prescribing drugs, performing surgery, measuring refraction and prescribing glasses.

optacon, device which converts print, letter-by-letter, into a pattern of moving pins, sensed by one finger. The print is photographed by a small camera, and the image processed by an electronics unit, which actuates the pins.

The optacon gives a blind reader access to non-Braille material, its great advantage. There are two main problems. First, the device is as yet expensive. Second, reading is slow: the user requires good tactile discrimination; language proficiency, such as some familiarity with the syntax of written language, also helps. An average reading speed of forty words per minute has been quoted, which is several times slower than that obtained on the Kurzweil reading machine, though the latter's spoken output imposes some restrictions on its use.

Reference:

Chapman, E.K. and Stone, J.M. (1988) *The Visually Handicapped Child in Your Classroom*, London, Cassell.

OPTIC (Observing Pupils and Teachers in Classrooms), schedule used to evaluate the effectiveness of *BATPACK*. Observations are made of teachers' comments to pupils, using a two-by-two classification as positive or negative, social or academic.

Observations are also made of pupils' on-task/off-task behaviour. Use of the schedules suggests that information on the quality of teacher comments can be useful. Doubts have been raised about the value of on-task behaviour as an index of successful education: scores would be high in low-level, repetitive exercises, but low in exercises such as class project work, where greater freedom is encouraged. Yet the latter should be more educationally effective.

This point applies to all schedules using on-task behaviour as an index. That the behavioural approach has value is not denied by this comment: but results based on it have to be interpreted with care.

Reference:

Martlew, C. and Reason, R. (1987) 'Making SENSS of OPTIC', Newsletter No. 25, Division of Educational and Child Psychology, *British Psychological Society*, 31–5.

optometrist, non-medical specialist in eye function. In particular the optometrist measures refraction, prescribes glasses and may carry out vision training.

ORACLE project, Observational Research and Classroom Learning Evaluation, studied what went on in primary classrooms, including the consistency of pupils' behaviour when they changed classes in the primary school and on transfer to secondary school. The project was active from 1975 to 1980.

ORACLE was not specifically concerned with special education, but it did draw attention to the limited amount of individual attention that pupils receive. While on average 80% of a primary teacher's time is spent in interacting with pupils (considerably more than in secondary schools), conversely only 2% of a pupil's time is spent in individual interaction with teacher. Although pupils with special needs received on average more attention than others, nevertheless the time available was still low. This can be regarded as an argument for better teacher–pupil ratios, or for the provision of classroom assistants, to support integration in the primary school.

Reference:

Galton, M., Simon, B. and Croll, P. (1980) *Inside the Primary Classroom*, London, Routledge and Kegan Paul.

oral–manual controversy, long-standing debate over the method to be used for helping the hearing-impaired to communicate. Although the debate has at times been passionate, and threatened to divide the world of deaf education, nevertheless proponents of both sides share the aim of helping children with hearing impairment attain the highest possible levels of speech and language.

Many teachers believe that all children, no matter how seriously hearing-impaired, should be educated orally. Oral education implies making the maximum use of any residual hearing through early diagnosis and amplification, with the aim of developing lip-reading and intelligible speech. In its purest form the use of gesture is proscribed, on the argument that gesture is the easy way out, and that the great prize of proficiency in oral communication, and the integration opportunities it confers, requires single-minded concentration on speech and lip-reading. Children acquire language as any child does, but require much more experience and training, which must start as early and intensively as possible. Other oralists allow natural gestures, though still concentrating on teaching though the medium of speech.

Manualists argue that many children, particularly the more profoundly deaf, never acquire convincingly satisfactory standards of commmunication through the oral method alone. No matter how hard gesture is proscribed, most children will revert to it as a natural means of communication. Where hearing impairment is severe, the manualists advocate teaching a non-verbal communication system, such as a sign language, alongside speech, from an early age, arguing that this helps the child acquire a language more easily, with consequent improvement in lip-reading skills and possibly in intellectual development too.

The debate has not been resolved, since there is no clear evidence that one method produces better mastery of language and academic progress than another. Research has now begun to focus on the quality rather than the mode of communication as children and adults interact, in order to help account for differences in children's progress.

See *total communication.*

References:

Reed, M. (1984) *Educating Hearing-Impaired Children,* Milton Keynes, Open University Press.

Webster, A. and Wood, D. (1989) *Children with Hearing Difficulties,* London, Cassell.

Wood, D., Wood, H., Griffiths, A. and Howarth, I. (1986) *Teaching and Talking with Deaf Children,* Chichester, Wiley.

oral stage, see *Freudian theory.*

Oregon Direct Instruction Model, title given to the development of the Bereiter-Engelmann work, on moving to the University of Oregon, under the direction of Engelmann and Becker. It was the basis of the well-known Direct Instruction materials.

The Oregon model was one of nine different approaches to teaching disadvantaged children which were evaluated in the USA in the 1970s. On a measure of attainment in basic skills over the years from school entry to age nine years, the Oregon model scored highest. It also achieved the highest effect on a self-esteem measure, and did well on other criteria. Its success has been attested by the popularity of direct instruction methods in current work with children with learning difficulties.

See *Bereiter and Engelmann program, Direct Instruction.*

Reference:

Hare, B.A. and Hare, J.M. (1977) *Teaching Young Handicapped Children,* New York, Grune and Stratton.

orthofunction, see *conductive education.*

orthoptist, person who investigates and treats defective vision through exercises, usually in conjunction with an ophthalmologist. Thus a child with a squint may be given exercises to realign the axes of vision of the eyes.

Orton-Gillingham method, see *Gillingham method.*

Oseretsky test, see *Bruininks-Oseretsky Test of Motor Proficiency.*

osteogenesis imperfecta, see *brittle bones.*

Otis-Lennon School Ability Test (OLSAT), classic USA group test of cognitive development. The authors avoid describing it as a test of intelligence, preferring to provide a 'school ability index', or SAI, which with a mean of 100 and a standard deviation of sixteen points is effectively a deviation IQ masquerading under another name.

Technically, the test is well produced. It covers the full range of compulsory education (in the USA) in five different versions, with parallel forms available at each level. One interesting feature is the provision of different norms for children assessed in the spring and the fall (autumn).

It is not designed specifically for use with special populations, but is an acceptable screening instrument (in the USA).

Reference:

Salvia, J. and Ysseldyke, J.E. (1985, 3rd edn.) *Assessment in Special and Remedial Education,* Boston, Houghton Mifflin.

otitis media, inflammation or infection of the middle ear, often accompanied by pain, fever, and giddiness. It is the most common cause of a *conductive hearing loss* in children.

There are many different forms of otitis media, not all of which are painful, but all of which may lead to conductive deafness through various routes. The inflammation can prevent the ear from functioning properly, either through filling the middle ear with sticky fluid (*glue ear*), or through altering the air pressure in the middle ear, so affecting the vibration of the eardrum. In either case there is a hearing loss, usually temporary.

Since the inflammation often follows an upper respiratory tract infection – heavy cold, runny nose, etc. – a condition which frequently recurs in some young children, particularly in winter, the conductive deafness fluctuates. It may be present for a few days, and then hearing may return to normal, until the next bout. Teachers should therefore be alert to the possibility of some conductive deafness in pupils after heavy colds. The educational effects are those of any conductive hearing loss, i.e. most clearly seen in a child's language development, and although they are not permanent if the hearing loss is tackled, they can be long-lasting.

References:

Webster, A. (1988) 'Glue Ear', *Special Children*, 20, 26–8.

Webster, A and McConnell, C. (1987) *Children with Speech and Language Difficulties*, London, Cassell.

outer ear, see *ear*.

Outreach, umbrella description of programmes which provide expertise in settings away from their normal base. Programmes work both ways. In the school sector, the work of special school staff in ordinary schools, collaborating with mainstream colleagues in teaching pupils with special needs, has been described as outreach work. As the links between special and ordinary schools have developed in both directions and grown in strength, so outreach work can be subsumed under the general concept of integrating the special and ordinary school systems.

In the further education sector, outreach has been applied to college staff moving into the community to offer educational opportunities for young people and adults with special needs. This occurs most commonly through teaching in adult training/social education centres, though education is also provided for people with special needs in hospitals and elsewhere.

In effect, any outreach provision is a particular form of a *link scheme*.

oval window, see *ear*.

over-correction, behaviour therapy technique in which undesirable behaviour is immediately followed by a requirement to restore – and improve on – the status quo. Thus a child who makes a mess will be required to clean it up (restitution) and then spend some time in additional cleaning (improvement). Over-correction has to be applied regularly and systematically, and for a set period or periods. Note that unlike most behaviour therapy used with children, it contains an element of punishment, since an aversive stimulus (in the example, time and effort spent in cleaning) is used. But its advocates argue that unlike most punishment, over-correction does substitute a desired behaviour (in the example, cleaning) for undesired behaviour. Note too that it constitutes an example of time-out procedures, since during over-correction other activities are denied.

Over-correction is most often used in work with children with severe learning difficulties and serious behaviour problems, though it is readily recognisable as a procedure in occasional but unsystematic use in many familiar settings.

Compare *extinction*, operant *conditioning*.

Reference:

Porter, J. (1986) 'Beyond a Simple Behavioural Approach', in Coupe, J. and Porter J.

(Eds.) (1986) *The Education of Children with Severe Learning Difficulties*, Beckenham, Croom Helm.

P

PAD, see *Preventive Approaches to Disruption.*

Paget-Gorman Sign System (PGSS), system of non-vocal communication, designed to help deaf people develop correct language patterns. PGSS was based on the argument that the predominant language of the deaf, British Sign Language, had evolved into a system with a linguistic structure sufficiently different from English possibly to impair the ability to understand spoken English (e.g. through lip-reading) and to use written English. To circumvent this, PGSS is constructed to correspond as closely as possible to the English language. The user signs every word in a sentence, and also signs tenses, affixes, suffixes, possessives, etc., so mirroring the grammar, syntax and morphology of spoken English as closely as possible. The signs are designed on a logical basis, one hand giving the central concept, and the other the identifying detail. Thus all foods have identical signs with one hand, but different signs with the other.

on

sleep

The correspondence between PGSS and spoken English means that speech and signing can be used simultaneously and precisely.

There is some evidence to support the claim that children using PGSS do produce written language that is grammatically more mature and more correct than those produced by deaf children taught by an 'oral' method. On the other hand the latter seem to produce written language more easily.

Since the PGSS requires some ability to understand grammar, it has the reputation of not being as easy to learn as other non-vocal systems, such as Makaton. Nevertheless it is in use in some schools for children with severe learning difficulties and communication problems. It does require good hand coordination in order to be signed properly, but again pupils with poor coordination are able to produce understood approximations.

See *sign language, total communication.*

References:

Brooke, M.V. (1986) 'Written Syntax in Deaf Children and the Paget-Gorman Sign System', *British Journal of Special Education*, 13, 2, Research Supplement, 67–8.

Kiernan, C., Reid, B. and Jones, L. (1982) *Signs and Symbols*, London, Heinemann for Institute of Education, University of London.

Rowe, J. (1981) 'The Paget-Gorman Sign System', *Special Education: Forward Trends*, 8, 4, 25–7.

paired number, is based on similar principles to paired reading, though the comparatively limited development of paired number has not defined the field as clearly.

One of the few experiments included the following elements: regular home–school liaison; regular parent–child sessions at home; loosely structured tasks; regular recording by parents; an involvement contract; a relaxed attitude on the part of participants.

The results were limited, but encouraging.

References:

Arora, A. and Bamford, J. (1986) 'MATHS – Multiply Attainments Through Home Support: Piloting 'Paired Number' in an Infant School', *Educational and Child Psychology*, 3, 3, 68–74.

paired reading, originally a method of teaching reading in which a child who needs reading help is paired with a fluent reader. The tuition is said to be based on behavioural principles whose simplicity has enabled the technique to be learnt easily by non-specialists, notably parents.

Paired reading has two phases. In the first, reading together, parent and child simultaneously read aloud reading material chosen by the child. In behavioural terms the child receives a model, and continuous prompting. The second phase involves the child reading alone. The transition from the first phase is under the child's control; when confidence is right, the child gives a non-verbal signal, for example a knock, the parent ceases reading and the child carries on alone. After a mistake, or a few seconds' hesitation, the parent reads the correct word, the child repeats it, and simultaneous reading is reintroduced until confidence returns again. Reinforcement through praise, pats, etc., is given throughout.

There are many pieces of evidence testifying to the success of paired reading schemes, though so far few have been well-designed experiments, and most results refer to short-term gains. Although any gains are valuable, and those reported from paired reading projects seem better than most, many methods of reading help produce short term gains which are reduced or lost over time.

Many variations to the original paired reading formula have been instituted, and not everyone has accepted that behavioural theory is the only explanation for their success. Their advantages include the involvement of parents in their children's education; the positive, encouraging attention that a child gets from a parent; the amount of reading practice that a child gets in addition to that given at school; the pleasure many children feel at controlling their own learning (choice of material; decision on going solo). Whether any of these factors, alone or in combination, may be responsible for the success of a technique which is both promising and inexpensive, remains to be elucidated.

See *Haringey experiment, Pause, Prompt and Praise.*

References:

Pearson, L. and Lindsay, G. (1986) *Special Needs in the Primary School*, Windsor, NFER-Nelson.

Topping, K. and Wolfendale, S. (Eds.) (1985) *Parental Involvement in Children's Reading*, London, Croom Helm.

Wolfendale, S., Topping, K. and Hewison, J. (1986) 'A Review of Parental Involvement in Children's Reading', *Educational and Child Psychology*, 3, 3, 55–63.

Young, P. and Tyre, C. (1983) *Dyslexia or Illiteracy?* Milton Keynes, Open University Press.

palmar crease, single crease which replaces the usual flexion creases across the palm of the hand. It is said to be one of the characteristic physical signs of Down's syndrome, but the palmar crease is not invariably found nor only found in individuals with Down's syndrome.

parallel forms, alternate forms, equivalent forms of the same test, covering the same mental processes though using different items. The difficulty levels are intended to be as similar as possible, and the two forms will have been standardised on the same population, and cover the same age-range.

Parallel forms are particularly valuable when a child has to be retested within a short time interval, for they reduce substantially the practice and memory effects which apply when the same test is re-used.

Parallel forms are also useful for assessing the reliability of a test. For the reasons just mentioned, the two forms can be given to the same samples with only a short interval between administrations, so reducing the error associated with variation across occasions which occurs when the same test is repeated after a reasonable time interval.

Reference:

Anastasi, A. (1982, 5th edn.) *Psychological Testing,* New York, Macmillan.

paranoia, serious personality disorder, characterised by chronic suspicion, jealousy, and delusions of persecution. A paranoid personality shows some of these features though not so obviously as to result in a serious distortion of personality. Both are more likely to occur in adults and older adolescents.

paraplegia, inability to use the lower limbs. This may be a result of *cerebral palsy, muscular dystrophy, spina bifida,* or for other reasons, e.g. accident. The kind of care needed in school depends on the cause, and whether there are associated problems, e.g. incontinence. In most cases special attention has to be paid to avoiding pressure sores in children confined to a wheelchair for long periods, particularly since pain sensation in the lower limbs may be absent.

Medical advice on these issues will be needed, as will suggestions for suitable aids to help overcome the limitations on access to normal classroom facilities and equipment.

Reference:

Russell, P. (1984, 2nd edn.) *The Wheelchair Child,* London, Souvenir Press.

PARC case, see Pennsylvania Association for Retarded Children v. the Commonwealth of Pennsylvania.

parents, play an increasingly important role in special education, though there is still much room for development. Recent changes rest in no small measure on a much more sensitive appreciation of and reaction to the feelings and views of parents of a child with special needs. These feelings are initially closely linked to the way in which parents have been told that their child is handicapped: if this has been handled sensitively then there is more chance of positive feelings developing towards the child. Studies of parental feelings towards mentally handicapped children some time after they have been made aware of their child's condition have commented on reactions such as guilt, over-protection, and rejection. But with good early services and growing experience in child-rearing, most parents develop more positive attitudes.

Many children with learning difficulties come from impoverished homes, and several successful compensatory education programmes offered training in basic parenting skills, in order to improve children's learning. This approach, which later spread more widely through the institution of parental workshops, tends to emphasise the expertise of the professional and the inexperience of parents.

Later work recognised the importance of the parent as a collaborator. This is reflected in the theme 'parents as partners', proposed in the Warnock Report and given practical expression in collaborative exercises such as paired reading and the Portage project. The Education Act 1981 gave this view legal backing, extending parents' rights to participate in assessing special needs and in formulating statements.

The current phase is perhaps best described as 'parents as consumers'. In a society where the consumer reigns, the Education (No. 2) Act 1986 has increased the presence of parents on school governing bodies at the expense of the local education authority. The 1988 Act gives the revised governing body more power still through the regulations relating to local management of schools. While this legislation is not formulated with special education in mind it does apply to special education pari passu.

This does not mean that all parents of children with special educational needs now determine their children's education. Much depends on their personal interest and on the encouragement given by the education service. In many schools, some parents are not deeply motivated. Many parents do not attend meetings arranged by the school, are unaware of their representatives on the governing body and do not know their rights. In special schools, which draw from a wide catchment area, difficulties can be partly explained by practical problems such as distance from school, parents not owning cars, living in homes without telephones, etc. On the other hand there are many parents who feel very strongly that they want a greater say in their children's education than is currently the case, that their undoubted expertise in their child's development is being neglected and that the cry of 'parents as partners' is rhetoric, not reality.

References:

Cunningham, C. and Davies, H. (1985) *Working with Parents*, Milton Keynes, Open University Press.

Lunt, I. and Sheppard, J. (Eds.) (1986) 'Participating Parents: Promise and Practice', *Educational and Child Psychology*, 3, 3 (whole issue).

McConachie, H. (1986) *Parents and Young Mentally Handicapped Children: a review of research issues*, London, Croom Helm.

Mittler, P. and Mittler, H. (1982) *Partnership with Parents*, Stratford-upon-Avon, National Council for Special Education.

partially-hearing, used to refer to pupils who had sufficient hearing for their language development to follow a normal, if slow, pattern, given special teaching. Since the abolition of categories following the Education Act 1981, the term has lost its legal status, but is still used to refer to some educational facilities, e.g. partially-hearing units.

See *hearing impairment.*

Reference:

Reed, M. (1984) *Educating Hearing-Impaired Children*, Milton Keynes, Open University Press.

partially-sighted, used to refer to pupils with useful vision, but needing aids, special teaching and materials, to manage school. With the abolition of categories, following the Education Act 1981, the term no longer has legal status as far as education is concerned. The term is still in use, however, to describe some educational facilities, e.g. classes for the partially-sighted.

Partial sight is defined for welfare purposes as vision falling between 3/60 and 6/60 after correction; if the field of vision is also affected, as in hemianopia, for example, these criteria are varied.

See *visual impairment.*

References:

Corley, G., Robinson, D. and Lockett, S. (1989) *Partially Sighted Children,* Windsor, NFER-Nelson.

Fitt, R. and Mason, H. (1986) *Sensory Handicaps in Children,* Stratford-upon-Avon, National Council for Special Education.

pastoral care, aims to promote the personal, vocational and educational development of individual pupils. These are three of the aims of good education anywhere, but to be effectively pursued, teachers have to be in close contact with pupils. With the growth of large comprehensive schools, this 'personal touch' became harder to find; and a pastoral care structure was introduced. Responsibilities for pastoral care were given to form tutors, to Heads of years, to support teachers and in a few instances to full-time school counsellors.

The three aims require the pastoral care teacher to be able to offer sensitive understanding to pupils with the personal problems of adolescence; to offer wise and sensible counsel over career possibilities at a time when career choice is a critical question; to help with educational difficulties which may need modifying a curriculum, or learning effective study skills to cope with the existing one.

To fill these roles effectively requires some special training, as well as experience of teaching adolescent pupils. One of the criticisms of the pastoral care structure is that it has been introduced with minimal opportunity for the pastoral care staff to train for their new responsibilities. Another is that pastoral specialists spend a disproportionate amount of time dealing with discipline problems. A third criticism is that the 'hidden agenda' for its introduction was the need to offer an alternative promotion ladder for teachers who were not successful in the existing departmental career structure.

Yet whatever the covert reasons for introducing pastoral care to schools, it does make sense to attempt to strengthen a school's activities in this area. Major problems need the specialist support services – the school psychological service; the career service, etc. But other difficulties do not need such expensive and sophisticated treatment: they are part of the school's own responsibilities towards its pupils. Moreover, a school has responsibilities for the well-being and interests of its own staff, and a good pastoral care system offers support from senior staff to teacher colleagues, too, any of whom may have personal or career problems at times. When many of the differences between the attainment and behaviour of school pupils are being ascribed to differences in school climate, a good pastoral care system can play an effective part in creating that important but sometimes elusive objective, the warm yet efficient atmosphere of a good school.

See *counselling.*

References:

Baynes, A. (1987) 'The Pastoral Role', in Hinson, M. (Ed.) (1987) *Teachers and Special Educational Needs,* Harlow, Longmans in association with National Association for Remedial Education.

Galloway, D. (1985) *Schools, Pupils and Special Educational Needs,* London, Croom Helm.

Lowe, P. (1988) *Responding to Adolescent Needs; a pastoral care approach,* London, Cassell.

Pause, Prompt and Praise, technique for teaching reading which rests heavily on the the belief that self-correction of reading errors is the key to improvement.

It originated in New Zealand, and is a form of *paired reading,* the pupil being tutored by parents or peers. Reading material which can be read with an accuracy of between 80% and 90 % (compare *informal reading inventory*) is provided, and the tutors give feedback to the learners.

It is the method of providing feedback which is the key to Pause, Prompt and Praise. Tutors have to pause for five seconds before attempting to correct an error. This is to give the learner time to appreciate that an error has been made and to attempt to self-correct. If no attempt at correction has been made after five seconds, then the tutor has to prompt the learner, perhaps by asking a question which helps with the correction. When the word has been read correctly, the learner is praised.

These are simple techniques; yet when applied correctly and in accordance with the advised procedures, very real improvements in reading skills have been shown. It has been argued that tutoring without previous training in the technique is characterised by substantially less pausing (so allowing less time for self-correction), substantially less prompting (so again reducing the opportunity for self-correction) and very much poorer reinforcement with praise.

Like paired reading, this technique requires pupils to receive regular personal tutoring beyond that which a teacher can usually give. When peers are used as tutors, it has been shown that the reading level of the tutors shows significant improvement, as well as that of the learners.

See *companion reading.*

Reference:

MacNaughton, S., Glynn, T. and Robinson, M. (1987) *Pause, Prompt and Praise: Effective Tutoring for Effective Reading,* Cheltenham, Positive Products.

Merrett, F. (1986) 'Peer Tutoring of Reading using the Pause, Prompt and Praise Techniques', *Educational and Child Psychology,* 5, 4, 17–23.

Peabody Language Development Kits (PDLK), aim to improve self-expression, communication and reasoning ability in children with mental ages between three and nine-and-a-half years. There are four kits which between them cover the age range.

The kits originate in the USA, but have been used in this country, notably in compensatory education programmes aimed at improving the language development of young disadvantaged children. The materials were interesting to the children, but the scripted lessons were less attractive to the teachers.

Reference:

Dunn, L., Smith, J. and Horton, K. (1981) *Peabody Language Development Kits*, Windsor, NFER-Nelson.

Peabody Rebus Reading Program, an introduction to reading in which words are represented by pictures. Some pictures are directly representational (e.g. a picture of a cow standing for 'cow'), others stand for the sound of the word (e.g. a picture of a tin can for the auxiliary verb 'can'), yet others are quite arbitrary (e.g. the symbol for the definite article, 'the').

As with other rebus systems the Peabody scheme offers children the opportunity to gain meaning from symbols without having to manage the alphabet code; they feel they can 'read', and develop a positive attitude towards reading. Normal print is introduced later through a controlled, gradual transition.

The Peabody scheme was constructed in the USA, where it has been used in prereading activities with groups of children with learning difficulties: it may not be so easy to use it alongside a different reading scheme in an integrated classroom. But it has been used in this country with children with severe learning difficulties, where associated improvements in other language skills have sometimes been reported.

See *rebus.*

References:

Kiernan, C. (1983) 'The Exploration of Sign and Symbol Effects', in Hogg, J. and Mittler, P. (Eds.) (1983) *Advances in Mental Handicap Research*, Chichester, Wiley.

Devereux, K. and Van Oosterom, J. (1984) *Learning with Rebuses*, Stratford-upon-Avon, National Council for Special Education.

peer tutoring, has been defined as 'more able pupils helping less able pupils in cooperative working pairs carefully organised by a teacher'. The amount of individual tuition that pupils can normally receive in class is limited; peer tutoring offers a method of substantially extending individual tuition, though from peers, rather than from teacher, who controls the arrangements.

Successful peer tutoring needs careful organisation. Principles for matching pairs, pretraining for tutors, choice of materials, monitoring and evaluation, structure of sessions – all these and other points need planning beforehand.

Yet there is good evidence to show that peer tutoring is effective in raising attainments. Moreover there is some evidence that it can also have beneficial effects on the tutor, both on personality (increased self-esteem) as well as attainment.

Recently experiments have been reported in which children with special needs have been used as tutors. For example mentally handicapped pupils have taught sign language to their non-handicapped peers. Again there is some evidence of both academic and social gain for the tutors.

See *Pause, Prompt and Praise.*

References:

Topping, K. (1988) *An Introduction to Peer Tutoring,* Educational and Child Psychology, 5, 4, 6–16.

Topping, K. (1988) *The Peer Tutoring Handbook,* London, Croom Helm.

Pennsylvania Association for Retarded Children v. the Commonwealth of Pennsylvania (PARC case), a landmark in the achievement of education for all handicapped children. When the case was brought, it was legal for children with mental ages lower than five years to have their entry to the Pennsylvania school system deferred. In effect, this meant that some children with severe learning difficulties were permanently denied education. The court ruled in 1971 that the State had to provide free public education for all children, regardless of the degree of handicap.

Reference:

Lippman, L. and Oldberg, I.T. (1973) *Right to Educate,* New York, Teachers' College Press.

percentile rank, index of a position in a distribution ranging from 0 to 100. Some tests transform raw scores into percentile rank scores. Thus a percentile rank of 82 means that 82% of scores (of the standardisation sample) fall below that level.

Percentile ranks are thus useful for comparison purposes. But note that they are not equal interval scores: an improvement in performance from say, the 82nd percentile to the 92nd percentile may represent a very different gain from that measured by an improvement from the 45th to the 55th percentile, though both represent a change of ten percentile ranks.

See *deviation quotient* illustration.

perceptual disorder, difficulty in interpreting information gained through the senses. Note that a perceptual disorder is not the same as a sensory impairment: a child with intact senses may nevertheless suffer from a perceptual disorder. Thus a child with good hearing may still have difficulty in interpreting speech; although the sounds are heard, the meaning of their relationship is not easy to grasp.

Perceptual disorders clearly affect learning. Children with problems of visual perception will have some difficulties in learning to read, for while the print may be seen perfectly, interpreting the patterns as meaningful symbols may present problems. For this reason various attempts have been made to train perceptual skills, particularly visual perception and perceptuo–motor skills, in the hope that learning would improve. In the educational context, the results have been disappointing. Perceptual disorders may relate to single senses, or the relationship between senses, perceptual integration, may be affected.

See *Developmental Test of Visual Perception, perceptual–motor ability.*

Reference:

Tansley, J. and Panckhurst, J. (1981) *Children with Specific Learning Difficulties: a Critical Review of Research*, Windsor, NFER.

perceptual span, the area from which a reader can receive information during a single eye fixation. For print, the perceptual span varies between individuals, ranging from two to twenty characters, approximately, and bears some relationship to speed of reading.

Reference:

Pavlidis, G.Th. (1981) 'Sequencing, Eye Movements and the Early Objective Diagnosis of Dyslexia', in Pavlidis, G.Th. and Miles, T.R. (Eds.) (1981) *Dyslexia Research and its Application to Education*, Chichester, Wiley.

perceptual–motor ability, ability to coordinate motor and perceptual skills. This is basic to learning: for example, eye–hand coordination, central to the infant's exploration of the world, depends on the ability to perceive visual information and relate hand movements to it. This ability then underlies educational skills ranging from catching a ball to writing an essay.

Where perceptual–motor skills have been damaged, there are special educational needs. How best to meet these needs is not easily answered. As with single perceptual disorders, there have been many attempts to train perceptual–motor skills, often based on teaching the normal developmental sequence of motor skills and matching visual training to them. Results from such programmes are controversial.

See *clumsy child.*

References:

Burr, L.A. (1984) 'Perceptual Motor Disorders', in Levitt, S. (Ed.) (1984) *Paediatric Development Therapy*, Oxford, Blackwell.

Hallahan, D.P. and Kaufman, J.M. (1988, 4th edn.) *Exceptional Children: Introduction to Special Education*, Englewood Cliffs, Prentice Hall.

Kavale, K. and Forness, S. (1985) *The Science of Learning Disabilities*, Windsor, NFER-Nelson.

performance test, assesses competence at practical tasks not involving spoken or written language, e.g. manipulating blocks, arranging pictures in a sequence. The instructions may be given through language, which distinguishes a performance test from a non-language test, and helps to explain why the factorial structures of some performance tests show a significant loading on the v.ed group factor.

A score on a performance test is sometimes compared with a score on a verbal test to provide diagnostic information for assessment purposes, but great care has to be taken with this procedure if the standardisations are not similar.

See *Wechsler Intelligence Tests.*

Reference:

Mehrens, W.A. and Lehmann, I.J. (1978, 2nd edn.) *Measurement and Evaluation in Education and Psychology*, New York, Holt, Rinehart and Winston.

peripatetic teacher, see *support services.*

Perkins Brailler, most common machine used by blind pupils for producing Braille. Its advantage over earlier machines is that it produces the embossed dots by pressure from below; pressure from above, though simpler, produced a reverse image, so complicating the process of learning to write braille.

Using the Perkins Brailler in class does need a little more working space than usual.

See *Braille.*

Reference:

Chapman, E.K. and Stone, J.M. (1988) *The Visually Handicapped Child in Your Classroom*, London, Cassell.

perseveration, continuing to respond in an inappropriate way. Thus a child may continue to engage in an activity after its usefulness is over. Once committed to wearing a coat for going outside, a child may continue with the dressing routine, putting on gloves, scarf, hat, etc., even if these are not needed. In class a child may perseverate with a drawing for example, continuing to elaborate it long after it is time to move on to another activity: or a child may write the same word many times over.

This unusual difficulty some children have in accepting change and in demonstrating normally flexible responses may occur for many different reasons. Children with neurological damage can demonstrate perseveration; but it would be wrong to infer neurological damage from the behaviour alone. Alternatively, perseveration may occur because of the reinforcement a child receives from carrying on with an activity, perhaps particularly true of some behaviour patterns of some children with severe learning difficulties.

personal construct theory, model for understanding how we perceive and make sense of things, developed by G.A. Kelly. Each person has a unique (but neither totally independent nor unchanging) set of principles or constructs used in characterising the world around us. Thus one mother might characterise (or construe) her children in terms of whether they learn well or not, whether they are healthy or not, etc. Another may construe her children in terms of whether they are healthy or not, whether they are lovable or not, etc.

Personal construct theory has developed simple techniques for elucidating the constructs people use. Unlike other theories it does not attempt seriously to seek the causes of constructs, either in terms of early experiences or reinforcement systems; it is descriptive rather than explanatory. This is helpful in understanding how a parent views a child with special needs, or how a child views a professional, for example. Given this understanding, a basis is established for attempting to readjust constructs through counselling. In special education it is probably in relation to helping parents of children with serious handicaps come to terms with their situation that personal construct theory has had its greatest application.

References:

Cunningham, C. and Davies, H. (1985) *Working with Parents: Frameworks for Collaboration*, Milton Keynes, Open University Press.

Button, E. (Ed.) (1985) *Personal Construct Theory and Mental Health*, London, Croom Helm.

personality disorder, can be used in several different ways. It usually covers a group of conditions less serious than the psychoses or neuroses, but which nevertheless can be disabling. Thus a socially undesirable personality trait might be classified as a personality disorder.

This is a medical (psychiatric) approach. To the special educator it would be more useful to have an accurate description of the behaviour and the circumstances under which it is evoked.

Reference:

Barker, P. (1988, 5th edn.) *Basic Child Psychiatry*, Oxford, Blackwell.

personality test, any test which assesses psychological characteristics other than abilities and attainments, e.g. interests, relationships, traits, personality dimensions, etc.

A personality test is usually constructed by one of two methods; either by factor analysis or a criterion-group approach. In the first case, items thought to measure particular personality traits are given to a trial population, the results factor-analysed and items not loading on (adequately fitting) the traits being measured are discarded. Tests constructed by this method usually have acceptable technical data and tend to be used in large-scale research projects where objectivity is important. In the criterion-group approach, items are given to two groups of people, one with a particular personality characteristic, e.g. schizophrenia, and the other not. Items which differentiate the two groups are then incorporated in a test of schizophrenia. Tests constructed in this way are often weak on technical data, and tend to be used in clinical assessments, where the test data and other information are subjectively interpreted.

In practice, personality tests are often classified by the ways in which responses are made and interpreted. This leads to them being grouped as projective tests, rating scales, sociometric techniques, observation schedules, personality inventories, etc. Recently, more emphasis has been placed on techniques that assess observable behaviour rather than those which measure personality variables. The former approach has much clearer application to classroom problems.

Reference:

Salvia, J. and Ysseldyke, J.E. (1985, 3rd edn.) *Assessment in Special and Remedial Education*, Boston, Houghton Mifflin.

Perthe's disease, deformity of the head of the femur, seen most frequently in boys between the ages of four and six years, causing pain and limping. Treatment involves relief of strain through bedrest, crutches, hip splints or traction. There are no special educational implications other than those following from the use of these appliances in a school situation.

petit mal, see *epilepsy*.

phenylketonuria (PKU), inherited metabolic disorder caused by a recessive gene. The enzyme which converts phenylalanine into harmless products is missing, and unless the condition is treated, severe learning difficulties result.

The incidence is about one per ten thousand to fifteen thousand births. Screening shortly after birth for PKU is now a standard procedure, and on detection, a special diet prevents the intellectual deterioration occurring: the earlier the diet is instituted the better the outcome. Very few children with PKU now need special education.

Reference:

Powell, R.M. (1984) 'Medical Screening and Surveillance', in Lindsay, G. (Ed.) (1984) *Screening for Children with Special Needs*, Beckenham, Croom Helm.

phobia, persistent irrational fear of objects or situations. The phobias are usually classified as anxiety conditions, i.e. a subgroup of the broad category of neurotic behaviours. Simple phobias, a child's irrational fear of a single class of objects, e.g. dogs, are often amenable to the behavioural therapies. Some children show irrational fears of several different sorts, perhaps accompanied by other neurotic behaviours, e.g. nightmares, eating disorders, etc. These may well represent a more deep-seated emotional disorder, and therapeutic education may be beneficial, alongside other treatments.

See *school refusal*.

Reference:

Barker, P. (1988, 5th edn.) *Basic Child Psychiatry*, Oxford, Blackwell.

phoneme, minimal sound unit of a language. For example, the long 'o' sound is a phoneme, represented by a number of different graphemes, as in toe and boat. English is said to use forty-four phonemes, but additional sounds can be distinguished.

Most children have acquired the full sound patterns of vowel and consonant phonemes by the time they are seven years old, though some phoneme contrasts may not be properly learnt until even later. This is a point that should be borne in mind in considering the early teaching of reading. Children are then beginning to read, i.e. to relate the phonemes to the graphemes, the characters of the written language, and clearly the ability to discriminate the phonemes is a prerequisite. Learning grapheme–phoneme correspondence is at the heart of the reading, spelling and writing processes and an adequate mastery of the phonemes is essential for progress.

See *initial teaching alphabet, phonic method.*

References:

Crystal, D. (1982) *Child Language, Learning and Linguistics,* London, Arnold.

Young, P. and Tyre, C. (1983) *Dyslexia or Illiteracy?* Milton Keynes, Open University Press.

phonic method, describes the phonic approach to teaching reading that relies on learning the relationship of written symbol to spoken sound, i.e. grapheme–phoneme correspondence. At its simplest, this might start with learning the sounds of the letters.

Since English is not phonetically regular, there have been attempts to improve its grapheme–phoneme consistency. Colour coding and diacritical marks are examples, and the initial teaching alphabet carried this principle to its logical conclusion by rewriting the alphabet and modifying spelling.

Improving consistency provides an aid the price of which is paid at the unavoidable transition to the irregularities of the normal language. Even with perfectly regular languages, children have reading difficulties, for example with syllabification: grapheme–phoneme correspondence is not the whole answer to reading problems.

Nevertheless the phonic method, applied to normal English does provide a logic to enable many new words to be attempted. But it would be a committed advocate who would argue the case for phonics alone when confronted with words like 'quay' and 'yacht' – though even here knowledge of phonics provides clues which can be added to those the reader gains from context, etc.

The phonic method is often contrasted with the *look-and-say method*: there is some evidence that for some children with language difficulties, for children from deprived backgrounds, and for children said to be dyslexic, an approach emphasising phonics is more successful. But results from studies based on groups may not necessarily apply to individuals: the heart of the issue is not whether the phonic method is better, but when to introduce it, to whom and in what way.

References:

Goodacre, E. (1978) 'Methods of Teaching Reading', in Chapman, L.J. and

Czerniewska, P. (Eds.) (1978) *Reading: from Process to Practice*, Milton Keynes, Open University Press.
Herbert, D. and Davies-Jones, G. (1983) *A Classroom Index of Phonic Resources*, Stafford, National Association for Remedial Education.
Reason, R. and Boote, R. (1986) *Learning Difficulties in Reading and Writing: a Teacher's Manual*, Windsor, NFER-Nelson.
Young, P. and Tyre, C. (1983) *Dyslexia or Illiteracy*, Milton Keynes, Open University Press.

phonology, the study of the pronunciation system of a language. Note the difference from phonetics, which studies the physics and physiology of the production of human sounds, irrespective of the language spoken.

Many articulation disorders of childhood involve phonological problems and require skilled analysis to determine the phonological contrasts that the child can and cannot make.

Reference:

Crystal, D. (1988, 2nd edn.) *Introduction to Linguistic Pathology*, London, Cole and Whurr.

physically handicapped, children with disabilities limiting their mobility, but not necessarily associated with sensory impairments. Physical handicaps are broadly distinguished from mental handicaps, though many children may suffer from conditions which result in both.

The many congenital conditions, such as cerebral palsy, or spina bifida for example, comprise one group of causes of physical handicap: accidents and injuries are another.

Children with physical handicaps have traditionally been more easily accepted in the ordinary school than children whose special needs arose for other reasons, e.g. sensory or mental handicaps. This is probably because their handicaps had no necessary bearing on their educational progress. Access to the curriculum, particularly in secondary school, might have been hindered by their condition, but adapting the building, providing aids and modifying subject choice could go a long way towards meeting educational needs. These arrangements did nothing for any social problems, however, which were sometimes neglected.

Since the Education Act 1981, better arrangements for support have enabled more children with physical handicaps to be educated in ordinary schools. Many authorities now provide a classroom assistant, sometimes as a result of a Statement of special needs. While this is helpful, both academically and socially, it has been argued that providing a classroom assistant on a one-off basis for each physically handicapped child is not the most effective way to offer help. Clustering a small group of children in one school, designated for the purpose, with suitable physical facilities and appropriately staffed with classroom assistants, is one method adopted. Attaching classroom assistants to the support service for special needs gives them a base and somewhere to turn for guidance. Job descriptions and guidelines for the classroom assistants' work are additionally useful in improving the way in which teachers can be helped to help pupils with physical handicaps fit into the regime of the ordinary school, and enjoy the promised access to the *National Curriculum.*

See *COHI.*

References:

Cope, C. and Anderson, E. (1977) *Special Units in Ordinary Schools,* London, University of London Institute of Education.

Darnborough, A. and Kinrade, D. (1988, 5th edn.) *Directory for Disabled People,* Cambridge, Woodhead Faulkner.

Halliday, P. (1989) *Children with Physical Disabilities,* London, Cassell.

Moses, D., Hegarty, S. and Jowett, S. (1988) *Supporting Ordinary Schools: LEA Initiatives,* Windsor, NFER-Nelson.

Riddick, B. (1990) 'The Education of Children with Physical Impairments: Curriculum Developments, Integration and Prospects', in Evans, P. and Varma, V. (Eds.) (1990) *Special Education: Past, Present and Future,* London, Falmer Press.

Russell, P. (1984, 2nd edn.) *The Wheelchair Child,* London, Souvenir Press.

physiotherapists, carry out physical treatments to help improve posture, mobility and physical condition generally. They work within the health service, and are based in hospitals or in the community health services. Paediatric physiotherapists specialise in work with children, which may start from the earliest months, and continue throughout schooldays, often involving them in visits to schools to observe, assess and treat.

Like all remedial therapists, they are in short supply, and many children who could benefit are probably not receiving their services. For this reason, they are increasingly working in an advisory mode, calling on parents and teachers who are in daily and prolonged contact with children, to help with the exercises they prescribe. Physiotherapy is a skilled activity, with training requirements quite different from teaching. But note that *conductive education* is an example of a development which attempts to blend the two roles in the interests of the child.

Reference:

Hegarty, S. and Pocklington, K. (1981) *Educating Pupils with Special Needs in the Ordinary School,* Windsor, NFER-Nelson.

Levitt, S. (Ed.) (1984) *Paediatric Developmental Therapy,* Oxford, Blackwell.

Piagetian theory, is essentially a stage theory of *cognitive development.* Jean Piaget proposed that cognitive development could be considered as an invariant progression through the stages summarised below, the ages given relating to normal development and being approximate only.

In the sensorimotor stage, birth to two years, the infant starts to manipulate objects and to explore the environment, so learning that objects and other persons have a separate existence. This is followed by the pre-operational stage, from two to seven years, in which children learn to identify objects by name, to recognise attributes of objects, such as colour, but are unable to grasp abstract concepts; reasoning is still largely on a trial-and-error basis. At about the age of seven, children move into the concrete operations stage. In this stage, children will have learnt to conserve, i.e. to appreciate that some properties of materials, e.g. volume, number, etc., remain unchanged irrespective of configuration: they can think flexibly and they can classify, so laying the foundations of logical thought.

The final stage, from eleven years onwards, Piaget calls the formal operations stage. Here the child demonstrates the power of adult logic, using the 'if A then B' argument as required.

Note that the stages are divided into substages: note too that for Piaget the age at which children move through the sequence is less important than the fixed nature of the sequence that everyone follows.

Although Piaget's original work was based on observations of children of at least normal ability, his theory has had application to children with learning difficulties, particularly in the field of mental handicap. Thus studies have located many children with severe learning difficulties at the sensorimotor or pre-operational stages: less severe learning difficulties can be placed at correspondingly later stages. Using the qualitative Piagetian model is an advance on describing children in terms of IQ, since it gives a view of the next stage in the development of thinking, and allows exercises aimed at fostering these competencies to be developed. To this extent the Piagetian approach takes an opposite tack from many environmentalists, who argue that fostering language and environmental experiences will improve cognition: Piaget focuses on cognition, arguing that this is the bedrock on which other competencies can be built.

But Piagetian programmes have not been obviously successful in either accelerating the rate at which pupils pass through the Piagetian stages, or raising the stage at which thinking development ceases. At the same time recent work has challenged some of the basic tenets of Piagetian theory, arguing for instance that under certain conditions logical thought is demonstrable at a much earlier age than Piaget described. The social conditions of learning, neglected in Piagetian theory, are more important than he thought.

References:

Child, D. (1986, 4th edn.) *Psychology and the Teacher*, London, Holt, Rinehart and Winston.

Donaldson, M. (1978) *Children's Minds*, Glasgow, Fontana.

Hogg, J. (1987) 'Early Development and Piagetian Tests', in Hogg, J. and Raynes, N.V. (Eds.) (1987) *Advances in Mental Handicap*, Beckenham, Croom Helm.

Lloyd, P. and Swann, W. (1985) 'Piaget and After', Unit 5 of Open University Course E206, Milton Keynes, Open University.

Webb, R. (1983) 'Can Adaptive and Cognitive Behaviour Really be Increased by Sensorimotor Training'? in Hogg, J. and Mittler, P. (Eds.) (1983) *Advances in Mental Handicap Research*, London, Wiley.

pica, persistently eating substances other than food. Young children might eat paint, cloth, dirt, etc. Pica may be associated with mental handicap, or due to a mineral deficiency, or due to poor supervision. Children showing pica should be referred to a paediatrician or to a child guidance clinic. There is always the danger of illness resulting from ingesting poisonous substances, e.g. lead.

Reference:

Barker, P. (1988, 5th edn.) *Basic Child Psychiatry*, Oxford, Blackwell.

pictogram, see *calligram*.

picture vocabulary tests, are widely but misleadingly used as measures of intelligence. In fact, as the name suggests, they measure vocabulary, and in particular oral comprehension vocabulary.

Granted this limited purpose, they are very useful instruments. Essentially they present a child with a selection of pictures, one of which represents the word spoken by the examiner. The child simply has to point to the correct picture. The tests are quick to give. Utilising words and concepts of increasing difficulty enables a wide age-range to be covered with the same procedure and, since the response can be modified to accept a nod instead of pointing, even children with serious language and physical impairments can be assessed.

Most picture vocabulary tests quote high reliabilities, but high values given in manuals are sometimes achieved by using a wide age-range: with restricted age-ranges reliabilities will be lower.

See *British Picture Vocabulary Scale*.

Reference:

Salvia, J. and Ysseldyke, J.E. (1985, 3rd edn.) *Assessment in Special and Remedial Education*, Boston, Houghton Mifflin.

PKU, see *phenylketonuria*.

PL entries, see *Public Laws*.

place of safety order, can be issued by a magistrate or by a juvenile court to protect children in an emergency. An order authorises the removal of a child to a place of safety for a period of up to twenty-eight days. A place of safety is defined as a community home, a controlled community home, any police station, any hospital, surgery, or other suitable place where the occupier is willing temporarily to receive the child.

Under the Children Act 1989, the protection of children will be safeguarded by means of an *emergency protection order* and a *child assessment order*.

See *child abuse*.

play therapy, method of treating young children's emotional and behavioural difficulties, based originally on psychoanalytic principles. Freud believed that children's psychological immaturity made it difficult if not impossible to use psychoanalytic techniques to help them. Certainly orthodox interpretations of dreams, free association methods, etc., can hardly be applied with very young children. Melanie Klein and Anna Freud both believed that children's play expressed their conflicts and difficulties just as clearly as orthodox techniques did with adults. By acceptance of the feelings and relationships revealed in play, followed by skilled and sensitive interpretations of the play situation, usually over a series of regular sessions, they believed that children's problems could be understood and conflicts resolved.

Children's play itself has of course long been recognised as an activity with intrinsic therapeutic and developmental effects, most obviously appreciated in nursery and infant schools, where it is usually an important part of the curriculum. But play therapy is not play, but a highly skilled treatment, and play therapists require long training. They usually work at some child guidance clinics, more often with individual highly disturbed children, but sometimes with small groups. Nevertheless the use of play therapy has been called into question, alongside other treatment based on psychoanalytic principles. The cost of a lengthy series of sessions is an obvious criticism, but the efficacy of the treatment has also been questioned. Moreover the play therapy model is largely a medical model, locating the problem within the child, to be solved by helping the child to change. This may be a valid approach for some problems. For many others it is more effective to see the problem in terms of its context, which for the young child is nearly always the family. Here techniques such as family therapy may be more effective, possibly in combination with behaviour therapy.

See *child guidance, Freudian theory.*

References:

Axline, V. (1971) *Dibs: in Search of Self,* Harmondsworth, Penguin.
Landreth, G.L. (Ed.) (1982) *Play Therapy,* Springfield, C.C. Thomas.

Plowden Report 1967, 'Children and their Primary Schools,' report of the Central Advisory Council (England). It called for the establishment of educational priority areas and devoted a chapter to the education of handicapped children in ordinary schools, including a recommendation for their early identification and for a full-scale enquiry into their needs.

The Plowden Report was enormously influential in shaping English primary education in the 1970s and 1980s. The full-scale enquiry into the education of handicapped children which it recommended was set up in 1974, when the Warnock Committee was formed.

See *Gittins Report.*

Reference:

Department of Education and Science (1967) *Children and their Primary Schools,* London, HMSO.

Plunket nurses, provide a preventive health service in New Zealand for infants and preschool children, and are responsible for identifying many young children with special needs. They see mothers and their children at home and at clinics, on the model of health visitors.

Reference:

McGee, R. and Silva, P.A. (1982) *A Thousand New Zealand Children: their Health and Development from Birth to Seven,* Wellington, Medical Research Council of New Zealand.

Portage project, home-based intervention scheme for helping the development of young children with special needs. The scheme originated in Portage, Wisconsin, but has spread widely in the UK. It offers a teaching package that is based on behavioural theory.

The family is visited at home for about an hour each week by a trained member of the Portage team – a volunteer, or a health visitor, psychologist, physiotherapist, or other professional. The visitor helps the parent (usually mother) first complete a developmental checklist covering the child's social, language, cognitive, self-help and motor skills, then choose a teaching target, and express it in behavioural terms. Task analysis is used to break this down into stages, and a programme of teaching activities, manageable in a week or so, is then worked out.

The Portage pack includes cards linked to the developmental items and offering suggestions for teaching activities. The visitor models for the parent some of the techniques of reinforcement, prompting, shaping, etc., used, and a system of recording the progress made in the short daily sessions is instituted.

The visitor returns after a week or so to discuss progress and plan the next week's activities, and there is usually a built-in structure of meetings between the various Portage workers in an area team.

Portage was designed for preschool children with moderate learning difficulties, but in the UK it has also been widely used with children with severe learning difficulties. In this context, some items are not quite so readily applicable. There are also some reports of better progress with children from deprived environments. A more important criticism is that Portage concentrates on the child to the exclusion of the environment in which the child is developing. It can be argued of course that the very use of Portage will in itself effect a change in the family, even though it was designed as a child-centred technique.

These criticisms apart, Portage is often the most suitable and sometimes the only feasible arrangement for offering education to very young preschool children with special needs. It should ensure that preschool children are brought to the attention of the education authorities as soon as they are able to profit from more orthodox educational provision. But its key feature is the way it capitalises on the wish of many parents of children with special needs to help their child learn. It does this by removing the mystique of the professional, who gives expert skills to the parent. It is the prime example of parents in partnership with professionals.

See *home tuition, parents.*

References:

Cameron, R.J. (Ed.) (1982) *Working Together: Portage in the UK*, Windsor, NFER-Nelson.

Cunningham, C. and Davis, H. (1985) *Working wih Parents: Frameworks for Collaboration*, Milton Keynes, Open University Press.

Portage Early Education Programme: available from NFER-Nelson, Windsor.

positive discrimination, see *discrimination.*

positive reinforcement, see *reinforcement.*

postlingual deafness, severe hearing impairment that has been acquired after the child has gained some competence in spoken language. Since the child has learned at least some of the rhythms, intonation, and linguistic structure of speech, communication ability and hence educational prospects generally are much better than for a child with a similar hearing loss acquired prelingually. The great effort required to learn to communicate means that many profoundly deaf children with a prelingual hearing loss leave school with very limited achievements. The postlingually deaf child should reach much higher standards. However, the quality of the child's speech will gradually deteriorate, since feedback will be missing, but speech therapy helps to maintain this.

Obviously the later the hearing loss is acquired, the less the overall effect, but even the experience of living in a hearing world for a relatively short time makes a substantial difference to later progress. This emphasises the importance of knowing the age of acquisition of a hearing loss in making any recommendations about the education of children with *hearing impairment.*

pragmatics, the use of language in social situations. Children may have a good grasp of the mechanics of language, but still have problems in appreciating the conventions and usages which govern its use in conversation in particular. These children are just as language-disabled, though in a different way, as children whose command of vocabulary and grammar, for example, is weak.

Odd and even bizarre use of language is a characteristic of some serious disabilities, such as autism. But whatever the condition, regular exercises designed to give practice in coping with the use of language in social situations, perhaps using techniques such as role-play, are needed. Collaboration between teacher, psychologist and speech therapist is important.

Reference:

Beveridge, M. and Conti-Ramsden, G. (1987) *Children with Language Disabilities*, Milton Keynes, Open University Press.

precision teaching, system for analysing the effects of teaching, by frequent and accurate measurement of pupils' learning. Precision teaching uses behavioural techniques to analyse teaching into successive steps. These usually include:

- specifying attainment targets in behavioural terms;
- recording performance daily;
- graphing results;
- recording teaching method used;
- analysing data to determine whether progress is satisfactory, and if not, the teaching changes needed.

Teacher sets the mastery level for the skills being taught, and also the rate at which the child is expected to progress, so that actual progress charts can be compared with targets.

The daily assessment is based on short five-minute 'probes', teacher-constructed criterion-referenced tasks. Since the target behaviour has been set behaviourally, progress can be assessed by counting or measuring (e.g. number of sentences read correctly; number of sums completed per minute, etc.). Sometimes special graph-paper is used so that the progress graphs can be interpreted with more insight.

Precision teaching has proved useful with children with learning difficulties. Although the techniques appear time-consuming, advocates of the method insist that they are easy to learn and uncomplicated to apply. They are clearly child-centred: attention is focused on the learning of an individual child and the effects of teaching are brought home in an immediate and curriculum-related way. If progress is slow, it is the teaching approach that has to be altered: responsibility for any shortcoming is not thrust on the pupil.

Feedback for teacher is also feedback for pupil. Many pupils take great interest in their own progress and the target objectives and rates of attainment can prove helpful incentives.

See *behavioural objective.*

References:

Sabatino, D.A. and Miller, T.L. (Eds.) (1979) *Describing Learner Characteristics of Handicapped Children and Youth,* London, Grune and Stratton.

Solity, J. and Bull, S. (1987) *Special Needs: Bridging the Curriculum Gap,* Milton Keynes, Open University Press.

prelingual deafness, see *postlingual deafness.*

prematurity, birth before thirty-seven weeks of gestation, irrespective of weight.

Prematurity is associated with a higher risk of handicapping conditions than full-term delivery, and the lower the birth weight the greater the risk. There is an association with physical, sensory, and neurological damage, leading to impaired cognitive development. To give one example, the incidence of sensorineural hearing loss in the general childhood population is about 0.5%; studies report incidences of between 4% and 18% in populations of very *low birth weight* babies who survive the neonatal period. Behaviour may also be affected – perhaps because the separation from mother in the immediate post-natal period does not permit normal bonding to take place.

These points have implications for education. Thus the Isle of Wight Study found a higher prevalence of children born prematurely (though using a slightly different criterion of prematurity) in an intellectually retarded group, a reading retarded group and a special schools group than in a control group. With advances in medical technology a higher proportion of premature infants are surviving, leading to greater demands on the special education service later.

References:

Rutter, M., Tizard, J. and Whitmore, K. (1970) *Education, Health and Behaviour*, London, Longman.

Tucker, I. and Nolan, M. (1984) *Educational Audiology*, London, Croom Helm.

pre-operational stage, see *Piagetian theory.*

pre-reading activities, activities introduced before a child starts a first reading scheme and intended to prepare for it. There is no clear boundary between these and reading itself: the one stage shades gradually into the other. The activities include listening pleasurably to stories, expressing experiences, enjoying stories told in pictures, learning the meaning of book, page, letter, line, bottom, top, etc., i.e. learning the vocabulary of reading, recognising words and identifying letters.

These are some examples of the many activities that young children enjoy and which help the transition to becoming 'book-bound'. Note too that they can just as easily be described as activities to develop language as activities to prepare for reading.

References:

Department of Education and Science (1975) *A language for Life*, London, HMSO (Bullock Report).

Reason, R. and Boote, R. (1986) *Learning Difficulties in Reading and Writing: a Teacher's Manual*, Windsor, NFER-Nelson.

pre-school education, narrowly defined as education in nursery schools and classes provided by the local education authority (LEA), but often an umbrella term, including classes provided otherwise, and also experiences in playgroups, combined nursery centres, home visiting schemes, etc.

Research into the long-term effects of pre-school education has rarely yielded robust findings, the recent report from the *Child Health and Education Study* (Osborn and Milbank, 1988) being perhaps excluded. Nevertheless many earlier enquiries, even if open to methodological criticism, also suggest that pre-school education improves children's cognitive development, and that the effects last. Social development improves, too. These are just two reasons why provision for the under-fives with special needs was accorded priority in the Warnock Report.

Legally, for pre-school children with statements, LEAs must provide the education stipulated. Note that while LEAs have a duty to assess and provide for the special needs of children over the age of two years, for those under two, the LEA can only proceed with the consent of or at the request of the parent.

Pre-school children with statements are often children with significant visual and hearing impairments and with severe disabilities, known to the support services. Priority admission to LEA classes and schools is often available. But for the less readily identifiable child, the chances of pre-school education are not good. Many young children with mild learning difficulties, growing up in poor circumstances, will miss pre-school education entirely.

While pre-school education is good, for children with special needs it undoubtedly could be better. Surveys point to the need for training in special needs for the staff involved. While financial stringency rules, home visiting schemes such as the Portage project, in which resources are targeted at children most in need, and parents provide the day-to-day educational input, will continue to have considerable attractions.

See *nursery education, pre-school playgroups*.

References:

Birchall, D. (1984) 'Services for the Pre-school Child with Special Needs: a Review of Research', *Highlight*, 58, London, National Children's Bureau.

Chazan, M., Laing, A.F., Bailey, M.S. and Jones, G. (1980) *Some of our Children*, London, Open Books.

Clark, M.M. (1988) *Children Under Five: Educational Research and Evidence*, London, Gordon and Breach.

Osborn, F. and Milbank, J.E. (1987) *The Effects of Early Education: a Report from the Child Health and Education Survey*, Oxford, Clarendon Press.

Robson, B. (1989) *Pre-school Provision for Children with Special Needs*, London, Cassell.

pre-school playgroups, aim to extend young children's experiences and widen social contacts through play. Groups, which usually charge for admission, are run by voluntary organisations, or by the local community, or by the local authority, and there is a thriving Pre-school Playgroups Association. Although the need for playgroups may be greatest in deprived areas, they tend to be found more frequently elsewhere. Some playgroups, sometimes called opportunity groups, cater mainly for handicapped children, but most parents want their child to attend the neighbourhood group. Admission depends on the attitude of the leader, often influenced by other parents, though the attitudes are usually positive.

There is a widely-held view that play-group attendance improves both language and social skills, though conclusive evidence for this is not easy to find: pre-school playgroups are held to be a particularly valuable educational experience for children with special needs. What the groups usually lack is the educational expertise in designing suitable experiences for young children with special needs. What they offer, apart from the integrative experience itself, is the presence of a large number of willing adult helpers.

See *nursery education, preschool education.*

References:

Chazan, M., Laing, A.F., Bailey, M.S. and Jones, G. (1980) *Some of our Children*, London, Open Books.

Robson, B. (1989) *Pre-school Provision for Children with Special Needs*, London, Cassell.

prevalence (of special needs), the number of children with special needs in a defined population over a given period. Prevalence rates usually refer to the general population, and are essential in planning services.

Prevalence is distinguished from incidence, which is effectively prevalence of new cases. Note, too, the importance of the phrase 'given period'. Thus the prevalence of special needs in the UK over the period of compulsory schooling was estimated as c.20% (one in five): at any one time it was estimated as c.16% (one in six).

The prevalence of special educational need due to physical conditions, with clear criteria for diagnosis, can be determined more reliably than prevalence of socially determined conditions, such as learning difficulties and behavioural difficulties, which depend on relativities. Here surveys based on teachers' opinions have been used alongside psychometric methods to arrive at prevalence rates.

Some authorities prefer to give prevalence ranges, rather than exact rates. Others point out that quoted prevalence rates may be partly determined by political and social factors: the service provided depends on the prevalence estimate, but the prevalence estimate may also depend on the service provided. Nevertheless, a number of developed countries publish overall prevalence rates for special educational needs of between 10 and 20% of the school population.

See *incidence.*

References:

Department of Education and Science (1978) *Special Educational Needs*, London, HMSO. (Warnock Report).

Hallahan, D.P. and Kaufman, J.M. (1988, 4th edn.) *Exceptional Children: Introduction to Special Education*, Englewood Cliffs, Prentice Hall.

Galloway, G. and Goodwin, C. (1987) *The Education of Disturbing Children: pupils with learning and adjustment difficulties*, Harlow, Longman.

Ward, J. (1982) 'Special Education in Australia', *The Exceptional Child*, 29, 2, 137–47.

Preventive Approaches to Disruption (PAD), package of materials intended to be used in school-based inservice training. The materials aim to avoid classroom disturbance by improving skills in lesson organisation, pupil management, and teaching skills generally. They include practical activities, a video, observation guides, etc. Although designed for secondary schools, the materials have application to primary schools.

The pyramid model of training used in the Education of the Developmentally Young (EDY) programme and Special Needs Action Programme (SNAP) is advocated, with the psychologist introducing the materials to a school.

References:
Chisholm, B., Kearney, D., Knight, G., Morris, S. and Tweddle, D. (1986) *Preventive Approaches to Disruption*, Basingstoke, Macmillan.
Knight, G., Chisholm, B., Kearney, D., Little, H. and Morris, S. (1989) 'Developments in the Use of Preventive Approaches to Disruption', *Educational Psychology in Practice*, 5, 3, 148–59.

primary reading skills, see *higher-order reading skills.*

profile analysis, interpreting the pattern of scores on subtests in order to help with diagnosis and prescription for teaching. An example is the 'cocked hat' profile on the Wechsler intelligence scales, a characteristic pattern of performance sub-test scores, which suggests that hearing should be checked, since it is often found in children with hearing impairment.

However, profile patterns are based on differences between subtests. Subtest scores are inevitably less reliable than full scores, and differences between them usually have to be substantial to reach significance. This is not to say that they should be ignored, but rather that they should be interpreted with great caution, and with an awareness of their reliability – or unreliability.

Reference:
Berger, M. and Yule, W. (1987) 'Psychometric Approaches', in Hogg, J. and Raynes, N.V. (Eds.) (1987) *Assessment in Mental Handicap*, Beckenham, Croom Helm.

profiling, assessing, reviewing and recording pupils' performance, usually in consultation with them.

In secondary schools, profiles provide pupils with an ongoing graphical record of their achievement which is material testimony to their achievement at school, and which can be taken with them on leaving.

For pupils with learning difficulties, the ability of the profile to record achievement in non-academic areas, including personal qualities and out-of-school activities, is a great advance over the usual school report system. It enables positive attributes to be recorded and helps improve a pupil's self-image. The involvement of the pupil in negotiating those attainments and qualities to be profiled often helps in relationships with staff. Significant improvements in pupils' behaviour have been reported after the introduction of a profiling system.

In primary schools in particular, profile analysis is a qualitative and quantitative method of describing a child's assets as well as difficulties, educational needs, and continuing development. It complements the narrowly-focused regular recording of daily progress by providing a more rounded picture. The main problem in introducing a profiling system is the need for staff training beforehand and for time to ensure that it is managed in the spirit intended. For pupils with special needs, a properly managed profile system is usually only beneficial.

See *Records of Achievement.*

Reference:

Baynes, A. (1987) 'The Pastoral Role', in Hinson, M. (Ed.) (1987) *Teachers and Special Educational Needs,* Harlow, Longman in association with National Association for Remedial Education.

Wolfendale, S. (1987) *Primary Schools and Special Needs: Policy, Planning and Provision,* London, Cassell.

profound retardation, implies a level of intellectual functioning so impaired that a child will need care and supervision throughout life. In the USA this description is usually reserved for individuals with an IQ of less than 20–25, the range allowing for clinical judgement at the borderline between profound and severe retardation. In the UK the term is also applied to adults with a mental development of less than that of a three-year-old, effectively a similar description.

Many children with profound retardation also suffer from additional handicaps. They may not walk or talk, and normal social relationships may be difficult to sustain. Most are educated in special care units. These are usually attached to special schools for children with severe learning difficulties, but sometimes to schools for other needs. The quality of the provision is variable, and the lack of adequate support for the teaching staff is striking, perhaps a reflection of the intensive adult–pupil ratio that these children demand.

See *mental retardation, special care provision.*

References:

Evans, P. and Ware, J. (1987) *Special Care Provision,* Windsor, NFER-Nelson.

Sebba, J. and Hogg, J. (Eds.) (1988) *European Journal of Special Education,* 3, 4, Dec. 1988.

Progress Assessment Charts (PAC), developed by Gunzburg for assessing the personal and social development of people with mental handicap. Different charts are used for different age-groups and there is one specifically designed for use with individuals with Down's syndrome.

Information is provided by someone familiar with the individual's behaviour, or by direct observation. The charts provide a visual profile of competencies, which permits comparisons with peers.

See *adaptive behaviour.*

References:

Raynes, N.V. (1987) 'Adaptive Behaviour Scales', in Hogg, J. and Raynes, N.V. (Eds.) (1987) *Assessment in Mental Handicap,* Beckenham, Croom Helm.

Shakespeare, R. (1970) 'Severely Subnormal Children', in Mittler, P. (Ed.) (1970) *The Psychological Assessment of Mental and Physical Handicap*, London, Methuen.

projection, see *defence mechanism.*

projective techniques and tests, methods of studying personality characteristics by providing the child with a relatively unstructured task and analysing the response.

Projective techniques are based on the belief that an open task allows freedom for individuals to respond in ways that reflect their concerns and personality. More specifically, adherents of psychoanalytic theories believe that projective techniques allow individuals to reveal unconscious feelings and attitudes, often disturbing feelings that the individual finds it hard consciously to acknowledge. Unlike most standardised measures of personality, they do not attempt to assess single traits or personality factors, but offer a means of coming to understand the dominant elements in a whole personality.

Asking a child to draw a picture is an example of a simple projection technique, for the drawing can then be interpreted by the clinician. Other techniques involve telling stories to pictures, describing inkblots, completing sentences, etc. These more formalised approaches permit some comparisons between frequently made responses and unusual ones, so beginning to introduce an element of objectivity into an area in which it is notably absent.

Overall, most projective techniques are characterised by poor standardisation, poor reliability and questionable validity. Yet they continue to be widely used, perhaps because of the insights they can sometimes offer to the skilled user. For classroom use they are rarely of much value, but they are frequently used in clinical settings with emotionally disturbed children.

See *personality tests.*

Reference:

Anastasi, A. (1982, 5th Edn.) *Psychological Testing,* New York, Macmillan.

prompt, an extra stimulus which helps to generate the required response, provided when the main stimulus is ineffective. The use of prompts is stressed in behavioural approaches to teaching. The obvious analogy is the actor's prompt in the theatre. Like this, the teaching prompt is dropped as soon as the main stimulus (the preceding line) is effective.

See *cueing.*

References:

Alberto, P.A. and Troutman, A.C. (1986, 2nd edn.) *Applied Behavior Analysis for Teachers,* Columbus, Merrill.

Wheldall, K. and Merrett, F. (1984) *Positive Teaching: the Behavioural Approach,* London, Allen and Unwin.

psychoanalysis, see *Freudian theory.*

psychodrama, method of group psychotherapy which uses the techniques of the theatre to treat emotional and interpersonal problems. Situations are played out on the stage, with the therapist as director. Where music, lighting, sound effects, etc., are available and lend verisimilitude, these are used. Usually the situation enacted depicts a personal problem of one of the group members, who helps the other players portray the other dramatis personae as accurately as possible.

When the play begins, the director may vary the situation, change the characters, reverse roles, etc., in an effort to identify the emotional blocks in the central character's life. Once identified, the drama proceeds to attempt to resolve them, using the support of the group.

Psychodrama requires a highly-trained and sensitive therapist. Its main use in special education has been in schools for older children with serious emotional and behavioural difficulties, usually due to relationship problems.

Reference:

Van Meerts, M. (1983) *The Effective Use of Role-Play: a framework for teachers and trainers*, London, Kogan Page.

psychologist, person with a training and higher education qualification in psychology recognised by the appropriate professional organisation (in the UK the British Psychological Society). There are many different kinds of psychologist: those that are recognised as professionally qualified are titled *chartered psychologists*. *Educational psychologists* employed in school psychological services are most closely involved in special education, though hospital-based *clinical psychologists* also see children with developmental difficulties.

Information available from:

British Psychological Society, St Andrews House, 48, Princess Rd. East, Leicester, LE1 7DR.

psychoneurosis, see *neurosis, neurotic behaviour*.

psychopaedic hospital, hospital in New Zealand which serves people who are mentally handicapped. The term was coined in an effort to find a name which avoids any stigma associated with a title such as 'hospital for the mentally retarded' and yet distinguishes such a hospital from one for the psychiatrically ill. Psychopaedic nurses and psychopaedic training officers cover duties with mental handicap similar to their counterparts in the UK.

Reference:

Singh, N.N. and Wilton, K.M. (Eds.) (1985) *Mental Retardation in New Zealand*, Christchurch, Whitcoulls.

psychopathic disorder, one of the four legal categories of mental disorder, defined in the Mental Health Act 1983 as a persistent disorder or disability of mind (whether or not including significant impairment of intelligence) which results in abnormally aggressive or irresponsible conduct.

Note that this is a legal definition, describing psychopathic disorder in terms of persistent antisocial behaviour. This is the behaviour for which offenders without psychiatric labels are sent to prison; those with are admitted to hospital.

Clinically, 'psychopathic personality' is a term often used to describe a person unable to give or to respond normally to affection, with an undeveloped conscience and lack of guilt at antisocial acts. Bowlby and other child psychiatrists have argued that the basis for this maldevelopment is severe deprivation in infancy, in particular the inability to form bonds with a parent or parent-figure – or indeed any person – during this critical period.

References:

Gostin, L. (1983) *A Practical Guide to Mental Health Law*, London, MIND.

Rutter, M. (1981, 2nd edn.) *Maternal Deprivation Reassessed*, Harmondsworth, Penguin.

psychosis, psychotic behaviour, the most serious group of psychological illnesses. The main characteristic is a lack of contact with reality; bizarre, disordered thought and behaviour.

Psychoses can be classified as the schizophrenias, toxic confusional and delirious states (as in serious drug abuse), dementias (due perhaps to neurological or organic damage), and brief reactive psychoses (sudden appearance of psychotic symptoms at times of severe stress). Psychoses are rare in childhood. After puberty, the prevalence of the first two groups increases, and medical or psychological advice should be sought if bizarre behaviour appears in pupils. Reliable prevalence figures are not easy to obtain because diagnostic criteria vary, but figures of less than one per thousand have been quoted.

Psychotic illnesses can be managed and in some cases cured, though the outlook must always be uncertain for such serious conditions. Drug treatments, behaviour therapy, psychotherapy, milieu therapy, etc., are all used, depending on the individual child and the views of the person in charge of treatment. There is no best method. Providing suitable educational facilities, often in special units or schools, may be the most helpful course of action. Here, in a therapeutic community, education and treatment can merge.

See *schizophrenia*.

References:

Barker, P. (1988, 5th edn.) *Basic Child Psychiatry*, Oxford, Blackwell.

Simon, G.B. (1984) *A Teacher's Guide to Medication for Children with Special Needs and to Drug Misuse by Young People*, Stratford-upon-Avon, National Council for Special Education.

psychotherapy, treatment by psychological means, nearly always treatment of emotional and behavioural difficulties. Normally the term is applied more narrowly, i.e. only to those therapies that are rooted in the psychodynamic tradition. It is then contrasted with behaviour therapies, based on learning theories, cognitive therapies, based on the importance of having to think about behaviour, and humanistic therapies, based on self-concept development.

In its normal, psychodynamic usage, psychotherapy assumes that conflicts underlie a person's difficulties, and then attempts to resolve them. Classic Freudian psychotherapy posits that these conflicts result from repressed infantile sexuality, and that the orthodox techniques of psychoanalysis – interpretation of dreams, free association, etc., must be used first to identify them, then to bring them to consciousness and then to deal with the repressed emotion through catharsis.

As psychoanalytic theory ramified, different therapies developed. Some granted more influence to experiences later than infancy. Others developed techniques for working with much younger children than hitherto. Still others modified the one-to-one relationship with the therapist by developing family therapies and group therapy. All these are derivatives of classic psychotherapy.

One point is clear. None of these approaches offers much help to the teacher in the ordinary classroom: therapists are highly-trained professionals, who offer an intensive and expensive service to a very small number of children, usually in an office or clinic away from the ordinary school community.

Moreover there is considerable controversy over the efficacy of classical psychotherapy. Studies find little difference between the success rate claimed and natural remission – though this is an oversimplification of a complicated debate. Consequently, in the school situation, other approaches – behaviour therapies (e.g. behaviour modification), humanistic therapies (e.g. non-directive counselling) etc. – are used. Here clear differences between control groups and experimental groups of children with behavioural difficulties can be shown, one study reporting improvement rates of 70–80% for these therapies as opposed to 50+% remission rate for the controls.

But for very disturbed children the picture may be different, and psychotherapists and play therapists do work at some schools and units for very disturbed children, where psychotherapy is one of the essential weapons in the treatment armoury, sometimes used in conjunction with others.

See *Freudian theory, play therapy.*

References:

Greben, S.E. (1987) 'Psychotherapy Today', *British Journal of Psychiatry*, 151, 283-287.

Kolvin, I., Garside, R.F., Nicol, A.R. MacMillan, R., Wolstenholme, F. and Leitch, I.M. (1981) *Help Starts Here*, London, Tavistock.

Public Law (PL), the equivalent in the USA to an Act of Parliament. Each Public Law is designated by two hyphenated numbers: the first identifies the Congress that passed the bill and the second is the bill number within that Congress. Thus PL 94-142 is the 142nd bill passed by the 94th Congress.

There are many Public Laws which affect special education. They have assumed increasing importance in recent years, with the increasing tendency for parents to challenge the providers of education in the courts. They offer the opportunity to use the legal process to make special education more accountable. The following entries refer to some of the more influential laws commonly encountered in the literature.

PL 93-112, aimed to terminate discrimination against handicapped individuals. It provided that no-one should be denied participation in any activity funded by federal grant on grounds of handicap. This specifically applied to employment, health, welfare, and social services, as well as to education. The interesting point is that the education provisions resemble those of the much better known PL 94-142, which was passed some two years later.

Reference:

Taylor, J. (1981) *Speech Language Pathology Services in the Schools*, New York, Grune and Stratton.

PL 93-380, contained a number of provisions relating to special education, many of which foreshadowed PL 94-142. But the most well-known section, the Buckley Amendment, relates to records and reports. This gave parents (and students over eighteen) the right to inspect all relevant official records relating to the students, and to have them altered if incorrect. The law also placed limits on the release of student data without parental permission. This second stipulation did cause some difficulties to researchers, but the first was hailed as an important step in parents' right to freedom of information.

Reference:

Taylor, J. (1981) *Speech-Language Pathology Services to Schools*, New York, Grune and Stratton.

PL 94-142, Education for all Handicapped Children Act, brought together earlier provisions for special education in the USA, strengthened and extended them, and offered increased federal support.

The two key features of PL 94-142 that have attracted most attention are requirements that:

(1) all children should be educated in the *least restrictive environment*, usually but not necessarily interpreted as mainstreaming; in fact this provision has not substantially increased the proportion of handicapped children educated in the mainstream;
(2) all handicapped children should have a written *individualised education program (IEP)* prepared. This has some similarities to the Statement of special educational needs in the UK. One difference is a time-limit

stipulation – thirty days between identification of need and implementation of the IEP. The time-limit is not always met, but it does result in a much speedier process.

In addition, PL 94-142 placed responsibilities on education agencies to identify all children with handicaps, to make available a free and appropriate public education, to ensure due consultation with parents, and to ensure that parental access to records was granted. These provisions are similar in principle to some of the provisions in the *Education Act 1981*, but with some interesting differences. For example appeals by parents against recommended educational programs are not heard by representatives of the education service, but by neutrals. Another significant difference lies in the assessment procedures. While the requirements for multidisciplinary evaluation are not dissimilar, PL 94-142 states that assessment must not be biased by language or cultural characteristics, a protection against discrimination in assessment that is not present in the UK legislation. But the effect of this provision has not always met its intentions: it has been argued that some school districts have been reluctant to label minority children as handicapped, so depriving them of appropriate education, for fear that the assessment procedures could not be defended.

Possible difficulties of this nature notwithstanding, PL 94-142 has been a landmark in USA special education legislation, and an Act which has been influential in many other countries.

References:

Carrier, J. (1984) 'Comparative Special Education: Ideology, Differentiation and Allocation in England and the United States', in Barton, L. and Tomlinson, S. (Eds.) (1984) *Special Education and Social Interests*, Beckenham, Croom Helm.

Gordon, M. (1986) 'Lessons from America', *Support for Learning*, 1, 2, 3–7.

US Department of Education (various dates) *Annual Reports to Congress on the Implementation of Public Law 94-142*, Washington, US Department of Education.

PL 94-482, considerably increased the funding for vocational education for handicapped persons by requiring states to match the federal contribution. In many cases this doubled resources, resulting in a substantial increase in the number of programs (courses), and in personnel to service them.

Reference:

Brolin, D.E. (1982, 2nd edn.) *Vocational Preparation of Persons with Handicaps*, Columbus, Merrill.

PL 95-561, Gifted and Talented Children's Act, provided funding for improving educational services for the gifted and talented. The services supported include projects for developing innovative methods for delivering education as well as providing teaching materials and courses for teachers.

References:

Alexander, P.A. and Muia, J.A. (1982) *Gifted Education: a Comprehensive Roadmap*, London, Aspen Systems.

PL 95-602, provided services to support independent living for those whose disabilities make work impossible.

Reference:

Brolin, D.E. (1982, 2nd Edn.) *Vocational Preparation of Persons with Handicaps,* Columbus, Merrill.

PL 99-457, extended PL 94-142 to children aged three to five years in states that do not offer free education for children in that age group. These states were previously exempt from its application to these children. Consequently, from 1990–91, when the provisions come into force, every handicapped child in the USA is entitled to an appropriate education from the age of three years. PL 99-457 also encouraged the development of early intervention programmes for younger children and infants.

These provisions can be compared with the duties laid on education authorities in the UK to identify children with special needs from the age of two, and from birth if the parents request this, specified in the Education Act 1981.

Reference:

Hallahan, D.P. and Kaufman, J.M. (1988, 4th edn.) *Exceptional Children: Introduction to Special Education,* Englewood Cliffs, Prentice Hall.

Pudenz valve, see *shunt.*

punishment, is used in at least two different senses. To most people, punishment is an act of retribution, to be enforced when behaviour infringes an agreed code. This view rests on the belief that the infringer can choose to behave in certain ways, and that punishment is to be expected when the wrong or antisocial choice is made. This view raises many philosophical questions – for example, what is the age at which children can reasonably be expected to make deliberate choices?

The second view of punishment is that held by the behaviourists. They take a functional view, defining punishment as any stimulus which results in a decrease of the behaviour preceding it. Thus sending a child to his room for misdemeanours will be seen by the behaviourist as a punishment only if the misdemanours decrease thereafter; the parent probably classes it as a punishment notwithstanding its effect.

Behavioural therapies usually avoid punishment, emphasising the more productive effect of reinforcing wanted behaviour, or reinforcing behaviour which is incompatible with the unwanted behaviour. Where punishment is applied, it can either take the form of withdrawing a reward, as in time-out, or in applying a stimulus which causes pain, e.g. corporal punishment. Aversion therapy is a technique which makes controlled use of this latter method. But it should be noted that corporal punishment is now illegal in schools in Britain.

Note the difference between punishment and negative reinforcement: the former is aimed at reducing unwanted behaviour, whereas the latter is aimed at increasing wanted behaviour.

There are legal and ethical issues for teachers who consider applying aversive stimuli – e.g. should parental agreement be obtained? Moreover the situation is complex: how it is done may be as important as what is done. Behaviourists have argued that applying aversive stimuli may be effective in the short term, but long term effects are more doubtful: they may alienate rather than educate.

See *aversion therapy, reinforcement.*

References:

Alberto, P.A. and Troutman, A.C. (1986, 2nd edn.) *Applied Behaviour Analysis for Teachers*, Columbus, Merrill.

Docking, J.W. (1986) 'The Effects and the Effectiveness of Punishment in Schools', in Cohen, A. and Cohen L. (Eds.) (1986) *Disruptive Behaviour: a Sourcebook for Teachers*, London, Harper and Row.

pupil–teacher ratios, were recommended by the Department of Education and Science in circular 4/73. The ratios depended on the categories of handicap then in force, and varied from 2–3 for blind children using Braille, to 11–13 for children with moderate learning difficulties. These recommendations were used for special schools, special classes and units.

The Education Act 1981 abolished categories, and advocated increased integration. This has thrown the pupil–teacher guidelines into the melting-pot. The welcome development of closer links between the staffs of special and ordinary schools has further complicated the issue. The ratios for children with special needs in ordinary classrooms need to be rethought. One approach to the problem is to reduce class size where children with special needs are involved. Another is to increase the provision of outreach teaching services from staff based in special schools. Or both methods can be used. Current proposals suggest allocating teacher time per pupil, depending on the intensity of demand made by pupils on teachers. The teacher time might vary between 0.1 teachers per pupil to 0.2 teachers per pupil, according to learning difficulty. But these figures are proposals, not recommendations at this stage.

Note that classroom assistants, important though they are, are counted in adult–pupil ratios, not in pupil–teacher ratios. Nor should the staff of the advisory services, who usually work with teachers, not directly with children, be counted in the pupil–teacher ratio.

See *classroom assistant.*

References:

Department of Education and Science (1990) *Staffing for Pupils with Special Educational Needs*, Circular letter 10.1.1990, London, Department of Education and Science.

Hogg, B. (1988) 'Circular Saw', *Times Educational Supplement*, 14.10.1988.

Sayer, J. (1987) *Secondary Schools for All? Strategies for Special Needs*, London, Cassell.

Purdue Perceptual–Motor Survey, assesses proficiency in five areas, namely balance and posture; body image and differentiation; perceptual–motor match; ocular control; form perception. Scoring is qualitative, in that the examiner selects a statement that best describes a child's performance.

The survey was standardised on children in grades one to four inclusive (aged seven to ten approximately), but is applied more widely.

Physiotherapists use the survey for evaluating children's physical performance. It has also been used as the basis for remedial exercises, on the assumption that improving perceptual–motor skills will help with learning difficulties, but this is a controversial area.

Reference:

Faas, L.A. (1981, 2nd edn.) *Learning Disabilities: a Competency-based Approach*, Boston, Houghton Mifflin.

pure-tone audiometry, see *audiometry.*

Pygmalion effect, self-fulfilling prophecy, the belief that a prediction is fulfilled simply because it is made. In education, this was investigated in relation to intelligence by Rosenthal and Jacobson, who claimed that a teacher's expectations about a child's intelligence actually affected that intelligence, and that the effect could be measured by changes in test scores.

Rosenthal and Jacobson's original work has been criticised, and replications have not always found the effects claimed. Findings on the Pygmalion effect differ, depending on variables such as the context, the pupils, the teacher, and whether academic or social behaviours are involved.

See *labelling.*

References:

Rogers, C. (1990) 'Teachers' Expectations and Pupils' Achievements', in Entwistle, N. (Ed.) (1990) *Handbook of Educational Ideas and Practices*, London, Routledge.

Rosenthal, R. and Jacobson, L. (1968) *Pygmalion in the Classroom*, New York, Holt, Rinehart and Winston.

Q

quadriplegia, see *cerebral palsy.*

Quality and Equality, abbreviated title of a report of the Australian Schools Commission, produced in 1985. While the report applied to Australian education generally, it made a number of recommendations aimed at strengthening the responses of individual States to meeting special educational needs, through modifying and improving funding arrangements for approved educational objectives. Special programme funds were also recommended for improving special education support services, early special education, etc. (Full title: Quality and Equality – Commonwealth Specific Purpose Programmes for Australian Schools.)

Reference:
Martens, M.-H., (1986) 'From the President's Desk', *Australian Journal of Special Education*, 10, 1, 4–5.

Quota Scheme, legal requirement that every employer of twenty or more persons should employ a prescribed percentage (set at 3% in 1946) of the work force from a register of disabled persons. Where a firm is below quota it must take on a suitable registered disabled person to fill a vacancy, unless permitted by the Employment Service (within the Department of Employment) to engage someone who is not disabled.

An employer can apply for special exemption if the quota of disabled persons cannot be filled because no suitable candidate is available, or because the work is not suitable. Bulk permits can be obtained covering six-month periods: effectively, employers can escape their obligations to the register by a twice-yearly application for exemption.

The impact of the legislation in securing employment opportunities for the disabled has been minimal.

Government departments and the National Health Service are exempt from the quota requirements, but have accepted them on a voluntary basis. This attempt to set a moral lead has not been particularly successful.

See *Disabled Persons Register.*

Reference:
Darnborough, A. and Kinrade, D. (1981) 'The Disabled Person and Employment', in Guthrie, D. (Ed.) (1981) *Disability – Legislation and Practice*, London, Macmillan.

Quirk Report 1972, 'Speech Therapy Services', concluded that about 3% of children in ordinary schools suffer from some kind of speech disorder, but only about 2% were in need of speech therapy. In preschool children Quirk raised the estimate of those needing speech therapy to 3%. For children with special needs of various kinds, the prevalence of speech problems increases. Thus the report estimated that 50% of children then described as severely educationally subnormal needed speech therapy.

As with all estimates of prevalence, the rate given depends heavily on the criteria used. But using these estimates, which were based on a review of the available research, the report was able to point to the acute shortage of *speech therapists* and to the consequent limitations placed on the services needed by children with language disorders.

Since the Quirk Report, there has been an increase in the number of speech therapists in post, but newer and better methods of working require extra time, and the increase has not satisfied demand.

References:
Crystal, D. (1988, 2nd edn.) *Introduction to Language Pathology*, London, Cole and Whurr.
Department of Education and Science (1972) *Speech Therapy Services*, London, HMSO (Quirk Report).

R

radio aids, overcome many of the problems associated with conventional hearing-aid systems, offering a better signal-to-noise ratio at the child's ear. A radio system comprises a microphone and transmitter unit worn by the speaker, whilst the child wears the radio receiver. What the speaker says is picked up by the microphone, converted into a radio signal and then broadcast on a permitted radio frequency range. The child's radio receiver is tuned to the transmitting frequency and picks up the signal, which is amplified by the child's own hearing-aids and fed directly into the child's ears. There is thus no noise interference and a clear signal is received over a distance of up to 100 metres, regardless of background noise.

Radio systems are a major factor in the successful integration of severely deaf children into mainstream schools, since children receive clear speech signals, even in difficult listening conditions. However, they are not a panacea and must be used selectively and with expert oversight.

Ralphs Report 1973, dealt with the work of an *education welfare officer* (ewo). It noted that some 70% of the ewos' time was concerned with work of a social nature. It argued that ewos should be trained in social work skills, but that their work should continue to be carried out in an educational setting. In this latter respect it advocated a different point of view from the earlier Seebohm report, which believed that the ewos should be part of a local authority's personal social services.

Not all of the report's assumptions have been followed: it expected that there would be a need for specialist ewos, with specialist functions, but services have continued to operate mainly with generalist staff. But it has set the broad pattern and direction of ewo work for over a decade.

Reference:

Local Government Training Board (1973) *The Role and Training of Educational Welfare Officers*, Luton, Local Government Training Board.

Rampton Report 1981, interim report of the Committee of Enquiry, chaired by Sir Anthony Rampton, on the educational needs and attainments of children from ethnic minorities. One of the reasons for establishing the Committee was the strong feeling of parents and others on the preponderance of pupils from families of West Indian cultural background in special schools and classes for children with learning and behavioural difficulties. This proved a predictably thorny issue, and after the production of this interim report the Committee was reconstituted under a different chairman.

The Committee argued that the major determinants of the underachievement of West Indian pupils were difficult social conditions leading to poor preschool care, parental attitudes, as well as 'unintentional racism', negative attitudes and low expectations on the part of some teachers. It noted that Asian children did as well as or better than white children.

The Committee aimed at creating a multicultural education system, in which the cultures of ethnic minorities would be valued and racial bias reduced. Its recommendations dealt, inter alia, with preschool provision, content of books and teaching materials, school–community links, and arrangements for special education, including the ethnic mix of special schools for pupils with learning difficulties.

See *Swann Report.*

Reference:

Department of Education and Science (1981) *West Indian Children in our Schools,* London, HMSO (Rampton Report).

Rasch Model, method of item analysis used in constructing some tests. The Rasch model is a fairly recent development. Unlike other methods it aims to identify items which fit the model and which differ from each other in difficulty. A Rasch scale aims to be unidimensional. The items can be assigned difficulty estimates, so permitting test scores to be regarded as scores on an equal interval scale.

Perhaps the best known uses of the Rasch model have been in the preparation of the British Ability Scales, and in the measurement of some aspects of attainment.

References:

Elliott, C.D., Murray, D.J. and Pearson, L.S. (1983) *Manuals to the British Ability Scales,* Windsor, NFER-Nelson.

Pumfrey, P.D. (1987) 'Rasch Scaling and Reading Tests', *Journal of Research in Reading,* 10, 1, 75–86.

ratio IQ, see *intelligence quotient.*

ratio reinforcement, see *reinforcement.*

rationalisation, see *defence mechanism.*

Raven's Progressive Matrices, intelligence test developed by J.C. Raven between 1938 and 1958. The test was originally held to measure 'g'. Factorial studies have suggested that while this is largely true, it is to some extent a measure of spatial and other abilities too. The standard form consists of sixty designs arranged in groups of twelve. Each design has a piece missing; the missing piece has to be chosen from a number of possibilities. The correct choice depends on perceiving increasingly difficult logical relationships. There is a coloured form suitable for five- to eleven-year-olds or individuals who are mentally handicapped, and an advanced form for the very able.

Raven's matrices are simple to give. Children with many different special needs can be assessed, since responses can be made by pointing, or gesture.

They have been widely used with children whose mother tongue is not English, but even an apparently neutral test like the Matrices is open to criticism when used cross-culturally, perhaps particularly with non-Western populations. The greatest criticism is usually directed at the poverty of the test construction data, which give little or no information on item selection, reliability, validity, etc. However, its worldwide currency testifies to its usefulness, and several local norms have been produced, including a British restandardisation in the 1970s, and ones in Australia and Hong Kong in the 1970s.

References:

de Lemos, M.M. (1984) 'A Note on the Australian Norms for the Standard Progressive Matrices', *ACER Bulletin for Psychologists*, 36, Nov. 1984.

Kyle, J.G. (1977) 'Raven's Progressive Matrices – 30 Years Later', *Bulletin of the British Psychological Society*, 30, Dec. 1977.

readability index, the level of difficulty of a text, usually assessed by a formula and expressed as a reading age or grade. Note that the technical term does not cover interest level, which is often included in the everyday usage, e.g. 'a readable book'. A knowledge of the readability of texts is important, if only to make sure that reading schemes and curriculum materials generally are pitched at an appropriate level for the children. Many measures of readability, or readability formulae, have been devised for this purpose, for publishers' estimates, if available, can be inaccurate!

Most formulae rely on two indices, a semantic index (e.g. a measure of word difficulty) and a syntactic index (e.g. a measure of sentence difficulty). These are combined, as in the *Fog index*, to produce a readability score – a grade equivalent or reading age. More complicated formulae add little to the validity of the measures for most texts.

Two aids to calculation should be noted. Graphs and charts enable a readability score to be determined visually, as in the *Fry readability formula*. Computer programmes enable several different readability figures to be obtained from the same piece of text.

But to make an accurate estimate of the readability of a book, the whole book should be assessed: readability formulae take samples, and all samples are subject to sampling error. More importantly, a key question is the criterion against which the readability score is validated. This is usually a reading age score on a comprehension test, which at once raises questions about the standardisation date, population, etc. Readability measures are useful, but not set in stone. As in so many instances, decisions on the suitability of texts should not be based on a measure alone: judgement should also be used.

Cloze procedure is a variant on the formula method, and overcomes the uncertainties of the formulae by requiring the child to interact directly with the material. The sampling problem remains, but cloze procedure does give a measure of how well the child follows the text, a direct and immediate criterion.

References:
Harrison, C. (1979) 'Assessing the Readability of School Texts', in Lunzer, E. and Gardner, K. (Eds.) (1979) *The Effective Use of Reading*, London, Heinemann.
Klare, G.R. (1982) 'Readability', in Mitzel, H.E. (1982, 5th edn.) *Encyclopaedia of Educational Research*, New York, Free Press.

reading age, reading performance measured against the average reading standards of children of different ages, as assessed by a standardised reading test. Thus a ten-year-old with reading difficulties may read at the level of a child of seven years four months: this is his/her reading age.

Like mental age, this is another example of an *age equivalent* score, with all the associated drawbacks. But reading age has proved a more tenacious concept. The apparent ease of testing, often based on only a graded word reading test, together with the apparent simplicity of interpretation, means that it was for a long time the most widely used classroom index of children's reading performance, preferred to the statistically more satisfactory deviation quotient. However, this unsatisfactory measure is increasingly being replaced by criterion-referenced tests and measures of functional literacy.

Reference:
Davies, P. and Williams, P. (1974) *Aspects of Early Reading Growth*, Oxford, Blackwell.

reading comprehension, see *comprehension.*

reading difficulties, because the reading process is a complex one, determining the causes of pupils' difficulties in learning to read is a complex and sensitive task. The difficulties may lie within the child, and arise from visual or auditory perceptual problems or their integration, which may have affected, too, the child's language acquisition; if the child's intellectual development is inadequate for the task of comprehending the language encountered in print which, unlike speech, is unsupported by situational referencing, the child will have difficulty in understanding what is read; children from deprived linguistic and cultural backgrounds may also have difficulties in reading; memory defects, whether general, or specifically for visual or auditory information, will affect the ability to learn, while some children with attentional, motivational or other difficulties may find all learning difficult.

In all these dimensions, quite mild defects which have little effect on a pupil's other functioning may disproportionately delay the acquisition of reading skills, e.g. an intermittent hearing loss caused by colds or middle ear infection may cause uncertainty and confusion about language as well as distort or reduce auditory input. Similarly, emotional and motivational factors, often reinforced by poor self-image and failure may affect the acquisition of new skills such as reading. Social and cultural factors, especially those which may delay language development or place a low value on literacy are not only significant for beginning readers, but also for older readers, when peer-group pressures may militate against success in school activities, whilst task avoidance may cover for a lack of competence. Educational factors, such as frequent changes of teacher, mistaken beliefs of teachers who have been told that children will pick up reading when they are ready, school absence, inadequate variety and inadequate provision of books appropriate to the abilities and interests of children, which may adversely affect both the most and the least able, and low expectations on the part of teachers and/or parents, are also common causes of difficulties.

In the early years of schooling, the slower maturation of boys accounts for the disparity in reading achievement between the sexes: if this lag is ignored and early efforts not introduced to compensate for it, then some boys may continue to be retarded. Similarly, as all pupils learn in different ways and at different rates, difficulties arise in pupils for whom the methods of teaching are inappropriate: this is particularly common in schools which stick rigidly to one method and one reading scheme, or in which there is no method. Where some infant teachers cannot spend more than thirty seconds at a time in helping individual children, as one enquiry found, many children will enter the junior school at the level of word recognition, and with other reading skills, such as appropriate use of contextual clues, not properly developed.

These difficulties aside, all of which need to be identified and dealt with quickly and appropriately, there remain the difficulties presented by the children. On-task diagnosis of these specific difficulties must also be carried out, with particular emphasis on determining what the pupils are able to do, together with more detailed analyses using diagnostic tests and diagnostic teaching techniques. These will be most successful if pupils with reading difficulties are returned to a level at which they are successful and if the instruction is in the form of games and activities based on the reading material, wherever possible.

See *dyslexia, remedial education, specific reading difficulty.*

References:

Department of Education and Science (1975) *A Language for Life*, London, HMSO (Bullock Report).

Gulliford, R. (1985) *Teaching Children with Learning Difficulties*, Windsor, NFER-Nelson.

Ravenette, A.T. (1968) *Dimensions of Reading Difficulties*, Oxford, Pergamon.

Young, P. and Tyre, C. (1983) *Dyslexia or Illiteracy?* Milton Keynes, Open University Press.

reading readiness, stage when a child has developed sufficiently to be able to learn to read easily. The doctrine of reading readiness was derived from ideas of physical (usually visual) and psychological (usually intellectual) maturity needed to manage the reading process. At one time this was expressed simplistically as normal visual acuity and a mental age of six years; later workers took many other factors into account, for example motivation, perceptual skills, interest in print, etc.

Readiness for what? This question was usually answered as readiness for formal reading teaching, perhaps through introducing the child to a reading scheme. Tests of reading readiness were devised, measuring skills such as visual and auditory discrimination, use of symbols, etc. But as reading skills have been increasingly seen as part of a broader pattern of language and communication competencies, the idea of the 'teachable moment', inherent in the concept of reading readiness, has lost its appeal. The ability to make sense of symbols is obvious at least from the day a child understands a road sign or recognises the caption on a favourite television programme. Reading a first book is but one step on a long road to literacy that begins far earlier than the supporters of reading readiness advocated.

See *Harrison-Stroud Reading Readiness Profiles.*

Reference:

Chazan, M. (Ed.) (1970) *Reading Readiness*, Swansea, University College of Swansea Faculty of Education.

Reading Recovery, an early intervention scheme, introduced originally in Auckland, which has since been implemented in every Education Board area in New Zealand.

Marie Clay, the director of the project, believed that reading difficulties were largely due to incorrect strategies, not knowing how to learn from each encounter with print. Hence the project teaching was not concerned with the technicalities of what sight words to teach, or which phonic skills to introduce, or which perceptual training programme to use, but rather with the use of meaning, sentence structure, initial letter cues, etc.

The project worked with six-year-olds, on the argument that at that age recovery should be easier to effect than later. And the project recognised that this approach, successful though it proved to be, would not work with every child: there would be a 'hard core' of children needing expert teaching over a long period, at least a year or more.

The key features of the reading recovery programme are the screening at six years of age, the use of contextual strategies, the emphasis on learning to read by reading, not by exercises, and the central place allocated to the specialist teacher: there seems to be little acknowledgement of the possible contribution of parents.

See *miscue analysis.*

References:

Clay, M.M. (1979) *The Early Detection of Reading Difficulties*, London, Heinemann.

Tansley, P. and Panckhurst, J. (1981) *Children with Specific Learning Difficulties: a Critical Review of Research*, Windsor, NFER-Nelson.

reading scheme, series of books and other materials designed to provide a controlled gradient of reading difficulty for children learning to read. Schemes usually provide a reading age level as an indication of the difficulty of the books, but this is only one of the considerations in choosing a scheme for a child or a school. The story content, the interest, the size and length of the individual books, the illustrations, the extent of repetition, etc., are some of the various points to be borne in mind.

See *basic reading scheme.*

Reference:

Saunders, R. (1981) 'Choosing a Reading Scheme', in Somerset Education Authority, *Ways and Means 2,* Basingstoke, Globe Educational.

reality therapy, form of psychotherapy which advocates the use of reasoned argument in helping children face the reality of the social world to which they belong. The effects of undesirable behaviour are discussed and the children are encouraged to take responsibility for their actions. The approach is forward-looking: like behaviour therapy, reality therapy takes no heed of possible causes in past history. Unlike behaviour therapy the therapist is not interested in modifying the environment so as to effect behaviour change: the children have to suggest ways in which they themselves can change unacceptable behaviours. Reality therapy advocates an encouraging, interested attitude on the part of the therapist. Punishment has no part in the treatment, for a positive relationship between child and therapist is important. Reality therapy can be used by teachers and school counsellors in dealing with behavioural difficulties, particularly with older pupils. It has the great advantage of being directly applicable to school and classroom.

References:

Glasser, W. (1969) *Schools without Failure,* New York, Harper and Row.

Laslett, R. (1982) *Maladjusted Children in the Ordinary School,* Stratford-upon-Avon, National Council for Special Education.

rebus, picture puzzle usually offering an easily recognisable representation of an idea – an object, or an instruction, or an action, etc. e.g. = house; = ship, etc. Some rebuses are not immediately recognisable without teaching; for example in rebus reading schemes + is often a symbol for 'and': this has to be learnt. Sometimes, rebuses are used to represent individual syllables within a single word.

Rebuses have been used to develop language skills in children with severe learning and communication difficulties. They can be used as a communication system for children without speech. They prove useful in helping children appreciate that meaning can be conveyed by symbols, the essence of reading. For this reason rebuses can be a useful introduction to reading for children whether with or without special needs, and there are published reading schemes using them.

See *Peabody Rebus Reading Program.*

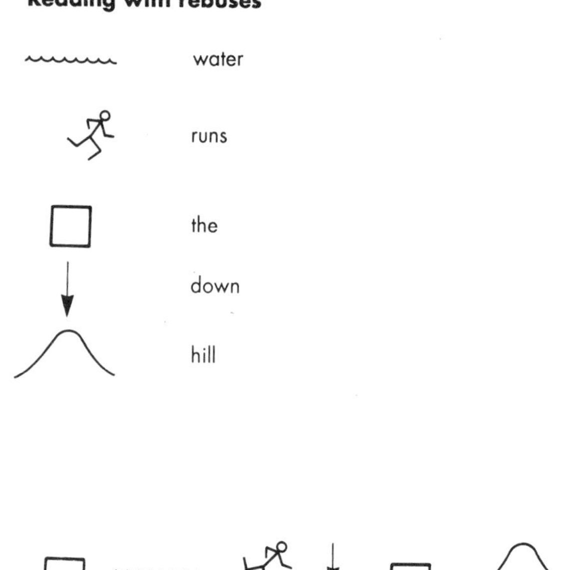

Reference:

Devereux, K. and van Oosterholm, J. (1982) *Learning with Rebuses*, Stratford-upon-Avon, National Council for Special Education.

receptive language disorder, receptive *aphasia,* impairment of the ability to comprehend language. The impairment is central, and is usually associated with damage to Wernicke's area.

This however is an oversimplification. There are different levels of receptive aphasia: in some the ability to comprehend speech is impaired; in others reading cannot be interpreted; in others some facility for both skills is present, but particular language structures give difficulty.

Moreover receptive aphasia implies a separate category from expressive aphasia: yet in reality both may coexist, and to different degrees, depending on the nature of the central damage. Most aphasias are caused by accidents, particularly by strokes in elderly people. Aphasias in children are sometimes classified as acquired (i.e. accidental, as from a head injury) or developmental (i.e. effectively present from birth.) These last are children who are not mentally handicapped, have no hearing impairment, nor emotional problems affecting language, yet have always had difficulty in comprehending language. Hence they are held to suffer from developmental aphasia, on the assumption that there must be neurological damage present, even though there is no medical evidence for this. This diagnosis by exclusion is debatable, and some prefer to call this condition a developmental language disorder.

Whatever might be the cause, these are children whose problems are not medical, but primarily educational. They have to learn to comprehend, and specialised teaching is required. Sign systems sometimes have to be introduced. The prevalence of children whose receptive communication difficulties are severe enough to require a place at one of the few special schools catering for this kind of need is very small, and social as well as language issues need to be considered before such a recommendation is made.

See *dyslexia.*

Reference:

Crystal, D. (1988, 2nd edn.) *Introduction to Language Pathology*, London, Cole and Whurr.

recessive gene, see *gene.*

Record of Achievement, method of assessment which was introduced into secondary schools after pilot projects in the early 1980s. Unlike traditional school reports, which are largely confined to performance in academic subjects, records of achievement include assessments of a pupil's personal qualities, including activities and experiences outside school.

They are intended to encourage motivation and personal development through promoting practical and social skills as well as academic performance. The record is intended to be cumulative, being built up by the pupil in consultation with the school staff as the pupil moves on through the years of secondary schooling. School leavers can present the document to future employers and trainers.

The non-academic qualities and experiences included on the record offer considerable opportunities for children with special educational needs to gain a document which reveals strengths that an orthodox school report form would not mention. The formative profiling that is usually involved helps encourage pupils' motivation. The negotiation involved in compiling the document can help to ease the relationship between teachers and pupils, and may reduce disaffection.

It remains to be seen whether the Education Act 1988 will affect the growth of the movement to introduce records of achievement.

See *formative assessment.*

References:

Department of Education and Science (1987) *Records of Achievement: a Progress report for Teachers*, London, Department of Education and Science.

Department of Education and Science (1989) *Records of Achievement: Report of the National Evaluation of Pilot Schemes*, London, HMSO.

Green, P. (1987) 'Records of Wider Achievement', *British Journal of Special Education*, 14, 4, 141–3.

Sawyer, J. (1987) *Secondary Schools for All?* London, Cassell.

Record of Need, equivalent, in Scottish legislation, to a *Statement* (*of special educational needs*) in England and Wales. While there are slight differences of emphasis in the official guidance, like the Statement the Record is opened when a child has special needs which are severe, complex and unlikely to be short-term.

There is evidence of considerable variability between the Scottish education authorities in the practice of recording pupils, and in the threshold used. Moreover it has been suggested that the process of opening a Record has been reserved for pupils for whom a conscious decision to recommend segregated education has been taken.

References:

Scottish Education Department (1982) *Annex 2 to Circular 1083*, Edinburgh.

Thomson, G.O.B., Ward, J. and Gow, L. (1988) 'The Education of Children with Special Needs: a Cross-cultural Perspective', *European Journal of Special Education*, 3, 3, 125–39.

Reed Test, a simple screening test for the early detection of high-frequency hearing loss. The child is presented with a series of cards, each carrying four pictures of objects whose names differ in high-frequency consonants only, e.g. bus, duck, cup and jug. For each card, the child has to point to the picture named by the examiner.

The number of errors is an index of difficulty in discriminating high-frequency speech sounds, suggesting the need for a hearing investigation.

Since the child has only to point, quality of speech plays no part in the responses. The drawback is the absence of a standardised loudness level of presentation. There is also a danger that a loss in one ear might be missed, since the child uses both ears to respond. The test's advantages are that it is easy to give, enjoyed by children, and is a useful screening device for schools.

Reference:

Available from the Royal National Institute for the Deaf, 105 Gower St., London WC1.

Register of Congenital Malformations, is held by the Registrar-General at the Office of Population Censuses and Surveys. All infants with congenital malformations have to be notified by the medical authorities within seven days of birth.

The register provides information on the incidence of some conditions for which special education may be needed later.

Reference:

Powell, R.M. (1984) 'Medical Screening and Surveillance', in Lindsay, G. (Ed.) (1984) *Screening for Children with Special Needs*, London, Croom Helm.

Register of Disabled Persons, see *Disabled Persons Register.*

regression,

(1) regression to the mean, the tendency for a predicted score to be closer to the mean than the score used for predictive purposes. This is generally true since no two measures are perfectly correlated. If two measures bear no relationship to each other at all, then whatever the score on one, the best prediction of an individual's score on the other would be the mean, since this is the most probable value. If the correlation between the two measures were to be perfect, then the best prediction of an individual's score would obviously be the same as the score obtained on the first measure (assuming that both tests have the same mean and standard deviation). The weaker the correlation, the more the predicted score regresses, or falls back towards, the mean. If a child's score on a reading test is substantially above average, then we would expect the score on a related test to be above average, but not to the same extent: if the first test score is substantially below average, then this time the expected score on another test would be closer to the average score than previously.

This principle is particularly important in special education research, where experimental populations are often below average. An experiment which measures the effect of, say, a teaching procedure on children with reading difficulties would expect scores on a retest to move towards the mean through the regression effect. This should be allowed for in the experimental design by the appropriate use of regression equations, or randomising allocations to experimental and control groups; otherwise incorrect inferences can be (and have been!) made.

Note too that the common phrase 'regression to the mean' is technically incorrect. Regression occurs to the most probable measure, the mode. It so happens that most educational measures are constructed so as to give normal distributions, where the mode and mean coincide. But in the general case, the phenomenon might be more appropriately called 'regression to the mode'.

Reference:

Rowntree, D. (1981) *Statistics without Tears: a primer for non-mathematicians*, Harmondsworth, Penguin.

(2) regression analysis, statistical technique for analysing correlations between sets of variables in order to try to identify their relative importance. It can produce a regression equation, enabling one score to be predicted from scores on other variables; their relative contributions to the predicted score are signified by the regression weights attached to each.

Reference:

Ahlgren, A. and Walber, H.J. (1975) 'Generalised Regression Analysis', in Bynner, J. and Stribley, K.M. (Eds.) (1978) *Social Research: Principles and Procedures*, Milton Keynes, Open University Press.

(3) regression (in development) reversion to behaviour typical of an earlier stage, as when a ten-year-old throws a temper-tantrum.
(4) regression (in reading), see *eye movements.*

Regular Education Initiative (REI), an integration movement which seeks to educate all pupils in the USA in the regular (i.e. ordinary) school system. This means the abolition of special schools.

The supporters of REI argue that the presence of a separate special school system leads to a loss of interest in the progress of pupils with special educational needs in the ordinary school. They further argue that the special school system is not cost-efficient. They believe that educating all pupils in the mainstream, given the resources to improve provision, including appropriate support services, would better meet the educational needs of all children.

This view is disputed by other educators, not least on the grounds that it lacks operational detail. Nevertheless the movement may succeed in stimulating the development of new approaches to the delivery of services to pupils with less severe difficulties.

See *integration.*

Reference:

Lowenthal, B. (1989) 'The United States Regular Education Initiative', *European Journal of Special Needs Education,* 4, 3, 180–4.

REI, see *Regular Education Initiative.*

reinforcement, the central principle of operant *conditioning;* following a behaviour with an event that increases the likelihood of that behaviour recurring.

Behaviour modification, probably the most widely applied behaviour therapy in schools, is built on reinforcement. Learning, whether of academic skills or acceptable social responses, can be managed by suitable reinforcement. Reinforcement may be positive or negative. Positive reinforcement is most frequently used in the classroom, and involves rewarding desired behaviour. Negative reinforcement is the removal of an aversive stimulus, again so as to increase behaviour. For example, children may be required to tidy their desks before being allowed to go to play. Desks will be cleared so that the aversive stimulus of missing play is avoided. Note the difference between negative reinforcement and punishment, in which the intention is to decrease undesirable behaviour by following it with a painful consequence.

In positive reinforcement the nature of the reward is important, for what may be rewarding to one person may be much less so to another. In the school situation the reward may be simply praise, or a token exchangeable for a privilege, or a more tangible reward such as a sweet, etc.

Reinforcement is given in two main ways. In ratio reinforcement rewards are received in accordance with the number of behaviours, as when a pupil is given a star for every ten words spelt correctly. In interval reinforcement, rewards are received in accordance with length of time for which a behaviour extends, as when a child is praised after every five minutes of quiet working.

Both these methods of reinforcement can be further classified, depending on whether the rewards are given according to a fixed schedule, or variable schedule. The two examples given above are of a fixed schedule: a variable schedule might involve giving the star after ten words, then after the next twenty, then after fifteen and so on.

There are three main criticisms of reinforcement – and of operant conditioning generally. The first questions its ethics, and asks what right has anyone deliberately to attempt to control another's behaviour. The second questions its effectiveness, arguing that it may be dealing with superficial symptoms and not underlying causes. The third draws attention to its limitations, pointing out that reinforcement may work for simple skills, but how can creative behaviours be explained by conditioning when by definition they are one-off events?

The validity of these points is debatable. But the fact remains that reinforcement techniques continue to be widely and successfully applied to children's special needs.

References:

Alberto, P.A. and Troutman, A.C. (1986, 2nd edn.) *Applied Behaviour Analysis for Teachers*, Columbus, Merrill.

Wheldall, K. and Merrett, F. (1984) *Positive Teaching: the Behavioural Approach*, London, Allen and Unwin.

reliability, the consistency with which a test measures. Most simply, giving a test twice to the same sample of children and correlating the scores is one obvious measure of reliability, though there are many others. Perfect agreement represents perfect reliability and would be represented by a correlation coefficient of +1.00. Reliabilities of this level are, of course, unattainable in practice. Most well-constructed tests of attainment ought to achieve reliabilities better than +0.90. Tests of personality are for various reasons less reliable, and values over +0.80 are acceptable for many purposes. Values for at least one of the different forms of reliability should be quoted in every test manual.

There are many caveats against taking reliabilities at their face value. One particular point is the effect of the range of the sample from which the reliability figure was derived. The wider the range, the higher the reliability. For example, if the reliability of a test of vocabulary is derived from a test-retest of 100 individuals, from five to fifteen years old, the spread of scores (or variance) is so wide that few if any individuals will have changed position between the two administrations. In this circumstance the correlation, or reliability will be very high. In contrast, if the reliability figure is derived from a test-retest of 100 individuals all of the same age, the spread of scores will now be much narrower and doubtless several individuals will have changed position between the two administrations. The correlation, or reliability will then be lower.

This effect of range is important to consider in evaluating test reliabilities. It has particular importance for special education, where tests may be used for populations of restricted range. In these circumstances reliabilities may well be lower than those quoted in the test manual, which nearly always relate to a normal distribution, even if not artificially extended by widening the age-range, as in the example.

References:

Anastasi, A. (1982, 5th edn.) *Psychological Testing*, New York Macmillan.

Child, D. (1986, 4th edn.) *Psychology and the Teacher*, London, Holt, Rinehart and Winston.

remedial education, or remedial teaching, special teaching for children who are not progressing as well as expected. Originally, remedial education was conceived as special help for able children with reading problems, and provided through remedial centres or through withdrawal groups in the ordinary school, initially serviced by peripatetic teachers. Remedial reading was offered to retarded children, not backward children; these latter were taught in full-time special classes and schools.

Later, full-time remedial classes were organised in the larger secondary schools, established following the movement towards comprehensive education. The division between the backward and remedial classes became harder to sustain, and secondary schools developed remedial departments, concerned with all children with learning difficulties in the school.

During the 1970s, there was a call for remedial teaching to be extended to all areas of the curriculum, not just the basics of reading and arithmetic. At the same time, pressures for integration were growing, not just between the special and ordinary school, but within the ordinary school itself, where children in the remedial department could be segregated, to all intents and purposes. These twin forces culminated in the movement to replace remedial teaching with *support teaching.*

See *whole-school approach.*

References:

Bines, H. (1986) *Redefining Remedial Education*, Beckenham, Croom Helm.

Gulliford, R. (1985) *Teaching Children with Learning Difficulties*, Windsor, NFER-Nelson.

Smith, C. (Ed.) (1985) *New Directions in Remedial Education*, Brighton, Falmer Press.

remedial gymnast, therapist specialising in exercises designed to help individuals with physical difficulties. Remedial gymnasts are usually physiotherapists with additional training and qualifications, and usually work in hospitals rather than schools.

Remploy, a public, non-profit making company which offers *sheltered employment* for handicapped people. There are several full-time paid directors and some part-time directors who have industrial experience and are interested in the problems of disabled workers.

Remploy runs units which are involved in light manufacturing and services, and is Britain's largest employer of people with disabilities. People may work there temporarily, in order to gain confidence in their capacity for working, before seeking employment elsewhere.

Details are available through Disablement Resettlement Service via local jobcentres.

repression, see *defence mechanism.*

residence order, see *custodianship order.*

residential care for children is provided in establishments such as children's homes, various kinds of community homes, residential care homes, nursing homes, etc. The Children Act 1989 will govern the regulation of residential care for children in these establishments, and will also apply where children are accommodated by a health authority or a local education authority for a period of at least three months. In all cases there will be a duty to ensure that the child's welfare is safeguarded and promoted. A similar duty applies where a child is in an independent school; the local authority where the school is located will also have duties to the children in this case. Private children's homes run for profit have not previously been subject to control, but they will become registered children's homes under the provisions of the Act.

'Home Life: a Code of Practice for Residential Care' sets out the general principles upon which care should be provided, with added recognition of the special needs of particular groups, such as children and young persons, and people who are disordered and mentally handicapped. Further discussion of the needs of children in residential care is to be found in the report of the Wagner Committee.

See *residential special education, special school.*

References:

Centre for Policy on Ageing (1984) *Home Life: A Code of Practice for Residential Care*, London.

National Institute for Social Work (1988) *Residential Care: a Positive Choice*, London, HMSO (Wagner Report).

residential special education, enjoyed a rapid growth in popularity in the years following the implementation of the 1944 Education Act. Education authorities ascertained an increasing number of handicapped pupils, but were not sure how to provide suitable education for the educationally subnormal and for the maladjusted in particular. A residential school was one answer, and many authorities purchased country houses and refitted them as schools.

The disadvantages of this course of action gradually became clear. Children were isolated from their local community; often cut off in the countryside, their experiences were restricted; the education was expensive; links with families were difficult to sustain, since visiting often involved a day's expedition or more – and the period of full-time return to the family for the holidays was often traumatic. These considerations led to growing unease and to an increasing emphasis on day provision. Between 1973 and 1983 virtually all residential provision decreased, except that for the maladjusted, which rose slightly.

There are arguments for residential education. Rare conditions, needing very special teaching, but not prevalent enough to enable a group to be assembled in one locality, comprise one case. So do children with complex disabilities, who may need an intense educational experience throughout the waking day. Children who need to be afforded relief from intolerable home conditions may comprise another, though here a foster placement through the social services together with attendance at a local school is an alternative. Each child's needs are different, and residential special education offers an extra possibility which in some circumstances may prove to be the best solution.

See *special school.*

Reference:

Cole, T. (1986) *Residential Special Education,* Milton Keynes, Open University Press.

resource room, neither a special class nor a remedial class, but a learning centre, usually offering the expertise of a resource teacher (UK support teacher). The size and location varies: it may be a room in a resource suite, or it may be a 'cupboard'.

Its functions vary, too. As well as being the resource teacher's room, it may also serve as a source of materials and equipment, a meeting-place for case conferences, a base for the authority's visiting support staff, etc. It offers a flexible arrangement, school-based, for providing support to pupils with special needs, and to teachers.

Reference:

Hallahan, D.P. and Kaufman, J.M. (1988, 4th edn.) *Exceptional Children: Introduction to Special Education,* Englewood Cliffs, Prentice Hall

respite care, offers relief on an occasional or regular basis to parents of children with demanding special needs. At present, respite care schemes are often organised by local authority social services departments, though schemes are also run by voluntary groups, including self-help schemes run by parents themselves. Under the provisions of the *Children Act 1989,* local authorities will be under a duty to give support to *children in need* and their families, which can include help to enable child and family to have a holiday.

There are four main types of respite care:

- residential care, in an institution, such as a boarding arrangement in the child's own school, a bed in a hospital ward, etc.;
- family-based care, usually involving placing a child with an approved respite foster home;
- care in the child's own home, from a trained care worker;
- holiday schemes, in which play-group facilities are provided during the school holidays.

Each variant fulfils a different function. But in every case there are issues such as legal responsibility, insurance cover, which need to be resolved beforehand, preferably using the experience of the local authority's social service department.

The arrangement for separating the child and the family, even for a short holiday period, has to be done sensitively and constructively. On the other hand, the much-needed relief that respite care affords to hard-pressed families also enables the child to stay in the parental home for longer.

See *family support unit.*

Reference:

Furneaux, B. (1988) *Special Parents,* Milton Keynes, Open University Press.

retardation, discrepancy between potential and performance; attainments below expectations based on ability as measured by an intelligence test. Thus a child with a mental age of ten years and a reading age of eight years would be two years retarded in reading.

Retardation is distinguished from *backwardness,* since attainment is compared with ability, not chronological age. Note that if the child mentioned above had a chronological age of ten years, then backwardness and retardation would both be held to be present. Note too that a child could be functioning well above average for the age-group, but still be retarded; e.g. an eight-year-old with a mental age of twelve years and a reading age of ten years.

The reduced use of intelligence tests, the growth of curriculum-based assessment, doubts over the logic underlying the concept of retardation (see *ability–attainment controversy*), the absence of allowance for *regression* effects in simple retardation calculations, are all reasons why the idea of retardation, though inherently attractive to many teachers, has become suspect.

Reference:

Tansley, P. and Panckhurst, J. (1981) *Children with Specific Learning Difficulties; a Critical Review of Research,* Windsor, NFER-Nelson.

retinitis pigmentosa, progressive disease of the retina, usually inherited. Vision undergoes a gradual deterioration, often first noticed as night blindness and tunnel vision.

In some adolescents, the disease may have progressed sufficiently to pose educational problems, e.g. difficulties in locating work on the blackboard, mobility problems, etc. Awareness that a transition from print to Braille may have to be made is a source of concern, and can be a difficult decision to take during school years, when the adolescent is involved in courses leading to examinations. Sympathetic counselling is often needed.

Reference:

Chapman, E.K. and Stone, J.M. (1988) *The Visually Handicapped Child in Your Classroom*, London, Cassell.

retinoblastoma, congenital, malignant tumour of the retina, usually inherited. Treatment may involve removal of the eye, in which case an artificial eye may be fitted.

retrolental fibroplasia (RLF), often called retinopathy of pregnancy (ROP), disease of the retina, leading to visual impairment. It was first associated with premature infants who had been given uncontrolled supplies of oxygen. Reducing the oxygen levels reduced the incidence of RLF, but the condition still occurs, though less frequently, and almost always associated with prematurity: for this reason it is sometimes called retinopathy of prematurity.

The vision of children with RLF, and hence their educational need, depends on the location and extent of damage to the retina. Some will have light perception only and will need to communicate through Braille; others will have relatively good vision, though over part of the retina only.

Reference:

Chapman, E.K. and Stone, J.M. (1988) *The Visually Handicapped Child in Your Classroom*, London, Cassell.

reversal, usually applied to a transposition of the shape of a letter (e.g. 'b' for 'd'), or the letters in a word (e.g. 'was' for 'saw'), or a numeral (e.g. '23' for '32'). Reversals can occur in reading, writing, or mathematics. Reversals also occur in speech (e.g. Spoonerisms) but have been much less studied.

They represent a difficulty common to most children in the early stages of their schoolwork. But some children continue to reverse until well into their junior school career and in some cases beyond, when reversals are said to be one of the features of dyslexia.

Reversals are said to be associated with the problem of learning directionality: the left–right concept, important if reversals are to be avoided, is said to be inherently more difficult to learn than other pairs of terms. Leftness and rightness depend upon position; something on one's left when facing one direction is on one's right when facing the other way: left and right are thus said to have fluctuating referents.

Most children can surmount this problem. It has been speculated that those who find it peculiarly difficult may not have established hemispheric dominance: other suggestions have attributed reversals to less specific problems of perceptual organisation. But programmes aimed at improving reading and writing skills by concentrating on perceptual–motor activities have not achieved obvious success. Reversals can be minimised by good teaching, i.e. emphasising those characteristics of print that are important for making the correct directional attack for both reading and writing.

See *mirror-writing*.

References:

Clark. M.M. (1974) *Teaching Left-handed Children*, London, Hodder and Stoughton.

Miles, T.R. and Ellis, N.C. (1981) 'A Lexical Encoding Deficiency II: Clinical Observations', in Pavlidis, G.Th. and Miles, T.R. (Eds.) (1981) *Dyslexia Research and its Application to Education*, Chichester, Wiley.

reverse chaining, see *chaining*.

reviews (of Statements), must take place at least annually, in accordance with the provisions of the Education Act 1981, Schedule 1, Part II, para 5. The purpose of the review is to monitor the arrangements made for pupils with Statements. Local education authorities are expected to take account of reports prepared by the school, which should be related to specific educational aims and objectives for the child, and should include assessments made under the Education Act 1989 in relation to the National Curriculum. Parents should be given a written invitation to participate in the review procedure, an opportunity to help in assessing their child's progress and to set further goals. Where possible the child should also participate in reviewing progress and in goal-setting.

Reviews may result in a 'reassessment' of a child's needs – though a reassessment can of course take place at any time that there appears to have been a significant change in a child's circumstances. The Education Act 1981 requires that a reassessment takes place when a pupil with a Statement of special needs is between the ages of twelve years six months and fourteen years six months, in order to prepare for the period of transition from school to work or to other education. Similar arrangements apply in Scotland, where a recorded child has to be reassessed during the second last year of compulsory education.

References:

Adams, F. (Ed.) (1986) *Special Education*, Harlow, Councils and Education Press for Longman.

Department of Education and Science (1989) *Circular 22/89 Assessments and Statements of Special Educational Needs: Procedures within the Education, Health and Social Services*, London, Department of Education and Science. (Joint circular with Department of Health.)

Department of Education and Science (1983) *Circular 1/83*, London, Department of Education and Science.

Scottish Education Department (1982) *Circular 1082*, Edinburgh, Scottish Education Department.

Reynell Developmental Language Scales, assess linguistic functioning in the age-range one to seven years, providing an expressive language scale and a receptive language scale. Receptive language is measured by assessing verbal comprehension, while expression is assessed by measuring use of language for descriptive and ideational purposes. A separately administered reception scale, using eye-pointing responses, is provided for children with physical or emotional difficulties.

The scales have been criticised on the grounds that they assess a limited selection of language skills only; thus grammatical maturity is not covered. They do provide a norm-referenced comparison of the relative development of aspects of reception and expression, and so offer a useful first exploration of young children's language functioning. Speech therapists in particular use them widely.

Reference:

Webster, A. and McConnell, C. (1987) *Children with Speech and Language Difficulties*, London, Cassell.

Reynell-Zinkin Developmental Scales for Young Visually Handicapped Children, provide a guide to development in six different areas of particular importance to children with visual impairment. These areas are social adaptation; sensorimotor understanding; exploration of environment; response to sound and verbal comprehension; expressive language; communication.

The scales provide standardised scores for both a blind and a partially-sighted population, as well as for a sighted population, between the ages of nought and five years. The resulting profile enables a programme of early teaching activities to be planned. The tests are restricted in use to professionals (paediatricians, teachers, psychologists, etc.) working with the visually impaired.

Reference:

Levy, P. and Goldstein, H. (1984) *Tests in Education*, London, Academic Press.

rheumatoid arthritis, is normally considered a disease of adults, but a form of the condition (Still's disease or juvenile rheumatoid arthritis) does affect children. A 70% recovery rate has been quoted.

Apart from the psychological stress of being ill, and in a painful and possibly deforming way, the main educational problems arise from the periods away from school for treatment, the restricted mobility around the school, the possibly limited fine motor control, leading to difficulties with writing, for example, and the therapy (exercises, etc.) that may be required during school time.

Reference:

Russell, P. (1984, 2nd edn.) *The Wheelchair Child*, London, Souvenir Press.

RLF, see *retrolental fibroplasia.*

role-play, technique based on the contributions of J.L. Moreno. Acting an appropriate role enables a pupil with emotional difficulties to express feelings which might otherwise be repressed. In this application role-play is a form of therapy, used in psychodrama.

Role-play is also used in less emotionally charged situations. Thus in social skills training it can be particularly valuable in helping a child acquire insights into appropriate and inappropriate responses in social situations.

The main disadvantages of role-play are the demands it makes on time and resources. As a therapeutic technique it requires a suitably-trained therapist and in this case in particular the size of the group participating will be small.

See *psychodrama.*

Reference:

Van Meerts, M. (1983) *The Effective Use of Role-Play: a handbook for teachers and trainers*, London, Kogan Page.

room management, method of organising the work of adult personnel in a classroom, so as to gain the maximum advantage for children's learning. In the UK, room management was developed for work with people with mental handicap, and has been widely applied in schools and classes for children with severe learning difficulties.

The key to room management is the activity period, a time of perhaps an hour or so when two or more adults are in the classroom simultaneously. During this period one adult, the individual helper, devotes time to teaching individual pupils. The work will have been pre-planned and there will be a rota of children to be taught so that no-one is omitted. Another adult has the role of room manager, who rewards the other children carrying on with their tasks, ensures that they have adequate materials, are suitably seated, etc.

This principle of specialisation of function within the classroom lends itself to extension, particularly if more adults are available, and there are many variants on the original room management proposals. Thus a third adult has taken on a toileting/hygiene role. Roles can be exchanged during the activity period, too.

It is claimed that room management procedures increase the time that children are constructively engaged with materials, or participating in activities with teacher. Whether this is so for the least responsive children has been challenged – but this is only one of several criteria by which room management can be judged.

It is also an attempt to sharpen and make more precise the various activities that are involved in 'teaching', and there is a case for extending this specialisation of function to other areas of education. Indeed it could be argued that well-planned support teaching offers an example of room management in operation in the ordinary secondary school.

References:
Hinson, M. (Ed.) (1987) *Teachers and Special Educational Needs*, Harlow, Longman in association with National Association for Remedial Education.
Thomas, G. (1985) 'Extra People in the Classroom: a key to integration?' *Educational and Child Psychology*, 2, 3, 102–7.
Thomas, M. (1985) 'Introduction to Classroom Management', in Farrell, P. (Ed.) (1985) *EDY: its impact on staff training in mental handicap*, Manchester, Manchester University Press.
Ware, J. and Evans, P. (1987) 'Room Management is not Enough?' *British Journal of Special Education*, 14, 2, 78–80.

Rorschach test, probably the best-known projection test, consisting of ten cards, each bearing a picture of an inkblot. The subject has to say what each blot represents and the responses are analysed to reveal aspects of the subject's personality.

Considerable time is needed for the analysis, and lengthy and detailed training is said to be needed to be able to interpret Rorschach responses effectively. The use of the Rorschach with children is more specialised still. These considerations limit its use to complex clinical applications. Moreover many attempts to establish the validity of Rorschach diagnoses have led to inconclusive results. However, some psychiatrists, particularly those working within a psychoanalytic framework, find it a useful tool. More objective scoring methods are now available.

Reference:
Anastasi, A. (1982, 5th edn.) *Psychological Testing*, New York, Macmillan.

rubella, German measles, mild viral illness, which nevertheless can have catastrophic effects on the foetus if the mother contracts the illness during pregnancy, particularly during the first three months. The earlier in pregnancy the more damaging the effects, which can include hearing and visual impairments, as well as mental handicap and heart defects. It has been estimated that the chance of having a normal infant after contracting rubella in the first eight weeks of pregnancy may be as low as one in three. At one time rubella was held to be the leading prenatal cause of deafness, and a prime cause of dual sensory impairment. Vaccination programmes for girls and young women, together with pregnancy counselling, have reduced the incidence of rubella-damaged children. Further improvement can be expected from the introduction of a combined measles/mumps/rubella vaccine for pre-school children.

References:
McInnes, J.M. and Treffry, J.A. (1982) *Deaf-Blind Infants and Children: a developmental guide*, Milton Keynes, Open University Press.
Tucker, I. and Nolan, M. (1984) *Educational Audiology*, London, Croom Helm.

Rudolf Steiner schools, cater for children with some of the most complex and severe handicaps, offering an education based on the principles of *curative education*. Independent schools, such as these are, now have to be placed on the approved list of the Department of Education and Science before local education authorities (LEAs) can place children there without special permit. Since most teachers at Rudolf Steiner schools have followed a course of curative education, rather than an orthodox teaching qualification, this has posed some difficulties. But the contribution of the Steiner schools to special education is so valued that LEAs have been advised to continue to seek to use the schools until this anomaly has been dealt with.

See *Camphill movement.*

Reference:

Department of Education and Science (1985) *Special Education Letter* (85)4, London, Department of Education and Science.

Rutter's Behaviour Questionnaires, comprise two scales, one completed by teachers and the other by parents, with a number of overlapping items. The teacher's scale has been widely used as a quick screening device for emotional and behavioural difficulties in children aged seven to thirteen years of age. It consists of twenty-six statements of behaviour, each with a three-point scale, effectively 'yes' (score 2), 'somewhat' (score 1), and 'no' (score 0), which teacher checks.

The total score provides a measure of maladjustment (score of nine or more), and two subscales permit a diagnosis of neurotic or antisocial behaviour to be made.

The Rutter scales provide no normative data. Their validity was established by demonstrating the extent to which they discriminated between a sample of children with psychiatric problems and a normal sample. Acceptable reliability figures have been quoted.

Many research investigations (e.g. the Isle of Wight Survey) have used them as a quick device for measuring behavioural difficulties of large samples, and they have also enjoyed wide use in surveys designed to identify children at risk of emotional and behavioural difficulties. Results from the scales alone would be quite inappropriate for drawing conclusions about an individual child: further clinical enquiry is needed before action can be taken.

Reference:

Levy, P. and Goldstein, H. (1984) *Tests in Education,* London, Academic Press.

S

's', specific factor, the other component which along with 'g', comprised any human ability in Spearman's model of the structure of intellect.

While this model proposes only one 'g', permeating all abilities to greater or lesser degree, there is a different 's' for every different ability. This simple model has long since been overtaken by other, less restricted ones. Its main interest lies in the fact that it resulted from the first application of the statistical technique of factor analysis to explain the interrelations between performances of different skills.

See *'g', intelligence.*

Reference:

Child, D. (1986, 4th edn.) *Psychology and the Teacher*, London, Holt, Rinehart and Winston.

saccades, see *eye-movements.*

sanctuary, unit for children with *emotional and behavioural difficulties.* A sanctuary is often a short-term refuge, where a child in a disturbed state, for whatever reason, can remain in school in a less stressed atmosphere, usually in a small group of perhaps no more than five or six children, with a teacher whose style is understanding, rather than punitive. When the immediate situation has cleared, the aim is to return the child to a suitable (though perhaps modified) programme as soon as possible.

The term sanctuary is sometimes applied to a unit which children attend long-term. In this case, as with all units of this nature, there are problems of providing a broad curriculum with no more than two or three teaching staff.

See *disruptive behaviour.*

Reference:

Felsenstein, D. (1987) 'Strategies for Improving School Attendance', in Reid, K. (Ed.) (1987) *Combating School Absenteeism*, Sevenoaks, Hodder and Stoughton.

savant, formerly idiot savant, individual who is mentally handicapped (idiot was formerly a term used for a person with an IQ less than 20) and who possesses a remarkable facility in a particular area, perhaps in mental arithmetic, remembering dates, or playing a musical instrument.

Reference:

Hall, A.L. (1978) 'Savants: Mentally Retarded Individuals with Special Skills', in Ellis, N.R. (Ed.) (1978) *International Review of Research in Mental Retardation*, 9, 277–98, London, Academic Press.

schedules of reinforcement, see *reinforcement.*

schizoid personality, see *schizophrenia.*

schizophrenia, the classic adult psychosis, characterised by delusions (e.g. delusions of persecution), thought disorders (e.g. broken chains of thought, with ideas following each other in an apparently unrelated sequence), hallucinations (e.g. hearing voices), inappropriate emotions (e.g. reacting to a distressing event with amusement rather than sympathy), loss of willpower, stereotypical behaviour, etc.

Schizophrenia in childhood has been a focus of some professional debate. Different diagnostic criteria mean that reliable estimates of incidence are difficult to establish. Most authorities now agree that it is a different condition from *autism*, with which it was once confounded. One of the main distinguishing features is the age of onset: autism occurs early in development, whereas the overriding feature in schizophrenia is a loss of contact with reality in children who have previously been well.

Schizophrenia is also distinguished from schizoid personality, which describes a sensitive, isolated individual, unable to form social relationships easily, and given to daydreaming and solitary interests. But children with schizoid personalities are in touch with reality, though aloof. Given a sympathetically structured education and emotional support, they should cope. Schizophrenia, however, is a serious illness. It may require treatment as a hospital inpatient, and the treatment may involve drug therapy or one of the psychotherapies. Children out of hospital may need a special school for serious emotional disturbance until they are well again, and they will continue to need psychiatric care for a long time. Their families need support as well, for having a schizophrenic child in the family can be a harrowing experience.

References:

Barker, P. (1988, 5th edn.) *Basic Child Psychiatry*, Oxford, Blackwell.
Cantor, S. (1984) *The Schizophrenic Child*, Milton Keynes, Open University Press.

Schonell reading tests, battery of four tests of reading attainment and three diagnostic tests. The attainment tests assess between them word recognition, speed and comprehension, in the context of reading aloud single words, or reading prose passages aloud or silently. The diagnostic tests assess aspects of phonic skills, directional attack and visual discrimination.

These tests were first published in the 1940s. In spite of attempts to modernise the norms, by present-day standards they are not well constructed and psychometric details are poor. The attainment tests provide *age-equivalent* scores, with their attendant weaknesses. The diagnostic tests are dated. Over the last forty years, the graded word recognition test, Schonell R1, may well have been the most widely-used test ever. The continued use of the Schonell tests even today is a tribute to their easy administration and simple interpretation.

References:

Levy, P. and Goldstein, H. (1984) *Tests in Education*, London, Academic Press.
Pumfrey, P. (1985, 2nd edn.) *Reading: Tests and Assessment Techniques*, Sevenoaks, Hodder and Stoughton in association with UKRA.

school counsellor, see *counselling*.

school governors, have had their functions extended considerably in recent years. Under the Education Act 1981, they are expected to ensure that where a pupil has special educational needs, those needs are provided for and are made known to the teachers involved, and that the school staff as a whole is aware of its responsibilities to cater for special educational needs (Section 2(5)).

The Education (No. 2) Act 1986 laid down the composition of governing bodies and the Education Act 1988 placed increased responsibilities on them under those sections of the Act dealing with local financial management of schools. This means that governors can have considerable influence in determining the amount of support provided by the school for pupils with special needs.

This last Act also introduced the National Curriculum, to which all pupils are entitled, but with provisions for pupils with special needs to be exempted from part or all of it. Under some circumstances the exemption decision rests with the Head of the school, but there are provisions for parents to appeal against a decision to the governing body.

In short, governors are now much more potent than before in determining their school's approach to and support for pupils with special educational needs.

References:

Department of Education and Science (1989) *School Governors: A New Role*, London, HMSO.

Goacher, B., Evans, J., Welton, J. and Wedell, K. (1988) *Implementing the 1981 Education Act*, London, Cassell.

Wallis, E. (1989) 'Governors and Special Needs', *ACE Bulletin*, 27, Jan.–Feb. 1989, 9–12.

school health service, provides health care for pupils through the community health services of the District Health Authority (DHA). This is distinguished from hospital-based care. The school health service provides medical examinations, immunisations, dental care, eyesight and hearing tests, etc. Usually each school has a named school nurse and doctor, responsible for carrying out specific screening tests and available for consultation about particular problems. The DHA is normally also responsible for delivering therapy services, such as speech therapy and physiotherapy, sometimes provided at special schools themselves, but otherwise often at hospitals.

Note that this arrangement for providing health care normally works well, but can pose problems. The local education authority may be required to implement a statement of special needs, which includes a request for speech therapy for the child. The DHA provides therapy services, but is not under the same legal obligation as the education authority; it may feel that it has other, more pressing demands for its therapy services than the child in question. The assessment of needs will have been made by a multidisciplinary team, whereas responsibility for meeting needs is divided, and the education authority is legally responsible for a duty that it may be powerless to discharge.

This particular problem did not arise when both health and education services were provided by the local authority.

See *community medical officer.*

school phobia, see *school refusal.*

school psychological service (SPS), part of the local education authority (LEA)'s service; organisation in which nearly all *educational psychologists* work. The SPS is often known as the Educational Psychology Service.

As schools have grown more familiar with the work of educational psychologists, so demand for the SPS has grown. In addition, the extension of the LEA's responsibilities to seriously mentally handicapped children – Education (Handicapped Children) Act 1970 – and the raising of the school leaving age to sixteen in 1972 both resulted in an increase in demands on the SPS. The Education Act 1981 led to a further significant increase.

Although the service works extensively with the learning and behavioural difficulties of children and young people of all ages, the Wedell and Lambourn survey showed that it was most frequently involved with middle junior school pupils. Before 1983, when the Education Act 1981 was implemented in England and Wales, the nature of the work was already altering in the direction of the philosophy of the *Warnock Report,* in particular towards retaining pupils in ordinary schools, rather than placing them elsewhere.

The 1981 Act affected the work of the SPS in a variety of ways, two of which in particular deserve mention. First, the Act required that educational psychologists should be involved in the statementing process, formalising a situation which had previously existed in relation to the old ascertainment procedures in many but not all areas. This strengthened the image of the service as being primarily concerned with assessing children. Yet over the years educational psychologists had sought to modify this image, through a growing use of more sophisticated evaluation techniques, not necessarily dependent on standardised tests, a greater involvement in treatment procedures, and an increasing emphasis on preventive work through influencing teachers and parents.

Moreover many local education authorities expected that the SPS would collate the contributions of the various professionals involved in statementing, so requiring the service to shoulder additional administrative responsibilities.

The future position of the SPS is difficult to forecast, given the major changes that the Education Act 1988 will effect. One of the issues is the relationship between the SPS and *support services* for special education. Here, the main point of distinction is probably the emphasis placed by the SPS on working with children, while the other services work primarily with teachers – though this is an oversimplification of a complex situation. But at a time when surveys reveal that the most common complaint about the SPS is that the schools do not see enough of their educational psychologist, the demand for it looks likely to increase.

See *Summerfield Committee.*

References:

Atkinson, J.R. and Lucas, D.J. (1989) 'Promoting Psychology in the Local Authority', *Education and Child Psychology,* 6, 4, 5–18.

Department of Education and Science (1990) *Educational Psychology Services in England 1988–9,* London, HMSO.
Dessent, T. (1978) 'The Historical Development of School Psychological Services', in Gillham, B. (Ed.) *Reconstructing Educational Psychology,* London, Croom Helm.
Lucas, D.J. (1989) 'Implications for Educational Psychology Services of the Educational Reform Act 1988', *Educational Psychology in Practice,* 4, 4, 171–8.
Moses, D., Hegarty, S. and Jowett, S. (1988) *Supporting Ordinary Schools,* Windsor, NFER-Nelson.
Wedell, K. and Lambourn, R. (1980) 'Psychological Services in England and Wales', *Occasional Papers of the Division of Educational and Child Psychology,* Vol. 4, Nos. 1 & 2, Leicester, British Psychological Society.
Wright, H.J. and Payne, T.A.N. (1979) *Evaluation of a School Psychological Service,* Winchester, Hampshire Education Department.

school refusal, inability to attend school, often associated with sickness, stomach pains, and other psychosomatic symptoms when the time for morning departure approaches. At a conscious level the child wants to go to school, but feels unable to. These points are the main features distinguishing school refusal from truancy, where the child chooses not to attend, where the neurotic symptoms are absent, and where the parents may not always be aware of the problem, let alone centrally involved in it.

School refusal is most common in adolescents aged eleven to thirteen, often in the first few terms of starting secondary school, though it can occur at any age. Many children have similar difficulties starting infant school, though at that age the problem is usually more easily managed than when it occurs in older children, and in most cases the children are not referred to a specialist service. A prevalence of 1 to 2% has been reported in schoolchildren, but quoted prevalence rates are usually obtained from referral rates to child guidance clinics and school psychological services: an unknown number of unreferred cases may mean that the true prevalence of the condition is higher. In addition, surveys of the general population show a higher prevalence of similar but less acute symptoms, not resulting in the classic picture of great distress and often longstanding non-attendance.

Notwithstanding the name, many authorities prefer to interpret school refusal as a problem of separation from mother rather than a problem connected with attending school as such. But school problems – e.g. bullying, attitude of teachers, etc. – can also play a part. The presence of additional symptoms may place school refusal as part of a more pervasive depression.

The treatment depends on the cause: conditions at school can be changed; psychotherapy with the child and family can help; behaviour therapy is also used; a place at a small special unit for pupils with emotional disturbance sometimes helps to effect an immediate return to schooling. While there is no consensus on what is the most effective method of management, the outcome is usually good.

References:

Barker, P. (1988, 5th edn.) *Basic Child Psychiatry*, Oxford, Blackwell.

Blagg, N. (1987) *School Phobia and its Treatment*, London, Croom Helm.

Hersov, L. and Berg, I. (Eds.) (1980) *Out of School: Modern Perspectives in Truancy and School Refusal*, London, Wiley.

scoliosis, curvature of the spine. In itself there are no educational implications, though the exercises or surgery that may be required may involve some loss of school time, and a brace, if worn, will impose some physical needs.

screening, assessing a whole population in order to identify those individuals for whom some intervention in development would be beneficial. An obvious medical example is the process of screening all neonates for a metabolic disorder such as phenylketonuria. A simple urine test is carried out, enabling a dietary treatment programme to be instituted for babies found to be suffering from the condition.

Similar principles have been applied to special educational needs. Here, two types of screening can be distinguished, immediate screening to identify an existing need, and predictive screening intended to identify (and so prevent) a future need.

An example of immediate screening is a survey to identify all eight-year-olds with reading problems, the kind of operation that many local education authorities carry out. Here the criterion might be a reading age of six years or less; all children with lower scores to receive some form of special help. Although this seems a simple enough operation, it is not quite straightforward, for no test is perfectly reliable and the extent to which the test discriminates at the six-year reading level is crucial. The procedure could be improved by using additional criteria, but the extra effort involved for all children has then to be balanced against the increased accuracy of identification of the few. This problem can be eased by introducing multi-stage screening, as exemplified in some programmes for identifying hearing loss. A simple first screen for all, e.g. group audiometry, is followed by a more complex screening for the few.

This raises the validity of the first screen. The greater the number of *false negatives* and false positives, the less effective the screen. Moreover, apart from the statistical poverty of a procedure with a high proportion of false identifications, there is the ethical problem of the unnecessary concern raised in the minds of parents and children.

The second type of screening, predictive screening, has been the philosopher's stone of special education. The advantages of early identification of special needs have led to a search for effective methods of identifying young children who would have special educational needs in the future. Special programmes could then be instituted to prevent needs that would be likely to arise were no early intervention instituted.

Much work has centred on identification shortly after school entry, for this is the earliest that the whole child population is easily accessible. Schedules, tests, questionnaires, etc., have been devised, usually in the hope of identifying children who, for example, would be having serious reading difficulties at the age of seven or eight. Very few of these instruments have been adequately validated. It can also be argued that since academic attainment is so obviously dependent on the environment – including teaching skill – and on variations in individual development, predictions of this sort are bound to be hazardous. Predictive screening is best seen as just one stage in a continuous process of monitoring children's educational development so that appropriate help can be given as soon as possible.

References:

Drillien, C. and Drummond, M. (1983) *Developmental Screening and the Child with Special Needs: a Population Study of 5,000 Children*, London, Heinemann.

Gipps, C., Gross, H. and Goldstein, H. (1987) *Warnock's Eighteen Per Cent: Children with Special Needs in Primary Schools*, London, Falmer Press.

Lindsay, G. (Ed.) (1984) *Screening for Children with Special Needs*, London, Croom Helm.

seizure, see *epilepsy.*

self-fulfilling prophecy, see *Pygmalion effect.*

self-injurious behaviour (SIB), e.g. hair-pulling, head-banging, self-biting, i.e. repetitive, stereotyped behaviour which actually causes physical injury. A broad definition of SIB includes such actions as rocking and hand-movements, but the more common, narrower definition, limits it to those actions resulting in direct bodily harm.

SIB is a particular problem in the severely mentally retarded and the schizophrenic populations. Prevalence rates of up to 14% in the former and 40% in the latter have been quoted.

Various causes have been proposed. The specific form of self-mutilation associated with the Lesch-Nyhan syndrome may indicate a biochemical abnormality, genetically determined. The positive reinforcement (attention) generated by SIB may also explain its occurrence. So may negative reinforcement, when SIB is a means of escape from a demanding activity. So may a need for adequate levels of stimulation, provided by SIB in the absence of alternatives. Several or all of these mechanisms may be operating concurrently. As there is no one agreed cause, so there is no recommended treatment. Behavioural methods, including aversion therapy, are said to offer some success. The ethical objections to aversion therapy have to be set against the damage to the child that SIB incurs.

Reference:

Gunter, P.L. (1984) 'Self-Injurious Behaviour: Characteristics, Aetiology, and Treatment', *The Exceptional Child*, 31, 2, 91–8.

self-stimulating behaviour, see *stereotypic behaviour.*

semi-literacy, see *literacy.*

SENIOS, Special Educational Needs in the Ordinary School.
See *integration, whole-school approach.*

SENNAC, Special Educational Needs National Advisory Council, coordinating body consisting of representatives of eight of the main organisations concerned with special education in the UK. It publishes occasional pamphlets, and has held conferences.
Further information from:
Hon. Sec., SENNAC, Hillside, 271 Woolton Rd., Liverpool, L16 8NE.

sensorimotor stage, see *Piagetian theory.*

sensori-neural hearing loss, hearing loss caused by damage to the inner ear and/or the neural apparatus. This can be congenital, in which case the condition could be inherited, or caused by maternal illness such as rubella during pregnancy, or by hypoxia during birth. Alternatively sensori-neural loss can be caused post-natally, for example by a severe bout of some viral illnesses, most commonly meningitis. But in many instances it may not be possible to identify the cause.

Sensori-neural hearing loss is usually more serious than conductive hearing loss, since there is little that medical treatment can so far offer, and a heavy responsibility is placed on the education service. Fortunately, the prevalence of sensor-ineural loss is low, and an estimate of less than one child per thousand with severe hearing loss for this reason has been made.

Unlike *conductive hearing loss,* the whole hearing spectrum is rarely uniformly impaired, and often hearing for the higher frequencies is more affected. A high frequency loss results in distorted hearing; the child will usually be able to appreciate rhythm, intonation, stress, etc., and to hear most vowels, but many consonants will be inaudible. Assessment for a hearing aid is essential, of course, but an aid can only offer limited help with the distortion.

The effects on a child's education depend not only on the extent of the hearing loss, but also on other factors such as whether the child is intellectually damaged as well, the kind of support given by the parents, and the age at which the loss was diagnosed. As with all hearing impairments, speech and language suffer, and as these are the main educational media, extra support, whether education proceeds in the ordinary classroom or in a special unit or school, is required. And although nearly all hearing losses of this nature are detected before school age, it is still essential that teachers should be alert to the possibility of a child with an undiagnosed hearing loss in their classes.

See *hearing impairment, high frequency hearing loss.*

References:
Fraser, B. and Chapman, E. (1983) 'Children with Sensory Defects in School', *Special education: Forward Trends*, 10, 4, 36–8.
MacCarthy, A. and Connell, J. (1984) 'Audiological Screening and Assessment', in Lindsay, G. (1984) *Screening for Children with Special Needs*, London, Croom Helm.
Webster, A. (1986) *Deafness, Development and Literacy*, London, Methuen.
Webster, A. and Wood, D. (1989) *Children with Hearing Difficulties*, London, Cassell.

sensory aphasia, see *aphasia.*

sensory deprivation, occurs most obviously in children with visual and hearing impairment. Normal sensory input is restricted: where the restriction is severe, there are devastating effects on learning in general and communication and mobility skills in particular. Sensory deprivation also occurs in children with other handicaps. For example, the child with motor impairment may not be able to explore the environment efficiently, and the consequent limited opportunity for touching objects, appreciating shapes, experiencing the world around, is sometimes considered to be an example of sensory deprivation, though different in kind.

Sensory deprivation may also occur for social reasons. Children who have been institutionalised for long periods will have had limited experiences of social activities, as well as a restricted physical environment: extreme cases have been recorded where children have been incarcerated in attics, perhaps for years. They too have been described as sensorily deprived and one of the controversial issues is the extent to which the effects of such early and severe deprivation can be ameliorated by special education programmes.

Here, the converse view, that the greater the sensory stimulus, the better the learning environment, is too facile an inference. Just as important as the amount of stimulation is its nature. This is as true for early development as it is for teaching later.

See *cultural deprivation, maternal deprivation.*

References:
Clarke, M. and Clarke, A.D.B. (1976) *Early Experience – Myth and Evidence*, London, Open Books.
Hunt, J.M. (1961) *Intelligence and Experience*, New York, Ronald.
Skuse, D. (1984) 'Extreme Deprivation in Early Childhood II: Theoretical Issues and a Comparative Review', *Journal of Child Psychology and Psychiatry*, 25, 4, 543–72.
Schaffer, R. (1977) *Mothering*, Douglas IOM, Fontana/Open Books.

separation anxiety, unrealistic worry amounting sometimes to panic when a child is separated from a parent, or other attachment figure, or even from familiar surroundings, particularly home. Often other anxiety symptoms are present, e.g. psychosomatic stomach-aches, sleep disturbance, etc.

Most preschool children are anxious about separation on occasion. But after the first year or so in school these worries usually subside. Separation anxiety is then most often shown in relation to school, sometimes developing into *school refusal*. The child should be referred to a child guidance clinic or school psychological service. Difficulties with school are not usually implicated, though school can assist by offering a reassuring atmosphere and collaborating in any therapeutic programme suggested.

Reference:

Bowlby, J. (1969, 1978 and 1980) *Attachment and Loss: Vol. 1, Attachment; Vol. 2, Separation Anxiety and Anger; Vol. 3, Loss Sadness and Depression*, Harmondsworth, Penguin.

setting, see *ability grouping*.

severe learning difficulty, describes an inability to manage the normal curriculum, to the extent that even simple reading will be a skill that many children will not achieve by the usual school leaving age. Children with severe learning difficulties were the last group to be admitted into the education system, following the Education (Handicapped Children) Act 1970. Many children in this group suffer from organic damage, perhaps a chromosomal abnormality, or biochemical disorder, or neurological damage. With the run-down of the mental handicap hospitals and the emphasis on community care, more severely damaged children are being admitted to the special schools where children with severe learning difficulties are mainly educated.

Educational programmes concentrate on developing adaptive behaviour, aiming to help children develop a degree of independence, so that they might later be able to achieve, with support, a place in the community. Reconciling these purposes with the entitlement of all children to the National Curriculum, with its emphasis on academic subjects, is a difficult issue.

The emphasis on later integration has been one argument for seeking greater integration for these children at the school stage. This is another difficult issue, for the detailed educational and curricular needs of these children are very different from those of children in the mainstream. Yet investigations show that it is schools for children with severe learning difficulties that are most active in developing links with mainstream schools, 80% of them in a recent survey having links of one sort or another in operation. These links can involve regular exchanges both of pupils and staff, often programmed into each other's timetables. This is not full integration, but it does represent a move in that direction which has been achieved with minimal resource and maximum goodwill and effort. In many areas of special education, provision in special schools has later been followed by provision in units attached to the ordinary school. This move has been proposed as a natural next step in the education of these children.

See *learning difficulties*.

References:
Coupe, J. and Porter, J. (1986) *The Education of Children with Severe Learning Difficulties*, London, Croom Helm.
Jowett, S., Hegarty, S. and Moses, D. (1988) *Joining Forces; a Study of Links Between Special and Ordinary Schools*, Windsor, NFER-Nelson.
Mittler, P. and Farrell, P. (1987) 'Can Children with Severe Learning Difficulties be Educated in the Ordinary School?' *European Journal of Special Education*, 4, 2, 221–36.
Ware, J. (1990) 'Severe Learning Difficulties and Multiple Handicaps: Curriculum Developments, Integration and Prospects', in Evans, P. and Varma, V. (Eds.) (1990) *Special Education: Past, Present and Future*, London, Falmer Press.

severe mental impairment, one of the four categories of mental disorder specified in the Mental Health Act 1983. In this Act, severe mental impairment is defined as 'a state of arrested or incomplete development of mind, which includes severe impairment of intelligence and social functioning and is associated with abnormally aggressive or seriously irresponsible conduct'.

See *mental impairment.*

Reference:
Gostin, L. (1983) *A Practical Guide to Mental Health Law*, London, MIND.

severe mental retardation, see *mental retardation.*

sex education, has been a taboo subject for many children with special needs, particularly those with serious handicaps. Young people whose intellectual development is limited, or who need caring and support for other reasons, are sometimes assumed to be children in every way; yet they usually have the emotional and physical needs of all young people of their chronological age. Their need for sex education is perhaps particularly great; some worry about their attractiveness to the opposite sex, while others may have unrealistic ambitions about having children and enjoying a normal family life. But the main point is that the right to love is a basic human right, which extends to all members of society and from which those with special needs should not be excluded.

References:
Craft, A. (Ed.) (1986) *Mental Handicap and Sexuality: Issues and Perspectives*, Tunbridge Wells, Costello.
Greengross, W. (1976) *Entitled to Love: the Sexual and Emotional Needs of the Handicapped*, London, Malaby Press.

sexual abuse, see *child abuse.*

shaping, see *behaviour shaping.*

sheltered employment, employment arrangements designed to offer work for people whose disabilities are such that they are unable to gain open employment. The Disabled Persons Employment Acts provide legislative support. There are three main providers, local authorities, who run sheltered workshops, voluntary bodies, who run a range of different schemes, and *Remploy.*

Sheltered employment workshops may be involved in furniture-making, light engineering, basket-work and many other activities, sometimes as sub-contractors to industry and sometimes on their own account. The hours of work, conditions, rates of pay, etc., match those in open employment as closely as possible. This helps workers become accustomed to normal work routines, for one of the purposes of sheltered employment is to help people who are disabled learn skills that will enable them to gain open employment later. This may sometimes be in conflict with managers' desire to retain their better workers.

An enclave scheme, in which small groups of workers with disabilities work together under supervision within a normal business is a kind of half-way house between sheltered and open employment, operated as a collaborative scheme between the employer and a local authority or voluntary body.

For information on these arrangements for school-leavers and others the Disablement Resettlement Service should be consulted, via the local job-centre.

See *Quota scheme.*

References:

Hutchinson, D. (1982) *Work Preparation for the Handicapped,* London, Croom Helm.
Thomson, M. (1986) *Employment for Disabled People,* London, Kogan Page.

shunt, surgically implanted valve used to control *hydrocephalus* through shunting excess cerebrospinal fluid into the bloodstream. There are various versions, but two of the most commonly used are the Holter and the Pudenz valves.

SIB, see *self-injurious behaviour.*

siblings, play an important part in a child's development: the increasing emphasis on integration within the community means that more children with serious special needs will live at home, and the repercussions on siblings may become a greater subject for concern.

The nature of these repercussions varies, and the evidence is conflicting. Jealousy over the extra attention required by the child with special needs is often mentioned, yet some studies find this not to differ from jealousy between siblings in ordinary families. There seems little doubt that at least as far as siblings of children with mental handicaps are concerned, there is a restriction on normal social activities. Effects of this nature depend on various factors. As with any children, sex and age make a difference: very broadly, the more distant the sibling the less the effect. The position of the sibling in the family is also important; it has been shown that when the child with special needs is the youngest of a large family, effects on the siblings are less than when the child is one of only two children, for example.

The nature of the special need also plays a part; children with a mentally handicapped sibling are less likely to show jealousy than children with a sibling whose handicap is physical – in fact there is evidence that they show particularly caring attitudes. But these are all general findings, based on group studies: each individual family is different. For example, where a mother has had to give up work, and there are serious financial losses for which disability allowances do not compensate, the resulting stress may outweigh any of the points mentioned above. But probably the most important factor in a complicated set of possibilities is the attitude of the parents: a sensible, honest attitude enables siblings of children with special needs to gain from their experience, too.

References:

Andersson, E. (1988) 'Siblings of Young Mentally Handicapped Children and their Social Relations', *Research Supplement of British Journal of Special Education*, 15, 1, 24–6.

McConachie, H. (1986) *Parents and Young Mentally Handicapped Children: a Review of Research Issues*, London, Croom Helm.

sight vocabulary, see *basic sight vocabulary.*

sight word, word that children are expected to recognise immediately, i.e. as a whole and without requiring analysis. In the early stages of learning to read, children are often taught to recognise 'at sight' a number of words occurring frequently. These words constitute a basic sight vocabulary.

sign language, any system that uses gestures of hands and fingers as well as eye and body movements, to communicate. Deaf communities in virtually every country have developed their own version of a sign language: for example, in the UK, British Sign Language (BSL) is the most widely-used sign language, whereas in the USA, Ameslan, or American Sign Language is used. *Makaton* is essentially a simplified form of BSL, used widely with children with both hearing impairment and mental handicap.

Although it used to be held that sign languages convey meaning less precisely than spoken and written languages, they are now acknowledged as languages in their own right, with their own grammars, lexicons, etc. They do not obey the same linguistic conventions as the English that the hearing-impaired will need to master at least in written form, and which have to be learnt. For these reasons attempts have been made to increase the correspondence between sign languages and English through the development of sign systems which differ from the traditional language of the deaf. Signed (Exact) English, or SEE, is an example of a system with greater correspondence. This embodies natural signs from the deaf which are used in spoken English word order, with additional signs and finger spelling to indicate such features as tense and plural endings, so that a complete visual representation can be given alongside speech.

The *Paget-Gorman Sign System* is a logically-constructed system that mirrors English grammar, morphology and syntax, by signing plurals, tenses, prefixes, etc. Its signs differ from BSL and it has the reputation of being difficult to learn.

In Signs Supporting English, SSE, only some of the features of spoken English are illustrated with signs, giving some additional clues to aid understanding.

While sign languages can be modified or sign systems constructed to provide correspondence with English for children with severe hearing loss, communication skills are tackled differently with children whose hearing enables them to comprehend speech, albeit imperfectly. Apart from the information gained from lip-reading, signs can be used to improve comprehension. The most common system of signs here is that used in *cued speech,* which is a system of single hand shapes around the lips to differentiate speech sounds which are unseen or look alike on the lips.

The decision over whether to use a sign system, and if so which one, is very much a matter for the expert, in consultation with the parents. For the profoundly deaf, it is argued that both a sign system and English must be acquired. Many authorities believe that while signing, words must always be spoken to the child, no matter how severe the hearing loss. Every opportunity to use additional information channels should be taken. The goal, however achieved, is to give children the ability to communicate with as many people and in as many different contexts as possible.

See *oral–manual controversy, total communication.*

References:

Kiernan, C., Reid, B. and Jones, L. (1982) *Signs and Symbols,* London, Heinemann for Institute of Education, University of London.

Miles, D. (1988) *British Sign Language: a Beginner's Guide,* London, BBC Books.

van Uden, A.M.J. (1982) 'Hearing Impaired/Deaf, Education of', in Mitzel, H.E. (Ed.) (1982, 5th edn.) *Encyclopaedia of Educational Research,* New York, Free Press.

Wilson, A.R.S. (1983) 'The Use of Manual Communication with Deaf-Blind Mentally Handicapped Children', in Hogg J. and Mittler, P. (Eds.) (1983) *Advances in Mental Handicap Research,* Chichester, Wiley.

Signed (Exact) English (SEE), see *sign language.*

significant living without work, view that there are some young people with special needs who will never be able to work, and who must be prepared for a life without paid employment.

Such children raise the question of the aims of education in a peculiarly acute way. A central aim of most education programmes is to enable a child to go out into the world as an independent adult: that means earning a living. If it is clear that this will be impossible, then there are direct and inescapable implications for the curriculum. For children with severe learning difficulties, the notion of a developmental curriculum, concentrating on acquiring the skills of daily living, has been broadly accepted. But intelligent though severely disabled children pose different questions. Some argue that their education should be primarily education for leisure, aiming at personal fulfilment through recreation, or through lifelong education; preparation for a job that will never be available is as irrelevant as it is dishonest. These are issues which may have to be faced by many others than the severely handicapped, as societies alter the value previously placed on lifelong, full-time employment for all.

References:

Bookis, J. (1983) *Beyond the School Gate: a Study of Disabled Young People*, London, Royal Association on Disability and Rehabilitation.

Hutchinson, D. (1982) *Work Preparation for the Handicapped*, London, Croom Helm.

Signs Supporting English (SSE), see *sign language.*

simultaneous method, see *total communication.*

six-hour retarded child, was used in the 1970 report of the President's commission on mental retardation in the USA. It described children who had learning difficulties in school, but who functioned normally in home and community. These are children whose learning difficulties seem to relate primarily to the demands of the school curriculum.

Reference:

Van Etten, G., Arkell, C. and Van Etten, C. (1980) *The Severely and Profoundly Handicapped*, St. Louis, Mosby.

sleeper effect, effect which appears after some time has elapsed; delayed effect. Perhaps the best-known example is to be found in the *Head Start* literature. When the first national evaluation of the Head Start project was reported in 1969, some four years after its start, serious doubts were raised about the efficacy of the project. Any benefits were seen to be modest and short-lived, far out of keeping with the vast investment of resources. But a later re-evaluation of a small group of well-controlled studies showed that while the immediate benefits indeed seemed to have 'washed out' shortly after the early intervention ceased, there was evidence of benefits re-emerging in high school.

This phenomenon was dubbed a 'sleeper effect'. Note that it describes a phenomenon; it produces no model to explain why the effect was dormant, nor to suggest whether maturation, changing school demands, or whatever, caused it to reawaken. A sleeper effect on its own is description, not explanation.

Reference:

Woodhead, M. (1985) 'Early Intervention', Unit 25 of Open University Course E206, Milton Keynes, Open University.

slicing, technical term for breaking down tasks into smaller, more manageable teaching units. It is a feature of *task analysis* used in the behavioural approach to teaching. The purpose of slicing is to extract tasks of roughly equivalent but lesser difficulty from the main objective.

For example, an objective might be that the pupil learns to spell correctly three-letter phonically regular words to a set criterion (thirty-six correct out of forty on a ten-minute presentation, say). This could be sliced into five equal tasks, each requiring the pupil to spell correctly eight three-letter words with identical central vowels (seven correct on a two-minute presentation, say). Each sliced task would use a different vowel. The sliced tasks are each easier than the main objective.

Finally the pupil could be tested on the main objective.

Note that the sequence in which the sliced units are taught is not critical. This distinguishes slicing from other behavioural techniques such as chaining and behaviour shaping, in which the sequence in which the behaviour units are taught is all-important.

Reference:

Ainscow, M. and Tweddle, D. (1981) 'The Objectives Approach: a Progress Report', in Somerset Education Authority, *Ways and Means 2,* Basingstoke, Globe Education.

SMOG index, or Simple Measure of Gobbledygook, *readability* measure devised by McLaughlin. SMOG is based on the number of words with three or more syllables (polysyllable count) in thirty sentences, sampled from the beginning, middle and end of the text.

The SMOG grade level = 3 + square root of polysyllable count. This can be transformed into a reading age by adding 5 to the grade level.

SMOG is probably the easiest readability formula to use, provided the user is unworried by square roots! It also agrees well on average with teachers' estimates of readability levels. But the price of ease is accuracy, and at plus or minus 1.5 years, the standard error of the SMOG measure is somewhat higher than that of other measures.

References:

Harrison, C. (1979) 'Assessing the Readability of School Texts', in Lunzer, E. and Gardner, K. (Eds.) (1979) *The Effective Use of Reading,* London, Heinemann.

Klare, G.R. (1974) 'Assessing Readability', in Chapman, L.J. and Czerniowska, P. (Eds.) (1974) *Reading: from Process to Practice,* London, Routledge and Kegan Paul.

SNAP, Special Needs Action Programme, structured approach to helping schools respond effectively to children's special needs. The main aims of the SNAP project are to encourage Heads to develop identification procedures, to assist teachers to provide suitable curricula, and to coordinate the work of the support services. SNAP, which was developed in Coventry, was originally aimed at the primary school; a version for secondary schools has been produced since.

The core of SNAP is a series of modules to be used for inservice education, originally in a series of six workshops. Each participating school provides a coordinator for special needs for the SNAP course, whose task thereafter is to make colleagues aware of their responsibilities for children with special needs, to coordinate the developments in their schools and generally to assist their colleagues. SNAP is therefore an example of a cascade or pyramid model of inservice training.

The emphasis in the SNAP materials is on the relativity of special needs; since learning difficulties are situation-specific, it is up to each school to devise those procedures and programmes that suit the context in which its pupils are being educated. The modules follow an objectives approach to learning difficulties, and include presentations on children with sensory impairments and behavioural difficulties.

The original SNAP project was evaluated positively by the participants, who, as well as enjoying the course, particularly appreciated the discussions with colleagues that operating SNAP entailed. A follow-up two years later was somewhat hampered by the fact that the majority of coordinators had moved to new posts, but the continuing SNAP activity in the schools is one measure of the success of the programme. One of the main problems had been the lack of non-teaching time for the coordinators to use for SNAP activities, but a later arrangement to provide cover temporarily for one afternoon a week helped to maintain the impetus.

References:

Moses, D. (1988) 'The Special Needs Action Programme', in Hegarty, S. and Moses, D. (Eds.) (1988) *Developing Expertise: INSET for Special Educational Needs*, Windsor, NFER-Nelson.

Muncey, J. and Ainscow, M. (1983) *Launching SNAP in Coventry*, Special Education: Forward Trends, 10, 3, 8–12.

Snellen chart, simple method of measuring visual acuity. It consists of a number of lines of letters of descending size of type face. The type size on each line is appropriate to the distance at which a person with normal acuity can read it correctly. Depending on how far away from the chart the person stands and the size of the letters read, visual acuity is described by a fraction: the upper figure represents distance from the chart, the lower figure the size of the letters. A person stands at a distance of six metres from the chart. If he or she can read the tiny, six-metre line of print correctly, his or her vision is described as 6/6, i.e. normal vision; if the smallest print size read correctly is the twelve metre line, then vision is 6/12. Thus 6/60 vision means that a person can only read the largest of the letters at six metres, although someone with normal vision would be able to read them from sixty metres away.

As a rough guide, children with a Snellen ratio of 6/36 AFTER CORRECTION in the better eye are likely to need low vision aids, and a ratio of 3/60 is the boundary for registration as blind, when sighted methods of learning may not be suitable. Note that in the USA Snellen ratios are given in feet, not metres; thus normal vision is expressed as 20/20; the legal definition of blindness (which is different from the UK) is given as 20/200. The Snellen chart is simple to give and to interpret. However, it measures visual acuity only, and important though this is, there are many other aspects of visual functioning which determine how well a person 'sees'. It is not an ideal measure for educational purposes; since it measures distance vision, it is not necessarily a good predictor of the ability to read print, for example. But it is the most widely used quick assessment of visual ability recorded for school children.

References:

Fitt, R.A. and Mason, H. (1986) *Sensory Handicaps in Children*, Stratford-upon-Avon, National Council for Special Education.

Chapman, E.K. and Stone, J.M. (1988) *The Visually Handicapped Child in Your Classroom*, London, Cassell.

social class, has been widely but controversially used as an explanatory principle in special education research. Many studies show that the prevalence of special educational needs in children increases the further one goes down the social class scale, in which social class is measured as the *occupational classification* of the family's main bread-winner. A good example of this relationship is found in the research conducted for the Plowden Report.

This relationship has been explained in various ways. The higher prevalence of physical and sensory impairment in children from lower social class groups has been attributed to a lack of care at the prenatal and immediate postnatal stages. While it is true that mothers from the lower social classes make below-average use of the prenatal and child care services, to ascribe this to a feckless attitude may be to overlook the possibility that it may stem from the practical difficulties of attending clinics without the use of a car and with a number of other children, for example. In these straitened circumstances, it may be that the service delivery is inadequate, not the mother.

Similarly, the higher prevalence of learning difficulties in children from lower social class groups has been attributed to inadequate language development; it has been argued that children in these families have less verbal stimulation and consequently develop an inadequate and inferior set of language skills. Others argued that the language and culture of the poorer classes was not inferior but different; the learning difficulties of the children stem not from their class but from the inability of the education system to appreciate the culture and values of a low-status group.

These are complicated and politically charged issues, with implications for the heredity–environment debate. Many would feel happier to abandon the concept of social class and concentrate on the social factors which are undoubtedly and less controversially associated with learning difficulties.

See *language code.*

Reference:
Barton, L. and Tomlinson, S. (Eds.) (1984) *Special Education and Social Interests*, London, Croom Helm.

social competence, equivalent to *adaptive behaviour*. The term is sometimes used in the narrower sense of personal interaction skills only, i.e. social behaviour.

social education centre, new name for *adult training centre*. The change of name is intended to reflect the change in objectives, as the centres emphasise their educative rather than their occupational purpose.

Social Services Authorities, together with the National Health Service, are the major organisations supporting the education service in meeting children's special educational needs. There are four main situations where a local Social Services Authority (SSA) might be involved.

The first arises when a child is assessed with a view to providing a Statement of special educational needs. At this point the local education authority (LEA) must inform the SSA, though consultation with it is permissive, not mandatory. This is a different position from that which obtains with the District Health Authority, from which the LEA is legally obliged to seek medical advice. Many feel that both health and social service advice should have been obligatory, even though this would have interposed an extra link in an already long operation.

The SSA is also involved in its role as the agency in which parental rights for children in care are vested. This is an important function, for among children in care, there is a higher proportion with special educational needs than in the general population. Here there may be a divergence of views. For example, the SSA policy for children in care may favour fostering or adoption, whereas the assessment team may advise the LEA that a place at a residential special school is desirable. In this situation the SSA is in fact acting as a parent, rather than collaborating with another local authority department.

The third situation occurs where the SSA is a provider of services which are used by families of children with special needs. Thus the SSA may provide respite care for families of children with severe learning difficulties. The SSA may also be responsible for organising a preschool playgroup for very young children with special needs, a facility which offers great opportunities for the LEA to collaborate in the provision of early education, either directly or through working through parents.

The fourth situation arises at school-leaving, when a number of young people with special needs will attend facilities provided by the SSA, most obviously social education centres. Here again there are opportunities for the LEA to play a part, perhaps through providing links with the school to ensure an easy transition, perhaps through providing education at the centre, or perhaps through supporting outreach courses from the local college of further education.

Apart from these activities the social workers on the staff of the SSA may well have other contacts with parents of children with special needs, giving them help over completing statutory forms, counselling them over their family problems, advising them about their child's rights, and in many other ways. For all these reasons it is important that the LEA and the SSA collaborate at all levels, from the personal level of teacher and social worker upwards, as extensively and intensively as possible.

The *Children Act 1989* has considerable implications for the provision of services for children with special needs and their families.

References:

Adams, F. (Ed.) (1986) *Special Education*, Harlow, Councils and Education Press for Longman.

Goacher, B., Evans, J., Welton, J. and Wedell, K. (1988) *Policy and Provisions for Special Educational Needs: Implementing the 1981 Education Act*, London, Cassell.

social skills, those adaptive behaviours that are concerned with making effective interpersonal relationships. They are skills which most children acquire through learning from their parents and peers, but which may have to be taught to children with marked learning difficulties and emotional problems.

Social skills training programmes usually follow behavioural principles. They deal with problems such as excessive aggression, withdrawn behaviour, disruptive behaviour, unassertiveness, etc. Encouraging results have been obtained.

See *behaviour therapy*.

Reference:

Herbert, M. (1987) *Behavioural Treatment of Children with Problems: a Practice Manual*, London, Academic Press.

social worker, member of a profession which has among its concerns helping people cope with disabilities and associated emotional, social and economic handicaps. This remit includes children with special needs and their families, and some social workers specialise in this field.

Most, but not all social workers are employed by local Social Services Authorities. One of their functions is to coordinate services, a task which together with assessment will become increasingly important when the recommendations of the White Paper 'Caring for People' are implemented.

Social workers may undergo professional training leading to a Certificate of Qualification in Social Work (CQSW), or Certificate in Social Service (CSS). Within the next few years the CQSW and the CSS are to be replaced by a single qualification, to be known as the Diploma in Social Work.

The activities of social workers in relation to children with special needs have increased since the Education Act 1981. The main situations in which social workers interact with the special education system are described in the *Social Service Authorities* entry.

The cry for collaboration between the education and social services is frequently heard. But the implicit conflict between the social worker's responsibility to the individual client and the teacher's responsibilities to the whole school community may make cooperation difficult. There is little sign that the training for either profession is yet able to provide adequate understanding of the constraints on the other's style of working. There are inevitable tensions between different professions with different concerns and different priorities. Yet tensions can be creative as well as destructive, and special education does offer some splendid examples of the cooperation that is so often advocated from afar.

References:

Craig, B. (1984) 'The Social Worker: Front Line and Last Ditch', in Lindsay, G. (Ed.) (1984) *Screening for Children with Special Needs*, London, Croom Helm.

Wingham, G. (1987) 'Social Workers and the Special Education System', National Council for Special Education, *Research Exchange*, Issue 8, Sept. 1987, p.4.

sociodrama, similar to psychodrama in that role-play techniques are used, but different in that it is used to explore problems of social groups, rather than of individuals. Thus an issue might be the attitude of the police to minority groups. Discussion would lead to a specific example, from which a scenario could be constructed and acted. The players would be asked to discuss their feelings, and the whole exercise would be used to give greater insight into the problem and the behaviour of the participants. Sociodrama aims to clarify, rather than cure.

Reference:

Van Meerts, M. (1983) *The Effective Use of Role-play: a Handbook for Teachers and Trainers*, London, Kogan Page.

socioeconomic status (ses), individual's standing in society, usually measured by *occupational classification*. Studies of the relationship between social class and prevalence of special needs often use ses as a measure of social class. A five-category scale is commonly used: professional; intermediate; skilled; semiskilled; unskilled. The 'skilled' category is sometimes sub-divided into 'manual' and 'non-manual' groups. The classification of an individual's occupation into these five groups is usually based on the current Registrar General's Classification of Occupations, published by HMSO.

sociogram, see *sociometry*.

sociometry, technique for investigating social relationships in a group by asking group members to express their preferences for each other. Thus pupils might be asked to provide (in confidence) the name of the classmate with whom they would most like to work on a project. The pattern of

Sociogram for project work, two choices per pupil

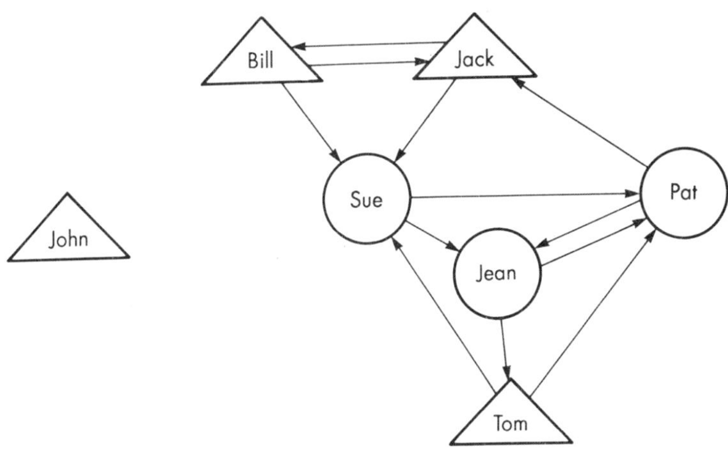

Note John is an *isolate*

choices can be represented in different ways. The most popular method is to map the choices on a diagram, or sociogram. This enables the investigator to locate internally cohesive teaching groups; stars, or popular choices; neglectees, pupils who make choices but are not themselves chosen; and isolates, pupils who neither receive nor make choices. The sociomatrix and sociometric index are other methods of handling the data obtained, less visually obvious in impact, but slightly more sophisticated.

Sociometry can be used as part of a screening procedure for identifying children with relationship difficulties: neglectees and isolates are the key individuals here. It can also be used to assess cross-group relationships, as in exploring the extent to which friendship patterns cross racial boundaries. Methods have been developed for using sociometry with children who cannot write – young children or children with mental handicaps.

Sociometry is not without problems. The extent to which nominated preferences match observed preferences is one. Another is the problem of handling data, which for a large class can be horrendous: for this reason the smaller the group with which the technique is used initially the better. For the same reason it is usual to restrict the number of choices requested to a maximum of two.

See *sociogram* illustration.

References:

Cohen L. (1976) *Educational Research in Classrooms and Schools: a Manual of Materials and Methods*, London, Harper and Row.

Marsh, G.E., Price, B.J. and Smith, T.E.C. (1983) *Teaching Mildly Handicapped Children*, St.Louis, Mosby.

soft neurological sign, neurological sign whose significance is unclear, i.e. it does not indicate major neurological damage, but may suggest minor neurological impairment, e.g. mild speech impairment or poor fine motor skills.

solvent abuse, deliberately inhaling the fumes given off by volatile substances in order to achieve intoxication. Glue sniffing is a common example.

Surveys suggest that up to 8% of the secondary school population have tried solvent sniffing, though truants, among whom the prevalence may be higher, might not have been included. Moreover the prevalence varies considerably from district to district. Within these figures it is possible to identify three separate groups, the experimenters, who will not continue for long; the regular users, perhaps a tenth of the experimenters, who may continue sniffing for a few months; and the habitual long-term users.

Sniffing is undoubtedly dangerous, and in 1984 it caused eighty-one deaths in the UK. Within schools, prevention strategies emphasise providing basic information about solvents and drugs generally, as well as techniques for resisting peer-group pressure. As with drugs, collaboration with specialist advice from the Health Service should be sought in order to ensure that a sound prevention strategy is instituted.

See *drug abuse.*

Reference:

Ives, R. (1986) 'Solvent Misuse', *Highlight*, 43, London, National Children's Bureau.

SOMPA, System Of Multicultural Pluralistic Assessment, controversial USA attempt to provide an assessment of learning potential that is independent of ethnic background or sociocultural group. Instead of trying to construct a culture-fair test, the authors of SOMPA accept that tests are culturally loaded in favour of children from the white middle classes, and aim to provide a correction factor for others. SOMPA provides standardised measures of adaptive behaviour and Estimated Learning Potential (ELP); a set of 'medical' measures, assessing qualities such as fine motor control, physical development, sensory acuity, etc.; and a measure of sociocultural background. These three measures are intended to provide a comprehensive assessment system, to be used diagnostically.

SOMPA is predicated on the authors' belief that any differences between ethnic and socioeconomic groups on educational and psychological tests of ability are artefacts of the tests: there are no inherent differences between the groups. Thus a 'true' measure of an individual's ability is only gained after the score obtained has been weighted to allow for the relationship between the scores of the group of which he or she is a member and the test norms. This principle is applied to produce the ELP scores. While there are some criticisms of the technical level of the SOMPA subtests, the main point of controversy is the principle of correction used. In SOMPA, a score on the WISC-R is used to provide a measure of ELP. A child's ELP is based on regression equations which use ethnic group membership (Hispanics, Whites, and Blacks) and a sociocultural background score to weight the obtained WISC score. The effect is to equalise the means and (partly) the distributions of transformed WISC scores for ethnic and socioeconomic groups. These transformed scores comprise the ELP.

This approach is based on an article of faith: how far the compensated scores are 'true' scores, and how valid is the principle on which the compensation is based are both matters of conjecture. By raising ability scores in this way, adverse labelling may be reduced, and self-images may be enhanced, but the question of the kind of educational programmes needed remains.

Reference:

Salvia, J. and Ysseldyke, J.E. (1985, 3rd edn.) *Assessment in Special and Remedial Education*, Boston, Houghton Mifflin.

Southgate Reading Tests, two group tests, each designed to enable teachers to assess an aspect of children's reading performance without hearing them read aloud. Test 1, which has two parallel forms, assesses the ability to recognise a word spoken by the tester through selecting it from a multiple-choice format. Test 2, which has three parallel forms, tests comprehension through completing a sentence correctly, again by choosing a word from a multiple choice format. The tests are technically satisfactory, though the standardisation is elderly, and they have been widely used in screening children between six and nine years of age for reading difficulties.

Reference:

Pumfrey, P.D. (1985, 2nd edn.) *Reading: Tests and Assessment Techniques*, Sevenoaks, Hodder and Stoughton in association with UKRA.

spasticity, increased muscle tone in one or more limbs, leading to resistance to stretching.

See *cerebral palsy*.

special care provision, in England and Wales is established for children who are profoundly mentally handicapped, with IQ levels usually below 20 points and/or other handicaps. Most cannot walk or talk, show few self-help skills and may be at the earliest stages of human development. There are many different medical conditions accounting for their very severe difficulties. They attend special care units or special schools. Some may be educated in hospital schools, though the number of children in long-stay hospitals for individuals with mental handicap is falling in the UK. There is considerable overlap between the populations attending these three kinds of provision, and whether a child is placed in one or other may depend heavily on local circumstances.

Special care units are classrooms in schools for children with severe learning difficulties (SLD). A report of a survey (Evans and Ware) has articulated concern over the low level of support given to these arrangements. Pupil–teacher ratios were slightly higher than in the SLD schools, although the overall pupil–staff ratio was slightly better: visiting by other professional staff was infrequent. Morale among teaching staff was low. Like the characteristics of the children themselves, the provision was extremely variable.

The experiences of teaching special care children over the last two decades has raised again the question of their educability: others would express this as a question of the meaning of 'educability', for some development since birth has occurred and some skills have been learnt. What is clear is that since the impetus of the Education (Handicapped Children) Act 1970, this area of education has been neglected.

References:

Department of Education and Science (1978) *The Education of Children in Hospitals for the Mentally Handicapped*, London, HMSO.

Evans, P. and Ware, J. (1987) *'Special Care' Provision*, Windsor, NFER-Nelson.

HM Inspectorate (1983) *A Whole Community – the Education of Educationally Subnormal (Severe) Children in Wales*, Cardiff, Welsh Office.

special care schools, the Northern Ireland title for schools for children with severe learning difficulties. Until 1987, these schools were controlled by the health authorities; thereafter responsibility for them was transferred to the Northern Ireland education service.

A survey at the time of transfer has reported inferior staffing ratios and inadequate resources in comparison with similar provision in England and with schools for children with other handicaps in Northern Ireland. Improvements have followed.

See *Education Order (Northern Ireland) 1984.*

References:

Dwyer, E. and Conliffe, C. (1990) 'A Survey of Facilities in Northern Ireland Schools for Children with Severe Learning Difficulties: The Effects of Legislative Change', *European Journal of Special Education*, 5, 2, 79–86.

Dwyer, E. and Swann, W. (1987) 'Educational Services for Mentally Handicapped Children in Northern Ireland: a Survey of Provision', *European Journal of Special Education*, 2, 1, 25–44.

special care unit, see *special care provision.*

special class, class attached to the ordinary school, enrolling children with special needs. The special class developed in particular after the second world war, when it was seen as an alternative to the *special school*, offering less seriously handicapped children the advantages of education in a more natural environment, and the possibility of some integrated activities. Special classes usually admitted children with the same category of handicap. Most special classes catered for children with learning difficulties. Where the handicap was sensory or physical, the group was often called a unit rather than a class, and though attached to an ordinary school, the unit often felt itself to be organisationally distinct, under the wing of the school for administrative purposes, but linked to the advisory services for curriculum matters and admission and discharge of pupils.

Although most schools left curriculum in special classes to the discretion of the teacher, unlike units the class was much more clearly part of the organisation of the school. This made sense, partly because a special class often served one school only and partly because children with learning difficulties were not felt to need such specialised support services as those whose special educational needs were due to physical or sensory impairments.

At the primary stage, one of the main educational disadvantages of special classes (not present in special schools) was the lack of progression for the children: a seven-year-old admitted to a primary school special class would remain in that class, with the same teacher, until eleven years of age. To help to meet this, there was a move in the 1960s to attach two special classes to the same primary school. This gave progression, but at the expense of a wider catchment area, meaning that some children had to travel to a different school – albeit not the special school – from their friends.

As pressure for integration increased, and remedial and special class teachers began to switch to a support teaching role, so children with less demanding special needs were absorbed into the ordinary streams. At the same time, some children from special schools were placed in special classes in the ordinary school, with the effect that special classes may now deal with more complex special needs. Some children with severe learning difficulties, at one time deemed ineducable, then educated in special schools, are in some authorities now being educated in special classes in the ordinary school, at least at the infant stage.

There is little definitive research on the relative educational value of special classes as opposed to special schools, partly because the criteria adopted vary from investigation to investigation. Moreover there are inherent design problems which are difficult to eradicate: for example one study found little difference between the attainments of pupils in special schools and special units for children with physical handicaps – but the pupil–teacher ratios were substantially better in the units than in the schools. Opportunities for integration are of course very much better in the units, and as in so many educational issues, the interpretation of findings depends on the values attached to different criteria.

One striking feature in recent special class provision has been the growth in units for disruptive pupils, particularly at the secondary stage. The advantages and disadvantages of this type of provision have been well-discussed: very broadly the pupils appreciate the more liberal atmosphere and the pupils and schools are both afforded relief from a stressful situation. On the other hand, these are segregated arrangements, and the record of return to the ordinary school is not good. More importantly, the curriculum on offer is restricted, and in the light of the 1988 Education Act, either the National Curriculum will have to be modified or disapplied, or better arrangements for delivering it will have to be made.

See *emotional and behavioural difficulties.*

References:

Brennan, W.K. (1987) *Changing Special Education Now*, Milton Keynes, Open University Press.

Cope, C. and Anderson, A. (1977) *Special Units in Ordinary Schools*, London, Institute of Education, University of London.

Fish, J. (1985) *Special Education: the Way Ahead*, Milton Keynes, Open University Press.

Hodgson, A., Clunies-Ross, L. and Hegarty, S. (1984) *Learning Together: teaching pupils with special educational needs in the ordinary school*, Windsor, NFER-Nelson.

Topping, K.J. (1983) *Educational Systems for Disruptive Adolescents*, London, Croom Helm.

special education department, see *support teaching.*

special education support/advisory service, see *support services.*

special educational need, key concept underpinning the right to special education, as stated in the *Education Act 1981*. It replaced membership of a category of handicap, the determining principle of previous legislation. A prevalence of one in six children with special educational needs at any one time has been widely accepted. (Department of Education and Science 1978, para. 3.16.)

The relative definition of special educational need which was adopted by the drafters of the Education Act 1981 has been welcomed as a move away from a medical model, but criticised on the grounds of ambiguity. Thus the 1981 Act states that a child has a special education need if s/he has a learning difficulty for which special educational provision is required. The two key terms are learning difficulty and special education provision. Learning difficulty is defined as a learning difficulty significantly greater than that experienced by the majority of children of the same age, irrespective of the cause, or a disability preventing or hindering use of educational facilities generally available to children of a similar age. Note that there can be difficulties of interpretation: should 'difficulty' be interpreted relative to children from a particular school, or family, or area, or more widely? How much greater is 'significantly greater'? Note too that this usage is different from that proposed in the Warnock Report, where learning difficulty is used more narrowly, as a replacement for the old educationally subnormal and remedial education concepts.

Special educational provision is defined as provision additional to or different from that generally made for the age group by the local education authority (and any educational provision made for a child under two years old). The Warnock definition was much more precise, describing special education in terms of one or more of three criteria, *viz.* access to an appropriately qualified or experienced teacher; access to other appropriately trained professionals; and an environment with the necessary aids, equipment and resources.

Although the Act defines special educational need imprecisely, it is quite specific on one contentious point. Learning difficulties which arise because the language of instruction is different from the language used at home are excluded from the special needs legislation. This point has direct relevance to children from many ethnic minorities, to some immigrants, and to children in bilingual areas such as parts of Wales and Scotland. But note that this exclusion does not affect an education authority's responsibilities for providing suitable education under other legislation.

See *Statement*.

References:

Adams, F. (Ed.) (1986) *Special Education*, Harlow, Councils and Education Press for Longman.

Brennan, W.K. (1985) *Curriculum for Special Needs*, Milton Keynes, Open University Press.

Cox, B. (1985) *The Law of Special Educational Needs*, London, Croom Helm.

Department of Education and Science (1978) *Special Educational Needs*, London, HMSO (Warnock Report).

special school, the supreme example of segregated folly, or of sensible educational policy, depending on the values one holds. Probably no sector of education has been the centre of such a tempest in recent years as the special school sector. Yet it is no stranger to controversy: debate over its place in the education system is long-standing, with attitudes changing with the times.

Special schools fall into three types, according to how they are run: maintained schools, provided by local education authorities; non-maintained schools, provided by voluntary bodies and which are non-profit-making concerns, eligible for certain grants from public funds if approved for the purpose; and independent schools. Recently, in the decades following the second world war, there was a steady and substantial increase in the number of places available in maintained special schools, both day and residential. For children with learning and behavioural difficulties, pressure for places always exceeded availability, so much so that local authorities were often forced to use the non-maintained or independent sectors when their own schools were full.

When the Warnock Report argued in favour of greater integration, the apprehension that many special schools felt over their future was tempered by proposals to use their skills as centres of research and of support and advice to the ordinary school system. In fact this development has been slow to materialise, while at the same time the decline of the special school sector has not occurred to the extent predicted. While on the one hand, numbers of children from special schools have been integrated in the ordinary schools in accordance with the spirit of the times, on the other, there has been an increase in the number of children surviving with complex and serious impairments. This, coupled with the move to community care, has led to more requests for special school places. But while special schools have survived, the special school population has changed in character.

In addition, the special schools have changed their outlook. Many schools now operate link schemes with neighbourhood schools, which permit exchange of staff and pupils. This development preserves the protection of the segregated educational base, but allows some integrated experiment to proceed. It certainly brings the special school sector more into the ambit of the rest of the education service, and lessens the isolation of staff and pupils.

Special schools have to be approved by the appropriate Secretary of State. The arrangements for approval are covered in Sections 11, 12 and 13 of the Education Act 1981. Circular 6/83 sets out the position in greater detail. Section 14 of the 1981 Act sets out altered procedures for closing special schools, giving more protection to the interests of pupils and parents. Circular 3/82 applies.

References:

Brennan, W.K. (1987) *Changing Special Education Now*, Milton Keynes, Open University Press.

Cole, T. (1986) *Residential Special Education*, Milton Keynes, Open University Press.

Cole, T. (1989) *Apart or a Part?: Integration and the Growth of British Special Education*, Milton Keynes, Open University Press.

Department of Education and Science (1982) *Circular 3/82, Section 14 of the Education Act 1981, Discontinuance of Maintained Special Schools*, London, Department of Education and Science.

Department of Education and Science (1983) *Circular 6/83, The Approval of Special Schools*, London, Department of Education and Science.

Jowett, S., Hegarty, S. and Moses, D. (1988) *Joining Forces: a study of links between special and ordinary schools*, Windsor, NFER-Nelson.

special unit, see *special class.*

specialist careers officer, offers careers guidance for young people with disabilities: the crucial link between school and work for the disabled school-leaver.

The work differs from that of most careers officers in two ways. One is the difficulty of finding employment for the clients. This emphasises the need for specialist careers officers to possess other skills, such as leisure counselling and giving non-vocational guidance. The other is the need to work collaboratively with many colleagues from other disciplines, who will be able to contribute constructively to an appraisal of the young person's potential (though links with the *Disablement Resettlement Service* do not seem to be exploited as fruitfully as they could be). Both these points highlight the need for insisting on providing training additional to that normally required by careers officers.

The Warnock Report recommended that one specialist careers officer should be employed per 50,000 school population.

Reference:

Bookis, J. (1983) *Beyond the School Gate: a Study of Disabled Young People*, London, Royal Association on Disability and Rehabilitation.

specific learning difficulty, one of the four kinds of *learning difficulty* mentioned in the Warnock Report. A specific learning difficulty describes the condition of children who perform perfectly satisfactorily in most school activities, but who have problems with one area. These children have been marginal to special educational legislation in many countries until fairly recently. The most common condition is a specific reading difficulty, but other conditions, such as specific mathematical difficulty are met, too.

The important point about specific learning difficulty is that it is no more than a description of an educational state: it makes no assumptions about causation, leaving this controversial area to the research worker. Terms such as dyslexia, dysgraphia, acalculia, etc., can all be subsumed by it. The label is not as important as the need to introduce the best educational programme.

This approach differs from that usually followed in the USA, where the nearest equivalent term is learning disability. This term excludes individuals whose learning difficulties are due to mental retardation, sensory, physical and emotional handicaps, etc., but is clearly intended to include diagnoses of minimal brain damage, aphasia, dyslexia, etc. It sets out to represent a group of neurological conditions. There is an interesting discussion on the two approaches in the Cadman Report, which ended by recommending the use of the term learning difficulties without qualification.

In the UK, educational arrangements for these children have usually been provided through remedial education, now being replaced by support teaching.

See *dyslexia, mathematical difficulties, reading difficulty.*

References:

Elliott, C.D. (1990) 'The Definition and Identification of Specific Learning Difficulties', in Pumfrey, P.D. and Elliott, C.D. (Eds.) (1990) *Children's Difficulties in Reading, Writing and Spelling*, London, Falmer Press.

Gulliford, R. (1985) *Teaching Children with Learning Difficulties*, Windsor, NFER-Nelson.

SPELD (1979) *Interim Statement on Educating Children with Specific Learning Disabilities*, SPELD, Christchurch, NZ.

specific learning disability, alternative term for *learning disability.*

specific reading difficulty, probably the most common specific learning difficulty. Some concern has been expressed over whether the concept is a statistical artefact, or if not, whether it could be distinguished from backwardness in reading. Enquiries support the view that the condition occurs more frequently than might be expected on the basis of test parameters, and that there are differences between the two groups suggesting that the two conditions are differently caused. Thus children with reading backwardness (i.e. reading significantly lower than chronological age) are more likely to show signs of neurological disorder and to come from families of lower income, whereas children with reading retardation (i.e. reading significantly lower than predicted on the basis of age and measured intelligence) are more likely to be boys. Both groups tend to come from large families and to have associated speech and language disorders.

Much debate has centred on the relationship between this concept and *dyslexia*. The Tizard Report preferred the term 'specific reading difficulty', but some of the heat has been taken out of the argument by the learning difficulties approach used in the Warnock Report and the Education Act 1981.

References:

Tansley, P. and Panckhurst, J. (1981) *Children with Specific Learning Difficulties; a Critical Review of Research*, Windsor, NFER-Nelson.

Young, P. and Tyre, C. (1983) *Dyslexia or Illiteracy?* Milton Keynes, Open University Press.

speech audiogram, see *audiogram*.

speech disorder, any kind of speech difficulty that interferes with normal communication. If speech should be clear and unambiguous, so should be the terminology used in its study: unfortunately this is not so. Since speech is spoken language, speech disorders are sometimes described as language disorders, though terminology here is not always consistent. Some authorities like to distinguish between disorders of language and of speech. The argument is that a child's language, in the sense of grammar, sequence, etc., may pose no problems, although speech, perhaps through stuttering, may. Conversely a child may speak entirely adequately, yet there may be language problems present, perhaps a severely restricted vocabulary. But the interpenetration of speech and language disorders makes this distinction difficult to sustain, perhaps particularly in relation to children, where speech and language develop together and speech and language problems often co-exist.

Granted this issue, speech disorders can be classified according to whether the cause is related to reception or expression, though other classificatory systems are used.

On the receptive side, poor speech can be due to hearing loss. There may be nothing at fault with the speech organs as such; the implication is that hearing should always be checked when a child appears to have a speech problem.

Alternatively, the reception problem may be central: damage to those brain structures concerned with receiving sound signals may be responsible for language difficulties in a child whose hearing and speech organs are both functioning normally. The sufferer hears the sounds, but has difficulty in constructing meaning from them. This condition is sometimes described medically as receptive aphasia (or dysphasia), normally associated with damage to Wernicke's area. Other terms used for variants of this condition are auditory agnosia and word deafness.

Expressive problems start centrally. If there is neurological damage at Broca's area of the frontal lobe, then the person may comprehend perfectly, but have reduced ability to express himself or herself, although again the speech organs may function perfectly. The common medical term is expressive aphasia (or dysphasia).

Much the most common speech problems in children are associated with the speech organs and speech mechanism itself. There are two main groups of problems here, those concerned with the production of sounds, and those concerned with the articulation of sound into speech. The first group of disorders are known as phonation and resonance disorders; these are usually due to impaired functioning of the larynx and associated structures. They might be recognised as an unusual voice quality – perhaps an unusually quiet or breathy voice, or a voice with a very nasal quality. Dysphonia or aphonia (literally no voice at all) are the usual medical terms.

Virtually all children produce articulatory errors when learning to speak: these become articulatory disorders when the standard speech sounds are not consistently produced correctly after the age when most children can do so. Obvious examples are lisping and lalling, but some articulation disorders are much more serious: the various organs – lips, tongue, teeth, palate – involved in phoneme production are not articulated correctly and the speech which results can range down to the virtually unintelligible. These articulation disorders are sometimes called dysarthrias or anarthrias. Dyslalia is another term sometimes used for articulation disorders.

Stammering and stuttering are usually classed as fluency disorders.

Two issues cannot be stressed too strongly. First, attempts to classify speech disorders anatomically, developmentally, linguistically or in any other way run the risk of missing the point that speech disorders are often interlinked – the same neurogical damage that causes receptive aphasia may also cause both expressive aphasia and damage the muscular control of the speech organs. Second, speech is part of the process of human communication, and speech disorders must be set in a psychological and social context – *pragmatics* is an obvious example.

Since there is no agreement over the boundary between normal speech and a speech disorder, prevalence figures vary. As a rough guide, it has been estimated that about 5% of children enter school with serious communication difficulties, though if less stringent criteria are used, figures as high as 20% have been found. An overall prevalence of 10% of the school population with disorders sufficiently serious to pose a regular problem to adults is sometimes regarded as a reasonable middle-of-the-road figure. Irrespective of these variations, some inferences can be drawn.

First, the prevalence figures tend to be highest among preschool children. The need for guidance on speech development for parents of children in this age-group is acute.

Second, while a few children with very severe speech disorders are educated in residential special schools, the great majority are on the rolls of ordinary schools. This means that every teacher should be alert to their presence and ready to seek help from the specialist services – for even if staff shortages prevent regular treatment for all but the more serious problems, at least advice can be sought. A speech disorder affects a child's confidence and self-image, and teachers should be sensitive to this.

Third, surveys show that the most common speech problems in children are articulation disorders: these account for about half of the total prevalence, with fluency disorders accounting for about a further tenth, and all other problems the remainder.

Fourth, there is a higher prevalence of speech disorders in boys than girls. For articulation disorders a two-to-one ratio has been reported.

Fifth, the prevalence jumps sharply in most special populations: in special schools for children with moderate learning difficulties a figure of 32% with speech disorders has been reported: articulation problems have been reported in 75% of children with cerebral palsy. This has implications for the provision of specialist help. If speech therapy services can offer regular sessions at schools, then units and schools for children with special needs are effective places to concentrate help. Greater integration demands that service delivery be rethought.

References:

Crystal. D. (1988, 2nd edn.) *Introduction to Language Pathology*, London, Cole and Whurr.

Crystal, D. (1984) *Language Handicap in Children*, Stratford-upon-Avon, National Council for Special Education.

Feinmann, J. (1990) 'Children with Speech and Language Difficulties', in Evans, P. and Varma, V. (Eds.) (1990) *Special Education: Past, Present and Future*, London, Falmer Press.

Hallahan, D.P. and Kaufman, J.M. (1988, 4th edn.) *Exceptional Children: Introduction to Special Education*, Englewood Cliffs, Prentice Hall.

Webster, A. (1988) 'The Prevalence of Speech and Language Difficulties in Childhood: some brief research notes', *Child Language Teaching and Therapy*, 4, 1, 85–91.

Webster, A. and McConnell, C. (1987) *Children with Speech and Language Difficulties*, London, Cassell.

speech reading, see *lipreading.*

speech tests for hearing, unlike pure-tone audiometry, assess what a child can hear of spoken language at different levels of intensity. In one approach, a child may be asked to listen to a live voice in free-field. A more controlled test is to present word or sentence lists (with a controlled spread of vowels and consonants, or familiar vocabulary) through loudspeakers or headphones. The child is asked to repeat what is heard, and from the proportion of correct responses a speech audiogram can be completed, showing success at different sound levels. This is an important piece of information; the ability to hear the complex pattern of sounds involved in speech represents a different and more practical index of hearing than that provided by pure tone measurement.

It is important to produce speech which is definitely within the child's comprehension. For this reason speech tests are not usually used until a child is over two years of age. Various games – identifying toys, pointing to pictures, etc. – are the basis of most tests until the child is old enough to be able to repeat words presented by the examiner.

See *audiometry.*

Reference:

Tucker, I. and Nolan, N. (1984) *Educational Audiology,* Beckenham, Croom Helm.

speech therapist, specialises in the assessment and treatment of communication disorders. Entry to the profession is by a three-year diploma course or, increasingly, a four-year degree course. Since 1974, speech therapists in the public service have been employed by the National Health Service, whereas previously some were employed by education authorities. They can work with adults or children.

The profession's title is in fact misleading: speech therapists' work is neither limited to speech (for it includes work in language and communication generally) nor to therapy (for it includes a teaching role). In the USA attempts to recognise this have led to a variety of different titles being used, some of which are speech and language clinician, communicologist, and perhaps the most common, speech-language pathologist.

The teaching element has sometimes led to a role conflict with teachers, particularly teachers of language-impaired and hearing-impaired children, for although the training for each group of professionals carries a different emphasis, communication, language and speech feature prominently in the activities of all three, yet can be the prerogative of none.

Under the 1981 Education Act, statements of special educational need appear to amount to a legal obligation on Education authorities to provide speech therapy services where these are indicated. This is a difficult point, for speech therapists, even those working in schools, are employed in the Health Service, which will have other demands for them and other priorities. Resolution of this point highlights clearly the issue of the speech therapist's position, described in the *Quirk Report* as a professional standing between medicine and education, and drawing on and serving both.

Communication difficulties affect so many children with special needs that an effective speech therapy service is vital. Yet speech therapists are in extremely short supply. Previously, the service delivery was concentrated on special education facilities such as language units and special schools for children with learning difficulties. The move to greater integration means that speech therapy services, if school-focused, have to be delivered to many more schools, so exacerbating the shortage. This problem is being tackled in two ways. The traditional activity of offering speech therapy sessions to individual children is being partly replaced by a consultancy role, in which parents and teachers, the adults in closest contact with the child, are advised on the kind of exercises, etc., needed. In addition, speech therapists are increasingly pooling resources by working in teams; multiprofessional teams with educational colleagues are one way forward.

References:

Crystal, D. (1988, 2nd edn.) *Introduction to Language Pathology*, London, Cole and Whurr.

Humphries, C. (1987) 'Speech Therapy Services: the Effects of the 1981 Education Act on the Provision of Speech Therapy Services', *Newsletter No. 5*, Policy and Provision for Special Needs, Project, Institute of Education, University of London. p.8.

Taylor, J.S. (1981) *Speech-Language Pathology Services in the Schools*, New York, Grune and Stratton.

SPELD, Specific Learning Difficulties Association, a prominent organisation in New Zealand and Australia, concerned to advance the education and general wellbeing of individuals with learning disabilities.

spelling difficulties, are held to be one characteristic of dyslexia, but are better considered as an indication of a specific language difficulty. Some authorities suggest that an error rate of 10% of written output constitutes a spelling difficulty severe enough to justify special action.

Spelling difficulties are rarely given the attention devoted to reading difficulties, with which they are often closely associated. The role of spelling in early reading is currently a lively research field, some arguing that spelling practice is a significant factor in developing reading skills. Yet the two skills differ, reading being primarily dependent on recognition and decoding, spelling primarily on retrieval and encoding language in print. The use of context, a mark of a fluent reader concentrating on meaning, is of little help to successful spelling, which demands concentration on accurately memorising the detail of individual words. Hence some good readers are relatively poor spellers.

Spelling is an underrated skill. Although spelling dictionaries, spelling check programmes, etc., help, if children have to concentrate on spelling details, they are unlikely to be able to enjoy fully the pleasure of communicating through writing, nor to display fully their talents for it. Spelling is often taught through learning word-lists, either related structurally or thematically, and effort in learning the code cannot be avoided. But diagnosis of a child's particular difficulties, usually categorised as visual or phonic errors, though each category covers various discrimination and sequencing problems, helps in the design of suitable remedial programmes. Children with spelling difficulties will usually be best helped by learning the patterns of letters in spelling when learning the patterns of letters in handwriting and by, initially, saying the letters or words as they write them.

See *calligrams, onomatopoeic words.*

References:

Cataldo, S. and Ellis, N. (1990) 'Learning to Spell: Learning to Read', in Pumfrey, P.D. and Elliott, C.D. (Eds.) (1990) *Primary Pupils' Reading and Spelling Difficulties,* Basingstoke, Falmer Press.

Moseley, D. (1988) 'New Approaches to Helping Children with Spelling Difficulties', *Educational and Child Psychology,* 5, 4, 54–9.

Moseley, D. (1990) 'Suggestions for Helping Children with Spelling Problems', in Pumfrey, P.D. and Elliott, C.D. (Eds.) (1990) *Children's Difficulties in Reading, Spelling and Writing,* London, Falmer Press.

Peters, M. L. (1975) *Diagnostic and Spelling Manual,* London, Macmillan.

Reason, R. and Boote, R. (1986) *Learning Difficulties in Reading and Writing: a Teacher's Manual,* Windsor, NFER-Nelson.

spina bifida, congenital defect in which part of the spinal column has not closed properly, leaving the spinal cord indequately protected. The effects depend mainly on two factors, the location of the lesion, and the amount of damage to the spinal cord.

The most severe type, myelomeningocele, is also the most common. Nervous tissue and membranes protrude from the back in a sac-like bulge, or cyst. In meningocele the spinal cord itself is undamaged and the sac contains fluid and membranes only. Hence this form of spina bifida is usually less handicapping. A third type of spina bifida, spina bifida occulta, is less serious still and may well be undetected.

The incidence of spina bifida is usually quoted at three to four per thousand births, but there is considerable geographical variation: in some of the South Wales valleys the incidence is approximately twice as high. Since spina bifida is a condition that can now be detected by antenatal testing, the rate dropped substantially in the 1980s. Another factor that affects the amount of educational provision needed is the attitude taken towards the survival of severely handicapped neonates. In the 1960s and early 1970s virtually all babies born with spina bifida were treated, but for some the quality of life was so poor and the damage to family life so great that this policy was reconsidered, and thereafter in many hospitals only the more lightly affected were treated. Thus a group of older pupils and college students with spina bifida may include some more seriously handicapped individuals than a group of younger pupils. The main problems in school are toileting and mobility, for many spina bifida pupils are incontinent, and unable to walk. A nurse or classroom assistant may be needed to help over these problems – and also for other reasons, such as adjusting body position to avoid pressure sores.

Adolescents are more prone to emotional problems such as depression, loneliness and apathy, and there are obviously stresses on the family which may need sensitive discussion and counselling.

The mean intelligence test score of groups of spina bifida pupils is often reported as 20 to 30 points below average, but this will vary with the age group for the reasons given, and in any case the population will include some able pupils. At the same time some will have severe learning difficulties, most likely to occur in the presence of hydrocephalus, which affects up to four-fifths of spina bifida infants. Like intelligence scores, educational attainments tend to be below average, and there is some evidence of particular difficulties with arithmetic and skills such as writing and drawing.

Children with spina bifida, like all children, should have as full an access to the National Curriculum as possible, whether a child's needs are best met in the ordinary school, a special unit or a special school. For these children, intellectual abilities, emotional adjustment and physical competencies must always be kept in mind in considering the most helpful educational provision.

References:

Anderson, E.M. and Spain, B. (1977) *The Child with Spina Bifida*, London, Methuen.

Gillham, B. (1986) 'Spina Bifida', in Gillham, B. (Ed.) (1986) *Handicapping Conditions in Children*, London, Croom Helm.

Dinnage, R. (1986) *The Child with Spina Bifida*, Windsor, NFER-Nelson.

Dunning, D. (1987) *Children with Spina Bifida and/or Hydrocephalus at School*, London, Association for Spina Bifida and Hydrocephalus.

stammering, interruption of fluent speech by involuntary blocking or hesitation at sounds and words. It used to be contrasted with *stuttering*: the stammerer has difficulty in starting, whereas the stutterer has difficulty in stopping.

See *speech disorder*.

Standard Assessment Tasks (SATs), national tests of competence in each subject of the *National Curriculum*. The SATs are intended to measure progress towards the attainment targets proposed for each subject at the key stages of seven, eleven, fourteen and sixteen years of age. The assessments will be criterion-referenced against ten levels of performance, and will be reported in profile form. Individual children will of course progress through the levels at different rates.

The SATs are intended to be suitable for or adaptable to children with special educational needs. In addition the National Curriculum Task Group on Assessment and Testing recommended that SATs should be so designed that teachers could curtail them discreetly or give recorded assistance where children with special educational needs were taking them.

Reference:

National Curriculum Task Group on Assessment and Testing (1988) *A Report*, London, Department of Education and Science and the Welsh Office.

standard deviation, one measure of the spread of data, the extent to which a set of scores deviates from the mean. Knowing the standard deviation (and mean) of a distribution enables any score to be interpreted, for in most distributions approximately two-thirds of the scores fall between ± one standard deviation of the mean score. Since most normative educational tests are standardised to a mean of 100 and a standard deviation of 15 points, two-thirds of scores fall between 85 and 115, and one-third outside these limits, a sixth above and a sixth below. Consider a score of 85 points. Five-sixths of scores fall above it and one-sixth below. Tables enable any test score to be interpreted in this way, provided the mean and standard deviation of the distribution are known.

Reference:

Aiken, L.R. (1986, 4th edn.) *Psychological Testing and Assessment*, New York, Allyn and Bacon.

standard error (of measurement), sem, is the estimated standard deviation of the range of test scores associated with any 'true' test score. In conventional test theory, an 'obtained' test score comprises two elements: a 'true' test score component and an 'error' score component. The latter accounts for chance changes in 'obtained' test scores from one testing to another.

The sem is an estimate of the 'obtained' score confidence limits. The larger the sem, the more caution is needed in accepting the reliability of an 'obtained' test score.

The scores used for these limits are often + one sem and − one sem. Two-thirds of an individual's test scores fall between these limits. If a child obtains a score of 90 on a test with a sem of five points, there is a 66% chance that the 'true' test score corresponding to the 'obtained' test score of 90 lies between the limits of 85 and 95. A higher confidence level can be attached to a wider range. Thus we can be 95% certain that the 'true' test score lies between two sems on either side of the 'obtained' test score, i.e. between 80 and 100.

The use of the sem illustrates the dangers of making decisions about a child's education on the basis of single obtained scores on an educational test. It underlines the point that such 'obtained' scores can vary from occasion to occasion due to chance (error) effects.

The formula for the sem is relatively simple.

sem $= s\sqrt{(1-r)}$, where s is the standard deviation of the test and r its reliability. The sem for a test with the usual standard deviation of 15 points and a reliability of $+0.96$ is given by:

sem = 15√(1 − 0.96) points
sem = 15 x √0.04 ,,
sem = 15 x 0.2 ,,
sem = 3 points

Reference:

Guilford, J.P. and Fruchter, B. (1978, 6th edn.) *Fundamental Statistics in Psychology and Education*, New York, McGraw Hill.

Standard Reading Tests, set of twelve tests. The first test is a measure of reading accuracy, offering an assessment of reading performance up to a nine-year level in terms of seven 'standards'. Nine diagnostic tests follow. Test eleven is a spelling test, and the last test is a sentence completion exercise which can be given in group form and which offers norms from six to fourteen years.

There are serious technical flaws in the tests, which were first produced in 1958. The underlying philosophy of the 'seven standards' has also been criticised, though its emphasis on qualitative rather than quantitative assessment appeals to many teachers.

The convenient book form in which the tests are available also make them attractive to teachers and, in spite of the problems mentioned, a recent survey showed that Test 12 was the most widely-used reading test for identifying slow-learning pupils at entry to secondary school.

References:

Clunies-Ross, L. and Wimshurst, S. (1983) *The Right Balance: Provision for Slow-learners in Secondary Schools*, Slough, NFER-Nelson.

Pumfrey, P.D. (1985, 2nd edn.) *Reading: Tests and Assessment Techniques*, Sevenoaks, Hodder and Stoughton in association with UKRA.

standard score, alternative name for *z-score*.

Stanford-Binet Intelligence Scale, the classic individual test of intelligence, developed from the original Binet-Simon scales. The first version was published in 1916, since when several new versions and restandardisations have been released, the fourth and latest version appearing in 1985. Like its predecessors it offers age scores and an overall IQ score. In addition it incorporates many new items, allowing four separate scores to be obtained, each for a different cognitive area, viz. verbal reasoning, quantitative reasoning, abstract/visual reasoning and short-term memory. This partly meets previous criticisms of its high verbal content, particularly at the older age levels.

Its former pre-eminence for use with children in this country, notwithstanding its USA standardisation, has been eroded by the development of the family of Wechsler tests and by the British Ability Scales. Since it has a test floor of two years it has been found useful in assessing individuals with profound retardation. As with all individual intelligence tests, sound administration and sensible interpretation require a trained examiner.

stapes, one of the three small bones in the middle ear which transmit sound vibrations from the ear-drum to the cochlea.

See *ear.*

Statement (of special educational needs), description of a child's educational needs made by a local education authority (LEA) under the *Education Act 1981,* for children whose special needs cannot be met informally using normal resources. In practice this is often taken to be the minority of children with more serious special needs, about 2% of the school population and a smaller proportion of the preschool population.

The statement is intended to protect the rights of the child to an educational programme based on a proper assessment of needs and the rights of the parents to involvement in its preparation. Protection is ensured by the legislation, which stipulates the procedures which have to be followed.

Two main criticisms have emerged in practice. The first relates to the detail of the procedure. The checks and safeguards are time-consuming. First, the LEA decides to assess the child with a view to preparing a statement. At this point the parents must be informed, and are given a period of twenty-nine days in which they can make representations. The parent then has to be notified of the next step, usually assessment, which requires a teacher, a medical officer, an educational psychologist and possibly others to produce reports for the LEA.

These reports are then collated and usually a draft Statement is prepared. (If no Statement is to be prepared, there are set procedures for notifying the parents.) The draft Statement should include the form of special educational provision to be made, specifying the facilities, equipment, staffing, and curriculum needed by the child. The Statement must also specify the school or other arrangement required, and any non-educational provision needed.

This draft Statement is then sent to the parents who, if they disagree, have a period of fifteen days to make representations. The Statement can then be modified, and if the parents still disagree, they have a second period of fifteen days to make their views known. Thereafter the LEA can issue a Statement which hopefully is in a form acceptable to the parents and to the authority. The LEA is then under a legal obligaton to meet the needs in the manner set out by the Statement.

This is a brief outline of Statementing. There are many points at which parents have to be informed of their rights of access to reports, of access to the assessing professionals, of appeal, etc. The effect of a procedure as cumbersome as this is to interpose lengthy delays between deciding that a child may have special needs and starting to meet them in an agreed way.

Surveys have shown that on average LEAs require eight to nine months to complete the Statementing process. This is an unacceptably long time in the educational life of any child, let alone a child with special needs – and in half the instances a longer period is needed!

The second main criticism refers not to procedure, but to content. The Statement places a legal obligation on the LEA to deliver the educational services specified. Yet it is completed by officers of the LEA. While as professionals the needs of the child must be uppermost in their minds, nevertheless they would be only human if at the same time they wished to avoid committing their colleagues to providing resources which are unavailable or very difficult to deliver in a particular place – e.g. the ordinary school. The ideal and the practical may be in conflict.

With the *Education Act 1988*, the Statement may assume a different role. Since all children must follow the national curriculum unless exemption is approved, the Statement may well become the instrument through which exemption, or disapplication can be approved. This gives it a role for which it was not intended.

There is a second possibility, too. With the advent of Local Management of Schools, formulae for financing schools have to be agreed. Where a school has a high proportion of children with special needs, it is equitable that allowance for the extra resources needed should be made. Will Statements be the evidence?

These questions will not be answered until the 1988 Act is fully operational and its effects fully appreciated. The introduction of the Statement, admirable though its purposes were, has had quite unforeseen consequences. Yet although the problems of procedure and content are irritating, the Statement is still serving its original purpose of protecting the interests of child and parent. But in the future, not only its method but also its purpose may be queried, for it may develop as an unexpectedly useful tool of policy, used for purposes for which it was unintended.

See *appeals, reviews*.

References:

Adams, F. (Ed.) (1986) *Special Education*, Harlow, Councils and Education Press for Longman.

Department of Education and Science (1983) *Circular 1/83, Assessments and Statements of Special Educational Needs*, London, Department of Education and Science.

Department of Education and Science (1989) *Circular 22/89, Assessments and Statements of Special Educational Needs: Procedures within the Education, Health and Social Services*, London, Department of Education. (Joint Circular with Department of Health.)

Dessent, T. (1989) 'To "Statement" or not to "Statement"', *British Journal of Special Education*, 16, 1, 5.

Goacher, B., Evans, J., Welton, J. and Wedell, K. (1988) *Implementing the 1981 Education Act*, London, Cassell.

Steiner, Rudolf, see *Camphill movement, Rudolf Steiner schools.*

stereotypic behaviour (stereotyped behaviour), repetitive, motor behaviour that appears to meet no purpose, yet its persistence suggests that it is pleasurable. Examples are hand-waving, rocking, head-rolling, masturbation, tooth-grinding, eye-poking, etc.

Behaviours of this sort can be found in any population of children, but they are most common in special groups, such as children with profound mental retardation, children with autism and children with multisensory deprivation.

The behaviours appear to be self-reinforcing and so are difficult to eliminate, though behavioural methods offer some success. This is advised not least because the persistent action interferes with the acquisition of new skills. Where the behaviour actually causes physical injury, as in hair-pulling, it is described as *self-injurious behaviour*. The pressure to eliminate the behaviour is then correspondingly greater.

Stern apparatus, see *structural apparatus*.

stigma, effects of negative *labelling*.

Still's disease, see *rheumatoid arthritis*.

strabismus, or squint, occurs when the eyes are not parallel to each other. The effects can be serious. Thus young children may suppress one of the two separate images received, and if the defect is not corrected soon, good vision from the one eye may be lost permanently. If strabismus occurs later in childhood, then the child may be coping with the stress of double vision.

Obviously correction should be instituted as soon as possible, and if a child develops a squint in class, the medical authorities and parents should be informed. If the treatment includes covering the good eye with a patch, so as to force the use of the weaker eye, then initially vision in this eye may be particularly poor, with effects on the child's responses in the classroom. Note too that in some groups of children with special needs, perhaps particularly children with cerebral palsy, the prevalence of strabismus is unusually high, rates of over 40% having been reported.

Reference:

Chapman, E.K. and Stone, J.M. (1988) *The Visually Handicapped Child in Your Classroom*, London, Cassell.

streaming, see *ability grouping*.

structural apparatus, rods, cubes and other solid objects, made of wood or plastic, and designed to help children understand number and number relationships. Some systems (e.g. unifix) are interlocking, some (e.g. Stern apparatus) are colour coded. Manipulating them builds mathematical models which help children with arithmetical difficulties learn the language of mathematics, develop confidence in counting, understand the four operations of number, and in many other ways.

Reference:
Taylor, R. (1981) 'Structural Apparatus', in Somerset Education Authority *Ways and Means 2*, Basingstoke, Globe Education.

stuttering, dysfluent speech, characterised by frequent involuntary repetitions, hesitations, blockages, etc. At one time stuttering, difficulty in stopping speech, was distinguished from stammering, difficulty in starting speech, but nowadays the distinction is regarded as artificial and the two terms as synonymous.

About 1% of the school population are still stuttering at adolescence and the prevalence in younger pupils ranges up to about 3%. At least twice as many boys are affected as girls. Because there is such a strong social-psychological component to the condition, it can be a significant handicap in school – reading aloud, or responding to teacher in the presence of other children can be painful in the extreme. Teasing by peers does not help.

Many different methods of treating stuttering have been advocated, from breathing and relaxation exercises, to delayed auditory feedback and behavioural methods. Where stuttering has started after a traumatic event, psychotherapy may be indicated. In every case the advice of a speech therapist should always be sought.

See *speech disorder.*

References:
Barker, P. (1988, 5th edn.) *Basic Child Psychiatry*, Oxford, Blackwell.
Webster, A. and McConnell, C. (1987) *Children with Speech and Language Difficulties*, London, Cassell.

Stycar tests, screening tests for young children and retardates. There are three Stycar tests, for vision, hearing and language. In the 1950s, Mary Sheridan was aware of the importance of early *screening* for sensory disorders and of the absence of standard procedures for this. She therefore devised these sets of screening tasks, since then revised several times.

The vision and hearing tests can be used with children as young as six months, and the language test from a year old. The tests are based on using familiar everyday objects and activities – for example the hearing tests include observation of the child's responses to a human voice, to rattles, spoons, etc. – to assess whether more sophisticated investigation is necessary.

The tests have been criticised on the grounds of poor reliability, though at such young ages the reliability of most assessments can be queried. Since usually another adult has to be present as well as the tester, they have been called labour-intensive, but again this point applies to most work with very young children. Notwithstanding these issues, and the development of more sophisticated techniques, the Stycar tests continue to be used, for example, by health visitors screening infants and by psychologists and others investigating the development of older children with severe and profound mental handicap.

References:
Jennings, K. (1984) 'The Role of the Health Visitor', in Lindsay, G. (Ed.) (1984) *Screening for Children with Special Needs,* Beckenham, Croom Helm.
Sebba, J. (1987) 'Assessments of Physical Development, Hearing and Vision that can be used by Educational and Care Staff', in Hogg, J. and Raynes, N.V. (Eds.) (1987) *Assessment in Mental Handicap,* Beckenham, Croom Helm.

substance abuse, see *drug misuse, solvent abuse.*

summative assessment, assessment intended to establish a pupil's current attainments. Perhaps the best example is a public examination at the end of a course. A school leaving report can also be regarded as a summative assessment.

Summative assessment is contrasted with *formative assessment,* which aims to help a pupil's development. The distinction is not always clear-cut; for example, an end-of-term examination (normally thought of as summative) can also be used formatively, for the pupil may be placed in a different teaching situation the following term, depending on the result.

Summerfield Report 1968, 'Psychologists in Education Services' was produced by a working party set up to consider the field of work of *educational psychologists,* their qualifications and training, and numbers required. This was the first government report concerned specifically with educational psychologists as a professional group. It sprang from a growing awareness of the central role played by the profession in the ascertainment and education of children with special needs – handicapped children then – and of increasing demands by local education authorities for their services.

Some of the issues which exercised the working party were the changing relationships between the new profession and established medical services, the place of a new organisation, the *school psychological service,* in relation to the established *child guidance clinic,* and the place of training and experience as a teacher in preparation for work as an educational psychologist.

The Report recommended a ratio of one educational psychologist to a school population of 10,000 children, representing a doubling of the profession's size. This, like other recommendations, has long since been overtaken by events. The Summerfield Report was influential in the context of a new profession, seeking recognition at a critical time in its growth. That time has now passed, but for school psychological services, the Summerfield Report was a turning point.

Reference:
Department of Education and Science (1968) *Psychologists in Education Services,* London, HMSO (Summerfield Report).

Sundberg declaration, statement produced by a 1981 UNESCO conference, and named after a participant who died at the conference. The declaration affirmed the right of every person who is handicapped to education, training, cultural activities and information. In meeting these rights there should be measures to reduce the handicapping effects of disabilities and to maximise integration. Those who are disabled should be consulted in planning services, and in making decisions.

References:

Fish, J. (1985) *Special Education: the Way Ahead*, Milton Keynes, Open University Press (p.3).

UNESCO (1982) *Report of World Conference on Actions and Strategies for Education, Prevention and Integration, 1981*, Paris, UNESCO.

supervision order, places a child under the supervision of a local Social Services Authority or, possibly, a probation officer. Usually supervision orders are made either in care proceedings under the Children and Young Persons Act 1969 or as the result of criminal proceedings. In either case the order can last for a maximum period of three years and places upon the supervisor the general duty to advise, assist, and befriend the supervised person. A person under supervision must keep in touch with the supervisor and inform him or her of any change of address (or employment). In addition, a supervision order may contain requirements such as participation in an Intermediate Treatment scheme.

Under the *Children Act 1989* the grounds on which a court may be able to make a supervision order will be the same as those governing a *care order* and the same principles will be applied by the court. A supervision order will impose obligations not only upon the supervised child but also on a 'responsible person', i.e. a person with parental responsibilities for the child or with whom the child is living.

See *education supervision order.*

support services, are provided by local education authorities (LEAs). Many have grown out of the remedial reading services which LEAs began providing in the 1950s to help primary school pupils with reading difficulties. As then, present-day support services are still largely based on the education office and not the school, and still work mainly with ordinary schools, rather than special schools and units. But vast changes have occurred.

The field of work has broadened. LEAs now provide some specialist support for the education of all children with special needs. This may be offered through separate services for the hearing-impaired, the visually-impaired, for children with learning difficulties, etc.; but the trend is to provide an integrated special needs advisory and support service, however titled.

The age-range served has widened. Staff increasingly serve secondary as well as primary schools; work with preschool children, hitherto the particular province of the hearing-impaired specialist, is developing; colleges, too, are starting to ask for help from the service. Establishments have increased, both in number and nature. A survey conducted in 1984 and reported in Moses *et al.* (1988) found the modal establishment to be twenty to thirty staff. To the peripatetic teachers have been added advisory teachers, advisors and other support staff.

There has been a change too in the mode of working: the familiar pattern of the withdrawal group, in which the peripatetic teacher withdrew a small group of children from their classes for intensive reading tuition is being increasingly replaced by a *support teaching* model, in which the peripatetic teacher works with the children in their ordinary lessons, in collaboration with their own teacher. The content of the work has extended to cover curricular areas other than reading.

The advisors carry a different set of responsibilities. The thrust of their work is with teachers, not children: they offer suggestions on teaching methods and materials, content of the curriculum, staffing arrangements, etc. In addition, unlike advisory teachers, they have administrative responsibilities for inservice education, for policy matters, for preparing Statements, for inspecting schools, etc. But the scope of their duties does vary from one LEA to another, as does the pattern of activity of the different services.

These changes have not been achieved without difficulty. One issue has been the extent to which the senior staff can carry a role which is at times that of an inspector, with loyalties to the LEA, and at times that of an advisor, with loyalties to the school and its pupils. Another issue has been the relationship of the service to the school psychological service. Both organisations are concerned with pupils with special needs, and in each LEA an arrangement ensuring that they act complementarily, rather than competitively, has had to be made.

Most importantly, the future of support services in the light of the Education Act 1988 has yet to be determined. The LEA continues to carry ultimate responsibility for ensuring that children's special needs are met, but schools with budgetary responsibilities may have to decide what support services they wish to buy. This dilemma remains to be resolved. It will take some time before new patterns of working, with their relative advantages and disadvantages, become clear.

References:

Hegarty, S. (1987) *Meeting Special Needs in Ordinary Schools,* London, Cassell.

Moses, D., Hegarty, S. and Jowett, S. (1988) *Supporting Ordinary Schools; LEA initiatives,* Windsor, NFER-Nelson.

support teaching, has grown out of remedial teaching. In essence it involves providing support to children who work in their ordinary classes, rather than withdrawing them for special tuition, part-time or full-time.

The idea of remediation carries the implication of a deficit within the child, somehow to be put right; this was one of the reasons leading in the 1980s to the change of title. There was also dissatisfaction with the mode of working. The equation of remedial teaching with remedial reading led to a very narrow approach, which did not touch the difficulties some children had with other aspects of the curriculum. Moreover, peripatetic teachers from the 'remedial' services, withdrawing children from class, were not demonstrating the principle of integration. Nor was integration illustrated by the 'remedial departments' of secondary schools, which offered a basic curriculum to children with learning difficulties, largely taught in non-examination classes, separated from their peers. For both groups of teachers, moving from a remedial to a support model brought both children and teachers into the main stream of education. But the change was not accomplished without difficulties.

One is the spread of subjects with which the support teacher has to be familiar. This is not a problem in the primary school, and in the secondary school it can be met by some specialising among the group of teachers in the support department, though there may be timetabling complications.

There have been worries that helping the child in the ordinary lesson identifies and stigmatises the child with learning difficulties just as effectively as withdrawal did. Experience shows that if the support teacher operates in a sensitive way, realising that occasionally any child may need help, this worry is largely unfounded.

There are two concerns of substance in this model of support teaching and both involve the relationship between the teacher and the support teacher. Responsibilities for a lesson in which two colleagues are present in the classroom must be planned carefully if the lesson is to be a success. Both teachers can make constructive suggestions about materials and methods. But there must be enough non-teaching time for effective planning.

The second concern touches on status: no teacher will want to feel downgraded to a form of classroom aide, and these feelings must be taken into account. It is for this reason that 'team teaching' is sometimes preferred to support teaching as a description for this work, though it must be remembered that support in this context is intended as support for the child, not a colleague.

In short, operating a support teaching model requires a different set of skills. Not everyone possesses these, nor does every child necessarily respond better to one model than the other. Hence in many schools the new model co-exists with the old.

See *room management.*

References:

Bines, H. (1986) *Redefining Remedial Education,* London, Croom Helm.

Ferguson, N. and Adams, M. (1982) 'Assessing the Advantages of Team Teaching in Remedial Education: the Remedial Teacher's Role', *Remedial Education,* 17, 1, 24–30.

Garnett, J. (1988) 'Support Teaching: Taking a Closer Look', *British Journal of Special Education,* 15, 1, 15–18.

Hinson, M. (Ed.) (1987) *Teachers and Special Educational Needs,* Harlow, Longman in Association with National Association for Remedial Education.

Swann Report 1985, 'Education for All,' report of a committee set up to review the needs and attainments of children from ethnic minority groups, to consider arrangements for monitoring their educational progress and to establish the role of education in a multi-racial society. The committee produced an interim report, the Rampton Report, in 1981. One impetus for these enquiries came from the fierce concern expressed by the parents of West Indian children at the high proportion of their children being educated in schools and units for pupils with learning and behavioural difficulties.

The Swann Report considered neither assimilation nor separation of ethnic groups to be a satisfactory principle. It noted major areas of concern in teaching English, which should be provided within the mainstream; in teaching the mother tongue; in teaching religious education and in training teachers. It also established clearly the existence of substantial under-achievement among children from some ethnic groups, but concluded after an exhaustive survey of the research literature that any group differences in inherited intelligence could safely be ignored as explanations for these learning difficulties.

See *ethnic minorities, Rampton Report.*

References:

Department of Education and Science (1985) *Education for All,* London, HMSO (Swann Report).

Vallender, I. (1985) 'Education for All', *Highlight,* 66, London, National Children's Bureau.

Swansea Project, 1967–72, Schools Council Project in compensatory education, which developed screening techniques to identify children in need of early educational support, studied the emotional development and response to school of children aged four to eight, constructed teaching programmes for culturally deprived infant school children and studied the special problems of Welsh-speaking infants.

The project was a child of its time, generated by the social concerns of the 1960s. It produced the Swansea Test of Phonic Skills, the Swansea Infant Evaluation Profiles and a book of suggestions for teaching language skills, as well as various research reports.

Reference:

Chazan, M. and Williams, P. (Eds.) (1978) *Deprivation and the Infant School,* Oxford, Blackwell.

Symbolic Play Test, is used to assess early understanding of symbols and early concept formation in children aged from one to three years. The most useful part of the test is not the set of toys provided, but the set of guidelines for observing child play. These are useful in assessing the development of children with delayed language, for they help determine whether the child can represent the world in symbols – such as toys – even though linguistic symbols (words) are absent.

Reference:

Beveridge, M. and Conti-Ramsden, G. (1987) *Children with Language Disabilities*, Milton Keynes, Open University Press.

System of Multicultural Pluralistic Assessment, see *SOMPA.*

systematic desensitisation, alternative name for *desensitisation.*

T

tactile perception, sensory input from any external part of the body, not, as is often thought, from contact with hands and fingers solely.

Tactile perception is vitally important in the education of multi-sensory deprived children. Its dimensions of stability, area, strength (pressure) and duration are the characteristics through which meaning can be carried, and start to illustrate how much more there is to touch than just contact. Tactile perception in the narrower sense of input from finger sensation is also one of the components of multisensory methods of teaching reading to children with difficulties. In short, every sensory channel ought to be considered when teaching children with special educational needs, and the sense of touch should not be neglected.

See *dual sensory impairment, Fernald method.*

Reference:

McInnes, J.M. and Treffry, J.A. (1982) *Deaf-Blind Infants and Children, A Developmental Guide*, Milton Keynes, Open University Press.

TASH, see *The Association for Persons with Severe Handicaps.*

task analysis, breaking down a defined task into its component steps, or teachable sub-goals.

Task analysis should be seen as part of a precise, behavioural approach to education, focusing as much on the curriculum as on the child. Interest in task analysis grew in response to disenchantment with the limitations of the norm-referenced testing of abilities, a feature of the mental measurement movement. The 1970s, in particular, were marked by the widespread adoption of techniques such as *curriculum-based assessment,* an objectives approach and *precision teaching.* Much of the lead in pioneering this change of approach was taken by those working with children with severe learning difficulties.

Task analysis involves three main steps. First, the *terminal behaviour* itself has to be described in behavioural terms. The hierarchy of skills involved in mastering the task is then identified and sequenced. Finally, these skills are sliced into teaching tasks appropriate to a child's learning pace, with specified objectives. Note that task analysis is not a method of teaching: it specifies a set of tasks or skills that have to be mastered in order to reach the terminal behaviour required. It is in effect the blueprint for the teacher to use. Notwithstanding the improvements in educational efficiency claimed for this strategy, it too has limitations. Not all areas of the curriculum are amenable to hierarchical analysis, and even those that are are not always easily analysed into a suitable set of skills. Good task analysis requires time and careful preparation.

See *behavioural objective, slicing.*

References:

Ainscow, M. and Tweddle, D. (1981) 'The Objectives Approach: a Progress Report', in Somerset Education Authority *Ways and Means* 2, Basingstoke, Globe Educational.

Solity, J. and Bull, S. (1987) *Special Needs – Bridging the Curriculum Gap,* Milton Keynes, Open University Press.

Van Etten, G., Arkell, C. and Van Etten, C. (1980) *The Severely and Profoundly Handicapped,* St. Louis, Mosby.

TAT, see *Thematic Apperception Test.*

Taylor Report 1977, A New Partnership for our Schools, report of a committee of enquiry into the management and government of maintained primary and secondary schools in England and Wales. It proposed that the local education authority, members of the local community, the teachers and the parents should all have equal representation on the governing bodies of schools. These bodies were to have new duties, in particular to help establish a school's objectives, including the curriculum, with access to professional guidance. The committee's terms of reference excluded special schools, but the extension of its proposals to special schools was broadly endorsed by the 1978 Warnock Report, on the grounds that apart from their intrinsic worth, greater similarity between ordinary and special schools was only to be encouraged. The *Education Act 1980* went only part way to meeting these recommendations and it was not until the *Education (No. 2) Act 1986* that changes in the composition of governing bodies which met the spirit of the Taylor Report were introduced.

See *Education Act 1988, school governors.*

Reference:

Department of Education and Science/Welsh Office (1977) *A New Partnership for our Schools,* London, HMSO (Taylor Report).

teacher training, see *initial training, inservice education and training.*

team teaching, two or more teachers working together to take a lesson. Originally it described a situation in which the teachers combined their pupils for a given lesson, so that each teacher could play to his/her pedagogic strength. This principle of specialisation of function also underpins *room management.*

More recently, team teaching has been applied to any situation where two or more teachers work together. Some prefer to use it to describe *support teaching,* for it implies that a partnership exists between the teachers, and neither is 'in charge' of the other. The key to any lesson is careful planning. This applies with even greater force to team teaching: well-prepared it can be most effective, but ill-prepared a disaster.

terminal behaviour, technical term for the behaviour that a student will have mastered at the end of a teaching sequence: the task that the teacher has specified in behavioural terms.

See *task analysis.*

Test of Motor Impairment (TOMI), aims to detect impairment of motor function in children from five years upwards. It assesses such skills as manual dexterity, balance, ball skills, etc. There are eight tasks for each of four age-bands, five and six years, seven and eight years, nine and ten years, and eleven years upwards. As well as providing norm-based scores and subtest scores, emotional and motivational hindrances to performance are recorded and there are additional checklists for the systematic observation of specific motor difficulties which may be responsible for failure.

The test was revised in 1984, and is usually used in clinical settings.

See *motor impairment.*

Reference:

Sugden, D. and Wann, C. (1987) 'The Assessment of Motor Impairment in Children with Moderate Learning Difficulties', *British Journal of Educational Psychology,* 57, 225–36

Test for the Reception of Grammar (TROG), assesses the extent to which children aged four to thirteen years understand grammatical structures and contrasts of the singular–plural, active–passive type. Understanding is assessed by requiring the child to indicate which one of four pictures illustrates a sentence spoken by the examiner. TROG is a standardised test, enabling a child's grammatical understanding to be compared with the age-group, and so identifying weaknesses to be targeted in teaching.

Reference:

Webster, A. and McConnell, C. (1987) *Children with Speech and Language Difficulties,* London, Cassell.

Test of Scholastic Abilities (TOSCA), New Zealand standardised group test which measures 'those verbal and numerical reasoning abilities which are judged to be essential components in school-related intellectual functioning'. The test constructors identified items which could be placed in each of nine cells of a three-by-three content-process matrix. The three content areas are numbers, words and sentences; the three process areas are conceptualisation, convergent reasoning (classification) and convergent reasoning (operational). Over forty different types of items were generated. There are three forms, each containing seventy items, designed for primary, intermediate and secondary schools in New Zealand. TOSCA provides a quick measure of learnt and developed abilities, which should be interpreted in the light of the child's previous experience.

Reference:

Reid, N., Jackson, P., Gilmore, A. and Croft, C. (undated) *Test of Scholastic Abilities: Teachers' Manual*, Wellington, New Zealand Council for Educational Research.

Thackray Reading Readiness Profiles, group test for children aged four years eight months to five years eight months, i.e. reception class children. The four subtests measure vocabulary, visual discrimination, auditory discrimination, and general ability, claimed by the authors to be the four most important skills contributing to readiness for reading. The manual gives guidance on the interpretation of the profiles and some suggestions for activities.

The use of a child's drawing of 'Mummy' as the basis for the assessment of ability is a well-established but questionable procedure. Otherwise, unlike many screening devices for infant-school entrants, these profiles, traditional in conception, are technically acceptable, well-produced, and widely-used.

Reference:

Levy, P. and Goldstein, H. (1984) *Tests in Education*, London, Academic Press.

The Association for Persons with Severe Handicaps (TASH), national (USA) organisation for helping with the educational, occupational, legal, social, medical, and other problems faced by people with severe handicaps. Membership includes parents, teachers, students, college personnel, legal advocates, government personnel, speech and language therapists, psychologists, social workers, etc. The Journal of the Association for Persons with Severe Handicaps (JASH) is published quarterly and emphasises reports and reviews of original research, and papers offering ideas on new directions, assessment and intervention strategies, and service delivery programs.

Thematic Apperception Test (TAT), projective technique designed for adults and adolescents and from which the *Children's Apperception Test (CAT)* was developed. Like the CAT, it employs the same principle of telling a story to a picture, and then interpreting the story form and content to gain an insight into personality structure. Although the TAT is found useful in many clinical settings, it is open to the various criticisms levelled against *projective techniques* in general.

Reference:

Anastasi, A. (1982, 5th edn.) *Psychological Testing*, New York, Macmillan.

theta wave, see *electroencephalogram.*

Thomas Report 1963, 'The Handicapped School Leaver', noted that many handicapped children left school with an unsatisfactory standard of education. The report recommended that local education authorities should review and improve facilities for advanced and technical education for handicapped young people. In this respect it foreshadowed some of the recommendations of the Warnock Report some fifteen years later.

Reference:

British Council for the Rehabilitation of the Disabled (1963) *The Handicapped School Leaver*, London, British Council for the Rehabilitation of the Disabled (Thomas Report).

Thomas Report 1985, 'Improving Primary Schools', report of a committee set up by the Inner London Education Authority (ILEA). Recommendations with relevance to special needs included a plea for the investigation of reading difficulties early, and no later than eight years of age. The report also argued for the use of diagnostic tests rather than standardised tests, and advocated that parents and other volunteers should be encouraged to visit schools to help children with their reading.

References:

Birchall, D. (1985) 'Improving Primary Education: a summary of the Thomas Report', *Highlight*, 68, London, National Children's Bureau.

ILEA (1985) *Improving Primary Schools*, London, ILEA (Thomas Report).

tic, recurrent, involuntary, rapid movements, most commonly of the eyelids or facial muscles.

The prevalence is difficult to establish since duration is a criterion which is not always mentioned. But surveys of school children have reported prevalence figures of between 10 and 24% who have experienced tics at some time: at any one time the prevalence rate will be much lower. They appear about three times as frequently in boys as girls. Tics are exacerbated by stress, and eased when stress is removed. Various treatments have been tried: behaviour therapy and medication are said to be the most effective. In school, child ticquers could be referred to the school psychological service, though undue concern over the condition may make it worse.

References:

American Psychiatric Association (1980, 3rd edn.) *Diagnostic and Statistical Manual of Mental Disorder*, Washington, American Psychiatric Association.

Barker, P. (1988, 5th edn.) *Basic Child Psychiatry*, Oxford, Blackwell.

time-out, separating a child from the chance of reinforcement; short for 'time out from positive reinforcement'.

Time-out is often thought to be placing a disruptive child in a separate (time-out) room. This is too simple a conception. The first point is that the situation from which the child is separated must contain the possibility of reinforcement if time-out is to be effective. Removing a child from a boring lesson can in itself be rewarding!

Second, removing a child to a time-out room is only one of various options. Thus activity time-out involves barring a child from an enjoyable activity, while permitting watching it – e.g. standing on the edge of a game. Other forms of time-out might involve a period of social isolation within the room. The old practices of standing a naughty child in the corner, or on a desk, illustrate the principle.

Third, if room time-out is to be employed, it is important that the time-out room used is non-rewarding.

Time-out tends to be employed with younger rather than older children. Time-out periods should be short – periods of between three and fifteen minutes are suggested, depending on age. As with all behavioural procedures, pupils should be aware of when it is to be used and its use should be consistent. It is effectively a form of *punishment*, since it involves denial of the opportunity of reward, and for that reason behaviourists prefer as far as possible the more productive approach of reinforcing desired behaviour – with which time-out can be used concurrently.

References:
Alberto, P.A. and Troutman, A.C. (1986, 2nd edn.) *Applied Behaviour Analysis for Teachers*, Columbus, Merrill.
Herbert, M. (1987, 2nd edn.) *Conduct Disorders of Childhood and Adolescence: a Social Learning Perspective*, Chichester, Wiley.

Tizard Report 1972, 'Children with Specific Reading Difficulties', report of a subcommittee of the then Advisory Committee on Handicapped Children. The Secretary of State for Education and Science asked it to consider whether local education authorities needed guidance on the education of children said to be suffering from *dyslexia*.

The main issue was the existence or not of a separate condition called dyslexia, requiring special educational provision above that offered by the remedial services then working with children with reading difficulties.

The report concluded that a minority of children did suffer from severe reading (and sometimes associated number and language) difficulties. But it also concluded that the term dyslexia was used in too loose and misleading a way to be useful and proposed that it should be replaced by 'specific reading difficulties'.

This conclusion did not satisfy the dyslexia lobby. The controversy did not die down until the Warnock Report argued that all children, whether previously seen as 'remedial' or 'special', should be considered as children with special educational needs.

References:
Department of Education and Science (1972) *Children with Specific Reading Difficulties*, London, HMSO (Tizard Report).
Young, P. and Tyre, C. (1983) *Dyslexia or Illiteracy?* Milton Keynes, Open University Press.

TMR, see *trainable mentally retarded.*

t.o., see *traditional orthography.*

tokens, are used as secondary reinforcers, exchangeable for a variety of rewards. The advantage of tokens, instead of the primary reinforcement, is that they can offer a choice of reward: tokens can be exchanged for any one of a number of material rewards, such as sweets, collectables, etc., or privileges such as extra play, later bed-times, etc. This enables the child to choose a more effective and thus more motivating reinforcer. Their use is not limited to the classroom, for they can be offered in any setting. In addition, since tokens should be easily dispensed, behaviour can be reinforced frequently, a point which is important for some pupils.

Tokens take many forms: stars and points are often used, though more tangible tokens such as plastic discs can be employed. It is important that they are not easily forged and that an accurate recording system is used.

Tokens are widely used in education generally, but their use has probably been most developed in special schools. Here, some schools are run as token economies, with the whole school operating on agreed exchange rates. The system has to be clearly understood by all pupils and has to be implemented fairly. Although open to the criticisms levelled against *behaviour modification* in general, it has proved a successful way of motivating pupils and encouraging desired behaviour.

References:

Alberto, P.A. and Troutman, A.C. (1986, 2nd edn.) *Applied Behavior Analysis for Teachers*, Columbus, Merrill.

Burland, J.R. (1979) 'Behaviour Modification in a Residential School for Junior Maladjusted Boys: an overview', *Journal of the Association of Workers for Maladjusted Children*, 7, 65–79.

TOMI, see *Test of Motor Impairment.*

top-down approaches to reading, consider reading primarily as a process for obtaining meaning, using experience and context in order to predict the flow of text. On this view, the details of single letters and individual words, which 'bottom-up' theorists regard as essential to correct reading, need be sampled only: comprehension depends on the child's informed guesses, which become more accurate as reading skills improve. In a nutshell, 'children learn to read by reading.'

This view is in contrast to that held by proponents of a phonic approach and, to a lesser extent, by the advocates of a look-and-say method. However, there is evidence that skilled readers do use individual letters and graphemic skills and do fixate virtually every content word in a text. This is not to deny the importance of the use of hypotheses based on contextual clues and previous expectations. It is simply to point out that reading is a complex skill, that children interact with text in different ways, that no one method offers a royal road, and that every approach has value.

See *bottom-up approaches.*

References:
King, C. and Quigley, S. (1985) *Reading and Deafness*, London, Taylor and Francis.
Sheldon, S. (1985) 'Learning to Read', Unit 13, Open University Course E206, Milton Keynes, Open University.

TOSCA, see *Test of Scholastic Abilities.*

total communication, aims to provide a language environment for hearing-impaired children which includes normal speech, optimal use of residual hearing and hearing aids, lip-reading, a manual sign language, together with finger-spelling and other communicative modes such as print.

Total communication has to be seen in the context of the *oral–manual controversy*. The advocates of these two main approaches to communication for hearing-impaired children each used to argue for the use of their one method alone: learning to communicate was difficult enough without mixing methods, and schools followed either an oral or manual approach. But in practice children, like everyone else, use whatever information helps communication. Some teachers of the hearing-impaired now accept the need for some more severely hearing-impaired children to use supportive and additional methods of communication, which include both signs and speech.

Others see total comunication as a broader concept, as defined at the start of this entry, using both these approaches and any other method of communication that helps improve competence in comprehension and expression – reading, writing, sign systems of every kind.

Three further points need to be made. First, children who sign in mainstream school situations will be restricted in their social and linguistic interactions, unless others are taught the system. Few schools in the UK offer sign language to hearing students or adults and the presence of signing interpreters in the schools is uncommon, although this situation is changing and contrasts markedly with other countries. (In the USA Ameslan is often taught as a second language in schools.)

Second, oral language is a necessary means of gaining access to hearing society. But many deaf people feel that deaf children should be taught sign as well as speech so that they can also identify with the deaf community.

Thirdly, decisions about choice of communication are controversial, highly-specialised and should always take into account the views and circumstances of the families and children involved.

References:
Twiss, D. (1987) 'Aided and Unaided Alternative Communication Systems', in Mitchell, D.R. and Singh, N.N. (Eds.) (1987) *Exceptional Children in New Zealand*, Palmerston North, Dunmore Press.
Tucker, I. and Nolan, M. (1984) *Educational Audiology*, Beckenham, Croom Helm.

touch-sensitive screen, device for feeding information into a computer without using the keyboard. The child merely has to touch an appropriate symbol or image on the screen with the finger. An infra-red beam is broken, the computer calculates the point of break and treats this as input.

It is argued that avoiding the keyboard removes the need to appreciate the abstract link between keyboard and screen, and hence makes the computer more accessible to children with severe learning difficulties. Children with motor and some visual impairments also find this an effective way to interact with a computer programme.

Reference:

Elf, B. (1988) 'Use of the Touch-sensitive Screen with Children who have Special Educational Needs', Research Supplement, *British Journal of Special Education,* 15, 3, 116–18.

toy library, centre for lending toys to children. The centres fill a particular need for children who are living away from home. They can be a useful resource for teachers, psychologists, social workers and others who work with residential establishments and with children living in deprived circumstances.

Further details from:

National Toy Libraries Association, 68 Churchway, London NW1 1LT.

trainable mentally retarded (TMR), used in the USA (but not in the UK) to describe individuals who are placed in a class which concentrates on teaching adaptive behaviour skills. The curriculum may also include some academic work, depending on intellectual development, as with the curriculum for children with severe learning difficulties in the UK.

TMR pupils are distinguished both from children who are described as *educable mentally retarded* and are taught basic academic subjects, as for pupils with moderate learning difficulties in this country, and from children with *profound retardation.*

Note that the tripartite classification of mental handicap into individuals who are educable, trainable or profoundly retarded, is basically an educational classification, and is a parallel system to that used by the American Association on Mental Deficiency (AAMD). The AAMD system classifies into four groups, viz. mild, moderate, severe and profound, based on severity of mental handicap and not on education needed.

See *learning difficulties, mental retardation.*

Reference:

Hallahan, D.P. and Kaufman, J.M. (1988, 4th edn.) *Exceptional Children: Introduction to Special Education,* Englewood Cliffs, Prentice Hall.

Transactional Analysis (TA), approach to counselling and therapy developed by E. Berne. Essentially it is a technique for analysing the transactions or exchanges that take place between people.

Berne believed that people normally assume one of three ego-states, behaving as a parent (emphasising rules), as a child (swayed by feelings), or as an adult (taking decisions). The well-adjusted personality is a balanced mixture of all three states.

Berne called the plans or programmes by which people structure their lives, their 'scripts'. The habitual ways in which people structure their interpersonal relations in order to derive satisfaction, he called 'games'.

The counsellor working within the TA framework seeks to understand the interplay of the client's ego-states, the script guiding the client's life at that time, and the games played. The object is then to offer these insights to the client who is expected to develop a better and more satisfying pattern of social transactions.

TA is derived from the psychoanalytic tradition; it adopts a psychodynamic approach to people's personality problems. Its great strength is its advocacy of the view that for most problems there is no need to rely on specially trained professionals: people can take care of and control their own behaviour.

TA is primarily an approach for adults. It has been tried in school counselling, but there is little available published work here.

Reference:

Berne, E. (1964) *Games People Play: the Psychology of Human Relationships*, New York, Grove.

transition programming, used in the USA to describe the preparation given to pupils with mental handicap for their move from school to work. It involves bridging an administrative divide through coordinating school-based and post-school services.

Reference:

Hallahan, D.P. and Kaufman, J.M. (1988, 4th edn.) *Exceptional Children: Introduction to Special Education*, Englewood Cliffs, Prentice Hall.

translocation, chromosome abnormality in which genetic material is rearranged in various ways. For example, a part of one *chromosome* may be added to another; or two chromosomes may exchange portions; or two chromosomes may fuse.

The abnormal chromosome formed by translocation can reproduce itself, and hence an individual who inherits it can be a carrier. The most obvious implication for special education occurs in relation to Down's syndrome: 4% of children with Down's syndrome owe their condition to a particular translocation, and not to the more usual trisomy.

See *genetics*.

triarchic theory, conception of *intelligence* associated with Sternberg, based on an information-processing approach. He believes that previous attempts to provide a structure for intelligence relied too heavily on limited data, such as test scores. He uses evidence from cognitive psychology to develop a model of intelligence resting on three supports; the contextual, involving adaptation to the environment; the experiential, involving handling novel and routine information; the componential, involving the mental mechanisms underlying intelligent behaviour.

The theory offers some insights into mental retardation, which Sternberg relates to inadequacies in the componential activity, specifying the particular processes involved. This may lead to the development of training programmes aimed at improving the intellectual functioning of children with learning difficulties.

Reference:

Sternberg, R.J. (1985) *Beyond I.Q.: a Triarchic Theory of Human Intelligence*, Cambridge, Cambridge University Press.

triplegia, see *cerebral palsy.*

trisomy, kind of *chromosome* abnormality in which a pair of chromosomes is replaced by a triplet. Individuals with a trisomy show developmental abnormalities, the nature of which depends on the particular trisomy involved: some lead to a very brief life expectancy. An exception is trisomy at chromosome 21, which is responsible for about 95% of children with *Down's syndrome.*

See *genetics.*

TROG, see *Test for the Reception of Grammar.*

truancy, any unlawful absence from school – though some studies restrict the term to absenteeism from school without the parents' knowledge. Persistent truancy is usually considered to be a conduct disorder, increasing in the secondary school to a peak in the final year of compulsory attendance. It is more prevalent in boys than girls, and is an offence for which parents can be brought to court, though this is a last resort.

Unlike *school refusal,* the truant usually chooses to follow another activity, rather than go to school. One factor associated with this is lack of interest in school on the part of the parents: a minority of parents may collude with the pupil, who may be asked to stay at home to help with home and family duties. This is not invariably the case, and some truants come from homes with a very positive – perhaps too positive – an attitude to school.

Just as important as family attitudes are school factors. Among schools with similar catchment areas there can be substantial differences between truancy rates, pupils demonstrating their view of the relevance of a school's curriculum and care in the clearest way possible.

Whereas school refusal is usually a matter for the educational psychologist, truancy is normally referred to the education welfare officer, who would certainly want to involve the home. Where truancy rates are high, however, there is a case for collaboration between the school, the advisory services and community organisations in order to try to improve matters.

See *units for disruptive pupils.*

References:

Galloway, D. (1985) *Schools and Persistent Absentees*, Oxford, Pergamon.
Her Majesty's Inspectorate of Schools (1978) *Truancy and Behavioural Problems in Some Urban Schools*, London, Department of Education and Science.
Hersov, L. and Berg, I. (Eds.) (1980) *Out of School: Modern Perspectives in Truancy and School Refusal*, Chichester, Wiley.
Reid, K. (1985) *Truancy and School Absenteeism*, London, Hodder and Stoughton.

TVEI, Technical and Vocational Education Initiative, programme of vocational and general education, often with work exerience, funded by central government. It supported suitable projects for pupils aged fourteen to eighteen years in secondary schools and colleges.

TVEI was intended to cover the needs of young people across the whole ability range, emphasising preparation for work in a technological society. As far as pupils with special needs are concerned, those integrated in the mainstream of schools and colleges have had most ready access to TVEI projects. Special school pupils have had fewer opportunities to participate, though there are exceptions.

Reference:

Cooper, D. (1987) 'TVEI: Across the Ability Range?' *British Journal of Special Education*, 14, 4, 147–9.

Twenty-twenty vision, see *Snellen chart.*

tympanic membrane, eardrum. See *ear.*

type-token ratio, index of vocabulary development used in some simple analyses of young children's speech. It is the ratio of different words to total words in a sample of speech.

$$\text{Type-token ratio} = 100 \times \frac{\text{No. of different words}}{\text{Total words}}$$

typogram, see *calligram.*

U

unit, see *special class.*

units for disruptive pupils, have grown substantially in number in recent years, particularly in the secondary sector. This development has not passed unchallenged. Removing a pupil from the mainstream to a separate unit runs contrary to the integrationist philosophy which is supposed to inform the education system. Yet pupils by and large settle well in units, preferring their small groups and informal approach, and schools are relieved to lose some of their more troublesome members.

The opponents of the unit system point to the restricted curriculum that a unit, usually staffed by two or three teachers only, can offer, and to the finding that return to the main school after a period in a unit usually leads to a reappearance of the difficult behaviour. They also argue that removing a child from an admittedly unsuitable school environment should be an action of last resort: in a good school the caring systems (pastoral care, counselling) and the ethos of the school should be able to modify arrangements sufficiently to support many of the children currently being transferred to units. If 'disruptive' pupils are not disruptive in the context of the unit, the problem may not lie with them, but with the environment of the main school. Finally, they argue that integration is valuable for all children, not merely those with special needs.

The introduction of a national curriculum may have significant consequences for units for disruptive pupils, for the power of Heads to disapply the full curriculum for pupils is limited. Whatever the future of units, it is important that their aims and functions are clear, and understood by staff and pupils alike. The closer the links that can be retained with the main school the better.

See *emotional and behavioural difficulties.*

References:

Chazan, M. (1990) 'Children with Emotional and Behavioural Difficulties', in Entwistle, N. (Ed.) (1990) *Handbook of Educational Ideas and Practices*, London, Routledge.

Mortimore, P., Davies, J., Varlaam, A. and West, A. (1983) *Behaviour Problems in Schools*, London, Croom Helm.

Williams, P. (1985) 'Troubled Behaviour', Units 18/19 of Open University Course E206, Milton Keynes, Open University.

V

VAKT method/system, see *Fernald method.*

validity, the extent to which a procedure assesses what it is intended to assess. It is the basic issue to be examined in evaluating any procedure – experiment, interview, survey, test, etc. Thus validity is an essential principle of research enquiries. For example, if a comparison of two teaching methods is badly designed, the difference between groups obtained in the experiment may not be due to the teaching method but to uncontrolled influences. The experimental results are then invalid.

Validity is a key – the key – criterion for evaluating educational and psychological tests. If the test does not measure what it purports to measure, it is invalid. Perfect validity is an ideal, and the extent to which a test is valid is given by comparisons with accepted criteria: for example, a test designed to screen children for hearing loss can be validated against the results of clinical examination. Validity – preferably several forms of validity – should be reported in the manual of every published test.

Note that the other key criterion for evaluating assessment measures, *reliability*, has a bearing on validity. If a test is unreliable, then it cannot be valid, for its results are untrustworthy by definition. But if a test is reliable, then it is still not necessarily valid. A reliable group test of mathematics, where children have to read the items, may be entirely valid for most classes, but if given to children with serious reading difficulties it will also be measuring reading performance. A child with good mathematical ability who cannot read the questions then obtains a poor score. In this situation the test is invalid, but still reliable, for results will be consistent on retest.

This illustrates the point that a test which is valid for one population may not be valid for another. Finally, concerns about test validity are eased, though not removed, when *criterion-referenced assessment* procedures are introduced.

References:

Anastasi, A. (1982, 5th edn.) *Psychological Testing*, New York, Macmillan.

Child, D. (1986, 4th edn.) *Psychology and the Teacher*, London, Holt, Rinehart and Winston.

Levy, P. and Goldstein, H. (Eds.) (1984) *Tests in Education*, London, Academic Press.

v.ed, verbal-educational ability, one of the two major groupings of abilities, or group factors, in the hierarchical model of human abilities advanced by British psychometrists.

Since the educational system is so heavily verbal, scores on v.ed tests are very good predictors of educational success (and vice versa!). The traditional view that the test scores represented an index of innate verbal ability has given way to a realisation that perhaps more than any qualities, these are developed abilities. The similarity between some tests of verbal abilities, heavily loaded with v.ed, and some tests of competence in major curricular areas such as English, for example, illustrates this. Yet scores on verbal tests continue to be used in assessment and programme planning, whether or not the user accepts the model of the structure of human abilities that is implied by the v.ed factor, to which so many such tests in the UK owe their origins.

Reference:

Child, D. (1986, 4th edn.) *Psychology and the Teacher*, London, Holt, Rinehart and Winston.

verbal–performance discrepancy, the contrast between a child's performance on the two main measures, the verbal quotient and the performance quotient, often derived from the Wechsler tests.

Although it is just one example of a difference between test scores, this particular difference is often reported as a psychologically and educationally meaningful score in its own right, since the Wechsler tests are used so regularly.

Its interpretation is governed by the constraints that govern any difference score, namely the standard errors of the two measures and their intercorrelations. Tables are available to determine the significance of obtained differences. For example, for non-extreme verbal and performance scores for ten-and-a-half-year-olds on the WISC-R, differences of less than twelve points can occur through chance variations alone. Even if a reliable difference is obtained, indicating that the child is consistently better at one set of abilities than the other, the question of the rarity of a given discrepancy remains. In the example given, a level of 3% could be set as sufficiently rare to justify taking the discrepancy seriously: 3% of children at this age have verbal quotients at least twenty-nine points greater than performance quotients.

Thus very large discrepancies have to be reached before they become statistically significant. This does not necessarily mean that smaller differences should be ignored. In clinical work, any reliable verbal–performance difference, even if it occurs fairly frequently in the population, is a piece of evidence to use in testing hypotheses about a child's special needs. A substantially lower verbal quotient may raise questions about language experiences, for example, and in conjunction with other evidence lead to suggestions for a particular kind of educational programme.

References:

Chazan, M., Moore, T., Williams, P. and Wright, J. (1974) *The Practice of Educational Psychology*, London, Longman.

Berger, M. and Yule, W. (1987) 'Psychometric Approaches', in Hogg, J. and Raynes, N.V. (Eds.) (1987) *Assessment in Mental Handicap*, Beckenham, Croom Helm.

Versabraille, electronic Brailler which stores text on cassette or disc. It can display written material on a twenty-character Braille display, and print text in Braille or normal typeface. Text can also be typed in via an ordinary computer keyboard, and reproduced as Braille.

The advantages for educating older blind children are obvious. But the Versabraille is expensive, which will limit its availability for blind children being educated in the ordinary classroom, which is where it would probably be at its most useful.

Reference:

Chapman, E.K. and Stone, J.M. (1988) *The Visually Handicapped Child in Your Classroom*, London, Cassell.

Viewscan, *low vision aid*, particularly useful for reading. It consists of a camera, which moves along a line of print, connected to a screen on which the print is displayed at a magnification and contrast chosen by the viewer.

The Viewscan is portable. The operation of the camera has to be learnt, and it is probably most suitable for secondary pupils.

Reference:

Chapman, E.K. and Stone, J.M. (1988) *The Visually Handicapped Child in Your Classroom*, London, Cassell.

Vincent work-station, system for producing hard copy, either in Braille or normal typeface, from a Perkins Brailler via a BBC computer and printer. This permits a pupil to produce an immediate copy of work in a form that a non-Braille teacher can use, so facilitating the integration of blind children, through making ordinary lessons much more accessible.

There is a speech synthesiser, which enables work in progress to be checked, and which is useful for children learning Braille.

Reference:

Chapman, E.K. and Stone, J.M. (1988) *The Visually Handicapped Child in Your Classroom*, London, Cassell.

Vineland Scale, originally developed as a measure of social maturity, the 'Vineland' in its different editions was in wide use for half a century. It was an age-scale, used to assess the competence of individuals in areas of social competence such as self-help in eating and dressing; communication, locomotion, etc.

The latest revision (1984) changed the title to 'Vineland Scale of Adaptive Behaviour', and improved the content and organisation. Like the earlier versions, information on behaviour is gained from a parent or care-giver, and not by direct observation. The results, though available as standard scores, can still be transformed to age-equivalents. The age-equivalent score is a most useful attribute of the Vineland. It provides an assessment of the development of older children with severe learning difficulties whose performance on tests designed for their age-group might be well below the test's floor level, and hence of little meaning.

Reference:

Raynes, N.V. (1987) 'Adaptive Behaviour Scales', in Hogg, J. and Raynes, N.V. (Eds.) (1987) *Assessment in Mental Handicap*, Beckenham, Croom Helm.

visual discrimination is an essential component of reading: if a child cannot discriminate between different letter shapes, then teaching reading is impossible. It is for this reason that tests of visual discrimination are usually included in diagnostic reading tests.

However, visual discrimination is not a simple skill. One component must be visual acuity, for if this is poor, then so will be visual discrimination, unless the visual impairment is corrected. Another must be the skill of perception, for a child may have good acuity, yet readily confuse similar letter shapes, such as 'b' and 'd'. Could this be an orientation problem? Might there be a memory problem present? Or is it simply a question of the child needing good teaching?

Similarly, a child may have difficulty in recognising individual letters or shapes in a background of other shapes or letters. Is this figure-ground confusion the result of or cause of the difficulties?

In short, visual discrimination is a complex of subskills. If visual discrimination of letter shapes is found to be poor, this is the beginning of an investigation, not the end. It is perhaps because training exercises designed to improve visual discrimination have not taken a more precise, analytic approach, that they have not proved as successful as was first hoped.

Reference:

Downing, J. and Thackray, D.V. (1971) *Reading Readiness,* London, University of London Press.

visual half-field tests or tasks, have been devised to investigate how pupils with severe reading difficulties perform when stimuli are presented to the half-fields separately, so comparing effects of right hemisphere and left hemisphere processing. The investigations derive from concern about the possible damage to or lack of maturation of the cerebral hemispheres of these pupils. As with *dichotic listening tests* the results so far are inconclusive, if suggestive.

Reference:

Tansley, P. and Panckhurst, J. (1981) *Children with Specific Learning Difficulties; a Critical Review of Research,* Windor, NFER-Nelson.

visual impairment, damage to sight, up to and including blindness, resulting in special educational needs of varying severity. Since it has been estimated that 80% of school tasks are based on vision, the importance to education of adequate vision cannot be overstated. The prevalence of children with special needs due to visual impairment is said to be dropping; in the early 1980s a figure of about three-and-a-half per 10,000 pupils was reported, but this does refer to children categorised as blind or partially sighted under the pre-1983 legislation: there are undoubtedly others with visual handicap not included in these returns.

Apart from loss of colour vision, which should be checked if there are any suspicions of difficulty, visual impairments fall into two main categories, defects of acuity, or sharpness of vision, which glasses can often but not always correct, and limitations of field, or area seen. There are many visual conditions which can lead to one or both of these, e.g., glaucoma (pressure behind the cornea), retinitis pigmentosa (one of a number of diseases leading to retinal degeneration), etc. etc. Some visual conditions are associated with other problems: for example, children whose mothers contracted rubella in pregnancy may suffer from mental handicap and hearing impairment as well as visual impairment. For reasons such as this, the prevalence of visual handicap among the mentally handicapped is many times that in the rest of the population – one estimate suggests a multiplying factor of ten, but different criteria provide different ratios. But it is essential that children's vision should be particularly carefully checked if other special needs are detected.

Children with visual impairments will need an assessment of their functional vision, as well as an assessment of their acuity and field of vision. The functional vision determines their educational needs, and the specialist teacher/adviser of the visually handicapped will be able to translate the test results into an educational programme, taking into account considerations such as the child's level of intellectual development, motivation, family support, etc.

Visual impairment is a specialised field, reflected in a number of ways. For example, the educational advice which has to be sought when assessing a child's special educational needs must be provided in consultation with a qualified teacher of the blind if it is thought that a child is visually handicapped. This point, which features in the regulations following the introduction in 1983 of the Education Act 1981, has been instrumental in persuading many of even the smaller local education authorities to establish advisory services for the visually impaired.

Children with visual impairments have traditionally been taught in schools for the blind and partially-sighted. As the numbers of children with severe visual handicaps has tended to decrease, special schools serve increasingly large areas, and hence have tended to become residential establishments. Moreover, an increasing number of children with visual handicaps are now being educated in ordinary schools, either in special classes, or as individual pupils. Here, there is a demand for a network of support centres for the visually handicapped, established in designated ordinary schools, and able to act as bases from which pupils could be gradually introduced to mainstream classes, with support from the specialist staff at the centre. Where such close support is not available, and a visually handicapped child is being educated in a neighbourhood school, the peripatetic service has to offer it for child and school alike. For the teacher in the ordinary class, the special adviser should be able to provide, based on the child's Statement or otherwise, information on the kind of illumination needed, the low-vision aids and other equipment required, details and sources of any suitable teaching material, preliminary opportunities for the pupil to become familiar with the school layout and organisation, and above all planned opportunities for information from and discussions with the advisory service.

See *blindness, partially-sighted.*

References:

Chapman, E.K. and Stone, J.M. (1988) *The Visually Handicapped Child in Your Classroom*, London, Cassell.

Corley, G., Robinson, D. and Lockett, S. (1989) *Partially-sighted Children*, Windsor, NFER-Nelson.

Hodgson, A. (1985) 'How to Integrate the Visually Impaired', *British Journal of Special Education*, 12, 1, 35–7.

Low, C. (1983) 'Integrating the Visually Handicapped', in Booth, T. and Potts, P. (Eds.) (1983) *Integrating Special Education*, Oxford, Blackwell.
Moses, D., Hegarty, S. and Jowett, S. (1988) *Supporting Ordinary Schools*, Windsor, NFER-Nelson.
Tobin, M. (1990) 'Integrating Visually Impaired Pupils: Issues and Needs', in Evans, P. and Varma, V. (Eds.) (1990) *Special Education: Past, Present and Future*, London, Falmer Press.

visual perception, ability to attach meaning to what is seen. The essential point is that visual perception is different from vision. The visual apparatus may be excellent; colour vision, acuity, field, may all be perfect, yet a child may have problems with perception. The ability to make sense of the difference between similar figures, such as a square and a diamond, and to recognise the difference between similar but not identical letters, such as 'b' and 'd', for example, are both examples of perception. These skills rely on the organisation and structure of the representation of the signals from the visual apparatus.

There are clear educational difficulties for children with problems of visual perception. For this reason various tests have been constructed to identify these difficulties, so that perceptual training programmes can be instituted. But the evidence for the success of this approach is weak.

See *Developmental Test of Visual Perception.*

visual reinforcement audiometry, technique for testing the hearing of infants from six months to three years of age, which overcomes the problems of *distraction tests* and *cooperative tests.* The child is trained to look in a certain direction whenever a sound stimulus is heard. This is done by rewarding the looking response with sight of an animated toy or illuminated puppet. As the child turns in response to sound, the puppet or toy is presented close to the sound source. The test provides fairly precise information about hearing across the frequency range, but requires fixed apparatus such as loudspeakers.

visuo-motor ability, particular kind of *perceptuo–motor ability,* in which the focus of interest is the coordination of visual perception and motor activity. An example is writing, for which good hand–eye coordination is needed. Some children – some with cerebral palsy, for example – have visuo–motor abilities damaged, and need lengthy and skilled training, aimed at improving their competence in them.

vocabulary development, traditionally the main index of children's language growth, and thus held to be a useful tool for diagnosing delayed language development. Early texts in this field contained illustrations of vocabulary growth over the years of childhood, listing oral vocabulary sizes expected at different ages. Perhaps the most obvious criticism of this technique is the difficulty of deciding what is to be counted as a 'word': do tenses of the same verb count as one or several words? What about singulars and plurals? The word-counting approach may nevertheless seem to be effective when a child has a very few words, but even then it can be questioned. One child may use the same word with different meanings, depending on context, whereas another may not. Does the count refer to words expressed, or words comprehended?

For these reasons, dimensions of language growth other than vocabulary development have proved more fruitful in investigating children's language disorders, and measures of vocabulary have been superseded by assessments of the development of language structures.

See *language development.*

Reference:

Crystal, D. (1976) *Child Language, Learning and Linguistics,* London, Edward Arnold.

vocabulary of reading, the words that a child needs to understand in order to profit from reading instruction from a teacher. The vocabulary is short: it includes words like 'line', 'word', and 'first', needed when teacher says 'Look at the first word on the line.' One suggested vocabulary consists of the words 'line, word, first, last, top, bottom, front, back, under, over', but this can clearly be extended – e.g. 'page, letter'.

This is simply an exemplification of the age-old educational principle of not teaching beyond the level of understanding of the pupil. Before starting to teach children to read, it is easy to forget that some pupils will not understand the simple instructional vocabulary used, and will first need help with this.

Reference:

Reason, R. and Boote, R. (1986) *Learning Difficulties in Reading and Writing: a Teacher's Manual,* Windsor, NFER-Nelson.

vocational guidance, see *careers guidance.*

vocational training, the traditional route into employment for many young people with special needs. Some of the major voluntary bodies (e.g. the RNIB) have pioneered vocational training, often by setting up residential colleges for people with particular disabilities.

As well as the voluntary bodies, centrally funded provision for training exists through the Employment Rehabilitation Centres. Information on the opportunities available can be obtained through the Disablement Resettlement Service, via the local jobcentre.

Reference:

Hutchinson, D. (1982) *Work Preparation for the Handicapped,* London, Croom Helm.

voice disorders, alternatively known as phonation and resonance disorders, see *speech disorders.*

vowel digraph, see *digraph*.

W

Warnock Report 1978, 'Special Educational Needs', report of the Committee of Enquiry into the Education of Handicapped Children and Young People, whose recommendations have since had a significant effect on special educational policy and practice.

The report argued that the scope of special education should be widened, and services based on the assumption that about one in six children at any one time and one in five at some time during their school career will need some form of special education; that most special education should take place in ordinary schools; that parents should be more involved in the practices and procedures of special education. Given these principles, the report went on to identify three priority areas, teacher education, special education in the pre-school, and special education for the sixteen to nineteen age group. The first of these areas reflected the importance attached to making the whole educational community aware of special educational needs: the second and third areas effectively extended the view of special education, which had previously been confined to the age-limits of compulsory education, i.e. five to sixteen years.

The report made many more recommendations, some sweeping, others more detailed. Some of the more important included the idea of special educational needs itself, as opposed to a mainly medical diagnosis, the consequent abolition of categories of handicap, the use of learning difficulties to point to the needs of both those children who had previously been diagnosed as educationally subnormal and of those who were in remedial education, the proposals for a structured system of assessment, the continued existence of special schools for children with some severe and complex disabilities, the designation of a named person, etc.

The Report was generally welcomed by most interested parties. Probably the most contentious set of recommendations were those dealing with the difficult issue of integration, where some believed that the report should have advocated a much more integrationist policy. At the same time, some special school teachers felt that the report undervalued the contribution of segregated education and feared that the effects of Warnock would lead to far too many school closures.

Probably the greatest disappointment associated with Warnock was the response of government. Whilst accepting most of the report's recommendations, the government was prepared only to endorse those that were expensive, and to legislate only where the financial obligation was minimal. Thus the recommendations covering the three priority areas were welcomed and then largely ignored: on the other hand the recommendations relating to the abolition of categorisation were given legal force. Even then, it was not until 1981 that the government produced legislation that was intended to respond to the Report, and not until 1983 that the legislation came into effect.

But the report had a major effect on special educational policy throughout the UK, and was influential abroad. The education community demonstrated its support for the spirit of the Warnock recommendations, notwithstanding the limited official response.

Reference:

Department of Education and Science (1978) *Special Educational Needs*, London, HMSO (Warnock Report).

Wechsler Intelligence Tests, range of intelligence tests produced by David Wechsler, a clinical psychologist in the USA. The tests are based on Wechsler's conclusions that intelligence is not a single entity, for which precise tests can be developed, but rather a global quality, for which a sampling of different abilities will give the best measure. Notwithstanding their American origins, the tests are widely used in many countries.

The original test and model for later developments is the Wechsler Adult Intelligence Scale, or WAIS, since revised as the WAIS-R. This was a noteworthy instrument: it was an individual test, based on Wechsler's views on intelligence. Like the main instrument then in use, the Stanford-Binet test, it gave an IQ. It differed from the Binet in that it was not an age-scale; items were not organised by age-level, but by ability being measured: thus all vocabulary items were grouped into a single subtest. Subtests themselves were organised into two main groups, the verbal group and the performance group.

This meant that the WAIS could provide both a verbal quotient and a performance quotient, as well as a 'global' IQ. Moreover standard scores were provided for each subtest, so permitting a profile of subtest scores to be constructed. The *verbal–performance discrepancy* and the subtest profile both introduced greater possibilities for differential diagnosis than were available through the Binet. This was a major reason for the popularity of the WAIS.

Wechsler then developed intelligence tests for children, constructed on similar principles and offering similar advantages. The first of these, the Wechsler Intelligence Test for Children, or WISC, revised as the WISC-R, now covers the age range six to seventeen. Later, the Wechsler Preschool and Primary Test of Intelligence, or WPPSI, was produced, covering the age range four to six-and-a-half. Both the WISC-R and the WPPSI contain verbal subtests measuring information, ability to identify similarities, arithmetic, vocabulary, comprehension, and a subtest measuring memory. The performance subtests both contain a picture completion subtest, requiring the child to identify missing parts of a picture, a mazes test, a block design test, a test measuring the child's ability to 'code', and one testing the child's skill at tracking through a maze. In addition the WISC-R includes a subtest requiring the child to assemble objects, and one requiring pictures to be arranged in a logical sequence. The WPPSI has now been itself revised (WPPSI-R) to produce a subtest structure similar to the WISC-R.

The range of abilities sampled by these tests is thus quite wide. Some studies of the structure of the tests show that the subtest relationships can be explained on the basis of a general factor, with evidence of a verbal factor additionally characterising performance on the verbal subtests in particular. Scores on the performance subtests are not easily explained by a single factor in addition to the general factor.

The technical details of reliability, standardisation, etc., are adequate and the tests have been adapted for British use. They have been an essential part of the educational psychologist's toolkit. The development of the British Ability Scales, combined with the change to a less test-dependent mode of working, may reduce their use in future.

See *profile analysis.*

References:

Anastasi, A. (1982, 5th edn.) *Psychological Testing,* New York, Macmillan.

Berger, M. and Yule, W. (1987) 'Psychometric Approaches', in Hogg, J. and Raynes, N.V. (Eds.) (1987) *Assessment in Mental Handicap,* Beckenham, Croom Helm.

Salvia, J. and Ysseldyke, J.E. (1985, 3rd edn.) *Assessment in Special and Remedial Education,* Boston, Houghton Mifflin.

welfare assistant, see *classroom assistant.*

Wepman auditory discrimination test, see *auditory discrimination.*

Wernicke's area, part of the temporal lobe of the brain, involved in the reception and perception of spoken language. The effects of damage to Wernicke's area are described as a *receptive language disorder*: the child can hear what is said but cannot make sense of it. The reverse relationship, i.e. inferring brain damage from evidence of problems with language reception is illogical. Neurological evidence is a prerequisite.

Note that if neurological damage does exist, other abilities are not necessarily affected.

See *brain, Broca's area.*

whole-school approach, slogan which is sometimes described as meaning all things to all men, yet which has proved an influential call in determining a school's policy for children with special needs. If the school is a whole school, and not a school which considers special needs as an additional responsibility, an appendage to its central purposes, then certain consequences follow. One group of consequences relates to the children. In a whole school approach, all pupils have access to the whole curriculum, all pupils are seen to contribute usefully to the life and work of the school, and all pupils are encouraged to respect individual differences.

Another group of consequences relates to the teaching staff. All teachers should be sensitive to the range of needs existing in their classrooms, all teachers should be responsible for using teaching materials appropriate to the needs of all their pupils, and all teachers should have access to specialised help for children with special needs in their classes.

A third group of consequences relates to senior management. Senior staff should ensure that these objectives are known and pursued by teachers, governors and parents alike, that resources are allocated for them, that adequate and appropriate inservice training, focusing on special educational needs in the ordinary school (SENIOS) is developed, and that the success of these policies is kept constantly under review.

Whether or not this approach entails adopting a particular kind of school organisation is a matter of debate. Some argue that as far as possible an unstreamed organisation is needed; others that the organisation is immaterial. In the end commitment to such a policy should be the overriding factor, and if this is so, then any organisation that proves not to be in harmony with it will be changed.

References:

Ainscow, M. and Florek, A. (Eds.) (1989) *Special Educational Needs: Towards a Whole School Approach*, London, Fulton in association with National Council for Special Education.

Galloway, D. (1988) 'INSET and the Whole-school Approach', *British Journal of Special Education*, 15, 4, 173–5.

Hinson, M. (Ed.) (1987) *Teachers and Special Educational Needs*, Harlow, Longman in association with NARE.

Sayer, J. (1987) *Secondary Education for All?* London, Cassell.

whole-word method, see *look-and-say.*

Williams Intelligence Test for Children with Defective Vision, set of 100 verbal and performance items, culled largely from an early version of the Stanford-Binet Scale, and standardised on a sample of children whose visual acuity did not exceed 6/36 on the *Snellen chart.* Its results are expressed as an IQ, norm-referenced to the standardisation population of course and not to a sighted population.

This is the only British standardised test for children with visual impairment, covering the age range five to fifteen years, though a version of the British Ability Scales is being developed for this purpose.

The Williams Test has been used since 1956. The technical data were adequate then, but need improving to meet modern standards. The main criticism is based on lack of knowledge of the extent to which the characteristics of the visually-impaired population might have changed since 1956. For both these reasons, a restandardisation would be valuable.

Reference:
Levy, P. and Goldstein, H. (Eds.) (1984) *Tests in Education*, London, Academic Press.

withdrawn behaviour, sometimes called avoidant disorder of childhood, one of the group of neurotic, as opposed to antisocial behaviours. Children who are solitary may well be individualists, content with their own company. But when they are in addition timid, clinging and sometimes excessively tearful, then they do have emotional difficulties. Their special needs can easily be overlooked, for they do not present teachers with the problems of management and of learning difficulties that aggressive, disruptive children do.

There are various causes of withdrawn behaviour. Some children appear to be temperamentally shy. Others develop withdrawn behaviour after a traumatic event, such as a bereavement, or a separation from a central figure, often mother. The start of school is often a time at which withdrawn behaviour occurs. Some psychiatrists see withdrawn behaviour as the outward manifestation of anxiety, or of a depressed state. Transient examples of withdrawn behaviour are shown by most children, but when it is sustained, it should not be ignored. Both psychodynamic and behavioural approaches can be helpful, particularly where the parent can be involved. Referral to a school psychological service is a natural step.

Reference:
Laslett, R. (1982) *Maladjusted Children in the Ordinary School*, Stratford-upon-Avon, National Council for Special Education.

word recognition, the ability to identify words correctly, usually assessed through pronouncing them correctly.

A test of word recognition, requiring a child to pronounce single words, is often used as a quick index of a child's reading competence. This is hazardous, for while word recognition is a fundamental reading skill, it has to be considered alongside others, such as comprehension, the ability to use context, phonic skills, etc.

See *graded word reading test.*

Reference:
Davies, P. and Williams, P. (1974) *Aspects of Early Reading Growth: a Longitudinal Study*, Oxford, Blackwell.

Words in Colour, method of teaching reading in which forty-eight different colours are used to provide additional, consistent clues to grapheme–phoneme correspondences in the early stages of reading. The colours are used in wall-charts, from which the child practises reading: the child's own reading materials are printed in normal black-on-white format.

Methods of teaching reading relying heavily on the use of colour have not proved as successful as their authors have suggested. In this particular example the narrow differentiation between some of the forty-eight colours has not helped.

See *colour coding*.

Reference:

Cattegno, C. (1970) *The Problem of Reading is Solved*, Harvard Educational Review, 40, 2, 283–6.

writing difficulties often occur in pupils with neuromuscular problems such as cerebral palsy, and may be so severe that wordprocessors/typewriters operated by breath or other means are essential.

Agraphia (inability to write) and dysgraphia (difficulty in writing), both neurologically caused, may also occur in pupils who have suffered head injuries, or cerebral tumours.

Apart from these pupils with special needs, writing difficulties are also found in the generality of pupils. Lack of muscular control in the fingers or hand, or excessive grip, may both make writing, with its fine motor movements, difficult. In both cases, which are rare, medical advice and therapy should first be sought.

More common are maturational difficulties and clumsiness. The former may need little more than patient understanding and encouragement, but in both cases tracing and copying exercises will help, as will the provision of lines to guide pupils and help develop the proportions of letters with their ascenders (e.g. b, d, f, h), descenders (e.g. g, j, p, y) and capitals. These pupils will also be helped from the early stages by indications of the starting points for a letter's formation and the directions in which letters are formed. Many writing difficulties arise from inadequate supervision, so that children begin forming letters of the right shape and size, but with the wrong sequence and direction of strokes.

See *expressive language disorders, handwriting*.

References:

Reason, R. and Boote, R. (1986) *Learning Difficulties in Reading and Writing: a Teacher's Manual*, Windsor, NFER-Nelson.

Snowling, M. (Ed.) (1985) *Children's Written Language Difficulties*, Windsor, NFER-Nelson.

Y

Ypsilanti-Perry Preschool Project, classic 1960s programme of the *Head Start* genre, aimed at improving the educational development of young black children from poor families. The programme was unusual in that it was based on Piagetian theory. Its strength lay in the involvement of mothers through weekly home visits, the use of intensive intervention – a daily preschool programme for two years – with the children, and an acceptable experimental design.

It has probably been better monitored than most similar programmes, the children having been followed up until they left high school. The results were in keeping with recent Head Start evaluations: the young people who had been enrolled in the preschool programme were more successful educationally, more successful in gaining employment, and more successful in avoiding brushes with the law.

Reference:

Woodhead, M. (1985) 'Early Intervention', Unit 25 of Open University Course E206, Milton Keynes, Open University.

Z

z-score, a score transformed into standard deviation units. Thus on a test standardised to a mean of 100 and a standard deviation of 15, a score of 115 would be represented as a z-score of +1.0, a score of 90 as a z-score of −0.67, etc.

Transforming score values into z-scores allows comparisons to be made between performances on tests with different means and standard deviations: this is a major advantage of such scores.

See *deviation quotient illustration.*